MW01517420

A Manual Of Mediaeval And Modern History

M. E. Thalheimer

A MANUAL

OF

MEDIÆVAL AND MODERN

HISTORY.

BY

M. E. THALHEIMER,

FORMERLY TEACHER OF HISTORY AND COMPOSITION IN THE PACKER COLLEGIATE

INSTITUTE, BROOKLYN, N. Y.

WILSON, HINKLE & CO.,

137 WALNUT ST.,   28 BOND ST.,

CINCINNATI.   NEW YORK.

PREFACE.

The following pages contain a sketch of fourteen centuries, from the fall of one Empire at Ravenna to the establishment of another at Berlin.

To give perfect literary form to such a mass of details would be a task beyond either the power or the ambition of the present writer, even were it not complicated by the necessity of bringing the work within certain material limits adapted to the wants of students. Our humbler attempt has been to convey some impression of the continuity of the civil history of Europe and its dependencies, under the successive leadership of the Goths and the Franks, the Empire and the Spanish power, France and England, until the supremacy of the Teutonic tribes at the opening of the period finds its counterpart in the predominance of the new German Empire and the Anglo-Saxon race, at its close.

This object has been sought through a simple narration of events. Larger generalization might have been more interesting to the mature reader, but students will only be able to form and rightly to estimate theories when they are in thorough possession of the facts.

In the grouping of incidents, two methods lay open to the writer. By presenting the States of Europe in a series of separate histories, greater completeness of execution could have been combined with the easy flow of a continuous narrative. But these advantages would have been neutralized by the lack of any comprehensive view of Europe as a whole—a whole, complex, indeed, but possessing, under all its superficial diversities, several grand principles of unity, whose workings, if we succeed in making them apparent, are of more value than the mere annals of any or all the individual States. The confluence of German ideas and customs with Roman civilization and religion must be studied in almost every country in Europe, from the subjugation of Gaul, Spain, and Italy, and the "missions" of Gregory the Great, to the recent rivalries of northern statesmen and prelates, and the correspondence of Bismarck with the Vatican. The religious unity of mediæval Europe, which alone could have produced the great tidal movements of the Crusades, is not broken by the Teutonic Reformation before another and very different sort of unity, formed and fostered by diplomacy, has been already three quarters of a century in growth. The new relations arising from discoveries, colonization, and

(iii)

consequent extension of commerce, lead, of necessity, to improvements in international law—a science which if perfected would realize and surpass the unjustly derided dream of Henry IV, by knitting all Christendom into a commonwealth of sovereign States, where reason should take the place of force, and the ultimate interests of each, be recognized as identical with the interests of all.

No apology is offered for the space allotted to Europe as compared with Asia, Africa, or America. In a natural history of mankind, Fijians and Hottentots would of course claim an equal share of attention with Englishmen. The philosopher who studies distinctions of race, as revealed in language, literature, or mythology, can by no means neglect the ancient and high civilizations of India, China, and Japan. Our task is limited to the civil history of man, and still more narrowly to those nations whose laws or customs have more or less intimately affected our own. It is conceivable that Hindus or Chinese, through their literature or by immigration, may become so important an element in our society, that acquaintance with their national history may be essential to a liberal education. But the time has not come, nor are materials yet accessible. On the other hand, the history of our own country is so universally taught in our schools of every grade, that we anticipate a ready pardon for occupying our limited space chiefly with details less familiar, though in a large view not less essential to a thorough understanding of our national institutions.

Whatever want of continuity may result from the arrangement which we have adopted, will be obviated, it is hoped, by the Review Questions at the end of each Book, and by the Index which with this view has been made as copious as possible. The lack of chronological tables has been supplied partly by the lists of sovereigns in the Index, and partly by references to pages on whose margins the dates will be found. The Recapitulations following each section will aid teachers in passing lightly over certain periods whenever the exigencies of the class may require it, while students at leisure may be guided to a more liberal course of reading by the list of books at the end of the volume. The twelve maps, copied from Spruner's new Historical Atlas, afford an invaluable supplement to the text—filling a want which has been lately deplored by one of the ablest living historians as accounting for much of the popular confusion of ideas on historical questions. (Freeman's Historical Essays, pp. 162, 163.)

It only remains to express the author's sincere and profound gratitude for the kind reception accorded to the "Manual of Ancient History," with the hope that an equally lenient judgment may await the present more difficult and, therefore, perhaps, more presumptuous enterprise.

BROOKLYN, N. Y., *April*, 1874.

CONTENTS.

BOOK II.—THE MIDDLE AGES.

PERIOD I.—*The Crusades.*

BOOK III.—THE MODERN ERA.

From the Discovery of America to the Close of the Thirty Years' War.

CONTENTS.

CONTENTS.

BOOK IV.—MODERN ERA CONTINUED.

From the Peace of Westphalia to the French Revolution.

PAGE

BOOK V.—MODERN ERA CONTINUED.

The Age of Revolutions.

CONTENTS.

MAPS.

INTRODUCTION.

MEDLÆVAL HISTORY covers the thousand years which divide the breaking up of the Roman dominion in the West from the formation of the modern European States-system, near the close of the fifteenth century. This interval between the old order and the new may, however, be conveniently viewed in two widely contrasted periods. During the first six hundred years, the forces which tend to anarchy and dissolution were apparently the stronger, excepting while they were held in check by the genius of Charlemagne. These six centuries are known as the Dark Ages. Their chief events were the migrations of the northern tribes; the repulse of the Saracens, who aimed to annex Europe to the dominion of the Caliphs; the revival of the Western Empire, and the rise of the Feudal System.

The next four centuries are more properly called the Middle Ages. They are marked by greater activity of the tendencies to order and civilization: tribes settle into nations, the remnant of the migratory impulse expending itself in pilgrimages and crusades; languages are developed and improved; chivalry refines the manners of the warrior, but itself declines, as feudal chiefs become subject to consolidated monarchies; learning is diffused, and industry attains something of its just dignity and importance.

Modern History may with equal advantage be divided into three parts, comprising respectively the Rise, Establishment, and Dissolution of the Balance of Power in Europe; the first period nearly coinciding with that of the discoveries and explorations upon the western continent, and

(13)

the opening of maritime traffic with the eastern; the second with the founding, and the third with the emancipation, of the greater number of European colonies in America.

This Manual includes, therefore, five Books:

I. The Dark Ages, A. D. 476–1096.

II. The Middle Ages, A. D. 1096–1492.

III. Discoveries in America, and Rise of States-system in Europe, A. D. 1492–1648.

IV. From the Peace of Westphalia to the Beginning of Revolutions in Europe, A. D. 1648–1789.

V. From the French Revolution to the Rise of the German Empire, A. D. 1789–1871.

BOOK I.

THE DARK AGES.
A. D. 476-1096.

PERIOD I. FROM THE FALL OF THE WESTERN EMPIRE TO THE RISE OF THE CARLOVINGIAN POWER, A. D. 476–732.

GEOGRAPHICAL SKETCH OF EUROPE.

1. THE field of Ancient History comprised only the shores of the Mediterranean and a part of Western Asia, the seat of empire having been gradually removed westward from Nineveh to Rome. Mediæval History is concerned with Europe and the adjacent coasts of Asia and Africa. Only within the Modern period have improvements in navigation, together with the increase of enterprise and intelligence, drawn the whole world within the circle of national and commercial intercourse.

2. Europe, though the smallest and least fertile of the continents, is the nursery whence art, learning, and civilization have been transplanted to the remotest regions of the globe. Its position at the center of the land-hemisphere, its varied coast-line deeply indented by inlets of the sea, and its islands richly endowed with metals and other valuable productions, have made it, if we may so say, the most sociable of the continents, inviting at every point the entrance of influences from abroad. Its climate is most favorable to human energy; the moderate fertility of its soil has developed the skill, industry, and strength of its inhabitants, while intensifying the idea of property, so essential to civilization, but always lacking in races which live indolently upon the bounties of a more indulgent Nature. That least favored of the European countries, formed by the marshy and sandy deltas of the Rhine, the Meuse, and the Scheldt — partly below the level of the ocean, and preserved from inundation only by incessant vigilance and toil — became, in fact, five centuries ago, the richest and most populous portion of the continent.

(15)

3. It is only needful to sketch those natural features of Europe, which have had an important influence upon its history. The three great southern peninsulas were, almost of necessity, for more than two thousand years its most civilized portion. Several ranges or systems of mountains, including the Pyrenees, Cevennes, and Alps, the Carpathian and Caucasian ranges, form a nearly continuous wall separating the scenes of the old civilization from those peculiar to the new. Northward of these mountains begins an immense plain, bounded on the west by the Atlantic and German Oceans, and the mountains of Norway; on the north by the Arctic Ocean, and on the east by the Ural Mountains and the Caspian Sea. The western portion of this plain is traversed by many small but important rivers, of which the Loire, Seine, Rhine, Elbe, Oder, and Vistula are chief.

The central and eastward portion is divided by a range of low hills, which separate the head-waters of the Dwina and Petchora, on the north, from those of the Volga, Don, and Dnieper, on the south. The northern section is an almost barren waste, marshy in summer and frozen in winter. The southern is fertile in grain, excepting the steppes bordering the Black Sea, which produce only a coarse grass. This great inland plain, though the scene of many interesting events between the ninth and the twelfth centuries, has only within the last two hundred years had any important share in the general interests of Europe.

4. Among European islands, we need only mention the most important of all, the British group. Situated in the current of the Gulf-stream, and thus endowed with a mild and equable climate, England is the home of the most vigorous race on the globe. Her natural gifts are those which stimulate and aid, instead of superseding, enterprise. The tin mines of Cornwall and the Scilly Isles first drew Phœnician mariners to explore those remote seas; and innumerable manufactures, supported by native coal and iron, have made England the great commercial center of the world. Her part in history before the Norman Conquest was comparatively unimportant. During the wars and tumults of the Dark Ages, Ireland, protected by her stormy seas, afforded the most secure and peaceful refuge for piety and learning; and the spirit of independence, nurtured by their insular position, has ever since made these islands an hospitable asylum for victims of oppression in other lands. The channel which separates England from the continent, though narrow, is sufficiently dangerous of navigation, owing to its variable winds and currents, to have formed a usually effective barrier against hostile invasions.

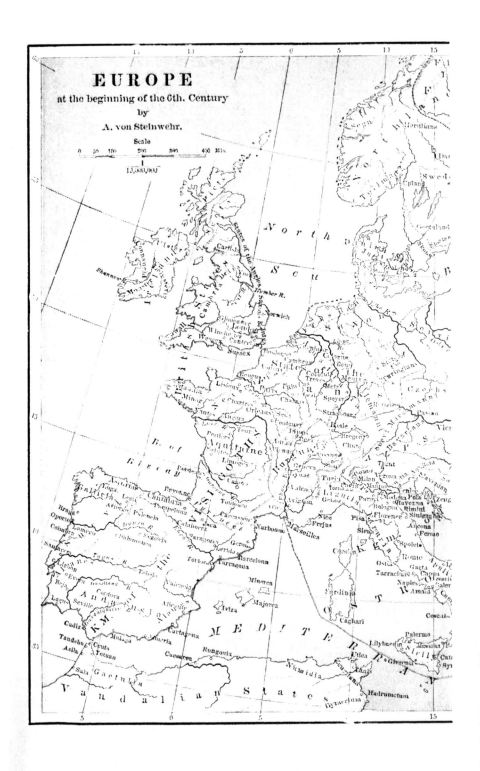

EUROPE
at the beginning of the 6th. Century
by
A. von Steinwehr.

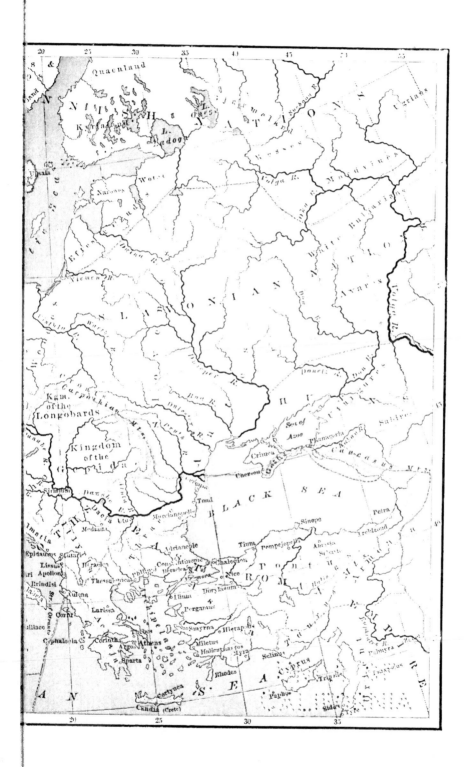

SETTLEMENTS OF THE NORTHERN NATIONS.

5. When Odoacer,* assuming the royal title, ended the illusory reign of Romulus Augustulus, the Teutonic or German race was already predominant in Europe. The *Visigothic* kingdom of Euric covered all Spain, and that part of Gaul which is bounded by the Loire on the north and by the Rhone on the east. His court at Arles was a center of learning and refinement, and nations even as distant as the Persians acknowledged by their embassies his preëminence among European sovereigns. His weaker descendants were driven south of the Pyrenees, but their kingdom in Spain lasted two hundred years, until it was overthrown by the Saracens, A. D. 711. The *Suevi* in north-western Spain were tributary to Euric. The *Ostrogoths* were at this time between the Danube and the Adriatic. The *Franks*, who soon by their conquests gave a new name to the greater part of ancient Gaul, were still mostly beyond its limits. Of the many tribes bearing this common name, the Ripuarians were on the Rhine near Cologne, and the more powerful Salians were between the Seine, the Meuse, and the Scheldt. The *Burgundians*, in the country comprising the valley of the Rhone and the Swiss lakes, had impressed their name on that great dominion which as kingdom, duchy, or county, though often dismembered and sometimes subdued, was yet for a thousand years to rival the power of the French kings.

6. Great numbers of the *Saxons*, whose piratical craft had vexed the coasts of Europe for a century, were now settled among the wooded inlets of northern Gaul, and with their kindred allies, the Angles, had made the important conquest of southern Britain. Of their eight kingdoms in that island, Wessex (West Saxony) became ultimately most powerful, and its chiefs were the ancestors of all English sovereigns but five, since the ninth century. The continental Saxons occupied the country from a little northward of the Rhine to the Baltic. The *Alemanni* possessed southern Germany, with Alsace and northern Switzerland. The *Thuringians* were between the head-waters of the Danube and those of the Elbe. The *Gepidæ* possessed the region now covered by Moldavia, Wallachia, and eastern Hungary. The *Vandals*, beside their original seats south and east of the Baltic, had been, since A. D. 459, masters of northern Africa, with Corsica, Sardinia, and the Balearic Isles.

7. In contrast with all these German tribes, colonies of Bretons, expelled from their native island by the Saxons, were mingled with the original Celtic inhabitants of north-western Gaul, and occupied the peninsula between the mouths of the Seine and Loire, which still bears their name. Scotland, Ireland, and the mountains of Wales were also inhabited by unconquered Celts. A fragment of the ancient empire was still main-

---

* See Anc. Hist., p. 361.

tained in the heart of Gaul, by Syagrius, who called himself "King of the Romans." In the great plains eastward from the Elbe dwelt the Slavonians, a pastoral people, more numerous but less powerful than the Teutons—ancestors of the modern Poles, Bohemians, Bulgarians, Illyrians, and a very large proportion of the Russians. The Finnish tribes occupied the frozen marshes to the northward. In the south-east, the Eastern or Greek Empire covered nearly the present dominion of the Turks.

8. The Germans, from whom most of the nations of Europe are in a greater or less degree descended, were described by Tacitus as distinguished from the degenerate races of the south by their huge and robust frames animated by unbounded energy, by their respect for the sacred dignity of women, and by "a sense they called honor, which led them to sacrifice their life rather than their word." In the time of Tacitus they were divided into fifty tribes, but these were united into five confederations: the Saxons, Franks, Alemanni, Burgundians, and Goths. The Saxons on the continent had no kings except in war, when the nobles chose by lot one of their own number to be their leader. The other tribes had each a royal family supposed to be descended from Odin, from which the king was elected by a free vote of his comrades; as the Ostrogoths had the Amals, the Visigoths the Balti, the Franks the Merovings, etc. The affairs of the Franks were settled in an assembly of all the warriors or freemen, held every year in March, or afterward in May.

9. In their northern forests the German tribes worshiped Odin as supreme, with Freya, his wife; Thor, the thunderer, their son; Baldur, the sun-god, and others of less importance. At the commencement of our period a majority of the Teutonic race was still pagan, but the Goths, Vandals, and Burgundians were Arian Christians. The Anglo-Saxons were instructed in Christianity by an embassy of monks, sent, A. D. 592, by Pope Gregory I.; and Winifrid of Devonshire became, in turn, the Apostle of Germany, to whose intrepid zeal 100,000 continental Saxons owed their conversion. He is better known by his Roman name and title, as St. Boniface.

10. THE FRANKISH KINGDOM. Chlodwig, or Clovis, succeeded his father as king of the Salian Franks, A. D. 481, and became the first German ruler of all France. He drew to his standard the other Frankish tribes, extinguished the remnants of Roman power in the person of Syagrius, and conquered the Alemanni in a great battle at Zülpich, A. D. 496. It was in consequence of this victory that he renounced the worship of Odin. His wife, a Burgundian princess, was a Christian; and his confidence in the sincerity of her faith led him to invoke "Clotilda's God" in the heat of the battle. He was subsequently baptized at Rheims, with 3,000 followers. The conversion of Clovis gained him the powerful support of the clergy, both against the pagan tribes and against the Arian

Goths and Burgundians. He defeated the latter A. D. 500, and, in 507, broke the power of the Visigoths by a battle near Poitiers.

The alliance of the Church with the Frankish monarchy made each, in its own sphere, preëminent in France. The clergy, representing Roman culture, and alone, as a class, skilled in the Latin language, served not only as mediators with the people, but as embassadors to foreign courts. The civil government south of the Loire was chiefly in their hands. On the other hand, French kings, from Clovis down, have vaunted their title of "Eldest Sons of the Church." All the barbarian sovereigns in Italy, Spain, and Gaul acknowledged the superiority of the Court of Constantinople; and it was therefore no unmeaning compliment when Anastasius, Emperor of the East, sent to Clovis the purple robe and diadem of a consul, thus raising his dignity, in the eyes of his Gallo-Roman subjects, to that of a lieutenant of the empire. By the murder of many Merovingian princes, Clovis made himself, toward the end of his life, sole monarch of the Franks.

11. The four sons of Clovis, upon his death in A. D. 511, divided his dominions among them. Theodoric, the eldest, reigned at Metz over the north-eastern country. The fourfold division into Austrasia, Neustria, Burgundy, and Aquitaine was effected somewhat later. Theodoric, while himself pursuing a savage career of violence, caused wise men, versed in ancient customs, to frame separate codes of laws for his Ripuarian, Alemannic, and Bavarian subjects, substituting Christian for pagan principles where these prevailed. Theodebert, his son, received gifts both from the Emperor Justinian and from Vitiges, king of the Italian Goths, as the price of his alliance in their war against each other. He defeated both armies near Pavia, A. D. 539, and then ravaged the peninsula, until famine and disease had destroyed two-thirds of his forces, and he withdrew beyond the Alps. To avert similar incursions in future, Justinian resigned the claim of the Eastern empire to the sovereignty of Gaul, and thenceforth the German kings placed their own instead of the imperial image upon their coins.

12. The fierce dissensions of the family of Clovis fill some of the darkest pages of history. Sigebert and Chilperic, his grandsons, married two daughters of the king of the Visigoths in Spain. Galswintha, the elder, was soon murdered by Fredegonde, a low-lived favorite of her husband, Chilperic, who rewarded the crime by raising the murderess to the throne of Neustria. Brunehaut, the wife of Sigebert, stirred him to revenge upon his brother the death of her sister; and the mutual hatreds of the two queens distracted the Frankish dominion, not only during the reigns of their husbands, but during the long minorities of their children and grandchildren.

The personal strife was aggravated by the rivalry between Neustria and

Austrasia, i. e., between the Romanized and the purely German party among the Franks. The people near the Rhine, continually reinforced by fresh arrivals of their countrymen, kept their German habits almost unmixed with Roman influences; while the Franks of the interior, though conquerors, were so far outnumbered by the Gallo-Roman population, that they soon adopted the language and culture of their subjects. Brunehaut, though queen of Austrasia, belonged to the Roman party, through her ardent love for literature, art, and Christianity. She was a friend and correspondent of Pope Gregory the Great, whom she aided in his scheme for the conversion of the Anglo-Saxons; and though herself a prey to cruel passions, she warred for fifty years against barbarian misrule, in the interests of Christian civilization. She was defeated at last by the Austrasian nobles, led by Pepin of Landen, and aided by the forces of Neustria and Burgundy. Falling into the hands of Clotaire, son of Fredegonde, the aged queen suffered three days of torture, ended by a brutal death.

13. Clotaire II. reigned as sole king of the Franks, A. D. 613–628. Under his son Dagobert the Merovingian race reached its greatest extent of dominion, only to sink immediately into indolence and incapacity. For a hundred years the kings bear no higher title in history than those of *fainéants*, or do-nothings, and *insensati*, or idiots. The real power was exercised by the bishops and great nobles, especially by a class of officials called Mayors of the Palace. Among these Pepin of Heristal, grandson of Pepin of Landen, became chief ruler in Austrasia, vanquished the Neustrian nobility in a decisive battle at Testri, A. D. 687, and made himself master of France, which he governed twenty-seven years with great prudence and success. The Merovingian king, a mere phantom of royalty, was shown to the people once a year at the Field of March; at other times he was held in a sort of mild captivity.

Charles Martel, the still more powerful son of Pepin, established his authority over the three kingdoms of Burgundy, Neustria, and Austrasia. He divided many rich lands of the Church among his followers, on condition of military service, and thus laid the foundation of the feudal system in France. (See §§ 76, 78.) The great crisis of the Arab invasions — soon to be described under the history of the Saracens — led to the rise of his family into an important dynasty of kings.

RECAPITULATION.

At the fall of the Western Empire, Europe was largely governed by Teutonic tribes, of which the Goths, Franks, and Saxons were most powerful. The few unconquered Celts were on the west, and the yet uncivilized Slavonians on the east of the Germans; while the Finns occupied the north, and the Greek empire a part of the south of Europe. The German worshipers of Odin and Thor were superior in virtue, though inferior in civilization, to the Romans. England was Christianized through the teachings of Augustine; Germany, through those of St. Boniface. Clovis, king of the Franks, allied himself with the Church, and received the consular dignity from the emperor of the East. The crimes of his successors produced a century of anarchy and misery in the Frankish dominions. The Merovingians then sinking into incapacity, the "Mayors" gained power, and the Carlovingian race became supreme.

OSTROGOTHIC KINGDOM IN ITALY, A. D. 493–554.

14. In Italy the dominion of the Herulian Odoacer gave way, after seventeen years, to that of Theodoric, king of the East Goths. This great leader had been educated as a hostage at the court of Constantinople, where he added Greek discipline to Gothic energy; and under his firm and wise rule of thirty-three years, peace and prosperity returned to the half depopulated country. Though the Gothic soldiers received one-third of the lands of the peninsula, they equally shared the taxes and were forced to respect the rights of their Italian neighbors; and while the former were ready at any moment to follow their chiefs to war, the latter were encouraged and protected in the industrious arts of peace. Two consuls, of whom one was chosen by the emperor, the other by the Gothic king, preserved the venerated forms of Roman government. All the Teutonic nations looked up to Theodoric as their head. During the minority of his grandson, Amalaric, who was also a grandson of Euric, he became ruler of the West Goths, and his united dominions extended from Sicily to the Danube, and from Belgrade to the Atlantic. When Amalaric became of age, he was lifted upon the shields of the Visigothic chiefs, and became king of Spain, A. D. 522.

15. Himself an Arian, Theodoric protected all forms of religion among his subjects. The shops, synagogues, and dwellings of the Jews having been burnt in several cities during fanatical riots, the mobs were compelled to make good the property they had destroyed. This impartial justice turned their rage against the king; and the last days of Theodoric were imbittered by the proof that, while laboring for the best interests of his people, he had failed to win their love. Boëthius,* the most illustrious member of the Senate, and one of the brightest ornaments of the

* In his prison at Pavia, Boëthius wrote an admirable treatise on the "Consolation of Philosophy," which was afterward translated into Saxon by Alfred the Great.—— Cassiodorus, the learned secretary of Theodoric, founded at Ravenna the oldest of modern public libraries. After thirty years of high office at court, he retired at the age of seventy to a monastery which he established at Squillace; and during his thirty remaining years—for his life was prolonged to nearly a century—he gave an impulse to monastic learning which lasted through the Middle Ages. He expended large sums for manuscripts, which he encouraged the monks to copy; and during the tumults of the following centuries, convent libraries were the safe depositaries of the learning of the western world.

court, was put to death on a charge of plotting with the Eastern emperor for the expulsion of the Goths from Italy. The execution of his father-in-law, the venerable Symmachus, soon followed; but remorse for these acts hastened the death, also, of Theodoric, who died A. D. 526.

16. His grandson, Athalaric, succeeded to the Ostrogothic kingdom at the age of ten years, under the regency of his mother, Amalasontha. The reign of this Gothic queen, aided by the experience of Cassiodorus, was as wise and beneficent as that of her father; but her son disappointed the anxious care which she expended upon his education. He rebelled against her, incited by his barbarous companions, who taught him to despise the joint authority of a woman and a philosopher; and at the age of sixteen this last of the Amals died of intemperance. His mother, in spite of the Gothic law or custom which excluded women from the throne, plotted to retain sovereign power in her own hands, while conferring the name of king upon her cousin Theodatus, whom she married. But Theodatus, incensed at being made the tool of his ambitious wife, ordered Amalasontha to be strangled in her bath, A. D., 534.

17. The Emperor Justinian, now reigning at Constantinople, gladly asserted his supremacy by interfering as the avenger of Amalasontha. His great general, Belisarius, who had lately overthrown the Vandal kingdom in Africa, landed with a small force in Sicily, quickly subdued that island, and wrested southern Italy from the Goths. Rome was surrendered without a blow, by its senate and clergy, A. D. 536; but Vitiges, the successor of Theodatus, mustered a powerful army and besieged Belisarius more than a year in the Eternal City. The sepulcher of Hadrian, now the Castle of St. Angelo, was then first used as a fortress, and the beautiful Greek statues which adorned it were hurled down upon the heads of the besiegers.

In a single assault the Goths lost 30,000 men; and, at length, Vitiges was compelled to draw off his reduced army to Ravenna, leaving all Italy to Belisarius. Ten thousand Burgundians, who had come to the aid of the Goths, destroyed the splendid city of Milan; and the next year Theodebert, their Frankish sovereign, passed the Alps with 100,000 men, disguising his intentions until he fell, almost at the same moment, upon both the Gothic and the Roman army near Pavia, and gained a complete victory. (See § 11.)

18. Ravenna, which could not be taken by force, was at length reduced by famine. The Goths, weary of the unfortunate reign of Vitiges, begged Belisarius himself to become their king. He pretended to accept their offer; but as soon as the keys of the fortress were in his hands, he declared that he held them only as the faithful subject and lieutenant of Justinian. Vitiges exchanged his uncomfortable crown for the rank of senator, and ample estates in the Eastern empire.

19. Pavia alone, with its garrison of 1,000 Goths, still held out; but as soon as Belisarius had been recalled to Constantinople, the new king, Totila, commenced his rapid and triumphant march for the recovery of Italy. Many cities which had welcomed Belisarius as a deliverer, had now suffered long enough from the fraud and oppression of the Byzantine officials, to sigh for a return of the Gothic rule. Rome was retaken by Totila, A. D. 546; its senators were carried away to Campanian prisons, and its people were scattered in exile. Belisarius, returning, soon regained the city, and defeated the Goths in a decisive battle. But the great general was fettered by the ungenerous suspicions of his master. Totila, A. D. 549, again took Rome, following up his success by the conquest of Sicily, Sardinia, and Corsica, and the invasion of Greece. An embassy, undertaken by the Pope himself, now induced Justinian to send a sufficient force, under Narses, for the recovery of Italy. In a great battle near Tagina, Totila was slain, and Rome for the fifth time in one reign changed masters, A. D. 552.

20. Teias, the last king of the Italian Goths, implored aid from the German rulers of France, but before it could arrive he was killed in a battle at Cumæ, A. D. 553. The following autumn, 75,000 Germans crossed the Alps, and ravaged all Italy as far as Messina and the Straits of Otranto. But the Ostrogothic kingdom, after sixty years' duration (A. D. 493–553) had already yielded to the lieutenants of the empire, who ruled all Italy with the title of Exarchs of Ravenna. The Goths either emigrated in quest of fresh lands or became absorbed into the mass of the people. Narses, the first and greatest of the exarchs, reigned A. D. 554–568. The territories wrested from the Vandals were likewise erected into the exarchate of Africa.

21. THE LOMBARD KINGDOM, A. D. 572–774. The Ostrogoths, during the time of their power, effectually guarded the line of the Danube against fresh incursions of the northern barbarians; but during the long wars in Italy, the Gepidæ crossed the river and occupied many unguarded fortresses. To expel these intruders, Justinian called in the Lombards, or Long-Beards, a savage though Teutonic race, who were pictured to the terrified imaginations of the Greeks as drinking human blood with the mouths of dogs. With the aid of the Huns, a still fiercer horde of Asiatic savages, the Lombards, in thirty years, conquered and exterminated the Gepidæ. The Huns were rewarded with the territories now comprising Wallachia, Moldavia, Transylvania, and the parts of Hungary beyond the Danube, where their empire lasted 230 years. (See § 54.)

22. The Lombards, under Alboin their king, turned upon Italy. As if to further their plans, Narses had been degraded, and replaced by the incompetent Longinus. Though the strong walls of Pavia withstood a three years' siege, the rest of the country, as far as Ravenna and Rome, was easily conquered and divided into thirty duchies. Upon the death of Clepho, the successor of Alboin, the thirty dukes continued ten years (A. D. 574–584) to govern in council without a king. But this divided government was insufficient defense against the Greeks on the east and the Franks on the west.

Autharis, son of Clepho, receiving the crown, successfully withstood three Frankish invasions, and extended his kingdom from the Rhætian Alps to the southern extremity of Italy, where he founded the great duchy of Benevento. His widow, Theodolinda, was intrusted by the nation with the choice of his successor. She chose Agilulf, duke of Turin; reclaimed him, with many of his subjects, from the Arian to the Catholic faith, and was rewarded by Pope Gregory I. with the famous Iron Crown, which was said to have been forged from one of the nails of the True Cross.

23. Italy was now divided between the Lombard kingdom and the ex-archate of Ravenna — the latter including a great part of the recent states of the Church, beside Venice, Naples, and the Calabrian coast. The Lombards never mingled, as the Goths had done, on friendly terms with the Italians. The rude manners of the former and the cowardly self-indulgence of the latter were objects of reciprocal disdain. Nevertheless, the long-bearded monsters of the north had already acquired some of the best fruits of civilization: the system of laws framed by their king, Rotharis, is esteemed the best of the barbarian codes,* and their kingdom in Italy was more peaceful and prosperous than any other which had been formed from the fragments of the empire.

RECAPITULATION.

Theodoric the Great founded the second barbarian kingdom in Italy, and bestowed one-third of its lands upon his Ostrogothic followers. Peace, justice, and liberality were the glories of his reign, but its end was marred by criminal severity, and he died burdened with remorse. His daughter, Amalasontha, succeeded to the sovereignty, first as regent for her son, Athalaric, and afterward in the name of her husband, Theodatus. Her violent death was avenged in the invasion and subsequent conquest of Italy by Belisarius. Rome was thrice taken by the Eastern Romans, twice reconquered by the Goths. Vitiges was deposed, Totila and Teias slain, and the Gothic kings of Italy were succeeded by the Greek exarchs of Ravenna.

After the extermination of the Gepidæ, the Huns founded a kingdom near the Danube, while the Lombards proceeded to the conquest of Italy. Thirty Lombard dukes formed a feudal aristocracy. The laws of King Rotharis were the most civilized of the barbarian codes.

---

* Six codes of laws were in force among the Lombards: the Roman, Gothic, Salian, Ripuarian, Alemannic, and the Lombard of King Rotharis. Any man, when summoned into court, might declare by which code he lived and desired to be judged; but unless he could prove himself a member of a Teutonic tribe, the Roman law prevailed. The barbarian codes were all based upon the immemorial usages of the German race; but assuming their permanent form after the respective nations were Christianized, they were largely modified by the precepts of the Old and New Testaments.

THE EMPIRE.

24. Under the Roman name and forms, the empire at Constantinople maintained the splendor without the power of its great founder. After the death of Arcadius, A. D. 408, it was governed first by the minister Anthe'mius, then, during the long minority and after the death of Theodosius II., by his sister Pulcheria, whose able and peaceful reign continued forty years. Her husband, Marcian (A. D. 453–457), was succeeded in turn by Leo the Thracian, Zeno, Anastasius, and Justin; but the fifty years of their successive reigns present nothing worthy of our notice.

The last-named emperor was a Bulgarian peasant, raised to the throne by reason of his soldierly virtues. The reign of his nephew, Justinian, was long and eventful. Its first five years were A. D. 527–565. absorbed in a costly and unprofitable war with Persia, terminated by what was fondly called the "Endless Peace." At the close of this war, Constantinople was convulsed by a sedition, which, breaking out between the *blue* and the *green* factions in the hippodrome, came near to lay the whole city in ashes and to revolutionize the empire. A nephew of Anastasius was proclaimed; 30,000 persons were slain in the tumult; but at length, through the firmness of the Empress Theodora, and the energy of Belisarius, the imperial party was triumphant. To punish the mob, the games of the hippodrome were suppressed during several years.

25. In the year following the sedition, Belisarius conquered the Vandal kingdom in Africa, more than a century from its foundation by Genseric (A. D. 429–533). Gelimer, the captive king, and a long train of nobles, adorned the victor's triumph, which was the first ever celebrated in the city of Constantine. Sardinia, Corsica, and the smaller islands of the western Mediterranean became subject to the exarchs of Africa. The Italian Goths rejoiced in the overthrow of the Vandals, who had injured them in the person of Amalafrida, sister of Theodoric the Great, and wife of Thrasimond, the Vandal king. The conquest of Africa was, however, soon followed by that of the Gothic kingdom, which has been described in §§ 17–20.

26. During the same year with the capture of Ravenna by Belisarius, a vast horde of Bulgarians swept over the Grecian peninsula, destroying thirty-two cities, and dragging away 120,000 captives. Another horde crossed the Hellespont and ravaged Asia. Twenty years later, the Danube being frozen, a multitude of Bulgarians and Slavonians overran Thrace, and encamped almost within sight of Constantinople. In A. D. 559. the panic which filled the court and the capital, the aged Belisarius was called from his well-earned repose to assume command. By a swift and decisive movement of his forces, he again saved the empire. But the conqueror of two kingdoms, the defender of the throne against both Persians and barbarians, the faithful servant of an ungrateful and jealous sovereign, was now too popular to be secure. The shouts of joy and gratitude which welcomed his return to Constantinople, awakened the suspicions of Justinian. Three years later, Belisarius was thrown into a dungeon on a false charge of treason; his possessions were confiscated, and though he was restored to the light a few months before his death, this event was hastened by the harshness with which he had been treated.

27. During the reign of Justinian the culture of silk was introduced into Greece, the eggs of the silkworm concealed in a hollow cane having been secretly brought from China by two Persian monks. The production and manufacture of this curious material were eventually extended to Sicily, whence they spread into Spain, Italy, and France, and gave employment to many thousands of people.

The reign of Justinian was still more distinguished by the number and grandeur of his public buildings, among which the metropolitan church of Santa Sophia — esteemed by the emperor as rivaling the glories of Solomon's Temple — was the chief. More substantial monuments of the period are found in the multiplied fortifications, which, however, revealed the weakness rather than the strength of the empire. The Danube was guarded by more than eighty fortresses. Long walls protected the friendly Goths of the Crimea from their northern neighbors; and the "rampart of Gog and Magog," built from the Black to the Caspian Sea, at the joint expense of the Persian king and the emperor, served to protect the dominions of both from the barbarous hordes which overswept southern Russia. Beyond the Euphrates, the three fortresses of Amida, Edessa, and Dara defended the Persian frontier.

28. Justinian suppressed the schools of Athens, and abolished the consulship, which, from an august dignity, had descended into a mere useless and expensive show. The chief glory of his reign is derived from the Code, the Pandects, and the Institutes, which, compiled under his direction by the ablest lawyers of his time, form the foundation of civil law for all the European nations. The Institutes contained the elementary principles of law; the Code was a condensed and revised edition of the enactments of all the emperors since Hadrian; the Pandects were a digest of precedents and decisions of the wisest judges, which had been accumulating a thousand years since the preparation of the Twelve Tables, and now filled thousands of volumes, "which no fortune could purchase and no capacity could comprehend." To extend the advantages of the new system, law-schools were founded or newly endowed at Rome, Constantinople, and Beirût.

29. The later years of Justinian were marked by fresh and formidable movements among the northern nations. The TURKS, a tribe of iron-

forgers from the Altai, issued from their mountains and established a new empire in Tartary. They subdued the Huns or Avars on the Til. A remnant of the conquered people fled to the Caucasus, where, hearing of the Greek empire, they resolved to claim its protection and enlist in its service. Justinian received them with liberality, and encouraged them to invade the Bulgarian and Slavonian territories. Within ten years they destroyed many tribes, imposed tribute and service on the rest, and extended their camps to the Elbe. Though Justinian afterward renounced their friendship for the more powerful alliance of the Turks, they were able, in the reign of his successor, to conquer the present territories of Hungary and European Turkey, and establish the kingdom of their "Chagans" which lasted two hundred and thirty years. (See §§ 21, 54.)

30. Justin II. resigned his crown, A. D. 574, in favor of Tiberius, captain of his guards. Eight years later, this emperor was succeeded by Maurice, who, unable to deliver Italy from the Lombards at the request of the Pope, invited the Franks to be his substitutes. Childebert, grandson of Clovis, was the last of the Merovingians who crossed the Alps. Defeated in two expeditions, he was more successful in a third; but for want of support from the Greeks, he made no permanent conquests. A sedition arising in the Eastern army, Phocas was declared emperor, and Maurice, with his five sons, was murdered at Chalcedon. Heraclius, exarch of Africa, refused tribute to the usurper, and sent his son with a fleet to Constantinople. Phocas was dragged from his palace and beheaded, and Heraclius the Younger was crowned.

A. D. 602.

31. Chosroes II., now king of Persia, took advantage of the first revolution to invade the empire and subjugate all Syria, Egypt, and Africa as far as Tripoli; while another Persian army, advancing to the Bosporus, took Chalcedon, and maintained its camp ten years in sight of Constantinople. Heraclius, whose empire was thus suddenly reduced to a few maritime districts, conveyed his army by sea to the borders of Syria and Cilicia, and on the very spot where Alexander of Macedon had, nearly a thousand years before,[*] defeated the ancestor of Chosroes, gained a decisive victory over the Persian host. In a second expedition he penetrated to the heart of Persia, and forced Chosroes to recall his armies from the Nile and the Bosporus; in a third, by a battle fought above the buried ruins of Nineveh, he destroyed a great part of the Persian forces, A. D. 627. The glory of the Sassanidæ died with Chosroes.

---

[*] Battle of Issus, B. C. 333. Hallam well remarks: "That prince may be said to have stood on the verge of both hemispheres of time, whose youth was crowned with the last victories over the successors of Artaxerxes, and whose age was clouded by the first calamities of Mohammedan invasion."

He was murdered by his son, and the Second Persian Empire fell into a confusion only ended by the Mohammedan conquest.

32. The Eastern Roman Empire, exhausted by the extraordinary efforts of Heraclius, fell in his old age into a rapid decline. The Saracens seized the provinces which he had rescued from the Persians, and the boundaries of the empire were gradually narrowed until they included only Constantinople and its suburbs. Of the two sons of Heraclius, who received the title of Augustus during his life, the elder, Constantine III., only survived his father a few months, and the younger, Heracleonas, was deposed by

A. D. 641–668.

the Senate. Constans II. came to the throne; but having, a few years later, ordered the death of his brother Theodosius, he was overwhelmed with remorse and went into voluntary exile. He was murdered in Sicily by a slave. Constantine IV., his son, shared with his two brothers the name, but kept for himself the substance of imperial power.

33. Justinian II. (A. D. 685–711) outraged the people by the rapacity and cruelty of his ministers, and was driven into exile among the Tartars, while Leontius and Absimar successively occupied the throne. He returned after ten years to execute a barbarous revenge. Ravenna was plundered and its chief citizens massacred, and an army was sent to destroy the free city of Cherson, in the Crimea. These distant cities, whose wealth attracted the avarice of Justinian, were the principal emporia of the trade between India and Europe, and to the great commercial importance of their situations was owing their recovery from so great a calamity. But the last act had filled the measure of the emperor's iniquities. Exiles from many provinces assembled in the Crimea, and proclaiming a new emperor, sailed for Constantinople, where Justinian and his son were put to a sudden and violent death. With them ended the race of Heraclius, which had ruled the Eastern world a hundred years.

34. The six years between the fall of the Heraclian and the rise of the Isaurian dynasty were filled by the three reigns of Philippicus, Anastasius

A. D. 717–741.

II., and Theodosius III. Leo III., the Isaurian, then raised himself from the army to the throne, and by his great abilities arrested the tendencies to decline, earning the title of Second Founder of the Eastern Empire. The name Byzantine, which modern historians apply to the reformed empire, dates properly from his reign. Though Greek was henceforth the language of the court, the church, and the people, yet the control of the government was usually in the hands of Asiatics—particularly Armenians, who filled the highest military commands. The artisans and middle class were commonly Greek; the lowest orders, including porters and day-laborers, were Slavonian.

35. Leo's defense of Constantinople against the flower of the Moslem force (A. D. 716–718) was one of the most brilliant exploits of that war-like age, and formed a turning-point in the relations of the Eastern emperors with the caliphs. What his arms had saved from destruction, his wise government continued to consolidate and protect. The highest moral and material civilization of their time was found in the dominions of Leo and his successors. The unchangeable regularity of Roman law maintained that social security which is the vital breath of commerce; and the prosperity of the trading class, as well as a great increase of free labor upon the soil, contributed in turn to the stability of the reorganized empire.

36. An attempted religious reform led to the war of Iconoclasm, which for one hundred and twenty years agitated Christendom, and was a chief cause of the reëstablishment of the Western Empire. The use, and by degrees the worship, of images and pictures, had crept into the Christian Church, especially in the great cities where wealth and luxury encouraged art. The taunts of the Jews and Arabs were, however, echoed by the more simple and severe of the Christian sects, who heard with horror the charge of idolatry applied to the usages of the metropolitan churches. Leo III. had imbibed among his native mountains a hatred of images which made him the first of the Iconoclasts. The details of the controversy belong, however, to the ensuing period; for the great power which, issuing from the sandy deserts of Arabia, threatened, to all human view, to overwhelm Christianity itself, must for the moment take precedence of the strife which divided the Christian nations.

RECAPITULATION.

The Eastern empire kept its name and forms 1078 years after its separation from the Western. Under Justinian, the great general Belisarius gained important victories over the Persians, subdued the *Nika* sedition in the capital, conquered the Vandals in Africa and the Goths in Italy, and repeatedly put to rout barbarian invaders of the empire. Reign of Justinian was commemorated by many buildings and fortifications, but still more by his great works of jurisprudence, which still form the basis of the civil law of Europe. The Turks at this period first appear in history, driving the Huns into Europe, and fixing their own empire in Tartary. The emperors Justin II., Tiberius, Maurice, and Phocas preceded the rise of the Heraclian dynasty, which ruled the empire A. D. 610–711. Heraclius I. drove back the armies of Chosroes II., who had extended the Persian dominion nearly to its ancient western limits. From this point the Persian empire fell, and the Greek rapidly declined, until Leo the Isaurian, by a complete reorganization, gave it new vigor. He began the war against images, which ultimately destroyed the Byzantine power in Italy.

THE SARACENS.

37. Mohammed, the camel-driver of Mecca, in his journeys to the Syrian fairs, met travelers of all nations and religions. The Christian Church was at that time rent by schism and weakened by luxury; the

Jews had to a great degree lost their religious character in that of traders; the Persians were worshipers of fire; the Arabians still adored the sun, moon, and stars. Mohammed conceived the grand idea of raising upon the ruins of all these creeds the worship of One God, of whom he aspired to be considered the prophet and apostle. How much of his extraordinary career must be ascribed to sincere though fanatical enthusiasm, and how much to selfish ambition and willful deceit, can probably never be decided.

38. Three years were spent in privately winning fourteen converts, before Mohammed publicly claimed the office of a prophet; and he dwelt ten years more within the walls of Mecca, preaching to a slowly increasing congregation concerning his own mission, the sinfulness of idolatry, and the unity of God. The tribe of Koreish, to which he belonged, were incensed at his pretensions, and vowed neither to eat nor drink until they had slain the self-appointed prophet. Mohammed fled with his friend Abu Beker to Medina, where he had already a powerful party; and this Hegira, or Flight, A. D. 622, is the era from which Mussulmans still date their lunar year of 354 days.

39. Within seven years all Arabia submitted to Mohammed; and in the same year with the conquest of Mecca, A. D. 630, his forces first came into collision with those of the Eastern Empire, at Muta, near Damascus. The Prophet now opened to his followers a career of conquest, in which religious zeal sharpened and sustained their military valor. Its motives may be found in the Koran. * "The sword is the key of heaven and of hell. A drop of blood shed in the cause of God, a night spent in arms, is of more avail than two months of fasting and prayer. Whoever falls in battle, his sins are forgiven." The Moslems were assured that no man can die until the moment appointed him by Fate; at that moment he would fall dead in his house or expire in his bed; until its arrival he is safe under the darts of the enemy. Under such a system no peril can be feared or avoided; and the soldiers of Islam have been distinguished a thousand years for their reckless and dauntless bravery.

40. Within a hundred years, under the "caliphs," or successors of Mohammed, the Saracen empire had extended from the boundaries of India to the Atlantic, and embraced Persia, Syria, Egypt, Northern

A. D. 640.　　Africa, and Spain. Even Scythian shepherds burned their idols at the command of the Prophet. Alexandria, then the greatest commercial city in the world, was taken by a siege, bravely

---

* Mohammed claimed to have received from the archangel Gabriel a volume bound in silk and gems, written with a finger of light, and containing the Divine Decrees. He made known its contents only in successive fragments, which were written out by his disciples, on palm-leaves or on the shoulder-bones of sheep, to be distributed among the faithful. After his death they were collected and published by his successor, Abu Beker.

resisted for fourteen months. Twice during the next four years it was reconquered by the forces of the empire, but twice recaptured by Amrou, the Mohammedan general. More enlightened than his brethren of that period, Amrou would willingly have spared the Library, which since the days of Ptolemy Philadelphus — though partly burned during the visit of Cæsar — had been the glory of the Egyptian capital. But the caliph Omar interposed, with the narrow bigotry peculiar to ignorance. "If these writings of the Greeks," said he, "agree with the Koran, they are useless, and need not be preserved; if they disagree, they are pernicious, and ought to be destroyed." The inestimable manuscripts were distributed for kindling among the 4,000 baths of the city; and such was their multitude that six months were required for their consumption.

41. Constantinople was twice besieged, once for seven years (A. D. 668–675), and again for thirteen months (see § 35), by the Moslem hosts. It was only saved by Greek Fire, a compound of naphtha, sulphur, and pitch, which was either poured in death-dealing torrents over the ramparts, projected in red-hot balls, arrows, and javelins, or blown through tubes from the front and sides of ships, which thus assumed the appearance of fire-breathing monsters. It exploded with great noise, heavy smoke, and a fierce, almost inextinguishable flame. Ignorance increased the terror of its victims. The secret of its composition was said to have been revealed by an angel to Constantine the Great, and it was closely kept more than four centuries by the Greeks.

42. At the western extremity of the ancient empire, the Saracens gained a more sudden and easy victory. Count Julian, a Spaniard who commanded the African fortress of Ceuta, had been injured by his sovereign, Roderick, who has sometimes been called the Last of the Goths. Unable to revenge himself by his own arms, the faithless chief betrayed his trust, and led a Moslem host into the heart of Spain. This advanced guard ravaged the beautiful province of Andalusia, and the next year a still larger army of Arabs and Moors crossed the A. D. 711. strait. In a seven days' battle near Cadiz, the strength of the Gothic kingdom was broken. Roderick was drowned in the Guadalete, and in a few months the Saracens had overrun the peninsula from Gibraltar to the Bay of Biscay. A few brave Goths retired with their prince, Pelayo, to the mountains of Asturias, and became the founders of the modern kingdom of Spain.

43. Musa, the Saracen emir, jealous of Tarik, his victorious lieutenant, followed with yet greater forces, occupied all the principal cities, and made Cordova the seat of a kingdom which lasted in Spain nearly eight hundred years. Colonies of Moslems from Syria and Arabia flocked into the conquered country, and Spain became as completely Arab as it had before been Gothic, Roman, or Phœnician. Successive troops of invaders crossed the Pyrenees, and reduced all south-western France between the Garonne and the Rhone to the obedience of the Prophet. The new dominion which was ultimately to overthrow the Eastern empire, thus came face to face with that which was already rising upon the ruins of the Western.

44. The Merovingian monarchy was distracted between the weakness of the king and the strength of the nobles. Southern Gaul had never been thoroughly subdued by the Franks. Many territorial lords aimed to make themselves independent, and one of them, Eudes of Aquitaine, had even assumed the title of king. He defeated the Mussulmans in some of their earlier incursions; but returning in greater force, under Abderrahman, their ablest and most experienced general, they had now fixed their capital at Narbonne, while their cavalry overran the country as far as Lyons and Besançon, marking their progress with the smoking ruins of once flourishing towns.

It was their purpose, after conquering France and Germany, to follow the Danube to its mouth, overturn the Greek empire, and thus surround the Mediterranean Sea with one great Moslem dominion. To this end troops were collected from Syria, Egypt, and the Barbary states, as well as from Spain; while Charles Martel, son and successor of Pepin d'Heristal as Mayor of the Austrasian Franks, drew to his standard all the Teutonic tribes from the forests of Germany and the marshes of the North Sea.

45. Near the center of France, between Tours and Poitiers, the two hosts of Europe and Asia, Germans and Arabs, stood seven days confronting each other, only partial skirmishes foretokening the great battle which

A. D. 732.

was to decide whether modern Europe should be Mohammedan or Christian. At length the Saracen horsemen spurred against the German spears, which stood "like a wall of iron, a rampart of ice," to receive them. The combat lasted all day, and was renewed the next morning with unremitting fury; but at length the Arabs gave way; Abderrahman was slain; the other generals quarreled among themselves, and each sought his own safety by a separate and silent flight. Their deserted camp was found filled with the wealth of the East and the spoils of France. Charles with his Germans had gained one of the most complete and decisive battles in the world's history. Though retaining for twenty years their foothold in Septimania, the Saracens made no more serious attempts at conquest north of the Pyrenees.

46. The Empire of the Caliphs, soon divided in itself, was indeed unable to avenge its defeat. The house of Ommiyah, which had ruled

A. D. 661-750.

ninety years, was overthrown, and the Abbassides, descendants of the uncle of Mohammed, rose into power. Spain, however, revolted, A. D. 755, in favor of the last of the Ommiades—a youth named Abdalrahman, who, by a wonderful series of adventures,

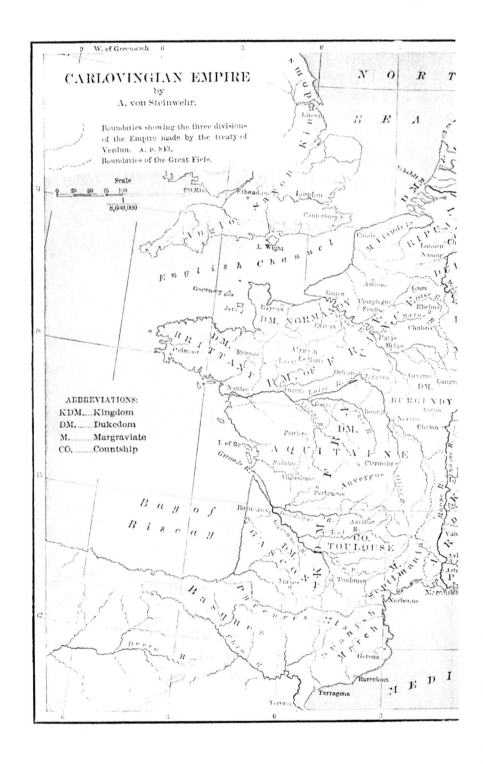

CARLOVINGIAN EMPIRE
by
A. von Steinwehr.

Boundaries showing the three divisions
of the Empire made by the treaty of
Verdun. A. D. 843.
Boundaries of the Great Fiefs.

Scale
0   25   50   75   100   200 Mls.
1
8,600,000

ABBREVIATIONS:
KDM....Kingdom
DM.......Dukedom
M........Margraviate
CO. ......Countship

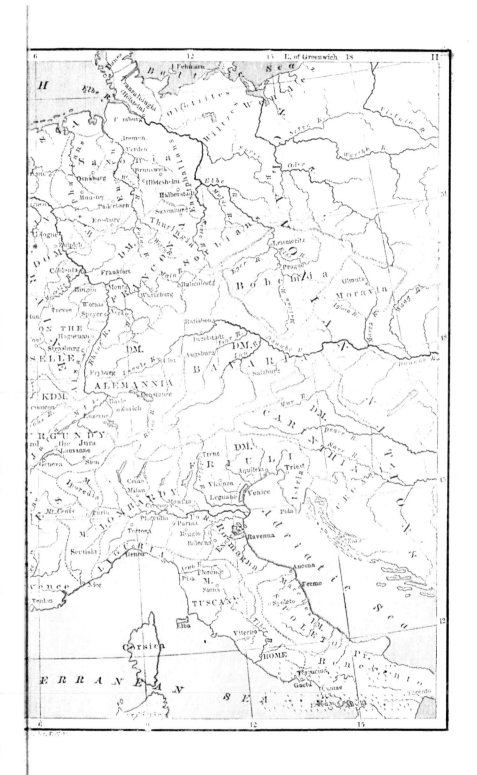

escaped the massacre which overwhelmed his family, and lived to establish an independent kingdom at Cordova. This kingdom, itself too weak to disturb the repose of Christian Europe, was a rampart against Saracen invasion on the side of Spain. The descendants of Ali, cousin and first convert of Mohammed, reigned at the same time in Persia and Mauritania; and the three dynasties — the Abbassides of Bagdad, the Ommiades and the Fatimites * — became the heads, respectively, of the *black*, the *white*, and the *green* factions, into which the Moslem empire was now permanently divided.

RECAPITULATION.

The Saracen Empire had its rise in fanaticism, and was extended by the sword, the Flight of Mohammed from Mecca to Medina being the era of its chronology. His successors reigned from the Indus to the Atlantic. Their conquest of Spain was aided by the treachery of Count Julian; but their progress in France was checked by the victory of Charles Martel, near Tours. Their empire was soon divided, the Abbassides obtaining the caliphate in Asia, the Ommiades in Spain, the Fatimites in Persia, Egypt, and northern Africa.

PERIOD II. FROM THE BATTLE OF TOURS TO THE BATTLE OF FONTENAYE, A. D. 732–841.

47. The tide of Saracen invasion having rolled back, two powers are seen arising in the West, whose varying relations with each other form the framework of Mediæval History. One is the restored Empire; the other, the temporal sovereignty of the popes.

48. While the exarchs of Ravenna were losing power in Italy, the bishops of Rome were often the only protectors of their people against barbarian incursions. The neglected duties and forfeited honors of the temporal rulers fell to them; and while still professing themselves the obedient subjects of the emperors, they began to be regarded as not only the spiritual but the civil heads of society. The war of the Iconoclasts completed the separation thus begun between Italy and the empire. Casting off the shadow of imperial authority, Rome A. D. 751. resumed the form of a republic, the bishop being the chief magistrate or prince of the city. Two successive popes, Gregory II. and III., excommunicated the agents who were charged with the destruction of the images.

The emperor sent forces to plunder Rome and arrest the latter pope.

So called from Fatima, the favorite daughter of Mohammed and the wife of Ali.

M. H.—3.

His fleet was defeated and destroyed off Ravenna, but the Lombards seizing the opportunity, besieged the papal city. Gregory III. appealed to the great mayor, Charles Martel—who had now extended his power throughout France by the conquest of Burgundy, Provence, and Aquitaine—offering him the titles of Patrician and Consul, and hinting that Rome was ready to revive the empire of the West in the person of its most powerful sovereign. Before the desired aid could be rendered, the pope, the emperor, and the mayor all died within one year, A. D. 741.

49. Pepin the Short, son of Charles, with the approbation of Pope Zacharias, exchanged his inadequate title of Mayor of the Palace for that of King of the Franks. Astolphus, king of the Lombards, had now seized Ravenna, put an end to the exarchate, 185 years from its foundation by Narses, and was threatening Rome. Pope Stephen II. crossed the Alps to implore the aid of Pepin, who the next spring led a powerful army into Italy, besieged Pavia, and extorted from Astolphus a promise to cede all the cities of the exarchate to the pope. As soon as the Franks had retired, the promise was forgotten. Astolphus ravaged the environs of Rome, and demanded the surrender of the chief pontiff himself.

With redoubled energy Pepin recrossed the Alps, and chastised the Lombard so severely that he was glad to buy peace with
A. D. 755.
a third part of his treasures and the keys of twenty-two towns, which were laid upon the altar of St. Peter. The sovereignty of these towns remained to the victor, but their rich revenues, with the feudal control of multitudes of vassals, went to the pope, who thus became the most powerful baron of Rome. The authority of the exarchs in the imperial city was transferred to the Carlovingian king, with the title of "Patrician." In his name money was coined, justice administered; and even the choice and consecration of the popes was subject to his supervision.

50. Since their overthrow by Charles Martel, the Arabs had kept possession of the province of Septimania; and by their superior skill in fortification, defended their capital, Narbonne, during a seven years' siege. It was surrendered at last, A. D. 750, by the treachery of some Goths within the walls, and the whole province was added to the dominion of Pepin. The great duchy of Aquitaine, comprising a fourth part of France, had cast off its allegiance to the Carlovingians, but it was reconquered in a long and obstinate war of ten campaigns. In the year of its surrender Pepin died, leaving to his two sons, Charles and Carloman, a well-compacted dominion reaching from the Rhine to the Pyrenees. Carloman survived his father only three years. The power of the family was raised to its highest degree by his brother, whose name

and honorary title have become inseparable in history as CHARLE-MAGNE. *

51. The heathen Saxons — only exasperated when not converted by the preaching of St. Boniface — had broken out into renewed rage during the long wars of Pepin in Aquitaine. By thirty-three years of almost unremitted warfare, Charlemagne subdued or scattered this fierce but freedom-loving people. Many times the humbled warriors sued for peace, and assumed the white robes of Christian converts, only to renew their ravages as soon as the Frankish chief was engaged in Spain or Italy. Many times his avenging armies desolated the Saxon country with fire and sword, on one occasion slaughtering 4,500 captives; on others, transporting thousands to settlements in France or Italy, and supplying their places with colonies of Franks.

Many bishoprics were established, not less as military posts than as centers of religious influence; while, faithful to his great plan for Christianizing all Europe, Charlemagne caused his Saxon hostages and prisoners to be diligently instructed in the true faith, that they might become the teachers of their people. In one, at least, of his forays, Charlemagne came in collision with the Northmen of the Baltic, who, though defeated in this first assault, became a most formidable scourge to the dominions of his descendants. The duchy of Bavaria, after existing two hundred years under one race, was absorbed into the dominion of the Franks.

52. In the mean time, Charlemagne made good his inherited title of Eldest Son of the Church, by crossing Mt. Cenis to the aid of Pope Adrian I. against Desiderius, king of the Lombards. Pavia was reduced by fifteen months' siege; Desiderius and his family were imprisoned for the remainder of their lives, and Charlemagne himself received the Iron Crown, the native dukes and counts being confirmed, as his vassals, in the possession of their estates. Within two years they conspired with the Greek emperor to crown the son of Desiderius. Charlemagne crossed the Alps in the depth of winter, took several cities by storm or siege, and effectually crushed the conspiracy, leaving his faithful Franks in all places of trust, instead of the Lombard nobles.

53. At the request of the emir of Saragossa, who besought his aid against the caliph of Cordova, Charlemagne invaded Spain, captured

---

* It may be said, once for all, that this Manual admits the common French names of the Frankish sovereigns only for the sake of uniformity, in obedience to a custom too long established to be easily changed. In strict accuracy, *Clovis* should have been written Hlodwig or Chlodwig (the original of Louis); *Charlemagne* is Karl the Great; *Eudes* is more properly Odo. The student can not too carefully bear in mind that both Merovingian and Carlovingian sovereigns were Germans, and were always regarded as foreigners by the Gauls and Romans whom they governed. The foundation of the modern French monarchy dates from the accession of Hugh Capet. See ¿ 85.

many cities, restored the emir, delivered the Gothic Christians from oppression, and extended his own dominion from the Pyrenees to the Ebro. Residing at Barcelona, the Frankish governor of the "Spanish March" held sway over Roussillon, Catalonia, and the infant kingdoms of Aragon and Navarre.

54. Italy and Aquitaine were erected into separate kingdoms for two sons of Charlemagne; and while he himself was conquering the tract between the Elbe and the Oder, the young king of Italy added to his dominion the provinces of Istria and Liburnia, on the Adriatic. Between the father and son lay the dense thickets of Pannonia, where the Huns had laid up in nine enormous "Rings," fortified by impenetrable hedges, the plunder of Europe and Asia since the time of Attila. During recent wars of Charlemagne, they had dared to extend their forays into Italy and Bavaria; and in a Diet held at Worms, A. D. 791, they were doomed to a signal revenge. Two armies entered Pannonia from the north and south, while a fleet descended the Danube. In one campaign the Huns were humbled and despoiled; and five years later the country, with its buried treasures, was added to the empire of the Franks. The defense of the long eastern frontier, from the Adriatic to the Baltic, was committed to noblemen called Margraves or Counts of the Border.

55. As Patrician of Rome, Charlemagne was called to protect Pope Leo III. against the assaults of his enemies within the city. He went to Rome, heard the accusations, and accepted the solemn oath of Leo as proof of his innocence. As he was offering his devotions on Christmas Day in the Church of St. Peter, the Pope suddenly placed upon his head a golden crown, hailing him at the same time with the ancient imperial titles: "Long life and victory to Charles AUGUSTUS, crowned of God, great and peace-giving Emperor of the Romans!" Clergy and people echoed the acclamation, and the king of the Franks was acknowledged as the successor of the Cæsars.

A. D. 800.

56. By the deposition of Romulus Augustulus, the Western empire had not been abolished, but only reunited with the Eastern; the exarchs represented imperial authority in Italy and Africa; and the proudest barbarian kings had their dignity increased by the patrician ornaments which marked them as lieutenants of the empire. But the throne of Constantinople was now usurped by Irene, a mere pretender, whose crime in supplanting her son, the lawful sovereign, neutralized her claims to allegiance. The supremacy which Rome had unwillingly relinquished to the younger capital was held to be rightly resumed, and Charles was declared the successor of Constantine VI., as temporal head of Christendom. Disregarding the insignificant series of emperors who had followed Theodosius in the West, he was numbered as sixty-eighth in order through the Eastern line from Cæsar Octavianus.

57. All the world hastened to recognize his greatness; Saxons of England and Goths of Spain sought his protection; and even from the banks of the Tigris, Haroun al Raschid sent, with other gifts, the keys of Jerusalem and the Holy Sepulcher, acknowledging the Western emperor as the official head of Christendom. During forty-six years of unexampled activity, as king and emperor, Charlemagne labored for the union and civilization of Europe. Germany at his accession was little more than a heathen wilderness, possessing no towns except those upon the Rhine and Danube which had been colonies of the Romans.

Under his vigorous administration, order and good government produced their just effects. Many schools yet existing owe their origin to him; and towns grew up as centers not only of commerce, but of intelligence and Christianity. Diets to which bishops as well as nobles were summoned, took the place of the ancient March- and May-fields of the Frankish warriors. The discussions were in Latin, and this circumstance alone gave a commanding influence to the clergy. The *Capitularies* of Charlemagne contain a great variety of general and special enactments, showing his minute attention to the details of government, and his sincere desire to guard the poor against the oppressions of the rich.

58. His favorite capital, Aix-la-Chapelle, was adorned with the fine marbles and mosaics of Italy, the sculptures of Greece, and enriched by an extensive library, a richly endowed college, and a school of sacred music. The first organs were by his order brought from Greece into northern Europe, and singers from Italy introduced the Gregorian chant. Learned men from all countries* were his favorite companions; and wherever his camp was pitched — on the ancient battle-fields of Italy and Spain, or amid the wilds of the Danube or the Baltic — their conversation was his constant delight. The empire of the West, revived in Charlemagne, lasted 1,006 years, until it was subverted by Napoleon. Its titles, stripped of most of their significance, are retained by the sovereigns of Austria.

59. Louis the Mild, though king of Aquitaine from his fourth year, and already associated in the imperial dignity before his father's death, was better fitted for a cloister than a throne. He reformed the court, sent commissioners throughout his realm to investigate and redress wrongs, raised the conquered Saxons to a level with his other subjects, repelled Norman invasions, and subdued revolts in Italy and other distant provinces. But in the necessary execution of the ringleaders of these revolts,

---

* Alcuin, the English philosopher, was his most familiar friend. He had previously been provost of the High School at York, in England, where was one of the few libraries then existing in Western Europe. Alcuin, at the request of Charlemagne, sent scholars to make copies of the books at York, as a foundation for the libraries which he attached to all the schools in Germany.

his sensitive conscience became burdened with remorse. He voluntarily underwent a public penance; and his turbulent and unscrupulous nobles, instead of being moved to follow his example, saw with contempt, in the humbling of the imperial dignity, an opportunity to augment their own. The power which his father had bestowed upon the Church was ungenerously used against the son.

60. As early as A. D. 817, Lothaire, the eldest son of Louis, was joined with his father in the empire, while his brothers, Louis and Pepin, received each an ample domain, with the title of king. Charles, the son of a second marriage, was afterward endowed with Switzerland and Suabia; and although this gift did not infringe their territories, it was made a pretext to draw the three elder sons into repeated revolts against their father, who was twice deprived of his crown by the rebellious princes, aided by the bishops.

At length the emperor, worn out by cares and sorrows, died upon a little island in the Rhine. His son Pepin had preceded him. Lothaire, according to the terms of his coronation, demanded the oath of allegiance from every subject of his father. He was supported by the Italians and the Austrasian Franks, who cherished the Roman idea of a united empire. His brothers, Louis and Charles, in claiming to hold their respective dominions in full sovereignty, were supported by the Germans, who had never been fully reconciled to the restored empire, and who insisted on referring the question of partition to the issue of battle, or, in the language of the times, to the "judgment of God." *

61. At Fontenay, near Auxerre, 300,000 men, representing nearly all the nations that had obeyed Charlemagne, met in unseemly strife, led by the three brothers. The battle was long, obstinate, and indecisive. At length Lothaire withdrew, leaving 40,000 of his soldiers dead upon the field. An equal number had fallen upon the other side. The flower of Frankish chivalry was destroyed, and the empire was left unprotected equally against the Scandinavian and Moorish pirates. By a subsequent treaty at Verdun, the dominions of Charlemagne were divided among his three grandsons. Italy, with a long strip of land extending from the Mediterranean to the German Ocean, between the Rhone and Meuse on the west, and the Alps and Rhine on the east, was assigned to Lothaire, that with the imperial crown he might also possess the two capitals, Rome and Aix; the coun-

A. D. 843.

* "Trial by battle," either single or general, was a common mode of determining disputes during the Middle Ages, because it was believed that Heaven would award the victory to the right, punishing a perjured man, or vindicating the innocence of one unjustly accused. Women and infirm old men, if accused of deadly crimes, were allowed to choose their champions; but if the champion lost the battle, the man was hanged or the woman burnt.

tries east and north of the Rhine were given to Louis the German; Gaul west of the Rhone and Saone, to Charles the Bald.

62. Germany dates her national existence from the Treaty of Verdun. Eastern or *Teutonic* was then forever separated from Western or *Latin France*, which in later times gained exclusive possession of the name, the heart of the Frankish dominions being known as *Franconia*. The oaths taken respectively by the armies of Louis and Charles show that the two languages were already distinct. The Frankish conquerors of Gaul were largely Latinized by intercourse with the former subjects of the Cæsars; and while the soldiers of Louis swore allegiance in Old German, the oath of Charles' army bore an almost equal resemblance to Latin, Provençal, and modern French. The Teutonic and Roman elements in European society and speech were from that moment separate.

RECAPITULATION.

The Carlovingian power having been confirmed by the victory near Tours, was increased by Pepin, and raised to its greatest height by Charlemagne, only to decline under the just but inefficient Louis, and to be permanently divided by his sons in the Battle of Fontenaye and the Treaty of Verdun.

Simultaneous with its rise was that of the civil power of the popes. The war of Iconoclasm separated Italy from Byzantine rule, and led to the revival of the Western Empire in the person of Charlemagne. Both Pepin and Charlemagne made war in Italy against the Lombards; the latter overthrew their kingdom and imprisoned its last native sovereign. The revenues of the exarchate — previously absorbed by the Lombards — went to the Pope, and its sovereignty to the Frankish king. Charlemagne subdued the Saxons; annexed Bavaria, the March of Spain, and the territory of the Huns; extended his dominion from the Mediterranean to the Baltic, and from the Atlantic and Ebro on the west to the Elbe and Theiss on the east. He civilized his German territories by Diets, in which the clergy had a voice, as well as by schools, libraries, and collections of art. By the Treaty of Verdun, the Germans east and north of the Rhine were separated from the Romanized Germans and the "Latin Race" on the west and south.

CONTEMPORARIES OF THE CARLOVINGIANS.

63. In the Saracen empire, the rude age of conquest was succeeded by a brilliant period of intellectual progress. Libraries and colleges sprang up in all the Moslem cities from Samarcand to Cordova, and the writings of the Greek philosophers were translated into Arabic. Arabian physicians had no superiors in the knowledge of botany, chemistry, and anatomy, and to their skill were intrusted the lives of many Christian princes. All sciences in their infancy are mingled with superstition. The Arabs were encouraged in their study of astronomy by the belief that they read human destiny in the stars; and they wasted long lives and ample fortunes in the researches of alchemy, hoping to discover the elixir of immortal youth, or the philosopher's stone, which could transmute all substances into gold.

64. Almansor, the second of the Abbassides, built Bagdad on the Tigris for his capital. Haroun al Raschid was the most magnificent and powerful monarch of his race; but his excessive cruelty to the people of the Eastern empire, whose lands he ravaged, and his murder of the Barmecides, his own intimate friends and faithful servants, make us doubt whether his surname of "the Just" was deservedly bestowed. Almamun, his successor (A. D. 813–833), was equally remarkable for his liberal patronage of science and literature. Learned men of all nations were welcome at his court. An accurate measurement of the earth's orbit evinced a degree of mathematical knowledge not previously attained.

It was during this reign that Crete was conquered by Arabian pirates, to continue nearly a century and a half their slave market, for the disposal of captives from all the shores of the Mediterranean. A rebellion against the Ommiad caliph of Spain had resulted in the exile of 15,000 of the insurgents. These took refuge in Egypt, but being expelled by the lieutenants of Almamun, they sailed to Crete, and commenced its subjugation by building the fortress of Candia, which ultimately gave its name to the whole island. The greater part of Sicily was conquered about the same time, and its ports became nests of pirates, who pillaged the neighboring coasts of Italy, and even twice assaulted Rome itself. The churches were robbed of their gold and silver, but the city was rescued and fortified by the valiant Pope Leo IV. He rebuilt the suburban villages, and inclosed with walls the Vatican quarter of Rome, which is still called in his honor the Leonine City.

65. The annals of the Byzantine empire during this period are full of important events. The war against images was begun, as we have seen, by Leo III. At his command the eastern churches abjured their idols, though not without tumult and bloodshed; his edict in the west was met with positive refusal by the popes, and a declared resolution by the people to "live and die in defense of the holy images." The son of Leo, Constantine V., was for a time expelled from his throne by the image-worshipers, and upon his return he punished the rebellion by a still more bitter and violent persecution. His reign was otherwise prosperous. The desolate shores of Thrace received new colonies; thousands of captives were redeemed from foreign slavery, and unusual plenty prevailed.

66. Leo IV. married Irene, an Athenian, whose remarkable talents raised her to the head of the empire. As regent for her son, Constantine VI., she undertook with zeal the restoration of the images. The monks, their most zealous promoters, reappeared from their hiding-places, and a general Council at Nice, A. D. 787, reversed the decision of that of Constantinople, A. D. 754, by declaring image-worship to be agreeable to Scripture and reason. As Constantine grew to manhood, the mother and son became the heads of rival parties which alternately possessed the throne. Irene at length prevailed, caused her son to be deprived of his eyes, and reigned in splendor five years alone. Her ministers then conspired against her, and Nicephorus, the treasurer, obtained the crown. His fiscal talents and experience enabled him greatly to increase the revenues from taxation; but excepting this kind of oppression, and in spite of his very bad reputation in history,* few crimes seem to have been justly charged upon him. He was tolerant of religious differences, and humane even to conspirators against his life.

His relations with Charlemagne were at first friendly, though their claims to universal empire were, of course, mutually destructive. A treaty concluded at Aix-la-Chapelle, A. D. 803, fixed the limits of the two empires in Italy. Venice, Istria, the Dalmatian coast, and the Calabrian cities remained to the Byzantine sovereign, while Rome and the exarchate of Ravenna were resigned to the Frank. Nicephorus suffered a humiliating defeat from Haroun al Raschid, A. D. 805, and ultimately lost his life in war with the Bulgarians, A. D. 811.

67. His son Stauracius had reigned but two months, when a new revolution compelled him to resign the throne to his brother-in-law, Michael Rhangabe. The mild virtues of Michael I. disgusted the army, and rather than preserve his crown by bloodshed, he retired into a monastery. Leo V., the Armenian, was saluted as emperor, and proved one of the best Byzantine sovereigns, though his accommodating policy concerning image-worship gave him the name of "Chameleon." During this reign the Bulgarian king, Crumn, repeatedly ravaged A. D. 813-820. the country to the very walls of Constantinople, and carried off in one expedition 50,000 captives. By the zeal and fidelity of these Christian slaves, many thousands of the Bulgarians were persuaded to accept Christianity. Nearly fifty years later their king Bogoris was baptized, and the entire nation soon renounced its paganism.

68. Leo V. was slain in a conspiracy by the adherents of his old friend and comrade, Michael the Amorian, who for repeated treasons had been sentenced to death by fire. Michael II. was snatched from his dungeon to be placed upon the throne, with the iron fetters still upon his limbs. Under the Amorian dynasty, the empire, though in its decline, far surpassed all other nations in wealth, owing to the extent of its commerce. In the Mediterranean the Greeks had a monopoly; and the trade between Europe and Asia has never been so concentrated in

---

* His most unpopular act—especially with the chroniclers—was a tax upon church property, monasteries, and charitable institutions. The prevailing fashion of endowing convents, in order to withdraw property from taxation, and provide a retreat for a whole family in case of misfortune, had greatly impaired the public revenues.

any one city as in Constantinople before the rise of the Italian republics. Central Asia was then more settled and civilized than now, since the ravages and conquests of the Tartar hordes. Rich cities rewarded the enterprise of merchants, whose caravans they entertained on the route to India or China. Throughout Europe and Asia, golden *byzants* were in circulation, furnishing for several centuries the only gold coinage on the former continent.

69. Theophilus, the son and successor of Michael II., was an able and magnificent sovereign, but he had many misfortunes in his wars with the caliphs of Bagdad, and his great revenues were used in adorning his capital with gorgeous buildings, rather than in fortifying his borders. Theophilus was an ardent Iconoclast, but his widow, Theodora, as regent for her son, Michael III., finally restored the images, and put an end to a war which had distracted the empire more than a century.

During the regency of Theodora and the reign of her son, the Paulicians—a heretical sect who professed themselves the obedient followers of St. Paul—were persecuted throughout the empire, and ten thousand persons are said to have been put to death under one commission. A greater number made armed resistance, and with the aid of the neighboring Saracen emirs, established themselves in an independent fortress at Tephriké, and in the mountainous region surrounding it, in the modern province of Roum. The new republic, like that of Holland and the American colonies in later ages, became, during the twenty-five years of its existence, a refuge for the oppressed of every name. With the reign of Michael III., a drunken and dissolute tyrant, the power of his family ended, and a greater dynasty arose.

70. The Gothic kingdom founded or preserved by Pelayo, in the north of Spain, was governed during this period by nine kings, most of whose annals are obscure. Alfonso the Catholic, A. D. 739–757, extended his dominion over one-fourth part of the peninsula, and established colonies of his Christian subjects in many places depopulated by his slaughter of the Arabs. The conquered lands were frequently lost and regained by his successors, and even when held were often under tribute to the Mohammedan sovereigns at Cordova.

71. Among the many Anglo-Saxon monarchs of the time, the most important were Cuthred (A. D. 740–754), who laid the foundation of the future supremacy of Wessex; Offa, king of Mercia (A. D. 755–779), who reigned over twenty-three of the modern English counties; and Egbert A. D. 827–836), who is still more distinguished as the first lord-paramount of all England. Exiled by the jealousy of his kinsman, King Brihtric, of Wessex, Egbert spent his youth at the court or in the camp of Charlemagne. He accompanied that great sovereign in his rapid expeditions throughout Europe, and drew inspirations for his own

subsequent reign from the enlightened and liberal policy of the founder of the new Western empire.

The privations and hardships of the prince proved beneficial both to himself and to his country. By the superior military science which he learned in the wars of Charlemagne, as well as by his wisdom and moderation, he either conquered or rendered tributary all the other Anglo-Saxon kingdoms, and gained decisive victories over the Britons. The only foes who could withstand him were the Danes, or Northmen, who were now infesting the coasts of Europe as the Saxons had done four centuries before. They once defeated the army of Egbert, but after their alliance with the Britons of Cornwall, the united forces were routed with great slaughter.

72. The countries on the Baltic, too sterile to support so numerous and active a race, sent forth the hardiest of their sons to a life of adventure, in which they had every thing to gain and nothing to lose; for no sovereign of the south cared to conquer the bare cliffs of Norway, the marshes and then impenetrable forests of Sweden, or the islands and peninsula inclosed in a tumultuous sea, which constituted Denmark. In addition to their usual ferocity, one class of Northmen cultivated a sort of brutal frenzy, in which they howled like wolves, gnashed their teeth like mad dogs, lashed themselves into a fury of superhuman strength, and then rushed, fearless of death, into scenes of atrocious slaughter, such as no sane mind even of a savage could endure. This "Berserker's rage" was in early times regarded with reverence, like the convulsions of inspired priestesses among the Phrygians and Greeks; but with the dawn of civilization it fell into disrepute and even abhorrence.

73. In the eighth century, Harald Harfagre, of Norway, united many petty sovereignties under his sway, and tried to clear his dominions of pirates. The nests being broken up, the marauders swarmed over Europe. Some, crossing the Scythian plains, reappeared upon the Hellespont, where the Byzantine sovereigns were glad to buy their services with liberal donations of gold; and these "Varangians," or exiles, became to the Eastern empire in its decline what the Franks and Goths had been to that of the West. A few years later, two successive bands of Northmen put an end to the Slavic kingdoms of Novgorod and Kiev, and thus laid the obscure foundation of the greatest empire of our own time. The Scandinavian conquerors, comparatively few in number, adopted the language of their subjects; but Ruric, the chief, imposed the name of his own Russian tribe upon the united nation.

A. D. 862.

74. Ragnar Lodbrog, king of the Danish isles, was expelled his dominions with the aid of the Franks. He retaliated by a raid upon France itself, sailed up the Seine to Paris, and plundered all the churches. Falling later into the hands of Ella, king of Deira, he was thrown into a dungeon and slain by the venom of innumerable serpents. Charlemagne had fortified the whole western border of his empire against the northern pirates, but while his grandchildren were destroying each other at Fontenay, these sea-robbers were left unchecked to ravage the coasts of Holland, France, and Spain.

RECAPITULATION.

The Saracens became distinguished for learning and high civilization. Almansor built Bagdad. Haroun al Raschid devastated the east, though he maintained friendly relations with the west. Arabian pirates conquered Crete and Sicily. Rome was only saved by Pope Leo IV.

War of Iconoclasm begun by Emperor Leo III.; continued by his son, Constantine V. Images restored by Irene, who supplanted her own son, but was in turn dethroned by Nicephorus I. Leo V. had long wars with the Bulgarians, who became Christianized through their intercourse with the empire. Great commercial prosperity under the Amorian dynasty. Theophilus renewed the war against images, but these were finally restored and the long contest ended by Theodora.

Gothic kingdom extended by Alfonso the Catholic over one-fourth of Spain. In England, Egbert of Wessex united all the Anglo-Saxon kingdoms under his own sway. The ravages of Scandinavian free-booters were increased by the consolidation of their states under Harald Harfagre. Many entered the imperial service at Constantinople; others, under Ruric, founded the Russian empire at Novgorod, while still greater numbers devastated the western coasts of Europe.

PERIOD III. FROM THE DIVISION OF CHARLEMAGNE'S DOMINIONS TO THE FIRST CRUSADE, A. D. 843–1096.

THE FEUDAL SYSTEM.

75. During the rapid decline of the Carlovingian family, the imperial crown passed during forty-five years from one to another of its three branches, which reigned in Italy until A. D. 888, in Germany until A. D. 911, in France until A. D. 987. No one of its members equaled their first imperial ancestor either in war or state-craft, or inherited his personal control over the princes and barons, whose estates covered almost the entire empire. Wherever special danger threatened, either from Magyars, Saracens, or Northmen, the burden of public defense fell upon local chieftains, who made war or peace on their own responsibility, and soon cast off the authority of the royal commissioners appointed by Charlemagne. Thus, on the west, the dukes of Aquitaine and Brittany, the counts of Anjou and Paris; on the east, the dukes of Saxony, Thuringia, Franconia, Bavaria, and Suabia; in Italy, the marquises of Friuli, Ivrea, Spoleto, and Tuscany, enjoyed wealth and power superior in almost every instance to those of their nominal sovereigns; and there was scarcely a city or castle in the whole empire which had not some other master than the king.

76. Estates were held upon a condition of military service, known as the "feudal tenure." Each year the great vassal, kneeling, placed his hands between those of his suzerain, and vowed to serve him with life and limb, faithfully and loyally, in consideration of the lands conferred. Beneath the great princes who held provinces directly from the king, were "rear vassals," who did homage to the count or duke for some portion of his domains; and these again might grant estates to smaller tenants, the whole territory being subject to a condition of service in time of war, or, as it was called, "held in fief." Even the absolute owners of land were often glad to secure the protection of some powerful lord by acknowledging his suzerainty; and thus during the ninth, tenth, and eleventh centuries, feudal holdings took the place of "allodial possession" throughout France, Germany, and a great part of Italy. Originally, the feudal grants were made only for a term of years or during the life-time of the vassal, but they gradually became hereditary. Upon the extinction of the family, or its failure to fulfill the oath of homage, the estate reverted to the superior; if of a great vassal, to the king.

77. The serfs who cultivated the soil were given away with it, and could claim nothing except protection for their families and cattle in time of invasion. So often was their humble industry broken up, not only by foreign inroads, but by the private wars of the nobles, that whole districts were sometimes depopulated by famine. The darkest period of the "Dark Ages" was comprised in the three centuries succeeding Charlemagne. The order and security restored by his great genius were replaced for a season by the wildest anarchy. "Fist-law" prevailed, and western Europe was more deeply sunk in ignorance and misery during the tenth and eleventh centuries than at any preceding period.

78. The Church was at this time the only protector of the weak; bishops and abbots were important vassals of the empire, and a great increase of power and wealth gave them the dignity of independent princes. Abbey-lands, being usually secure from ravages, were better cultivated, and the serfs attached to them more prosperous than those of secular estates. At length, in A. D. 1033, the French clergy were able to impose a check upon the private wars, which were a source of the greatest calamity to Europe. It was forbidden to engage in any warlike movement between sunset on Wednesday and sunrise on Monday of each week, or on any holy festival which might occur during the remaining days. This "truce of God," proclaimed as by direct revelation from Heaven, was observed throughout the countries which obeyed the Bishop of Rome.

79. From this glance at the general condition of Europe under the Feudal System, we turn to mark the rise of the several dynasties and nations. The Middle-Kingdom of Lothaire (see § 61) soon fell, under his sons, into its three natural divisions: Italy, Burgundy, and Lorraine. Louis II. at his father's death added to the Italian crown that of the Roman empire, and waged valiant war against the Saracens in Calabria. The kingdom of Burgundy, then comprising the country between the Rhone and the Alps, and known afterward as the kingdom of Provence or of Arles, was first to throw off the Carlovingian yoke and set up a native sovereign in Count Boso, son-in-law of the emperor Louis II., A. D. 877.

80. Charles the Bald outlived his brothers, and for a year claimed the whole dominion of Charlemagne. He continued the policy begun by Lothaire, of settling the barbarian invaders upon the lands they had devastated, by giving to Robert the Strong, probably a Saxon chief, all the lands between the Loire and the Seine, with the title of Count of Anjou. The wisdom of the grant was shown in the able resistance of Count Robert to the bands of Northmen who had in this reign plundered Rouen, twice stormed and sacked Paris, and massacred so many thousands of people that the islets of the Seine were whitened with their bones. Robert lost his life in battle with Hasting the Viking; but his son Eudes became the no less brave and able defender of Paris against a still more terrible assault. The siege lasted eighteen months. Charles III. (the Fat), who had once more united the dominions of Charlemagne, was A. D. 885, 886. absent and neglectful of his imperial duties. When at last he arrived before the walls of Paris, it was only to ransom the city with money, and suffer the half-conquered enemy to pursue his ravages as far inland as Burgundy.

81. Universal contempt for this conduct led to the deposition of Charles by a Diet of the empire at Tribur. His four kingdoms were divided. Germany chose for its king Arnulf, a grandson of Louis the German, who by defeating the Northmen at their fortified camp near Louvain, had already proved himself one of the most valiant of his race. The crown of Italy was bestowed upon Berengar of Friuli; but that of the empire was received by Guy of Spoleto, and upon his death, three years later, by Lambert, his son. Northern or Transjurane Burgundy became a separate kingdom under Rudolf I., while in western France, Count Eudes was called by general acclamation to the throne. Four years later, a rival party which adhered to the Carlovingians, crowned Charles the Simple, the last surviving descendant of Charles the Bald, who reigned north of the Seine until the death of Eudes, A. D. 898, and afterward nominally over all the country from the ocean to the Rhone and Moselle.

82. Western Europe still suffered from the ravages of the Danes. In England their piratical craft swarmed in all the rivers, while troops of corsairs scoured the country, pillaged York, London, and many other towns, and even forced Alfred, grandson of Egbert, to spend some months a homeless fugitive in his own realm, of which he was to become the civilizer and benefactor. Alfred, however, mustered a force to defeat them at Ethandune, and afterward, in pursuance of his liberal and peaceful policy, ceded to Guthrun, their leader, upon his baptism, the seven eastern counties north of the Thames in perpetual possession.

83. In A. D. 912, Charles the Simple, too poor to bribe and too weak to resist them, likewise ceded to Hrolf, or Rollo, their Norman leader, in perpetual fief, a large region of north-western France, with the feudal sovereignty of the duchy of Bretagne, on condition of his followers embracing Christianity and ceasing from their depredations. On the French side of the Channel this expedient proved effectual, for the Normans, now settling to the cultivation of the soil, formed a barrier against future incursions of their countrymen; and their province, which took from them the name of Normandy, became the richest and most orderly part of France. But in England, the Danes of the eastern border disclaimed all responsibility for the acts of their countrymen, who (A. D. 1003–1013) expelled Ethelred the Unready ten years from his realm; and at length *A. D. 1017–1011.* gaining sole possession of the kingdom, ruled it, under Knut and his two sons, Harold and Hardiknut, twenty-four years.

84. In France, the imbecility of Charles and the insolence of his low-born minister, Haganon, led to a war with the great vassals, by whom the king was defeated and imprisoned, with one brief exception, for the remainder of his life. Robert, duke of France, brother of Count Eudes, and Rudolph of Burgundy successively obtained the crown. The wife of Charles, with her infant son Louis, took refuge in England at the court of her brother Athelstan. Upon the death of King Rudolph, A. D. 936, three great nobles united to recall the young prince, who on account of his exile is known to history as Louis d'Outremer. Having been carefully educated by his uncle, Louis displayed more spirit and ability than were common to his declining family.

Hugh the Great, Duke of France and Burgundy and Count of Paris, had been chiefly influential in bestowing upon that prince a crown which he might as easily have obtained for himself. He resented the independent spirit of Louis, and at length, throwing off his allegiance, declared himself a vassal of Otho the Great, king of Germany. The duke of Normandy and other great feudatories followed his example. Otho invaded the country, and the French monarchy covered little more than the castle-rock of Laon, when, in A. D. 954, King Louis suddenly died.

85. Hugh the Great had the crown a third time at his disposal, but he bestowed it upon Lothaire, the son of Louis, and himself died two years later, having for thirty-three years exercised more than royal power, though without its insignia. Lothaire was succeeded, A. D. 986, by his

son, Louis V., with whom ended the Carlovingian line in France.
Charles, Duke of Lower Lorraine, only brother of Lothaire, was rejected
in consequence of his worthless character, and a great council of nobles
elected Hugh, Count of Paris, and eldest son of Hugh the Great, to be
their king. With his consecration at Rheims, July 1, 987, began the rule
of that illustrious dynasty which continued in unbroken succession to
govern France more than eight hundred years. Either from humility or
superstition, the new king habitually wore an abbot's cap instead of a
crown. To this circumstance he probably owes his surname *Capet*, which
is also applied to his family.

86. The accession of the count of Paris was a triumph of French nationality over what had always been more or less resented as the foreign rule
of the Carlovingians. The relation of the king to the great nobles was
merely that of precedence among equals; and even this slight authority
was sometimes disputed by the chiefs of the southern provinces, always
jealous rivals of those of the north. The marriage of Robert the Pious,
son and successor of Hugh, with a daughter of the Count of Toulouse, led
to more intimate relations between the two parts of the kingdom; and
though the clergy bitterly denounced the gay dress and easy manners of
the new courtiers, some advantage doubtless resulted from the infusion of
southern intelligence and refinement — partly retained in the Mediterranean provinces since the Augustan age, and partly derived from the Saracens, who were then the most cultivated people in Europe.

87. The munificence toward the Church, which distinguished both Hugh
and Robert, doubtless contributed much to the establishment of their dynasty, but did not preserve the latter from a cruel persecution on account
of his first marriage with his distant relative, Bertha. The kingdom was
placed under an interdict, which was enforced with extreme severity,
until the king, after several years' resistance, was compelled to yield.

A singular delusion which prevailed during this reign still further increased the power of the clergy. A prophecy widely circulated in Europe
foretold the end of the world one thousand years after the birth of Christ.
As the time approached no seed was sown, nor any worldly business
transacted. The terrified multitude thronged the churches, seeking by
prayer and penance to avert the worst features of their doom. The rich
and the great lavished their estates upon the monasteries; and many,
assuming the humble garb of penitents, hastened to the Holy Land, where
it was believed that our Lord would appear in person. Famine and untold
misery resulted from this extraordinary panic; and though industry was
slowly resumed after the fatal year had passed, yet the feeling of dependence upon the Church for the security of interests dearer than life, remained unabated in the minds of all classes.

88. The violent deeds which were characteristic of the time burdened

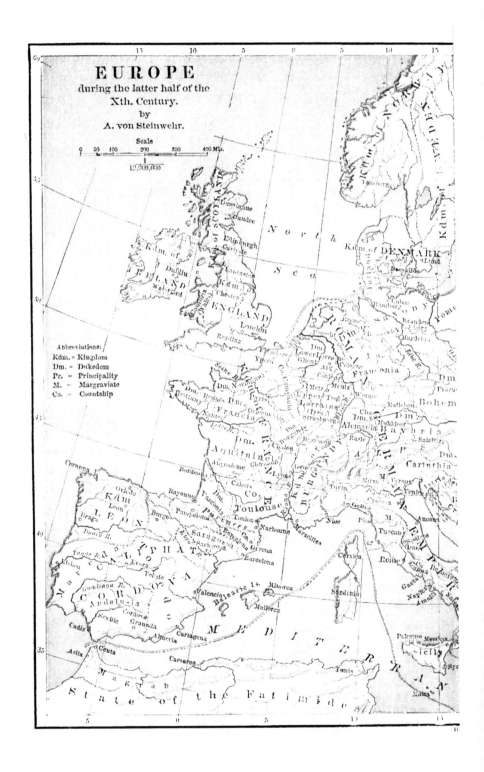

EUROPE

during the latter half of the
Xth. Century.

by

A. von Steinwehr.

Scale

0   50   100   200   300   400 Mls.

1:15,000,000

Abbreviations:

Kdm. = Kingdom
Dm. = Dukedom
Pr. = Principality
M. = Margraviate
Co. = Countship

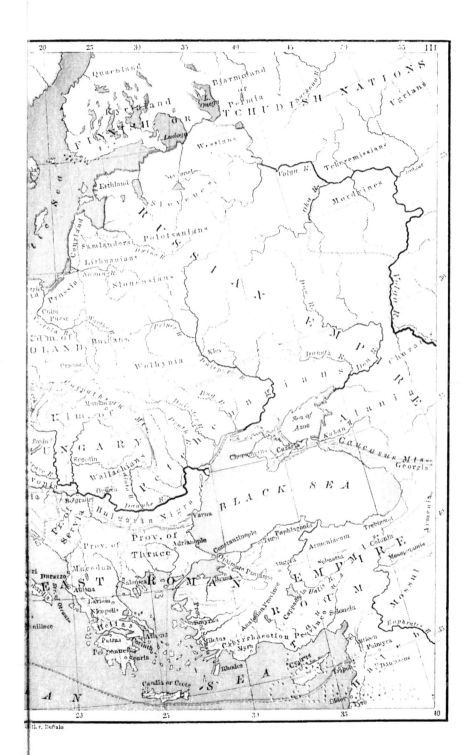

many consciences with remorse. The clergy taught that sin might be expiated by gifts to the Church, and thence arose the magnificent cathedrals and abbeys which constitute the principal ornaments of Europe. Many princes, among whom were eight or ten Anglo-Saxon kings, exchanged the cares and tumults of their regal state for the peace and seclusion of a monastery. A visit to the scenes of our Savior's life, teachings, and death was considered especially efficacious as an atonement for sin; and southern Europe was thronged with pilgrims, among whom the now Christianized Northmen were most numerous and zealous.

89. Duke Robert the Magnificent, the fifth from Rollo, filled with remorse for his unscrupulous and wicked life, abandoned his duchy after securing the allegiance of his barons to his young son William, and fulfilled his presentiment by dying in Asia Minor during his return from Jerusalem. William, becoming of age, proved one of the ablest princes of his line. He was cousin to Edward the Confessor, the last Saxon king of the family of Egbert; and on the death of that sovereign, without children, he claimed the English crown. Harold, son of the powerful Earl Godwin, was, however, made king, and for nearly a year defended himself against an invasion from Norway and the resistance of his own brother; but in September, A. D. 1066, William landed in the south of England with a formidable array of knights and gentlemen, and in the battle of Hastings ended the reign with the life of Harold.

90. The Norman Conquest, which introduced feudalism into England, was among the most decisive events in European history. The lands of the conquered island were bestowed in fief upon the followers of the duke; the abbeys and bishoprics, upon foreign churchmen. The language of the Conqueror — French as somewhat modified by the Northmen — was enforced in legal transactions; and not only the sovereigns, but most of the nobility of England, for eight hundred years have been of Norman blood. Some of the outlawed Saxons repaired to Constantinople, where they entered the service of the Eastern emperor, and soon enjoyed the opportunity of fighting their Norman foes during the Crusades. The greater number remained upon the lands as tenants or serfs of the conquerors, and their language, with a certain mixture of Norman words, became the predominant element in modern English.

91. In passing through southern Italy on their way to the Holy Land, the Norman pilgrims had not failed to remark the weakness of a country divided between Greeks, Lombards, and Saracens, who wasted their forces in petty wars. Joining one or another of these belligerent parties, they managed by stratagem or force of arms to possess themselves of great domains. Twelve Norman counts gained twelve cities with their territories in Apulia, and formed a military republic, with William of the Iron Arm at its head. They lived by

A. D. 1040.

M. H.—4.

brigandage, and so annoyed their neighbors that Pope Leo IX. persuaded the Eastern and Western emperors to join in a league against them. In A. D. 1053. a battle near Civitella the Normans were victorious; the Pope was made prisoner, and compelled to bestow upon his captors, as vassals of the Church, not only all the lands they had conquered, but all which they might yet obtain.

92. Robert Guiscard was the first duke of Apulia and Calabria. He not only drove from the maritime cities the last of the Greek magistrates, but conquered from the Lombards their three great principalities of Salerno, Capua, and Benevento, which had outlasted by three centuries the kingdom of their countrymen in the north of Italy. His brother Roger, meanwhile, with a few hundreds of Norman volunteers, conquered Sicily from the Saracens, and held it as a dependency of the duchy of Apulia. Thus arose the kingdom of Naples, or the Two Sicilies, which throughout its separate existence (until A. D. 1860) continued to be a "fief of St. Peter."

Not content with having founded, from the resources of a private adventurer, a kingdom which was to continue nearly eight centuries, Robert Guiscard aspired to conquer the empire of the East. He vanquished the Emperor Alexis Comnenus in a great battle before Durazzo, A. D. 1081, but was recalled to Italy by a rebellion of his subjects, and undertook, A. D. 1084, the protection of Pope Gregory VII. against the Western emperor, Henry IV. (See § 108.) He died A. D. 1085, and his dominions, after the death of his grandson, passed to the son of his brother Roger, who first of the family received the title of king.

93. The foundation of the Russian Empire by pagan Northmen, A. D. 862, has already been noticed. Many separate principalities were formed by successive chieftains, all of whom owned a sort of feudal allegiance to the family of Ruric. Christianity was early introduced by missionaries from Cherson and Constantinople; and in A. D. 955, Queen Olga, widow of the son of Ruric, and regent of the empire, was baptized in the latter city.

Vladimir the Great, after his baptism, established churches and schools A. D. 980–1015. throughout the empire, which he had enlarged by the conquest of Gallicia, Lithuania, and Livonia. After his death his dominions were divided by family wars similar to those of the Carlovingians; but they were reunited under Yaroslav (A. D. 1036), who contributed greatly to their civilization by reclaiming waste lands, multiplying towns, churches, and schools, ordering the translation of Greek books — especially the Holy Scriptures — into the Slavonian language, and compiling the first Russian code of laws. First of the Russian sovereigns, he allied himself with the western nations by the marriage of his three daughters with the kings of France, Norway, and Hungary.

RECAPITULATION.

During the decline of the Carlovingian empire, the power of the great vassals exceeded that of the sovereigns. Feudal System became prevalent. Misery of the serfs was only alleviated by the protection of the Church. The "truce of God" imposed a check upon private wars.

Alfred of England and Charles III. of France granted lands to the Danes, or Northmen, who in the latter country became settled and highly civilized. The efficient defense of France by the counts of Paris, and the incompetence of the kings, occasioned a revolution of nearly a hundred years, which at length overthrew the Carlovingian and established the Capetian dynasty in France.

The power of the Church, fostered by the first two Capetians, was increased by the terrors of the year of doom. Pilgrimages, monastic vows, and liberal ecclesiastical foundations relieved the burdened consciences of the great. The Normans, under their duke William, became the sovereign race in England; under Robert and Roger Guiscard, in southern Italy and Sicily; and under the descendants of Ruric, in Russia.

RISE OF THE ITALIAN REPUBLICS.

94. In the north of Italy, the three republics of Genoa, Pisa, and Venice were at this time most powerful. The latter claimed to be the eldest and only true daughter of the Roman Republic, having arisen, before the fall of the empire, from a population of Italians unmixed with the northern barbarians. (See Anc. Hist., Book V, § 249.) At first each island, peopled by a separate band of refugees, had its own tribune; but a more consolidated government was formed by the Assembly at Heraclea, A. D. 697, which elected for life a duke or doge, with all the powers of a king. Paul Luke Anafesta was the first doge of the united republic.

Pepin, son of Charlemagne, tried, in A. D. 809, to conquer Venice from the Eastern emperor, Nicephorus, who claimed it as a dependency. The citizens, concentrating themselves on the Rialto, defeated all his attempts to penetrate the winding and narrow passages between the islands; and as a monument of their success, built the ducal palace where it now stands. Twenty years later, the remains of St. Mark were brought from Alexandria and enshrined in the church which bears his name. The saint, or his emblematic winged lion, became the guardian of the republic, emblazoned on its standards, imprinted on its money, identified in every way with the state itself. By conquering the Dalmatian and Istrian pirates, the Venetians extended their dominion east of the Adriatic, and laid the foundation of the greatest commercial power of the Middle Ages. Alone of all the Italian republics, Venice never submitted to the German emperors, nor acknowledged any other secular authority within her walls.

95. Pisa was the first of the Tuscan cities to grow rich by commerce. The wealth of her merchants redeemed the marshes of the lower Arno, and made the whole region of the Maremma, now half deserted, a delightful garden. The islands of the Mediterranean being held by the Saracens, and Venice and Amalfi claiming all the commerce of that sea, Pisa gained her power only by continual strife. Sardinia was conquered, A. D. 1017–1021, by the allied Pisans and Genoese, from the Mohammedan corsairs, and was ultimately divided in fiefs among the Pisan nobles.

96. Genoa, sometimes the ally, but always the rival of Pisa, extended her power over the cities of the two *Rivieras* from Nice to Spezzia. Her constitution, like those of most of the Italian cities, was modeled upon that of the Roman Republic. The four or six chief magistrates were called consuls. At the end of their term of office they rendered a strict account to the people.

97. The fortifications of cities which, throughout northern Italy, had been destroyed by the Lombards, were rebuilt only by permission of the emperor, which included also the right to organize a citizen soldiery, and to take all needful measures for defense against the barbarians. The right of independent warfare belonged to municipalities as well as to barons, and the feuds of the Italian cities — especially of Pavia and Milan, the two capitals of Lombardy — fill a large place in mediæval annals. Pavia, situated in a fertile plain, held the control of all the rivers of Lombardy, and had been the favorite residence of the Lombard kings. Milan, seat of the Western Empire since the days of Diocletian, and of the first and greatest archbishopric in northern Italy, was richer, more warlike, and more powerful than her rival.

98. No period, even of the Dark Ages, is so dark as that which followed the dissolution of the Carlovingian power. Italy was overspread by the ravages of Saracens from the south and Hungarians from the north. The Arabian freebooters were the refuse and outlaws of their race, owing allegiance to neither of the Caliphates; while the Magyars, like their predecessors, the Huns, were regarded rather as wild beasts than as men. The Italian kings, absorbed in their rivalries, were unable to resist the marauders. Berengar's authority was divided successively with the emperors Guy and Lambert, and with Louis of Arles and Rudolph of Burgundy, who were crowned at Monza even during his life.

99. After the death of Berengar I., the Italian crown was bestowed upon Hugh of Provence, who proved an intolerable tyrant. He married Marozia (see § 103), but her son, Alberic, expelled him from Rome, and ruled that city many years as consul or senator. At length Berengar, marquis of Ivrea, being threatened by King Hugh with the loss of his eyes, took refuge in Germany. The crown of that country, after the failure of the Carlovingian line, had been conferred first upon Conrad of Franconia, and then upon Henry the Fowler, the first of the Saxon dynasty. This great sovereign restored and confirmed the power of the

German kingdom by his victories over the pagans on its eastern frontier. He wrested the mark of Brandenburg from the Slavonians, and at Merseburg, in Saxony, gained a great and decisive victory over the Magyars. His son, Otho, was now king of Germany.

A. D. 934.

100. Berengar returned with a large army of Italian refugees, A. D. 945, and was welcomed as master of Italy. Hugh retired into his own kingdom of Provence; his son, Lothaire, died A. D. 950, and Berengar was crowned king. But Adelaide, the widow of Lothaire, who had been imprisoned by Berengar for refusing to marry Adalbert, his son, escaped from her dungeon, found means of crossing the Alps, and threw herself upon the protection of Otho I. This sovereign, who was no less a brave knight than a generous king, descended into Italy, wedded the injured princess, and compelled her persecutor to hold his kingdom as a vassal of the eastern Franks. But the nobles were still discontented, and after ten years of Berengar's turbulent reign, the Pope invited Otho to restore peace and order to Italy by accepting the imperial crown. He was crowned with Queen Adelaide at Rome, in February, 962.

101. The "Holy Roman Empire," thus revived, continued to be inseparable from the German kingdom.* Its name indicates the deep place it held in the belief and reverence of the best spirits of the age. To a Roman emperor alone could men look for the reëstablishment of peace and justice in the place of anarchy and tumult, for Rome alone had ever yet united all civilized nations under her sway, and guaranteed order to the world. The emperor was by theory "lord of the world," the representative of the Divine Ruler in temporal, no less than the pope in spiritual affairs. Of course, the theory was little more than a dream, but it had its influence in elevating the views of the best of the emperors. It came to its fullest development in the Ghibelline or imperial party, hereafter to be described.

102. The existence of the Byzantine emperors, especially their supremacy in nearly one-third of Italy, was a continual protest against Otho's claim to be heir of the Cæsars. In a four years' war he gained many victories over Nicephorus Phocas and John Zimiskes, though he was not able to overthrow their Italian dominion. His son, Otho II., married the Greek princess Theophano, and renewed in her name the wars in southern Italy; but he was totally defeated at Basientello by a combined force of Greeks and Saracens, and narrowly escaped with his life. Otho III. became king of Germany when only three years of age, at his father's death, and at sixteen received the imperial crown at Rome. Instructed equally by his accomplished Greek mother and by the

---

* Emperors after Conrad II. received four crowns: the German at Aix, the Burgundian at Arles, the Italian at Monza or Milan, and the imperial at Rome.

wise and virtuous prelate, Gerbert of Aurillac, the young emperor had the most exalted ideas both of his dignities and duties. He aspired at once to make Rome the capital of the world, and to set up an ideal kingdom of righteousness and peace.

103. By appointing first his cousin, Bruno, and then his venerable tutor, Gerbert, to the papal chair, he sought to raise the character of the Roman bishops; for wealth and power had produced their too common effects in the Church, and even the pontiffs, who for centuries had been remarkable for the severity and purity of their lives, were now accused of every conceivable crime. For sixty years the wealth and influence of Theodora and Marozia, Roman ladies of high rank but degraded character, controlled all Roman affairs, and even disposed of the papal crown. Crescentius, a factious noble, by appealing to the miseries and the patriotism of the populace, managed to gain supreme power with the titles of consul, senator, and even emperor. Though ruling in the sacred names of freedom and justice, he was probably a mere demagogue, and was not undeservedly beheaded by order of Otho III., A. D. 998. But the young emperor was cut off in the dawn of his manhood, and the papacy reached its lowest depth of degradation in the sons and descendants of Theodora. Two antipopes disputed the title of Gregory VI.; and Henry III., the most absolute of the emperors, deposing all three, replaced them with Clement II. A succession of six German popes revived the credit, and in some degree the power of the Roman see.

104. Henry III. left his son and heir only five years old. During the long minority, Hildebrand, a Tuscan monk, produced, by his zeal, talents, and indomitable will, a strong reaction against the imperial power. He had secured the election of Victor II., and no less during the pontificates of Stephen IX., Nicolas II., and Alexander II., he was the "soul of the papal court." He obtained a decree against the marriage of the clergy, a custom which, though more or less discountenanced, had never been universally suppressed. The decree was nowhere cordially received, but it exasperated especially the Lombard priests, who felt justified in their domestic relations by the teachings of their great archbishop, St. Ambrose, and the example of two of his successors. Their resistance was punished as heresy, and thence arose the sect of the Nicolaïtes.

A still more severe struggle was for the right of investiture, which had been claimed by princes and nobles in churches which they themselves had founded. In France and Germany bishops were either nominated or confirmed by the sovereign; in England, by the parliament. Among other flagrant abuses of the age was the purchase of offices in the Church, and it was ostensibly to guard against this crime of "simony" that the Council at the Lateran prohibited clergymen to receive benefices from, or own allegiance to, laymen. But as more than half the lands in Germany had been granted to churchmen on condition of feudal obedience, this was evidently a mortal blow at the king and secular princes.

105. Hildebrand became Pope (Gregory VII.), A. D. 1073. Henry IV. was then twenty-three years of age. Though possessed of great talents and noble impulses, his passions were ill-regulated by a defective education, and his harsh measures had already driven nearly all the princes of the empire into revolt. He was prejudiced against the Church by the hostile movements of the clergy during his minority, and after a little diplomatic skirmishing war actually broke out. Gregory VII. was solemnly deposed by the Diet at Worms; Henry IV. by the Council at Rome. A sentence of excommunication absolved all the subjects of the latter from their allegiance, and declared it a crime to render him the slightest service. The papal authority — more respected in Germany than in Italy — encouraged Rudolph of Suabia, with other nobles and bishops, to make fierce and unrelenting war upon the emperor.

106. A diet was summoned at Augsburg, where the Pope was to preside, and to judge between Henry and his foes. If his excommunication was not then removed, a new sovereign was to be chosen. In this crisis, the emperor traversed some of the wildest passes of the Alps in midwinter, stood three days barefoot and fasting in the snow at the gate of the Castle of Canossa, where the Pope was then residing, and finally obtained a grudging removal of his sentence A. D. 1077. only by engaging to appear anew, at whatever time and place Hildebrand should appoint, and submit his imperial title to the decision of a diet. The Germans were indignant at this sacrifice of their emperor's dignity; and Henry himself had no sooner left the papal presence than he resumed the war with fresh fury, and gained a decisive victory over Rudolph of Suabia.

107. Gregory VII. owed much to the firm friendship and ardent zeal of Matilda, Countess of Tuscany, who consecrated her life to the service of the Church, and at her death left all her inherited estates, then the greatest of the Italian fiefs, as patrimony of St. Peter. Her first husband, the Duke of Lower Lorraine, had fought on the side of the emperor; but after his death, A. D. 1076, his wife maintained an independent court, reigned like a queen over Lombardy and Tuscany, and placed her armies and fortresses at the disposal of the Pope. Another source of strength to the pontiff was in the sympathy of the common people, who saw in him a man of their own rank, elevated to a power above that of kings or barons; able, and, as they long believed, willing to deliver them from their oppressors. The monks and clergy hailed him as the champion of their order against the secular power, so that numbers and intellect — the latter represented almost exclusively by the Church — were all on Hildebrand's side.

108. Rudolph of Suabia was chosen emperor by the German princes, and, after a victory over Henry at Mühlhausen, received the imperial crown from Gregory VII. Henry retaliated by procuring the election of Clement III., who crowned his patron as emperor in 1084. Gregory was now shut up in the Castle of St. Angelo, by the German army, which, with a multitude of Roman citizens, had for three years been besieging Rome. He was relieved by Robert Guiscard, the Norman duke of Apulia, who was encouraged by Gregory to expect for himself the crown of the Western Empire. He burned a large portion of the city and left it in a desolation from which it has never recovered.

Gregory VII. died, A. D. 1085, at Salerno, uttering curses against Henry with his latest breath. His successors continued his policy with equal zeal but inferior talents. They renewed the excommunication of the emperor, and persuaded his two sons, Conrad and Henry, successively, to rebel against him. His intention to abdicate in favor of the latter was anticipated by the indecent haste of the Diet of Mentz, which tore from him the crown and mantle, and loudly hailed his son as successor in the empire. The emperor, with the few friends that remained to him, gained one victory, but was afterward defeated in battle; and in the depth of poverty even begged in vain for the office of chorister in a church which

A. D. 1106.   he had himself founded at Spires. He died of grief, and his body remained five years unburied, until, in 1111, the excommunication was at last removed, and the long forbidden funeral was celebrated with unusual magnificence.

109. In the Byzantine Empire Basil I., a Slavonian groom, gained the crown, A. D. 867, by the murder of his patron, Michael the Drunkard. His grandson claimed for him a descent from the Arsacidæ of Parthia, and even from Alexander the Great; but impartial writers have refuted

A. D. 867–1057.   the assertion. His dynasty, which, with some interruptions, occupied the throne nearly two hundred years, bore, however, the name of Macedonian. The armies of Basil put an end to the little republic of the Paulicians, having slain its chief, Chrysochir, and demolished its stronghold of Tephriké. The expelled and wandering sectaries carried their doctrines into Europe, where they were found several centuries later among the Albigenses of southern France. Others joined the imperial army which drove the Saracens from the southern extremity of Italy and established the Lombard theme.*

The municipal republics of Gaëta, Naples, Sorrento, and Amalfi, renewed their formal allegiance to the Eastern Empire; though their

---

* The *theme* or military district of Lombardy will, of course, be distinguished from the earlier kingdom and later province of the same name at the other extremity of the peninsula.

"dukes," who had replaced the ancient tyrants, often allied themselves with the popes, or even with the Saracens, to make war with the Byzantine generals. The capture of Syracuse, A. D. 878, made the Mussulmans masters of the whole of Sicily, and their piratical craft swarmed throughout the Mediterranean. Even Thessalonica, the second city in the Eastern Empire, was seized by them, and the massacre of its population was among the chief calamities of the reign of Leo VI. (A. D. 886–911.) Twenty-two thousand of its youth, reserved from the slaughter, were sold into slavery.

110. Constantine VII. (Porphyrogenitus[*]) spent the first thirty-three years of his nominal reign in retirement, owing first to his minority, and afterward to the usurpation by Romanus I. and his three sons of the greater share in the imperial dignity. Constantine afterward reigned fourteen years alone, beloved by his subjects for his mild and equitable policy, though his studious and secluded life had deprived him of the knowledge of men, and subjected him to the impositions of unfaithful servants. His love of literature secured the preservation of many precious manuscripts; and his own works on the science of government, and on the life of the founder of his dynasty, contain the most valuable pictures of the state of the empire at that otherwise obscure period.

Romanus II., the son of Constantine, or rather his great general, Nicephorus Phocas, conquered Crete from the Saracens, an enterprise in which two emperors had signally failed. A. D. 960.
Nicephorus was raised to the imperial rank upon the death of Romanus, and ruled with great energy as guardian and colleague of the infant sons of his predecessor. He was murdered by his nephew, John Zimiskes, who likewise, with the imperial rank and dignity, held the place of prime minister to the young emperors Basil II. and Constantine IX.

111. The great event of John's reign was a war with the Scandinavian rulers of Russia, now a powerful dynasty, who harassed the shores of the Eastern Empire as seriously as their countrymen at the same time were vexing those of Western Europe. The emperor signally defeated them at Presthlava in Bulgaria, A. D. 971, and, after besieging their remaining forces in Dorystolon, made a treaty which added the kingdom of Bulgaria, lately conquered by the Russians, to the empire, thus extending its bounds again to the Danube. The peace was first broken, A. D. 988, by Vladimir the Great of Russia, who seized the important commercial city of Cherson, more lately known as Sevastopol. From its foundation as a Greek colony, it had retained its republican constitution until the reign

---

[*] This title, "born in the purple," belongs to most of the sons of Byzantine emperors, being derived from a porphyry-lined apartment in the imperial palace. It is applied more especially to Constantine VII., to distinguish him from his colleague, Constantine, son of Romanus I.

of Theophilus, and still boasted its independence in local affairs. Vladimir married a sister of the emperor, Basil II., and, having himself been baptized, took vigorous measures to complete the Christianization of his people.

112. Under Basil II. the empire reached its highest pitch of military glory. In a nearly forty years' war he conquered the Bulgarians and other Slavonian tribes of the Hellenic peninsula; but he disgraced his victory by a needless act of barbarity. Fifteen thousand prisoners were deprived of their eyes and thus sent back to their king, who died of grief and rage at the terrible sight. After the short and insignificant reign of Constantine IX., the fortunes of the empire were for nearly thirty years in the hands of the more or less wicked favorites of his daughters Zoe and Theodora, whose administrations need not here be detailed.

113. A new dynasty was then founded by Isaac Comnenus, a general of high birth, who was raised to the throne by his brother officers, A. D. 1057. Upon his resignation two years later, his brother John refused the crown, and four sovereigns of different families succeeded before Alexis I., son of John Comnenus, began his honorable but disastrous reign. His daughter, the princess Anna Comnena, has written the annals of her times, and has described the disasters which afflicted the declining empire. The victorious Turks had now spread from Persia to the Hellespont. The regions north of the Black Sea poured forth fresh swarms of barbarians; the Normans were invading Greece; and suddenly the first of a long series of events, soon to be described, "precipitated all Europe upon Asia," and threatened to sweep away the feeble remnant of the empire of Constantine.

RECAPITULATION.

Rise of Venice, Pisa, Genoa, and the Lombard cities. Italy devastated by Saracens and Hungarians. After the fall of the Carlovingians, the Italian crown is worn by Berengar I., Hugh, Lothaire, and Berengar II., until Otho I. unites it with that of Germany, and adds to both the diadem of the Cæsars. Rise of the Saxon line with Henry the Fowler. "Holy Roman Empire" implies the lordship of the world. Contest between the eastern and western Cæsars for supremacy in Italy. Otho III. inherits the claims and ideas of both, reforms the papacy, and overthrows Crescentius. Contest of Hildebrand (Gregory VII.) with Emperor Henry IV. Humiliation of the latter; his sons rebel against him, and he dies excommunicate. Basil I. founds a new dynasty in the Eastern Empire; conquers the Paulicians; establishes the Lombard theme in southern Italy. Syracuse and Thessalonica taken by Mohammedans; massacre in the latter city and captivity of its inhabitants. Virtues and literary works of Constantine VII. Conquest of Crete by Nicephorus Phocas. War of John Zimiskes with the Russians. Capture of Cherson by Vladimir the Great, and diffusion of Christianity in Russia. Military achievements and atrocious cruelty of Basil II. Rise of the Comneni and disasters of the reign of Alexis I.

QUESTIONS FOR REVIEW.

Book I.

BOOK II.

THE MIDDLE AGES.
A. D. 1096–1192.

PERIOD I. THE CRUSADES. A. D. 1096–1291.

THE CAPTURE OF JERUSALEM.

1. THE three Saracen empires on the eastern, southern, and western shores of the Mediterranean, now presented but a faint shadow of their former greatness. Wealth gained by conquest had destroyed the martial energy of the disciples of the Prophet, and the armies of the caliphs were recruited from the more vigorous tribes of Tartars which roamed over the great plains of central Asia. These northern barbarians, like the Gothic and Frankish mercenaries of Rome, became stronger than their masters, and aspired to raise and put down monarchs at their pleasure. At length the caliphs resigned all military command to the Sultan of the Turks, who bore the title of "Lieutenant of the Vicar of the Prophet," reserving to themselves only the spiritual duties and honors which belonged to the successors of Mohammed.

2. The first of the Turkish lieutenants was Togrol Beg, the founder of the Seljukian, and conqueror of the Ghaznevide dynasty of sultans. His nephew and successor, Alp Arslan, annexed Armenia and Georgia to his dominion, and, in four years' war with the Eastern empire, gained at last a decisive victory over Romanus Diogenes. His son, Malek Shah, the greatest prince of his time, reigned over a larger A. D. 1672–1092. empire than that of Cyrus, for it extended from Arabia to the borders of China. The Seljukian kingdom of Roum included all Asia Minor; and Nice in Bithynia, its capital, was a continual menace to Constantinople. But a still greater humiliation was the conquest of Jerusa- A. D. 1073. lem by the Turks, whose new zeal for the faith of Moham- med made them treat Christian pilgrims with ferocious barbarity.

3. So long as the caliphs, either of Bagdad or Cairo, governed Syria, their enlightened policy protected and encouraged European travelers. A quarter of Jerusalem was assigned for their use, and the keys of the Holy Sepulcher were in their hands; while in return the country was enriched by the money which they freely spent for relics and mementoes of the holy places. Syria, as the natural center of Mediterranean commerce, attracted multitudes of merchants, among whom the Greek inhabitants of Amalfi were most numerous and enterprising. Their ships conveyed western pilgrims to the ports of Palestine, and their liberality endowed the church and hospital of St. John of Jerusalem for their entertainment.

4. During the latter half of the eleventh century, the number of pilgrims was greatly multiplied, in spite of the increased peril, or rather, perhaps, in consequence of it. Seven thousand devotees, led by the primate of Germany and several of his bishops, braved the hostility of the Turks and visited Jerusalem, but they were glad to return by means of a Genoese fleet. Hildebrand himself prepared to lead fifty thousand volunteers to the rescue of Christian residents in the east from the hand of the infidel.

But it was reserved for Peter, a hermit of Picardy, effectually to kindle that flame of martial and religious zeal which was to burn two centuries in Europe. He returned from his pilgrimage, bearing letters from the patriarch Symeon, of Jerusalem, to Pope Urban II. and the whole multitude of Latin Christians, beseeching their aid. The Pope took counsel with Boemond, prince of Taranto, the son of Robert Guiscard. The Norman had inherited all his father's ambition; in the fanatical scheme of the hermit he saw his own chance of recovering the provinces of Illyria, Macedonia, and Greece, which, in his father's lifetime, he had wrested from the Eastern empire—as well as a victory for the pontiff over his rival, Guibert, who had been appointed by Henry IV., and for his comrades and followers, unlimited wealth and dominion in the spoils of the Saracens and Turks.

5. Peter preached the holy war throughout Italy and France, in streets, highways, and churches; in the palace and the cottage; and was everywhere received with a rapture of enthusiasm. The Pope himself set forth the claims of the East in the two councils of Piacenza and Clermont, where legates from the emperor, Alexis, also described the ravages of the infidel, and appealed to the chivalry of Europe for the defense of the only bulwark of Christianity in Asia. The crowd at Clermont responded with tears, groans, and the shout, "*Dieu le reut*" (God wills it), which became the battle-cry of the Crusades. Thousands of every rank and age placed the red cross upon their shoulders, and declared their purpose to die, if need were, in the Holy Land. Even the

A. D. 1095.

mountains of Wales, Scotland, and Norway heard the summons and sent forth their swarms of Christian soldiery. Europe forgot her private feuds; nobles sold or mortgaged their lands and castles; artisans and peasants, their tools and implements of husbandry; monks exchanged the cowled robe for armor of steel; serfs and debtors were released from bondage by their assumption of the cross; even robbers, pirates, and murderers renounced their lawless life, and believed that they could wash away its guilt in the blood of the infidels.

6. Unhappily, the first act of the Crusaders was a persecution and massacre of the Jews in the cities on the Rhine. In that dark age, hatred of unbelievers was deemed an essential feature of the Christian disposition, and the worst barbarities were committed against the Hebrews during the two centuries of the Holy Wars. The emperor, Henry IV., perhaps enlightened by his own experience of persecution, took these unhappy people under his protection, and ordered a strict restitution of their property.

7. Historians of the time assert that six millions of men, women, and children assumed the cross. The time of departure was fixed at August 15, 1096; but the ignorant and unwarlike rabble, who had deserted their industries without foresight of the means of subsistence, did not await the appointed day. Above 60,000 peasantry from the borders of France and Lorraine set forward under the guidance of Walter the Penniless, a brave though needy soldier; Peter followed with 40,000 more; and an irregular host of 200,000 without officers, guides, or the slightest knowledge of the way, pressed upon their heels. Failing of the miraculous supplies of food which they expected, they attempted to live at the expense of the countries through which they passed, and multitudes were put to death by the enraged inhabitants.

When the regular army of Crusaders arrived, a few months later, on the borders of Hungary, they found heaps of unburied corpses;—to their inquiries the King replied that the followers of Walter and Peter were certainly not disciples of Christ, and that their crimes of rapine and murder had only been justly avenged. The remnant who survived were kindly received by the emperor Alexis; but the ruined gardens, palaces, and even churches of Constantinople soon A. D. 1096. testified the barbarous ingratitude of his guests. Passing over into Asia, they were easily vanquished by Kilidge Arslan on the plains of Nice, and a pyramid of their bones was almost the sole remnant of this advanced guard of the crusading hosts.

8. Very different was the brave and brilliant array which, in four columns, for the sake of more abundant forage, set out in the autumn of 1096. The chivalry of Lorraine and north-eastern France were led through Germany, Hungary, and Bulgaria by Godfrey of Bouillon, duke

of Lower Lorraine and one of the noblest knights in Christendom. Raymond, Count of Toulouse and the greatest seigneur of southern France, led his host through Lombardy to Aquileia, and thence through Dalmatia and Slavonia. Prince Boemond of Taranto had a sufficient fleet to transport his army across the Adriatic. The remaining division was led by four royal princes — Hugh of Vermandois, brother of the King of France; Robert of Normandy, eldest son of the King of England; another Robert, Count of Flanders, and Stephen of Chartres and Blois, who had as many castles as there are days in the year. They traveled the length of Italy amid the applause of the people, and were intrusted by Pope Urban II. with the golden standard of St. Peter; but their army became scattered in the easy and triumphant march, and the four princes crossed the Adriatic in a less dignified array than that in which they had set out.

9. The emperor, Alexis, was overwhelmed by the numbers, and not a little incensed by the conduct of his allies. All his ingenuity was taxed to prevent a meeting of any two of their armies before the walls of his capital, and to expedite their departure for the Holy City. Their first operation was the siege of Nice, the Turkish capital of the kingdom of Roum, which was taken, June 20, 1097, and restored to the empire. The Turks were also defeated near Dorylæum in a hard-fought battle. Tancred, a kinsman of Boemond, and Baldwin, brother of Godfrey, were then sent forward with their horsemen. The former captured Tarsus. Baldwin, coming up after it was taken, desired to plunder the town in violation of its terms of surrender. His quarrel with the just and noble Tancred brought upon him the displeasure of all the crusaders, and, separating his own followers from the main army, he invaded Mesopotamia on his own account.

Edessa was then governed by a Grecian duke, who paid a heavy tribute to the Turks. Being childless, he adopted Baldwin, who as prince of Edessa threw off the Turkish yoke, made conquests among the hills of Armenia and the plains of Mesopotamia, and thus founded the first Latin sovereignty in Asia. That of Antioch was soon afterward gained by Boemond, Prince of Tarento. The city withstood a seven months' siege; and even when it was taken through the treachery of a Syrian renegade, the citadel held out, and a great reinforcement of Turks from Mosul reduced the Christian army, now exhausted by famine, to the verge of destruction. The timely discovery of a sacred lance, said to have been pointed out by a vision of St. Andrew, animated the crusaders to new and indomitable zeal; a fresh attack was made in twelve divisions in honor of the twelve Apostles, and the Turkish host was annihilated or scattered. The emperor Alexis rejoiced equally in the conquest of the Turks and the exhaustion of the Christians. A violent plague, aggravated by the summer heat, destroyed more than 100,000 of the crusading army.

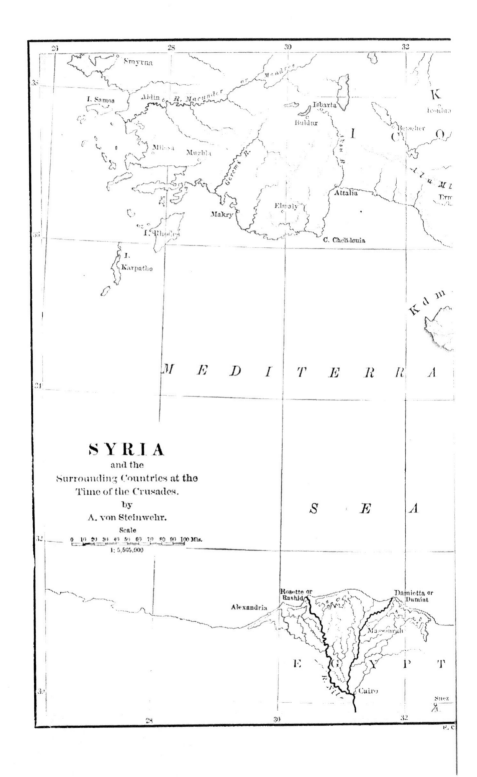

SYRIA
and the
Surrounding Countries at the
Time of the Crusades.
by
A. von Steinwehr.
Scale
0 10 20 30 40 50 60 70 80 90 100 Mls.
1: 5,565,000

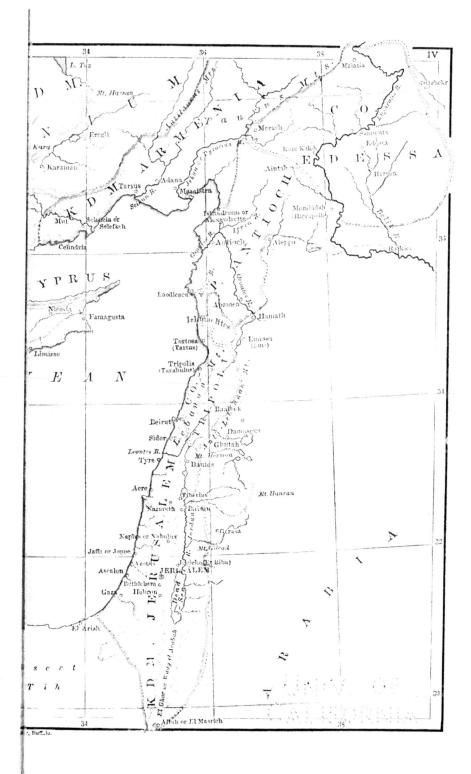

10. The Fatimite caliphs of Egypt had exulted in the victories of the Christians over their own enemies, the Turks, and had availed themselves of the abasement of the Seljukian power to repossess Jerusalem and all Palestine. Friendly letters and embassies were sent from Cairo to the Latin camp; but the leaders refused to make any distinction between the ferocious Turk and the courtly Saracen. They declared that the usurper of Jerusalem was their foe, whoever he might be; and early in the summer of 1099 the crusading host appeared before the Holy City. After three years' pilgrimage the first glimpse of Jerusalem was hailed with weeping and cries of joy. Their toils and sufferings were forgotten; casting themselves on the ground, the pilgrims gave thanks to Heaven, and "all had much ado to manage so great a gladness." The millions who had taken the vows were now reduced to 40,000 men; more than 850,000 had fallen by the way; of their princely leaders, two had returned to Europe and two were settled in their new principalities of Edessa and Antioch; but Godfrey of Bouillon, Raymond of Toulouse, Robert of Normandy, and Robert of Flanders pitched their respective camps on the northern and western sides of the city.

11. Wood for the assaulting engines was brought thirty miles from the forests of Sichem. The siege lasted forty days, during which the crusaders suffered intensely from want of water. The beds of the Gihon and Kedron were dry, and all cisterns had been destroyed by the Turks. The Saracens had now learned the use of Greek fire, and in the final attack for a day and a half victory seemed inclining toward the besieged. At length, however, on Friday, July 15, the victorious standard of Godfrey of Bouillon was planted upon the wall of Jerusalem, 460 years from its conquest by the Saracens. In the moment of victory the ferocious passions had sway — babes were torn from their mothers' arms to be dashed against the walls, and ten thousand Mohammedans were massacred in the Mosque of Omar. Then the soldiers of Christ remembered that they were pilgrims, and washing themselves of the blood they had so pitilessly shed, they walked in penitential procession to Mount Calvary, to weep and pray at the tomb of their Redeemer.

A. D. 1099.

12. Eight days after this great event, the army, by a unanimous vote, chose Godfrey of Bouillon to be king of Jerusalem and protector of Christian interests in the Holy Land. The office bore with it more of peril than of profit, and the great duke accepted it in all humility and faithfulness. He refused to wear a crown of gold in the city where his Savior had worn a crown of thorns, but he consented to be styled Guardian of Jerusalem and Baron of the Holy Sepulcher. A code of laws, called the Assise of Jerusalem, was prepared by the most competent of the Latin pilgrims and deposited in the Tomb on Mount Calvary. A few weeks

M. H. 5

after the capture of the Holy City, the Sultan of Egypt approached with an army to retake it. He was decisively overthrown at Ascalon, and his sword and standard were hung as trophies before the Holy Sepulcher.

13. The greater number of the crusaders, considering their vows accomplished, then returned to Europe, leaving Godfrey and Tancred with 300 knights and 2000 foot-soldiers to defend Palestine. The kingdom then consisted of only Jerusalem and Jaffa, with about twenty villages and towns lying in that region, but separated by fortresses of the Mohammedans. Godfrey survived his consecration but one year, and was succeeded by his brother, Baldwin. By successive conquests the Latin kingdom was extended east of the Euphrates and southward to the borders of Egypt. French law, language, titles, and customs reigned throughout the lands once governed by David and Solomon. Only four cities — Ems, Hamath, Damascus, and Aleppo — remained to the Mohammedans of all their Syrian conquests. The lands were parceled out, according to feudal custom, into the four great baronies of (1) Tripoli, (2) Galilee, (3) Cæsarea and Nazareth, (4) Jaffa and Ascalon.

14. The monks of the order of St. John rendered invaluable services to the crusading armies; and in A. D. 1121 they added military vows to those of the cloister, forming the first of three orders of chivalry which became the valiant defenders of the Holy Land. Nobles and princes hastened to enroll themselves as "Knights Hospitallers," and youth were sent from all countries to be trained in the Hospital of St. John to the practice of religion and knightly virtues; 28,000 farms and manors were bestowed upon them in various countries of Christendom, and they were able to support a large army of horse and foot from their own revenues. The Templars had their origin about the same time in the voluntary association of nine French knights, who added to the usual vows of the religious orders a fourth, binding them to the protection of pilgrims and the defense of the Holy Sepulcher. Originally poor, the Templars, like the Hospitallers, soon became distinguished by their wealth, numbers, and pride. Their grand master had the dignity of a sovereign prince, and, as the order owned allegiance to none but the Pope, it became an object of jealousy to the kings in whose realms it had possessions. The Teutonic Order was of somewhat later date.

15. When the glorious news of the capture of Jerusalem arrived in Europe, Hugh of Vermandois and Stephen of Chartres were filled with shame and regret at having so soon deserted their comrades. They hastened to retrieve their reputation by placing themselves at the head of a fresh swarm of French, German, and Lombard pilgrims who had now assumed the cross; 420,000 persons set forth in A. D. 1101, but nearly all perished in Asia Minor from plague, famine, and the arrows of the Turks.

Decline of Saracen and rise of Turkish power. Turks conquer Jerusalem and oppress Christian pilgrims. Appeal of Peter the Hermit to Western Europe seconded by the ambition of Boemond of Tarento. At Council of Clermont multitudes of all classes assume the cross. Massacre of the Jews. An unmilitary throng of crusaders, preceding the regular armies, perish by starvation and violence. Departure of the princes; they are received with scant courtesy by the emperor, Alexis; gain victories over the Turks. Baldwin becomes Prince of Edessa; Boemond, of Antioch. Jerusalem retaken by the Saracens of Egypt; is besieged and captured by the Crusaders. Godfrey of Bouillon chosen king. French law, language, and feudal institutions introduced into Palestine. Rise of the Hospitallers and Templars. Destruction in Asia Minor of a second crusading host under the French princes.

SECOND, THIRD, AND FOURTH CRUSADES.

16. Several causes in Europe and Asia combined to bring about a *Second Crusade.* The county of Edessa was conquered by Zenghi, a Turkish chief, and the eastern frontier of Palestine thus lay open to invasion. A. D. 1146-1149. Louis VII. of France, in war with his vassal, the Count of Champagne, violated his own conscience and the superstition of his subjects by ordering the burning of a church in which many hundreds of the surrendered people had taken refuge. Warned by illness, he resolved to expiate the crime by a pilgrimage to Jerusalem, in which he was joined by his queen, the celebrated Eleanor, heiress of Aquitaine. The marvelous eloquence of Bernard, abbot of Clairvaux, at the Council of Vezelay, stirred all ranks and classes to redeem the Holy Land from falling again into the possession of infidels. The emperor, Conrad III., yielded to the persuasions of the abbot, and his barons and people, who had taken little part in the First Crusade, followed in great multitudes. Towns were deserted, and only women and children were left, in many instances, to cultivate the land.

17. The emperor, Manuel Comnenus, received his allies with the same plausible but deceitful policy which had distinguished his grandfather, Alexis. Bread sold to the hungry armies was mixed with chalk; the guides, either by secret order from the emperor or through the bribes of the Turks, betrayed the crusaders to their enemies, or led them into the deserts to perish with hunger and thirst. The French king, meanwhile, was kept inactive by the false assurances of Manuel. When the truth became known, Conrad and Louis joined their forces for the march through Asia Minor. In a battle on the Mæander, the French were completely victorious; but in a narrow mountain pass between Phrygia and Pisidia, they were surprised and overwhelmed by the Mussulmans. With great difficulty, owing to the wintry snows, want of food, and the refusal of the Greeks to trade, the Franks arrived at Attalia, where the King of France embarked for Antioch, leaving the Count of Flanders to convoy the mass of pilgrims for whom no ships could be procured. Thousands were slaughtered by the Turks, and the count, seeing the case hopeless, escaped by sea, leaving his defenseless comrades to their fate.

18. The army which had set out from the Rhine and Danube exceeded in numbers that of Godfrey of Bouillon, but its leaders arrived at Antioch with only a shattered remnant of their forces. Their first enterprise was against Damascus, whose power and position threatened the kingdom of Jerusalem. The French, the Germans, and the two orders of knights vied with each other in deeds of unexampled bravery. The prize was within their grasp; but in disputes between the Count of Flanders and the barons of the Holy Land, the golden moment slipped away. The Saracens repaired their fortifications, and the crusaders, in sorrow and shame, retreated to Jerusalem. The emperor soon returned to Europe, and the French sovereigns, with all their knights and gentlemen, followed in a year. Thus ended the Second Crusade.

19. The Fatimite caliph of Cairo was dethroned, A. D. 1171, by a lieutenant of Noureddin, Sultan of Damascus, who was subject to the Abbassid caliph of Bagdad. Saladin, the most formidable foe of Christendom, was about to throw off his allegiance to Noureddin, when the latter died, and the aspiring young vizier made himself Sultan of Syria and Egypt. The kingdom of Jerusalem, which had owed its eighty-eight years' existence to the mutual enmity of the Saracens and Turks, was the first to feel his power. In a two days' battle on the Lake of

A. D. 1187.

Tiberias, the Christians were routed, and their king, Guy of Lusignan, with the grandmaster of the Templars, the Marquis of Montferrat, and others, were prisoners. Life was offered to the knights of the two orders only on condition of renouncing their faith, and 230 met a voluntary martyrdom. In consequence of the battle, Tiberias, Acre, Jaffa, Cæsarea, and many other towns fell into Saladin's possession. Tyre held out, under the command of Conrad of Montferrat. Jerusalem, after a long and desperate contest, was surrendered.

20. The news of the catastrophe of Tiberias and the fall of Jerusalem spread grief throughout Europe. The King of the Two Sicilies was first in arms. Philip Augustus of France and Henry II. of England met in Normandy to concert measures for the *Third Crusade*. The

A. D 1189–1193.

aged emperor, Frederic Barbarossa,* summoned a diet at Mentz, in which he himself, with his son and eighty-eight spiritual and temporal lords, assumed the cross. Throughout Europe a tenth of all movable property, known as the "Saladine Tithe," was levied upon Jews

---

* Frederic Barbarossa is the great hero of German romance. Popular tradition says he is not even now dead, but sleeping in a cavern near Salzburg, whence he will reappear when most needed.

and Christians for the expense of the wars. Passing the Hellespont without deigning to visit Constantinople, the Emperor Frederic defeated the Turks and captured Iconium, their capital; but he was drowned in the Cydnus, and the hardships of the march reduced the German host to one-tenth of its original numbers long before it arrived at Acre. Some soldiers of Bremen and Lubec, moved by the sufferings of their comrades here, converted their tents into a hospital; and the Duke of Suabia founded the Order of Teutonic Knights, who, A. D. 1190. combining the charities of the Hospitallers with the chivalric vow of the Templars, bound themselves to the relief of the sick and the defense of the holy places.

21. The Christians of Palestine had mustered all their forces for the recapture of Acre, which, as a strongly fortified port, was an important medium of supplies from Europe. Guy of Lusignan, whom Saladin had released from prison, perhaps on purpose to divide the counsels of the Franks, had at one time 100,000 men at his command; but the death of his wife and children, for whose sake alone the crown had been conferred upon him, undermined the authority which his crimes and weaknesses of character had always rendered irksome to his subjects. His sister-in-law, Isabel, a younger daughter of Almeric, married Conrad of Montferrat, now Prince of Tyre, a nobleman of great and deserved popularity, who became the successful candidate for the crown of Jerusalem.

22. The siege lagged until the arrival of the French and English forces, led by their respective kings. Richard I. had just received the crown of England upon the death of his father, Henry II., and the fame of his courage and strength gave new spirit to the besiegers. Two years from its investment, the city fell, July, 1191. The Duke of Austria planted his banner, in common with the French and English chiefs, on part of the walls, but Richard tore it down with his own hands and threw it into the ditch—an insult which led to a fierce and lasting quarrel between the two princes. The King of France, either disgusted by the superior fame of Richard, or really ill, as he alleged, soon returned to Europe, leaving a large portion of his forces with the Duke of Burgundy to serve under the English king. He solemnly swore that he would not molest the dominions of the latter during his engagement in the Holy Wars; but, pausing at Rome to be absolved by the Pope from this inconvenient vow, he had no sooner set foot in France than he began to plot with John—the brother of Richard and regent of England in his absence—to possess himself of the French counties and duchies for which Richard was his vassal, John being encouraged to assume the English crown as the reward of his compliance. Though rumors of these treacherous movements reached Palestine, the English king stayed to refortify Jaffa, Ascalon, and Gaza, working with his own hands like a common soldier, while bishops and the highest nobles, urged by his example, carried earth and mortar, and aided in building the walls. The united army approached within sight of Jerusalem where Saladin was posted; but the prudence or the treachery of the Duke of Burgundy prevented an attack, and Richard, covering his face with a shield, refused, with grief and shame, to look upon a city which he was unable to deliver from the infidel.

23. He consented to the crowning of Conrad of Montferrat as king of Jerusalem, indemnifying Guy of Lusignan, the deposed sovereign, by a generous gift of Cyprus, which Richard himself had conquered from Isaac Comnenus on his way to the Holy Land. Conrad died before his coronation, and Count Henry of Champagne succeeded to the empty title, which he bore, A. D. 1192–1197. On the eve of his departure for Europe, the English king signalized his valor by a new exploit, which terrified the Saracens and secured for the Christians a more advantageous peace. Saladin, by a rapid movement, had possessed himself of Jaffa. The great tower still held out, but the patriarch and knights had promised to surrender the next morning, unless succor should arrive. The English squadron appeared in time; Richard was the first to leap on shore, and so furious was his onset, that the Mussulmans broke up their camp and retreated some miles into the country. Learning with shame that they had been driven by only five hundred men, they endeavored in a night attack to regain their advantage, but Richard, with ten knights in full armor, issuing suddenly from the Christian tents, renewed the panic; and Saladin, now exhausted by the long series of battles, consented to an honorable truce of three years and eight months. The sea-coast from Tyre to Jaffa was surrendered to the Christians, and pilgrims from Europe were guaranteed safety and freedom from imposition in their visits to the Holy Sepulcher. The barons whose estates had been conquered by the Saracens were indemnified by grants of towns and castles.

24. Arriving in the Mediterranean, opposite the French coast, Richard learned that the feudal lords of that region had resolved to seize him if he landed on their territory. Unable to proceed to England in his unseaworthy vessel, he turned toward Germany, and, guided by some pirates, landed at Zara. He wished to traverse Germany in disguise, but he was identified and imprisoned by his old enemy, the Duke of Austria, who surrendered him the next spring to the emperor, Henry VI. Before the Diet at Haguenau, Richard was accused of several grave offenses, but he defended himself with such eloquence that all but the most prejudiced were convinced of his innocence. He received the investiture of the kingdom of Arles, and voted as a prince of the empire in the next imperial election. During his enforced absence from England, his brother made new efforts to seize the crown, while Philip of France invaded Normandy, and both perjured princes offered large sums of money to the

emperor, to keep Richard in perpetual captivity or deliver him into their hands. The disgraceful bargain might have been sealed, but for the indignant protest of the German princes, who compelled Henry VI. to accept the ransom offered by the English Parliament for the liberation of the king. He was released after long delays, and landed at Sandwich fifteen months from his capture and five years A. D. 1194. from his departure for the Holy Wars. The share of the Duke of Austria in his ransom-money went to enrich the newly founded city of Vienna.

25. During the captivity of Richard, his great enemy, Saladin, had died in Palestine, A. D. 1193. His three sons became sultans of Aleppo, Damascus, and Egypt; but his brother, Saphadin, ruled the greater part of Syria. A fresh crusade was undertaken by the German princes and bishops, who were joined on their march by the widowed Queen of Hungary. The dukes of Saxony and Lower Lorraine defeated Saphadin between Tyre and Sidon, thus liberating many cities and 9000 Christian captives. Another victory was followed by the news of the emperor's death, and the sudden departure for Germany of all the princes who, by vote or influence, could hope to affect the choice of his suc- A. D. 1197. cessor. Saphadin, rallying his forces, recaptured Jaffa, and put every inhabitant to the sword. The great expedition, having thus failed, is not commonly numbered among the Crusades.

26. A *Fourth Crusade* was proclaimed, A. D. 1200, by Innocent III., who imposed upon the clergy throughout Europe a tax for the expenses of the war. Princes and people joined their offerings. Those who could not go to Palestine in person commuted their service into money, and the treasury of the Vatican overflowed. Thibaud, Count of Champagne, brother of the late King of Jerusalem, was among the first to assume the cross, and a council of French barons met at Soissons to deliberate upon the means of fulfilling their vow. The horrors of a land journey into Asia were already too well proven; but the feudal lords had not, like Richard or Philip Augustus, the resource of a national navy. It was, therefore, resolved to engage the aid of Venice, then the greatest maritime power in Europe. A treaty was made between the deputies of the barons and the Grand Council of the republic for the transportation of the troops in Venetian vessels, Venice herself becoming an ally in the war and an equal sharer in the prizes.

27. Soon after Easter, A. D. 1202, the French crusaders crossed Mount Cenis and assembled at Venice. Some delay occurring in the prepayment of the transportation money, Doge Dandolo secured their aid in the recovery of Zara, on the Dalmatian coast, which had revolted to Hungary. Feeble and nearly blind, at the age of ninety-four, the Doge led the expedition in person and gained a complete victory. But a more brilliant enterprise tempted the French and Venetian arms. Isaac Angelus, Em-

peror of the East, had been dethroned, imprisoned, and deprived of his eyes by an unnatural brother, whom he had himself redeemed from Turkish slavery. His son, Alexis, escaped and found refuge with his brother-in-law, the Duke of Suabia. Appearing before the French and Italian leaders in their camp at Zara, the envoys of Alexis besought their aid in restoring his father to the throne, promising in return the coöperation of the Greeks in the conquest of the Holy Land.

28. The Pope forbade this diversion of forces which were consecrated to the deliverance of Palestine; but the knights resolved to turn so far aside from their original purpose in order to make good their character as champions of justice and avengers of wrong. By two attacks Constantinople was taken, and the blind old emperor was drawn from his dungeon and replaced upon the throne in partnership with his son, Alexis. The season being far advanced, the French and Venetians consented to winter at Constantinople, and aid to establish more firmly the power which they had restored. A brawl between the inhabitants and the Flemish soldiers ended in a conflagration, which continued eight days and consumed three miles of densely populated dwellings. Alexis, who was disliked by his own subjects for his alliance with the Franks, offended the latter by vacillation and delay in the payment of the promised subsidies, and a fresh war broke out. The guards of the palace set up an emperor of their own in the person of Alexis Mourzoufle, a kinsman of the imperial family distinguished for his hatred of the Latins. Alexis Angelus was imprisoned, and his blind father died of terror.

29. The French and Venetians now united for a second capture of the city. It was taken, and houses, churches, even the tombs of the emperors, were despoiled in a mad riot of pillage. Sculptures preserved from the golden age of Grecian art were destroyed by barbarians too ignorant to discern their value;—if of marble, they were hacked to pieces; if of bronze, they were melted into coin or household utensils. The Venetians, somewhat more civilized than the French, reserved the four bronze horses of Lysippus to adorn their church of St. Mark. After paying their long deferred debt to their allies, the French had a sum left from their share of the plunder which equaled seven times the yearly revenue of England at that time.

April, 1204.

30. Baldwin, Count of Flanders, was chosen by the two conquering nations to be Emperor of the East. Only one-fourth of the dominion of the Comneni fell to his share, the rest being divided between the Venetians, Lombards, and French. The Latin Empire at Constantinople lasted fifty-seven years, during which the Roman ritual superseded that of the Greeks in the churches, and the laws of Jerusalem were imposed upon the people in contempt of the code of Basil and Leo VI. Fragments of the conquered empire were erected into

A. D. 1204-1261.

rival states by members of the deposed family, who reigned at Nice, at Trebizond, and in northern Greece; and in A. D. 1261, Michael Palæologus, the Nicæan emperor, aided by the mutual rivalries of the Genoese and Venetians, expelled the sixth of the usurpers,* and recovered the throne of the Cæsars. Most of the Archipelago and Greece proper remained many years longer in the feudal control of the Latins.

31. Few of those who took arms for the Fourth Crusade ever reached the Holy Land; but the conquest of Constantinople so alarmed the Mussulmans, that Saphadin hastened by liberal concessions to secure a six years' truce.

The continuance of the fanatical spirit in Europe was shown by the Children's Crusade, A. D. 1211. A superstition gained ground, especially in Germany, that the princes and soldiery were forbidden to possess the Holy Land because of their sins, and that the great honor was reserved for the innocent and the weak. Ninety thousand children are said to have assembled from the various towns and hamlets, and, led only by a child, to have advanced as far as Genoa. Here they found the sea, of which they had never heard, and, separating, some took ship, only to fall into the hands of Moorish pirates, and the rest wandered about until they perished of hunger or fatigue. Probably not one of the deluded host ever reached Palestine, or even regained his home.

RECAPITULATION.

The King and Queen of France and the German emperor had part in the Second Crusade, which failed through the treachery of the Greeks and the rivalries of the Latins. Saladin, becoming Sultan of Egypt, defeated the Christians in the battle of Tiberias, and became master of Jerusalem. The emperor, Frederick I., led the van of a Third Crusade— soon followed by Philip II. of France and Richard I. of England, who combined their forces in a siege of Acre. Guy of Lusignan was deposed and Conrad of Montferrat appointed King of Jerusalem. Conrad dying, Henry of Champagne became king. Richard, on his return, was imprisoned fifteen months in Germany. In the Fourth Crusade, the French and Venetians established a Latin empire at Constantinople. The forces thus diverted never reached Palestine. Ninety thousand children perished in an attempted crusade, A. D. 1211.

---

* The Latin emperors were as follows: Baldwin I. died A. D. 1206, a prisoner of the Bulgarians. His brother, Henry, reigned, A. D. 1206–1216; and their brother-in-law, Peter de Courtenay, was appointed to succeed, but he died in captivity, A. D. 1219, before he could reach his capital. Robert de Courtenay reigned seven years, and was succeeded, A. D. 1228, by John de Brienne, guardian and father-in-law of Baldwin de Courtenay, the sixth and last of the line.

THE LAST OF THE CRUSADES.

32. By the death of Almeric of Lusignan and his wife, A. D. 1206, the shadowy crown of Jerusalem rested again upon a young girl's head; and as no nobleman in Palestine was judged worthy to share that slight but perilous honor, John of Brienne, a favorite of the King of France, was designated as the husband of Mary, daughter of Isabella and Conrad of Montferrat. He was accompanied from Europe by three hundred knights, the whole contribution of Christendom at that time toward the recovery of the Holy Sepulcher. England was absorbed by dissensions between her king and barons; France, by a crusade against her own people, the Albigenses of the south; and Germany, by the struggle between the emperor and the Pope for the dominion of Italy.

33. The new King of Jerusalem appealed for aid, and Innocent III. issued a stirring exhortation to all western Christendom. The eloquence of his preachers was seconded by the songs of poets, who had not only pious, but patriotic motives for urging the foreign expedition. Their sovereign and most munificent patron was the Count of Toulouse, with whom, as a protector of heretics, the King of France was at war; and they naturally desired to divert the assaults of bigotry from their own countrymen to the Saracens. The vanguard of the *Fifth Crusade* was led by the nation which had most obstructed the first. Andrew II. of Hungary, incited by his father's wish and his mother's example, took the cross, and was joined by all the lay and spiritual lords of southern Germany. But he accomplished personally little more than a multitude of pilgrimages and the collection of innumerable relics; and then, in spite of the entreaties of his allies, he returned to his impoverished kingdom.

A. D. 1217–1221.

34. Egypt was now the heart of the Moslem power, and thither a second army of Germans directed their efforts. They took the fortress of Damietta by assault, and besieged the town. Many obstinate battles were fought; the places of the exhausted besiegers were filled by recruits from England and the free cities of Italy; and at length the city was taken. A hideous spectacle met the eyes of the conquerors. Hunger and pestilence had reduced the 70,000 inhabitants to 3,000, and the survivors were more like animated skeletons than like living beings. In the attempt to complete the conquest of Egypt, the invaders were in turn vanquished by the great natural force which has served in all ages both for the nourishment and protection of that country. The rising Nile was turned into the Latin camp, tents and baggage were swept away, and all communication with Damietta cut off. In this perilous position the papal legate was reduced humbly to beg for far less favorable terms than he had once haughtily rejected. Damietta was surrendered; the starving hosts of

Christendom were fed from the granaries of the Sultan, and permitted to march into Syria.

35. The emperor, Frederic II., had been excommunicated for his delay in joining the crusade, and when in A. D. 1227 he at length embarked, he was excommunicated again for presuming to go without permission. He was welcomed, however, by the Teutonic knights, and cautiously joined by the Hospitallers and Templars. His personal influence effected more than even the battle-ax of Coeur de Lion: for Jerusalem, Jaffa, Bethlehem, and Nazareth were ceded to the Christians. Accompanied only by his courtiers and the Teutonic knights, Frederic crowned himself in the Church of the Holy Sepulcher, since no priest would perform that office. John of Brienne, with the hand of his daughter, Violante, had conferred upon the emperor his own right to the crown of Jerusalem; but returning to Europe he did not hesitate, in the service of the Pope, to ravage the Italian territories of his son-in-law.

36. The emperor being thus recalled from Palestine, the truce which he had made was disregarded, and on one occasion 10,000 pilgrims were massacred on the road to Jerusalem. The Templars sustained a severe defeat upon the death of the Sultan of Aleppo, with whom they were at peace. Every commandery in Christendom hastened to send reinforcements; a fresh crusade was announced by the Council at Spoleto, and the new orders of Dominican and Franciscan A. D. 1231. monks became the bearers of its decrees to all parts of Europe. The purpose was, as before, to fill the coffers of the Church with commutation money; and when Richard, Earl of Cornwall, brother of the English king, assumed the cross in sincerity, the Pope forbade his embarkation at Dover, and tried to intercept him at Marseilles. On the arrival at Jaffa of the English prince and nobles, the Sultan of Egypt sent to propose terms of peace. The greater part of Palestine was surrendered to the Christians; the walls of Jerusalem were rebuilt, and the churches reconsecrated. The objects of the expedition having been secured by peaceful negotiation, it is by most writers not reckoned in the number of the Crusades.

37. But another foe, equally terrible to Saracens and Christians, now appeared from the north-east, in the Tartar hordes expelled from Khorasmia by Zenghis Khan, and who, sweeping over Palestine, captured Jerusalem and murdered most of its inhabitants. The Templars called in their Syrian allies, and the combined armies fought for two days a fierce battle with the pagans, only to be overthrown and annihilated. The two grand masters of the Templars and Hospitallers were slain, and only fifty-two knights of all three orders remained alive and free. Barbacan, the Tartar chief, was slain, however, in a general battle, and southern Asia was relieved for the moment from its panic and distress.

38. The *Seventh Crusade* was led by the good king, Louis IX. of France, accompanied by his three brothers, the counts of Artois, Poitiers, and Anjou. Having wintered in Cyprus, Louis sailed to Egypt. Damietta, though strongly fortified, made no resistance, and all its magazines of grain were added to the stock of the crusaders; but in their march toward Cairo, the French were arrested by the canal of Ashmoum. The Count of Artois, discovering a ford, led his followers through, routed the Mussulmans who were posted on the opposite bank, and paused not until he had entered the half-deserted town of Massourah. Here the Moslems rallied and joined battle in the streets of the town. The concealed inhabitants flung stones, boiling water, and burning coals from their roofs upon the heads of the assailants. The arrival of the French king prevented a total rout; but the death of his brother, with the grand master of the Templars and a multitude of knights, paid the penalty of their rashness. The retreat was more disastrous than the battle. All the sick in the French camp were murdered by the Mussulmans; the king himself was made prisoner with his two remaining brothers, all the nobles, and 20,000 men of lower rank.

The city of Damietta was surrendered for the king's ransom. He then proceeded to Palestine, where he spent four years in seeking to establish that good order which his just and beneficent reign had already conferred upon France. No military successes attended his crusade. The death of the queen regent recalled him to his own kingdom; and he sacrificed his strong desire to visit Jerusalem to the feeling that a king in arms had no right to behold as a pilgrim what he could not possess as a conqueror.

39. If the Christians of Palestine could have remained at peace among themselves, they might have been victorious over the common enemy; but the Italian merchants of the various cities never forgot their rivalries, and the jealousy of the two military brotherhoods broke out, soon after the

A. D. 1259.　　Seventh Crusade, into actual war. The knights of St. John were the victors in a battle from which scarcely a Templar escaped alive. This shameful war was interrupted by the invasion of Palestine, by Mamelukes from Egypt (see ¿ 163). Ninety Hospitallers held Azotus, and died to the last man in its defense. The Templars at Saphoury were forced to capitulate; but, contrary to the terms of surrender, they were afterward required to choose between apostasy and death. The knights and garrison, to the number of 600 men, sealed their faith with their blood. Jaffa and Beaufort were taken; Antioch was surrendered after 17,000 of its people had been slain and 100,000 made prisoners.

40. The news in Europe of the fall of Antioch occasioned an *Eighth Crusade*. Prince Edward of England, with the powerful earls of Pembroke and Warwick, assumed the cross. King Louis of France heartily joined in the alliance; but his first, and as it proved his last, hostilities were directed against the Moors of Tunis. His brother, Charles, Count of Anjou, and now King of the Two Sicilies, urged this enterprise for selfish reasons, for northern Africa had formerly paid tribute to the Neapolitan kingdom. Carthage was taken and plundered, but the army was stricken by the plague, which carried off the king and one of his sons. Prince Edward arrived the next spring in Palestine, where the name of Plantagenet mustered around him all the European forces. Nazareth was taken, the Turks were defeated, and a truce for ten years was already concluded with the Sultan of Egypt, A. D. 1272. when the death of Henry III. in England required the return of the prince to assume his crown.

41. The last general effort for the deliverance of the Holy Land, though enrolling many great names, was feeble in its execution and disastrous in its results, and is not commonly numbered among the Crusades. Rudolph of Hapsburg, the new sovereign of Germany, Michael Palæologus, the conqueror and successor of the last Latin Emperor of the East, and Charles, the French King of the Two Sicilies, were partners in the enterprise. The latter received from Mary, Princess of Antioch, a surrender of her hereditary claim to the crown of Jerusalem. Hugh, King of Cyprus, was, however, crowned at Tyre, and disputes for this unsubstantial dignity had their part in defeating the counsels of the allies. Margat was captured by the Turks, A. D. 1280. Tripoli, the seat of the last remaining barony of the Christians in Asia, was taken, and its people murdered or enslaved. Acre was almost the only refuge of Europeans, and its several wards or districts were assigned to miserable fugitives from the lost cities and provinces, who could not forget their jealousies even in their common distress.

42. The Sultan of Egypt mustered all his forces to destroy this last nucleus of Christianity in the East, and 200,000 Mamelukes were assembled for the siege of Acre. The defense was long and obstinate; the principal entrance to the city was repeatedly lost and won, and each time at great expense of Moslem and Christian blood; but at length the grand master of the Templars, who had been intrusted with the command, was slain with most of his followers, the town was in flames, and the seven knights who alone survived of the Order of St. John, embarked for Europe. The unarmed people who could not escape by sea perished on the shore. Tyre, Beirût, and other towns surrendered. All Palestine was overrun by the Turks, and, after a few more efforts by the Templars, it was abandoned to the Moslem dominion.

43. Though the hope of delivering the Holy Land lingered several centuries in the minds of European princes, and though some private enterprises were undertaken with that purpose, no general and public effort was renewed. Fifteen years from the fall of Acre, a new crusade was proclaimed by Pope Clement V., but few of those who assembled at Brindisi knew its object, which was merely to conquer the island of Rhodes from the Greeks and Saracens for a permanent residence of the knights of St. John. The thousands of Europeans who remained in Palestine after the withdrawal of the princes and military orders, became so mingled with the Mohammedans that no distinction of faith or nationality was long to be perceived. The Venetians made a treaty of friendship with the Mussulmans of Egypt, and received in Alexandria a church, a magazine, and an exchange, where they carried on a disgraceful traffic in Georgian and Circassian slaves. The Genoese possessed extensive streets and warehouses in Constantinople, with the control of the commerce of the Black Sea.

44. Though failing in their immediate object, the Crusades had most important and widely reaching results. Europe, divided by the feudal system into a multitude of petty sovereignties, was then first united in the only bond that could equally hold kings, nobles, peasants, and priests. To defray the cost of their equipment, many princes had sold their estates, and these, though usually absorbed by the Church, were sometimes bought by common citizens, whose importance as individuals and as a class was thus greatly increased. On the crusaders themselves, contact with unfamiliar customs had something of its natural effect in enlarging the mind and rendering it tolerant of new ideas. Constantinople, then the grandest and most beautiful city in the world, produced, even in its decline, the same effect upon the western, that old Rome had upon the northern, barbarians — the impression of a society, though enervated and decaying, yet far more enlightened and advanced than their own.

45. In the historians who accompanied the several expeditions may be seen the contrast between the narrow views of the first crusaders and the more courteous and liberal sentiments of their successors. The earlier chroniclers describe the "infidel dogs" as monsters, and exult in the most inhuman atrocities inflicted upon their defenseless wives and children; the later writers mention some Mussulmans with admiration, and hold up the delicate generosity of Saladin as a rebuke to the barbarity of so-called Christians.

46. Extensive intercourse between the East and the West resulted from the Crusades. India and China, long the abode of high civilization, had hitherto contributed nothing of importance to the general stock of ideas and comforts, owing to their isolation at the extreme circumference of the land hemisphere (see Book I., § 2). The consequences of increased communication will very soon be seen in the adoption of eastern inventions, which changed the whole current of European life (§§ 142, 144). Mongol embassadors were seen in the cities of Europe; and Italians, French, and Flemings visited the court of the Grand Khan (§ 155). A Tartar made helmets for the French army of Philip the Fair. Venetian merchants— among them the father of Marco Polo—resided for years in China and Tartary, and established trade with Hindustan. The narrow circle of European ideas was widened to include the art and languages of Asia, and their influence may be traced in the rise of the modern literatures in Europe.

47. Of the three orders of knights founded during the Crusades, the Templars, having no longer use for their ample revenues, became luxurious, haughty, and dangerous to settled governments; the Hospitallers, being on garrison duty against the Turks, successively in Cyprus, Rhodes, and Malta, retained their chivalrous and active life; the Teutonic knights found a still more stirring field of combat with the heathenism of northern Europe. Prussia was still pagan, and her fierce warriors were even fanatical in their aversion to Christianity. Herman von Salza, the illustrious grand master, accepted with joy the invitation of the northern bishops. Building themselves a fort at Marienburg, the knights began their arduous task both by preaching and by fighting. More than half a century elapsed before the spirit of resistance was broken, and still another century before Christianity was firmly established.

In the intervals of war the knights redeemed the marshy country by embankments, and replaced the salt quagmires with grassy and fertile meadows. Meanwhile the order became the rallying point for all the chivalry of Germany. It absorbed into itself the Sword Brothers and other military fraternities, and was victorious not only in Prussia, but in Livonia, Courland, and Lithuania. Its near neighborhood to Pomerania and the kingdom of Poland led, however, to disastrous wars, and eventually to its decline.

RECAPITULATION.

The Fifth Crusade was occasioned by the appeal of King John of Jerusalem, seconded by the preaching of the friars and the songs of the troubadours. Andrew of Hungary led the van rather as pilgrim than soldier. Damietta was besieged and taken by the Germans, who were, however, defeated on their march toward Cairo. Frederic II. became King of Jerusalem, and gained an advantageous peace. Disorders which followed his recall to Europe suppressed by Richard of Cornwall, a nephew of Cœur de Lion. A Tartar horde overran Palestine, destroying Saracens and Christians alike. In the Seventh Crusade Louis IX. of France captured Damietta, but was defeated and taken prisoner near Massourah. After his release he spent four years in Palestine. Mutual strife of the military orders interrupted by their common foe, the Mamelukes of Egypt. In the Eighth Crusade, Louis IX. died at Tunis. Prince Edward of England defeated the Turks and made a ten years' truce. Two emperors and a king were defeated in a final effort to deliver Palestine. Acre was lost and the Holy Land abandoned to the Turks. The effects of the Crusades were seen in the increased humanity and culture of the Franks. The Templars became rich and indolent; the Hospitallers held the southern outpost of Europe against the Turks; the Teutonic knights conquered and civilized the pagan tribes of the Baltic.

GUELFS AND GHIBELLINES.

48. The two centuries of the Crusades were marked in Europe by a long and deadly strife between the emperors and the popes. Henry V., though he had been aided by Pope Paschal II. in A. D. 1106-1125. his shameful and perfidious rebellion against his own father, soon renewed the contest with the Church. Repairing to Rome to assume the imperial crown, he fought a battle within the very precincts of St. Peter's with the papal party; the pope and several cardinals were imprisoned, their territories ravaged, and they were released only upon the promise of Paschal to perform the coronation, and to resign to Henry the investiture of all bishops and abbots in the empire. Upon the death of Matilda, Countess of Tuscany, in 1115, Henry again entered Italy to claim her territories as fiefs of the empire, nor were the popes during his lifetime able to dispute the possession.

The next pontiff, Gelasius II., was seized during the ceremony of his consecration by a party of imperialists led by Cencio Frangipani, the head of a house which for centuries was among the most powerful and turbulent in Rome. After being imprisoned and brutally ill treated, he at length escaped into France, where he died at the abbey of Cluny, A. D. 1119. His successor, Calixtus II., was a descendant of the kings of Burgundy and a kinsman of the emperor. By his wise and dignified policy, the dispute concerning investitures was ended in the Concordat of Worms, A. D. 1122. Each party made just concessions. The election of each new bishop was to take place in the presence of the emperor or his delegate, who should present the scepter in token of the temporal power conferred upon the candidate; but the ring and crozier, the symbols of the spiritual office, were to be received only from the Pope.

49. The Franconian Line ended, A. D. 1125, with the death of Henry V., and Lothaire the Saxon was elected emperor. The "great man of the North," during this and the two following reigns, was Albert of Anhalt, commonly called the Bear. He possessed by inheritance or conquest all northern Saxony, with Lusatia and the margravates of Salzwedel and Brandenburg, in the latter of which he founded the city of Berlin about the same time that Leopold of Austria laid the foundation of Vienna (see § 24). But a greater power than that of either emperor or barons was exercised by St. Bernard, the great abbot who from his cloister at Clairvaux ruled all the courts of Europe by mere energy of will. Through his influence the emperor, Lothaire, with the kings of France, England, and Spain, acknowledged the papal authority of Innocent A. D. 1130. II., who had been elected with unseemly haste almost before the death of his predecessor, Honorius II. The antipope, Anacletus, though elected by a more numerous party of cardinals, was of Jewish descent, and commanded few adherents except in southern Italy and Aquitaine. The emperor accompanied Innocent to Rome, and received from his hands the imperial crown. But no sooner had Lothaire retired than Anacletus returned, and the acknowledged pontiff took refuge in Pisa. Several years later the emperor crossed the Alps with an army and reinstated the Pope. The antipope died, and the great Council at the Lateran, attended by a thousand bishops and innumerable abbots, reaffirmed the dignity of Innocent.

A. D. 1139.

50. Bernard gained an equal apparent, though less real, success over the philosopher, Abelard, the bold thinker who, in asserting the supremacy of reason, seemed to threaten the authority of the Church. He was silenced and his writings burnt by the Council of Soissons; but the excited throng whom his eloquence had drawn to Paris followed him into the wilderness, and around his thatched hut of osier twigs grew up a village of similar dwellings, forming a school rather than a monastery, to which Abelard gave the name of the Paraclete. Still followed by suspicion, he buried himself among the wild monks of St. Gildas de Rhuys on the coast of Brittany; but his books, to adopt the words of Bernard, were "flying abroad all over the world;" and their author was again summoned before the Council of Sens. He was condemned, and a confirmatory decree of Pope Innocent II. forbade all discussion of the mysteries of belief. Two years later Abelard died in seclusion, A. D. 1142.

A. D. 1121.

51. Upon the death of the emperor, Lothaire, A. D. 1138, the Hohenstaufen family came to the imperial throne in the person of Conrad III. Its great rival was the Guelfic house, which possessed not only the duchies of Saxony and Bavaria, but the vast hereditary domains of Matilda of Tuscany. In a battle near Weinsberg, A. D. 1140, were first heard the war-cries of "Guelf" and "Ghibelline," which were yet to ring through Europe from Sicily to the Baltic. Though both names belonged to Germany, the hostility of several successive popes toward the Hohenstaufen identified the name of Guelf with the papal, that of Ghibelline with the imperial party; and the whole controversy between the spiritual and civil supremacy was involved in these watchwords.

52. Frederic I., the nephew and successor of Conrad, is better known by his Italian surname, Barbarossa. No one of the German princes had a higher sense of his dignities and duties as emperor of the West. Having received the allegiance of the kings of Denmark, Poland, and Hungary, conferred the royal title upon the Duke of Bohemia, and made himself King of Upper Burgundy by marriage with the heiress, he proceeded to establish his authority over the rebellious cities of Italy. In his camp at Roncaglia the imperial shield was suspended from a high mast over his tent, as an invitation to all who had

A. D. 1152–1190.

suffered wrong to come and claim redress. He received the crown of the
Lombards at Pavia, and that of the empire at Rome. This
city had been for nine years under a republican government,
at whose head was Arnold of Brescia, a disciple of Abelard, a man of
pure, lofty, and ardent character, and a leader of the first organized
revolt against the high claims of the papacy as enforced by Hildebrand.
He had claimed the protection of the emperor in his opposition to the
Pope, but the two powers combined to crush the popular spirit, which
was equally hostile to both, and before the arrival of Frederic at Rome
Arnold was burned and his ashes thrown into the Tiber.

A. D. 1155.

53. Milan was the leader in the resistance to the emperor. In A. D.
1158, after a short siege, it was compelled to submit, and the imperial
eagle was placed upon the spire of its cathedral. A fresh attack upon
Frederic's officers gave occasion for more severe treatment. The proud
city was humbled by a siege of three and a half years, when the clergy,
nobles, and all the citizens marched out to the emperor's camp with
swords or halters suspended around their necks, and, casting themselves
upon the ground, begged for mercy. Their lives were spared, but they
were exiled to four villages, while the walls of their city were leveled
to the ground.

54. In his fifth visit to Italy, the emperor was detained seven months
by a fruitless siege of Alessandria, and was defeated in the battle of
Legnano, chiefly through the withdrawal from his army of Henry the
Lion, Duke of Bavaria and Saxony and head of the Guelfs. This great
prince had increased his territories by successful wars with the Vandals,
until they reached from the Danube to the Baltic and North seas, and
far surpassed the hereditary dominions of the emperor himself. He
aspired to be not only the conqueror, but the civilizer of the northern
regions, by means of schools, bishoprics, and courts of law. Peasants
dislodged from their homes in the Netherlands by an influx of the ocean
were conveyed at his expense into the new provinces of Holstein and
Mecklenburg, whose marshes and forests were soon transformed by their
industry into fruitful fields. Munich, the still magnificent capital of
Bavaria, was founded by Henry the Lion, A. D. 1157.

55. After Frederic had concluded at Venice, A. D. 1178, an advantageous peace with the Pope and the Lombard cities, he summoned Henry
the Lion to answer for himself before the Germanic Diet. Having disregarded four successive summons, the duke was declared an outlaw, and
in a two years' war was reduced to humble himself before the emperor and
beg for pardon. Frederic crowned a long and active life by leading his
armies against the Turks, and dying in Asia Minor, A. D. 1190.

56. His son, Henry VI., made himself master of Germany and Italy,
and raised the power of the Hohenstaufen to its highest pitch, but at the

cost of a series of tyrannical and cruel acts which made the name of Ghibelline detested. He gained the kingdom of Naples or the Two Sicilies in right of his wife Constantia, the last heiress of the Norman kings. At his early death, A. D. 1197, his son Frederic was but two years of age. He was educated in Italy, and Germany was for eighteen years torn by the contentions of the Guelfs and Hohenstaufen, the former of whom in the north set up Otho IV., a son of Henry the Lion, and the latter in the south, Philip, a brother of the late emperor. The Pope Innocent III., one of the greatest and most arbitrary of his order, espoused with zeal the Guelfic cause, but on the death of Philip of Hohenstaufen Otho became less obedient, and Innocent sent Frederic II. into Germany, choosing as the champion of the Church a prince whose whole life and reign were to be embittered by its hostility.

A. D. 1190–1197.

57. The young Hohenstaufen was crowned at Aix-la-Chapelle, A. D. 1215, and was universally acknowledged even before the death of his rival. As he grew older, however, his fondness for Arabic learning and his employment of Saracen troops,—above all, his great possessions in southern Italy which threatened the dominions of the popes, drew upon him the enmity of Gregory IX., who pronounced against him the severest censures of the Church, both before and during his crusade. (See § 35.) The emperor, returning, expelled the papal troops which were overrunning his kingdom of Naples, and devoted himself to the improvement of his favorite native land by a better code of laws, and by liberal patronage of art, commerce, and literature. The works of Aristotle and many of the Greek classics which had been preserved in Arabic versions by the Saracens, were by his order translated into Latin. The University of Naples was founded, and the far-famed college of medicine at Salerno newly endowed by him. Frederic was the most remarkable character of his time, uniting with the knightly energy and valor of his German ancestry the refined and subtle intellect of his native Italy, and excelling equally as lawgiver, poet, and warrior.

A. D. 1215–1250.

58. As king of the Two Sicilies he was a vassal of the Church, and his dispute with the popes involved all those questions of civil and spiritual authority which formed the main strife of the Middle Ages. The Ghibellines regarded the emperor as ordained of God, and denounced the Pope as antichrist for presuming to oppose him. The Guelfs declared that as Leo III. had taken the imperial crown from the Greeks and bestowed it upon Charlemagne, so every succeeding emperor had owed his power to the Pope, who conferred it in the ceremony of coronation. Gregory supported Milan and the Lombard cities in their rebellious league against the emperor, which was joined even by Henry, king of the Romans, who in his father's absence had been intrusted with the government of Germany. The undutiful prince ended his days in prison, but Frederic, whose affection had not been lessened by his son's ingratitude, lamented his loss in the words of David over Absalom.

59. In the great battle of Cortenuova, the Lombard League was defeated with enormous loss, and the emperor became master of Italy. Pope Gregory launched against him a fifth and if possible still more severe sentence of excommunication, depriving him of all his kingdoms, and proposing to bestow the imperial crown upon a brother of the king of France. St. Louis replied to these overtures by rebuking the "pride and audacity of the Pope which presumed to disinherit and depose a sovereign who had not his equal among Christians." It was at this crisis (see § 156) that the Tartar hordes of Zenghis Khan were devastating the borders of Germany and Poland; but the rival heads of Christendom had no force to spare against the common enemy. Gregory IX. died at nearly a hundred years of age, Innocent IV., the second of his successors, fled from Rome and took refuge in Lyons, a city which, though belonging to the empire, owned no government but that of its archbishop. Here a council was asembled which solemnly deposed Frederic and ordered the German princes to proceed to a new election. In accordance with its decree, Henry of Thuringia, and after his death, William, Count of Holland, were successively raised to the imperial dignity.

A. D. 1237.

A. D. 1245.

60. The death of Frederic II., A. D. 1250, was followed by great confusion. The Ghibellines every-where acknowledged his son Conrad IV. as emperor; and after the early death of Conrad, Manfred, another son of the great Frederic and of an Italian mother, became regent of Naples. Both brothers were excommunicated by Innocent IV., who hastened to offer the Sicilian kingdom successively to two English princes, and to Charles of Anjou, brother of Louis IX. of France. During the interregnum in the empire this prince held also the titles of senator of Rome and imperial vicar, which with his Neapolitan kingdom gave him the control of the entire peninsula. Manfred was defeated and mortally wounded in the battle of Benevento. His sons died in prison, and young Conradin, the son of Conrad IV., was the last of the Hohenstaufen. At sixteen years of age he went into Italy to claim his inheritance, but he was defeated and captured by Charles of Anjou, who, bent upon the utter extermination of the Ghibellines, caused him to be beheaded with five of his most faithful friends in the market-place at Naples.

A. D. 1266.

61. The French king and nobles treated the Two Sicilies as a conquered country. But their atrocious tyranny worked its own punishment. Conradin upon the scaffold had bequeathed his Italian kingdom to his cousin Constance, daughter of Manfred and wife of King Pedro III. of Aragon. John of Procida, a noble and physician who had been deeply in-

jured by the French, traveled in disguise from the court of Barcelona to that of Constantinople, and among the Ghibellines of Italy, every-where plotting vengeance against the usurper. At A. D. 1282. length in one eventful night, known as the "Sicilian Vespers," all the French in Palermo were massacred. Eight thousand of their nation perished in a few days, and the island of Sicily became an independent kingdom under Pedro III. of Aragon. The Pope—Martin IV., a slave of Charles of Anjou—declared Aragon itself to have been forfeited by Pedro, and bestowed it upon Charles of Valois, A. D. 1285. a nephew of the king of Naples. But in the same year, died the four chief actors in the dispute: Martin IV., Charles of Anjou, Philip III. of France, and Pedro III. of Aragon.

62. After the death of Conrad IV., in 1254, and of his rival, William, in 1256, no German prince would accept the imperial crown. One party, therefore, offered it to Alfonso the Wise of Castile, who never visited Germany for his coronation, while the other elected Richard of Cornwall, brother of Henry III. of England, who was crowned at Aix-la-Chapelle, in 1257; but his title, "King of the Romans," brought with it no real power, and the period from A. D. 1256 to 1273 is known as the Interregnum. The choice of the princes then fell upon Rudolph of Hapsburg, a brave knight who had won the highest esteem A. D. 1273-1291. by his noble and virtuous character, but who was so poor that even when emperor, he sometimes mended his doublet with his own hands. His energetic measures soon restored the honor of the imperial name. Ottocar, the powerful and rebellious king of Bohemia, was defeated and slain in battle, and his provinces of Austria, Styria, Carinthia, and Carniola enriched the house of Hapsburg.

RECAPITULATION.

Continued strife between emperors and popes, reclamation of waste or pagan countries on the Baltic by the great German princes, and the foundation of three royal capitals, belong to the period of the Crusades. Names of Guelf and Ghibelline, the former belonging to the Bavarian dukes, the latter to the Hohenstaufen, became watchwords of the papal and imperial parties. Frederic I. received feudal homage from kings of Denmark, Poland, Hungary, and Bohemia, and himself added the crown of Burgundy to those of Germany, Italy, and the Empire. He aided to suppress the Republic at Rome by the death of Arnold of Brescia, and crushed the rebellion of the Lombard cities by the destruction of Milan. He died during his crusade. Henry VI. conquered the kingdom of Naples and established his power throughout Germany and Italy. During the minority of his son Frederic, Otho of Saxony and Philip of Hohenstaufen were rival emperors. Frederic II. having received the imperial crown from Innocent III. was ever after the object of papal persecution, which stirred against him the rebellion of the Lombard League and even of his own son, and finally procured the election of rival emperors. Henry of Thuringia and William of Holland. Frederic was succeeded by his son, Conrad IV., who died A. D. 1254. Nearly twenty years interregnum followed, during which Alfonso of Castile and Richard of Cornwall bore the imperial name without the power. Manfred the brother and Conradin the son of Conrad IV. both perished in Italy, the one in the battle of Benevento and the other by order of Charles of Anjou, to whom the Pope had given the kingdom of Naples. The tyranny of the French was avenged by the "Sicilian Vespers" and by the revolt of Sicily to the House of Aragon, now sole representative of the Hohenstaufen. The interregnum in Germany was ended by the election of Rudolph of Hapsburg.

Great men of this period: Bernard of Clairvaux; Abelard; the Emperors Frederic I. and II.; Arnold of Brescia; Innocent III.—next to Hildebrand the greatest of the popes; Albert the Bear of Anhalt; Henry the Lion of Bavaria; Ottocar king of Bohemia.

ENGLAND AND FRANCE, A. D. 1100–1285.

63. In ENGLAND during the same period, the two great contests for civil and religious independence were in progress; namely, the strife of the kings with the popes for the appointment of prelates, and that of barons and kings for personal and feudal rights. Two sons* and a grandson of the Conqueror completed the elder Norman line which had governed England, A. D. 1066–1154. The Angevin house of Planta-

A. D. 1154–1189.

genet then succeeded in the person of Henry II., whose mother, the Empress† Matilda, daughter of Henry I. and granddaughter of the Conqueror, had vainly contested with her cousin Stephen the possession of the crown. Beside the throne of England, Henry inherited in France the great fiefs of Normandy, Maine, Touraine, and Anjou, and with his Queen, Eleanor, the discarded wife of Louis VII. of France, he received Aquitaine and Poitou. His French dominions thus exceeded by far the immediate possessions of the French king himself, who might well tremble in receiving the homage of his powerful vassal.

64. Crowned at the age of twenty-one, Henry Plantagenet set himself with vigor to the work of substituting justice and order for the lawless violence of Stephen's disputed reign. Ireland was added by conquest to his dominions, and the captive king of Scotland acknowledged the feudal supremacy of the English king. The long conflict between Church and State came to its height in the seven years' quarrel between Henry and his former chancellor and confidential friend, Thomas à Becket, whom he had raised to the primacy. It ended only with the murder of Becket at

A. D. 1170.

the altar of his cathedral church at Canterbury, but the victory remained with the prelate, who was worshiped as a saint, while the king was forced by the superstition of the age, perhaps by his own, to make a penitential pilgrimage to the tomb of his victim, where he humbly confessed his fault and submitted to be scourged.

---

* William II. (Rufus) A. D. 1087–1100; Henry I.—1135; Stephen of Blois—1154.

† Her first husband was the Emperor Henry V., who died A. D. 1125. She then married Geoffrey of Anjou.

65. Richard I., the valiant son and successor of Henry, spent only four months in England of the ten years (A. D. 1189–1199) that he wore its crown. The reign of his wicked and worthless brother John was productive of two great benefits to the kingdom. The A. D. 1199–1216. loss of most of his French dominions turned the attention of his successors to their duties as English sovereigns, while it heightened the feeling of nationality in their vassals, and the Great Charter, wrested by the Norman barons from the incompetent John, was the first guarantee of constitutional freedom, not only for themselves but for the Anglo-Saxon race. The kingdom was five years under an interdict, owing to the resistance of John to the investiture of Stephen Langton as archbishop of Canterbury; and even this harsh measure failing to move his obstinacy, Pope Innocent III. called upon all Christian princes to join in a crusade to dethrone him.

66. Philip II. of France who had already seized the greater part of the continental dominions of John, willingly mustered his forces for the conquest of England; but at this point the humbled and terrified king yielded more than was asked of him, by surrendering his kingdoms of England and Ireland to the Holy See, to be held by himself only upon payment of homage and tribute as a vassal. The wrath of both prelates and barons at this sacrifice of the national dignity led them to assemble in arms and demand the Great Charter, which was signed June 15, 1215, at Runnimede, on the Thames. The faithless king lost no time in breaking his oath and ravaging his kingdom with an army of Flemish mercenaries. The barons then offered the crown to Prince Louis of France, who swore to rule according to the laws established at Runnimede; but his triumphs ceased with the sudden death of John and the appointment of the Earl of Pembroke, the chief promoter of the Charter, as protector of the kingdom.

67. Henry III. was as weak and nearly as wicked as his father. Fifty-six years of misrule were partly compensated by renewed guarantees of the privileges of the people, which A. D. 1216–1272. they extorted from the ever recurring necessities of their king. In 1258 twenty-four barons formed themselves into a commission for the better government of the realm. At their head was Simon de Montfort, Earl of Leicester, one of the greatest men of his age. Seven years of civil war were the result. In the battle of Lewes the barons were triumphant, and the king, his brother Richard, king of the Romans, Prince Edward, and his cousin Prince Henry were made prisoners. In the name of the king, Simon de Montfort summoned the first English parliament properly so-called, for it included two knights from each county, two burghers from each city or borough, with eleven prelates and twenty-three peers. In the battle of Evesham, A. D. 1265 Prince

Edward, having escaped from prison, was victorious, the king was set free, and De Montfort and his son Henry were slain.

68. Edward I. was recalled from Palestine (§ 40) to assume his crown. His chief aim was to unite the island of Great Britain under one scepter by the conquest of Wales* and the marriage of his son with the heiress of Scotland. The death of the latter, A. D. 1290, delayed for three hundred years the union of the kingdoms, and the Scottish crown was left to be disputed by thirteen claimants. Edward, as lord-paramount, decided in favor of John Baliol, and five years later, upon some act of disobedience, he placed the kingdom under the regency of one of his own barons. William Wallace organized a revolt, A. D. 1297, defeated the English at Stirling Bridge, and became guardian of Scotland in the name of King John. He was, however, defeated at Falkirk, and after seven years guerrilla warfare was taken and executed at London, A. D. 1305.

69. FRANCE, during the Crusades, underwent still greater changes. At the commencement of the period the royal domain included only five cities with their territories, and the road between Paris and Orleans was controlled by a rebellious noble. The prudence of the Abbot Suger, the first of the great churchmen who have governed France, increased the power of the crown and depressed that of the nobles.

A. D. 1108–1137. Louis VI.† at his suggestion protected the leagues of the common people against the barons; and thus arose the *communes* or free charters of the towns. The cities of southern France, as of Spain and northern Italy, had never lost the municipal privileges bestowed by the Romans. They asserted those privileges during the twelfth century by choosing their own magistrates and arming for the common defense.

70. Louis VII. multiplied the communal charters, protected mer-
A. D. 1137–1180. chants, and founded "new cities"‡ for the reception of serfs who escaped from the tyranny of their masters. On his return from the Holy Land (§§ 16–18) he parted from his Queen, the Duchess of Aquitaine, who very soon transferred her vast domains to her second husband, Henry II. of England. The life-long enmity thus occasioned between the two kings, led Louis to shelter the exiled primate, Thomas à Becket, and even to aid and abet the rebellion of Queen Eleanor and her three sons against Henry.

---

* His son, afterwards Edward II., was the first English prince of Wales.

† Henry I. (A. D. 1031–1060) and Philip I. (—1108) were the third and fourth of the house of Capet.

‡ Hence the great number of French towns still bearing the names *Villeneuve* and *Villefranche.*

71. Philip Augustus both enlarged and consolidated his kingdom by the depression of the great nobles and the conquest of all except Aquitaine of the continental possessions of the English kings. His war against his own vassals in the Mediterranean provinces was only too successful. The Count of Toulouse—the almost independent sovereign of the most civilized country in Europe—refused to persecute his non-Catholic subjects, to whose opinions he was indifferent, but whose skillful industry and orderly habits made them good and valuable members of the community. The Pope thereupon proclaimed a crusade against Raymond VI. and his people, promising to all who would join it the same indulgences as if they were fighting against the Saracens, beside the more substantial reward of a share in the lands to be conquered.

A. D. 1180-1223.

The most active and fierce of the crusaders was Simon de Montfort, lord of great estates in Normandy and Earl of Leicester in England—the father of that earl who led the English barons in their opposition to Henry III. He bore for years, by the authority of the Lateran Council, the title of Count of Toulouse. The war raged from A. D. 1203 to 1229. Every-where fertile fields were laid waste, towns and villages depopulated, the refined diversions of music and poetry suppressed, together with the heresy which had sprung from intellectual freedom; and the very language of the Provençals, the first in modern Europe to be improved by a native literature, fell into a sudden and fatal decline. On the part of the king, this crusade against the Albigenses was perhaps less a religious than a political movement. It was a struggle of feudal with municipal France—of German with Roman institutions.

72. The war continued through the short reign of Louis VIII., A. D. 1223-1226; and was ended during the minority of Louis IX. by the submission of Raymond VII. of Toulouse. The greater part of his estate was annexed to the crown, and by the Mediterranean ports thus gained France became an important maritime power. The reign of Louis IX. is a new era in French history—an era in which the regular and equal action of law began to replace the turbulent misrule of the feudal ages. The baronial courts were suppressed; uniform coins and statutes prevailed throughout the realm. To prevent delays of justice, the king held courts in the open air—sitting under a tree in the forest of Vincennes—whither any man might bring his suit without ceremony. The sovereign appeared in his true character as the refuge of the oppressed, the source of justice, and avenger of wrong. The separation of France and England was made complete by a law of Louis IX., A. D. 1244, forbidding any vassal of his to hold estates under another crown. Before this, almost every English baron had fiefs in France, and might be punished by one king for lawful serv-

A. D. 1226-1270.

ices rendered to another. The two crusades of Louis have already been described. (§§ 38–40.)

73. His son Philip III., by inheritance or marriage, added to his

A. D. 1270–1285. dominions the counties of Champagne, Toulouse, Valois, and Alençon, and the kingdom of Navarre. The chief events of his reign were connected with the claims of his uncle, Charles of Anjou, upon the kingdom of the Two Sicilies, and those of his brother, Charles of Valois, upon Aragon. (See § 61.) The policy begun by the justice of St. Louis was continued by the ambition of his successors; and the 102 years dating from the beginning of his reign have been called the Age of the Lawyers—a century in which the legal powers of the crown subordinated without destroying the claims of the feudal chiefs.

74. During the crusades, notwithstanding the great waste of blood and treasure, many arts flourished, and architecture especially achieved some of its grandest works. The great cathedrals were the work of a society of masons which existed throughout Europe, the members being known to each other and distinguished from the uninitiated by peculiar signs and customs. Poetry also received a new impulse from the stirring incidents of the times; and the troubadours of Aragon and Provence, the minnesingers of Germany, and the poets of the Sicilian court of Frederic II. ushered in the dawn of modern literature. All the Suabian emperors were themselves poets. The Nibelungen Lied—the great German epic of the migration of nations—as well as the Book of Heroes, received from the house of Hohenstaufen the same service which Homer owed to Pisistratus. Their scattered portions were collected, edited, and made accessible to scholars.

75. The Church partook in great measure the movements of the age. On one side we find warrior-bishops, like Christian of Mentz, building fortifications, leading armies, storming or besieging towns; on the other, kings of the cloister, like Bernard of Clairvaux, who, refusing worldly rank for themselves, and blinding their eyes even to the splendors of the natural world, exercised almost absolute control over the turbulent spirits which governed secular affairs. The monastic life received a fresh impulse from the multiplication of new orders. The monastery of Monte Cassino in southern Italy, (founded by St. Benedict of Nursia, A. D. 528,) was the cradle of the first great organization of this kind. The Benedictines have benefited the world by the diligent scholarship which led them during the dark ages to preserve and multiply copies of the treasures of ancient literature; and, since the invention of printing, to compile great historical works such as require far more than one lifetime for their achievement.

76. The order of the Carthusians was instituted by St. Bruno, A. D. 1084, upon a desolate rock near Grenoble, with a discipline as severe and unattractive as its place of abode. Four years later was founded the monastery of Citeaux, which became the parent of 3600 similar convents of its own Cistercian order. The Carmelites, founded in Palestine, migrated to Europe in 1238, and assumed both the rule and name of St. Augustine. All these and other orders grew to be rich and powerful, both by the gifts of the great and by the sale or pledge to them of the estates of Crusaders. Many of these proprietors never returned; others came, broken with disappointment, to bury themselves in the cloister and leave their property to the brotherhood. The wealth and luxury of the monks became a reproach. As a protest against their corruption, two orders of mendicants, one founded A. D. 1210, by the Italian, Francis of Assisi, and the other in 1215, by Dominic Guzman, a Spaniard, bound themselves to acquire no property beyond the walls of their monasteries, and to subsist only by begging. Choosing a life of intense activity instead of the indolence of the cloisters, they were the first of all the brotherhoods to devote themselves to preaching. Speaking all languages, penetrating all countries, they constituted the standing army of the popes, to whom alone they rendered obedience, and whose power they contributed immeasurably to increase and prolong.

77. The reign of Innocent III. was equally signalized by the rise of the Inquisition, a secret tribunal charged with the detection and punishment of heresy, apostasy, and all crimes against religion. A. D. 1198–1216. Among the first inquisitors was the founder of the Dominicans; and these friars, with their secular brethren, the Familiars of the Holy Office, planted the terrible institution in France, Italy, and Spain. The accused person was snatched secretly from his home, and either never appeared again in the light of day, or only on his way to the flames. No counsel was allowed, nor any reading of the articles of accusation, which might be wholly new to the prisoner. To be suspected was almost certainly to be condemned. The tribunal first received its complete organization at the Council of Toulouse, A. D. 1229. It continued in southern Europe and the Spanish colonies in America until the beginning of the present century, when advancing civilization put an end to its barbarities. In the Spanish countries alone, more than half a million of persons had suffered in various ways, of whom more than 32,000 were burned at the stake.

78. No less characteristic of the Middle Ages was the *Vehm-gericht*, or secret secular tribunal, which established itself in Westphalia, but extended its power throughout Germany. Its members numbered several thousands of all classes, who could prove themselves "free, irreproachable, and honorable men;" they were bound by solemn oaths of secrecy, and recognized each other by signs known only to themselves. If any accused person failed after three citations to appear before them, he was

sentenced* to death, and each member of the court was bound to pursue
him until his punishment was accomplished. Even if he were the
father or a brother of a member, it was forbidden to warn him; and
wherever he was found—in his house, on the high road, or in the
forest—he must be hanged to the nearest tree or post. As a proof that
he was not a victim of lawless violence, his property was left untouched,
and a knife was planted near him in the ground. However irregular
such a tribunal may appear, it was a powerful supporter of justice in a
turbulent age, when the slow and uncertain action of other courts was
wholly inadequate to the suppression of violence. It was able either
to inflict instant and terrible punishment, or to track the offender to
the most obscure and distant retreat. Its authority, though for the last
two centuries confined to Westphalia, was only legally repealed in
A. D. 1811.

RECAPITULATION.

Elder Norman line of English kings is succeeded by the Plantagenets descended from
Count Geoffrey of Anjou. Henry II. has great dominions on the continent, for which he
is vassal to King of France; conquers Ireland and enforces his suzerainty over Scotland;
quarrels with Becket, Archbishop of Canterbury, but after Becket has been murdered,
does penance at his tomb. Richard I. is chiefly known as a crusader. John loses his
French inheritance; is excommunicated for opposing the investiture of Langton as primate; incurs the wrath of the barons by surrendering his kingdom to the Pope, and is
forced to sign Magna Charta. Henry III. renews privileges which his father has granted;
in his name the first English parliament is summoned. War with the barons led by
Simon de Montfort. The latter victorious at Lewes; defeated and slain at Evesham.
Edward I. conquers Wales and controls Scotland.

Rise of free cities in France under Louis VI. and VII.; conquest by Philip II. of Normandy, Maine, Touraine, and Anjou; crusade against the Albigenses lasts from his
reign to that of his grandson. Age of the Lawyers begins with Louis IX., the most
just of French kings. Several important provinces added to the kingdom by Philip
III. Flourishing period of mediæval art and literature. Increased power of the
Church; foundation of Carthusians, Cistercians, Carmelites, and the Mendicant Orders of St. Dominic and St. Francis. Rise of the Inquisition. Supremacy of the Vehm-
gericht in Germany.

---

* The form of the sentence is curious as showing the ideas of the time: "As now N.
has been cited, prosecuted, and adjudged before me. . . . who is so hardened in evil
that he will obey neither honor nor justice, and despises the highest tribunal of the
Holy Empire, I denounce him here by all the royal power and force, as is but just. . .
I deprive him, as outcast and expelled, of all the peace, justice, and freedom he has
ever enjoyed since he was baptized; and I deprive him henceforward of the enjoyment
of the four elements which God made and gave as a consolation to man, and denounce
him as without right, without law, without peace, without honor, without security; I
declare him condemned and lost, so that any man may act towards him as with any
other banished criminal. . . . And I herewith curse his flesh and blood, and may his
body never receive burial, but may it be borne away by the wind, and may the ravens
and crows and wild birds of prey consume and destroy him. And I adjudge his neck to
the rope, and his body to be devoured by the birds and beasts of the air, sea, and
land; but his soul I commend to our dear Lord God, if he will receive it."

PERIOD II. *From the Last Crusade to the Discovery of America.*
A. D. 1291–1492.

79. The two centuries following the Crusades were a period of rapid development throughout Europe. New thought revolutionized old opinions; powers which had only existed in the germ sprang to maturity; the learning of the ancient world was revived at the fortunate moment when western genius was able to be stimulated by it, not depressed into lifeless imitation; the art of printing came to diffuse among the middle and lower classes the treasures thus amassed; and the discovery of a hitherto unknown continent gave a new direction and unlimited scope to the quest of wealth, knowledge, and dominion.

80. We glance briefly at the condition of the several nations of Europe at the close of the thirteenth century. The Emperor Rudolph of Hapsburg was succeeded, A. D. 1292, by Adolph of Nassau, who was in turn deposed by the electors, defeated and slain by a new emperor, Albert of Austria, eldest son of Rudolph, A. D. 1298. Albert, unlike his father, was a stern and overbearing tyrant. His cruelties excited revolt in his own provinces of Austria, Styria, and Switzerland, and while he was marching to execute vengeance upon the latter, he was murdered by his nephew, John of Hapsburg, whom he had unjustly deprived of his estates.

81. France was ruled by a grandson of St. Louis, Philip the Fair, whose constant want of money led him to ruthless persecutions of Jews, Churchmen, Flemish merchants, and finally of the Knights Templars. His quarrel with Pope Boniface VIII. will soon be described. England, under the vigorous reign of Edward I., was extending her power over Scotland, and protecting the Flemings against the French king, their feudal lord. The Spanish peninsula contained the five Christian kingdoms of Aragon, Navarre, Castile, Leon, and Portugal, beside the two Moorish sovereignties of Cordova and Granada. Italy was divided between the kingdom of Naples, the States of the Church, and the free cities of Tuscany and Lombardy, which, while owing a nominal allegiance to the emperor, were usually governed by a podestà or some chief citizen, resembling the "tyrants" of ancient Greece. The Neapolitan kingdom was still in dispute between the houses of Anjou and Aragon, the latter having inherited the claims of the Suabian family. Frederic of Aragon, the bravest prince and ablest captain of his time, defended Sicily many years against the entire Gallic and papal force; and even against his own elder brother, King James of Aragon, after the latter had made peace with the French. By a treaty in 1302, Sicily and the smaller islands were erected into a separate kingdom, called Trinacria, for Frederic and his descendants, while the House of Anjou retained only the peninsular dominion.

82. Celestin V., a pious hermit but incompetent sovereign, was persuaded (A. D. 1294) to resign his tiara, by the Cardinal of Anagni, who himself became Pope with the name of Boniface VIII. Under this turbulent and ambitious prince, the papacy reached its highest pretensions, only to fall, at his violent and disgraceful death, into a long humiliation and depression. Over the greatest monarchs in Christendom, Boniface claimed the authority of a Roman Censor, to punish and even depose for private and personal offenses. Over the smaller kingdoms of Naples, Sicily, Aragon, Portugal, Hungary, Bohemia, Scotland, and England, he asserted the absolute power of a feudal chief, having bought a recognition of his supremacy by favoring one or another of rival claimants to those thrones, or extorted it from a weak sovereign by terror of spiritual penalties. (§ 66.) In the King of France, Boniface met a nature as proud and unyielding as his own. After a violent war of words, the pontiff was attacked and seized in his native city, Anagni, by Sciarra Colonna, a Roman prince whose family he had bitterly wronged, and William of Nogaret, a French lawyer whose ancestors had been slain by the Inquisition. Overcome by rage at this humiliation, he died a few weeks later at Rome, A. D. 1303.

83. In the north of Europe the petty principalities of the Baltic had become consolidated into the three modern kingdoms of Norway, Sweden, and Denmark. Christianity had slowly but surely conquered the ancient paganism, and with its milder teachings, letters and other arts of civilization had been introduced by the Benedictine monks. Waldemar II. (A. D. 1202–1241) governed not only Denmark and Sweden, but a great part of the present kingdom of Prussia. Before his death his empire fell to pieces, and its southern territories were soon conquered by the Teutonic knights.

84. Within twenty years from the signing of Magna Charta in England, the Hungarian barons extorted from their king, Andrew II., a similar document called the "Golden Privilege," which included even the right of armed resistance to the sovereign, in case of his failure to fulfill his obligations. With his grandson the family of Arpad became extinct in the male line in A. D. 1301, and the crown, becoming elective, was conferred in expectancy upon Charles of Naples, a descendant by his mother's side from the old Hungarian kings. Charles died before his accession; but intercourse with Italy had meanwhile been productive of great advance in the civilization of Hungary. The wastes of Transylvania were converted into fruitful fields and thriving villages by the labor of multitudes of Flemish and German colonists. Bohemia, though lately one of the most powerful monarchies in Europe, was at this time depressed by the losses and death of King Ottocar; while Poland, not yet recovered from the ravages of the Mongols, and further weakened by several disputed reigns, gave no promise of the greatness it was soon to attain under Ladislas I. and Casimir the Great.

85. Upon the death of Pope Benedict XI., the successor of Boniface VIII., the King of France secured the election of Bertrand de Goth, a Gascon, and thus a subject of the King of England, but, as it proved, the obedient servant of Philip himself. He assumed the name of Clement V., and removed the seat of the papacy from Rome to Avignon,* where it remained nearly seventy A. D. 1309–1378. years, in what was called by Italian writers of the time a Babylonish captivity. With this Pope, Philip IV. concerted his scheme for the extinction of the Templars. The admiration of Christendom during two centuries had loaded the order with wealth; and instead of nine poor knights, 15,000 of the most splendid chivalry in the world excited at once the fear and envy of the king. Their fortresses were among the strongest in Europe, and by the terms of their institution they were independent equally of the civil and the ordinary ecclesiastical power, owning allegiance only to the Pope. Even from him a sentence of excommunication could not strike the order; but when surrounding territories suffered under an interdict, their church-bells sounded, the dead were buried, and the living absolved as usual.

86. Three quite incompatible charges of idolatry, atheism, and Mohammedanism were laid against them; but their real crimes were their power and wealth. Their dealings with the Saracens had doubtless worn away the prejudices with which the Holy Wars began; and the Templars—mostly men of generous breeding—had learned to treat with liberality a foe whose mental culture they could not but respect; but in a bigoted age tolerance is a crime, and they were accused of yielding equal reverence to Mohammed and to Christ. The witnesses, most of them renegades from the order, were tortured, and the confessions wrung from them by insufferable agony seemed to admit the justice of the accusations. But when these confessions were read in open court, many of the sufferers indignantly denied their truth, and were sentenced to be burned as apostates: 113 thus suffered in Paris alone, and the number in the provinces can not be estimated. Jacques de Molay, the Grand Master, was immured seven years in a dungeon, until his intellect became disordered by long suffering and deprivation of light. His defense was then refused, and he was sentenced with two companions to the stake. From the midst

---

* Avignon with its territory, the Venaissin, had been a papal possession since 1273, being the share claimed by Gregory X. of the spoils of the Albigenses. It belonged to the popes till 1789.

of the flames he summoned the Pope and the King of France to meet him ere long at the bar of God. Both died within the year 1314.

87. England, governed by the weak and worthless Edward II., a son-in-law of Philip, followed the example of France in the suppression of the Templars. In the Neapolitan kingdoms and the Papal States similar confessions were obtained by torture; but in northern Italy most of the witnesses were firm in asserting the innocence of the Knights, and in Spain and Germany they were triumphantly acquitted. Their lands, however, were transferred to the Knights of St. John, while their movable treasures went to enrich the several sovereigns, especially their arch persecutor, the king of France. In Portugal alone a remnant of the order still exists, under the name " Chevaliers of Christ."

88. The rise of the Swiss Republics is among the important events of the beginning of the fourteenth century. The germ of their confederation may be found in the alliance of the three Forest Cantons, Schwytz, Uri, and Unterwalden, August 1, 1291; but it is usually dated from the Conjuration of Rütli, A. D. 1308; in which three men from the same three cantons, swore to each other under the open heaven to live and die for the defense of fatherland. Each chose ten confidants from his own canton, and the thirty-three repeated the oath. The people exhausted by the oppressions of Albert of Austria seized all his bailiffs and their satellites, and drove them from the country. The death of the emperor occurred on his march into Switzerland, but his son Leopold exacted a pitiless and bloody vengeance from the peasants of the Waldstätten, most of whom had no part in the oath of Rütli. He was defeated by a few hundred men in the narrow pass of Morgarten, November, 1315, with the loss of many of his highest nobility, and he himself only escaped death by a disgraceful flight. The three Forest States (Waldstätten) maintained their rights as distinct members of the Empire; and became the nucleus of the Federal Republic,* whose independence was first acknowledged by the Treaty of Westphalia, 1648.

89. Meanwhile, Henry VII. of Luxembourg was restoring order to the empire, and securing to his own house, by the marriage of his son, the vast revenues of the Bohemian kingdom. He visited Italy, whither no emperor had gone since Conrad IV., and where he was warmly welcomed by the oppressed Ghibellines. He earnestly endeavored to heal the long strife of parties, compelling all cities to recall their exiles, whether Guelf or Ghibelline, and appointing imperial vicars for the maintenance of justice and order. He died soon after his coronation at Rome, A. D. 1312, not without suspicion of his having been poisoned by means of sacramental wine administered by a Dominican monk.

A. D. 1308-1313.

---

* For the development of the Swiss Republic see Appendix.

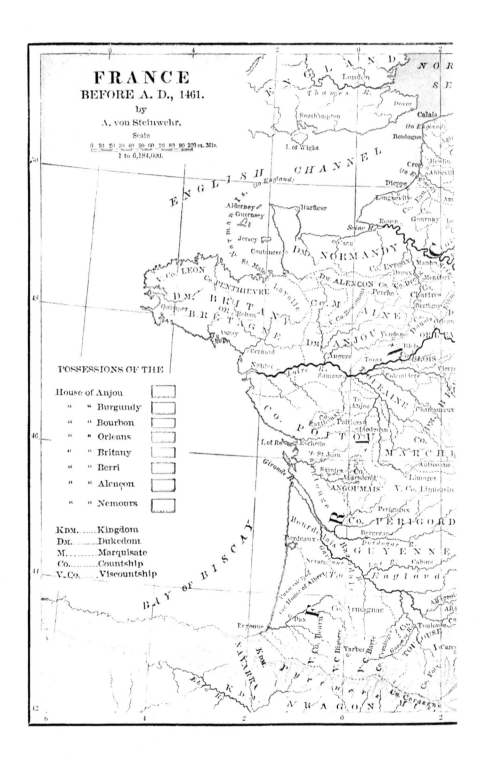

FRANCE
BEFORE A. D., 1461.
by
A. von Steinwehr.

Scale

0 10 20 30 40 50 60 70 80 90 100 st. Mls.

1 to 6,184,000.

POSSESSIONS OF THE

House of Anjou

"   "   Burgundy

"   "   Bourbon

"   "   Orleans

"   "   Britany

"   "   Berri

"   "   Alençon

"   "   Nemours

KDM. .... Kingdom
DM. .... Dukedom
M. .... Marquisate
Co. .... Countship
V. Co. ..... Viscountship

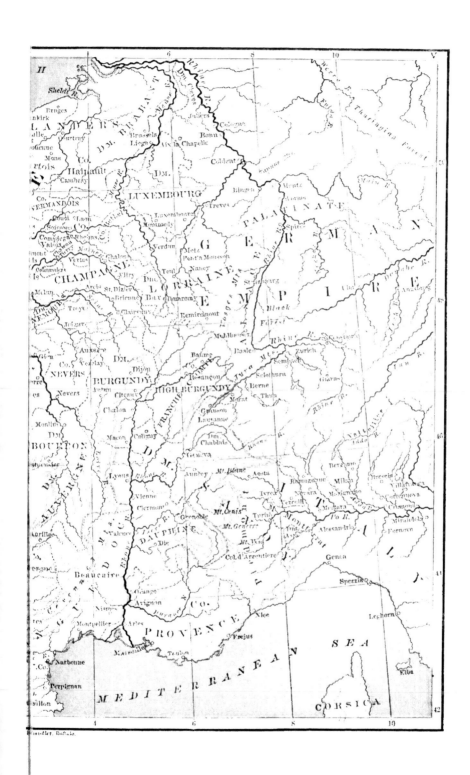

90. The German princes failed to unite in the choice of his successor; and the division extending through the empire occasioned an exhausting civil war of thirteen years. The primate, the towns, and common people preferred Louis of Bavaria; most of the nobility, led by the Archbishop of Cologne, were for Duke Frederic of Austria. In the battle of Mühldorf, A. D. 1322, Frederic became the prisoner of his victorious rival. Even then the enmity of several princes and of two successive popes made the reign of Louis IV. a continual scene of discord. King John of Bohemia, a true knight-errant, traversed A. D. 1314–1347. Germany, Italy, and France fomenting the hostility of all parties to the Bavarian emperor. At length, A. D. 1346, Charles of Luxembourg, the son of King John, was chosen by some of the German princes as their head, and the death of his rival, the next year, led to his general recognition as the Emperor Charles IV.

91. The year of his election was signalized by the battle of Crecy between the English and the French. The direct succession of the descendants of Hugh Capet was broken for the first time, A. D. 1316, after continuing from father to son more than three centuries. Popular opinion favored the daughter of Louis X., who died in that year, but the feudal principle, which demanded active military leadership in the suzerain, prevailed; and after the accession of Philip V., the brother of Louis, the States-general enacted for the first time a law definitely excluding women from the throne. Philip was likewise succeeded by his brother Charles, A. D. 1322; and as the latter left no sons, Philip of Valois, his cousin, came to the throne. Edward III. of England preferred a nearer claim through his mother Isabella, who was a daughter of Philip IV. The Flemings, now ruled by Jacques van Artevelde, the brewer of Ghent, in revolt against Philip of Valois, hailed Edward as King of France; and the Emperor Louis IV. appointed him imperial vicar in the Netherlands.

92. His invasion of France came to its most decisive issue at Crecy, where he was completely victorious, and King John of Bohemia, now old and blind, was left dead upon the field, together with a crowd of French chivalry. The sea-port and fortress of Calais, soon after taken by eleven months' siege, continued for two centuries in the English possession. King John of France, who succeeded his father, A. D. 1350, attempted to avenge himself upon Edward the Black Prince, who from his English territory of Aquitaine, was ravaging the western provinces. The battle of Poitiers was a still more remarkable victory for the English, their numbers being less than one-seventh of those A. D. 1356. of their enemies. King John was a prisoner, and 2500 knights and nobles were among the slain.

93. During the four years' detention of King John in Bordeaux and

M. H.—7.

London, the dauphin, as Regent, had to deal with a rebellion in Paris and a general revolt of the peasantry. These poor creatures were not apparently actuated by a hope, still less by a rational scheme for gaining their liberty, but rather by a blind fury of despair under oppressions too grievous to be borne. The castles of the nobles were demolished or burnt, and their inmates massacred. This ignorant warfare could not long maintain itself against the trained tactics of the ruling class. The peasants were defeated before Meaux with a loss of seven thousand of their number, and the scattered fugitives were hunted down like beasts. The "Jacquerie" was suppressed by the depopulation of vast districts. Unhappy France suffered at the same time from a three years' pestilence and from the ravages of the disbanded soldiers, who, thrown out of pay and released from discipline, roamed over the country, plundering and burning at their pleasure.

94. By the treaty of Bretigny, A. D. 1360, King John was liberated upon his renouncing all his sovereign rights over Aquitaine and several adjoining counties, and engaging to pay a ransom ruinous to his exhausted dominions. To raise the first installment, he condescended to marry his daughter to the heir of the Visconti, the rich and powerful lords of Milan. The celebrated Petrarch, who visited Paris on this occasion, describes it as a desert overgrown by brambles and grass. The royal dukes of Anjou and Berri, who were hostages for the fulfillment of the treaty, violated their parole, and their father voluntarily returned to London, where he died a prisoner, A. D. 1364.

95. Under the dauphin, now King Charles V., war with the English was indirectly renewed in the support by either nation of the rival claimants to the duchy of Brittany, and to the throne of Castile. The former contest is sometimes called the Ladies' War, because the rival dukes having been one imprisoned and the other slain, their wives carried on hostilities with equal energy. In both cases the English party was victorious, De Montfort being recognized as Duke of Bretagne, and Pedro the Cruel as King of Castile; but the last success was too dearly purchased by the incurable illness of the Prince of Wales, contracted in his Spanish campaign, and even suspected to have resulted from poison received from his jealous and ungrateful ally. Pedro was defeated by the French, A. D. 1368, and killed a few days later by his half-brother, Henry of Trastamare, who was able to retain the crown for himself and his descendants. The death of the Black Prince, A. D. 1376, was shortly followed by that of his father; and Charles V. by prudent and skillful management soon recovered from the English more than King John had lost.

96. Within three years the kingdoms of France and England were placed in curiously similar circumstances. Two minor princes, Richard II.

in England (1377) and Charles VI. in France (1380) came to the throne, each under the control of three* ambitious and powerful uncles, who used the royal resources for the furtherance of their own schemes of home and foreign dominion. John of Gaunt, Duke of Lancaster, having married a daughter of Pedro the Cruel, claimed the crown of Castile in her right, but his repeated attacks upon the country resulted only in failure. To understand the Duke of Anjou's attempts upon the kingdom of Naples, we must glance at the previous condition of Italy. King Robert of Naples, grandson of Charles of Anjou, was succeeded, A. D. 1343, by his granddaughter, Joanna, who at the age of sixteen was already married to her cousin, Andrew of Hungary. (§ 84.) The boorish manners of the king-consort and his attendants shocked the elegant court of Joanna, while his assumed claim to the crown in his own right alarmed her counsellors. Andrew was murdered, A. D. 1345, by the adherents, though, it may be hoped, without the connivance of his wife. His brother, Louis the Great of Hungary, avenged his death by invading the kingdom, while Joanna took refuge in the States of the Church.

97. Rome, deserted by its bishops, was a prey to the lawless violence of its nobles. Two princely and hostile families, the Colonna and Orsini, carried on their wars in the very streets of the city, or in the surrounding country, where their strong castles enabled them to defy justice. In this crisis Cola di Riénzi, a man whose genius and patriotism were fired by recollections of the glory of ancient Rome, proposed to the people a restoration of the "Good Estate," *i. e.*, suppression of private wars, enforcement of law even upon the proudest patricians, and the arming and drilling of citizens for the defense of their rights. He himself, refusing a senatorship, was chosen Tribune — by that name recalling the self-sacrificing efforts of the Gracchi.

A. D. 1347.

98. For a few months the den of robbers was transformed into a scene of peace and prosperity. The envoys of Rienzi, armed only with the white wand of their office, traversed Italy, Germany, and France, summoning cities and monarchs to acknowledge the ancient supremacy of Rome. The King of Hungary and the Queen of Naples submitted their cause to his arbitration, and the republics of northern Italy sought his protection. He cited the Emperor Louis to appear and submit his election, as of old, to the choice of the Roman people, and he summoned the Pope and cardinals to return to their lawful seat. But the Tribune was spoiled by prosperity. He indulged his personal vanity by kingly pomp, and burdened the people with oppressive taxes, while he debased

---

*The Dukes of Lancaster, York, and Gloucester in England; of Anjou, Berri, and Burgundy in France.

his acts of justice by needless cruelty, and by his extreme measures caused even the Colonna and Orsini to unite against him. He was forced to abdicate his authority and to spend six years in exile or in prison at Avignon, while Rome was left to the fury of the barons and the successive tyrannies of two self-styled tribunes, Cerroni and Baroncelli. Pope Innocent VI. at length released Rienzi from prison, and sent him to Rome with the title of senator. The people received him with joy, but the enmity of the nobles was not appeased, and after four months he was killed on the steps of the Capitol.

99. The earlier years of Rienzi's exile were marked by a calamity which for a time surpassed all the other sufferings of that disastrous period. A plague known as the "Black Death" was brought from Asia into Europe by Italian merchants. In the year 1348 it spread through Italy, Savoy, Provence, Burgundy, and Catalonia. The next year it covered all Barbary, Spain, England, and France. In 1350 it overran Germany, Hungary, Denmark, Sweden, and even Iceland. Some cities lost three-fifths, others even seven-tenths of their inhabitants, and throughout France it was estimated that one-third of the people had perished. As if this visitation were not enough, several countries were harassed by the brigandage of the "Free-Companies," and the common people, seeking some object more wretched than themselves on which to avenge their misery, accused the Jews of having produced the plague by poisoning the wells. A ruthless persecution was the result, and hundreds of Israelites chose to burn themselves and their families in their own houses rather than fall into the hands of the enraged and ignorant mob.

100. Pope Gregory XI. ended the "Babylonish Captivity" by returning with his cardinals to Rome; but his death was followed by the great "Schism of the West"—two, and at one time even three, popes reigning simultaneously in different countries. Urban VI. disgusted the conclave which had elected him, by his harsh and violent measures, especially by appointing at once twenty-six new cardinals, thus throwing the rest into a hopeless minority. These, retiring to Fondi, declared the former election null, and chose the warlike Archbishop Robert of Geneva, who, as Clement VII., was acknowledged by France, Naples, and Scotland, and ultimately by the Spanish kingdoms of Castile, Aragon, and Navarre; while the rest of Europe adhered to Urban VI. Queen Joanna of Naples had aided the election of the antipope. Urban VI. in revenge bestowed her kingdom upon Charles of Durazzo, nephew of the King of Hungary, and crowned him at Rome, A. D. 1381. Charles had the hereditary claim, for the old Angevin line was to expire with Joanna; but the childless queen, incensed at this disposal of her kingdom before her death, adopted Louis of Anjou, uncle of Charles VI. of France, as her

heir. Clement VII., at Avignon, hastened not only to crown the French prince as King of Naples, but to assign him a new "kingdom of Adria" from the States of the Church. Charles of Durazzo was first in the field. Joanna was captured, and murdered in her imprisonment—a long cherished revenge on the part of the King of Hungary for the death of his brother. In order to prosecute his claims, the Duke of Anjou seized the treasures of the French kingdom immediately upon his brother's death. But his great preparations ended only in disgrace. The greater part of his army fell victims to the plague, and he himself died near Bari, A. D. 1384. French claims upon the Neapolitan kingdom were cause of war for more than a century without ever resulting in permanent conquest.

RECAPITULATION.

Increase of mental activity in Europe after the Crusades. Rise of the House of Hapsburg. Extortions of Philip the Fair; supremacy of England among the British Isles. Seven kingdoms in Spain; rise of the *podestas* in the free cities of Italy; separation of Sicily from kingdom of Naples. Pontifical arrogance of Boniface VIII. met by the haughty resistance of Philip IV. Civilization of the northern kingdoms and of Hungary. Papal court at Avignon 69 years. Suppression of the Templars, A. D. 1307-1322. The "Conjurators" at Rütli lay the foundation of the Swiss Republic. Leopold of Austria defeated at Morgarten, 1315. Henry VII. restores imperial power in Italy. Contest between Frederic of Austria and Louis of Bavaria; the latter victorious, but superseded before his death by Charles of Luxembourg. Accession of the Valois in France; counter-claims of Edward III. of England. English victories at Crecy and Poitiers. Captivity of King John of France, and war of the peasantry. Wars of the French and English in Brittany and Castile. Minorities of Richard II. and Charles VI. Claims of John of Lancaster to Castile and of Louis of Anjou to Naples. Murder of Andrew of Hungary. Tribunate of Rienzi at Rome. Ravages of the Great Plague, depredations of the Free Companies, and a persecution of the Jews complete the disorders of Europe. Return of the popes to Rome, followed by a division in western Christendom. Rival popes favor rival candidates to the kingdom of Naples. Joanna put to death, the kingdom remains to the Hungarian line.

FRANCE AND ENGLAND, A. D. 1384-1493.

101. Despoiled by the unscrupulous ambition of Louis of Anjou, France had still more to suffer from the insanity of her king, and the mutual hatreds of the remaining princes of the royal blood. The Duke of Burgundy, by marrying the heiress of Flanders, had become lord of the Netherlands, and thus richer and more powerful than any sovereign prince then reigning in Europe. This circumstance, with his premiership among the peers of France, gave him a controlling power in the French court, but a rival party was led by the Duke of Orleans, brother of the king. John the Fearless, succeeding to the duchy of Burgundy, resorted to more unscrupulous measures than his father. After swearing reconciliation and friendship with his cousin of A. D. 1407. Orleans, he caused the latter to be murdered in the streets of Paris, and extorted from the imbecile king a pardon for the crime. A few years later John of Burgundy was himself assassinated in open day in the presence of the Dauphin.

102. Henry V. of England was already in the country, having availed himself of the miserable dissensions of the princes, to prosecute the ancient claim of his house to the French crown. The son of the murdered duke—known in history as Philip the Good—joined the English and contributed materially to their great victory at Agincourt, where the French, though four times as numerous as their enemies, were as signally defeated as at Crecy or Poitiers. A general reason for these victories of the English may be found in their employment of large companies of paid archers—precursors of modern infantry—while the French had as yet only feudal armies, consisting of independent nobles and their retainers. They learned, however, a lesson by their disaster, which made them before the end of the century a leading power in Europe. Charles VII. organized the first standing army, except the Janizaries (see § 160), which Europe had seen; and his regularly drilled troops soon superseded the feudal militia, which could only be called out for a limited time, and quitted the camp, after a few weeks' service, to resume the ordinary industries.

Oct. 1415.

103. Henry V., having married a daughter of Charles VI., was crowned at Paris with his infant son, and was duly recognized as regent and heir-expectant of the French kingdom. His sudden death occurring the same year with that of his father-in-law, cut short his plans of conquest; but the English interests were ably maintained by his brother and other great nobles, while the French were still a prey to hopeless dissensions, and Charles VII., their rightful sovereign, was driven south of the Loire and even meditated a flight into Spain. At this lowest point in the humiliation of France, unexpected relief appeared in the person of a young peasant girl from Domremy in Lorraine, who believed herself commissioned and inspired by Heaven. Her faith, and the superstition of both French and English soldiery, sustained the illusion, if such it was. She defeated the English before Orleans, and forced them to raise the siege of that city. Again defeating them at Patay, and taking by storm the two towns of Jargeau and Troyes, she conducted the Dauphin in triumph to Rheims, where alone he could be anointed with the holy oil used in the consecration of all kings since the days of Clovis.

A. D. 1422.

104. Her mission thus ended, Joan d'Arc desired to return to her sheepfolds, but the king refused to dismiss her, though the bitter jealousy of his counselors and his own apathy already indicated her approaching fate. At the head of the army she captured one of the suburbs of Paris, but was repulsed and wounded in an attack upon the city itself. She was subsequently captured by the Burgundians in a battle before Compiègne and basely sold to the English, who caused her to be tried, not as a prisoner of war, but as a sorceress, and burned in the market-place of Rouen. The King of France, who owed her his crown, made no effort to save her life. "Charles the Victorious" has been more truly styled the "Well-served," for the great successes of his reign were independent of his own efforts or abilities. The dissensions of the English princes dissolved that dominion in France which the brief career of Henry V. had built up; and the Duke of Burgundy, offended in many ways by his foreign allies, made his peace with the king, ending the long war with the Armagnac or Orleans faction, which had desolated the whole country during twenty-eight years.

105. England, meanwhile, was the scene of important events. Richard II. (see § 96 and Appendix) had been deposed A. D. 1399, and probably murdered in Pontefract Castle, by order of his cousin, Henry of Lancaster, who assumed the crown. The energy of Henry IV. and the military fame of his son suppressed or silenced the claims of the elder line of descendants from Edward III.; but the imbecility of Henry VI. and the violent policy of his brilliant but unscrupulous consort, Margaret of Anjou (see § 125) hastened the ruin of their house. The Duke of York was recalled from his regency of France, and seized the opportunity to assert his right to the English crown. A. D. 1455.
The "Wars of the Roses" — so called because a white and a red rose were the badges respectively of the parties of York and Lancaster—filled England for thirty years with confusion and bloodshed. The great Earl of Warwick, called the "King-maker," was at first a devoted adherent of the house of York, but having been deeply injured by Edward IV., the first sovereign of that family, he embraced the cause of Henry VI., whom he restored for a few months to the throne. He fell, however, in the battle of Barnet; the young prince, Edward of Lancaster, having been defeated at Tewkesbury, was brutally murdered in the presence of his conqueror; Henry VI. met a secret death in the tower of London, and the York party remained in the ascendant.

106. The two young sons of Edward IV. were murdered after his death by their uncle, the Duke of Gloucester, who himself assumed the crown as Richard III. He was defeated after two years at Bosworth Field; and Henry Tudor, a descendant of A. D. 1485. John of Gaunt, became the founder of a new line of English sovereigns. The battle of Bosworth, which overthrew the feudal system in England, was a no less important event than that of Hastings which introduced it. Many great families were ruined by the civil wars. In England, as in France, royal power increased as that of the nobles declined; and the Tudors were the most absolute of English kings.

107. Louis XI., who received the French crown upon his father's death, in 1461, had been an efficient ally of the Lancastrians, while his great vassal, Charles of Burgundy, married the sister of Edward IV., and espoused the cause of the Yorkists. This was but one of many points of enmity between the elder and younger branches of the Valois.* As dauphin, Louis had been banished for high misdemeanors to his own province of Vienne, where with extraordinary vigor he set in operation the same policy which afterwards distinguished his reign in France. He stopped the private wars of the nobles and cultivated the friendship of the people; he summoned a parliament at Grenoble and founded a university at Valence; he raised an army, coined money, and made treaties with foreign states in his own name.

Threatened by his father with an armed invasion of the rebellious province, he took refuge in Burgundy, and requited the generous hospitality of Philip the Good by studying the weak points in his dominion and sowing dissensions between the duke and his son, the future Charles the Bold. The two young princes became, a few years later, the chief actors in the events of their time. Their characters present the strongest possible contrast. Charles was haughty but impetuous, ready to risk all for glory and power; Louis was sly, cautious, insinuating, tenacious of his purpose, but willing to compass it by slow and secret approaches. His pride never interfered with his interests, and his cruelty was unchecked by either pity or honor.

108. The great effort of his reign was to consolidate the royal power at the expense of the nobles and the Church. One important step was the establishment throughout the kingdom of a system of posts by which swift and constant intelligence was received at the capital. The king's hostile measures provoked the great vassals to unite in a " League of the Public Weal," which had at one time 100,000 men on foot. It was joined even by the Duke of Berri, the only brother of the king, and its armies under Count Charles of Charolais, the heir of Burgundy, gained a doubtful victory at Mont l'Héri; but the wily king compassed its dissolution more by arts than arms. He excited rebellions in the Flemish provinces of the Duke of Burgundy, and by separate treaties he induced the several members of the League to forget the "public good" in their own advantage.

The success of the League would probably have made France what Germany has been until our day, a cluster of almost independent dukedoms and principalities. Its failure laid the foundation of a compact and powerful monarchy. The death of Charles du Maine, last heir of the Angevin claims and possessions, added to the crown-lands, Anjou,

---

* For a table of the royal and ducal houses of Valois, see Appendix.

Maine, and Provence, the latter with its ports making France for the first time a great maritime power, while the fatal bequest of his pretensions to the kingdom of Naples proved in three later reigns a source of almost unmingled disaster.

109. Charles, Duke of Burgundy, is known in history as the Terrible, the Bold, or the Rash; and though his career was illuminated by great talents and generous impulses, his disastrous end best justifies the latter epithet. Having failed to dismember France by the war of the Public Weal, his yet greater ambition was to overpower it by reviving the Middle Kingdom of Lothaire, (see Book I., §§ 61, 79.) To this end he purchased Guelders and the county of Zutphen from the aged Duke Arnold; obtained Alsace and large territories in Suabia from Sigismund of the Tyrol; and by seizing and imprisoning the young duke, Réné of Lorraine, established his power for a short time over that duchy. As Duke of Burgundy and Count of Artois and Flanders, Charles was a vassal of France. As Count of Burgundy, (or Franche-Comté,) Duke of Brabant, and lord of a dozen or more German and Netherlandish sovereignties, he was a prince of the Empire. No king then living possessed so many rich and flourishing cities, or could command such resources both for raising and sustaining armies.

But his hopes of royalty proved unsubstantial shadows. When all was ready for his coronation at Trèves, the Emperor Frederic III. suddenly changed his mind and left the city in the night. The gold and persuasions of the King of France stirred up the hostility of the Swiss, who invaded the territories of Charles, and defeated him at Granson and Morat with enormous loss of men and treasure. A few months later he lost his life at Nancy, in a battle with the Duke of Lorraine. As he left no son, the duchy of Burgundy was seized by the King of France; but the rich inheritance of the Low Countries was transferred to the house of Austria by the marriage of the young Duchess Mary with Maximilian, heir of that family, and afterwards emperor. The ambitious schemes of Charles the Bold were partly fulfilled by his great-grandson, who wore the imperial crown, and was a life-long rival of the King of France. A. D. 1477.

110. Louis XI. survived his great rival but six years. The cruelty and perfidy of his policy were signally avenged by the wretched suspicions which haunted his declining years. He shut himself up in the castle of Plessis-les-Tours, guarded by triple fortification of moat, rampart, and palisades, and by crossbowmen who shot at every living thing that approached. Into this gloomy abode the king scarcely admitted his own children, but confined himself to the company of a hangman, a barber, an astrologer, and a physician, who ruled him through his superstitions and satiated their avarice at his expense. He died, A. D. 1483.

His only son, Charles VIII., was but fourteen years of age, and weak both in body and mind. The government was therefore entrusted to his elder sister, Anne the Lady of Beaujeu, whose mental character so far resembled her father's, that he had called her the "least foolish woman in existence."

111. Her regency was disturbed by a fresh league of the nobles, aided by several foreign powers. Its two most important members were Francis Duke of Bretagne, the last of the Montforts, and Louis Duke of Orleans, brother-in-law of the French king. The Breton war was decided by the battle of St. Aubin, in which the army of the regent was victorious, the Duke of Orleans and the Prince of Orange being prisoners. Francis de Montfort soon died, and his daughter Anne, scarcely twelve years of age, inherited his sovereignty. The Duchess Mary of Burgundy had now been six years dead. Maximilian was regent of the Netherlands for his son, and was already crowned King of the Romans. In 1489 he was married by proxy to the young Duchess Anne, while his daughter Margaret was betrothed to the French king, and sent to Paris for her education. Tempted, however, by the hope of annexing the great duchy of Bretagne to the monarchy, Charles VIII. negotiated for himself a treaty of marriage with Anne, and thus deprived the future emperor at one blow of a wife and a son-in-law. The combined injury and insult drove Maximilian into a war in which though aided by Henry VII. of England, his resources were far less than his needs; but Charles was too anxious to depart on his invasion of Italy, to push his advantages in the north. By the Peace of Senlis, the Princess Margaret, and her rich Burgundian dowry, were restored to her father; the English king received a large sum in reimbursement of his expenses, and the provinces of Cerdagne and Roussillon—held in pledge by Louis XI.—were freely given back to Spain.

RECAPITULATION.

France, during insanity of Charles VI., is distracted by quarrels of the royal princes. Duke of Orleans murdered by his cousin of Burgundy, who is himself assassinated in turn with the connivance of the dauphin. His son in revenge joins the English, who gain a great victory at Agincourt under Henry V. Paid standing armies begin to supersede feudal forces. Henry V. crowned in Paris—dies the same year with Charles VI. French interests retrieved by Joan d'Arc, the inspired peasant-girl of Domremy. English dominion in France falls almost as rapidly as it has risen.

England ruled in succession by three Lancastrian and (nominally) three Yorkist sovereigns. Wars of the Roses only ended by the Battle of Bosworth and the accession of Henry Tudor.

Louis XI. of France, as dauphin and king, exalts royal at the expense of feudal power. League of the Public Weal defeated by his arts. His rivalry with Charles of Burgundy, who desires to restore the Middle Kingdom, but is defeated and slain at Nancy and his dominions dismembered. Miserable death of Louis XI. Regency of his daughter. War with Bretagne; that duchy united with the French crown by the marriage of Charles VIII. with the Duchess Anne.

Progress of the Empire.

112. To resume the history of the Empire: The principal act of Charles IV. was the "Golden Bull,"* which defined the powers and privileges of the seven Electors, and the mode A. D. 1346–1378. of imperial election at Frankfort and of coronation at Aix-la-Chapelle. The choice of the German princes was declared sufficient to constitute a true and lawful "Emperor of the Romans;" but until crowned by the Pope he bore only the title of emperor-elect. Charles himself was crowned at Rome, 1355, but by previous agreement he left that city on the same day, and never revisited it. Wenceslaus, son of Charles, became "King of the Romans," and succeeded peaceably upon his father's death in 1378. His drunkenness and indifference to the interests of the empire gave free course to the disorderly elements of the time. The cities of Suabia, like the cantons of Switzerland, leagued themselves to resist the tyranny of the nobles; and these, on the other hand, united to maintain by violence the interests of their order.

113. The most formidable of these armed societies consisted of 167 nobles with their retainers, who followed Duke Leopold of Austria in his vengeance against the Swiss. These confederates mustered 1400 men on the heights of Sempach; the army of the duke numbered several thousands even before his infantry arrived. Though magnificently mounted, his horsemen could not maneuver in the narrow mountain-pass, and he therefore ordered knights and nobles to dismount and charge the peasantry on foot. The latter were on the point of being surrounded by an impenetrable wall of steel, when Arnold of Winkelried, A. D. 1386. crying out "I will open a way to liberty," sprang into the midst of the Austrians, gathered into his bosom as many as he could seize of the enemy's spears, and instantly falling, made a path for his comrades over his dead body. The Austrians gave way; Duke Leopold seized his own banner, after four in succession of its brave bearers had fallen, and plunging among the enemy found the death he sought. More than 650 counts, barons, and knights, with thousands of their vassals, lay dead upon the field. The battle of Sempach resulted in an honorable peace, by which the Swiss were secured in the possession of all which they had gained.

114. The burghers of south Germany, who, encouraged by the victory of the Swiss, undertook a similar contest against the knights and barons,

---

* The decrees of popes and emperors were called *bulls* from the pendent *(bulla)* of gold, silver, or lead, which was affixed to the seal.—The seven Electors, now first confirmed in their offices, were, the three archbishops of Mentz, Trèves, and Cologne, and four lay-princes, the King of Bohemia, the Duke of Saxony, the Margrave of Brandenburg, and the Count-palatine of the Rhine.

were less fortunate. They were many times defeated; their families and
movable goods were crowded into the cities; but throughout the
country their houses and villages were destroyed. Wenceslaus resided
chiefly in his own kingdom of Bohemia, never concerning himself with
his imperial duties. In A. D. 1400, the dissatisfied electors declared
him deposed, and chose Rupert, Count-palatine of the Rhine, to be
emperor. The ten years' administration of Rupert, in spite of his energy
and ability, was too short to remedy the disorders of Germany. He was
succeeded, A. D. 1410, by Sigismund, King of Hungary, brother of Wenceslaus, and the most illustrious of the Bohemian princes.

115. Church and State were now equally in want of wise government.
The return of the popes to Rome had been followed by the Great Schism,
and three nominal heads of Christendom, in Italy, France, and Spain,
were launching the thunders of excommunication, each against his two
rivals and all their adherents. The damaging truths uttered during this
heat of controversy, naturally lessened the reverence in which the
hierarchy had been held; and the notorious unworthiness of many high
prelates impressed on the foremost adherents of the papacy a sense of the
need of reform. In England, near the end of the fourteenth century, the
preaching of Wicliffe, and above all, his translation of the Holy Scriptures into the popular tongue, had led many thousands of people to
doubt or deny the authority of the Church. In Bohemia, Milecz, Von
Zanow, and John Huss had begun a similar revolution, even before the
latter was reinforced and encouraged by the writings of Wicliffe. The
marriage of Anne, sister of King Wenceslaus, with Richard II. of England promoted a free interchange of opinion between the two countries
at this supremely important crisis. Scholars traveled back and forth
between the now famous universities of Oxford and Prague. Wicliffe
and Huss, the ablest doctors in their respective universities, spoke with
clearness and force the language of the common people; and their cogent
reasonings exposed the terrible abuses springing from the luxury of the
clergy and the pretensions of the mendicant orders.

116. The first care of Sigismund was the convening of a general council for the union and reformation of the Church and the suppression of
heresy. Eighteen thousand clergy, including patriarchs, cardinals, and
bishops, hundreds of learned men from the universities, sovereign princes
or their embassadors, and delegates from the free cities, met at Constance
near the end of A. D. 1414. During the following year Pope John
XXIII. from Rome — "a man charged, at least, with every imaginable
crime" — presided, and the Emperor Sigismund arrived soon after his
coronation. Though avowedly convened for purposes of reform, one of
the first acts of the Council was to condemn and burn a reformer. John
Huss, having been cited to answer for his teachings, had come to Con-

stance under the imperial safe-conduct. He was, nevertheless, cast into prison, and after repeated trials was compelled to choose between death and recantation. He manfully chose the former, and was burnt in the presence of many prelates of the Council. His friend Jerome, a professor of theology at Prague, suffered the same punishment eleven months later.

117. The Council having deposed all three of the existing popes, elected in their place Otto Colonna, who took the name of Martin V. Though himself of blameless morality, Martin evaded all the proposed measures for limiting the license of the clergy, so that the Council proved a failure so far as the highest of its purposes was concerned. The papal states were now wholly in the power of Braccio Montone, one of those captains of free companies who were seizing sovereignty by the strong hand in many of the cities of Italy. To expel the usurper, the Pope employed a still more famous and unscrupulous adventurer, Giacomuzzo Sforza, then in the service of Joanna II. of Naples, but whose immediate descendants became lords of Milan.

118. The death of Huss and Jerome of Prague excited an open revolt in Bohemia, where the ex-emperor, Wenceslaus, yet reigned as king. The zeal of the Hussites passed all bounds of reason; Prague was seized, the surrounding country ravaged, monks and friars every-where put to death. Their fury reached its height when by the death of Wenceslaus, A. D. 1419, his brother Sigismund — held guiltiest of all for the betrayal of the Bohemian martyrs — became rightful king of the country. All his attempts, supported by the whole force of the Empire, to regain his inheritance, were ignominiously defeated, and the desolating torrent of war swept over Saxony, Brandenburg, Franconia, Bavaria, and Austria. At length the Council of Basle by wise and just concessions, brought all the reasonable followers of Huss into peace with A. D. 1431–1449. the Church. The two extreme sects of Taborites and "Orphans," (so called in reference to their leader, Ziska, whom they had lost,) were defeated at Lepan, A. D. 1434, with the loss of their great general, Procopius, and Sigismund obtained his Bohemian kingdom only a few months before his death, in 1437.

119. The Council at Basle carried forward the movements toward reform proposed at Constance, and especially affirmed the voice of the whole Church, speaking through such an assembly, to be superior to that of the Pope. Eugenius IV., the new pontiff, finding himself unable to control the transalpine Council, summoned a rival one at Ferrara, under the specious pretext of receiving the eastern Emperor John Palæologus, with the Patriarch of Constantinople and a most important embassy of Greek clergy. His narrowing empire being more and more closely hemmed in by the Turks, that sovereign stooped to buy the succor of western Christendom by acknowledging the supremacy of the Roman

bishop and yielding the doctrinal points which for centuries had been
in dispute between the two Churches. The mercenary
A. D. 1438, 1439.
union was signed and sealed at Florence, whither the
Council had been adjourned; but it was indignantly repudiated at Constantinople, and fifteen years from the emperor's return, that city was
surrendered to the Turks.

120. The Council of Basle, meanwhile, unheeding its excommunication
by Pope Eugenius, declared him deposed, and elected for his successor the
abdicated Duke Amadeus of Savoy, who, weary of sovereignty, had retired to a hermitage on Lake Geneva. He assumed the name of Felix
V., and was crowned with great magnificence at Basle, A. D. 1440.
Æneas Sylvius Piccolomini, the historian of the Council, was the most
active spirit of the time. Changing his allegiance to suit his interest,
he became secretary successively to the anti-pope Felix, to the new emperor Frederic III., to Eugenius IV., and his successor; and it was chiefly
owing to the diplomacy of the wily Italian that Germany was led to
disown the Council and return to the obedience of Eugenius. The Pope
died a few days after this event, and by the wisdom of his successor,
Nicholas V., the Council was dissolved, and the anti-pope reduced to a
cardinal.

121. Nicholas V. was perhaps the best of the pontiffs. Instead of heap-
ing wealth and honors upon his family, his ambition was to make Italy
a home of letters and arts. His agents ransacked Europe and south-
western Asia for copies of Greek authors wherewith to enrich the new
library of the Vatican, and a crowd of emigrant scholars, driven from the
east by the progress of the Turks, were magnificently received at Rome
and Florence. The Jubilee of 1450 drew a countless throng of pilgrims
and a great influx of wealth to the papal city; but scarcely
A. D. 1453.
had the joy of that event subsided when all Christendom
was thrilled with fear and consternation by tidings of the fall of Constantinople.

122. Already under Mohammed I. (A. D. 1413–1421) the Turks had
become possessed of the entire territory of the Eastern Empire with the
exceptions of the Morea, a few insignificant places on the Propontis, and
the capital itself, within whose walls they established a colony, coined
money, and carried on Mohammedan worship, under the very eyes of
the emperor. In their attacks upon Hungary, long the bulwark of
Christendom against Islam, they were less successful. Their seven
months' siege of Belgrade, A. D. 1440, resulted only in failure and a loss
of 17,000 men. John Huniades, a Wallachian noble, defeated them on
many fields; his most decisive victory was gained at Kunobitza, where their
forces were nearly annihilated. Pope Eugenius IV. sent a French and
German army, under Cardinal Cesarini, which procured the treaty of

Szegedin, A. D. 1444, on terms humiliating to the Turks and honorable to the crusaders. But no sooner had the Turkish host departed into Asia, than the papal legate, against the indignant remonstrances of Huniades, resolved to break his word and recommence hostilities. The result was the fatal battle of Varna, in which King Ladislaus of Poland and Hungary, the Cardinal Cesarini, and thousands more, lost their lives. Huniades as regent of the kingdom for the infant Ladislaus, son of Albert II. of Germany, was again defeated by the Turks in a three days' battle on the plain of Cossova, A. D. 1448.

Nov. 1444.

123. The fall of Constantinople, though to discerning eyes long certain to take place, sent a shock of grief and terror throughout Europe. Thousands of affrighted fugitives from the captured city reported the watchword which was wont to pass between the sultan and his janizaries: "Farewell, until we meet in Rome!" Nicholas V. proclaimed a new crusade. The "Turk's bell" sounded at noon in every parish in Europe, calling the faithful to pray that the progress of the infidel might be arrested. Æneas Sylvius lent his great talents and energy to the arming of Christendom; and John of Capistran, a Franciscan friar, traversed Italy and Germany, every-where by his wonderful eloquence rousing the enthusiasm of the crowds. The irregular force which he raised, added to that of the Hungarians, was able to relieve the fortress of Belgrade, again besieged by the terrible artillery of the Turks; but the death of Huniades damped the rejoicings of Europe at this triumph.

A. D. 1456.

124. On the death of the young Ladislaus, Matthias Corvinus, the son of Huniades, was elected king of Hungary, and during his long reign he was the ablest champion of Christendom against the Turks. In the year of his accession, Æneas Sylvius became Pope Pius II. The Council of Mantua, A. D. 1459, raised (upon paper) an army of 88,000 men, of which the emperor was declared generalissimo; and the Pope, notwithstanding his years and infirmities, resolved to take the field in person. He died A. D. 1464, while still vainly awaiting at Ancona the arrival of the Venetian forces. The age of crusades was past. Although Venice, in defense of her commerce, waged a fifteen years' war with the Turks, (A. D. 1464-1479,) little or no aid was afforded by the other European states; and the Mohammedan power was gradually confirmed over all the territories of the Eastern Empire. In 1479, the Venetians, now more hostile to King Ferdinand of Naples than to the Turks, even invited the latter to invade the Italian dominions of the former, by representing that Otranto, Brindisi, and Taranto were parts of the Eastern Empire, and as such belonged to Mohammed. The invitation was too readily accepted; Otranto was taken and its citizens treated with atrocious cruelty. The sudden death of the Sultan, how-

A. D. 1458-1490.

ever, cut short the Italian conquests; and, pressed by famine, the Turks abandoned this westernmost point of their European dominions, little more than a year from its first occupation.

RECAPITULATION.

Golden Bull of Charles IV. settles the constitution of the Empire. Leopold of Austria, with his league of nobles, is defeated at Sempach by the Swiss; but the knights and barons are victorious over the Suabian peasantry and burghers. Wenceslaus deposed and Rupert made emperor, A. D. 1400.

Religious reformation in England and Bohemia. The Emperor Sigismund calls the Council of Constance, to end the schism and suppress heresy. John Huss and Jerome of Prague burned; three popes deposed and Martin V. elected by the Council. Twenty years' war of religion in Bohemia. Council of Basle declares against Eugenius IV., and elects Felix V. as anti-pope. A rival Council at Ferrara and Florence receives the Emperor and Patriarch of Constantinople, and attempts the reünion of the eastern and western Churches. Western Christendom again united under Nicholas V., a munificent patron of letters and all the arts. The Turks, long withstood almost single-handed by John Huniades, at length capture Constantinople and overturn the Eastern Empire. A crusade led by John of Capistran relieves Belgrade. Matthias Corvinus becomes king of Hungary. The westward progress of the Turks is arrested at Otranto, A. D. 1481.

ITALY AND SPAIN.

125. Of the many powers which divided Italy, only six now retained any importance: the three sovereignties of Naples, the States of the Church, and Milan; and the three Republics of Venice, Florence, and Genoa.

Queen Joanna II. of Naples, daughter of Charles of Durazzo, called to her aid Alfonso V. of Aragon and Sicily, who received the title of Duke of Calabria as heir-expectant of the Italian crown. The queen, however, changed her mind, and adopted Louis III. of Anjou as her heir. The French prince died in 1434, and Joanna herself the following year. Count Réné of Anjou, brother of Louis, had been named in her will, but he was captured and detained in the north by a rival claimant to the duchy of Lorraine; and the Neapolitan nobles called in Alfonso again. The forces of Genoa and Milan fought for Anjou, and gained a most bloody victory over the Catalan fleet in the Mediterranean, Alfonso, his brother, and many of their attendant nobles being prisoners. The personal qualities of the King of Aragon gave him, however, the final victory over the accomplished and amiable, but inefficient Réné, who retired from public contests to devote himself to the more congenial pursuits of poetry and painting. Two of Réné's children were strongly contrasted with him in energy of character: Margaret, who in England so long and valiantly maintained the Lancastrian cause against the house of York, and John, Duke of Calabria, who displayed no less genius and determination in the pursuit of his lost inheritance.

126. The death of the last of the Visconti, A. D. 1447, was followed by an attempt to restore a republic in Milan. If Venice and Florence had taken the generous part, this effort might have been successful, and northern Italy, united and free, might have become invincible to the foreign foes, who too soon found out her weakness and her wealth. But of the two neighboring republics, one was jealous of Milanese power, and the other was becoming indifferent to her own freedom and hostile to that of others. Francesco Sforza, a soldier of fortune, who had married a daughter of the deceased duke, succeeded in making himself master of the city and its territory. The disposal of the duchy, according to feudal law, could rest only with the emperor; but it was also claimed by Charles, Duke of Orleans, in the right of his mother, Valentina Visconti; and by King Alfonso of Naples, who had been designated by the will of the late duke. The four opposing claims gave rise to long and important wars, to be described in the next period.

127. Placed midway between the east and the west, Venice enjoyed almost a monopoly of the commerce of the Levant with western and northern Europe. Beside its extensive territories on the Italian mainland, it held, before the end of the century, the sovereignty of Crete, Cyprus, and the Morea, with many towns and fortresses on the Grecian islands. A curiously complex constitution made Venice the strongest oligarchy on record. The Doge or Duke, though nominally supreme, was really only a puppet of the Council of Ten. Every year as the representative of the state, he cast a consecrated ring into the waters of the Adriatic, saying: "We betroth thee, O Sea, in sign of our lawful and perpetual dominion!"

128. Genoa, having a far less strong and settled government than Venice, was at various times compelled to place herself under the protection of the Empire, of Naples, of Milan, or of France. The enterprise and energy of her merchants, made them, however, formidable rivals of the Venetians, whom they nearly excluded from the ports of the Black Sea, and thus gained a monopoly of the trade with the interior of eastern Europe. The naval wars between Genoa and Venice can not here be detailed. They ended usually in favor of the latter.

129. The inland republic of Florence has left a deeper impress upon the character of Italy and the literature and art of the world than either of her maritime sisters. Far more popular than that of Venice, her government rested upon the industries of her citizens. Chief magistrates could only be chosen from members of the "Arts" or trades' unions, which were the same as the "Guilds" of England and the Netherlands. These officers were chosen every two months and the grand Council of State every four months, so that the whole mass of citizens possessing the qualifications for office, was elevated in turn to public trust. No magistrate received any reward for his services. During the supremacy of the Guelfs, Florence conquered the ports of Pisa and Leghorn and half of Tuscany, while

M. H. 8.

the wealth of her great bankers, merchants, and woolen manufacturers established her commercial fame in Europe.

130. From 1434 to 1464, Cosmo de Medici held the supreme power in Florence, and his family continued for more than three hundred years, first as chief citizens, and then as grand-dukes, to control the destinies of the state. The power of Cosmo and of his grandson, Lorenzo the Magnificent, resembles that of Pisistratus and his family at Athens; it was simply that of citizens, first among equals; and though supported, especially in the case of Cosmo, by the control of a rich money-lender over needy borrowers, it seemed to rest on the esteem and affection of the people. The public entertainments which they gave rendered life in Florence a perpetual scene of gay and brilliant festivity. In judging their claims, it must be remembered that their patronage of literature gave the Medici the advantage of being favorably reported to posterity. Their policy exalted the intellectual fame of Florence at the expense of her freedom, and their influence among the states of Italy was often, as in the case of Milan, thrown on the side of despotism. Still, to their liberal and enlightened tastes, Florence, in great measure, owes her title of Mother of Modern Art.

131. Castile and Leon, during the long minority and reign of John II., (A. D. 1406–1454,) became subject to the sway of Alvaro de Luna, constable of the united kingdoms, and one of the most powerful vassals that Europe has known. His own retainers made an army of 20,000 men, and he held his court with all the pomp of sovereignty. The king at length joined with the other nobles against him, and caused him to be executed at Valladolid. Henry IV., son of John II., was succeeded, A. D. 1474, by his sister Isabella, whose marriage with Ferdinand, heir of Aragon, Catalonia, and Valencia, led to the union of all the Spanish kingdoms under one sovereign.

132. Aragon, by the acquisition of Catalonia in 1137, had become the third naval power in Europe, being excelled only by Venice and Genoa. The Catalans, a hardy and adventurous race, were the best of sailors, and their bravery contributed much to the extension of the Aragonese dominions. The power of the king was even more limited than in Castile. The law-making power in both kingdoms resided in the *Cortes* or national assembly, which consisted of clergy, nobles, and deputies of the towns; but so far from cherishing this guarantee of their freedom, the citizens seem to have grudged the expense of maintaining their representatives, and the number of towns summoned had dwindled in 1480 to seventeen.

133. Alfonso V. (A. D. 1416–1458) resided chiefly in his Italian kingdom, (see § 125,) while his brother, John II. of Aragon, acted as his viceroy in Spain, and ultimately inherited the crown. John II. acquired Navarre by marrying its heiress, but this increase of dominion was the occasion of many crimes. Upon the death of Queen Blanche, her son Charles was the rightful ruler of Navarre, but his father, jealous of his popularity, refused him the crown. Charles took refuge with his uncle in Naples, and after Alfonso's death went into a humble and studious retirement in Sicily. He was called into Spain by false but flattering promises, and died, there is reason to believe, from poison administered by the new queen, Joanna. The kingdom of Navarre now rightly belonged to his sister Blanche, but it had been promised by treaty to the Count of Foix, who had married the next younger sister, Eleanor. The unhappy Blanche was betrayed into the keeping of her sister, who caused her to be poisoned, A. D. 1464. The brave and free-spirited Catalans, attributing some, at least, of these crimes to Joanna, the second wife of John II., refused to take oath of allegiance to her son Ferdinand, and a civil war of eleven years was the result. The Catalans submitted at last, and John dying, A. D. 1479, Ferdinand became king.

134. The reign of Ferdinand and Isabella was signalized in both kingdoms by the reëstablishment of order and justice in place of the lawless violence of the nobles. According to the good old custom of their respective realms, the sovereigns presided in person once a week in courts of law, for the especial benefit of their poorer subjects who could not afford the expense of ordinary litigation. A heavy blot, however, rests upon their reign, in the tribunal of the Inquisition, erected, A. D. 1480, as a royal court for the punishment of heresy and kindred offenses. The Dominican Inquisition had been merely an ecclesiastical court, and both Jews and heretics had been more mildly treated in Spain than in any other country. Many of the former had been raised to the highest offices in the state, even intrusted with the tutorship of royal princes, and their wealth as bankers made them indispensable to many a needy king. The just and merciful Isabella long resisted the arbitrary policy of her husband and the bigotry of her confessor, but at length she yielded, and obtained from Pope Sixtus IV. a bull for the establishment of the terrible tribunal in her own kingdom of Castile. In the year 1481, two thousand persons were burned alive in Spain, while no fewer than 17,000 were, in the phrase of the court, "reconciled," *i. e.*, subjected only to fine, imprisonment, or other lighter penalties.

135. A nobler enterprise awaited the Spanish sovereigns in their wars with the Moors of Granada. In arts and learning this Arab race was far in advance of its Christian neighbors; the greatest European scholars had studied at Cordova, and Arab physicians were in demand at many courts. Architecture was earlier developed in the Moorish cities than in central Europe, and travelers still wonder at the airy grace of the ruined arches of the Alhambra. Dissensions among the Moors themselves hastened the fall of their kingdom. Boabdil (Abu Abdallah) rebelled against his aged father the Caliph; but having made a treaty with the Spaniards, was in turn opposed by his uncle, Abdallah the Valiant. While the Moorish kingdom was thus weakened by civil strife, the combined armies of Castile and Aragon steadily advanced. Malaga was taken by a three months' siege in 1487. In 1491, Granada, the capital, after a still more obstinate defense, surrendered, and all Spain was reünited under Christian rule.

126. All Christendom received the news with joy, regarding the overthrow of the Moslem dominion, after nearly eight centuries duration in the south-west of Europe, almost as an offset to the establishment of the Turkish empire in the south-east. The triumph of the sovereigns was sullied by a cruel act of persecution. In spite of the terrible warnings of the Inquisition, the great mass of Jews in the kingdom were still firm in their faith. An order was now extorted by the clergy from the covetousness of Ferdinand and the mistaken piety of Isabella, for the expulsion of the whole Hebrew race from the country in which they and their fathers had lived for centuries. The best authorities tell us that 300,000 — some say even 800,000 — refused to barter their religion for the privilege of remaining. The harrowing incidents of this sudden and enforced emigration must be read elsewhere. Uncounted thousands died from shipwreck, starvation, or diseases arising from the fatigues and exposures of the voyage. A mother was seen to kill her little child rather than endure the sight of its misery. Some of the more hardy and enterprising found new homes, where they speedily acquired wealth by their industry or fame by their learning. The Turkish Sultan, Bajazet II., said derisively of Ferdinand, "You call this a wise sovereign, who impoverishes his own kingdom to enrich mine!" The example of Ferdinand and Isabella was followed by their son-in-law, the King of Portugal, who to his edict for the expulsion of the Jews added a still more barbarous order, that all Hebrew children under fourteen years of age should be torn from their parents and dispersed throughout his kingdom.

An account of the discovery of America — the greatest glory of the Castilian Queen — is reserved for the modern period.

RECAPITULATION.

House of Aragon becomes supreme in Naples, the Sforzas in Milan, and the Medici in Florence. Commercial rivalry of Venice and Genoa. Florence conquers the Tuscan ports, becomes celebrated for wealth, freedom, and progress in art.

Castile subject nearly half a century to the great Constable, Alvaro de Luna. Catalan sailors make Aragon a great naval power. By the untimely death of Prince Charles its crown descends to his brother Ferdinand; and the marriage of this prince with Isabella of Castile and Leon unites all the Spanish kingdoms. Their reign signalized by establishment of the Spanish Inquisition, conquest of the Moors of Granada, expulsion of the Jews, and discovery of America.

CONDITION OF EUROPE.

137. In a review of the thousand years now traversed, great social changes will readily be perceived. During the Dark Ages, scarcely more than two secular classes, those of warriors and serfs, could be said to exist. Early in the twelfth century cities began to multiply, and a middle class, including artisans and traders, became important by its wealth. The increasing power of this class may be seen in the rise of municipal constitutions in Italy, of the *cortes* in Spain (A. D. 1188), the parliament in England (1265), the states-general in France (1302), and the first representation of the free cities of Germany in the Diet (1309). The wealth of the Flemish merchants enabled them especially to purchase many popular privileges from sovereigns always in need of money.

138. A great increase of commerce followed the Crusades. The Italian ships which transported armies of pilgrims, brought back gems, spices, perfumes, and costly armor from the Asiatic countries. Sugar was first introduced into Europe by crusaders. The fertile plain of Lombardy was found well adapted to the growth of the cane. Its culture spread to Sicily, Spain, the Canary and Madeira Isles, and thence, after the great discoveries at the end of the fifteenth century, to the West Indies and to America.

139. The importance of their commercial interests led the cities of northern Germany to join in what was called the Hanseatic League for common defense. Most of the German knights and many of the highest nobles lived by plunder, issuing from their strong castles to rob unoffending travelers, and finding refuge within their walls from the pursuit of justice. The League, at its greatest extent, included all the trading towns between Livonia and Holland; its power was feared and its alliance courted by sovereign princes. Its fleets and armies controlled the Baltic; it conquered successively two kings of Norway, deposed a king of Sweden, and gave his crown to a duke of Mecklenburg.

140. The four foreign factories of the League were at London, Bruges, Bergen, and Novgorod. The voyage from the Mediterranean to the Baltic was too long to be accomplished in one summer, by the imperfect navigation of those times. Italian vessels were therefore unladen at Bruges, where German ships were waiting to receive the products of Asia and the south in exchange for the timber, hemp, fish, and other naval stores of the northern countries. Richly laden merchant-trains passed overland from the northern cities to Novgorod in Russia, then the abode of 300,000 people, and an important center of the art, learning, and industry of Europe and Asia. Italian merchants had a monopoly of commerce in the southern half of Europe, and from handling the money of all nations, naturally became the universal bankers. They were com-

monly called Lombards; and the chief banking street in London still
bears their name.

141. With the increase of intelligence and enterprise in western
Europe, manufactures were improved and extended. Italy became noted
for her silks, glass, fine woolens, and jewelry. Spain, beside making
steel armor, paper, sugar, cotton, and silk, produced and manufactured the
finest wool. The woolen fabrics of the Netherlands were celebrated as
early as the twelfth century; they were woven from English fleeces, and
were usually coarser and heavier than those of the southern countries.
Edward III. invited many Flemish weavers into England; by their
industry the cloth manufacture of that country was founded, which now
supplies markets never dreamed of in the Middle Ages. The peculiar
industry of Holland was the packing and exportation of herrings—a
trade of immense importance at a time when all the world abstained from
eating flesh during more than one-fourth of the year.

142. Among the new mechanical arts which contributed most to bring
in the modern era, were the manufacture of gunpowder, of linen paper,
and of movable types for printing. The first undoubtedly originated in
the East. Roger Bacon, an English, and Berthold Schwarz, a German
monk, were the first Europeans who understood the nature of gunpowder;
but they had learned chemistry from the Arabs, who collected their
information from the widest extent of the Mohammedan dominions.
The Chinese used detonating mixtures in fire-works, ages before we have
any definite account of their employment in war; but very ancient traditions in the East describe the discomfiture of enemies by artificial thunders
and lightnings launched from the walls of cities. Missiles of stone or
iron projected by gunpowder quickly superseded the use of Greek fire,
(see Book I., § 41,) as they could be made effective at longer range. The
first cannon in Europe were employed by the Moors in their Spanish wars.

A. D. 1346.
They were used by the English in the battle of Crecy, but
so clumsy was their contrivance, that they served for little
more than to frighten the horses of the French chivalry. Within
that and the following century, however, the use of fire-arms had
wrought a social and political revolution no less marked and momentous than that in military tactics. Hitherto the knight on his war-horse,
both encased in steel, had been more than a match for a hundred
unarmed peasants; and his stone castle on the hill had defied all assaults
save those of hunger and thirst. The term of his service in war could
not exceed forty days, except at his own option. Kings, accordingly, were
debarred from long and distant wars, for a feudal army was always on the
point of crumbling to pieces, even at the most decisive moment.

143. We have seen the rise of standing armies even before the invention of fire-arms; and under Louis XI. in France they had already

contributed greatly to the consolidation of royal power. The use of gun-powder took away still more power from the nobles, to add it to the kings. Except to officers in high command, war became a game of chance rather than of skill, attended with more danger and less glory than when its success depended on the personal prowess of the warrior. Above all, the robber-castles yielded to the storm of cannon-balls directed by the armies of the Hanse-towns and of the cities on the Rhine. Trade became more secure; and burghers and nobles met in battle on equal terms. On the other hand, standing armies soon became what they have ever since been, the instruments of despotism, enabling kings to gratify their ambition at the expense of the blood and treasure of their subjects.

144. The manufacture of paper from linen rags was a humble but essential antecedent to the art of printing, for the costliness of parchment or vellum was as effectual a barrier to the multiplication of books as the labor of transcribing. The first Saracen conquerors learned the art of paper-making at Samarcand; but it was many centuries before some European genius discovered that linen would serve for the purpose as well as cotton, which was then far more expensive. Printing from solid wooden blocks, long common in China, was first introduced into Europe for the manufacture of playing cards. The invention of movable types, each representing a letter, was the great event which led to the universal diffusion of literature. It is variously ascribed to one Dutch and two German mechanics near the middle of the fifteenth century; but the merit may be pretty accurately divided between them. Laurence Koster of Haarlem invented wooden types, and printed from them the *Speculum Humanæ Salvationis*, A. D. 1438; John Gutenberg of Mentz *cut* types from metal, and began to print the first edition of the Bible, in 1444; Peter Schœffer of Gernsheim *cast* metallic types in 1452. John Fust made some improvements in Koster's invention, and aided both Gutenberg and Schœffer by his wealth. Within a very few years printing presses were found in England, France, Italy, and Spain. Aldus Minutius of Venice became especially famous by the elegance of his editions of the Latin classics.

145. During the darkest periods of the mediæval centuries, votaries of learning had not been wanting. The schools of divinity attached to the cathedrals and monasteries nurtured some of the greatest intellects of any age; but unhappily the prodigious acquirements of the Schoolmen*

---

*The greatest of the Schoolmen were Albert the Great, called the "Universal Doctor;" Thomas Aquinas, the "Angelic Doctor;" Bonaventura, the "Seraphic Doctor;" Duns Scotus, the "Subtle Doctor;" and William of Ockham, the "Invincible Doctor." Dean Milman says, "The tomes of scholastic divinity may be compared with the pyramids of Egypt . . . commanding, from the display of immense human power, yet oppressive, from the sense of the waste of that power for no discoverable use. Whoever penetrates were wasted in subtle disquisitions on subjects which had no possible bearing on human life. A few philosophers, like Albert the Great and Roger Bacon, studied physical as well as mental science, but the bigotry of their age denounced them as sorcerers. Their geometric circles and triangles were believed to be charms to compel the attendance of evil spirits: the Greek, Hebrew, and Arabic which they had mastered, were easily imagined by the ignorant to be the languages of those spirits. Bacon spent the last ten or fifteen years of his life in the dungeon of his monastery.

146. Long before the close of the Crusades, the Universities of Oxford, Paris, and Bologna were at the height of their fame. The lectures of Abelard are said to have drawn 30,000 students to Paris; those of Roger Bacon and later of Duns Scotus, attracted an equal number to Oxford; and Bologna counted 10,000 law-students during the twelfth century. The possession of a long-lost MS. of Justinian's *Pandects*, which was discovered at Amalfi, A. D. 1137 — together with the lectures of Irnerius or Werner — made the fame of Bologna as a school of jurisprudence. Most of the great German universities were founded during the fourteenth and fifteenth centuries. The exclusive prevalence of Latin as the language of the learned, enabled scholars to avail themselves of the schools of various countries, and in these pilgrimages for knowledge, they were under the especial safe-conduct of the emperor. The gown of a scholar was as effectual a security against violence as that of priest or monk ; and the license, very commonly received, to support themselves by begging, shows poverty to have been the ordinary condition of a life devoted to study.

147. All the languages now spoken in Europe had reached something nearly approaching their present form, before the end of the Middle Ages. The Saxon of England was among the first of the Teutonic dialects to be enriched by a literature, and it was much improved by the efforts of the great Alfred (A. D. 871–901) both as scholar and as king. He himself made many translations from the Latin, both of portions of the Scriptures and of other books, and he provided for the education of his people by establishing schools in all the principal towns, to which every Englishman owning a certain portion of land was required to send his sons. The Norman conquest brought a new language into polite society, but the mass of the people held fast their mother-tongue ; and it was only after three centuries that the two elements of speech became blended into modern English, as found in the curious travels of Sir John Mandeville, the sermons of Wicliffe, and the poems of Chaucer.

within, finds himself bewildered and lost in a labyrinth of small, dark, intricate passages, devoid of grandeur, devoid of solemnity ; he may wander without end, and find nothing."
— *Latin Christianity*, IX.: 118.

148. The Provençal language, formed from Latin as learned and spoken by the Burgundian conquerors, possessed the first of the modern literatures of Europe. Its improvement dates from the accession of a count of Barcelona as king of Arles, and the consequent introduction of a refinement of taste learned from the Arabs of Spain. The songs of the troubadours derived a new inspiration from the Crusades; the heroes of the holy wars—among whom Richard Cœur de Lion is preëminent—were scarcely less proud of their fame as poets than as knights. A hundred years later than the troubadours, the *trouvères* of northern France originated those tales of chivalry which afforded almost all the secular reading in the Middle Ages. Their language differed from the Provençal as much, probably, as the Burgundian dialect differed from that of the Franks. Both were called *Romance*—a name which passed in time from the language itself to the class of compositions most characteristic of the first French writers;—but the *Romance Wallon* spoken north of the Loire, was also known as the *Langue de Oui*, while the *Romance Provençal* was the *Langue d'Oc*; just as the Italian of that day was called the *Langue de Si*, and the German the *Langue de Ja*, the affirmative particle being taken as the point of comparison. The student must pursue elsewhere the attractive study of the romances of chivalry—works in which the adventurous spirit of the Normans is not less clearly displayed than in their conquests in Russia, Italy, and England.

A. D. 1092.

149. Modern Italian received its first literary form at the Sicilian court of Frederic II., whose chancellor, Peter de Vinea, wrote the earliest sonnets; but its perfection is due to the three great Florentines, Dante, Petrarch, and Boccaccio, A. D. 1290–1365. The last two seem neither to have known nor heeded the influence which they were exerting upon their native speech, for the works upon which their fame now rests were those which they themselves esteemed the least; and their chief enthusiasm was given to the revival of the ancient languages. To this end Petrarch ransacked the dusty libraries of the convents for lost manuscripts of the Roman authors, and spent many laborious days in bringing together scattered fragments and transcribing with his own hand the treasures thus secured. The first professorship of Greek at Florence was founded A. D. 1360, at the instance of Boccaccio. The ardent pursuit of ancient learning, stimulated by the example of these great men, delayed the progress of their own Italian language more than a century, until Lorenzo de Medici, himself a poet and not less celebrated for his genius than for his political power and influence, gave a fresh impulse both to the literature and art of Florence. He, too, was a zealous collector of ancient MSS., gems, and statuary, which he placed liberally at the service of all students, and thus became the founder of the new school of Italian sculpture, wherein

A. D. 1469–1492.

Michael Angelo holds the highest place. Matthias Corvinus, King of Hungary (1458–1490) kept for years a secretary in the library of Lorenzo, copying rare manuscripts, and all Europe was benefited sooner or later by the wealth, zeal, and liberality of the Florentine citizen.

150. The revival of ancient learning in the west, of which some scattered traces may be perceived during the Latin occupation of Constantinople, but which was greatly accelerated by the fall of that city into the hands of the Turks and the escape of scholars with their literary treasures, was one of the most efficient causes which brought in the modern era. European intellect, long trammeled by the philosophy of the schools, learned to take a wider range. The "New Academy" founded by Lorenzo de Medici, substituted (at least so far as its influence went) the philosophy of Plato for that of Aristotle, which had hitherto reigned supreme. The arts of painting, sculpture, and architecture shared the general impulse. Four great artists who are considered as the revivers of modern art, were at work in Florence near the beginning of the fifteenth century. Each was almost equally skillful as architect, painter, sculptor, and worker in bronze. They were Ghiberti, Brunelleschi, Masaccio, and Donatello. The first labored forty-nine years upon the bronze doors of the baptistery of St. John; the second, by studying the Roman Pantheon, learned to construct the wonderful dome of the Florentine cathedral, and became the first great master of the architecture which in Italy superseded the Gothic. Then followed the triumvirate of modern art, the three whose works taken together have never been surpassed: Leonardo da Vinci, Michael Angelo, and Raphael. Their chief productions belong, however, to the next century; and in any case our limits barely admit a mention of their names. The subject may be pursued in the biographies of the several artists, and in many books concerning the history and criticism of art.

RECAPITULATION.

Increased importance of the middle class through multiplication of cities and extension of commerce, distinguish the last four centuries of the media-val period. Products of the East enrich western Europe after the Crusades. Power and extent of the Hanseatic League. Bruges its chief center of trade with the south; Novgorod with the east. Italians the merchants and bankers for a great part of Europe. Importance of the woolen manufacture in Spain, Italy, England, and Flanders. Use of gunpowder brought from China by the Saracens, leads to the decline of the feudal system in Europe. Manufacture of linen paper and invention of printing effect a revolution in the literary world.

Learning of the Schoolmen contrasted with the ignorance of the masses. Rise of the great universities: Paris noted for theology; Oxford for philosophy; Bologna for law. Privileges and poverty of students. Anglo-Saxon language improved by Alfred; Anglo-Norman by Wicliffe, Mandeville, and Chaucer; Provençal by the *troubadours*; French by the *trouvères*; Italian by poets of the Sicilian court, and later, by Dante, Petrarch, and Boccaccio. Revival of ancient learning and art in Italy during 15th century; influence of the Medici; Florence the scene of the *Renaissance*.

The Mohammedan Empires.

151. For the sake of brevity, we insert here a connected view of the principal Mohammedan empires in Asia, though they embrace a period both earlier and later than that which we have reached. 1. The Gaznevides, Gaurides, Afghans, and Moguls in India; 2. The remaining Mongol or Mogul dominions of Zenghis Khan and Timour; 3. The Seljukian dynasties; 4. The Ottoman or present Turkish power.

152. The Gaznevides took their name from Gazna, a town on one of the branches of the Indus, where their founder, a rebellious governor of Khorassan, took refuge with his followers, A. D. 961. Mahmoud, the third of the line, not only extended his power westward to the Tigris and the Caspian, and received the title of Sultan from the Caliph at Bagdad; but by twelve expeditions into Hindustan, established the first Mohammedan empire in that great peninsula. He destroyed the pagoda at Sumnaut, whose pillars were covered with gold and resplendent with jewels. The huge idol of this temple was formed of a single stone fifty cubits in height, and the traditions of the Brahmins declared that it had been worshiped on that spot between four and five thousand years. Fifty thousand devotees sacrificed their lives in its defense, but the image was at length broken in pieces and found to contain untold wealth in diamonds and rubies. The demolition of hundreds of pagodas and thousands of idols between the Indus and the Ganges bore witness to the stern iconoclasm of Mahmoud.

153. Within two hundred years from its foundation, the Gaznevide Empire was dismembered, and a great part of its Indian territories conquered by Mohammed of Gaur, who plundered A. D. 1183. Benares, the most holy place of Hindu superstition, and fixed the seat of Moslem dominion at Lahore. Upon his death a new Afghan dynasty gained the greater part of India, and removed the capital to the more central city of Delhi. The second of the Afghan emperors conquered Bengal, but lost his Persian and Tartar dominions to the successors of Zenghis Khan. For two centuries the wealth of the emperors at Delhi drew upon them continual attacks from the Mongols; but the most destructive inroad of these invaders was led by Timour* in A. D. 1399. Crossing the Hindu Kush, with 90,000 horsemen, this Tartar chief penetrated to the plain of Delhi; conquered the city in a great battle and gave it over to his followers, who loaded themselves with its enormous wealth; 100,000 captives, who had impeded his march, had already been massacred in cold blood; and multitudes of unarmed pilgrims to the Ganges fell victims to the wanton cruelty of his followers.

---

*Often called Tamerlane — Timour Lenk, or the Lame.

154. Timour founded no permanent empire in India. The Afghan dynasty ended fourteen years after his invasion, with the death of Mah-moud. The several governors of provinces set up independent sovereign-

A. D. 1530.

ties, and it was reserved for Baber, a descendant of Timour, to unite them all in the great Mogul Empire. His grand-son Akbar, by his wise, liberal, and beneficent policy, gained and de-served the title, "Guardian of Mankind." By Shah Jehan, one of his descendants, Delhi was restored to its former magnificence; but it was under Aurungzebe (A. D. 1658–1707) that the Mogul Empire reached its greatest power and extent. Its rapid decline began with his death. Nadir Shah, the usurper of the Persian throne, was invited into Hin-dustan by conspirators against the house of Timour, and subjected Delhi to a massacre which surpassed the most horrid scenes in the career of his predecessors. Like Timour he founded no dynasty, but left the Mogul Empire to perish by its own weakness.

155. Zenghis Khan (A. D. 1154–1227) one of the most remarkable of the Scythian adventurers, founded an empire, which, under his descend-ants, extended over nearly all Asia, and a great part of eastern Europe, forming the most extensive dominion that the world has ever seen. The

A. D. 1279.

conquest of China was completed by his fourth descend-ant, Kublai Khan, who also conquered Burmah, Cochin China, and Tonquin. At his court the Venetian, Marco Polo, was liber-ally entertained; he received also an embassy from the Pope, and per-mitted Christian missionaries to establish themselves in China. The Mongol dynasty was overthrown, A. D. 1368, by a revolution following a famine in which 13,000,000 of people are said to have perished. A Buddhist monk managed to put himself at the head of the movement, and founded the Ming dynasty, which reigned 276 years, until it was overthrown by the Mantchoo Tartars, 1644. The present dynasty, which is still considered foreign by the mass of the people, is of the Mantchoo race.

156. In the west, the descendants of Zenghis had meanwhile over-thrown the Abbassides of Bagdad and extended their forays to the Adriatic, the borders of Germany, and the frozen shores of the Arctic

A. D. 1211.

Ocean. Kiev, Moscow, Cracow, and Lublin were burned; and in the great battle of Liegnitz, the Duke of Silesia, the Polish Palatine, and the Grand Master of the Teutonic Knights were defeated. Moravia, Silesia, and Hungary were laid waste, and Russia became tributary to the "Golden Horde." Towards the end of the thirteenth century the Mongol Empire in the west was broken up into many distinct sovereignties. It was reünited for a season by Timour, whose career of conquest was only second to that of Zenghis himself. He subdued the various Tartar tribes of central Asia, reduced Persia to submission, and came in collision with the Ottoman Empire near the Euphrates.

157. But Bajazet for a time found a nearer interest in the siege of Constantinople—Timour in the conquest of Syria; and it was not until July, 1402, that the two Moslem powers encountered each other upon the plains of Angora. Bajazet was defeated and a prisoner, and there is reason to believe that he passed the few months which intervened between his capture and his death in an iron cage. No proof of Timour's cruelty could appear incredible to those who saw the pyramids of human heads which marked the scene of his victories. A rebellion in Bagdad was avenged by the slaughter of 90,000 human beings. Yet this savage delighted in the conversation of learned men, and in the elegancies of art with which he adorned his capital, Samarcand. At this magnificent city in the wilderness, embassadors from Europe and Asia were constantly in attendance on the great sovereign, whom they propitiated by costly gifts.

158. The Seljukian dominion was short-lived, its flourishing period covering little more than half the eleventh century; but during that time twelve hundred subject kings or princes A. D. 1038-1092. surrounded the throne of the Sultan, and prayers were offered for him in the mosques of Jerusalem and Mecca, as well as at Ispahan, Samarcand, Bokhara, and Kashgar. Seljuk, a Turkish chief, about A. D. 980, drew to his standard the disaffected members of many tribes north and east of the Caspian, and set up an independent court at Samarcand. His grandson, Togrol Beg, (see § 2,) gained a great victory at Zendecan, A. D. 1038, over the Gaznevide sultan, Massoud, and conquered Persia and Korasmia. By defending the caliph at Bagdad against the Fatimite sovereign of Egypt and the rebellious emirs of Syria, Togrol gained the high-sounding title of "Lieutenant of the Vicar of the Prophet," a title which bore with it all temporal sovereignty in the Abbassid dominions. The Tartar chief was indeed better able to wield the sword for the common defense than his reverend but feeble superior. He made plundering forays into Georgia and Armenia, and invaded the Greek Empire, but the conquest of these provinces was reserved for his nephew and successor, Alp Arslan.

159. In three campaigns the emirs of this sultan were beaten by the Emperor Romanus, but when Alp Arslan took the field in person, the emperor was in turn defeated and made a prisoner. He was treated with the respect and sympathy due to his character and misfortunes, and was released with great generosity; but his subjects refused either to pay his ransom or to acknowledge a captive for their sovereign; and the king of Armenia, in whose cause Romanus had engaged in the war, imprisoned him in a monastery for the rest of his days. The victorious career of Alp Arslan was ended by the dagger of an assassin, and his son, Malek Shah, received the titles of Sultan and Commander of the Faithful. This descendant of Scythian nomads was the greatest prince of his age. Not only mosques, but roads, bridges, colleges, hospitals, and asylums for every sort of misfortune, were among the results of his enlightened and beneficent reign. He reformed the Moslem calendar which had fallen into confusion; and twelve times made the entire tour of his dominions to administer justice and redress wrongs. In his wars with the Byzantine emperors, Malek was once a prisoner, and once had his opponent in his own hands; but he freely dismissed him and sent him with an honorable escort within the Greek lines. The conquest of Asia Minor was effected by Solyman, an officer and kinsman of Malek, who permitted him to govern it as "King of Roum." His capital was first at Nice, afterwards at Iconium. (See §§ 9, 20.) Jerusalem was captured by the lieutenants of Malek, but it soon fell under the independent sovereignty of the emir Ortok, then was retaken by the Fatimite caliphs, and lastly by the crusaders. The Seljukian empire rapidly declined after the death of Malek, and its fragments were ultimately absorbed into the dominion of Zenghis Khan.

160. The Khorasmian or Ottoman Turks are the latest arrived among the ruling races of Europe; yet the empire which they erected on the three continents which surround the Mediterranean has been more lasting than that of any of the more splendid Moslem dynasties. At the beginning of the 14th century they entered Asia Minor, and enlisted in the service of the sultan of Iconium. Othman, the son of Orthugrul, was the real founder of the empire which bears his name. Having conquered the cities of Nicomedia, Nice, and Brusa, he made the latter his capital, and adorned it with a mosque, a college, and a hospital. Professors of Persian and Arabic learning, drawn thither by his patronage, showed that civilization had already made progress among the barbarians from the Tartar plains. Orchan, son of Othman, captured Gallipoli on the opposite shore of the Hellespont, and Amurath I., his successor, conquered Thrace and fixed the capital of his European dominions at Adrianople.

A. D. 1360-1389.

The city of Constantine, thus surrounded, seemed an easy prey, but Amurath first subdued the Slavonian nations of Bulgaria, Servia, Bosnia, and Albania; and by the institution of the Janizaries, laid a firm foundation for the future extension of his empire. From his multitudes of Christian captives he selected the strongest and most beautiful youth to be trained for his armies. Thus arose the first regular infantry in Europe; and their constant and rigorous discipline made them long the most effective soldiery on any field. Trained from childhood or early youth in the Mohammedan religion, and treated with marked favor by the sultans, the Janizaries were usually unswerving in their new allegiance; but in some instances they turned against their captors the weapons which they had gained in their service.*

161. Bajazet I. (1389–1403) bore the surname *Ilderim*, or the Lightning. His fame filled Europe with terror, especially when in the battle of Nicopolis he had defeated and slain the bravest chivalry of Christendom. An army of 100,000 men, led by Sigismund, then king of Hungary, afterwards emperor, was hopelessly overthrown; but the precarious existence of the Eastern Empire was prolonged by the defeat and death of Bajazet himself in his war with Timour. (See ¿ 157.) Mohammed I., the youngest son of Bajazet, retrieved the fortunes of his family; Amurath II. again defeated the combined forces of Christendom at Varna and Cossova; and under Mohammed II., the empire of the eastern Cæsars was finally overthrown. Not only Constantinople, but the Greek islands and peninsula became the prey of the Asiatic hosts.

A. D. 1396.

A. D. 1453.

162. For more than a century, from Mohammed II. to Solyman the Magnificent, the Turks were ruled by a rare succession of able princes, whose power was a perpetual menace to the peace of Europe, while they maintained within their own borders a vigorous and orderly discipline. The most intolerable of their impositions upon their Christian subjects was the child-tribute, which recruited the ranks of the Janizaries, after the supply of captives taken in war became insufficient. With Selim, the successor of Solyman, the Ottoman dynasty began to decline, and the Janizaries were commonly the real rulers of the empire, until, within our own century, their power was broken by a terrible slaughter. The main events of modern Turkish history will be indicated in their proper places.

163. In Egypt, the line of Fatimite caliphs ended, A. D. 1171, with the rise of Saladin. (See ¿ 19.) A later sultan, Malek Sala, bought a large number of captives from Zenghis Khan, and trained them, under the name of Mamelukes for his own body-guard. But the Mamelukes dethroned his successor, and set up their own leader, Ibeg, in his place.

---

* The most noted example was George Castriot, the son of an Albanian prince, who with his brothers became in childhood a captive to the Turks, and was educated as a Mussulman. His Turkish name, Scanderbeg, (Iskender Beg, meaning Lord Alexander,) indicates the military fame which gained him the favor of Amurath II. (A. D. 1421–1451.) At the age of 44, however, he suddenly abjured Mohammedanism and the service of the sultan, resumed his Christian name, and declared himself the avenger of his family and people. With his hereditary subjects between the mountains and the Adriatic, and an army of French and German adventurers whom he attracted by his valor and fortune, he held out twenty-three years against the Ottoman Empire; but died at last a fugitive in the Venetian territories, A. D. 1467. His nation ended with his life. Not so his fame, for the Turkish soldiers who rifled his tomb, made amulets of his bones, which, they believed, conferred invincible courage on whomsoever possessed them.

The first line of these military sovereigns were called Bahree or River Mamelukes, from having been trained upon an island in the Nile. They took into their pay another band of Georgians and Circassians, called Borghees, who in turn deposed the Bahree sultan, and raised Barkook, their commander, to the throne, A. D. 1387. The Borghees ruled until 1517, when they were deposed by the Ottoman Turks, and Egypt became a dependency of Constantinople. But Mameluke Beys were intrusted with the government of twenty-four provinces, and by their numerous guards retained the real power, while the viceroys or pashas enjoyed only the shadow.

RECAPITULATION.

Gaznevide and Gauride dynasties successively destroy the idols and enrich themselves with the wealth of the Hindus. Afghan emperors, succeeding, make Delhi the capital— are defeated and plundered but not dethroned by Timour. After the dissolution of their dominion, his descendant, Baber, establishes the great Mogul Empire, which culminates in Aurungzebe and suddenly declines at his death. Zenghis Khan and his family found the most extensive empire which the world has seen. Kublai Khan conquers China; the Golden Horde desolate eastern Europe. Timour conquers the Ottoman Bajazet and imprisons him in an iron cage.

The Seljukian dominion of great extent but short duration. Malek Shah the most powerful monarch of his time.

Ottoman Turks conquer all the territories of the Eastern Empire, while the Cæsars still reign in the capital. In the battle of Nicopolis they destroy the bravest and noblest defenders of Christendom. Corps of the Janizaries formed of Christian captives. Constantinople taken, A. D. 1453.

Dominion of the Mamelukes in Egypt gives way only nominally to that of the Turkish viceroys.

QUESTIONS FOR REVIEW.

Book II.

HOUSES OF YORK AND LANCASTER.

EDWARD III.

Edward, Black Prince.   Lionel, d. of Clarence.   John, d. of Lancaster.   Edmund, d. of York.

RICHARD II.   Philippa, m. earl of   HENRY IV.   John Beaufort, earl of
                   March.   Somerset.
              Roger Mortimer, earl   HENRY V.   John Beaufort, duke of
                 of March.   Somerset.

Edmund.   Anne, m. (2d) son of d. of York.   HENRY VI.   Margaret, m. Edmund Tudor,
                                                 earl of Richmond.
        Richard, d. of York.   HENRY VII (Tudor).

EDWARD IV.   RICHARD III.   George, d. of Clarence.

EDWARD V.   Richard, d. of York.   Elizabeth, married King Henry VII.

BOOK III.

THE MODERN ERA,

FROM THE DISCOVERY OF AMERICA TO THE CLOSE OF THE THIRTY YEARS' WAR.

A. D. 1492–1648.

DISCOVERIES AND EXPLORATIONS.

1. OUR study has hitherto been confined to the Eastern Hemisphere, and mainly to that small north-western portion of its vast extent which is covered by the continent of Europe. We now approach the unveiling of lands long hidden from the civilized world, though vague surmises concerning them may be found in ancient literature, and during the Dark Ages several adventurous seamen doubtless reached their shores— never, however, to return and increase the general knowledge by a record of their observations.

2. The few existing traces of the earliest inhabitants of the New World may well engage the ingenuity of antiquarians, but form at present no part of history. The structure of the American continent would seem to have insured its being discovered and introduced to the rest of the world by inhabitants of Europe rather than of Asia. The precipitous mountain barriers of the western coast are strongly contrasted with the broad and gradual slope, the deep bays, excellent harbors, and numerous navigable rivers of the eastern. That part of America which most resembles Europe lies nearest to it, and seems to have invited discovery. An Icelandic colony was formed in Newfoundland near the end of the tenth century; but all intercourse with the parent country having ceased, the settlers must have become absorbed into the native tribes; and when the renewed enterprise of the sixteenth century again brought Europeans to that region, their descendants, if any survived, were undistinguishable, either in color or customs, from the native savages of the coast.

3. The polarity of the magnet, and its application in the mariner's compass, were known in western Europe early in the twelfth century; but it was reserved for the fifteenth, with its extraordinary reäwakening of human thought and enterprise, to commence the great era of maritime discovery. The Portuguese, as was natural, from their western position looking out upon the Atlantic, were pioneers in the exploration of unknown seas. The Catalans had, indeed, preceded them by passing, A. D. 1346, the hitherto impassable point of Cape Non; and French seamen from Dieppe had penetrated, in 1364, to Sierra Leone and Rio Sestos. About the same time the Spaniards, partly by accident, discovered the Fortunate or Canary Islands, which were conquered and settled in successive expeditions from 1393 to 1495.

4. Prince Henry, fourth son of John I. of Portugal, gave to Europe the first example of a truly royal patronage of nautical science. At his residence near Cape St. Vincent, where the waves of the mysterious ocean almost washed the base of his observatory, he called together learned men from all countries, especially those who were skilled in astronomy and the mathematics of navigation, and consulted them concerning his favorite schemes. His liberal enterprises were rewarded by the discovery, A. D. 1419, of the Madeiras, and later of the Azores and Cape Verde Islands and the coast of Guinea.

5. The Roman pontiffs, as heirs of the Cæsars, claimed the right to dispose of all islands and newly discovered lands. At the request of the king of Portugal, Pope Eugenius IV. published a bull, adding to that monarchy all the countries between Cape Non and India! Hitherto the products of Asia had been brought into western Europe by Venetian vessels from Alexandria. The Portuguese now surmised a sea route to India, and in 1487, Bartholomew Diaz actually passed the "Cape of Storms," which from this happy success received its new name of "Good Hope." The great admiral, Vasco de Gama, following the same course, was the first European to enter the Indian Ocean. In spite of many difficulties and dangers, he explored the Malabar coast, and returned to Portugal, bearing not only a precious cargo of gold and spices, but wonderful reports of the wealth and civilization of that populous region.

A. D. 1497

6. The hostility of the Mohammedan rulers of India compelled the newcomers to put forth all their naval force in order to obtain a foothold and a share in the trade with the tribes of the interior; but the fort and factories established at Cochin soon became the cradle of a great commercial empire, whose power was felt from China to the Red Sea. Its most flourishing seat was the Isle of Ormuz, where semi-annual fairs transformed the salt and barren rock into almost the fabled splendor and luxury of an Oriental palace. Goa, the more permanent capital of the

Portuguese dominion, still displays in its stately churches, warehouses, and deserted dwellings, a remnant of that magnificence which gave it the title of "the Golden." The opening of the maritime route to India, though of less historical interest, was of greater immediate importance than the discovery of America. It revolutionized the commerce of Europe and contributed more than any other cause to the decline of Venice.

7. It is remarkable that the two great maritime republics of Italy furnished the two discoverers of the western continent, and by opening the navigation of the Atlantic gave another fatal blow to their own Mediterranean commerce. Christopher Columbus, a native of Genoa, spurred to emulation by the success of the Portuguese, conceived it possible to reverse their route and reach India by sailing westward. Bits of carved wood, logs, and even two human bodies of unfamiliar complexion washed up by the waves upon the shores of Madeira and the Azores, convinced him that some unknown continent was not far distant. The spherical form of the earth—though denied by the Church, and distinctly affirmed by only a few bold thinkers, like the Archbishop of Cambray—afforded the basis of his calculations.

8. Many painful years were spent in imploring aid from the governments of Genoa, Portugal, England, and Spain. At last, Isabella of Castile exclaimed, "I will undertake the enterprise for mine own crown, and if it be needful I will pawn my jewels to defray the expense." Columbus was made High Admiral and Viceroy of all the lands which he might discover, and secured in one-tenth of the net profits of trade with the same. Three small ships were placed at his disposal, and he set sail from Palos, Aug. 3, 1492. After stopping at the Canaries to refit, the little squadron pushed westward into those unknown regions which were peopled with indescribable terrors for the ignorant and superstitious seamen. Just as their discontent was breaking out into dangerous mutiny, the glad sound of "Land ahead!" was heard. They were approaching one of the Bahamas, now known as St. Salvador. Reverently kneeling on the shore, the great discoverer gave thanks for safety and success, and took possession of the land in the name of the Spanish sovereigns.

9. The larger islands of Hayti and Cuba were discovered during the subsequent four months. Believing that he had arrived in the Indies, Columbus called the natives Indians, and these names qualified by the epithet "West," are still applied to the islands and people. Having built and garrisoned the little fort of La Navidad in Hayti, the Admiral sailed for Europe, carrying with him plants, animals, and some of the native men as proofs of his success and specimens of the products of the newly discovered countries. A storm drove him into the Tagus, where King John II.—though mortified by his own former rejection of an enterprise which had now proved so gloriously successful—received the Admiral

with distinguished honors. Seven months and eleven days from his departure, the ships of Columbus reëntered the port of Palos. All the bells of the village rang joyously, while its entire population accompanied the Admiral and his crew to the principal church; and thanks were offered as for persons rescued from the grave. Their progress through Spain was marked by the joy and wonder of all the people, and their entry into Barcelona, then the residence of the court, was like a Roman triumph. Multitudes thronged to see the discoverer of a "new world." The sovereigns received him with honors never before paid to mere intellectual greatness, unsupported by rank, fortune, or military renown. The natives in his train were immediately baptized, and the hope of extending to their race the blessings of Christianity was the strongest motive which engaged the pure and lofty spirit of Isabella in the further prosecution of discoveries. Letters of the time describe the impulse suddenly given to the imagination of all Europe by the great and unexpected event. Men congratulated each other on having lived to see a day when the bounds of human knowledge were widened by the opening of such vast new fields for observation.

10. An India-house was immediately established at Seville and a Custom-house at Cadiz, under the direction of a new Board of Trade. The Pope, Alexander VI., magnanimously conferred upon the Spanish sovereigns all lands then or thereafter to be discovered in the western seas; which territories were to be divided from those of Portugal by an imaginary line passing due north and south, a hundred leagues west of the Azores. The possibility of the Spaniards in their westward voyages coming into collision with the Portuguese who sailed toward the south and east, did not disturb the calculations of his Holiness.

11. Detaining by skillful diplomacy a fleet which King John of Portugal was sending forth in the hope of retrieving his mistake, Isabella hastened the departure of Columbus on his second voyage. Seventeen ships were now at his disposal, and from the multitude of applicants for enrollment in his service, it had been difficult to exclude all but fifteen hundred. With high hopes cheered by the acclamations of the crowd, this fleet sailed from Cadiz, Sept. 25, 1493. The treaty of Tordesillas, concluded with Portugal the following June, removed the partition line between the foreign possessions of the two nations to 370 leagues westward of the Azores—a most important transaction, since it confirmed the Portuguese in their subsequent claims to Brazil.

12. The second voyage of Columbus was rewarded by the discovery of Jamaica and of many of the Caribbee Islands. His colony in Hayti had been cut off by the natives in just vengeance for unprovoked outrages; but he planted a new town, which received the name Isabella, in honor of the queen. The fatal discovery of gold dust in **Hayti**,

diverted the attention of the Spaniards from agriculture and regular trade; and eventually brought to the West Indies an indolent and worthless crowd of adventurers, who sought only to repair their wasted fortunes at the expense of the unfortunate natives. These mild and friendly people, who in their ignorance had welcomed the first white men as messengers from heaven, were soon undeceived. The tax of a certain quantity of gold dust imposed upon each was an unjustifiable extortion; but it was only changed for the iniquitous system of *ripartimientos*, by which a number of natives was assigned to each settler, and compelled to render personal service in lieu of tribute. Feeble in body and mind, accustomed to live indolently upon the spontaneous products of the soil, and strangers to the consuming thirst for gold which animated their masters, the people rapidly sank under the labors of the mines. At one time their intolerable sufferings drove them into a revolt in which several hundreds of thousands perished. In the space of fifteen years, the population of Hayti was reduced by disease or violence from 1,000,000 to 60,000.

13. In his third voyage Columbus touched the American continent near the mouth of the Orinoco, and coasted the provinces since called Para and Cumana. But the grandeur of his A. D. 1498. discoveries only increased the envy and hatred of the Spanish cavaliers, whose misconduct would long before have destroyed the colony but for the severe coërcive measures of the Admiral. Such loud complaints reached the Spanish sovereigns that a commissioner with full powers was sent to investigate the affairs of the colony. The narrow mind of Bobadilla was unbalanced by a little brief authority, and without a show of justice he caused the Admiral to be seized and sent to Spain in irons! The noble queen hastened to soothe the wounds which this insolence had inflicted, by reïnstating Columbus in all his honors, and assuring him in many delicate ways of her unshaken confidence and gratitude.

14. His fourth voyage was undertaken in the hope of finding a passage from the Atlantic to the Pacific Ocean, which might afford a westward route to India. After coasting through the Gulf of Honduras, he was compelled by storms and the mutinous spirit of his men to abandon his design. He was subsequently shipwrecked upon the coast of Jamaica; and returning to Spain had the grief to find A. D. 1504. that his faithful friend, the queen, was upon her death-bed. Her husband, the covetous and ungrateful Ferdinand, evaded the payment to Columbus of his just share in the reward of his labors, until the great Admiral, worn out with disappointments, died in poverty at Valladolid. His tomb at Seville bore, by order of Ferdinand, the inscription: "To Castile and Leon, Columbus gave a New World." His remains were

afterward removed to the hemisphere he had discovered, to rest in the cathedral at Havana. The continent, almost by accident, received the name of a Florentine adventurer, Amerigo Vespucci.

15. The singular achievements and misfortunes of Columbus have merited a more detailed description than can be afforded to the other explorers. One year before the discovery of the South American continent, Sebastian Cabot, the son of a Venetian merchant, though in the service of Henry VII. of England, explored the North American coast from Lat. 67½° to 38.° The Portuguese Cabral in A. D. 1500, having taken an unusually westerly course in a voyage to India, discovered the rich and fertile country of Brazil, and took possession in the name of King Emmanuel I. It had been previously visited by Pinzon, a friend and former companion of Columbus, but in pursuance of the treaty of Tordesillas, above mentioned, it was resigned by the Spaniards. In the service of the same king of Portugal, Gaspar Cortereal explored the Gulf of St. Lawrence and the coast of Labrador to the entrance of Hudson Bay.

16. Diego Columbus, being invested in 1509 with his hereditary viceroyalty of the New World, projected the conquest and colonization of Cuba, which were accomplished in 1511. The next year the veteran Juan Ponce de Leon undertook at his own cost an explora-

A. D. 1512.

tion of the mainland, being led by a romantic tradition to seek there a fountain of perpetual youth. Near the present town of St. Augustine, he reached a coast which, either from its flowery appearance or from the circumstance of his arrival on Palm Sunday, he called *Florida.* In 1513, Vasco Nunez de Balboa, with 290 Spaniards, crossed the Isthmus of Darien, and, first of Europeans, looked upon the Pacific from its western border. Advancing in full armor into its waters, he vowed as a true knight to conquer and defend them for the king of Spain.

17. Six years later Hernando Cortez, with less than 600 men, undertook the conquest of Mexico. The wealth, luxury, and high civilization of this empire were strongly contrasted with the rude manners of the barbarous tribes on the north as well as of the indolent natives of the coast. Its populous cities were guarded by a well-ordered police; in their markets were found as great a variety of merchandise as in any European fair. The capital city was situated in the midst of an immense salt lake, and though itself many thousand feet above the sea, was surrounded by mountains of far greater altitude. Its temples were remarkable for their architectural grandeur, and were adorned with delicate and curious carvings in stone and wood. A race of hereditary emperors was regarded with almost religious veneration.

First subduing the warlike republic of Tlascala, and drawing from it 6,000 auxiliaries, Cortez advanced to the important town of Cholula. Here the officers of Montezuma entertained him with a show of friendship, while secretly laying plots for his destruction. But Cortez detected the treachery and revenged it by a massacre of several thousands of citizens.

18. The feeble Montezuma, unable to resent this violence, received the Spaniards with great magnificence in his capital; but his efforts at conciliation were unavailing to save either his kingdom or his life. He was seized and detained in the Spanish quarters as a hostage, and was slain during an attack, by a missile from the hand of one of his own subjects. The Spaniards were forced to withdraw for awhile from the capital, but returning with fresh reinforcements, they captured the new emperor, Guatimozin, and soon became masters of the whole empire. The possession of fire-arms and of horses had given the mere handful of Spaniards a comparatively easy victory over thousands of brave but defenseless natives. Armies of missionary monks completed the conquest which force had begun. The Mexicans, convinced that the gods of their fathers had either deserted them or had themselves been conquered, flocked in such numbers to embrace the new faith, that thousands were baptized in a single day. The humane efforts of the missionaries, especially of the good Las Casas, preserved the Mexicans in great measure from the cruel fate which Spanish conquest had brought upon the natives of the islands; and they were rewarded by the ardent attachment of that people to the Roman Church.

19. A more disgraceful tale of deceit and violence might be told of the conquest of Peru, A. D. 1531–1536. The mineral treasures of this great empire had been described to Balboa by the natives of the Isthmus; but the magnificence of the court and capital of Atahualpa far surpassed all that had been told. After buying his life with a room full of gold, the unhappy Inca was nevertheless condemned to be burned at the stake; and the utmost indulgence which he could obtain by a profession of Christianity, was death by a halter before the flames were kindled. Quarrels among the Spaniards themselves delayed the establishment of their power. Pizarro, the commander, was slain by one of his subordinates, but the rebel Almagro was in turn put to death, and order was restored by a new governor, Vaca de Castro. By a most cruel system of oppression, the Peruvians were driven in gangs to the mines, which they were compelled to work for the benefit of their conquerors; and it is said that four-fifths of the laborers died under these exactions.

20. In the mean while Magalhaens or Magellan had passed the southernmost point of the American continent, and in his attempted voyage around the world, crossed the Pacific and discovered that important group of islands which afterward received the name Philippine, in honor of Philip II. of Spain. He was killed in those eastern seas, and his squadron, completing the circumnavigation of the globe, arrived in Spain under another commander. The western coast of North America was explored by the Spaniards, Coronado and Cabrillo, A. D. 1540–42. Ferdinand de Soto undertook to colonize that fertile and attractive region which Ponce de Leon had discovered; but the Florida Indians proved themselves, what their descendants have since been found, the most difficult to subdue of all the natives of the coast. Failing in this enterprise, De Soto pushed on into the interior, and reached the Mississippi River not far from the present town of Memphis. Descending that river, he entered the Arkansas and explored its basin. He died in the wilderness, leaving neither settlement nor permanent conquest to preserve the memory of his toils.

21. The discovery of silver in Bolivia and Buenos Ayres quickened the Spanish enterprises in South America. The towns of Quito, Guayaquil, Santiago, and Buenos Ayres were all founded within five years; but two centuries of war in Chili failed to subdue the brave and freedom-loving Araucanians. Several captaincies were established in Brazil by the Portuguese; and in A. D. 1549, these were united under a Governor-General whose capital was Bahia.

A. D. 1535–1540.

22. The French were among the last to compete with other Europeans in the search for undiscovered lands; but the fisheries on the Banks of Newfoundland early attracted the bold seamen of Brittany, and there is even some evidence of their presence there before the discovery of the mainland by Cabot. King Francis I., envying the wealth and dominion of his hated rival Charles V. in the New World, and pursuing his favorite policy of patronizing Italian genius, gave a commission to Verrazzano, a Florentine navigator, to seek a westward passage to Cathay. Though this expected opening was not found, Verrazzano explored the Atlantic coast of America from Lat. 34° to 50°, and was the first European to visit the harbors of New York and Newport. The misfortunes of Francis I. interrupted these enterprises, but they were resumed in 1534, when Jacques Cartier, a Breton of St. Malo, made a slight examination of Newfoundland and the mouth of the St. Lawrence. The next year he returned with greater force, and ascended the river beyond the present sites of Quebec and Montreal — even then the centers of a large population. Five years later, he made another expedition to the New World, as lieutenant of the Sieur de Roberval, who followed with additional forces in 1542. This time a colony was planted in Nova Scotia, but its brief existence affords nothing worthy of mention. The fisheries and the trade in furs and marine ivory still engaged the enterprise of the French; but their colonization began only at the opening of the seventeenth century, with the daring advent-

A. D. 1524.

ures of Samuel de Champlain and the establishment of the feudal sovereignty of De Monts.

RECAPITULATION.

The western continent received one or more European colonies before its discovery by Columbus. Exploration of the Atlantic begun by the Catalans, greatly promoted by Prince Henry of Portugal. The Portuguese open a sea-route to India, and thus revolutionize European commerce. Goa the Golden becomes capital of their empire in the east. Columbus, believing the sphericity of the earth, crosses the Atlantic under patronage of Isabella of Spain ; discovers San Salvador, Hayti, and Cuba. Pope Alexander VI. divides the heathen world between Spain and Portugal. Haytians perish by hundreds of thousands under *ripartimiento* system of the Spaniards. Columbus discovers the continent in his third voyage, is shipwrecked in his fourth, and dies in poverty. North America discovered and explored by Cabot for Henry VII. of England; Brazil by Cabral for Emmanuel of Portugal. Cuba colonized by Diego Columbus. Florida discovered by Ponce de Leon — the Pacific by Balboa. Mexico conquered by Cortez, Peru by Pizarro. The globe first circumnavigated by the fleet of Magellan. Cabrillo and Coronado explore the western, De Soto the eastern side of the North American continent. Silver discovered and towns built by the Spaniards in South America. French fishermen on the Banks of Newfoundland. Verrazzano visits the harbors of New York and Newport. Colonies attempted by Cartier and Roberval.

RISE OF THE EUROPEAN STATES-SYSTEM.

23. From the new continent, the exploration of whose bays and rivers was engaging the most active spirits of an adventurous age, we turn to resume the thread of European history at the beginning of the modern era. The common interests of the several states had been greatly multiplied by the progress of civilization ; certain events were felt to affect all nations alike — especially the progress of the Turks and the growth in every country of opinions contrary to the doctrines of the established Church. The new art of printing increased the interchange of ideas ; and the establishment of colonies in Asia and America led to more intimate commercial dealings between the parent states. All these causes conspired to develop the European States-system — a confederacy of powers independent and widely various in their local constitutions — whose relations are determined and maintained not by authority but by diplomacy, or by the still incomplete, though constantly maturing, science of international law.

The preservation of the "balance of power," *i. e.*, of the independence of all the states, by preventing any from acquiring a preponderance which would threaten the general security, became a chief object, and demanded from every government a vigilant attention to the affairs of other nations. Thence arose many alliances and counter-alliances and much diplomatic activity. States of inferior rank, like Savoy, Lorraine, and the Swiss Republics, were protected by their more powerful neighbors, as convenient smaller weights in the balance.

24. Among the great nations of Europe, *Spain* was clearly predominant at the opening of the sixteenth century. Since the conquest of the Moors, all the peninsula except Portugal obeyed Ferdinand and Isabella, and the important Aragonese dependencies, Sardinia, and the kingdom of the Two Sicilies, were soon permanently reünited to the crown, while the extension of Spanish dominion in the New World promised unlimited increase of wealth and power. *France* had equal European advantages, though destitute of colonial possessions. Bretagne was recently annexed to the crown by marriage, and Burgundy, the last of the great fiefs which had threatened the sovereign power, was absorbed into the kingdom upon the death of Charles the Bold. *England* was likewise consolidated and pacified by the blending of rival claims to the crown in the marriage of Henry VII. with Elizabeth of York, and by the extinction of some formidable families in the Wars of the Roses.

25. *The Empire*, no longer Roman except in name, was henceforth almost an hereditary appanage of the House of Austria. The theory of the universal supremacy of the Cæsar had vanished with the discovery of a hemisphere unknown to Augustus or his successors. Maximilian I. was a great ruler, but it was as Archduke of Austria, Count of the Tyrol, Duke of Styria and Carinthia and Regent of the Netherlands, rather than as emperor. The multitude of petty German sovereigns had collectively far more power than their nominal head. Still the empire continued for two centuries to form an essential part of the system of European states—"important to all, but dangerous to none." The *Ottoman* power came to the height of its greatness under Solyman II., A. D. 1520–1566. His fleet nearly controlled the Mediterranean, and his Janizaries—then the most effective infantry in the world—were equally formidable on land.

26. Charles VIII. of France no sooner found himself in possession of sovereign power, than he prepared to prosecute the claim to Naples derived by his father from Charles of Maine. Though full of grand schemes of conquest, the young king was diminutive and deformed in person and weak in mind. His army, which had cost ruinous sacrifices to equip, waited for him at the foot of the Alps until he had spent in tournaments and festivities the entire sum provided for the war; and he could only proceed by borrowing 50,000 crowns from a Milanese merchant. Having entered Italy he borrowed and pawned the jewels of the Duchess of Savoy and the Marchioness of Montferrat, in order to prosecute his enterprise. His chief ally was Ludovico Sforza, uncle of the reigning duke of Milan, and one of the most unscrupulous plotters of the age. He had invited the French into Italy in the hope of being protected by them in the usurpation of the duchy; and his nephew died about this time under strong suspicion of having been poisoned by Ludovico.

27. The Florentines were ancient allies of the French, but their present ruler, Piero de Medici, was bound by a treaty to Alfonso II. of Naples. A sedition arose against Piero, who, driven by his fears to an opposite extreme of policy, voluntarily offered to put Charles VIII. in possession of all the Tuscan fortresses, and to furnish him with a loan of 200,000 florins. Enraged by this degrading submission, the Florentines expelled the Medici from their city, confiscated their goods, and offered a price for their heads. The Dominican reformer, Savonarola, who had foretold the coming of the French as ministers of divine vengeance upon the corruptions of Italy — especially the notorious wickedness of the Pope and his family, the Borgias — now came to the head of affairs. Appearing before Charles VIII. at Lucca, he prophesied for him earthly victory and heavenly glory, on condition of his protecting the liberties of Florence. The king took up his residence in the Tuscan capital, but upon his proposing to tax the city and recall the Medici, the people rose as one man in defense of their rights, and he was compelled to retire.

28. Charles entered Rome with an army of 50,000 men and a train of artillery. The personal wickedness of Alexander VI. was deepened in the view of his contemporaries by his close but unnatural alliance with the Turkish sultan, Bajazet. Zizim, a younger brother and hated rival of Bajazet, had taken refuge with the Knights of St. John at Rhodes. For greater security he was sent to France, A. D. 1483, and remained several years in various fortresses belonging to the order; while Bajazet, well satisfied to have him out of the way, paid a liberal yearly allowance for his maintenance. Later, the unfortunate prisoner was committed to the keeping of the Pope, and Alexander now made use of so valuable a prize in his negotiations with Bajazet. Charles VIII. was well known to aim at the conquest of the Turks and a restoration of the Eastern Empire, the title to which he had purchased from Andrew Palæologus, nephew of the last reigning emperor. The Pope now sent word to the sultan that Charles was scheming to get possession of Zizim in furtherance of his plans against the Ottomans. Bajazet replied by offering 300,000 ducats for the murder of his brother, and as Zizim died within a few months, his death was commonly imputed to a slow poison administered by order of the Pope.

29. As soon as the French army entered the Neapolitan dominions, the people rose against their king, Alfonso II., a harsh and odious tyrant. Seized with remorse and terror, the king abdicated in favor of his son; but the virtues of Ferdinand II. were unable to retrieve the desperate fortunes of his family. His infantry threw down their arms at the approach of the French; one of his principal officers betrayed Capua to Charles, and the city of Naples rose in revolt. Ferdinand burned or sank most of his fleet, placed his available troops in the fortresses near Naples, and retired to Sicily with fifteen ships. The king of France entered the capital the next day amid the acclamations of the people; the fortresses soon surrendered, and in a few weeks the entire kingdom had fallen into his hands almost without a blow.

30. This undeserved success turned the weak head of Charles. He treated the Neapolitans as a conquered people; and instead of rewarding their nobles and generals, whose influence had mainly secured his triumph, he confiscated their hereditary lands and offices to bestow them upon his own idle followers. The first extensive league known to European history was now formed against him by the arts of Ludovico Sforza, who had gained all he could hope from the presence in Italy of the French, and was alarmed by the nearness of the Duke of Orleans, the rightful heir of the Visconti. A treaty was signed at Venice in March, 1495, by representatives of the Pope, the Emperor, King Ferdinand of Spain, the Venetian Republic, and the Duke of Milan. A Spanish army was soon landed in Sicily and a Venetian fleet appeared on the Apulian coast.

Disappointed of a coronation by the Pope, Charles consoled himself by a magnificent entry into Naples, clothed in the robes of an eastern emperor, bearing a globe in one hand and a scepter in the other. The next week he left his southern capital unprovided with either money in its treasury or food or ammunition in its fortresses. As a contrast, however, to the poverty in which he had entered Italy, he was followed in

July, 1495.　　　his northward march by an immense baggage-train loaded with treasure. At Fornovo in Lombardy he was met by the army of the allies, which nearly four times outnumbered his own. All might have been lost for the French, but that their rich plunder diverted the attention of the enemy, whose disorderly ranks were easily put to flight. The king then made a new treaty with Sforza, who acknowledged himself the vassal of Charles for Genoa, and promised to take no part in any of the movements of the allies against France.

31. Meanwhile the French dominion in Naples was falling as rapidly as it had arisen. The king of Aragon sent an army to the aid of Ferdinand II., who landed at Reggio within a week of Charles' departure. His forces were defeated at Seminara; but the people of the capital, now weary of their new masters, rose in revolt and welcomed their natural sovereign with shouts of joy. All the southern coast declared for Ferdinand. The French king's cousin and viceroy, the Duke of Montpensier, made some efforts to continue the war, but, no aid arriving from France, he was forced to conclude a treaty, in which little more was granted to the French than permission to depart for home. While awaiting transports, a pestilence broke out, which destroyed the viceroy himself and great numbers of his men. The Constable d'Aubigny was defeated about the same time in Calabria, by Gonsalvo de Cordova, whose career of uninterrupted victories won him the title of the Great Captain. Ferdinand II., dying in 1496, was succeeded by his uncle Don Frederic, a prince of great talents and popular disposition, who soon destroyed the last traces of French domination.

32. The chief result of the wild expedition of Charles VIII. was a fatal thirst for distant conquests excited in the sovereigns and people who had been drawn into his wars; and unhappy Italy, weakened by her own dissensions, suffered many years from the display of her helplessness and wealth. To the refined and enervated Italians, the invasion by the French was like a new irruption of northern barbarians; for the carnage wrought by the well-served artillery of Charles, presented a murderous contrast to the Italian battles of the day,* in which "the worst that a soldier had to fear was the loss of his horse or the expense of his ransom." Another and more important effect of Charles' Italian expedition, may be traced in larger views of national policy among the governments of Europe.

Several marriages negotiated about this time by the Spanish sovereigns had a controlling influence upon subsequent history. The Princess Margaret, daughter of the Emperor Maximilian, and discarded bride of Charles VIII., was married to John, Prince of Asturias and eldest son of Ferdinand and Isabella; while her brother Philip, heir of the Netherlands, became the husband of their second daughter, Joanna. Their eldest daughter, Isabella, was espoused to the king of Portugal; and their youngest, Catherine, to the heir of the English crown. The early deaths of the Infant of Spain, the queen of Portugal and her only son, left the inheritance of the Spanish monarchies to the eldest son of Philip and Joanna, who fills a most important place in the history of the sixteenth century.

33. The crimes and vices of the Borgias gave terrible energy to the preaching of Savonarola, who loudly summoned the princes of Europe to convene a council and depose the Pope. Alexander responded by excommunicating the Florentine prophet and all the members of his government. The fanaticism of the *Piagnoni*, or Weepers, who followed Savonarola, had strengthened two other parties in Florence; and it was by availing himself of their dissensions that the Pope procured the death of his bold adversary. Savonarola, with two of his disciples, was burnt in

---

* The manufacture of defensive armor during the 14th and 15th centuries, so far excelled that of the weapons of destruction, that war became almost as safe as the peaceful contests of the chess-board. It was chiefly carried on in Italy by mercenary companies of adventurers, who were hired out by their captains to any prince or city that offered the greatest pay or plunder; and it was the obvious policy of the leaders to keep their forces undiminished, as the material of future bargains. Machiavelli mentions two decisive battles, in one of which no man was injured, and in the other, one was killed only by the accident of falling from his horse and being smothered in the mud.

the market-place at Florence, May 23, 1498. But the pontiff did not thus escape the natural result of his crimes. His eldest son, the Duke of Gandia, had already been murdered by Cæsar Borgia, his own brother, who bore in the Church the high rank of Cardinal of Valencia. For a few days even Alexander VI. was struck with remorse. He openly confessed his sins and promised reformation; but he soon plunged more deeply than ever into violent and degrading courses. He not only forgave the murderer, but by releasing him from his vows as a prelate, prepared to make him a great secular prince.

34. Charles VIII. was preparing for a fresh invasion of Italy, when a sudden death cut off his designs. He left no son, and the French crown A. D. 1498. passed to the younger branch of the Valois, now represented by Louis, Duke of Orleans. The training which Louis had experienced in the stern school of adversity proved a benefit to his realm. No king since Louis IX. had shown so active a sympathy for his poorer subjects; and the fear of the courtiers that he might avenge himself for the slights and persecutions which he had suffered during the minority of his cousin, were silenced by his noble remark that "it ill became a king of France to remember the quarrels of a duke of Orleans." If his foreign policy had been equally mild and moderate, the nation might have had still greater reason to rejoice. But the fatal bequests of Joanna of Naples and Valentina of Milan were destined still to be the curse of the French people.

35. With Louis XII. began the ascendency of the Cardinal-statesmen, who, with little intermission, governed France 150 years. George d'Amboise, Archbishop of Rouen, had long been a faithful friend, and was now the trusted minister of the king, whose designs upon Italy he warmly favored, in the hope of succeeding to the papacy at the next election. Cæsar Borgia, won to French interests by the gift of the duchy of Valentinois, promised to insure this result by creating as many new cardinals as might be needed. He brought also to the king a dispensation from his marriage with the daughter of Louis XI., and permission to espouse the Duchess Anne, widow of Charles VIII., thus reännexing Bretagne to the French monarchy.

36. The king's next object was the prosecution of his hereditary claim to the duchy of Milan. All things being ready, an army of 23,000 men was sent across the Alps under three experienced generals. Venice was the ally of Louis. The success of the expedition was as sudden as that of Charles VIII. against Naples. The Milanese were disaffected with their duke, who, fearing violence, departed to the Tyrol to ask aid in person of Maximilian. In his absence, the city of Milan set the example of declaring for the French, and all Lombardy was annexed, without a battle, to the dominions of Louis. The king crossed the Alps to enter his new capital in triumph, and the Lombards were charmed with fair promises of a mild, paternal government. Scarcely, however, had he returned to France, when the extortions of Trivulzio, his lieutenant, and the rudeness of his soldiery, exasperated the people and revived the party of the exiled duke. Sforza now approached with an army which he had raised in Switzerland, and the French retreated to Mortara.

In April, 1500, the two armies met near Novara; but the infantry on both sides was Swiss—in the one case obtained by treaty with the government, in the other enlisted man by man. The recruits of Sforza had received orders from their Diet not to fight their countrymen; and immediately after the opening of the battle, they retreated, accordingly, into the town. Here they began a secret agreement with the French, promising to desert the duke and go home, on condition of a safe-conduct, which was readily granted. One private soldier surpassed the perfidy of his comrades by betraying Ludovico himself while trying to pass out in their ranks, disguised as a monk. He was carried into France and spent the remainder of his life in a dungeon. In spite of the perfidious crimes which mark him for condemnation, Ludovico Sforza had been in many respects a wise and beneficent sovereign. The great Lombard plain owes, to this day, much of its productiveness to the canal by which he completed its system of irrigation. Leonardo da Vinci, the greatest artist of the time, chose Ludovico for his patron and friend, and, as painter, sculptor, and poet, contributed much to the splendor of his court.

37. A counter-revolution now made Louis XII. again master of the Milanese, and opened the way for his march upon Naples. The cousin and natural ally of King Frederic—Ferdinand of Spain—had secretly turned against him, and made a treaty with the king of France, to divide the Neapolitan dominions between them. Under pretense of a crusade against the Turks, which was duly proclaimed by Pope Alexander, Ferdinand had a fleet and army ready in the ports of Sicily before the arrival of the French. Several towns and fort- A. D. 1501. resses which had been committed to him by his cousin as a friend and ally, were retained for his own possession. When the disgraceful plot became known, Frederic abandoned his kingdom rather than subject his people to a useless war; and surrendering himself to Stuart d'Aubigny, was conveyed into France. The military fame of Gonsalvo de Cordova is covered with disgrace by his obedience to a faithless king. He gained possession, by a false oath, of the son of King Frederic and heir to the kingdom, who was sent as a prisoner into Spain. Thus ended the Neapolitan branch of the House of Aragon, which had reigned sixty-five years in the Two Sicilies.

38. The fraudulent conquerors of Naples naturally quarreled in the division of their spoils. The French gradually gained the whole country,

M. H. 10.

excepting Barletta and a few towns on the south-western coast. A new fraud put the Spaniards again in possession. The Archduke Philip, on his return from Spain to the Netherlands, was commissioned to make a treaty with the king of France at Lyons. It was there agreed that the two sovereigns should bestow their newly acquired kingdom upon two children, Charles of Austria and Claude of France, who were to be married when they became of age. In the meantime Philip was to be regent for his infant son, and to govern at Naples, jointly with a commissioner from the king of France. Louis, relying on this treaty, ordered his generals in Italy to suspend hostilities; but Ferdinand, who had resolved not to be bound by it, sent secret commands to his Great Captain, who by a sudden and rapid movement surprised the French in their inaction. The two decisive battles of Seminara and Cerignola secured the kingdom to the Spaniards. Most of the towns, including Naples itself, opened their gates to Gonsalvo, and within three months the last Frenchman had quitted the dominion.

RECAPITULATION.

Opening of the modern era marked by great increase of diplomatic relations between the several states of Europe. Predominance of Spain; consolidation and increased power of England and France. The Empire still important in theory though reduced in effective force, and possessed almost exclusively by the Austrian princes. Culmination of Turkish power under Solyman. Invasion of Italy by Charles VIII. of France; occupation of Florence and Rome; conquest of Naples. League formed against the French; Naples recovered by the House of Aragon. Important alliances of the Spanish royal family. Martyrdom of Savonarola; crimes of the Borgias. Accession of Louis XII. in France; his conquest of the Milanese; end of the career of Ludovico Sforza. In alliance with Ferdinand of Aragon, the French again conquer Naples, but are outwitted by him, and finally expelled from the kingdom.

PROGRESS OF EUROPEAN STATES-SYSTEM.

39. The Borgias had availed themselves of the presence of the French to conquer, by force or fraud, many small sovereignties in central Italy, from which they intended to organize a new and powerful "kingdom of Romagna." But Alexander VI. was doomed to perish by his own wicked devices. Of the forty-three cardinals whom he appointed, the greater number bought their dignity with enormous sums of gold; but after they had become enriched by employments in the Church, very many were poisoned, that the papal coffers might again be filled by the confiscation of their estates and the sale of their high offices. Such a fate was designed for the Cardinal of Corneto, who was invited with Cæsar Borgia to the Belvedere, a favorite retreat of the Pope near the Vatican. A servant had been instructed to serve the guest with poisoned wine; by mistake the bottles were interchanged, and Alex-

A. D. 1503.

ander and his son, as well as their unsuspecting victim, partook of the fatal drugs. The vigorous constitutions of the younger men conquered the violent illness which ensued; but the Pope, now seventy-two years of age, died within a week.

40. The Cardinal d'Amboise now proved the worthlessness of that friendship which is bought with worldly favors. A French army, on its march to Naples, halted near Rome to influence the choice of a new pope; but perceiving that the election must nevertheless go against him, Amboise gave the votes of his party to the Cardinal of Siena. He was a good old man, but his elevation was owing chiefly to a mortal illness with which he was already prostrated, and which ended his life in less than a month. He had used the few days allotted to him in planning a general council for the purification of the Church. The second election was yet more destructive to the hopes of Amboise. Cardinal Julian della Rovera, an active and powerful man, received the votes of the conclave, and became Pope Julius II. His warlike reign was absorbed by two objects: the expulsion of foreigners from Italy, and the recovery of the alienated estates of the Church. The spiritual dangers which more and more threatened the papal supremacy failed to attract his attention. Cæsar Borgia was soon stripped of all his ill-gotten possessions, and immured in the same tower in Rome, where he had himself confined innumerable prisoners. When released, he availed himself of the safe-conduct of Gonsalvo de Cordova, and repaired to Naples, only to be betrayed by that general into the hands of his perfidious sovereign and consigned for three years to a Spanish prison. He escaped, and fell fighting in one of the civil wars of Navarre.*

41. Filled with resentment by the ill-faith of Ferdinand of Aragon and his Great Captain, Louis XII. had lost no time in fitting out three expeditions—one against Naples and two against Spain. The first was delayed, as we have seen, by the selfish schemes of Cardinal d'Amboise, until the lateness of the season rendered all its efforts futile. Heavy rains had converted the valley of the Garigliano into a noisome swamp; hundreds of the French died of malaria, while the army of Gonsalvo, better posted and more thoroughly fed and equipped, was able to take advantage of their misfortunes. The battle, or rather the rout, of the Garigliano,

---

* Macaulay has given in a few vigorous phrases the most favorable view of the character and career of Cæsar Borgia — " who emerged from the sloth and luxury of the Roman purple, the first prince and general of the age; who, trained in an unwarlike profession, formed a gallant army out of the dregs of an unwarlike people; who, after acquiring sovereignty by destroying his enemies, acquired popularity by destroying his tools; who had begun to employ for the most salutary ends the power which he had attained by the most atrocious means; who tolerated within the sphere of his iron despotism no plunderer or oppressor but himself; and who fell at last amid the mingled curses and regrets of a people, of whom his genius had been the wonder, and might have been the salvation."

Dec. 29, 1503, completed the conquest of Naples by the Spaniards. The two French expeditions against Spain were no more effective; and a peace between the two nations was negotiated by Frederic, the deposed and captive king of the Two Sicilies.

42. In A. D. 1504, died the good Queen Isabella, overwhelmed with grief for the loss of her family, and especially for the insanity of her daughter Joanna, the wife of Philip of Austria. King Ferdinand, in the absence of his daughter, became Regent of Castile, though he caused Philip and Joanna to be proclaimed as sovereigns. Encouraged by a party among the nobles opposed to Ferdinand, Philip wrote a discourteous letter requiring his father-in-law to withdraw into his own kingdom of Aragon. Ferdinand replied by inviting Philip to Spain; but he sought revenge by making a close alliance with Louis XII. of France, and marrying Germaine de Foix, a niece of that monarch. The French claims upon the kingdom of Naples were her dowry.

43. Early in A. D. 1506, Philip and Joanna set sail for Spain; but their Dutch and Flemish fleet was dispersed by a storm, and they themselves driven to take refuge in an English port. Henry VII. availed himself of their misfortune to extort from Philip a commercial treaty, which favored England at the expense of the Netherlands, and a promise of the close alliance of their families by two marriages, which, however, never took place. After several months' delay, the sovereigns were permitted to depart for Spain, where they received the allegiance of the Castilian cortes. Ferdinand resigned all authority in Castile, retaining only the West Indian revenues and the grand-masterships of the three military orders, which were secured to him by the will of Isabella, and set sail for Italy with his new queen. Before his arrival at Naples, he received tidings of the sudden death of Philip. Ferdinand was willing, however, to have his absence regretted by the ungrateful Spaniards, who, in fact, were thrown into great confusion and alarm by the unexpected event. He proceeded, therefore, to regulate at his leisure the affairs of his Neapolitan kingdom, and only returned to Spain in the summer of 1507.

44. The unfortunate Joanna, whose mental malady was aggravated by excessive grief, submitted herself wholly to her father's control, and during the remaining forty-seven years of her life, never consented to take any active part in public affairs. Her son, Charles, remained in the Netherlands, under the guardianship of his grandfather, the emperor. Margaret, daughter of Maximilian, now the second time a widow, was appointed regent of those countries. To her skill in diplomacy was due the treaty of Cambray, which united the Emperor, the Pope, the king of Spain, and the king of France against the Venetian Republic. It was negotiated by Margaret with the Cardinal d'Amboise, and was signed in the cathedral of Cambray, Dec. 10, 1508.

45. The wealth and power of Venice — lately confirmed by the capture of several Greek islands from the Turks — excited the fear and jealousy of her neighbors. Louis XII., as duke of Milan, wished to reclaim several Lombard towns which had been secured by treaty to the Venetians during his wars with Sforza. The Pope insisted upon the grants of Pepin and Charlemagne, securing Rimini, Faenza, and some other towns to the dominion of St. Peter. Ferdinand coveted Brindisi and other maritime cities which had been pledged to the Venetians by his cousin and predecessor, King Frederic, as security for their expenses in his cause. Padua, Vicenza, and Verona were claimed as belonging to the empire by ancient right; Roveredo, Treviso, and Friuli, to the House of Austria. The Duke of Savoy, as lineal descendant of Guy of Lusignan, claimed the Isle of Cyprus, which had been bequeathed to the Venetians by Catherine Cornaro, widow of its last reigning sovereign, and the king of Hungary desired to reännex the lands conquered by the Republic in Dalmatia and Slavonia.

46. Florence was drawn into the league by an act of the basest perfidy on the part of Ferdinand of Spain and Louis of France. Ever since the Italian expedition of Charles VIII., Pisa, previously the unwilling subject of Florence, had been bravely struggling for independence. Maximilian, as emperor, and therefore nominal sovereign of Italy, had been implored to undertake her cause, but his movements were so long delayed that "succor for Pisa" had become a proverb and by-word in Germany. The French and Spanish monarchs now agreed to place a garrison in Pisa, which would readily be received as friendly, but which should be instructed to open the gates at an appointed time to the Florentines. For this act of royal treachery, the king of France was to receive 100,000 ducats, and the king of Spain 50,000. The half-starved city was entered, June 8, 1509, by the soldiers of Florence, who, by a liberal distribution of food, showed greater generosity than their allies.

47. The League of Cambray is important as having been the first great coalition of leading European powers since the Crusades. It is said to have laid the foundation of public law, by raising the question whether ancient and hereditary right, the faith of treaties, or general considerations of the common good shall have precedence in controlling national affairs. The text of the treaty is deeply tinged with the hypocrisy of the time, for it declares the main object of the alliance to be a war against the Turks — as preliminary to which, it was necessary to put an end to the rapine, losses, and injuries caused by the insatiable cupidity and thirst for domination which characterized the Venetian Republic. Venice was, in fact, the strongest barrier of Europe against the Turks, and best able by her maritime power to oppose them in the seat of their dominion.

48. Pope Julius II. opened hostilities by a decree of excommunication against the Venetians, expressed in the bitterest terms of reproach. Louis XII. was the first in the field, and by a victory at Agnadello, gained all, and more than all that had been assigned to him in the treaty of Cambray; for he was able to send to Maximilian the keys of Verona, Vicenza, and Padua. The Venetians, reduced to desperation by the number and strength of their enemies, adopted the masterly plan of setting free all their Italian dependencies, throwing thus upon the subject cities the burden of their own defense, and narrowing the frontiers of the Republic to the islands at the head of the Adriatic which had been its earliest territories. They also surrendered to Ferdinand the Apulian towns which he demanded, and made dutiful professions of obedience to the emperor and the Pope. The barbarities committed by both French and Germans had, however, the effect of arousing the peasantry of all north-eastern Italy to take part with Venice. Padua was retaken and garrisoned by a Venetian force. It was presently besieged by Maximilian with an army of 40,000 men, but the defense was obstinate and at length successful; the emperor withdrew and disbanded his forces, and the Venetians again became masters of many cities.

49. The Pope had now gained all that he desired for the territories of the Church, and his mind reverted to the other great object of his ambition, the expulsion of the French from Italy. He re-

A. D. 1510.

lieved Venice from the interdict, and he made an alliance with the Swiss, who having quarreled with the king of France, agreed to furnish 6,000 or more of their best halberdiers to the service of the Church. The king of Aragon was propitiated by the feudal investiture of the kingdom of Naples, and the tribute formerly demanded from that realm was commuted into a yearly offering of a white horse, and an aid of three hundred lances in case of actual invasion of the States of the Church. The Duke of Ferrara had incurred the wrath of the Pope by yielding in every thing to the counsels of the king of France. The first signal of the change in the papal policy was the sudden dismissal from the Roman court of the embassadors of the king and the duke.

50. The allied French and German armies were still carrying on war in northern Italy with more brutality than success. Vicenza, which, after the imperial failure at Padua, had speedily returned into alliance with Venice, was now exposed to the vengeance of the Germans. All its people who could, removed their families and property to Padua; but the remainder, with the neighboring peasantry, took refuge in a vast cavern in the mountains not far from the city. The French soldiery filled the entrance of the cave with light wood, which they kindled into a flame, and thus smothered all who were within, to the number of six thousand. Porto Legnano and Monselice, two fortified places of immense strength, had just yielded to the allied armies, when the Pope's declara-

tion of war against the Duke of Ferrara, and a simultaneous attack of his Roman and Swiss forces upon Genoa and Milan, turned the scale against the imperialists. The Venetians, promptly availing themselves of the change, recovered Vicenza and many other places. The papal officers failed, however, to excite in Genoa a revolt against the French; and the Swiss who had descended upon the Lombard plain, finding themselves entrapped among the numerous rivers and harassed by the movements of their enemy, hastily retreated into their own country without approaching Milan.

51. Louis XII. was now deprived by death of the invaluable services of Amboise; but the French clergy, assembled at Lyons, peremptorily called upon the Pope to lay down weapons so unsuited to his spiritual dignity, and submit his complaints to a general council. A new treaty was signed at Blois between the emperor and the French king, which provided for the sending of French forces into the field. Only enraged by these movements, Julius II. pushed his warlike preparations with increased vigor. He was nearly taken captive by the French at Bologna, while confined to his bed by dangerous illness; but he managed to amuse their general by negotiations until a Venetian army, including a body of Turkish horsemen, came up. Untamed by his infirmities, the fiery old pontiff proceeded to besiege in person the fortresses of Concordia and Mirandola amid the snows of a most severe winter. Encased in armor, his white hairs covered by a helmet of steel, he appeared on horseback among his men, sharing all their hardships and perils, and encouraging them with the promise of rich plunder. When at length the place surrendered, he entered by a ladder at a breach effected by his guns, being too impatient to await the opening of the gates.

52. In a congress convened by Maximilian at Bologna, the Pope vainly tried to detach the emperor from the alliance of France; and peace was rendered impossible by the haughty bearing of the imperial secretary. The Pope, seized with panic, quitted Bologna, and his army, pursued by the French, lost its great standard, twenty-six cannon, and an immense quantity of baggage. The Bolognese received back the Bentivoglios, their former masters, and destroyed the bronze statue of Julius II., which was considered one of the greatest works of Michael Angelo.

53. A new alliance, called the Holy League, was formed against the French by the Pope, the king of Spain, and the Venetians. Oct., 1511. Henry VIII. of England and the Emperor were secret parties to the transaction; but they delayed the open avowal of their designs until the interests of each could be best secured. Henry was promised a reconquest of Guienne, and the title "Most Christian King," of which Louis XII. was to be deprived. The romantic mind of Maximilian was filled just now with an uncommonly visionary scheme.

The illness of the Pope had inspired the Emperor with the idea of taking holy orders and becoming himself a successor of St. Peter. While waiting thus to unite the two supreme dignities of the West, he assumed in advance the title of Pontifex Maximus, which the popes had inherited from the Cæsars.

54. By a singular contrast of characters and conduct, the spiritual head of Christendom combined the genius of a general with the ambition of a temporal sovereign; the king of France was holding ecclesiastical councils, and the Emperor began to sigh in his old age for the dignity of a pope and the life of a saint. Louis XII., the object of Julius' bitterest enmity, was the only prince who scrupled to fight against him, and voluntarily resigned advantages he had gained, rather than do injury to the reputed vicar of Christ; while Henry VIII., the future destroyer of papal supremacy in his own realm, was at present willingly bought with a few skillful flatteries by the head of the Church.

55. The French armies in Italy were commanded by Gaston de Foix, nephew of Louis XII. and brother-in-law of the king of Spain—a young nobleman of extraordinary genius, whose brief and brilliant career filled Europe with amazement, and gained for him the name of the "Thunderbolt of Italy." By a swift and resolute movement he threw his army into Bologna, then besieged by the allies. The forces of the League immediately decamped; and Gaston, leaving Bologna strongly guarded, marched with still greater rapidity into Lombardy, where he learned that two cities had expelled or imprisoned their French garrisons. He defeated the Venetians near Isola della Scala in a battle before day-break, with no light but that of the stars reflected from the snow. Brescia was taken by storm and given up to plunder and massacre. Bergamo escaped this terrible fate only by timely submission and the payment of a ransom.

56. Perceiving the strength of the combination against him, the king of France now ordered his kinsman to fight one decisive battle, which being gained, he was to march upon Rome, depose the Pope and dictate the terms of a peace. In pursuance of this plan, the viceroy moved toward Ravenna, the allied army retiring before him. The engagement which followed has been described as "one of those tremendous days into which human folly and wickedness compress the whole devastation of a famine or a plague." The French commander, who claimed the kingdom of Navarre, and regarded the king of Spain as his personal foe and rival, left his right arm bare, that he might bathe it in Spanish blood. The artillery of the Duke of Ferrara, from one end of the crescent-shaped line of the French, kept up a destructive cross-fire, which mowed down whole ranks of the Spanish and papal troops. In the cavalry-charge which followed, the French were victorious; but the serried ranks of the Swiss, bristling with the points of their long lances,

April 11, 1512.

like a Macedonian phalanx, had a more difficult conflict to sustain with
the short swords and Roman drill of the Spanish infantry. They were
only rescued from destruction by the French horsemen, led by the gallant
young viceroy himself, who dearly purchased a victory by the sacrifice
of his life. On hearing the fatal news, Louis XII. exclaimed, " Would
to God that I had lost all Italy, and that Gaston were safe!"

57. In the first panic of the allies, all Romagna surrendered to the
French. Rome trembled, and even the iron-hearted Pope was ready to
accept Louis' terms of peace. A few weeks changed the aspect of affairs.
The French soldiery were dispirited by the loss of their general ; the
German lancers were withdrawn, and the Duke of Ferrara negotiated
a separate peace with the Pope. The Council which met at Rome three
weeks after the battle of Ravenna opposed the terms offered by France.
The Pope, the Emperor, and the Swiss combined to place Maximilian
Sforza, son of Ludovico, upon the ducal throne of Milan. The French
general, La Palisse, retired before them, first to Pavia, and thence, after
a bloody battle, into his own country. Scarcely more than three towns
and three fortresses in Italy remained to Louis XII. at the end of
June, 1512.

58. The Holy League, however, when relieved from external pressure,
soon fell apart by its own dissensions. The Pope, bent upon enlarging
the States of the Church to their greatest former limits, seized the cities
of Parma and Piacenza from the new duke of Milan, and sent his nephew
to occupy the duchy of Ferrara, while he detained the now pardoned and
reconciled Alfonso as a prisoner at Rome. Maximilian sent his army to
prey upon the territories of his new allies, the Venetians; while the Swiss
reserved for themselves the three districts of the Valtelline, Locarno, and
Chiavenna, and levied forced contributions upon the subjects of Maximilian Sforza, whom they had deposed. The late allies agreed only upon
one point — the necessity of punishing Florence for her neutrality during
their wars ; and this was done by conferring power in the Republic upon
that party which could pay the highest price.

The Cardinal John de Medici had been a prisoner at the battle of Ravenna ; but he escaped in the confusion attending the retreat of the
French from Milan. He was now sent with a Spanish army to revolutionize Florence, and restore the dominion of his family. The suburban
village of Prato was taken and subjected to a brutal massacre and pillage.
The Florentine government, in consternation, deposed its chief magistrate,
and accepted all the terms of the allies, including a large payment in
money to the emperor and the Spaniards, and the restoration of the
Medici, though not as princes, but as citizens. Julian de Medici, youngest
son of Lorenzo the Magnificent, entered the city, followed shortly by
his brother, the Cardinal, who, in a packed assembly of the citizens,

obtained a complete reversal of the Republic and the establishment of a narrow oligarchy with Julian at its head.

59. The next year, upon the death of Pope Julius II., John de' Medici received the papal crown with the name of Leo X.

A. D. 1513.

Though he had been raised at the age of thirteen to the highest dignity but one which the Church could bestow, Leo had derived from his father and the brilliant freethinkers of the New Academy (see Book II., § 150) fully as much respect for pagan mythology as for the Christian faith. Though his spiritual qualifications for the pastorate of western Christendom were thus singularly deficient, his mind had been improved by travel and the conversation of the greatest and wisest men of his day; his taste in art was perfect; his court was distinguished at once by the highest elegance and the most profuse magnificence; and to all his accomplishments he added wonderfully winning and amiable manners. He differed from his stern and warlike predecessor no less in character than in principles of government. He dissolved the Holy League and made peace with France; and if he pursued Julius' favorite policy of expelling foreigners from Italy, it was only that he might unite the peninsula under the sway of his own house. Julian de' Medici, whose weak and pliant character ill fitted him for the control of a freedom-loving people, abdicated his government in favor of his nephew, Lorenzo II., and accepted from his brother the post of Captain-General of the Church. Unhappy Florence became the slave of a despotic master.

RECAPITULATION.

Poisoning of Alexander VI.; successive elections of Pius III. and Julius II. Fall of Cæsar Borgia. Defeat of the French in southern Italy. Death of Isabella of Spain and the Archduke Philip; regency of Ferdinand in Castile. League of Cambray against Venice an important landmark in European diplomacy. Success of the allies and humiliation of Venice. The Pope changes sides and forms a new league against the French. Gaston de Foix gains the battle of Ravenna; but the loss of his life ruins French interests in Italy. Restoration of the Medici in Florence; Cardinal de' Medici becomes Pope Leo X.

HENRY VIII. — FRANCIS I. — CHARLES V.

60. Meanwhile the English army which was to have been conveyed in Spanish vessels to the coast of Guienne had been landed by order of Ferdinand in his own dominions, where he strove to enlist the Marquis of Dorset, its commander, in his own schemes against Navarre. Though the English refused actual hostilities, their presence as allies of Spain so overawed the Navarrese, that the Duke of Alva was able to conquer the entire country. Navarre became part of the kingdom of Castile, while its native sovereigns, though still retaining their royal titles, were reduced to their little principality of Bearn, north of the Pyrenees.

61. In April, 1513, Margaret, regent of the Netherlands, concluded a new treaty at Mechlin, between the Emperor her father, Ferdinand of

Spain, Henry VIII. of England, and the Pope, by which the contracting parties bound themselves to invade France from four separate quarters, while still pursuing their combined hostilities in Italy against Louis. The French king hastened his preparations, and in the month of May, his generals, by a series of brilliant and fortunate actions, subdued all Lombardy except two towns. The Italians, now equally disgusted with the inefficiency of Sforza and the brutality of the Swiss, welcomed the French on every side. But the reaction was as sudden and rapid as the advance. Fresh arrivals of Swiss compelled the French to raise the siege of Novara, and within a few days they were defeated and driven beyond the Alps.

62. Henry VIII. arrived with his army at Calais, and was joined by the Emperor in the siege of Terouenne. The "Battle of the Spurs," in which the French cavalry were not so much defeated as put to flight, decided the fate of the city. It surrendered and was destroyed, to the great consternation of the Parisians. Not far from   A. D. 1513. the same time, James IV. of Scotland, the generous ally of Louis XII., who had vainly tried by an invasion of England to prevent the movements of Henry VIII. against France, perished in the disastrous battle of Flodden Field. The invasion of Burgundy by Swiss and German troops in the pay of the Emperor, was defeated by bribery. It was the most disgraceful period in the history of the Swiss republics, when their brave mountaineers, not content with once exchanging their blood for gold, sold themselves successively to the highest bidders.

63. The eventful year 1513 was destined to see still greater changes. Before its close, Louis was reconciled with the Pope and sought the friendship of the Emperor and the king of Spain, with a view to furthering his designs upon Milan. His consort, Anne of Brittany, dying in January, 1514, he allied himself with Maximilian by engaging to marry the Emperor's granddaughter, Eleanora of Austria, while his own daughter, Renée, was affianced to the Archduke Charles, heir of Spain and the Netherlands. But this projected union of families alarmed the Pope, by its threatened consolidation of Austria, France, Spain, and the Low Countries into one enormous state, which would inevitably have destroyed the newly cherished balance of power in Europe. With the aid of two English prelates, he substituted for it another marriage-treaty, by which Louis espoused Mary, sister of Henry VIII. This wedding took place at Abbeville, in October, 1514; but the consequent festivities were fatal to the already failing health of the king of France. He died on the first day of 1515. His eldest daughter, the Princess Claude, was already married to Francis, Duke of Angoulême, and representative of the younger branch of the House of Orleans — who, as Louis left no son, became at once the sovereign of the realm. The duchy of Bretagne remained henceforth a part of France.

64. The new king was twenty-one years of age, gay, brilliant, and equally fond of pleasure and of military glory. The cares of government fell into the hands of his mother, Louisa of Savoy, whom he made Duchess of Angoulême and Anjou. The queen-mother surrounded herself with ladies of the noblest families, and it was under her auspices that the French court first became noted for elegance and extravagant gayety. The penetrating wit of French women, vailing profound art with consummate grace, has ever since made its influence felt, for good or ill, in the affairs of France. The Chancellor Duprat and the Constable de Bourbon— elevated to their respective dignities by the favor of the queen-mother— played important parts in the history of the reign. Pedro Navarro, a noted military engineer, long in the service of Ferdinand of Spain, having been wronged by that sovereign, entered the armies of France; and from the recruits which he raised among the mountaineers of the Cevennes and Pyrenees, presented Francis with the invaluable aid of regiments formed upon the model of the Spanish infantry. The French king lost no time in assuming the title of Duke of Milan, and preparing to prosecute the claims of his house in northern Italy.

65. The history of the first half of the sixteenth century is largely occupied by three sovereigns, then all recently entered on the stage of active life. Henry VIII., the second of the Tudor kings of England, was the first who, in more than a hundred years, had ascended the throne of that country with an undisputed title. The three Lancastrian kings, Henry IV., V., and VI. (A. D. 1399–1461) had owed their crowns, first to a successful usurpation, then to the support of the Church and the popularity of the wars with France. The House of York (A. D. 1461–1485) had nearly been ruined by the reckless caprices of Edward IV. and the haughty assumptions of his brother, Richard III. Henry VII. (A. D. 1485–1509), who represented the Lancastrian line, had to resist two formidable rebellions, led by pretenders to the dignities and claims of the House of York; while his unbounded avarice exhausted at once the purses and the patience of his people. The ample treasures which he left, contributed largely, however, to the popularity of his son, who, while punishing the agents of his father's exactions, made no scruple of using the funds in furtherance of his own schemes. Inheriting from his mother the claims of the House of York, Henry began his reign with proofs of justice, intelligence, and liberality, which secured to him the unlimited affection of his people. His later history is clouded, as we shall see, with caprice, and stained with odious tyranny.

66. Charles, son of Philip of Austria and Joanna of Spain, replaced his aunt, Margaret, in the government of the Netherlands, during the same year that Francis I. received the crown of France. The next year the death of his grandfather, Ferdinand of Spain, gave him the government of that country; for his mother continued to her death in a state of mental incapacity, though her name, as rightful queen, was always associated with that of Charles. Three years later, upon the death of his paternal grandfather, Maximilian, Charles received the votes of the German electors, and added to all his other dignities the imperial crown. Nearly at the same time the victories of Cortez added the empire of the Montezumas to his dominions, and — what was of greater consequence to his European schemes — ships laden with Mexican gold and silver began to arrive in his ports. See pp. 136, 137.

67. Francis I., the third in this trio of youthful monarchs, was in many things the bitter rival of Charles, but especially in his aspirations to the imperial dignity. Beside this, Charles demanded the restitution of Burgundy, which had been confiscated from his grandmother, the Duchess Mary, by Louis XI.; he inherited the Suabian and Aragonese right to Naples, while Francis represented the House of Anjou; as emperor he became sovereign of the imperial fiefs in Italy, including the duchy of Milan, which Francis claimed as head of the House of Orleans. All these rival claims afforded so many pretexts for indulging the ambition and jealousy of the two princes.

68. They commenced their reigns, however, in close alliance, for Charles was at this moment on unfriendly terms with his two grandfathers, who were actively opposing Francis' operations in Italy. A Swiss army guarded the only western Alpine passes then deemed practicable — those of Mont Cenis and Mont Genèvre — or was stationed in the Italian plain to close the exits from the valleys. In this difficulty the French forces, consisting of 64,000 men, with 72 great and 300 smaller cannon, performed one of the most extraordinary transits recorded in history. Guided by chamois-hunters or Alpine shepherds, the two generals, Trivulzio and Lautrec, with the engineer, Navarro, pioneered a more southerly route over the Col d'Argentière. This path, scarcely passable by the sure foot and practiced eye of the mountaineer, was prepared by the skill and genius of Navarro for the transportation of heavy artillery. Bridges were thrown from one dizzy height to another; masses of rock were removed by charges of gunpowder; cannon were swung from peak to peak by means of ropes. Before the enemy were aware that the ascent had begun, the French army stood triumphant on the Lombard plain.

69. A small division of cavalry, crossing by another route never before trodden by horses, had meanwhile surprised Prosper Colonna, the Pope's general, at Villafranca, with 700 of his men. The main army proceeded by way of Turin, the Swiss retiring before them to Milan and Novara, while a detachment, turning southward, recovered Genoa and the whole region south of the Po by a bloodless victory. At Marignano, about ten miles from Milan, was fought a decisive battle, which transferred the

duchy from Sforza to Francis I. The Swiss, newly reinforced by 20,000 of
their countrymen, burst unexpectedly upon the French quarters, late in
the afternoon of September 14. The furious onset and no less fierce resistance rendered the issue doubtful; and only midnight and the going down
of the moon interrupted the combat for that night. The exhausted combatants threw themselves on the ground in a mingled throng of friends
and foes. The French king slept on a gun-carriage, and at day-break rallied his men with sound of trumpet. The victory was again doubtful,
until a small body of Venetians appearing upon the scene, the Swiss
drew off in perfect order. Francis received the order of knighthood on
the battle-field, from the hand of Chevalier Bayard — "the good knight
without fear and without reproach."

70. Sforza retired into France on a pension. With the aid of his
natural allies, the Florentines and Venetians, Francis might easily have
conquered the kingdom of Naples. But his false and shallow notions of
honor led him to consider manufacturers and merchants as unfit confederates for a great prince. He therefore made a close alliance with the
Medici, the oppressors of Florence; sacrificing most of the advantages of
his victory, and consenting, at the Pope's persuasion, to defer his attack
on Naples until the death of Ferdinand. At Geneva he made a treaty
of peace and alliance with the Swiss, by which he gained the important
right to levy troops in their country. Then disbanding most of his army,
and appointing the Constable de Bourbon his lieutenant in the Milanese,
he retired into France.

71. Before his departure, Leo X. was already conspiring with the
emperor and the kings of Spain and England, to invest Francisco
Sforza with the duchy of Milan; though his recognition of Francis in
that dignity had been almost the only article in the treaty of Bologna
which favored the French king. The league which had been promoted
by Ferdinand of Spain was, however, disconcerted by his sudden death in
January, 1516. The different estimates of this sovereign by his friends
and enemies are well expressed in his titles. "Spain called him the
Wise; Italy, the Pious; France and England, the Perfidious." When we
remember his ingratitude toward Columbus and Gonsalvo de Cordova, or
the base deception by which he deprived his cousin Frederic of the crown
of Naples, we can not but think the latter epithet the best-deserved. He
was, however, the most successful prince of his age, and even his avarice
and cunning laid the foundation for the brief ascendency of Spain, while
his narrow, persecuting policy introduced the elements of its sudden and
fatal decline.

72. In March, 1516, the emperor fulfilled his part in the treaty by
invading Lombardy with a large body of Swiss, German, and Spanish
troops. The French general, Lautrec, was forced to retire into Milan,

while the Constable de Bourbon burned the surrounding villages, to prevent their affording shelter to the enemy. Thirteen thousand Swiss in the army of the French refused to fight their countrymen, now approaching under the banners of Maximilian, and Bourbon was reluctantly compelled to dismiss them. But the emperor's good fortune deserted him when apparently within his grasp. As usual his coffers were empty and his soldiers unpaid: the Swiss colonel entering his bed-chamber one morning bluntly declared that he would lead his men over to the service of the French unless their pay was forthcoming. The emperor left his army and made a hasty journey to Trent under pretense of collecting money; but as he failed to return, his army fell to pieces, and its scattered companies consoled themselves for their arrears of pay by pillaging several unoffending towns. The threatening war-cloud dissolved itself in vapor, and Maximilian, conscious of the ridicule he had incurred, never again led an army to the field.

73. Upon the death of King Ferdinand, the Spanish prime-minister, Cardinal Ximenes, proclaimed the Archduke Charles at Madrid, then recently become the seat of government for the united kingdoms. The Navarrese made a fruitless attempt to restore the house of Albret; the Cardinal wreaked a terrible vengeance upon the country, destroying its towns, villages, and castles to the number of 2,000, reserving only Pampeluna and a few places on the upper Ebro, as military posts from which to hold the nation in awe. The exposed positions of Navarre and the Netherlands led Charles still to cultivate the friendship of the king of France. By the treaty of Noyon, he engaged to marry the infant daughter of Francis, who was to bring as her dowry all the French claims to the kingdom of Naples; and already by anticipation addressed that sovereign, who was scarcely older than himself, as "my good Father."

74. The Peace of Brussels between the emperor, the French king, and the Venetians (Dec., 1516) closed the wars which had sprung from the League of Cambray. The next autumn Charles visited his Spanish dominions for the first time since his accession, and the joy of the unexpected meeting dispelled for a moment the cloud which rested upon the mind of Queen Joanna. The Spaniards, however, were disgusted with the insolent rapacity of the Flemish courtiers who accompanied their king and absorbed his confidence. A continual stream of gold, drawn from their offices and pensions, flowed from Spain to the Netherlands. The aged minister, Ximenes, addressed from his sick-bed a letter to the king, begging a personal interview. The Flemings feared the ascendency of the great minister; by their persuasions Charles replied in terms which vailed under forms of courtesy the coolest and basest ingratitude; for they involved a dismissal from all his offices except that of bishop. This blow, from a prince whom he had served so faithfully and well, brought on a relapse of the fever, which had already subdued the iron frame of the Cardinal, and he died in his 81st year, only commending his university * at Alcala, with his last breath, to the favor of Charles.

75. To his zeal for learning and his great ability as a statesman, Ximenes added warlike talents, in which he was scarcely surpassed by Pope Julius II. In 1509 he undertook to chastise the Moors in Africa for their depredations on the Spanish coast. He personally took Oran by assault, and it was in pursuance of his plans that several important fortresses became permanent possessions of Spain. The darkest shade upon his character belongs more properly to the age in which he lived. During his eleven years' presidency of the Inquisition, he "permitted," says Llorente, 2,536 persons to be burned at the stake, while 51,167 suffered less aggravated punishments. The chancellorship vacated by his death was bestowed upon one Fleming, and his primacy upon another. The Castilian cities, early accustomed to a voice in national affairs, now joined to defend their rights, and addressed a petition to the king, in which they complained of the unlawful bestowal of high offices on foreigners, the increase of taxes, and the exportation of coin. Charles disregarded their complaints, but the "Junta" threatened at a later period to overthrow the monarchy.

76. The rapid progress of the Ottomans about this time demanded the attention of Europe. Selim, son of Bajazet II., by a successful revolt dethroned his father, whom he put to death, as well as two brothers and five nephews; and then subdued a great part of Persia and Mesopotamia, and the whole of Syria, Arabia, and Egypt. The death of King Ladislaus of Hungary and the long minority of his son, Louis II., left that country — already exhausted by a ruinous war of the peasantry — an easy prey to the victorious Turks. It was reprieved a few years by a revolt of the Janizaries, which absorbed the attention of Selim, and by his sudden death in 1520.

77. The result of the election, which followed the death of Maximilian in 1519, has already been stated. The seven electors, conscious of the enormous powers they were bestowing, required from Charles a solemn guarantee of all their privileges; and the Elector-Palatine, with the Archbishops of Mentz, Trèves, and Cologne, formed the "Electoral Union of the Rhine" for common defense. The new emperor, now in his twentieth

---

*The name of Ximenes is rendered illustrious by his Polyglot edition of the Bible — the grandest literary work of his age, and one of the chief glories of the University of Alcala. It was the work of nine scholars, deeply versed in the ancient languages, who were sustained by the patronage and guided by the counsel of Ximenes. The Old Testament contained the original Hebrew, with Chaldaic, Greek, and Latin versions; the New Testament, the Greek and Vulgate. The type was cast at Alcala under the eye of Ximenes, as none yet existed in the Oriental character. The most ancient Hebrew texts were found among the confiscated property of the exiled Jews.

year, showed little promise of the commanding character which afterward distinguished him. He was sluggish in mind and weak in body; but the motto, "*Non Dum,*" (Not Yet,) which he assumed at his first tournament, expressed, perhaps, some consciousness of unawakened power. His Spanish subjects were deeply offended by his acceptance of the imperial crown; and it was with difficulty that Charles obtained a grant of money from the Cortes, to enable him to make a suitable appearance in his new dignity.

78. On his way to Germany he visited the king of England in order to divert him from any alliance with France. Cardinal Wolsey was gained by gifts and promises; the king was already opposed to France by his desire to renew the conquests of Henry V. He proceeded, however, to that celebrated interview with Francis I., which is known as the Field of Cloth of Gold—so overladen with   June. 1520. costly display were the tents and trappings of the courtiers on either side; and in reading aloud his state-paper, prepared for the occasion, he is even said, by an affectation of courtesy, to have dropped his own customary title, "King of France." * The emperor waited at Gravelines for this visit to be over; and, subsequently, spent some days with Henry at Calais, in order to remove any favorable impression which the French king might have made.

Charles was crowned as emperor-elect at Aix-la-Chapelle, in October, 1520; and in the following January held his first Diet at Worms, where were transacted affairs of momentous importance, which must be related more in detail.

RECAPITULATION.

Ferdinand of Spain conquers Navarre; joins the emperor, Pope, and English king in hostility to France. Brilliant but transient conquests of the French generals in Italy in 1515. Battle of the Spurs lost by the French; Terouenne taken and demolished by Henry VIII. James IV. of Scotland slain at Flodden. Marriage of Louis XII. with an English princess; he dies and is succeeded by Francis of Angoulême. Henry VIII., as heir to the two lines of York and Lancaster, unites all parties in England. Charles, lord of the Netherlands, ultimately becomes king of Spain and emperor. The French armies, crossing the Alps by a new route, invade Italy and gain a great victory over the Swiss at Marignano; but their king relinquishes most of its advantages by his alliance with the Medici, including Pope Leo X. The Emperor Maximilian is prevented by his poverty from dislodging the French from Italy. Charles, succeeding his grandfather, Ferdinand, offends the Spaniards by indulging his Flemish courtiers, and the Castilian cities form a Junta in opposition. The prime-minister, Ximenes, punishes a revolt in Navarre with frightful severity; founds a university at Alcala, makes a famous edition of the Bible, conquers Oran for the Spanish crown. Under Sultan Selim, the Turkish power makes threatening advances. Charles, elected emperor, visits England and secures Cardinal Wolsey to his interests. The kings of France and England meet at the Field of Cloth of Gold. Four Electors form the Union of the Rhine for mutual protection against imperial usurpations.

* It was only within the present century that the English sovereign abandoned his old style, "King of England, *France*, and Ireland."

M. H. 11.

THE REFORMATION.

79. The reformation in religion, which led to the withdrawal of a large part of the Teutonic nations from the Roman Church, was among the most important events connected, either as cause or consequence, with the opening of the modern era. The luxury and venality of the papal court; its removal to Avignon, to the neglect of the Pope's especial diocese; the subsequent schism, during which the adherents of one pope were accustomed to ridicule and condemn the others; the notoriously evil lives of such pontiffs as Sextus IV. and Alexander VI., and the vices of their clergy; the wars of Julius II. and the quarrels of many of his predecessors with the emperors — these were but a few of the many causes which had broken up the old traditional reverence for the popes as vicars of Christ and fathers of the Church. There had, indeed, never been a time when the doctrines of the Church were not called in question in some part of Europe; but the invention of printing — now beginning to diffuse among the middle classes opinions and speculations which had hitherto existed only in cloisters or among the most learned — gave tremendous importance to the teachings of Luther.

80. This remarkable man was the son of a Saxon miner, and had been born at Eisleben, in 1483. Like other poor scholars, he earned his daily bread by singing from door to door; and thus cultivated that love and talent for music which enabled him afterward to move the heart of Germany by his sacred songs. His studies at the University of Erfurt disciplined and enriched his mind, while they inspired him with contempt for the frivolous technicalties which formed the greater part of the learning of the age. In 1507, deep religious impressions led him to abandon the profession of law, and become a monk of the order of St. Augustine. His experience in the monastery at Erfurt led him to suspect the insufficiency of the rites of the Church to give peace to the conscience; but a Latin Bible, which he found chained in the library, and then read for the first time, afforded more effectual comfort to his mind. His sus-

A. D. 1510.   picions were confirmed during a visit which he made to Rome on business connected with his order. The warlike pomp and ambition of the Pope, the avowed infidelity of the clergy, and their sacrilegious contempt for the mysteries of the faith, shocked his religious nature; in the midst of his ascent of the Holy Staircase, the words, "The just shall live by faith," flashed upon his mind and became the watch-word of the Reformation.

81. Before this time, in 1508, Luther had been appointed professor of Theology in the new university of Wittenberg, where his clear and vigorous style drew crowds of students to his lectures. Frederic the Wise, Elector of Saxony, was at once a devout member of the ancient

Church and a firm friend and protector of Luther, whom he prized as the chief ornament of his favorite university; and the esteem in which the Saxon prince was held throughout the empire secured a respectful hearing to the doctrines of the reformer. The sale of "indulgences" was just then attracting new attention in Germany. This traffic, from apparently innocent beginnings, had risen by successive degrees to be the principal source of income to the papal treasury. At first, remission of temporal penalties for sin was promised to all who took part in the Crusades — then to those who founded churches or monasteries, or paid a certain amount of money as a commutation for personal service. It was afterward to be obtained by the performance of pilgrimages, especially by visiting Rome during the years of Jubilee.

82. It was Alexander VI. who first assumed to remit the penalties of sin in a future life, in consideration of money paid or penances performed in this; but, in the sixteenth century, the affections as well as the hopes and fears of the faithful were enlisted by the promise of releasing the souls of their departed friends from the pains of purgatory. "At the moment when the money clinks in the chest, the soul flies upward." Germany, whether from the credulity or piety of its people, was the great market for the sale of indulgences; and the immense sums of money remitted on this account to Rome were there named "the sins of the Germans." So open was the management of this revenue, that the great Augsburg bankers, the Fuggers, farmed it like any other tax; and portions of it were sometimes granted by the Pope to temporal princes for limited times. Thus, Frederic the Wise had himself obtained the sale of indulgences in Saxony for the purpose of building a bridge over the Elbe; the king of Hungary, in 1508, received two-thirds of the proceeds in his kingdom for the prosecution of his wars against the Turks; and the emperor at one time permitted the sale only on condition of the payment of one-third into his treasury. The extravagance of the court of Leo X. demanded increased revenues, and the sale of indulgences was therefore pushed with greater energy than ever, during the years which followed Luther's return from Rome. Albert, Elector of Mentz and Primate of Germany — a young and dissolute churchman — had purchased his see at a ruinous price, and was aided by the Pope to pay for it, by a special dispensation of indulgences.

83. One John Tetzel, a Dominican monk, but a man of infamous character, was his agent, and traveling through the country offered not only remission of past sins, but indulgence for future transgressions at a regularly graded tariff of prices. Animated by his new and ardent belief in justification by faith alone, Luther preached with great energy against the traffic, and refused absolution to any of his hearers who should buy the wares of Tetzel. A more decisive act, which is celebrated as the

beginning of the Reformation, was the affixing to the door of the Castle

Oct. 31, 1517.

Church at Wittenberg, of ninety-five theses, in which Luther denounced the papal assumptions, and declared that every sincere penitent would receive the remission of his sins without the intervention of the Church.

84. Tetzel and others published replies, and news of the affair reached Rome; but the Pope, who cared little for doctrine, affected to regard the dispute as a mere monkish quarrel, and praised the genius of Luther in highly complimentary terms. Dr. John Eck, however, wrote a book to show the identity of Luther's heresy with that of Huss. Luther's reply showed so many weak points in the argument of Eck, that the latter, in revenge, spared no effort to excite the Pope to interfere. Luther was, in fact, summoned to Rome; but as the Elector of Saxony, his sovereign, forbade him to go, and demanded that he should be tried in Germany, Cardinal Cajetan was sent as papal nuncio to decide the case in the Diet of Augsburg. Appearing before this assembly, Luther declared his readiness to retract all his doctrines, provided that they were proved erroneous by comparison with Holy Scripture. The cardinal refused all discussion, and scornfully rejected the second offer of the Reformer to submit his theses to the four universities of Basle, Freiburg, Louvain, and Paris. Perceiving that a just judgment was out of the question, Luther drew up an appeal to the Pope, which he affixed to the cathedral of Augsburg, and, quitting that city, returned to his post at Wittenberg. Three-fourths of the German people were now on his side; and the most enlightened men of the age — poets, painters, and scholars — joined in doing honor to his piety and moral energy.

85. The war of opinions was interrupted a year or two by several political causes. Upon the death of Maximilian, the imperial crown was first offered to Frederic of Saxony, and though he refused it and recommended the young king of Spain, yet Charles, who owed him his crown, could not immediately offend the Elector by punishing a man who enjoyed his patronage and esteem. Charles, too, had quarrels of his own with Leo X., concerning the Inquisition in Spain, and purposely favored the Lutherans for the sake of annoying the Pope. These matters being

A. D. 1520.

settled, a papal bull was issued, requiring the reformer to burn his books and abstain thenceforth from preaching or writing. Luther, whose mind was now more free from superstition than when he began his work, publicly burned the bull before a gate of Wittenberg. The next month he and all his disciples were solemnly excommunicated from the Catholic Church, and the emperor summoned him to appear before the Diet then sitting at Worms.

86. His journey thither was a triumphal procession, for the people of many towns came a distance of miles to meet and escort him. Though

he was accompanied by an imperial herald and protected by a safe-conduct signed by Charles himself, his friends feared for his life; but Luther replied to their remonstrances: "Huss has been burned, but the truth has not been consumed with him; go I will, were there as many devils aiming at me as there are tiles upon the roofs." Entering Worms, he was escorted to his lodgings by a crowd of nobles and citizens. The next day he appeared before the Diet. As he entered the great hall, George Frundsberg, a noted military leader, tapped him on the arm, saying, "Little monk, little monk, thou art doing a more daring thing than I or any other general ever ventured on. But if thou art confident in thy cause, go on, in God's name, and be of good cheer, for He will not forsake thee."

87. In his examination before the Diet, Luther admitted that he had expressed himself concerning the Pope and the clergy with unbecoming violence, but he refused to retract any of his teachings unless they could be refuted from the Bible. Several princes desired to seize him, in spite of the safe-conduct; but the emperor replied to their petitions, "No, I will not blush like Sigismund at Constance!" He permitted Luther to depart, but warned him to expect henceforth the treatment due to a heretic. The Edict of Worms enacted that whoever sheltered the reformer, or printed, sold, bought, or read his books, should incur the penalty of outlawry. Soon after his departure from Worms, Luther was seized by a company of horsemen in masks, and shut up in a Thuringian castle. This, however, was not the act of his enemies, but had been ordered by the Elector Frederic as the only means of securing him from their violence. It was generally believed that he had been murdered; and the period of seclusion which followed was spent by Luther in the most important of all his works, the translation of the Scriptures into the German tongue.

88. During the same years with the German reformation, a kindred movement took place in Switzerland, under the influence of Ulrich Zwingli, a priest of Glarus. Born a few months later than Luther, Zwingli, like him, on coming to manhood, adopted the Scriptures as his only standard of faith; and when the sale of indulgences became infamously common in his country, he denounced it in no less energetic terms. As citizen of a republic, he took a more active part than Luther in national affairs; and strongly opposed the foreign enlistment of her soldiery, which had disgraced Switzerland for more than a half a century. Being transferred to Zurich, Zwingli obtained from the town-council of that place, an edict forbidding any thing to be A. D. 1520. preached, except what could be proved from the Word of God. Three years later, by the same authority, the veneration of images and relics was forbidden, and wine as well as bread was granted to the laity in the holy Communion. The reformation spread rapidly, especially in the western or French-speaking cantons of Switzerland, and its changes — owing, perhaps, to the freedom-loving character of the people — were more radical than in Germany. Luther desired to retain all the doctrines and practices of the Church which were not contrary to the Scriptures, while Zwingli desired to reject all that were not thereby expressly commanded or inculcated. This difference led to an unhappy controversy between the two great reformers, which, undoubtedly, checked the progress of reformation. In Switzerland the mingling of civil with religious questions occasioned a war between the Catholic and Protestant cantons, in which Zwingli ultimately lost his life. A. D. 1531.

89. Meanwhile the disappointment of Francis I., in the bestowal of the imperial crown, gave rise to that long series of wars between France and Austria, which was to continue, with only slight intermissions, nearly two hundred years — A. D. 1520–1715. Andrew de Foix, a relative of the deposed king of Navarre, invaded that kingdom, and, as its fortresses had been nearly all destroyed, (see § 73,) made a rapid and easy conquest of the whole territory. Encouraged by this success, he tried to form a junction with the Spanish insurgents, who had obtained control of the imbecile queen, Joanna, and sought, in her name, to expel the regent appointed by Charles. The demands addressed by the Castilian Junta to their king, show just views of the rights and interests of the common people. They required the sovereign to reside in Spain and to appoint no foreigner to any civil or ecclesiastical office — demanded an assembly of the *Cortes* once in three years, and guarded the independence of their members by a rule that no one of them should receive any place or pension from the king. Judges were to be supported by regular salaries, and forbidden to receive any part of the fines or forfeitures of persons whom they condemned; bishops to reside in their dioceses at least half the year; indulgences to be sold only with the consent of the *Cortes*, and the proceeds applied wholly to wars against infidels.

90. This bill of rights being rejected by Charles, the Junta proceeded to open war; but their army of 20,000 men was at length defeated and its leader executed. The attempted union with the French, above mentioned, had been prevented by the advance of the royal army; but when the French commander laid siege to a Castilian town, even the insurgents themselves turned against him, and compelled him to retire into

June, 1521.

Navarre, where, having been defeated and captured, he died a few days later of his wounds. Navarre was speedily recovered by the Spaniards. The petty wars carried on by the French king with Germany and the Netherlands had no more important results.

91. Leo. X., meanwhile, pursued a shifting policy, allying himself successively with either of the great princes who would aid or permit him

to seize the most valuable estates in Italy for the aggrandizement of his house. In this way the duchy of Urbino and the lordships of Modena, Reggio, Perugia, and Fermo had fallen into his possession. In 1521, he entered into a more important league with Francis I., to drive the Spaniards out of southern Italy, whence large additions were to be made to the States of the Church, and the rest bestowed in full sovereignty upon the second son of the French king. Some delay occurring in the ratification of this treaty, the Pope made a counter-alliance with the emperor, to expel the French from northern Italy. In return for being allowed to seize the Venetian territories, Charles promised to extirpate the heresy of Luther and his adherents; and this agreement was signed in the presence of the imperial Diet on the same day with the Edict of Worms.

92. Three months later, a conference was held at Calais between the representatives of the Pope, the emperor, and the kings of France and England. Henry VIII. had offered his services as mediator between Francis and Charles; and his great minister, Wolsey, was courted and flattered by both parties, who wished to gain him. The emperor's promises were the more magnificent; Wolsey was already his pensioner to the amount of 10,000 ducats yearly; and his vast influence was pledged to secure the papal crown to the English cardinal at the next vacancy. The claims of the rival sovereigns were, however, too many and too great to be reconciled. Francis demanded the two kingdoms of Naples and Navarre; Charles required the abandonment of Milan and Genoa by the French, the restitution of Burgundy, and the release of homage on his part for his possessions in the Low Countries. After all its grand pretensions, the Conference of Calais merely regulated some disputes concerning the herring fisheries of France and Flanders! The German and English sovereigns immediately after concluded a treaty, by which each engaged to invade France with 40,000 men; and the Pope, with his own weapons, took part in the enterprise by excommunicating Francis I., and releasing the French nation from its allegiance. In a subsequent treaty between Charles, Henry, and Leo, all agreed to proceed with rigor against heretics, and the English king, having lately published a book against Luther, was rewarded with the title, "Defender of the Faith," which is still borne by his successors.

93. The war which now broke out can not be related in detail. That part of the Navarrese kingdom which lies north of the Pyrenees was recovered by the Albrets, and never again lost. In the Netherlands, the French also gained the town and fortress of Hesdin, but lost Tournay. In Italy, which was to be the chief seat of war, Lautrec, an able general, but a cruel and rapacious tyrant, held the viceroyalty of Milan, and used it only as a means of enriching his family at the expense of the people. The dissensions of the Parisian court crippled the war-movements, and in

three months lost to France the Milanese duchy. Two hostile parties in the court were led, one by the king's mother, the other by the Countess of Chateaubriand, sister of the general, Lautrec. When a large sum of money was raised for the payment of the army, Mme. Louise of Savoy seized it for her own use; and the 20,000 Swiss commanded by Lautrec, discontented for want of pay, either marched home or went over to the imperial service. Lautrec was forced to shut himself up in Milan, but a night-attack being made by the Spanish infantry upon the Roman gate of that city, it was opened by the Ghibelline faction, who hated the French; and Lautrec with his brother sought safety in flight.

94. The fortress of Milan still held out; but the Lombard cities, with scarcely an exception, opened their gates to the imperial troops. Parma and Piacenza were likewise taken, and, in fulfillment of the treaty, were held for the Pope. The joy of these successes is said to have occasioned the death of Leo X.; other and more probable accounts ascribe it to poison. He died in the forty-sixth year of his age and the ninth of his pontificate. This event threw the affairs of the victorious allies into confusion. The papal army was disbanded for want of funds; Urbino, Perugia, and other places gladly received back their native rulers.

Dec., 1521.

95. After a long and violent contest in the conclave, Adrian, regent of Spain and former tutor of the emperor, was chosen to be pope. His narrow scholastic education made him a bitter opponent of Luther, though as an honest man he deplored the corruptions of the Church. He began his reign with stern efforts at reform; entered Rome bare-footed, in scornful rebuke of the luxury of his predecessors, and turned with horror from the rare sculptures which the taste of Leo had collected in the Vatican, exclaiming, "These are pagan idols!" One old servant provided as before for his humble household. The elegant courtiers of Leo looked on with disgust, which was increased when their new sovereign attempted to retrieve his ruined finances by abolishing many useless and expensive offices; but the common people regarded with reverent enthusiasm the self-denying humility of their pontiff.

A. D. 1522.

96. The French, having been once more defeated by the imperial army, withdrew from Italy, surrendering all but the three citadels of Milan, Novara, and Cremona. Genoa was taken by the Germans, and Antoniotto Adorno became doge.

The departure of the regent, Adrian, from Spain compelled the emperor to visit that discontented country. Visiting England on his way, he renewed his agreement with Wolsey by fresh promises, flattered the nation at large by making the Earl of Surrey his admiral, and induced the king to declare war against France.

97. Called thus to contend with the greatest powers of Europe, Francis I. secured his eastern frontier by a treaty with the Regent Margaret, by which he promised to make no wars in or against her territory of Franche Comté for three years. This treaty, often renewed, left the two Burgundies in the enjoyment of peace, industry, and prosperity for more than a century, while the Austro-French wars were raging around them. The three duchies of Savoy, Lorraine, and Bar were also neutral territories, which, with the county of Burgundy, completely covered the eastern side of France.

98. Fixing his residence in Spain, Charles won the hearts of his subjects by his lenity to those who had rebelled during his absence, by adopting the dress, language, and manners of the country, and by excluding all foreigners from employment in Church or State. At the same time he increased his own power at the expense of the popular liberties, by making the three estates of the *Cortes* meet in separate places, thus preventing a concentration of their strength; by gaining over individual representatives of the commons to his own interests; and by permitting no debate except in the presence of a presiding officer of his own appointment. His policy toward the Moors was as unjust as that of his grandfather toward the Jews. That refined and industrious people contributed not a little to the prosperity of Spain, while living in the exercise of their own religion, but in obedience to the laws of the land. Suddenly, in 1525, it was resolved to compel them to a change of faith. Their copies of the Koran were seized, their mosques shut up; all who were not baptized before a certain date were exiled from Spain; but to prevent their reaching Africa, all the ports, except Corunna in the extreme northwest, were closed to them. A subsequent and still harsher edict sentenced all who refused a change of religion to forfeit their goods and be sold into slavery. This atrocious treatment drove many into open revolt. Thousands were slain; 100,000, more fortunate than the rest, escaped to Africa; those who remained, conformed unwillingly to the rites, customs, and language of their conquerors; but they were deprived of all privileges and reduced to the condition of beasts of burden.

RECAPITULATION.

Dissensions and decay in the Church and diffusion of intelligence among the people lead to religious reformation. Luther, an Augustinian monk and professor of theology at Wittenberg, preaches against indulgences. His 95 theses rouse all Germany to controversy. He is tried before the Diet of Augsburg, is condemned by a bull of Leo X.—which he burns—and is denounced again by the Diet of Worms. Concealed for a time in Thuringia, he begins to translate the Scriptures into German. Zwingli moves reform in Switzerland; differing in some points from Luther, he is bitterly opposed by him. Series of Austro-Frankish wars begun by French invasion of Navarre. Bill of Rights presented by the Castilian Junta to Charles is rejected, and a rebellion ensues. Pope Leo X. plots alternately to drive the Spaniards from southern and the French from northern Italy; makes a compact with the Emperor at Worms to crush the Reformation. Conference at Calais fails to arrest the war, and is followed by a fresh league against France. Intrigues of the French court occasion defeat of Lautrec and loss of the Milanese. Imperial and papal arms triumphant in Italy. Leo dies and is succeeded by Adrian VI. Peace of Burgundy and the neutral duchies secured by treaty. Charles conciliates the Spaniards while stealing away their liberty; but cruelly persecutes the Moors.

WARS IN ITALY.

99. Europe was now threatened anew by the Turks. Solyman II, who succeeded Selim in 1520, concentrated his great military talents upon the conquest of Hungary and Rhodes. The small army raised in the south of Hungary could offer no effective resistance, and, in the summer of 1521, Sabatz, Semlin, and finally Belgrade, fell into the power of Solyman. The Isle of Rhodes was the stronghold of the Knights of St. John of Jerusalem. Its capture was undertaken by a force of 300 Turkish ships and 110,000 men. The knights, under their illustrious Grand Master, L'Ile Adam, fought long and valiantly, but at last they were compelled to surrender to overwhelming numbers. After several removals, the surviving members of the order were presented by the emperor with the island of Malta.

Dec. 21, 1522.

100. Unable to combine the Christian princes of Europe against the Turks, Pope Adrian formed a powerful league against the king of France, whose indifference was supposed to have thwarted the former attempt. The prompt invasion of Italy, with which Francis intended to meet and disconcert this alliance, was delayed by the sudden and fatal defection of his kinsman and most powerful subject, the Constable de Bourbon. This great vassal possessed by inheritance or marriage two duchies, four counties, and two viscounties, beside many smaller lordships in the center of France, and might even hope to inherit the crown itself in case of the king's dying without sons. His great military services had been rewarded with the highest dignities and revenues; but his cold and haughty temper ill suited the jovial disposition of the king, and the court favorites delighted to annoy so powerful a rival. Especially the queen-mother, whose vanity had been incurably wounded by the Constable, pursued him with unrelenting enmity. Representing an elder, though female, line of the House of Bourbon, she sued him before the Parliament of Paris for all the possessions of that duchy, and secured to herself the private revenues of Anne of France, his mother-in-law.

101. Under this load of insults and injuries, the proud heart of Bourbon resolved upon a bitter revenge. He opened negotiations with the emperor and the king of England, to betray into their hands the French kingdom, which was then to be divided among the three princes; the hereditary dominions of the Bourbons, with Provence and the territories of Lyons and Dauphiné, being erected into an independent sov-

ereignty for the Constable himself. The conspiracy seemed on the point of success. English forces landed at Calais, and, being joined by an imperial army from the Netherlands, advanced within thirty-three miles of Paris. But the invasions from the frontiers of Germany and Spain proved failures, and the discovery of the plot by the French king prevented the vassals and retainers of Bourbon from executing their part of the agreement. Bourbon himself, instead of appearing on the field of war as a sovereign prince, master of a great army and of many provinces, had to flee into Germany attended by only sixty gentlemen, and to present himself to the emperor like a destitute soldier of fortune.

102. At this crisis Pope Adrian died and was succeeded by the Cardinal Giulio de'Medici, who took the name of Clement VII. Wolsey, again disappointed, had to content himself with the rank of papal legate in England, to which were attached extraordinary powers. In the spring of 1524 Bourbon entered Italy as lieutenant-general of the emperor. The incompetent Bonnivet, then commanding the French forces, was forced by the allies to retreat into France. In a battle near Romagnano, the Chevalier Bayard was killed. An imperial army under Bourbon and the Marquis Pescara now invaded France by the Cornice Road, received the surrender of Aix and several other towns, and laid siege to Marseilles. Bourbon was disappointed, however, in his hope of French recruits, and thwarted not less by the jealousies of the imperial generals whom he outranked, than by the suspicions of the English king, who, moved by Wolsey's revenge, and, fearing that the emperor would gain more than his share of the spoils, delayed or refused the promised supplies of money. At length the allies were compelled to raise the siege and make a hasty retreat into Italy.

103. The French king speedily followed with a well appointed army of 30,000 men, and besieged Pavia. The Pope, under cover of neutrality, made a secret treaty with Francis, who, elated by this turn of affairs and the evident disorganization of his enemies, actually sent the Duke of Albany with an army to undertake the conquest of Naples. His rashness proved his ruin. The imperial army, now reinforced, moved from Lodi and encamped within a mile of the French lines before Pavia. A night-attack was planned in concert with the garrison, but day dawned before the preliminary movements were completed, and the French then coming up, the battle became general. The French artillery produced great havoc in the ranks of the enemy, until Francis, inconsiderately charging in advance of his guns, compelled his men to cease firing lest they should endanger him. The German reserves were now brought forward, while the garrison of Pavia prepared to attack in the rear. The French yielded and fled. The king himself, while endeavoring to rally his Swiss, was unhorsed and taken prisoner. He was recognized

Feb. 1525.

by an attendant of Bourbon, who besought him to surrender to the Constable; but the king scornfully refused to become the captive of his rebellious vassal, and calling for Lannoy, gave his sword into his hands. The French army was permitted to retreat, and, within a fortnight, the last soldier had crossed the Alps.

104. When the news reached Madrid, the emperor forbade all public rejoicings, and studied to dissemble the exultation which he might naturally be supposed to feel. France was filled with terror; Paris was guarded as if the enemy were already at the gates. The queen-mother, into whose hands the defense of the kingdom was thrown at this perilous crisis, had alienated by her intrigues those who should have been her best supporters. Of three chief princes of the royal blood, one was a declared traitor; another, the king's brother-in-law, had disgraced himself by cowardice at Pavia, and had since died of vexation and chagrin; and the third, the Duke of Vendôme, was an enemy to the queen-mother, and suspected of a secret understanding with Bourbon. He silenced this suspicion, however, by generously forgetting his grievances and joining Louisa at Lyons. The Count of Guise, founder of a family destined to play a still more important part in the history of France, rendered good service by suppressing a peasant-war which had spread from Germany into Lorraine, Champagne, and Burgundy. The Parliament of Paris, which had convened immediately upon the news of the king's captivity, presented a long list of wrongs, and insisted upon redress before granting supplies or taking measures for the public defense. Among the least offensive of their demands to the regent was that for the extermination of the Lutheran heretics, who were held responsible for all the misfortunes that had come upon France. Two of these pious and unoffending people were shortly burned at Paris.

105. Four months after the battle of Pavia, the royal prisoner was conveyed into Spain, where he was subjected to a severe and rigorous confinement. Vexation of mind threw him into a dangerous illness; and Charles, who had not hitherto deigned to visit his former "good father," "friend," and "brother," now feared that his prisoner would escape him without subscribing the hard terms which he desired to impose. He went to see Francis in his prison, and a few kind words so raised the spirits of the captive, that his health began to improve. His favorite sister, the recently widowed Duchess of Alençon, undertook an embassy to Spain, with full powers to negotiate a peace between the two monarchs, but she failed to obtain easier terms for France. Charles insisted upon a partition of that kingdom, by which he himself was to receive Burgundy, Picardy, and whatever else had belonged to Charles the Bold at his death; all the Bourbon possessions, with Provence, were to be conferred with a royal title upon the Constable, and Normandy, Guienne, and Gascony were to revert to the king of England. The dominion of Francis would thus have scarcely exceeded that of the first of the Capets.

106. Subsequently, the demands of Bourbon were reduced to a free pardon and restitution to his hereditary possessions. The towns of Picardy, so long in dispute between Louis XI. and Charles the Bold, were also abandoned by the emperor; and the Treaty of Madrid, thus modified, was sworn by Francis "on the word and honor of a king." He had previously stated in the presence of his embassadors, that he had acted under compulsion, and did not intend to execute the conditions which he was about to sign. The treaty was confirmed, however, by his betrothal with the emperor's sister, Eleanora, the widowed queen of Portugal, and the two sons of Francis were given as hostages for its fulfillment.

107. Once free and upon his own soil, he refused to ratify his engagements with the Spanish ministers at Bayonne, on the plea that he must first consult the Estates of France and Burgundy; and when these were assembled, they insisted, as had probably been prearranged, that the king could not annul his coronation-oath by any subsequent agreement. The Burgundian envoys also declared that they would resist by force of arms any attempt to sever them from France. The king then offered the imperial embassadors, who were present, two millions of crowns as a compensation for Burgundy, and promised in all other respects to fulfill the treaty. The emperor, when informed of this evasion, remarked that it was easy for the king of France to redeem at least his personal honor by returning into Spain; but the honor of Francis was of a different tone from that of Regulus, or even of his ancestor, King John.

108. Meanwhile, the Italians had been thrown into consternation by the too decisive victory of their ally at Pavia; for the whole peninsula seemed at the mercy of the emperor. Another Holy Alliance was formed against him by the Pope, the Venetians, the Duke of Milan, and the king of France. Francesco Sforza had been restored to his duchy only as a vassal, and his chancellor, Morone, now devised a plot for destroying at a blow the union and freedom of Italy. Pescara, Italian by birth, though Spaniard by descent, was known to be disaffected toward the emperor. He was informed by a trusty messenger that all the states of Italy were ready to unite in placing the crown of Naples upon his head; provided, that he would disband the imperial army, of which he had sole command, and thus aid in delivering the peninsula from the German yoke. Finding that this conspiracy was already known in Madrid, Pescara resolved to meet the advances of the Milanese with a counter-plot. He invited Morone to a personal interview, and took care to have Antonio de Leyva, the Spanish general, concealed behind the tapestry. When the unsuspecting chancellor had fully disclosed the plans of his master, he was seized, and found himself the victim rather than the partner of Pescara.

109. Francesco Sforza was deprived of all his dominions, which were then bestowed by the Emperor upon the Duke of Bourbon. Pescara died a few weeks later. Morone remained a prisoner in Milan, until Bourbon, wanting money, first sentenced him to death, and then sold him life and liberty for 20,000 ducats. The Milanese people, who had suffered new miseries at every change of masters, hailed the arrival of Bourbon in the hope of a firm and settled government. He promised to remove his army, which had been quartered upon the citizens, upon the payment of 300,000 crowns. But when that sum was raised, the soldiers still refused to move, and some of the Milanese, despairing of relief, put an end to their own lives.

110. The Pope was soon subjected to still greater misfortunes. Cardinal Colonna, a man of revengeful and lawless temper, an old enemy of Clement VII., with whom, however, he had been formally reconciled,

Sept., 1526.

suddenly raised an army of his own vassals and retainers, and marched upon Rome. The Pope shut himself up in the Castle of St. Angelo, but for want of provisions was compelled to surrender in three days. The freebooters who followed Colonna plundered the Vatican palace and the church of St. Peter. The kings of France and England hastened to send money and troops; and Clement was soon able to exact a terrible vengeance from the Colonnas. Their palaces in Rome were leveled with the ground, and their estates in the country were ravaged by the papal forces.

111. But a fresh calamity now threatened the Eternal City. Frundsberg, the famous Lutheran captain, marched from Germany at the head of 11,000 brigands, who had enlisted less in the hope of pay than of plunder. The papal capital was at once the richest and the weakest object that could tempt them, and, joined by the unpaid and hungry troops of Bourbon at Milan, they marched upon Rome. On the way they were met by a papal embassy proposing a truce; the soldiery, fierce for their promised prize, rose in open mutiny, and even leveled their spears at the breast of their own general, who was trying to pacify them. Stung by their ingratitude, Frundsberg fell into convulsions from which he never recovered; and the soldiers, too late struck with remorse, subsided into order, only reiter-

A. D. 1527.

ating their cry, "Rome! Rome!" On the evening of May 5, they arrived before the walls, and the next morning orders were given for the assault. Bourbon was placing a ladder with his own hands, when he received a ball in his side. Feeling that he must die, he covered his face with his cloak that he might not be recognized, and breathed his last, while his victorious followers were making their entrance into the city. The Prince of Orange was chosen by the troops to be their commander-in-chief.

112. Rome was seized with a panic. The Pope, with a crowd of cardinals, nobles, and citizens, took refuge in the castle of St. Angelo. The city was abandoned to the Spanish and German soldiery, and was filled for two weeks with horrid scenes of massacre, pillage, and desecration. The treasures, which for centuries had been flowing from all Christendom toward Rome, were now the prize of a starved and greedy multitude, whom neither fear nor conscience could restrain.

113. The Florentines availed themselves of the presence of the imperial army to expel the Medici, and, placing themselves under the protection of France, sought to restore the Republic which Savonarola had set up. Venice recovered Ravenna and Cervia, and the Dukes of Urbino and Ferrara revenged themselves for former disasters, by seizing several cities in the States of the Church. It was expected and desired by many that the Emperor would fix his residence in Rome, and thus restore to the Western Empire its ancient capital.

114. Charles affected the utmost humility and moderation. He attired himself and his court in mourning for the misfortunes of the Pope, and ordered prayers in all the churches for his deliverance. This was effected by treaty, six months after the capture of Rome. The pontiff paid a ransom of several hundreds of thousands of gold crowns, promised to assemble a general Council for the reformation of the Church and the suppression of heresy, and engaged never more to meddle in the affairs of Naples or the Milanese.

115. A French army under Lautrec was already in Italy; and a French fleet commanded by the great admiral, Andrew Doria, besieged Genoa, expelled the Ghibelline doge, Adorni, and set up a governor in the name of the king of France. Lautrec took Pavia by storm and gave it up to plunder, in revenge for its resistance to Francis and his consequent misfortunes in 1524. The Pope being now liberated, Lautrec proceeded to the siege of Naples, in which he was aided by a Genoese and Venetian fleet. The city must have been taken, had not the French king, intent only upon his own pleasures, withheld the needed supplies from his army, and at the same time offended the Dorias by most injurious treatment. Andrew Doria transferred his services to the Emperor, and, sailing to Naples, forced the French commander to raise the siege. Lautrec was already dead from a pestilence which had carried off the greater part of his army. This fourth invasion of Italy by the armies of Francis I. was a failure. The Prince of Orange was established as viceroy of Naples for the Spanish sovereign. The French were expelled from Genoa, and the republic reorganized under imperial protection. The old feud of Guelfs and Ghibellines was ended by a more just and efficient constitution; public affairs were intrusted to a Council of Four Hundred; and Genoa suffered no more revolutions until its conquest by the French in 1797.

116. The war between Charles and Francis, after dragging another year, was terminated by the treaty of Cambray, commonly called the "Ladies' Peace," as it was negotiated by the Emperor's aunt and the King's mother. Francis kept Burgundy, but surrendered all his claims in Italy, together with the feudal sovereignty of Flanders and Artois. The House of Bourbon was reinstated in its dignities and possessions. The sons of Francis were redeemed from their captivity, and were accompanied from Spain by the Emperor's sister, who soon became queen of France. The wars of the French in Italy had continued 36 years, from the invasion by Charles VIII.

RECAPITULATION.

Hungary invaded and Rhodes conquered by the Turks. Knights of St. John settled finally at Malta. League against Francis I. joined by the Constable de Bourbon, who plots the partition of France. Clement VII. (Cardinal Medici) becomes pope. Bourbon and Pescara drive Bonnivet from Italy and invade France. Francis I. in turn enters Italy and besieges Pavia; is taken prisoner and conveyed into Spain; being released, he evades the fulfillment of the treaty which he signed at Madrid, and joins a new league of the Pope and other powers against the Emperor. Plot of Morone for deliverance of Italy being discovered, leads to the fall of the Sforzas. Bourbon becomes duke of Milan. Rome twice captured and plundered, once by Cardinal Colonna and again by an imperial army under Bourbon. French recapture Genoa and Pavia, and besiege Naples, but are thwarted by pestilence, and the defection of the Dorias. Genoa becomes independent. Wars in Italy closed by the Treaty of Cambray, 1529.

PROGRESS OF THE REFORMATION.

117. The Reformation, meanwhile, had made only the more rapid progress, while the attention of spiritual and temporal princes had been absorbed by affairs in Italy. Luther was disturbed in his retreat at the Wartburg by news of violent and fanatical movements among his followers, which threatened discredit to the cause of religious freedom. Carlstadt, his substitute at Wittenberg, had nearly broken up the University by denouncing profane learning, encouraging the students to deface the churches, and himself resorting to the most ignorant persons for instruction in the Scriptures. Though still outlawed by the imperial edict, Luther returned to Wittenberg, and by preaching and writing, threw his great influence into the restoration of order and reason.

A. D. 1522.

118. Several causes were now disturbing the peace of Germany. In spite of the abolition of the right of private war, knights still scoured the country with their retainers, robbed merchants and rich travelers, and even cut off the right hands of their prisoners. Franz von Sickingen, the greatest of the Rhenish knights, became the head of a league formed by his order in hostility to the princes. The knights professed a bitter hatred of the priests, and claimed the support of Luther; but the

Reformer, who dreaded nothing so much as the propagation of his doctrine by the sword, only exhorted Sickingen and his companions to observe the peace of the empire. They declared war, nevertheless, against the Archbishop of Trèves, who was aided by the Landgrave, Philip of Hesse, and Frederic, the Elector-Palatine. Sickingen, after being deprived of many of his castles, was besieged at last in Landstuhl; and its massive walls being reduced to a heap of ruins by artillery, he was found in one of the inner apartments, mortally wounded. "What have I done," exclaimed the archbishop, as he entered the vaulted chamber, "that you should attack me and my poor people?" "Or I," said the Landgrave Philip, "that you should overrun my lands in my minority?" "I must answer," replied Sickingen, "to a greater Lord." Being asked to confess his sins, he said "I have already in my heart confessed to God." The princes knelt in prayer, while the chaplain administered the last religious rites, and their enemy expired. Twenty-seven castles of Sickingen and his friends, and most of the similar strongholds in Franconia, were soon dismantled or destroyed.

119. The following years were marked by a terrible revolt of the peasantry in Suabia, Franconia, Lorraine, Alsace, and the Palatinate. These unfortunate people believed that the "new religion" was to put a sudden end to all the grievances under which they had so long and bitterly suffered. They submitted to Luther their list of demands, the first of which was the right to choose their own religious teachers. Luther advised them to submit to their rulers, while he published an appeal to the latter, charging them with having occasioned the disturbances by their suppression of the Gospel. The peasants were joined by several nobles and knights, and gained some advantages   A. D. 1523-25. over the armies sent to oppose them; but they could not long withstand the cannon and thoroughly armed horsemen of their antagonists. They were defeated, and in multitudes of instances either hanged or tortured; 100,000 persons are said to have been destroyed and their fertile fields made desolate.

120. The fanaticism of one Thomas Münzer prolonged the commotions. He drew around him crowds of idle and unprincipled people by proclaiming community of goods, and leading them to the plunder of churches, convents, and even castles. A young nobleman, who was sent to treat with them, was brutally put to death; but in the battle which followed the disorderly crowd were slaughtered without mercy.

121. The Catholic princes, Duke George of Saxony, the Electors of Mentz and Brandenburg, and others, now united themselves more closely to oppose the Reformation, while the friends of the reformed   A. D. 1526. doctrines formed the League of Torgau, for mutual protection in case of attack upon their religion. Both parties were ready for

M. H.—12.

action in the Diet held at Spires, in June, 1526. The hostile relations between the Emperor and the Pope at this crisis, (see §§ 111–114,) and the pressing need of uniting all Germany against the Turks, led to a suspension of the Edict of Worms; and, during the few years of tranquillity which followed, the Reformation gained strength. In a subsequent Diet at Spires the adherents of the ancient Church secured a decree against all innovations in worship or doctrine; and the reformed party entered a solemn protest against this decree, which gave to them, and by derivation to all who have since held their essential doctrines, the name of PROTESTANTS.*

122. All Europe was now thrown into consternation by the movements of Solyman II., who, in the five years since his capture of Belgrade, had subdued Egypt, shaken the Persian kingdom to its foundations, and, turning toward Europe, declared himself emperor of the West as well as of the East, aiming to make Constantinople again the capital of the world. Hungary was his first point of attack; and that country was reduced by the wars of the great nobles to the last degree of weakness and poverty. The royal Council at Tolna were still disputing about means of resisting the Ottoman invasion, when the smoke of a burning town announced to them that the Turks, now numbering 300,000 men, had crossed the Drave and were in full march northward. King Louis II. awaited

Aug., 1526. them with only 20,000, in the marshy plain of Mohacz. His army consisted chiefly of heavily armed cavalry, while the Turk had availed himself of the latest improvements in fire-arms, and, beside his thoroughly drilled infantry, had three hundred well-mounted cannon in his camp. The dashing courage of the Hungarians was of little avail; the flower of their nobility soon lay dead upon the fatal field, and the young king — now only in his twentieth year — was drowned or smothered in the swamp in attempting to escape.

123. Solyman marched toward Buda, burning towns and villages in his way. After two weeks' residence in the capital he withdrew, carrying with him the valuable library collected by Matthias Corvinus, and several works of art which served to adorn Constantinople. The vacant crowns of Hungary and Bohemia were claimed by the Archduke Ferdinand, (brother of the Emperor Charles,) who had married a sister of King Louis. He was crowned at Prague, Feb., 1527; but in Hungary he had a powerful rival in John Zapolya, the lord of seventy-two castles and the

---

* These first Protestants may be here recorded: John, Elector of Saxony; Philip, Landgrave of Hesse; the Dukes of Grubenhagen, Celle, and Mecklenburg; Prince Wolfgang of Anhalt; two Counts of Mansfeld; George, Margrave of Brandenburg; and the cities of Magdeburg, Strasbourg, Nuremberg, Ulm, Constance, Reutlingen, Windsheim, Memmingen, Lindau, Kempten, Heilbronn, Isny, Weissenburg, Nördlingen, and St. Gallen.

greatest of the Hungarian magnates, who was supported, moreover, by the influence and money of the French king and the Pope. Zapolya received the crown of St. Stephen in November, 1526; but a party among the nobles declared for Ferdinand, who advanced with a large army from Bohemia, gained the battle of Tokay, and, together with his consort, was crowned in turn with St. Stephen's diadem.

124. Zapolya now made an alliance with the Sultan, who had conquered the greater part of Bosnia, Croatia, Dalmatia, and Slavonia, and advanced again in 1529 to the plain of Mohacz. Here Zapolya appeared and did homage for his crown, after which degrading ceremony he accompanied the Grand Turk to Buda and aided in putting its garrison to the sword. The entire Turkish army, supported by a fleet in the Danube, now laid siege to Vienna. All parties in Germany united in this moment of general danger, and the defense was as determined as the attack was formidable. The very number of the Turks, moreover, made it difficult to maintain them in a hostile country, and by the middle of October they commenced their retreat. Zapolya was left to conduct the civil war with Ferdinand on his own account.

125. The Emperor, who had resided eight years in Spain, visited Italy to restore the order so long interrupted by his wars with the king of France. The freedom of Florence, already sold by the Pope in his treaty with Charles at Barcelona, was now overthrown. Upon the refusal of the citizens to recall the Medici, the Prince of Orange was ordered to lay siege to the city. It was fortified by Michael Angelo, and valiantly defended by an army without the walls; but its best general having been slain in battle, and another proving a traitor, the city was compelled to receive an imperial garrison, to pay a heavy ransom, and agree to the hereditary rule of the Medici. The Prince of Orange was killed in the same battle; and his titles and dominions were transferred, by the marriage of his sister, to the House of Nassau.

126. The Emperor proceeded to Bologna, where he received from the Pope the iron crown of Lombardy and the imperial diadem. The German Electors were not invited to take their hereditary parts in the ceremony; the Duke of Savoy carried the crown, the Marquis of Montferrat, the scepter, and the Duke of Urbino, the sword. Charles V. was the last Emperor crowned in Italy.

127. Crossing the Tyrolese Alps into Germany, the Emperor repaired to Augsburg, where he had summoned a Diet to meet in May, 1530, for the two purposes of settling religious difficulties and concerting measures against the Turks. The threatening movements of Solyman compelled a more conciliating tone toward the Protestant princes; and thus the Moslem hosts became the unconscious allies of the Reformation. A statement of the Lutheran doctrines, known as the Augsburg Confession, had

been drawn up by Melancthon, a theologian of great learning, and firm devotion to the truth, though of a mild and gentle disposition. It was signed by all the Protestant princes and representatives, and has ever since been the standard of belief in the Lutheran churches.

128. In December of the same year, the League of Smalcald was signed by the same powers. Its leaders were the Elector of Saxony and the Landgrave of Hesse; and it included eventually seven princes, two counts, and twenty-four cities. To avoid leaving the government in the hands of the imperial vicars during his frequent absences from Germany, the Emperor had resolved to have his brother Ferdinand elected king of the Romans; and in spite of the protest of the Elector of Saxony, who was one of the vicars, the archduke was actually crowned at Aix-la-Chapelle in 1531. The Duke of Bavaria, hereditary rival of the House of Austria, allied himself with the Smalcaldic League in opposing the power of Ferdinand. The League was further strengthened by the alliance of Francis I., who, though himself engaged in burning heretics, rejoiced in every sort of opposition to the power of Charles. For the same reason he kept up his intimacy with King John (Zapolya) of Hungary, and even with Solyman, the Turk. The French king declared himself the protector of Christians in the Levant, and obtained from the Sultan for their use all the churches in Jerusalem, except the principal one, which was now a mosque. Henry VIII. of England also favored the League, for, though proud of his controversy with Luther, he had his own cause of enmity with Charles, which is soon to be described.

129. The progress of the Turks compelled the emperor to conclude the *first religious peace* at Nuremberg, in 1532. It was confirmed by the Diet of Ratisbon, and granted full liberty to preach and publish the doctrines of the Augsburg Confession. The same month, John the Steadfast died and was succeeded by his son, John Frederic, in the electorate of Saxony. In consequence of the peace, Charles was soon attended near Vienna by an army of 80,000 men. Solyman advanced into Hungary at the head of 350,000, and with a dazzling display of Oriental magnificence. Many fortresses sent him their keys, and his march was less like an invasion than a peaceful progress through his own dominions. At the little fortress of Güns, however, he met an opposition which severely wounded his pride. His whole army was detained more than three weeks by a garrison of only 700 men, who repulsed eleven assaults, and at last only permitted ten Janizaries to remain an hour in the place, to erect the Turkish standard. The operations of Andrew Doria in the Morea, and the defeat of his cavalry at the Sömmering Pass, further discouraged the Sultan, who hastily retreated, leaving only a force of 60,000 men at Essek, to support the interests of Zapolya. Peace was made the following year between the Empire and the Porte.

130. Important events had occurred meanwhile in western Europe. Pope Clement VII., having causes of offense with the Emperor, courted the alliance of the king of France, and negotiated at Marseilles the marriage of his niece, Catherine de' Medici, with Henry, Duke of Orleans, the second son of that monarch. By the subsequent death of his elder brother, Henry became heir to the French kingdom, and Catherine during the reigns of her three sons exerted a powerful and most baleful influence upon the fortunes of France.

131. Henry VIII. of England had married Catherine, youngest daughter of Ferdinand and Isabella of Spain, and the widow of his brother Arthur. All the sons born of this marriage had died in infancy, and only one daughter remained — the sickly Princess Mary, afterward as queen, to bear so melancholy a name in history. According to the notions of the age, Henry regarded the death of his children as signs of Heaven's displeasure with the marriage, and for several years had been petitioning the Pope to annul it. Clement, however, was embarrassed by the necessity of conciliating many powers. If he declared for Catherine, both France and England were ready to sever their connection with the Roman Church; if he favored Henry, Germany and the Netherlands were no less certain to become protestant. The queen of England was aunt of the Emperor Charles, who naturally supported her claims and those of her daughter. When imperial influence prevailed at the papal court, Clement refused the divorce; when the French king, who was in alliance with England, had the ascendency, a different decision was hinted as probable.

132. By the advice of Cranmer, then an obscure priest, Henry submitted the question to the universities of Europe. The balance of opinion was assumed to be in his favor, and, in June, 1533, Cranmer, now promoted to be Archbishop of Canterbury, solemnly pronounced the marriage with Queen Catherine annulled. The king was already married to Anne Boleyn, who had imbibed the reformed doctrines in the court of the French king's sister, Margaret of Navarre, and was considered by the English Protestants as a powerful ally of their cause. The famous parliament of 1534 abolished the papal authority in England, forbade the payment of "Peter-pence" or other tribute to Rome, and declared the king to be the head of the national Church. Though this decisive event was immediately brought about by personal and selfish motives, yet the reformation in England had a far deeper origin, and had only been hastened by the discussions concerning the king's marriage. The irresolution of the Pope shook the faith of many who would gladly have regarded him as inspired with unerring wisdom; and the question was heard: "If Pope Clement *will* not decide when England's welfare is at stake, where is his justice? — if he *can* not, where is his infallibility?" In spite of the law for the burning of heretics, now in full force, and illustrated by many executions during the reign of Henry VIII., the hearts of the common people were more and more alienated from the ancient Church.

133. Pope Clement VII. died in September, 1534. His pontificate had been marked by losses and calamities unknown to his predecessors: himself a prisoner, Rome plundered and desecrated, once by a prince of the Church and once by the forces of the Emperor; Denmark, Sweden, and England severed from their obedience to the Church, whose doctrines were also denied by a great part of Germany and Switzerland. Clement was succeeded in the papacy by Alexander Farnese, who took the name of Paul III.

134. The Mediterranean coasts were infested at this time by Mohammedan pirates, especially by the "flying squadrons" of Barbarossa, who, on the death of his brother Horuc, had become king of Algiers. The Sultan Solyman appointed this daring freebooter his admiral; from Gibraltar to Messina, along the borders of Spain, Italy, and France, no man slept securely; and on the African coast a multitude of captives were waiting to be ransomed, while reduced by their fierce and barbarous masters to a most degrading servitude. Barbarossa had recently taken possession of the kingdom of Tunis, from which he expelled its rightful monarch, Muley Hassan; and the terror of Europe was only heightened by this increase of his power.

135. Among the most famous and successful enterprises of the reign of Charles V. was a crusade against these corsairs. Mustering his forces at Cagliari, in Sardinia, the Emperor took command in person, and landed on the African coast near the ancient town of Utica. The fortress of Goletta, which protects Tunis, was taken by storm; Barbarossa was routed in a pitched battle, and, with the aid of the Christian captives, Tunis itself was taken. Muley Hassan was restored upon his engaging to suppress piracy, to protect all Christians in the exercise of their religion, and to pay the Emperor a yearly tribute of 12,000 ducats. Charles was preceded into Europe by thousands of liberated captives, whom he had caused to be clothed and equipped at his expense, and who spread his fame with ardent gratitude through their various countries.

136. The king of France now made a new pretext for war, by advancing a most unreasonable claim to the duchy of Savoy. The reigning duke was his uncle, but was nearly allied both by marriage and interest with the Emperor. Early in 1536, the French troops overran the duchy. All attempts at negotiation failing, the Emperor declared war, and armies were collected in Italy and the Netherlands for a double invasion of France. With that reckless cruelty which too often disgraced his policy, Francis caused the rich and beautiful region between the Alps and the Rhone, as far north as the Durance, to be made utterly waste. Towns, villages, and mills were destroyed, crops burnt, and wells poisoned. Only three places were left to be defended, and of these the Emperor chose to attack Marseilles. But the terrible plan of defense proved effectual; hunger and disease among his troops compelled him to raise the siege after sixteen days, and to retreat with a loss of 30,000 men. The invasion of Picardy was attended by no greater success.

137. Francis, elated by the discomfiture of his rival, now cherished great plans of conquest both in Italy and the Netherlands. He renewed his old alliance with the Turks, and engaged Barbarossa to land an army in the kingdom of Naples, while he himself should enter Lombardy with 50,000 men. These great preparations, however, came to nothing. The queen-regent* of the Netherlands, with her sister, the queen of France, arranged a truce, in July, 1537, which was prolonged by the negotiation of the sovereigns in person at Nice, 1538, and finally settled into a "perpetual peace" by the treaty of Toledo. Francis was left in possession of Savoy, Bresse, and half of Piedmont; A. D. 1539. the rest of Piedmont and the duchy of Milan remained to the Emperor. The Duke of Savoy, unjustly deprived of his dominions, had to content himself with the little county of Nice. Geneva, long subject, nominally, to the dukes of Savoy, but really to its bishops, now became an independent republic. It was ruled twenty-five years by John Calvin, through whose influence it became not only the stronghold of the Reformation in all the French-speaking countries, but a focus for all Europe of religious, political, and scientific progress.

RECAPITULATION.

Luther opposes the fanaticism of many reformers, the lawlessness of the knights, and the disorders of the peasantry. Many castles destroyed; 100,000 peasants put to death. League of Torgau unites the Protestant princes against a counter-alliance of the Catholics. *Protest* of the former in the Diet of Spires gives a name to their party. Advance of the Turks; Louis of Hungary and Bohemia slain at Mohacz; Buda taken and plundered. Archduke Ferdinand becomes king of Bohemia, and claims Hungary, which is held, however, by Zapolya, in alliance with the Turks.

Florence captured by an imperial army and the Medici restored. Charles receives at Bologna the crowns of Italy and the Empire. Augsburg Confession adopted by the Lutherans. Smalcaldic League unites the Protestant powers, and is favored by France and England. Archduke Ferdinand crowned King of the Romans. Third invasion of Hungary by Solyman attended with great pomp, but trifling results. Marriage of Catherine de' Medici with Henry of France. Separation of Henry VIII. from Catherine of Aragon and his marriage with Anne Boleyn favor the reformation in England. The king's supremacy in the Church declared by Parliament. Moorish corsairs ravage the European coasts of the Mediterranean. Charles V. takes Tunis and liberates a multitude of captives. Francis I. lays waste Provence. Charles besieges Marseilles without success. Peace being made, Geneva becomes independent.

*The Queen-dowager Mary of Hungary, widow of the young king, Louis II., who was slain at Mohacz, and sister of the Emperor Charles. She succeeded her aunt, the Duchess Margaret, as regent of the Netherlands, in 1530.

Reign of Charles V.

138. The highest military office in France had remained vacant since the treason of Bourbon. It was now filled by the appointment of Montmorency, a life-long companion of the king, whom he had served with distinguished merit, both in the field and the cabinet, especially in the negotiations for his release from the captivity in Spain. Under his influence, Francis I. broke off his friendship with the king of England and his alliances with the Lutherans and Turks, while he cultivated closer relations with the Emperor. A scheme was even proposed by the French embassador in England for the partition of that kingdom among Charles V., Francis I., and James V. of Scotland. This coming to the ears of Henry VIII., he resolved to league himself more closely with the confederates of Smalcald (see § 128) by marrying Anne, sister of the Duke of Cleves and of the Electress of Saxony. The duke was one of the greatest Protestant princes, having lately become heir to Guelders and Zutphen by the extinction of the family of Egmont, as well as to his father's duchy of Cleves and his mother's inheritance of Berg, Jüliers, and Ravensberg. His estates lay along the Rhine, from Cologne to the neighborhood of Utrecht, and from the Werre to the Meuse. The marriage, however, having been occasioned by a temporary policy of personal resentment, was soon annulled by the king himself, and, though Anne continued to reside in England, the failure of the alliance led to the downfall of the Protestant party at court.

139. The fleet of Barbarossa was again pursuing its ravages in the Levant and conquering nearly all the islands of the Archipelago. Venice

A. D. 1540.

not only lost these and several places on the mainland, but had to pay a ransom which exhausted her resources and left her dependent upon the protection of France. The Emperor, though master of Mexico and Peru, had great difficulty in meeting the expenses of his government, and the Spaniards, ill-content to be taxed for enterprises in which they had no concern, refused to vote supplies. Charles revenged himself by ceasing to convene the *Cortes*. The grandees shut themselves up in their palaces and country-seats, where they found consolation for the loss of political power by maintaining all the ceremony of royal courts and exercising sovereignty over thousands of vassals. Ruining their fortunes by extravagance, and losing all warlike energy and skill in a life of indolence, they ceased to be formidable to their monarch.

140. The Netherlands protested in their own way against the burdens of taxation. Ghent, the Emperor's native city, rose in revolt, and sent envoys to the king of France, acknowledging him as its sovereign. Francis being now on friendly terms with Charles, betrayed their confidence, and even invited the Emperor to pass through France on his way to punish the rebellion. He was entertained with great magnificence, but had no sooner set foot in his own dominions than he received from Francis a demand of the investiture of Milan as the price of his safe passage. It was refused, except upon conditions which the French king declined to accept; and the Milanese duchy was the same year bestowed upon the emperor's son Philip. Charles entered his native city on his birthday, 1540. All the principal citizens, with bare heads and feet, asked pardon on their knees. But no submission could soften the vengeance of the sovereign. Twenty magistrates were beheaded; the ancient abbey of St. Bavon and the Bell Roland, which, from its tower, had so often summoned a free people to arms, were destroyed; and from the fines of the citizens a fortress was erected upon its site. All the privileges of Ghent were abolished. The commercial prosperity of the town was transferred to Antwerp; its brave enthusiasm for freedom was inherited by the northern provinces, which were yet to wrest their independence from the son of Charles.

141. The French king, disappointed in his mercenary aims, now dismissed Montmorency and renewed his alliance with the Lutherans and the Turks. The former had gained strength by the accession in 1535 of Joachim II. as Elector of Brandenburg, and in 1539 of Henry the Pious as Duke* of Saxony, in the places of princes who had been bitterly opposed to the reformation. The people of these countries were already protestant at heart, and the reformed worship now prevailed from the Rhine to the Baltic. Conferences between Romish and protestant divines were held at Frankfort in 1540, and before the Diet at Ratisbon in 1541, bringing the two parties more nearly to agreement than ever before or after, but without producing peace.

142. The death of King John Zapolya of Hungary renewed the hostilities with the Turks. Before the troops voted by the Diet of Ratisbon could take the field, Solyman had a third time entered the Hungarian capital, where he now established both government and religion upon a Mohammedan basis, which continued nearly 150 years. In vain King Ferdinand sent embassadors offering to hold Hungary as a tributary of the Porte; Solyman haughtily replied by demanding a yearly tribute for the arch-duchy of Austria. The Elector of Brandenburg led a German army to the siege of Pesth, but he failed, and town after town fell into the hands of the Turks, until, in 1547, the Sultan desiring to turn his arms toward Persia, consented to a truce for five years. The government of the Turkish conquests was committed to twelve officers appointed by the Porte.

---

* It should be remembered that there were two branches of the Saxon family; the elder or Ernestine possessing the electoral, and the younger or Albertine, the ducal title. The latter had the territories of Meissen and part of Thuringia, including the cities of Dresden and Leipzig. Wittenberg was the capital of the electorate.

143. The Emperor Charles, meanwhile, had been overwhelmed with disasters in his expedition against Algiers. His landing on

A. D. 1541.

the African coast was accompanied by a tempest of wind and rain which spoiled his ammunition, swept away his tents and turned his encampment into a swamp. His fleet being wrecked, the provisions were destroyed; a pestilence carried away the greater part of the army; and at last the emperor, accompanied by the shattered remains of his splendid armament, arrived in December at the Spanish port of Cartagena. The French king, his late ally, received the news of his calamities, with unconcealed joy, and immediately sought to draw into his own alliance all who had any cause of complaint against the emperor. A rebellious party in Naples, the Duke of Cleves and the kings of Denmark and Sweden, entered the new league, but Henry VIII., incensed by the intrigues of Francis with the Scots, rejected his advances.

144. In the summer of 1542, five French armies were in the field, three of which were to operate against the Netherlands, one in Italy and one toward Spain. Luxembourg was unprepared, and many of its fortresses were taken by the Duke of Guise with a force under the nominal command of the second son of the king; but the young prince, hearing that his brother the Dauphin was planning a pitched battle in the south, disbanded a great part of his army and went to join him, leaving Luxembourg and Montmédy to be easily retaken by the Regent of the Netherlands. The siege of Perpignan by the Dauphin failed,

A. D. 1542.

through the incompetency of the engineers and the violence of the autumnal rains. The place was defended by the Duke of Alva with the coöperation of Andrew Doria. The king of France approached within forty miles, when, perceiving the hopelessness of the undertaking, he ordered the siege to be raised. His immense preparations — the greatest during his reign — had been dissipated in aimless or trivial enterprises, and only a few small places in Picardy and northern Italy remained as the fruits of his efforts.

145. An English army, during the autumn of the same year, devastated Scotland, and its victory at Solway Moss hastened the death of the Scottish king James V. His only daughter was but seven days old, and the king of England, in hopes of an alliance which might bring the whole island under one crown, recalled his forces and proposed a marriage between his son Edward and the infant queen. This union would have averted many miseries from both kingdoms; it was prevented by the opposition of Scottish nobles under the influence of France.

146. The emperor now passed into Germany, to punish the Duke of Cleves for his treacherous conduct in the recent wars. Francis left his ally to his fate. Charles took Düren by storm and caused every inhabitant of the place to be massacred. The duchy of Jüliers, whose strongest place had been chosen for this fearful example of vengeance, immediately submitted to the emperor; and the duke hastened to throw himself at the feet of his offended sovereign. Charles let him remain there without even looking at him for a time; at length he listened to terms which were sufficiently humiliating to the duke: Guelders and Zutphen were surrendered; the alliance of France and Denmark and the exercise of protestant worship were renounced, and all the ducal troops were transferred to the imperial armies.

147. The Turkish freebooters, who were the most disgraceful allies of the French, were now ravaging the south of Italy. They burned Reggio, destroyed all vineyards and olive-orchards near the coast, carried off all the people whom they could find, and, appearing at the mouth of the Tiber, threatened Rome. The French embassador interfering for the protection of the Pope, Barbarossa steered for Marseilles, where he found a ready market for the captives whom he had brought away from the Calabrian coast. He was enraged, however, to find the French unprepared for the grand enterprise in which he had been invited to coöperate; and to pacify him Francis gave orders for an attack upon Nice. This last stronghold of the Duke of Savoy might have fallen but for the opportune arrival of Doria's fleet and a Spanish army, which caused the combined force of French and Turks to retire. The city of Toulon was given up as winter-quarters to the latter, who converted it for the time into a Mohammedan town.

148. The imminent danger arising from the near presence of the Turks induced the emperor, at the Diet of Spires, to renew his concessions to the protestants, who in turn vied with the other A. D. 1544. members of the Empire in voting supplies for the war. Hostilities in Piedmont went on all winter with great energy; but as the successes of the French and imperial forces were pretty evenly balanced, they need not here be related. A large army was assembled in Lorraine by the emperor, who received the submission of Luxembourg and of several other towns in that province and Champagne. The siege of St. Dizier detained him several weeks, but he arrived in due time at Chateau Thierry, within two days' march of Paris. The king of England, by previous agreement, invaded France at the same time with a powerful army; took Boulogne by a two months' siege, and was marching upon the French capital, when he received the unwelcome news that Charles and Francis had made peace at Crespy without the least consultation with himself.

149. The king of France, having sacrificed all other alliances for that of the Turks, was now forced to rid himself of these unmanageable allies by the payment of nearly a million of crowns. The corsairs at Toulon had behaved as if in an enemy's land, seizing men even in the royal galleys for service in their fleet, and making slaves of whomsoever they

could capture in the surrounding country. Barbarossa had sailed in April for Constantinople, ruining and wasting the coasts of Italy as he went, and his late ally was now at liberty to conclude a treaty in which he promised to coöperate with the emperor not only in suppressing heresy, but in defending Christendom against the Turks.

150. In pursuance of the former object, Charles ordered certain doctors of the University at Louvain to draw up a Confession of Faith, which all his subjects in the Netherlands were required to accept under penalty of death. As an earnest of his resolution, a Calvinistic preacher, Peter du Breuil was burned alive in the market-place of Tournay.

Feb., 1545.

The same views were made apparent in the Diet of Worms, which met in March of the same year. The Pope, fearing that his dignity might be slighted by the consultation of temporal princes concerning the religious affairs of Europe, had issued a bull summoning at last the long delayed and eagerly demanded Council to meet at Trent in March, 1545. So short a time was suffered to elapse between the summons and the meeting of the Council, in order that the Italian prelates might have exclusive control of its arrangements. So few, however, were present at the first session, that it was necessary to adjourn until the following December, when the Council was really opened.

151. The king of France was signalizing his zeal for the faith by such a persecution of the innocent Vaudois as would have disgraced the worst of the pagan emperors of Rome. These simple people in their elevated Alpine valleys between France and Piedmont had retained, from the earliest times, the purity of their Christian faith and worship, unmingled with the materialistic rites which crept into richer and more luxurious churches. More recently they had hailed the doctrines derived by the reformers from the newly opened Bible, as agreeing essentially with their own; and this connection drew upon the obscure and hitherto unnoticed heretics an attention which they might otherwise have escaped.

152. On the first day of the year 1545, the king of France addressed a letter to the parliament of Provence, requiring the enforcement of its decree passed in 1540, but suspended hitherto by the intercession of the German protestants. This atrocious law enacted that all fathers of families persisting in heresy should be burnt, their wives and children made serfs, their property confiscated and their dwellings destroyed. The especial object of persecution was a colony of Vaudois settled among the mountains north of the Durance — a rugged region which their patient industry had converted into a fruitful garden. The Baron d'Oppède was the worthy instrument of the work of desolation; and his forces had been trained by the plundering and ravaging campaigns of the French in Italy. Bursting into the Vaudois country, they laid waste vineyards, orchards, and grain-fields, and massacred the people. The little town of Cabrières was induced to surrender by a promise that all lives should be spared. But no sooner were its inhabitants in the power of the conqueror, than they were put to death. Those who had fled to the higher mountains were hunted like wild beasts. Some of the strongest were chained in the royal galleys; the rest were destroyed. This persecution of the Vaudois sent a thrill of horror through the greater part of Europe, but the French clergy, who had demanded it of the king, deliberately avowed and sanctioned the atrocity. The flames of persecution spread throughout France, and persons were publicly burnt at Paris, Meaux, Sens, and Issoire. Meaux had received reformed doctrines twenty years before, from its good bishop, Briçonnet, and had become a chief seat of the French reformation. Among its martyrs was Stephen Dolet, a distinguished scholar and author, who was highly esteemed by the literary men of his time.

153. The prelates and theologians had not long been in session at Trent, when it became evident that the wounds of Germany lay too deep for them to heal. The emperor was vigorously, though as secretly as possible, preparing for war — mustering one army in Italy, another in Austria, and a third in the Netherlands. The Pope aided him not only by contributions of men and money, but by authorizing in Spain the sale of monastic property and a tax upon the clergy. The protestant princes and cities, though late in discerning the cause of these preparations, acted promptly; and their army, commanded by the Elector of Saxony and the Landgrave of Hesse, was first in the field. Charles, having first broken his coronation-oath by bringing foreign troops into Germany, violated the constitution of the Empire by pronouncing its ban — the highest penalty of treason — against the leaders of the Smalcaldic forces and all their followers. This sentence could only be legally published with the consent of the Diet; it declared the princes to be rebels and outlaws, absolved their subjects from allegiance, and confiscated all their possessions. The confederates replied by a declaration of war, in which they renounced all obedience to " Charles of Ghent, pretended Emperor," and the army of the city of Strasbourg hastened to occupy the forts of Ehrenberg and Kufstein, in order to prevent the papal forces from entering Bavaria through the passes of the Tyrol.

154. The first summer's campaign was indecisive, but in the autumn the execution of a deeply laid plot seemed to throw all advantage on the side of the emperor. Duke Maurice of Saxony (see note, page 185), though a protestant in belief, had withheld himself from the Smalcaldic League, and so far from being included in the ban of the Empire, enjoyed the secret confidence of Charles. He had been intrusted by his cousin, now at the head of the allies, with the defense and administration of the Saxon electorate, but, won by the imperial promises and flatteries, he betrayed his trust, and, aided by King Ferdinand, with an army of Hungarians and Bohemians, seized the territory for himself. By this unlooked for defection, the protestants saw their cause reduced to the verge of ruin. Their common treasury was exhausted; many of their troops deserted for want of pay, and their army was forced to retreat from Upper Germany. Most of the towns and princes in that region made their submission to the emperor, and bought peace with heavy fines.

155. In northern Germany the case was different. The elector John Frederic advanced with an army into his confiscated dominions, and not only dispersed the troops of Maurice, but overran the Saxon duchy, the people being so unanimously on his side as against the treason of their duke, that the latter dared not levy an army among them. King Ferdinand had no greater success in raising troops among the Bohemians, whom he had offended by attempting to change their elective monarchy into a hereditary possession for his family. The deposed elector, aided by subsidies from both France and England, might, apparently, have made himself emperor of the protestant part of Germany and, perhaps, king of Bohemia, if his energy in action had been equal to his general excellence of character. The situation was reversed by the sudden and rapid advance of Charles, who, with a fresh army, came upon John Frederic at Muhlberg and crossed the Elbe almost under his eyes, while the elector still imagined him many miles away. The resistance was well planned and resolute; but the elector was wounded and captured, and his forces put to flight. With the capitulation of Wittenberg, his capital, all his electoral and princely rights were surrendered to the emperor; his possessions, except a few towns, were divided between King Ferdinand and Duke Maurice. John Frederic remained in captivity at the imperial court, while his children became pensioners of their unfaithful kinsman. The new elector, Maurice, was solemnly invested with his dignities by the emperor himself, while the deposed and captive prince looked on the ceremony from the window of his lodgings.

April, 1547.

156. Duke Eric of Brunswick, with an imperial army, was compelled, during the spring of 1547, to raise the siege of Bremen, and was totally defeated near Drachenburg; but the news of the Wittenberg capitulation paralyzed the arms of the victorious Leaguers, and Lower Germany, with the exception of Magdeburg, was soon subdued. In his return to the south, the emperor received at Halle the submission of the landgrave, Philip of Hesse, who, begging pardon on his knees in the presence of the court, engaged to surrender his artillery, demolish all his fortresses but one, release the prisoners whom he had taken, and pay a considerable fine. By a most unworthy evasion of the terms of the treaty, he was even then held as a prisoner; and the captivity of two great princes of the Empire only increased the complaints of the more honest part of the nation. These events went far, however, to overawe resistance in Bohemia, where the protestant army was soon dispersed: the nobles hastened to join King Ferdinand, and Prague itself, after a short resistance, was surrendered. The result of the rebellion was only a firmer establishment in Bohemia and throughout Germany of the power of the House of Austria.

RECAPITULATION.

Francis I. allies himself with the emperor, Henry VIII. with the Smalcaldic League. Venice despoiled by the Turks. Spain deprived of freedom, and her nobles of power. Ghent punished for rebellion by the loss of all its privileges. Establishment of the Turks in Hungary. Failure of the emperor's attempt upon Algiers occasions a new league against him in Europe; but the great efforts of the French have little result. English victory at Solway Moss; death of James V. and accession of the infant Mary as "Queen of Scots." The Duke of Cleves severely punished for his part in the league. The Turks, as allies of the French, ravage the Mediterranean coast; set up a slave-market at Marseilles and a mosque at Toulon. Invasion of France by imperial and English forces, ended suddenly by the peace of Crespy. Persecution in the Netherlands. First meeting of the Council of Trent. Proscription and massacre of the Vaudois, and martyrdoms in northern France. Smalcaldic war in Germany. Treachery of Maurice of Saxony transfers the electorate to his branch of the family. The battle of Muhlberg lost by the rightful elector, and Wittenberg surrendered. John Frederic, with Philip of Hesse, become prisoners of the emperor, who considers himself "for the first time lord of Germany."

LAST YEARS OF CHARLES V.

157. Henry VIII. of England died in January and Francis I. of France in March of 1547. The former was succeeded by his youthful son, Edward VI., during whose minority a protestant regency established the English Church in nearly the same doctrines and usages which it still maintains. Henry II., the young king of France, resembled his father in grace and affability of manners and attractiveness of person; unhappily, also, in the recklessness with which he abandoned public affairs to selfish and unworthy favorites. Disregarding his father's dying advice, he recalled the constable Montmorency to court, and raised the family of Guise to the highest honors.

158. The Guises, who surpassed in their talents for intrigue all the members of the new court, were a younger branch of the house of Lorraine which owed allegiance only to the Empire. Claude, the first Duke of Guise, had married a French princess, and his daughter became the wife — soon afterwards the widow — of James V. of Scotland. During the long minority and absence of the young queen (see § 145), who was educated in France as the affianced bride of the Dauphin, Mary of Guise was the center of French influence in the Scottish court; and both in her person and that of her daughter, the beautiful but unhappy Mary

Stuart, the Guises may be said to have ruled Scotland. They claimed also the rights of the House of Anjou in Provence and the kingdom of Naples, being descended from old King Réné, whose daughter Yolande had married a duke of Lorraine.

159. Two sons of Duke Claude of Guise held important places in the Council of Henry II. — Francis, Duke d'Aumale, and Charles, Archbishop of Rheims, afterward better known as Cardinal of Lorraine. At the head of the Council were Henry d'Albret, king of Navarre, and his son-in-law, Antony of Bourbon, first prince of the royal blood. For a time, however, the chief ruler of the court was Diana de Poitiers, soon created duchess of Valentinois, who possessed the keys of the public treasury by causing one of her confidants to be appointed to high fiscal office. All ecclesiastical appointments in the kingdom were in her gift, and holders of rich benefices were undoubtedly in some instances removed by poison, in order that the proceeds of the sale might be the sooner in her hands. The realm which Henry II. had solemnly sworn to administer in the fear of God, was thus left a prey to unchecked robbery. A court so occupied gave no uneasiness to the other powers of Europe; and the emperor was able to pursue his dealings with the Pope and the princes, unembarrassed as formerly by the intrigues of France.

160. Paul III., too late alarmed by the growing power of the emperor, had withdrawn his troops from Germany, and, by favoring a sedition in Genoa, sought to substitute French for imperial influence in that city. The death of the chief conspirator, just when his presence would have given success to his party, thwarted the plan, and the Dorias remained in power. The dissension between the temporal and spiritual sovereigns was still more embittered by the murder of the Duke of Parma, a son of the Pope, and an Italian tyrant of the most odious type. The emperor, instead of punishing the crime, seemed almost to assume the responsibility of it, by occupying Placentia, where it had occurred, with his own troops, and refusing to invest the son of the murdered duke, who was his own son-in-law, with the duchy of Parma.

161. The Pope had already ordered the removal of the Council from Trent to Bologna, where it might be under his own control. The Spanish and Neapolitan prelates, obeying their temporal sovereign, remained at Trent; the other thirty-four passed into Italy; and the two Councils, instead of restoring peace and unity to Christendom, opened a war of words between themselves. The emperor resolved to settle the religious differences of Germany by his own authority. Three divines, belonging respectively to the old and new Catholic and the Lutheran parties, were appointed to draw up a Confession of Faith which should reconcile all differences, at least until a more generally acceptable Council could be convened. In allusion to its provisional and temporary nature, this paper was called the "Interim." In aiming to please all parties, it naturally contented none, and was attacked with equal violence at Magdeburg, at Geneva, and at Rome. It was presented, however, to the Diet at Augsburg, not for discussion but acceptance; and the Elector of Mentz, immediately rising, thanked the **May, 1548.** emperor for his efforts to restore peace to the Church, and declared the articles to be fully approved by the Diet. This unauthorized assumption was allowed on that occasion to pass unchallenged; but protests were soon entered, both by the actual and the deposed Elector of Saxony, as well as by several imperial cities. Magdeburg and Constance were the chief centers of opposition. Both were placed under the ban of the Empire; the latter was captured by the army of King Ferdinand, and, in defiance of its ancient privileges, annexed to the dominions of the House of Austria. Magdeburg sustained a longer resistance, and became the stronghold of the protestant faith.

162. Having, as he hoped, suppressed religious innovations by means of the Interim, the emperor proceeded to reform the Catholic party by a special edict characterized by great wisdom and moderation. At the same Diet, the seventeen provinces of the Netherlands* were incorporated with the Empire under the name of the circle of Burgundy.

The French king was now in Italy stirring up plots against the imperial interests in Parma, Genoa, and Naples; but he was recalled by a revolt excited by his tax-gatherers among the peasantry in Guienne. Fifty thousand rebels were in arms. They were easily put down by the disciplined troops of Montmorency and the Duke d'Aumale, and the vengeance inflicted by the former upon the citizens of Bordeaux was too frightful to be recorded.

163. The Guises, for their own interests, lost no opportunity to promote hostilities between England and Scotland, and especially to oppose the marriage-treaty which might so happily have united those two nations. The Scottish reformers and protestants were naturally in favor of the English alliance, while the Catholic party found its support in France. Its leader was Cardinal Beaton, a man of savage and bigoted character, whose overbearing insolence at length provoked his assassination. The 150 conspirators, who had accomplished his death, held the castle of St. Andrews against the Queen-mother, Mary of Guise, until the arrival of a French fleet and army to her aid. The regent Arran was soon after defeated by the English protector Somerset. French forces were constantly engaged in these actions, and in 1549 war was openly declared between France

* The Low Countries belonging to Charles V. either by inheritance or conquest comprised the *four* duchies of Brabant, Limburg, Luxembourg, and Guelders; the *seven* counties of Artois, Flanders, Hainault, Namur, Zutphen, Holland, and Zealand; the margravate of Antwerp; and the *five* baronies of Mechlin, Utrecht, Friesland, Overyssel, and Groningen.

H. M.–13.

and England. The young queen of the Scots, now six years of age, was sent into France, where she remained until after her marriage and widowhood. Somerset was soon overthrown by civil dissensions in England, and the Earl of Warwick coming into power signed a peace with France.

164. The French protestants lost, about this time, an invaluable friend and protectress in Margaret, Queen of Navarre, who died Dec. 21, 1549. The ambition of the Guises, the cruelty of Montmorency, the rapacity of all the courtiers, and especially the resentment of Diana of Poitiers, whose iniquities had been plainly dealt with by an honest reformer, all combined to fan the flames of persecution. Four Lutherans were burnt to heighten the festivities attending the coronation of the French queen, Catherine de' Medici, and in every province heretics were hunted like wild beasts.

165. Paul III. dying, Nov., 1549, the cardinal Del Monte became pope under the name of Julius III. He sought favor with the emperor by reöpening the Council at Trent; and Charles summoned a new Diet at Augsburg to devise means of compelling the protestant party to submit to its decrees. As the emperor grew older and his constitutional melancholy settled more heavily over his mind, he became more willingly a persecutor. In the Netherlands he had just established the Spanish Inquisition; and his cruel Edict of Brussels denounced the death-penalty against all who should buy, sell, or possess any protestant book, meet for the study of the Scriptures, or speak against any of the Romish doctrines. Men thus offending were beheaded, women were either burnt or buried alive.

166. By a vote of the Diet of Augsburg, Maurice of Saxony was intrusted with an imperial army for the siege of Magdeburg. But Maurice had now gained from the emperor all that his ambition could demand; he was alarmed by the stretch of prerogative which seemed to threaten his own princely rights, and, offended by the continued captivity of his father-in-law, Philip of Hesse, he resolved to retreat from his irksome and disgraceful position and resume his true place at the head of the protestant party. It was not easy to win back the confidence he had forfeited; but, while actually conducting the siege of Magdeburg to a

Jan., 1552.

successful termination, he concluded a treaty with France for combined war against the emperor. Among the articles was one engaging the French king to seize the towns of Metz, Toul, Verdun, and Cambray, and hold them as imperial vicar — an engagement under which the government of France, to a very recent date, claimed possession of these towns. The treaty was signed at the Castle of Chambord, near Blois, by Henry II. and Albert of Brandenburg.

167. The emperor, not alarmed by rumors of this event, had sent large detachments from his army to Italy and Hungary, and had posted himself with a mere guard at Innsbruck to watch the proceedings at Trent. Maurice published a manifesto in which he announced his determination to maintain the laws and constitution of the Empire, to protect the reformed worship, and to liberate the landgrave Philip. He then advanced upon Augsburg, which opened its gates to him without a blow. A small force which the emperor had collected upon the borders of the Tyrol was put to flight; the pass and castle of Ehrenberg were taken by storm; and Charles himself escaped by a hasty flight from Innsbruck through the cold and darkness of a rainy night, being carried in a litter over the snow-covered mountain roads into Carinthia. Maurice might probably have captured him, but desisted because he "had no cage big enough for such a bird." The Council of Trent made a no less sudden retreat, and only met again ten years later — in 1562.

168. The French forces had, meanwhile, seized Toul and gained possession, by stratagem, of the free imperial city of Metz. The same plan failed at Strasbourg, where the citizens were on their guard. Returning through Lorraine, Henry II. occupied Verdun; then, invading Luxembourg, captured several towns and bestowed their plunder upon his courtiers and high officers, to the equal discontent of the soldiers and the defrauded inhabitants.

169. The treaty of Passau ended the first religious war in Germany. It was willingly signed by King Ferdinand and the Catholic princes, who perceived that the emperor's schemes were not less hostile to the civil than to the spiritual rights of the members of the Empire. It was now agreed that both parties should enjoy the free exercise of their religion, and should be equally admitted to the Imperial Chamber. The deposed Elector of Saxony and the Landgrave of Hesse were set at liberty. The forces of the Smalcaldic League were either disbanded or enlisted in the war against the Turks.

Aug., 1552.

170. This had broken out afresh in Hungary, through a fancied slight received by Martinuzzi, Bishop of Waradin and guardian of the infant Zapolya, from the Sultan Solyman. The restless and warlike bishop offered to betray the interests of his ward by securing the province of Transylvania and the crown of Hungary to King Ferdinand, on condition of receiving for himself a cardinal's hat and the governorship of the province. The Turkish army, which immediately entered Transylvania, was opposed by the combined forces of Martinuzzi and Castaldo, the general of Ferdinand; but the arrogance of the cardinal became unbearable; the general accused him of a secret understanding with the Turks, and, with the consent of King Ferdinand, procured his assassination. The memory of this king is stained with many similar crimes of too little importance to our general purpose to be recorded.

171. The Turks now overran all southern Hungary; Temesvar and the other fortresses of the Banat fell into their possession, and their customs, both of government and worship, remained established there until 1716. The approach of the elector Maurice, after the Peace of Passau, compelled them to retire from Erlau, a little town in the north which had withstood three furious assaults, and so held them at bay until succor could arrive.

172. The emperor, with 100,000 men, undertook the recapture of Metz, which was defended by the Duke of Guise and all the chivalry of France. Albert of Brandenburg, who had hitherto refused to accede to the peace of Passau, and had been ravaging western Germany as an ally of the French king, now suddenly changed sides, defeated and captured the Duke d'Aumale, and made his peace with the emperor. The siege of Metz, though conducted with grim determination, made no progress, owing to the diseases and hardships incident to the severity of the winter, and the skill of the defense. The Spanish and Italian troops suffered most of all from the cold and from the heavy rains which made their camp uninhabitable. At length, in January, 1553, Charles, with tears of mortification, abandoned the enterprise. Metz became wholly French; Lutheran books were burnt and the reformed worship suppressed.

173. All this time the Turkish corsair Draghut was ravaging the Mediterranean coasts. From every cliff and castle along the shores of Italy an anxious lookout was kept for the sails of this marauder, and columns of smoke too frequently signaled his approach to the terrified inhabitants of the villages. Not only were richly laden merchantmen captured upon the sea, but the pirates often penetrated inland, carrying into slavery all the people whom they could seize. The island of Corsica, then belonging to Genoa, was attacked and several places taken; but here the Turks quarreled with their Christian allies, the French, and seized not only all the Corsicans who were fit to row in their galleys, but several French nobles, whom they detained for ransom.

174. In Germany the restless temper of Albert of Brandenburg involved him in a war with a new league of princes. In the long and obstinate battle of Sievershausen, victory at length decided for the league, but its general, the elector Maurice, received a mortal wound. He died two days later, in the thirty-second year of his age. His brother Augustus succeeded to the electorate, which, down to the dissolution of the Empire in 1806, and subsequently as the kingdom of Saxony, has remained in the Albertine branch of the family. Prince Albert of Brandenburg was again defeated near Brunswick, and spent the remaining years of his life as a dependent upon the court of France, or upon his brother-in-law, the Duke of Baden. Germany enjoyed a long interval of respose, during which it had little part in the general affairs of Europe.

175. On the side of the Netherlands, Terouenne was taken by an imperial army, and so completely destroyed that it ceased to be a town. Hesdin was also taken, and it was during its siege that Emmanuel Philibert, eldest son of the exiled Duke of Savoy, displayed those surprising talents which regained for him in due time his father's dominions. The duke died a few months later at Vercelli, which was seized and plundered by the French almost immediately upon his decease.

A. D. 1553.

176. During the same summer, the young king, Edward VI., died in England, and his sister Mary — daughter of the deposed Queen Catharine, and a bitter enemy of the party in church and state which had dethroned her mother — came to the throne. The ambitious scheme of the Duke of Northumberland, to obtain the crown for his daughter-in-law, Lady Jane Grey, a grandniece of Henry VIII., led to her destruction and his own. Mary took immediate steps to abdicate her supremacy in the Church, and submit her kingdom again to the control of the Pope. The latter wept tears of joy on the news of her accession, and dispatched Cardinal de la Pole — a member of the English House of York, and, therefore, a near relative of the queen — to complete the religious revolution.

177. The emperor, too, had his eyes upon England, and, with a view to extend his power in that direction, soon secured the marriage of Mary with his son Philip, whom he invested with the kingdom of Naples, that his rank might equal that of his bride. The marriage took place July 25, 1554. So unpopular was it in England that three insurrections broke out in different parts of the country, though Philip made liberal use of Spanish gold in attaching nobles and people to his interests.

178. The queen and her husband were perfectly agreed in the desire to extirpate the reformed faith and worship in England. Four months after the marriage an act of Parliament restored the nation to its obedience to Rome. The embassadors who were sent to take the oath of allegiance to Julius III., heard, on their way, of the death both of that pontiff and of his successor, Marcellus II., and finally fulfilled their mission to Paul IV.

John Peter Caraffa, who assumed this name, had been distinguished hitherto for piety, learning, and a simple and blameless life. He was a member of the Oratory of Divine Love, instituted during the reign of Leo X., and was one of the founders of the Theatins. At the age of seventy-nine he suddenly took on a new character, that of worldly ambition and overbearing tyranny. He appeared in public only in magnificent array of velvet and gold, and his daily life in the palace was ordered with princely pomp and ceremony. His ruling passion was hatred of the Emperor Charles, to whose jealousy of the popes he chose to ascribe the alienation of the Germans from the ancient Church. Paul, accordingly hastened to make a close alliance with France, and to magnify all his causes of disagreement with the emperor.

179. Charles was not long, however, to stand in the way of the papal schemes. For years the desire had grown upon him to throw off the burden of public affairs. His health had failed; the high hopes with which he had begun his reign were further than ever from their fulfillment; the Turks held the greater part of Hungary, and his heretical subjects in Germany, so far from being reduced to submission, had first put him to a disgraceful flight and then dictated their own terms of peace. The recent death of Queen Joanna, whom the Spaniards had always persisted in regarding as their sovereign, rendered it possible for Charles to dispose of the crowns of Castile and Aragon. In hours of prayer he fancied that he heard his mother's voice calling him away; and he resolved to spend the remainder of his days in retirement.

180. In pursuance of this design, he called Philip from England and first invested him at Brussels with the Grand Mastership of the Order of the Golden Fleece. Then, in the presence of all the estates of the Netherlands, the emperor conferred upon his son the sovereignty of the seventeen provinces; reviewed the events of his own reign, and begged the assembly to pardon all the errors which he might have committed; charged Philip to defend the Catholic faith, to do justice and to love his people. Queen Mary of Hungary, at the same time, laid down the regency which she had held twenty-five years, and the new sovereign of the Netherlands appointed the Duke of Savoy to succeed her.

Oct. 25, 1555.

181. A few weeks later all the Spanish nobles then in the Low Countries were assembled in the same hall to witness the abdication of the crown of Spain and its dominions in Asia, Africa, and America. The resignation of the imperial crown in favor of King Ferdinand, though addressed to the electors, princes, and estates of Germany in the autumn of 1556, was not accepted until the Diet of Frankfort in 1558; but the emperor sailed from Flushing immediately after he had committed that document to his trusted friends, the Prince of Orange and Chancellor Seld, and, accompanied by his two sisters, the dowager queens of Hungary and France, proceeded to Spain. Yuste, in Estremadura, was his chosen retreat, where for his accommodation apartments had been added to a monastery of the order of St. Jerome. Here it was his delight to join in the musical services of the monks, or in fine weather to cultivate his garden and orchard with his own hands. He spent many hours with the Italian mechanician, Torriano, in making clocks and watches or other delicate machinery. Still he followed with eager interest the movements of public affairs, and by his counsels constantly aided his daughter, who, during her brother's absence, was regent of Spain.

182. He was visited by two young princes who were destined to widely different parts in the great drama of European affairs: his own son, John of Austria, and the unfortunate Carlos, son of Philip and heir of Spain and the Netherlands. Two years after his retirement, the ex-emperor felt his end approaching, and was seized with a fancy for celebrating his own funeral. Clothed as a monk, he joined in the mournful chants of the brotherhood around an empty coffin which was placed in the convent chapel. Within a month the solemn farce was turned into reality. On the 21st of September, 1558, the great sovereign expired, worn out more by toils of state than by years.

183. The reign of Charles V. comprised one of the most momentous periods in the world's history. Religious beliefs and principles, especially in northern and central Europe, had undergone a remarkable transformation; but, beneath the outward and visible changes already described, a counter-revolution had begun, which not only arrested the progress of the reformation, but apparently neutralized its results in Austria, Hungary, Bohemia, Italy, and Spain; in a word, in all the countries subject to either branch of the House of Hapsburg. In part this was due to the strong moral reaction felt almost equally within and without the Roman Church against the old-time venality and corruption of the clergy. A number of virtuous prelates, among whom the greatest and best was Charles Borromeo, Archbishop of Milan, restored the respectability of the Church; and for more than three hundred years no pope has desecrated his office by the flagrant iniquities of an Alexander VI., or the refined voluptuousness of a Leo X. The amendments desired by Wicliffe, Huss, and the later reformers being thus apparently accomplished, the need for separation from the ancient communion became less strongly felt.

184. But the principal agency in the restoration of papal power was the Society of Jesuits, whose active and peculiar part in European affairs throughout this and the following period entitles it to a more detailed account. Its founder was Ignatius Loyola, a Spanish gentleman, who was wounded during the siege of Pampeluna in 1521. The serious reflections excited in him by a tedious convalescence formed themselves into a scheme which would appear as visionary as the wildest dreams of romance, had not its main features been realized through the consummate ability of the followers of Loyola and its fitness for the emergency at which it was presented to the world.

185. So ignorant was the founder of this great and learned society, that he had to begin his elementary education at the age of thirty-three; but, while pursuing his studies at Paris, he made disciples of six of his fellow-students, who bound themselves by a solemn oath to attempt the conversion of the Turks. The society was formally recognized and established by Paul III., with a constitution

A. D. 1540.

differing in several important respects from those of the other religious orders. Instead of wasting themselves in austerities, the Jesuits were encouraged to cultivate all their talents by the liberal pursuits of art, science, and general literature. Thus becoming the most accomplished instructors of youth, they acquired a controlling influence over the princes and leading minds in Europe at the most impressible period of life, and this influence is clearly to be discerned in the later policy of the House of Austria.

186. The General of the Order had unlimited authority in assigning to every member a sphere of duty adapted to his character and ability. While the superior talents of some found exercise in the subtle diplomacy of European courts, the pious zeal of others was employed in the most toilsome and self-denying missions among the forests of America, or the crowded cities of China and Japan. Jesuits were pioneers in the exploration of the great lakes of our northern frontier. In Paraguay they even obtained the civil government of the country, where they introduced agriculture, building, and the arts of social life, and taught the natives to exclude all other foreign influences.

RECAPITULATION.

Death of the two chief rivals of Charles V.; accession of Edward VI. in England and of Henry II. in France. Ascendency of the Guises in France and Scotland. Dissensions between the emperor and the Pope; removal of the Council from Trent to Bologna; publication of the *Interim* in Germany. Annexation of the Low Countries to the Empire. Violent opposition to religious reform in Scotland, France, and the Netherlands. Maurice of Saxony abandons the service, and nearly captures the person of the emperor. First religious war ended by Peace of Passau. Conquest of southern Hungary by the Turks. Failure of Charles in the siege of Metz. Death of Maurice at Sievershausen. Accession of Mary in England; her marriage with Philip of Spain, and submission of her kingdom to the Pope. Abdication, retirement, and death of Charles V. Counter-reformation in Europe and rise of the Jesuits.

AFFAIRS OF FRANCE AND SPAIN.

187. The accession of the Emperor Ferdinand I. was welcomed by the German princes and recognized by every European sovereign except the Pope. Paul IV. declared that as he alone had the power to crown and depose emperors, so he only could sanction their abdication; and ordered Ferdinand to resign his scepter, do penance for his presumption, and submissively await the pleasure of St. Peter's successor. These pretensions, which had been heard without surprise, though not without resistance, from the lips of Hildebrand or Innocent III., only excited ridicule in the greater part of Christendom, and the emperors thenceforth dispensed with the ceremony of a papal coronation.

188. In pursuance of his unrelenting hostility toward Charles and his son, Paul persuaded the French king to break his solemn engagements with the former in the truce of Vaucelles, 1556. He himself imprisoned the Spanish embassador and even laid Spain under an interdict. This excessive severity was deeply felt by Philip II., whose religious scruples were more intense than those of Paul. The latter was even making an alliance with the Turks, while Philip was wearying all his theologians for arguments to justify him in resisting the Pope. At length the Duke of Alva set his army in motion, and, overrunning the Campagna, appeared before the gates of Rome. Reverence forbade him to enter that holy city in arms; but no scruple of humanity prevented his putting to the sword the innocent inhabitants of the captured villages.

189. The following winter the Duke of Guise entered Italy with a numerous French army. Lombardy and Tuscany might easily have been conquered for France, but his own interests drew him to Rome, where he persuaded Paul to create ten new cardinals, in order to improve the prospects of the Cardinal of Lorraine. The movements of the French and Spanish armies resembled a stately minuet rather than actual war. They advanced and retreated, marched and countermarched, to the infinite discomfort of the poor people whose fields were wasted and whose homes desecrated by the brutal soldiery, but with no gain to either sovereign. At length Guise was recalled into France to meet a more pressing danger on the side of the Netherlands; and the Pope dismissed him with the following benediction: "Begone, then! you have done little for your king, less for the Church—nothing for your own honor!"

Peace was now necessary to the Pope; and Philip was glad to desist from what seemed to him an impious warfare. The Duke of Alva, in his own name and that of his sovereign, did penance and received absolution for the crime of invading the papal states. The territories belonging to Florence and Siena were united to form the grand-duchy of Tuscany, which was ultimately conferred upon Cosmo de' Medici, and continued in his family until 1737, when his last descendant expired.

190. In the Netherlands, Philip had mustered an army of 50,000 men, among whom were 10,000 English sent by Queen Mary against the resistance of the Parliament and the murmurs of the nation. With these forces, the Duke of Savoy inflicted a severe defeat upon the French near St. Quentin, and almost annihilated their army. Paris was only saved from capture by the obstinacy of Philip himself, who, joining the Duke of Savoy, forbade him to move farther until the town of St. Quentin and some insignificant places in the neighborhood had been taken. The French admiral Coligny, with his little garrison, held out bravely three weeks, and though the town was ultimately taken, as well as Ham, Noyon, and Chauni, the tide of success had meanwhile turned. The English, never cordial, insisted on going home, and the Germans mutinied for want of pay. While the ex-emperor, in his retreat, was calculating that his son must be in Paris, Philip had in fact retired to Brussels, disbanded part of his army and sent the rest into winter-quarters.

191. At this crisis the Duke of Guise returned from Italy and was invested by the French king with extraordinary powers. After a feigned movement toward Luxembourg, he suddenly appeared with his whole army before Calais. This last stronghold of the English in France was negligently guarded, as the surrounding marshes, always overflowed in winter, were believed to constitute an effectual defense. Its two forts were taken in the first day's attack, and after three bombardments, the town itself was carried by assault. Guines was taken two weeks later, and the English, after possession since the time of Edward III., more than two hundred years, were driven from their foothold on the continent. The discontent universally felt in England with the needless war was heightened into indignation by this unexpected loss; and the poor queen's death was hastened by her remorse and disappointment.

192. During the captivity of Montmorency, who had been taken at St. Quentin, the Guises ruled France. The duke was lieutenant-general, the Cardinal of Lorraine was minister of the interior and of finance, a third brother commanded the fleet, and a fourth the army in Piedmont. Their power was increased by the marriage of their niece, the young queen of Scotland, with the dauphin Francis in April, 1558. The constable was now permitted to open negotiations with his captors. Two

April, 1559.   treaties were signed at Cateau Cambrésis, one between France and Spain, the other between France, England, and Scotland. Queen Mary of England had died during the conferences, and Philip engaged to marry Elizabeth, eldest daughter of the King of France; while the Duke of Savoy, reinstated in his paternal dominions, espoused Margaret, sister of the same king. Most of the conquests made by either French or Spaniards were restored. The bishoprics of Metz, Toul, and Verdun — each, in fact, a principality — remained to the French, the emperor Ferdinand being too weak to reclaim them.

193. The treaty of Cateau Cambrésis is important as making a new division of the powers of Europe. National jealousies were forgotten in religious enmity. The kings of France and Spain ended their long contest in order that both might be free to destroy heresy in their respective dominions. England, under the firm and prudent rule of Elizabeth — or rather, perhaps, of her great ministers — assumed her place as the head of the Protestant states and the protectress of religious freedom in all the nations of Europe. Spain became equally the champion of papal claims, and in every nation the ruler who wished to coerce the consciences of his people, looked to Philip for aid. The invincible infantry and the reputed wealth of Spain made her unquestionably the greatest power in Europe at this period, though unwise and unjust restrictions upon commerce had already cast a blight upon her prosperity, and her decline, though yet unsuspected, was begun.

194. The Reformed Church of France had organized itself at Paris during the month following the treaty of Cateau Cambrésis. Its doctrines were derived from Calvin, whose rescripts, dated at Geneva, were received throughout protestant France with as much reverence as those of the Pope himself commanded from the adherents of the ancient Church. His disciples were numerous among the more intelligent classes, and included even bishops, clergy, and members of the monastic orders. The parliament of Paris had refused to register an edict for the establishment of the Inquisition in France; but proceedings in matters of faith were intrusted to two divisions or committees of the parliament itself, one of which was called the Burning Chamber, from the multitude of victims whom it had consigned to the flames. Its rigors were condemned by the parliament of 1559, but Henry II. personally interfered in the discussion, and ordered the arrest and imprisonment of seven members who advocated a more merciful policy. To the remonstrances of the reformed synod, he replied that he would witness with his own eyes the burning of one of these prisoners.

195. He was mistaken, for one month after his visit to the parliament, he died by accident in the prime of his life. The marriages of the two princesses were celebrated with great festivities and rejoicings; and among the ceremonies was a grand tournament held in the space between the royal hotel and the tower of the Bastile, where the members of parliament were confined. The king of France challenged the captain of his guard, a Scottish nobleman, to a tilt. In vain the queen protested, and Montgomery tried to excuse himself from the encounter. They met, and both lances were shivered; but that of the Scot entered the king's eye between the bars of his helmet. Henry sank into the arms of his son, and expired amid the alarm and confusion of the court.

196. The Guises for a year ruled both France and Scotland, and in both kingdoms their violent adherence to the policy of Rome compelled those of the reformed faith to organize themselves more closely in defense of their rights. The league of reformers in Scotland was called the Congregation. In France the name of *Huguenots* was now first applied. The young king, Francis II., was but sixteen years of age, of feeble health, and slight mental endowments. Antony of Bourbon, King of Navarre, and first prince of the blood-royal of France, was equally destitute of character; his younger brother, the Prince of Condé, was regarded as the head of the protestant party, but he had purposely been sent on an embassy to Brussels. Even the queen-mother could not yet assume the power which she afterward wielded.

197. The kingdom was divided no less by political than religious differences. On the side of the Huguenots were the old feudal nobility of France and the highest princes of the royal blood. Opposed to them were the Guises, still regarded as foreigners by most of the nation, the queen-mother, an Italian, and the strong influence of the Pope and of Philip of Spain. The national party, therefore, favored reform or at least general toleration in matters of faith; and resented the persecuting policy of their opponents, not only for its inhumanity, but as the impertinent interference of foreigners. An assembling of the States-General was urgently demanded; the government refused, and the Huguenots retaliated by the "conspiracy of Amboise," whose main objects were to get possession of the young king, to make Antony of Bourbon regent, to try the Guises for their mal-administration, and to summon the States. This plot was betrayed, and its only effect was to strengthen the opposite party.

198. Paul IV., before his death, gave the world a new surprise by suddenly entering on plans of reform. He dismissed his nephews, whose robberies, murders, and midnight riots had been the scandal of his court; introduced order and economy into his finances; and, to guard against injustice in his ministers, caused a chest to be put in a public place, with an opening into which every man might cast his petitions or complaints, the Pope himself having the only key. His reforms, however, were almost harder to bear than his previous extravagance; for his zeal took the direction of persecution, and his last days were spent in listening to the tales of the basest informers, and ordering arrests. He died in August, 1559, and the people instantly broke open the prisons and released his captives. His statue was thrown down, and its head, wearing the triple crown, was cast into the Tiber.

199. A different character was elevated to the papacy in Gian Angelo Medecino, who took the name of Pius IV. He was an active old man, of affable manners and amiable temper, himself no persecutor, but allowing the inquisitors to proceed in their dreadful work unmolested. His only near relative, his nephew, Charles Borromeo, was a clear and striking contrast to the nephews of other popes who have made *nepotism* notorious. Promoted to the see of Milan, he distinguished himself by the self-denying purity of his life, his toilsome and frequent visits to the humblest and remotest mountain recesses of his diocese, and his ministrations to the poor during a terrible visitation of the plague. Pius IV. differed from his predecessor in being a friend to the House of Austria; he therefore recognized the imperial title of Ferdinand I., and consented to the reassembling of the Council at Trent in 1562.

200. Philip II., meanwhile, had been recalled into Spain by the progress of the Reformation in that country. Bibles in the Castilian language were commonly possessed by the middle and higher classes, and the constant intercourse with Germany during the reign of Charles V. had afforded free entrance to the Lutheran doctrines. The rigorous edicts of Philip were only too effective in suppressing the spirit of inquiry. The fires of the Inquisition, formerly lit only for Jews and Moors, were now kept blazing for loyal and blameless Spaniards. With the last vestiges of free thought, the prosperity of Spain vanished. More printing-presses existed in that kingdom in 1550 than in 1850; a fact which can surely be paralleled by no other country in Europe.

201. The dominion of the Guises in Scotland was overthrown in the summer of 1560, by the surrender of Leith to a combined army of Scots and English, after a long and severe siege, during which the queen-regent had died. The French, in fulfillment of their treaty, evacuated Scotland, and Mary Stuart and her husband were compelled to drop the arms and title which they had hitherto assumed as sovereigns of England. Six months later the supremacy of the Guises in France was shaken by the death of Francis II., just as their deeply laid plot for destroying the Bourbon princes approached its fulfillment.   Dec., 1560.
Catherine de' Medici, now ruling in the name of her second son, Charles IX., spared the lives of the Bourbons, that by playing off one party against the other she might maintain her own ascendency.

202. The States-General met Dec. 13; but, startled by the enormity of the public debt, declared that they could do nothing, and were dissolved in January, 1561. The Edict of Orleans the same day granted most of the reforms which had been demanded; and, for a while, the queen, offended by the overbearing conduct of the Guises, courted the favor of the Huguenots. The constable Montmorency, always a friend of Spain, and a firm adherent of the old Church, now joined the Duke of Guise and the marshal St. André in what was called the Triumvirate, for the suppression of heresy. But the present drift of affairs was against them, and they retired from the court. The States-General met again in Aug., 1561, after a new election in which the reformed party was victorious. They confirmed the disposition already made of the government during the king's minority, but insisted that no cardinal should be admitted to the Council of Regency, because he was subject to a foreign sovereign, the Pope; no bishop, because the law required him to reside in his diocese; and no *foreigner*, which term was held to include the whole family of Lorraine.

203. An important conference of divines took place at Poissy, Sept., 1561, in the presence of the king, the queen-mother, the king and queen of Navarre, and many prelates and theologians. Theodore Beza of Geneva made so favorable an impression upon the court by his eloquence, fearlessness, and noble bearing, that he was requested by Queen Catherine to remain in France, in the hope that his presence might contribute to peace and a better understanding between the parties. The following

A. D. 1562.
January an Edict of Toleration, prepared by the Presidents and Councilors of the several parliaments of France, officially recognized the Reformed Church and permitted the Huguenots to meet unarmed by daylight for worship in the suburbs of towns, though not within the walls.

204. The Triumvirate resolved to oppose the edict by force; and Philip of Spain wrote his mother-in-law that she must cleanse her kingdom with fire and sword, or the pestilence of heresy would overspread Spain and the Netherlands. The weak-minded King of Navarre was drawn over to the same side by promises of the island of Sardinia or of a marriage with the widowed queen of Scotland. Hostilities were begun by an attack of the Duke of Guise's retainers upon a congregation of Huguenots who were assembled on a Sunday morning for worship in a barn. A frightful massacre ensued, which was the signal for similar scenes all over France. Beza hastened to the court to remonstrate. The king of Navarre was present and threw all the blame upon the Huguenots. The reformer replied in memorable words: "I admit, Sire, that it is the part of God's Church, in whose name I speak, to endure rather than inflict blows; but may it please you to remember that it is an anvil which has worn out many a hammer."

205. Both parties sought foreign aid in the war which both foresaw; but while the Prince of Condé and the Huguenots wore the colors of the king and declared their purpose to deliver him from captivity, the Triumvirate and their followers assumed the red scarf of Spain. Philip offered 36,000 men, but the Catholic leaders, alarmed by the scandal which such an invasion would bring upon their cause, besought money instead. The Duke of Savoy led his own troops, and the Pope contributed 100,000 crowns. Elizabeth of England sent an equal sum of money to hire German mercenaries for the Huguenots, and added 6,000 of her own subjects to their armies. Havre was given up to her officers as security for the restitution of Calais.

206. Many of the chief towns in France declared for the Huguenots. Orleans became their capital and was blockaded by the other party. The King of Navarre received a mortal wound during the siege of Rouen; in a battle near Dreux — the first of any magnitude in these unhappy wars — the leaders on either side, Condé and Montmorency, were taken prisoners. Coligny became leader of the Huguenots, and the Duke of Guise was alone at the head of the Catholic party. The latter even dreamed of succeeding to the throne of France, but his ambitious schemes were ended by assassination, Feb., 1563. The queen-mother was the chief gainer by his death, for her real reign now began. Peace was made with the Huguenots, and the Edict of Amboise secured freedom of worship to nobles and great vassals of the crown, with their retainers and subjects—a signal illustration of the aristocratic character of the reformation in France.

207. The Council of Trent held its last session Dec. 4, 1563. Instead of healing the schism in the Christian world, it had excluded nearly half the body of believers from the communion of the Church; but, by the reformatory measures adopted during its later sittings, it gave new vigor to that venerable body, and apparently set a bound to the protestant movement in Europe. A few months after its close the emperor Ferdinand I. died. His son, Maximilian II., had   July, 1564. already been crowned King of the Romans, as well as of Hungary and Bohemia. He succeeded peaceably to the imperial crown, and his justice and liberality long delayed the wars of religion which were destined in the next century to bathe Germany in blood.

208. The next year Pope Pius IV. also died and was succeeded by the Grand Inquisitor Ghislieri, who took the name of Pius V. His austere piety and unyielding will well qualified him to continue the reformation of the Church. Certain of his own rectitude, he was equally sure of the unpardonable wickedness of all who differed from him. New prisons were built to contain the multitudes of his victims, and blood flowed, or the smoke of his executions ascended, every day. He sent money and troops into France, with orders for the instant death of all heretics who could be taken.

209. The details of the civil and religious wars in France can not be fully recorded here. The queen-mother, personally indifferent to all religion, courted either party which for the moment seemed best adapted to serve her ends. In a battle near Paris, Nov., 1567, the veteran constable Montmorency was killed, though the Huguenots were defeated. By the battle of Jarnac, March, 1569, the Huguenots lost a hundred nobles, among whom must be reckoned the Prince of Condé. His son Henry, then very young, became afterward one of the most illustrious leaders in France. Henry of Navarre, his cousin, though but fifteen years of age, was placed at the head of the reformed party, while Coligny, his instructor in war, was in command of their armies.

210. A more decisive battle was fought at Moncontour, Oct. 3, 1569; the Huguenots suffered a terrible reverse, with the loss of 12,000 men. But the interests of Catherine now required peace, for she hoped to marry her third and favorite son, Henry, Duke of Anjou, to the queen of England. The masterly generalship of Coligny also threatened the capital; and in these circumstances the treaty of St. Germains was signed, Aug. 8, 1570. The Huguenots were guaranteed the free and public exercise of their religion, with the restoration of all their goods and offices; and as security for the execution of this treaty, four cities—La Rochelle, Montauban, Cognac, and La Charité—were assigned to them for two years.

RECAPITULATION.

Paul IV. opposes the accession of Ferdinand I., and makes war upon Philip of Spain. Alva ravages the Campagna and carries on a semblance of hostilities with the French forces of the Duke of Guise. Spaniards victorious at St. Quentin, but the English lose Calais. Peace of Cateau Cambrésis recombines the powers of Europe according to their religious affinities. England becomes the head of protestant, Spain of Catholic powers. Organization of Reformed Church of France. Attempt of Henry II. to suppress discussion in the parliament is shortly followed by his death. Ascendency of the Guises in France and Scotland ended only by the death of King Francis II. and of Mary of Guise. Foreign influences in France arrayed against the national or reform party. Paul IV. undertakes persecutions and reforms. Pius IV. recognizes Ferdinand I. and reassembles the Council at Trent. Philip II. crushes the reformation in Spain. Tolerant Edict of Orleans opposed by the French "Triumvirate." Reformed party predominant for a time in France. War begun; the Huguenots aided by England and protestant Germany, the Triumvirate by Spain and the Pope. Death of Antony of Bourbon, the Duke of Guise, Montmorency, and the Prince of Condé. Henry of Navarre becomes leader of the Huguenots. Close of the Council of Trent. Accession of Emperor Maximilian II. and Pope Pius V., the former a peace-maker, the latter a persecutor. Defeat of the Huguenots at Moncontour followed by Peace of St. Germains.

WARS OF RELIGION.

211. King Philip of Spain had, meanwhile, been carrying on a barbarous crusade against the Moriscoes, or nominally Christian Moors of the Alpujarras. By his edict of 1566, these people were forbidden the use of their native language, their Moorish names, or any of their most innocent national customs; and all their children between the ages of three and fifteen were ordered to be sent to Spanish schools. After a year of secret preparation, the people flew to arms, murdered the Christian inhabitants of that region with every circumstance of barbarity, besought aid from the Sultan Selim and their brethren in Africa; and chose for their sovereign a descendant of the Ommyad caliphs of Cordova. The war raged three years, with all the violence of vengeance on one side and desperation on the other. The fugitive people were hunted like wild beasts among their mountains, but at length their spirit was broken by a series of inhuman massacres, and in 1571 the last symptoms of revolt were extinguished.

A. D. 1568.

212. A more important maritime war was still in progress with the Turks in the Mediterranean. In 1565 they had besieged Malta in great force, and the defense of that island by the Knights of St. John was one of the most valiant operations known to history. The fort St. Elmo was taken, but that of St. Michael, commanded by the Grand Master La Valette, held out, until the Turks, exhausted by a series of desperate attacks, gave up their enterprise and sailed away to Constantinople. All the sovereigns in Europe rivaled each other in showering praises and gifts upon the Grand Master, and Valetta, the new capital of Malta, has ever since borne his name. Solyman was overwhelmed with rage and regret, which were hardly assuaged by his capture the next year of the far more fertile and valuable island of Chios.

213. The Sultan was that year making war in Hungary, under pretense of supporting the claims of John Sigismund, son of Zapolya, against Maximilian II. The fortress of Szigeth was at length taken by his forces; but the noxious air of the surrounding marshes proved fatal to Solyman himself, who died in September, 1566. His two elder sons had been put to death through the intrigues of Roxolana, his Russian wife, who thus prepared the accession of her own son, Selim II. The new sultan was weak and profligate, and only secured the allegiance of the Janizaries by largely increasing the donative, which, like the prætorian guards of Rome, they demanded at every change of masters. Making a truce with Maximilian, Selim turned his attention to the conquest of Cyprus. This island had been for eighty years a dependency of the Venetian Republic, whose power was now declining, while the severity of its rule made the Cypriots look even to the Turks as deliverers.

214. In the summer of 1570, a Turkish army of 50,000 was landed on the island, and the Venetians, abandoning the open country, shut themselves up in the two towns of Famagusta and Nicosia. The latter was taken in about two months, the former not until August, 1571. Pius V., always an ardent foe of the Moslem power, was now roused to the most strenuous exertions; and the Holy League, consisting of himself, the king of Spain, and the Republic of Venice, had soon in the Mediterranean a fleet of 300 vessels. The command was given to Don John of Austria, half-brother of the king of Spain, the most accomplished knight, and soon to become the most famous general, of his time.

215. The Turkish fleet, whose number somewhat exceeded that of the Christians, had taken its position in the Gulf of Lepanto, when the allies came in sight. The battle which followed was the most memorable naval conflict in modern times. The Turks not only lost 224 ships and 30,000 men, but the fame of their invincible bravery and fortune, which had reached its height during the career of Solyman the Magnificent, ceased to be a terror to the nations of Europe. The decline of the Ottoman Empire is dated from the battle of Lepanto. If the Christians by a closer union could have followed up their victory, Greece might have been delivered. But rival interests divided their forces, and the death of Pius V. for a time interrupted their movements. In 1573, Venice made a separate peace with the Turks, surrendering Cyprus and even consenting to pay a yearly tribute. Selim died the next year, but not until the first collision of his empire with Russia had begun that long series of contests for the possession of the Black Sea, which is not yet ended.

M. H.—14.

216. In western Europe religious divisions were still producing either open or secret hostilities. A bull of Pius V. in 1570 excommunicated Elizabeth of England and released all her subjects from allegiance. The favorite plan of the Pope and the king of Spain was to place the queen of Scotland upon the English throne; but Mary was at this time the prisoner of Elizabeth, owing to a train of circumstances which can only be briefly indicated.

The pupil, though of late years the rival of Catherine de' Medici, Mary Stuart had returned to her inherited kingdom at the age of nineteen, with a character singularly unprepared to encounter the stern spirits which now surrounded the Scottish throne. Beautiful, and endowed with wonderful fascination of manner, she had been trained at a court where pleasure was the chief end of life, and the pursuit of selfish interest the only wisdom. The Scotch reformers did not adorn their solid virtues with the graces or even the common charities of the Christian life; in their eyes the gaieties of the queen's household were heinous sins, and the religion in which she had been educated from her cradle was an idolatry to be resisted even unto death. It is difficult to say how much of the subsequent calamities sprang from crime, how much from the weakness of the queen, or how much from the inevitable hostility between herself and her circumstances; but the suspicion which attributed to her an active share in the murder of her second husband, Henry Darnley, was only confirmed by her speedy marriage with his murderer, the Earl of Bothwell.

217. She was imprisoned by her nobles in Lochleven Castle, escaped the following year, mustered an army, risked and lost the battle of Langside near Glasgow, and took refuge in England. The regent of Scotland for the young king James VI., came with a retinue to York, where the cause between the rebellious subjects and their queen was tried before the commissioners of Elizabeth in October, 1568. Mary was neither convicted nor acquitted of the murder of Darnley; but she was detained nineteen years in England, the occasion of innumerable plots against the government and life of Elizabeth, and was finally beheaded in 1587.

218. In the meantime a startling event had destroyed the balance of religious parties in France. For two years after the Peace of St. Germains (see § 210), the court favored the Huguenots. The death of the queen of Spain dissolved for a time the cordial relations between her husband and her brother, the king of France. The revolt of the Netherlands against the tyranny and persecution of Philip II. also tempted Charles IX. to annex the Walloon provinces, formerly fiefs of France, and thus extend his kingdom to the Scheldt. Though this secret scheme never led to open hostilities with Spain, yet Charles gave his security to a loan negotiated by Coligny and Louis of Nassau for the insurgents in the Netherlands.

219. La Rochelle was the capital of the Huguenots; there Queen Jeanne of Navarre held her court and the reformed church its synods, unmolested by the Guises or the government. The good-will of the latter was still further indicated by the proposal to marry the princess Margaret, third sister of Charles IX., to Prince Henry, heir of Navarre. Coligny was invited to court and loaded with wealth, honors, and assurances of the affectionate confidence of the king. He used the power thus intrusted to him by striving to consolidate all sects and parties in France against the overbearing influence of the king of Spain. He promoted naval enterprise and colonization in America. The first settlement within the present limits of the United States — near the mouth of the St. John in Florida — was under his patronage; but the colony was exterminated—men, women, and children being massacred by Spaniards from the more recent plantation of St. Augustine.

220. Shortly before the time appointed for the marriage of Henry of Navarre, his mother, Queen Jeanne, died at Paris, June, 1572. The marriage was celebrated Aug. 18. Four days later, Coligny was shot in the street, but not killed, by a man hired for the purpose by the Duke of Guise. The king and his mother visited the admiral in his sick-room, expressing great indignation and desire to punish the assassin; but meanwhile a greater crime was secretly but swiftly preparing. The Guises were summoned to court, and the several quarters of Paris were assigned to them for the general massacre of the Huguenots, which was now resolved upon. Word was passed through the city; at the sound of a great bell all "good Catholics" were to be in the streets, distinguished by a white badge on the left arm and a white cross on the hat.
A little after midnight, in the early morning of St. Bar- Aug. 24, 1572.
tholomew's Day, the dreadful signal was given, and instantly, as if a myriad of wild beasts had been let loose, the yells of the murderers and the despairing cries of their victims resounded through the streets.

221. The massacre went on eight days and nights in Paris, and spread in six weeks through all France. As usual, private interest or revenge asserted itself under cover of the reigning excitement. Office-seekers murdered those whose places they coveted, suitors their opponents, heirs-at-law their nearest relatives. The lowest number of lives thus sacrificed in France, as stated by historians, is 20,000.

222. This outbreak of savage atrocity filled all Europe with surprise, but excited very different emotions at the several courts. Philip of Spain is said to have laughed for the first time in his life. His cousin, the emperor Maximilian, wept over the crime. Elizabeth of England received the French embassador in a hall draped with funereal black. No word was spoken, but the discomfited nobleman, having advanced through silent rows of black-robed figures, had to depart as he came, without permission to offer his explanations. The Pope (now Gregory XIII., who had succeeded Pius V. in May of this year), celebrated the event as a Roman victory, and caused the Hall of Kings in the Vatican to be adorned with a fresco representing the massacre. On the other hand, the 24th of August was appointed at Geneva to be annually observed as a solemn fast.

223. The revolt of the Netherlands and the rise of the Dutch Republic —a series of events among the most remarkable in modern times—have hardly been alluded to, in order that their history might now be given without interruption. These rich and thriving countries—called in various languages the Low, Nether- or Hollow-lands of Europe—had been in great part reclaimed from the sea, and owed their wealth wholly to the industry of their people. The seventeen provinces (see note, page 193), differed from each other in language, customs, and laws, and though governed in common by the king of Spain, were only united by the occasional meeting of their deputies in the States-General. The four Walloon provinces which bordered France spoke its language, though in a dialect of their own. The people of the midland countries spoke Flemish, the northern, Dutch—both languages being a greater or less variation from the German. The Netherlands, as a whole, were not only the most prosperous, but the most generally enlightened portion of Europe; for it was rare to find even a peasant who could not read and write. Agriculture was carried on by the most careful and intelligent methods; manufactures employed multitudes of skillful and industrious artisans; and the commerce of the East and West Indies had raised Antwerp, Amsterdam, and Rotterdam to a rank among the richest European cities.

224. These free and intelligent people had given an early and extensive reception to the doctrines of Luther and Calvin, which Charles V., by eleven successive edicts and the establishment of the Inquisition, had vainly endeavored to suppress. The Flemish Inquisition was far more restrained and mitigated by the secular government than the Spanish; but during the reign of Charles several thousands of the people had been required to seal their faith with their blood.

225. In leaving the Netherlands for Spain in 1559, Philip II. had committed the regency to his half-sister, the Duchess of Parma. Her cabinet consisted of three Councilors: Granvelle, Bishop of Arras—afterward Archbishop of Mechlin and cardinal; Viglius, an experienced lawyer and statesman; and Count Barlaimont, an honest and loyal Flemish noble. The most important man in the Netherlands was William, Prince of Orange, a favorite of Charles V., but at that period little known except for his vast wealth and powerful connections. The House of Nassau, to which he belonged, had been for five centuries of princely rank in Germany, to which it had given one emperor; and was of older standing in the Netherlands than that of Philip himself. The principality of Orange had been lost in the French wars, but restored to William by the peace of Cateau Cambrésis. Before the conclusion of that peace, the prince was a hostage in Paris, where Henry II. made known to him in confidence the secret agreement between himself and the king of Spain to extirpate heresy in their respective dominions. William was then an adherent of the Roman Church, but his just soul revolted from the plot, and he was thus opportunely put upon his guard.

226. The creation of a great number of new bishoprics was the first step after Philip's accession which alarmed the more liberal party. Count Egmont, a Flemish nobleman of the highest distinction, was sent to Spain that he might represent to Philip in person the growing discontents of the Netherlands and ask redress. The count's head was turned, however, by the king's flatteries and gifts, and he returned to his anxious friends with golden opinions of the just intentions of the Spanish court. He was soon followed by letters of the king commanding the Inquisition to proceed without delay, and declaring that Philip would rather lose a hundred thousand lives, were they all his own, than permit the smallest deviation from the ancient standards of faith. The Prince of Orange, as governor of Holland and Zealand, together with several other governors of provinces, refused to consent to the burning of his countrymen. Wise Flemings took the alarm and sought shelter under better governments; 30,000 of them settled in England alone, and contributed their capital and skill in fine manufactures to the growing prosperity of that country.

227. Two thousand persons, including members of all sects and parties, now united for mutual defense. While denouncing the Inquisition, they reässerted their loyalty to the king, and their determination to keep down all tumult and rebellion. A list of demands was presented to the regent, who — alarmed by the number and powerful array of her petitioners — was reässured by one of her Councilors' branding them as "only a pack of beggars." The opprobrious term was seized by the petitioners as a party watchword; it was adopted the next day at a great banquet, where Count Brederode appeared carrying a wallet and a wooden bowl, which were passed around the table amid jovial shouts of "Long live the Beggars!"

228. The government replied to the petition by an edict which it called the Moderation, but as the only concession was in permitting heretics to be hung instead of burned, the people nicknamed the document the "Murderation." The excitement increased; thousands began to assemble, first in the woods and by night, but at length in daylight and upon the open plains, to listen to preachers who descanted upon the miseries of the country. As they grew bolder, cathedrals and churches were pillaged and

images were thrown down. At length the regent, a prisoner in her own capital, was compelled to sign a permission for protestants to meet for worship, so long as they met unarmed and did not molest those of a different faith. A. D. 1566.

229. Secret intelligence from Spain indicated that war must soon break out. A battle was fought near Antwerp (March, 1567), in which 1,500 of the "Beggars" were slain, and 300 more were afterward murdered. The Prince of Orange, after vainly trying to mediate between the parties, withdrew into Germany. The subjugation of the Netherlands was now committed by Philip to stronger and sterner hands than those of his sister. The Duke of Alva, a man of iron will and cruel inflexibility of

Aug., 1567.

purpose, arrived with a Spanish army at Brussels. He treacherously seized counts Egmont and Horn and threw them into a dungeon at Ghent, then proceeded to organize in his own house and by his own authority an infamous tribunal which soon justified its name, the "Council of Blood."

230. The Prince of Orange and the nobles with him in Germany were summoned before this tribunal; they replied by denying its authority. Count Buren, the eldest son of the prince, was thereupon torn from his studies at the university of Louvain and sent into Spain. The Duchess of Parma, thus superseded in command, retired into Italy, and Alva, adding her powers to his own, became Governor-General of the Netherlands. The calamities which followed seem rather the work of a madman than of a rational and responsible being. The entire population of the Nether-

Feb., 1568.

lands, with a few exceptions specially stated, were sentenced to death by a decree of the Inquisition, confirmed ten days later by a royal edict. The very extravagance of this decree showed that it was not meant to be literally executed; but it was made the warrant for innumerable atrocities. Common criminals were hanged, nobles beheaded, obstinate heretics burnt. At first the government derived a revenue from the confiscated property of its victims, but this was soon exhausted, and an arbitrary tax of one per cent upon all property, real or personal, five per cent upon all transfers of real estate, and ten upon all other articles sold, aroused the wrath even of the classes whom the persecutions had spared.

231. Commerce ceased; towns were deserted; people near the coast took refuge upon or beyond the sea, many in the interior fled to the forests and became the terror of travelers and of the neighboring villages. Many of the sea-farers obtained letters of marque from the Prince of Orange, and under their assumed name, "Beggars of the Sea," waged piratical warfare against the Spanish marine. The outlaws of the woods were called "Wild Beggars." The emperor Maximilian remonstrated with his cousin, and claimed the "Circle of Burgundy" as under his own protection; but Philip replied that he would rather not reign at all than reign over heretics, and that he would persevere in his present policy though the sky should fall. The Prince of Orange now mustered three armies from his own resources and the contributions of the Dutch and Flemish cities, and planned a threefold attack upon the provinces of Alva. Before taking up arms he published a "Justification," in which he denounced the Council of Blood and all the atrocious acts of the Governor-General, and charged King Philip with having forgotten not only the services of the prince and his ancestors, but all his own royal oaths as sovereign of the Netherlands. Two of the armies were defeated, but Count Louis of Nassau gained a decided victory over the Spaniards near Groningen. Adolph of Nassau, a younger brother of the prince, fell in the battle, and so did the Spanish commander D'Aremberg.

232. Counts Egmont and Horn were hastily tried by Alva's Council, and sent to execution. Both were Knights of the Golden Fleece, and had a right to be tried only by the statutes of their order. Egmont might also claim the privileges of his native country, Brabant, solemnly guaranteed by the king of Spain at his accession, while Horn, as a German count, was subject only to trial by the electors and princes of the Empire. But law and equity were now disregarded. Both noblemen were beheaded in the great square at Brussels on the 5th of June, 1568. Two years later the baron Montigny, brother of Count Horn, who had gone on an embassy to Spain in 1566, was privately garroted in the prison to which he had been illegally consigned.

233. After the executions of Egmont and Horn, Alva marched against Louis of Nassau, who suffered a defeat, with the entire loss of his army, at Emden, and escaped without followers into Germany. His brother, the prince, was soon afterward compelled to disband his troops, and both proceeded, with a few hundreds of horsemen, to the aid of the Huguenots in France, while waiting for a brighter day to dawn upon their own distracted country.

234. For four years the Sea-Beggars had carried their prizes into English ports, where they obtained water and provisions, though the country was nominally at peace with Spain. Elizabeth secretly supplied money to the Flemish patriots, while Philip sent gold, spies, and even assassins into England to foment plots against the queen. At length, however, the English sovereign, unwilling to declare war, and unable to continue her aid to the rebels without it, forbade her subjects to sell food to the Beggars of the Sea. De la Marck, one of the Flemish captains, thereupon sailed from England, with twenty-four vessels, to the northernmost island of Zealand, and seizing upon Briel, its capital, made it the stronghold of the privateers. Walcheren, Enckhuisen, and a multitude of towns in the northern provinces, hastened to throw off the despotic yoke of Alva. Deputies from the nobles and cities met at Dort, July 15, 1572, and de-

clared the Prince of Orange to be the lawful Stadtholder of Holland, Zealand, Friesland, and Utrecht, during the absence of Philip II. Thus Queen Elizabeth's order in council led indirectly to the rise of the Dutch Republic.

235. Alva was for the moment in despair. The French court seemed to have turned protestant and to be bent upon espousing the cause of the heretics in the Netherlands. Louis of Nassau was besieged in Mons, but his brother the prince, advancing with a German army, had captured Ruremond, Mechlin, Dendermonde, and Oudenarde, and was on the point of relieving him, when news of the St. Bartholomew massacres in France completely changed the aspect of affairs. A band of Huguenot soldiers, paid by Charles IX. to coöperate in the defense of Mons, were betrayed, and by their king's own recommendation to Alva, were slaughtered in cold blood after they were made prisoners. Mons surrendered upon honorable terms. All the towns of Brabant and Flanders were compelled to submit to Alva. Mechlin was abandoned to three days' pillage and massacre. The revolution in the southern provinces was ended in defeat, but in the northern it was triumphant, and the Prince of Orange returning to Holland was put in possession of the government.

236. During the winter of 1572–73, the Dutch fleet was frozen up in the harbor of Amsterdam. The Spaniards marched across the ice to attack it, but a troop of Dutch musketeers on skates made a successful defense. The siege of Haarlem was among the most obstinate actions of the war. Several hundreds of the most honorable women enrolled and armed themselves for the defense of their native city, and took part in several battles. Thousands of Spaniards perished from cold, hunger, and sickness; but the town surrendered at last, and between two and three thousand citizens were put to death. Alkmaar, warned by this example, made so resolute a resistance that the Spanish commander had to raise the siege. Alva was soon after superseded by Don Louis de Requesens, whose just and liberal character was a pledge of a more conciliatory policy. Wholesale robbery and murder were now suppressed, but the oppressive taxes continued to be levied, and the Council of Blood maintained its sittings. The patriots were every-where victorious at sea, but on land the invincible Spanish infantry kept its ancient renown. Louis of Nassau, marching with some German recruits to join his brother, was defeated and slain near Nimeguen, Feb., 1574.

237. The siege of Leyden, interrupted by his invasion, was soon resumed, and its heroic defense is one of the most wonderful events of the century. The garrison was small, but the resistance was mainly kept up by the valor and constancy of the citizens. Famine began to be felt in June, and it was the 3d of October before the city could be relieved. The Prince of Orange, anxiously watching the

A. D. 1574.

enemy from his head-quarters at Delft and Rotterdam, could not approach with his fleet without breaking the dykes on the Meuse and Yssel, and thus laying the country under water. The young grain was in the field; but the States consented to the sacrifice, and under the prince's direction, the dykes were cut. The starving citizens of Leyden watched from their towers the rising of the flood which was to bear them relief. A provision fleet of 200 vessels sailed from Delft; but twice the waters were driven back by an east wind, and it lay helplessly stranded, while the more feeble and desperate citizens were crowding around the burgomaster in Leyden, clamoring for either food or surrender. The magistrate replied: "I have taken an oath never to put myself or my fellow-citizens in the power of the false and cruel Spaniards; and I will rather die than break it. But here is my sword; plunge it, if you will, into my breast, and devour my flesh, if that will relieve your hunger."

238. The people were roused to new courage, and at length their patience was rewarded. A north-westerly gale set in on the 1st of October; the waters of the German Ocean came pouring in over the ruined dykes. The fleet, now fairly afloat, had a singular midnight combat with that of the Spaniards amid the boughs of orchards and the chimneys of submerged houses; but the determination of the enemy was at length worn out by the amazing constancy of the besieged, in whose cause the elements of wind and water seemed enlisted. Even the fall of a large portion of the walls of Leyden, undermined by the waters, only frightened the besiegers, who, hastily abandoning their two forts, sought safety in retreat. The Dutch fleet sailed up the Channel, distributing loaves of bread all the way into the eager hands of the crowd which lined the banks. As soon as the pangs of hunger were relieved, the whole population of the city walked in joyful procession to the principal church, where thanks were rendered for the great deliverance. The next day a north-easterly gale swept away the invading waters, and the dykes were soon repaired. Leyden was rewarded by the institution of a ten days' annual fair, and by the foundation of a university which has given many illustrious men to Europe.

239. Philip II., defeated in war and ruined in finance, at length consented to the mediation of the emperor which he had before so arrogantly refused. To this end, a three months' congress was held at Buda in 1575. The king, however, would make no concession, and the States, in any case, had no reason to believe his word, so that the war broke out again more furiously than ever. The death of Requesens in March, 1576, threw the country into yet greater confusion, for the unpaid soldiery, now in open mutiny, marched through the provinces, plundering and destroying at their own savage will. Alost, Ghent, Utrecht, Valenciennes, and Maestricht successively fell into their hands; and at last Antwerp, the richest city of the Netherlands, and then the financial center of all Europe, was subjected to a three days' pillage. A thousand houses were burnt and eight thousand citizens murdered.

240. In this disastrous condition of the southern provinces, the Prince of Orange persuaded the authorities at Brussels to summon the States-General; and when these were assembled, he complied with their request by sending several thousand troops to expel the Spaniards from Ghent. An alliance was now formed between the northern and the southern Netherlands, under the name of the Pacification of Ghent. It was agreed to summon the Estates of all the provinces to an assembly similar to that which had received the abdication of Charles V.; to expel all Spanish troops from the country and to provide for peace and toleration in matters of religion.

Nov. 8, 1576.

RECAPITULATION.

Subjugation of the Moriscoes in Spain. Gallant defense of Malta by the Knights of St. John. Death of Solyman during his wars in Hungary. Capture of Cyprus by Selim II. John of Austria, in command of the allied forces, gains a great victory over the Turks at Lepanto. Mary, Queen of Scotland, imprisoned at Lochleven, abdicates in favor of her son. Becomes the prisoner of Elizabeth of England, to whose throne she has a claim; is beheaded after nineteen years' captivity. Brief ascendency of the Huguenots in France. Murder of Coligny and general massacre of St. Bartholomew's Day. Prosperity of the Netherlands; establishment of the Inquisition under Charles V. Regency of Margaret of Parma. Popularity of William of Orange. Mission of Count Egmont to Spain. Persecuting edicts of Philip II. Remonstrances of the "Beggars." Arrival of the Duke of Alva as Governor-General. Establishment of the Council of Blood; death-sentence of the entire people; restrictions upon commerce. Prince of Orange publishes his Justification and takes up arms. Illegal execution of counts Egmont and Horn. Louis of Nassau victorious near Groningen, but defeated at Emden, joins the Huguenots in France, surrenders Mons upon receiving news of the St. Bartholomew massacres; is afterward defeated and slain at Nimeguen. Capture of Briel by the Sea-Beggars, union of four provinces under the Prince of Orange, forming the germ of the Dutch Republic. Fall of Haarlem; successful resistance of Alkmaar. Requesens replaces Alva as Governor-General. Siege of Leyden; its brave defense, and relief by the arrival of the fleet. Failure of Congress of Buda to restore peace to the Netherlands. "Spanish fury" at Antwerp and other places. Northern and southern provinces briefly united by the Pacification of Ghent.

WARS OF RELIGION.—*Continued.*

241. The same year died the emperor Maximilian, the first European sovereign who recognized the duty of universal toleration. In Austria and Bohemia, his hereditary dominions, he relaxed all religious despotism, though his policy was in some degree thwarted by his near connection with the Spanish branch of his house; for he had married a sister of Philip II., whose fourth wife was a daughter of Maximilian. The empress Mary was a devoted adherent of the Jesuits, to whose arts the emperor opposed an inflexible resistance. By treaty with John Sigismund of Hungary, all that kingdom, except Transylvania, was secured to

Maximilian, and he was about contesting the elective crown of Poland with Stephen Bathori, when he died at the age of 49. The imperial dignities were conferred upon his son Rudolph II., who had already received the title King of the Romans and the crowns of Hungary and Bohemia.

242. Charles IX. of France survived the crime of St. Bartholomew's less than two years; and his early death — for he was only twenty-three years of age — was apparently due rather to torments of conscience preying upon a feeble nervous constitution than to A. D. 1574. mere bodily disease. His brother Henry, now heir to the crown, was in Poland, having been elected king of that country a year before the death of Charles; but he had departed most unwillingly from Paris and gladly obeyed the summons to return. He quitted Poland like a thief, carrying with him the crown jewels, and was pursued sixty miles on horseback by a large number of the Polish nobility, who desired to secure the kingdom from the anarchy too certain to follow so sudden an abdication. The fugitive king had not concerned himself to make any disposition of the government; but after more than a year of confusion, Stephen Bathori received the votes of the nobles. A. D. 1575.

243. The condition of France would have taxed greater talents and energies than those of Henry III. The Huguenots, in spite of the efforts of the court, had been rather strengthened than defeated by the events of 1573. The middle party, consisting of just and moderate Catholics, led by the Montmorencies, were shocked by the crimes and alarmed by the foreign alliances of the Guises. The consolidated monarchy so cautiously built up by Louis XI., seemed ready to resolve itself again into its feudal elements. La Rochelle, Nismes, and Montauban were like independent republics; the provinces of Languedoc, Guienne, Poitou, and others in the south-west, united themselves in a confederacy, which raised taxes, administered justice, and ordered military movements like a sovereign state. All over France, governors of provinces, and even commandants of towns and castles, acted independently of the crown.

244. The points now in dispute were rather political than religious; for of the original leaders of the Huguenots the greater number were either dead, exiled, or apostate. Even the King of Navarre and the Prince of Condé reconciled themselves, though insincerely, the year after the massacre, with the Roman Church. The Duke of Alençon, the king's only remaining brother, declared himself the protector of the Huguenots, and joined their army in Poitou. The prince-palatine, John Casimir, also their ally, led an army of 18,000 men into France. No important battle was fought, but the result of the movement was the most favorable treaty that the Huguenots had ever obtained from the May, 1576. court. It was called *la paix de Monsieur,* this being already the conventional title of the king's eldest brother. Perfect freedom of worship was conceded throughout France, except at Paris and in the immediate precincts of the court, wherever it might be. The Duke of Alençon received Touraine, Berri, and Anjou in full sovereignty, and bore thenceforth the title of the latter duchy. Having gained all that he expected from his alliance with the Huguenots, he now deserted them, and subsequently commanded an army against them. The King of Navarre was restored to his government of Guienne, the Prince of Condé received that of Picardy, and all the leaders were reinstated in their offices and pensions.

245. The Guise party alone derived no advantage from the treaty, and their discontent led to the coalition of Catholic nobles known in history by preëminence as The League. The formula signed by all its members promised "unlimited obedience to its head without respect of persons" and without reservation of the royal supremacy. The treasonable nature of the organization was only made apparent at a later day when it placed itself under the protection of a foreign sovereign, Philip II. of Spain. A plot was, however, already formed at Rome to seize and arraign the Duke of Anjou, exterminate the Huguenots, shut up the incompetent king in prison like the *rois fainéants* of the Merovingian line, and place the Duke of Guise himself, as a descendant of Charlemagne, upon the throne of France. This plan was discovered among the papers of a lawyer named David, who died at Lyons on his return to Rome; but it was regarded as a malicious fabrication of the Huguenots until another copy, obtained from King Philip, was forwarded from Spain by the French embassador to that country.

246. Henry III., alarmed by this commentary on the real purposes of the League, knew of no better way to avert its enmity than to place himself at its head. The States-General were already summoned to meet at Blois early in the winter of 1577. The manifesto of the League, first cleared of all expressions which seemed to limit or contest the royal prerogative, was laid before the assembly for acceptance. Some of the deputies signed it; others refused. All were offended by the false and undignified position in which the king's cowardice had placed him, and they declined to vote supplies for a continuance of the war. The conditions of the "Peace of Monsieur" were in truth too favorable to have been sincerely guaranteed, and the Huguenots, even during the sitting of the States, had been pushing their conquests in the south-west.

247. A new peace was now concluded by the treaty of Bergerac, and the king, forgetful of the perils which still beset his throne, plunged more deeply than ever into base and frivolous amusements. The orgies of the court could only have been paralleled in the deepest degradation of the Roman emperors. Violence, as well as luxury, ran riot, and murders were the unmarked occurrences of almost

Sept., 1577.

every day. The hostility of the Guises made it necessary for the court
to remain at peace with the Huguenots. In the summer of 1578, Catherine
de' Medici, accompanied by her daughter, Queen Margaret, and a "flying
squadron" of court-beauties, visited the King of Navarre in his capital,
and spent more than a year in the south, using all her Italian arts to
pacify and conciliate his party. The treaty of Nérac (Feb., 1579) secretly
assured to the protestants greater favors than had been promised in that
of Bergerac. One wearies of detailing the alternations of faithless peace
with indecisive wars. In the spring of 1580, upon the slightest possible
pretext, hostilities recommenced. This time the affair was called the
"War of the Lovers," from its whimsical origin. It was the seventh in
the series of what are commonly, but to a great extent inappropriately,
called Wars of Religion. Peace was mediated by the Duke of Anjou,
who was now desirous to assume the protectorate offered him by the insurgents in the Netherlands; while the court saw reason for breaking its
friendly relations with the king of Spain in the sudden and alarming
increase of his power by the conquest of Portugal.

248. King Sebastian succeeded his grandfather, John III., at the in-
fantile age of three years. His long minority was ruled by Jesuits, who
instilled into his mind romantic dreams of conquest over infidels; and
at the age of twenty he set forth with high hopes to wage war against
the Moors of Africa. Little was accomplished by this first
attempt; but, four years later, he renewed the enterprise in A. D. 1578.
aid of the fugitive king, Muley Mohammed, who had been driven from
his throne by his uncle. In the battle of Alcazarquivir, Sebastian was
defeated and slain, and his army, including most of the nobles and prelates of his realm, was nearly annihilated. The king was succeeded by
his uncle, Cardinal Henry of Braga, who, however, reigned but two
years, and the crown was then contested by several claimants more or
less related to his family.

249. The most powerful, and therefore the successful, candidate was
Philip of Spain, who sent the Duke of Alva into Portugal, with 24,000
Italian and Spanish veterans, within a few months after King Henry's
death. Don Antonio, nephew of the late king, had been crowned at
Lisbon in June, 1580, but he was defeated and wounded in the battle
of Alcantara, and finding resistance hopeless, escaped, after some months,
into France. Alva set up in Portugal a similar reign of terror to that
which he had conducted in the Netherlands, but, instead of heretics, his
victims were now monks. The conquest being completed, Philip entered
the country to receive the homage of the Estates, and spent two years in
arranging the affairs of Portugal.

250. The other powers of Europe had been too much absorbed in their
own affairs to interfere with the progress of Philip. France and England

suddenly became conscious of the extension of the Spanish dominion, not only throughout the Iberian peninsula, but over the rich and undeveloped possessions of Portugal in Brazil, Africa, and the Indies. The French court sent two naval expeditions to the Azores, which had declared for Don Antonio. These islands were of the greatest importance as a refiting and watering station for vessels bound either for the East or West Indies; and a fierce combat for their possession was fought between the French and Spanish fleets. It resulted in the destruction of the former, and all the French prisoners were put to death as pirates. The power of Philip was firmly established in the islands.

251. The interference of France was avenged by a still closer alliance of the king of Spain with the Guises, who in his interest had watched and attempted to thwart the expedition to the Azores. This failing, Philip tried the other party, and repeatedly offered money to the King of Navarre to renew his wars against Henry III. His overtures were rejected, and the death of the Duke of Anjou only drew closer the relations between the two French princes, for Henry of Navarre, as head of the House of Bourbon, now became heir-presumptive to the throne of France. The same event occasioned a renewal of the League, under the protection of Philip of Spain. A formal treaty was signed by the heads of the League and the envoys of Philip, in December, 1584, in which the "extirpation of all protestant and heretical sects in the Netherlands, as well as in France, and the exclusion of heretical princes from the throne," were prominent articles.

June, 1584.

252. Alarmed by the movements of the League, but not daring to break with the king of Spain, Henry III. refused the petition of the States of Holland which besought his protection, and by the Edict of Nemours yielded all the points demanded in the manifesto of the Guise party. He revoked all former edicts of toleration, and warned adherents of the reformed doctrines to quit his kingdom within six months.

RECAPITULATION.

Accession of Henry III. in France, Stephen Bathori in Poland, and Rudolph II. in the Empire. Feudal elements in France opposed to centralized government. The Duke of Alençon protects the Huguenots and obtains for them a favorable peace. The League is organized by the Guises; Henry III. places himself at its head; the States-General disapprove. Treaties of Bergerac and Nérac. War of the Lovers followed by a peace demanded by the foreign relations of the court.

King Sebastian of Portugal perishes in a vain attempt against the Moors of Africa. Short reign of King Henry. The crown successfully claimed by Philip of Spain, who thus gains the rich colonial possessions, as well as the European territory, of Portugal. Defeat of a French fleet sent to support the cause of Don Antonio in the Azores. Death of the Duke of Anjou and Alençon makes Henry of Navarre heir to France. Edict of Nemours revokes all acts of toleration.

Affairs of the Netherlands.

253. We go back eight years to take up the eventful history of the Netherlands. Shortly before the Pacification of Ghent, John of Austria, the hero of Lepanto, was intrusted by his brother Philip with the government of these rebellious states; but so united were the people in their resistance, that he was compelled to enter even Luxembourg — the only province which had refused to join the Union — in the disguise of a Moorish slave. Unprovided with either money or troops, he had no choice but to yield all the points demanded by the insurgents, and swear to observe all the charters and customs of the country. These concessions were embodied in the *Perpetual Edict*, a name which seems intended for a mockery, when we learn the instructions of the court of Spain to the regent, recommending him to promise every thing but perform nothing. Even after his edict, Don John was refused possession of the citadel of Brussels. He revenged himself by treacherously seizing the fortress of Namur, and by capturing Charlemont and Marienburg. The citadels of Ghent and Antwerp were destroyed by the people of those places to prevent their falling into his hands.

Nov., 1576.

254. A rival to John of Austria was now set up by the Catholic nobles, in the person of the Archduke Matthias, brother of the emperor. The Prince of Orange recognized Matthias as Governor-General of the Netherlands and was named his lieutenant. A new Union of Brussels — a league of all the States for the common defense, on a basis of perfect religious toleration — drew more closely the ties between the northern and southern provinces. It was the last time that all the Low Countries were united, until the present century (A. D. 1814–1830).

255. Queen Elizabeth, about this time, discovered a plot of Don John to depose her, marry Mary Stuart, and reign over England — the plan being favored by the Pope and the Guises, but regarded with unbrotherly jealousy by the king of Spain. Moved by this state of affairs, she was inclined to render more effective aid to the people of the Netherlands, and early in 1578 her contribution of 6,000 men joined the army of the States. Philip had prepared for this combination by sending his nephew, Alexander Farnese, with reinforcements of Spanish and Italian veterans. The battle of Gemblours resulted in the sudden rout and almost total destruction of the army of the States; but the accession of Amsterdam a week later to the Union of Brussels more than consoled the patriots for that disaster. The following August, Don John was defeated at Rymenants, mainly by the English auxiliaries, and died two months later from disease. He was succeeded by Alexander of Parma — undoubtedly the greatest general of the age, though lacking that fascination of manner which occasioned the unbounded popularity of his predecessor.

256. Meanwhile the party which had set up the Archduke Matthias discovered that he was a useless puppet, and virtually deposed him by calling in the Duke of Anjou (see above, § 245). Anjou was a weak and insignificant character, capable of being flattered by the high sounding title, "Defender of the Liberties of the Netherlands." He hoped to obtain a crown by marriage with the queen of England, a hope which the subtle or wavering policy of Elizabeth neither indulged nor denied. Entering Hainault with a French army in September, 1578, he took several towns; then feigning submission to the will of Elizabeth, he retired into France. The queen's firm persuasion of the divine right of kings, made her averse to the independence of the Netherlands, though she desired that their hereditary sovereign should be compelled to respect their ancient rights. Her council, on the other hand, desired to see them severed from the Spanish crown even at the price of their becoming dependencies of France.

257. The union of the seventeen states was overthrown at last, not by foreign despotism, but by the riotous conduct of the popular party. Two noblemen, of radical principles and depraved character, excited an insurrection at Ghent, against the terms of the religious peace. They imprisoned its governor and set up a democracy in which the law-making power was intrusted to the deans of the guilds and the captains of militia, while the executive was vested in a council of eighteen citizens. Many other towns followed the example. The Archduke Matthias and the prince-palatine, John Casimir, were allies of the democracy, and the division between the reputed friends of freedom proved fatal to the interests of the country. The arms which were needed against the common enemy were turned against each other; the Walloon provinces were devastated by a Huguenot force, while the Walloons, aided by the French, ravaged the country up to the gates of Ghent.

258. These disorders, in which the destructive elements were mixed up with the Huguenot cause, effectually severed the Catholic provinces from the Union of Brussels. The Prince of Orange, who had vainly interfered to suppress the revolutionary movements by protecting the interests of the Romish priests and people, only succeeded in forming a perpetual confederation of the seven protestant countries* by a document called the Union of Utrecht. Nominal allegiance was still rendered to Philip II.; but it was resolved to drive all foreigners from the country, and to restore in each province its ancient and peculiar laws, customs, and privileges. A congress at Cologne, under the auspices of the emperor Rudolph II., and attended by the envoys of the Netherlands, France, England, several German states, Philip and the Pope, failed to procure the union and

---

* Holland, Zealand, Utrecht, Guelders, Overyssel, Friesland, and Groningen.

reconciliation of all the provinces, for though seven months were spent in busy diplomacy, no concession could be extorted from either side.

259. The four Walloon provinces resumed their obedience to Philip II. on condition of the withdrawal of the Spanish troops; and the Netherlands were thus divided into three parts: the protestant United States of the north; the middle or Flemish provinces, whose people belonged almost equally to the two communions; and the wholly Catholic Walloon provinces of the south. Maestricht, after three months' siege by Farnese, yielded at the end of June, and was given up to the brutal rage of the Spanish troops. The Prince of Orange restored order to Ghent and exacted a just restitution of property which had been plundered during the riots.

260. Cardinal Granvelle had now returned to power, and it was by his advice that Philip II. published his royal ban against the prince. The crimes of Cain and Judas were denounced against that illustrious and blameless patriot; a price of 25,000 gold crowns was set upon his head, and the murderer was moreover promised pardon for all crimes, however heinous, which he might have committed, and promotion into the proud ranks of Spanish nobility. William replied by one of his most remarkable state-papers, in which he treated the royal denunciation with the scorn which it deserved. He declared that all Philip's hereditary claims upon the Netherlands were canceled by the violation of his solemn oaths and the charters of those states, " not once only, but a million of times;" and indignantly flung back the charge of having fomented discord in those countries upon the king himself, whose atrocious cruelty had made his most loyal and peaceful subjects the victims of robbery and massacre. Ridiculing the attempt to terrify him by setting a price upon his head, he inquired whether Philip could suppose him ignorant of the many previous undertakings of paid poisoners and assassins. And affixing his name and seal, bearing the characteristic motto, "I will maintain," he sent the document to most of the European sovereigns.

261. Negotiations were now renewed with the Duke of Anjou, and the Archduke Matthias was permitted to retire on a pension. The French prince signed an agreement to reside constantly in the Netherlands; to assemble the States-General once a year, and strictly to observe the rights and privileges of the provinces. In return he was invested with full sovereignty in all the provinces, except Holland and Zealand, which were reserved for the Prince of Orange. On the 26th of July, 1581, the States-General at the Hague cast off their allegiance to Philip II. by a solemn Act of Abjuration, and proclaimed Francis of Valois as sovereign lord of the Netherlands. The paper was drawn up by Sainte Aldegonde, a friend of the Prince of Orange, and is the first distinct assertion of the natural right of a people to depose an unjust sovereign. It declares that princes

M. H.—15.

are appointed of God to rule for the good of their subjects, and that if they neglect their sacred duty — oppressing instead of protecting their people—the latter are no longer bound in law or reason to recognize their authority. It was the first of a series of charters of political freedom, which were only reënacted by our own Declaration of Independence.

262. Leading an army of 17,000 men into the Netherlands, the Duke of Anjou compelled Alexander of Parma to raise the siege of Cambray, and entered that city in triumph. A few months later he made his Joyous Entry into Antwerp, where he was invested by the Prince of Orange with the ducal cap and mantle, and duly proclaimed "Duke of Brabant, and Margrave of the Holy Roman Empire." Other provinces successively installed him in their respective sovereignties. But he was ill content with the limited power thus conferred, bitterly jealous of the superior influence of the Prince of Orange; and was already plotting with his worthless favorites to overthrow the liberties which he had solemnly sworn to maintain. He was never trusted by the Flemings, and when, under pretense of a review, he brought his army to take military possession of Antwerp, the people flew to Jan., 1583. arms, secured their streets with chains and barricades, and made so valorous a resistance that only half the French troops left the city alive. The "French Fury" of 1583 was less destructive to Antwerp than the "Spanish Fury" of 1576, chiefly because the soldiers of Anjou began to plunder before they killed, while the more methodical Spaniards first murdered and then took easy possession of the property of their victims. Baffled in his design, the new sovereign mounted his horse and fled toward Dendermonde. A dyke was opened upon his route, and a thousand of his followers were drowned. Having ceased by his own act to be the Protector of the Netherlands, Anjou retired to Dunkirk, and though a treaty of reconciliation was signed in March, he soon quitted the country never to return.

263. The wars in Portugal were now ended, and with fresh reinforcements, the Prince of Parma was able to resume active operations. Before the autumn of 1584, only three Flemish towns remained to the patriot party. But in July of that year the Netherlands sustained a far severer loss in the assassination of their brave and faithful leader, the Prince of Orange. Within two years five attempts upon his life had been made by agents of Philip of Spain. The first was so nearly fatal as to occasion indirectly the death of the princess, through her anxiety and suspense. The successful murderer was one Balthazar Gerard, a Burgundian, who, under pretense of obtaining a passport, gained admission to the household of the Prince. He was seized immediately after the fatal deed and put to death with a refinement of cruelty which has been well described as "a crime against the memory of the great man whom it professed to avenge." His parents received the promised reward from the estates of his victim; and three lordships in Franche Comté, with a title among the landed aristocracy of Burgundy, were the lasting badges of their shame.

264. To the self-denying and steadfast energy of William of Orange the Dutch Republic owed its existence, though he was not permitted to see its freedom established. The greatest statesman of his time, he possessed in singular measure the art of reading the purposes of others and concealing his own, and to this last accomplishment, rather than to unsocial taciturnity of manner, he owed his surname, the Silent. His immense fortune had been spent in the service of his country; and he had repeatedly refused the most magnificent offers of wealth and dominion, by which the king of Spain had sought to detach him from the cause which he had embraced. His imprisoned son should be restored; cities, estates, and sovereignties in Germany should be conferred; in short, he had only to name his terms for abandoning the often apparently hopeless scheme of reëstablishing the Netherlands in their ancient rights. "They well knew," afterward said the Prince, "that I would not for property nor for life, for wife nor for children, mix in my cup a single drop of the poison of treason."

265. The Count de Buren (see § 230) was still a prisoner in Spain— an alien not less from the faith and patriotism than from the home of his father. The second son, Maurice, though only eighteen years of age, was immediately named Stadtholder of Holland, Zealand, and Utrecht, and High Admiral of the Union.

The siege of Antwerp, continuing nearly a year, taxed all the consummate genius of the Prince of Parma, while its defense displayed not only the ability of Sainte Aldegonde, but the extraordinary valor and constancy of the citizens. Half a year was spent by the Spaniards in the construction of a fortified bridge or causeway below the city to cut off its connection with the maritime provinces. The besieged attempted in vain to destroy it by means of fire-ships, and, in seeking to open a new passage to the sea, they were defeated in a bloody battle fought upon the dykes. The city surrendered; its fortress was rebuilt from the ruins of private habitations; and with the entry of a foreign garrison and the Jesuits, "civilization and commerce departed." Where had been the banking center of all Europe, grass grew and cattle fed in the deserted streets; while thrift, intelligence, and industry sought other homes.

266. The queen of England, knowing herself to be the subject of a similar plot to that which had proved fatal to the Prince of Orange, now made a public alliance with the Hollanders, and sent men and money to their aid, justifying her conduct to the world by a state-paper in which she recited the iniquities of the Spanish government toward the Netherlands and its secret hostilities against herself. The States, in return, placed Flushing and Briel in her hands as security for the moneys expended, and conferred upon the Earl of Leicester, commander of the English forces, the title of Governor-General. The queen, who had herself repeatedly refused the sovereignty of the Netherlands when urged upon her by the States, was thrown into a tempest of wrath by the earl's acceptance of that dignity, and her sharp reprimand, read in the presence of the States-General, went far to undo all the advantage of the alliance, for it awakened strong suspicions — which, indeed, were not groundless — that she was secretly in correspondence with the king of Spain. On the other hand, Philip retaliated the queen's manifesto by seizing all English persons and property then in his dominions; and the Prince of Parma pressed hostilities in the Netherlands with redoubled vigor.

267. In September, Leicester besieged Zutphen, and in a skirmish before that place, Sir Philip Sidney, the most accomplished knight and gentlest spirit of his age, received a mortal wound. He had insisted on lending a portion of his armor to an older officer, who happened to be unprovided, and the exposure cost him his life. As he suffered from insupportable thirst, water was brought him, but at that moment he saw a wounded soldier carried by in his last agonies, who cast a longing eye upon the cup. "Take it, my friend," said Sidney, pushing it from his lips; "thy necessity is greater than mine." He died three weeks later at Arnheim. Leicester, finding at length that he had undertaken a task beyond his powers, returned to England at the end of the year 1587. The command-in-chief devolved upon Prince Maurice, Lord Willoughby having control only of the English troops.

268. One of the greatest of the popes, Sixtus V., had now succeeded to Gregory XIII. Bred in a Franciscan convent, Sixtus's mind had never been set free from the romantic dreams of youth by actual contact with the world; and he cherished designs of overthrowing the Turkish Empire, conquering Egypt, opening a maritime passage from the Mediterranean to the Red Sea, and transporting the Holy Sepulcher into Italy. Happily, more practicable schemes had their place in the mind of Sixtus. He improved the water supply of Rome, adorned it with new buildings, and exterminated the banditti, who, during the inefficient reign of his predecessor, had swarmed in the papal states. The number of cardinals, hitherto fluctuating with the avarice, ambition, or revenge of successive popes, was fixed by him at seventy, in memory of the elders who aided Moses with their counsels.

269. The execution of Queen Mary of Scotland at Fotheringay Castle (Feb., 1587) inflamed the enmity of Philip II. and the Pope against Elizabeth. The Spanish king, who had long meditated the conquest of

England as a stepping-stone to Holland, now proclaimed himself heir to the House of Lancaster and rightful sovereign of the former country. The depredations of Sir Francis Drake upon the Spanish possessions in America only heightened his resolution. San Domingo, Porto Rico, Santiago, Cartagena, and Florida had been plundered and ravaged. With his fleet of forty ships, Drake destroyed about a hundred Spanish vessels laden with military and naval stores under the very guns of Lisbon and Cadiz; and as another result of his enterprise, was able to report to his queen the preparations going on in the Spanish ports.

270. In May, 1588, the fleet of Philip, proudly called the *Invincible Armada*, sailed from Lisbon, and after a temporary dispersion in a storm, entered the English Channel. Her eyes once opened to the danger, the queen had made the most heroic exertions, and her spirit animated all her people. As soon as the appearance of the Armada was made known by a fishing-boat, which had been stationed to watch, Lord Howard of Effingham stood forth to meet it. No general engagement ensued, but seven days were spent in frequent skirmishes, in which the lighter English vessels had usually the advantage over the heavy and unmanageable Spaniards; while fire-ships drifted down with the tide into the midst of the Armada. The Duke of Parma, who had prepared a powerful fleet and army to coöperate, was blockaded in the Flemish harbors by the Dutch. Unable to retire to the southward, the Armada sailed through the German Ocean, designing to compass Scotland and Ireland and return by the Atlantic; but a tempest wrecked it among the Orkneys, and when the shattered remnants of his fleet had all arrived in Spain, Philip could count less than half the gallant armament which he had sent forth.

271. The next year the English retaliated by an invasion of Portugal, which, though it did not restore Don Antonio to the throne, gained possession of the suburbs of Lisbon, and of sixty Hanse vessels laden with supplies for a new armada. The Spaniards were discouraged from a fresh encounter with English bravery. In the Netherlands their movements were paralyzed by an exhausted treasury, for the soldiers of Parma were not only unpaid, but nearly starved, and the duke himself was soon ordered by Philip to lead his army into France, where a new state of affairs had been brought about by the accession of Henry IV. Prince Maurice, by his wise and victorious generalship, reunited the Seven Provinces, overran Flanders and Brabant, and established himself on the left banks of the Meuse and Scheldt. Alexander of Parma, to whose wonderful genius in war and state-craft Spain owed the preservation of the Flemish provinces, died in December, 1592; and was succeeded in the Governor-Generalship by the Archduke Ernest, brother of Matthias and son of Maximilian II.

WARS OF THE LEAGUE.

272. In France, the Eighth Religious War broke out in 1585, between the forces of the League on one side, and those of the King of Navarre, the Prince of Condé, and the Duke of Montmorency, on the other. Henry III., though nominally an ally of the League, dreaded its success even more than that of the Huguenots. The shallowness of his character was more than ever apparent; while his kingdom was torn with fierce dissensions, he was amusing himself with his dogs, monkeys, and parrots, or draining his already exhausted treasury by foolish and fantastic entertainments. Meanwhile Henry of Navarre gained a great victory over the royal troops at Coutras. A large German army was sent into France by John Casimir, the prince-palatine, but its leaders were surprised by the Duke of Guise in Anneau, and multitudes were killed. The exasperated peasantry joined with the duke in harassing their retreat and murdering all who fell into their hands.

273. The chiefs of the League had been forbidden to enter Paris. Guise came, nevertheless, and was received by the people with shouts of welcome. He had ever been the idol of the populace, and the city was now divided into two hostile camps, the Hotel de Guise being guarded by the mob as constantly as the Louvre by the royal troops. The advance of several thousands of Swiss mercenaries by the king's order, caused a general rising in the city, known as the "Day of the Barricades." The king escaped in terror to Chartres, and Guise, assuming dictatorial power, overawed the parliament, filled all military and civic appointments with his own people, and seized and fortified the towns in the neighborhood of Paris to prevent surprise. The revolutionary government thus established in the capital continued six years in force. Henry III. was compelled to sign, at Rouen, an Edict of Union, in which he granted all the demands of the League—among the rest an assembly of the States-General, which the duke intended should legalize his usurpation of power and place the king under his control.

274. But Henry had resolved to rid himself of this hated guardianship. Guise was summoned to the royal bed-chamber, and murdered by the guards in an anteroom. In the apartment beneath, Catherine de' Medici, the now aged queen-mother, lay dying. Henry hastened to her with the words, "Now, Madam, I am a king!" Startled by the folly, more, probably, than by the wickedness of his act, she was thrown into a state of anxiety which hastened her end. The Cardinal of Guise was murdered two days after his brother.

Dec., 1588.

275. Paris was in an uproar; the Sorbonne—the great ecclesiastical authority of the kingdom—declared the people released from their allegiance. The parliament, attempting to quiet the tumult, was imprisoned in the Bastile, only those members being subsequently released who promised to be the obedient tools of the Council of Sixteen. By this fragment of a parliament, the Duke of Mayenne, a brother of Guise, was appointed Lieutenant-General of the kingdom. Between the Huguenots in the south and the League in the north, the wretched king possessed only five or six towns on the Loire. The Guises refused to treat with him; the Pope summoned him to Rome to answer for having murdered a prince of the Church; his only refuge was in a treaty with Henry of Navarre. After a personal conference at Plessis-les-Tours, the two kings joined their forces for a siege of Paris. Terror increased the fanatical rage of the Parisians; and their priests declared that only the murder of one or both the kings could save religion. In this state of feeling, Jacques Clement, a Dominican monk, sought the camp of Henry of France, obtained an audience and stabbed the king. The assassin was immediately dispatched by the guards; his victim expired the following morning. With Henry III. ended the family of Valois, which had ruled France since 1328.

276. The House of Bourbon, descended from the second son of St. Louis, was now nearest to the throne. Its elder branch had been extinguished in the Constable de Bourbon, who died before Rome in 1527; the younger was represented by Henry of Navarre, to whom Henry III., in dying, had commended his army and his people. Five years of civil war preceded the establishment of Henry IV. in his kingdom. The obstacles to his accession seemed, indeed, insurmountable. He was a Huguenot; he had lately been allied with the murderer of the Duke of Guise, whose brother Mayenne was at the head of a numerous and well-appointed army. No fewer than eight claimants disputed the crown, of whom Philip II., the most powerful, possessed the ablest general and the most effective infantry in the world. He demanded to be named Protector of France in the right of his daughter, Clara Eugenia Isabella, who, by her mother's side, was a granddaughter of Henry II. To this end he recalled the Duke of Parma (§ 271), from the Netherlands in the summer of 1590 — a policy fatal to his own interests, but fortunate for the United Provinces, which were thus enabled to establish their independence.

277. Henry IV. had already gained two brilliant victories at Arques and Ivry over the Duke of Mayenne. He might have taken Paris by assault, but he refused to sacrifice the lives of his people. The king, who had already been twice a Catholic and twice a protestant, and probably had no very deep convictions in favor of either side, now resolved upon a change of his ecclesiastical relations, which promised to restore peace and harmony to his kingdom. He caused himself to be publicly "instructed" in the Romish faith; and on the 25th of July, 1593, he abjured protestantism and received the mass before a great assemblage in the cathedral of St. Denis. Two years later he was reconciled with the Pope. Rheims being in the possession of the League, he was crowned at Chartres, and was admitted into Paris the following month, by bribery of Brissac, the commandant. He lightly remarked that "so fair a city was well worth a mass!"

Feb., 1594.

278. The young Duke of Guise and the Duke of Lorraine made their peace, and in January, 1596, a treaty with Mayenne put an end to the League. Henry IV. had many of the qualities of a great prince; he could forgive and forget injuries, and his generous confidence was never narrowed by jealousy and resentment. Consequently, he was more faithfully served by men who had been his bitterest foes than are many kings by their life-long favorites and dependents. To reässure his Huguenot subjects, alarmed by his defection from their faith, Henry signed, in April, 1598, the celebrated Edict of Nantes, by which he guaranteed the unobstructed exercise of their religion. They were admitted, equally with Catholics, to all colleges, schools, and hospitals, and to all civil offices, without submitting to any oath or ceremony contrary to their consciences; and were permitted to publish religious books and found institutions of learning for their own exclusive patronage.

279. War was declared (Jan., 1595) between France and Spain; and Spanish armies entered France both from the north and the south. Cambray was surrendered, Oct. 2, and Calais taken by surprise in April, 1596. The queen of England, now fearing an invasion of her own dominion, hastened to make a treaty with the king of France, in which the Hollanders were included. A great English and Dutch armament fought an obstinate battle with the Spaniards in the harbor of Cadiz, resulting in victory to the allies and the destruction of thirty or forty Spanish merchantmen. The city and all its wealth was abandoned to the vic-

tors, and though they used their power with moderation, the fleet returned home with great spoil on board. A similar expedition the next year was defeated by a storm, but on the other hand, Philip II., who had raised a great *armada* for a second invasion of England, intending to place his favorite daughter upon the throne of Elizabeth, was thwarted by the same tempests. The English fleet, which had merely been driven back to port, then proceeded to the Azores, where it captured Fayal, Graciosa, and Flores, but failed to encounter the treasure-laden galleons from Spanish America, which had been the object of the enterprise.

280. The same year Prince Maurice gained a great victory over the Spaniards at Turnhout, chiefly by the then novel device of furnishing his cavalry with fire-arms. The town of Amiens, taken soon after by a stratagem of the Archduke Albert, was recaptured, in a siege of several months, by the forces of Henry IV. The king of Spain, now drained of resources, aged and infirm, consented to a peace with France, which the Pope had long been desirous of mediating, in order to direct the forces of Christendom against the heretics and the Turks. A treaty was signed at Vervins, by which the Spaniards restored all their conquests except the fortress of Cambray. In August May, 1598. of the same year the Infanta Isabella was acknowledged as sovereign of the Netherlands and Franche Comté. Albert of Austria, her destined consort, received an equal share in the government, and, to render their dignity identical, both were known as "the Archdukes."

281. Philip II. died in Spain, Sept. 13, 1598, closing a disastrous reign of forty-two years. No prince was ever born to more magnificent prospects. If his wisdom and justice had been equal to his diligence, his vast inheritance would have made him by far the greatest monarch in Christendom. But he crushed Spain, ruined Portugal, lost a great part of the Netherlands and drained the rest of their prosperity, and finally, with the wealth of the Indies at his disposal, died a bankrupt. His eldest son, Carlos, a youth of unhappy disposition, was driven to madness by his father's severity, and died in imprisonment. Philip III., the youngest and only surviving son, succeeded to the government of Spain, Portugal, the Two Sicilies and the Duchy of Milan.

282. Few events had taken place in Germany since the accession of Rudolph II. In consequence of his Spanish education and the continued influence of the Jesuits, he expelled all Lutherans from his hereditary dominions; and in Austria and Bavaria there ensued a strong reäction toward the ancient Church. The favorite studies of Rudolph were alchemy and astrology. By means of the latter, wiser men than he were encouraged to more reasonable researches; for the great astronomers, Kepler and Tycho Brahe, were successively entrusted with the superintendence of his observatory at Prague.

283. A singular event, which promised an extension of protestantism in Germany, really fixed more firmly the authority of Rome. The Arch-bishop elector of Cologne, wishing to marry the beautiful Agnes of Mans-feld, renounced the spiritual allegiance to which he owed his dignities, and openly adopted the Confession of Augsburg. He intended to secularize his province, as the Grand Master of the Teutonic Knights had already done; but Prince Ernest of Bavaria, his former rival for the appointment, was elected to succeed him; the protestant princes stood aloof, and the deposed elector spent the rest of his days in retirement at Strasbourg. For nearly two centuries the important see of Cologne was filled by members of the Bavarian family.

284. War between the Ottoman and German empires was begun by the defeat near Sissek of the Turkish governor of Bosnia, in June, 1593. Amurath III. immediately raised a great army, which captured Vesprim, but was in turn defeated by the Austrians. The next year Moldavia, Wal-lachia, and Transylvania revolted from the Turks, and allied themselves with the emperor. In his dismay, Amurath sent to Damascus for the holy

Jan., 1595.

standard which was supposed to insure victory over unbeliev-ers; but he died without having experienced its miraculous aid. His son, Mohammed III., secured his own succession with the usual barbarity of his race, by the murder of nineteen brothers. The campaign of 1595 was disastrous to the Turks. The Austrian army was ably com-manded by Count Mansfeld, who took the important town of Gran and received the submission of Wissegrad and Waitzen.

285. The next year Mohammed in person took the field. He captured Erlau, and, by a three days' battle at Keresztes, defeated the Christians, who lost 50,000 men, beside 100 guns and all their treasure. Terror seized Vienna and spread through Europe. But the Turks neglected to reap the fruits of their victory, and though the war continued ten years longer, its events were of too little importance to require detailed narration. The Ottoman dominion, though still among the most extensive that the world had seen, had passed the zenith of its power and had begun to decline.

Jan. 1, 1607.

The Peace of Sitvatorok was remarkable for the abatement it showed in the extravagant pretensions of the Porte. Ru-dolph II. was named with his full imperial titles instead of being slight-ingly alluded to as "King of Vienna;" and, in consideration of a large immediate payment, he was relieved of the degrading annual tribute hitherto exacted by the Turks. The territorial limits of the two empires remained nearly as in 1597.

286. At the end of the sixteenth century, France was the greatest, richest, and most populous kingdom in Europe, and Paris was, with the exception of Moscow, the largest capital. Venice had, even then, more inhabitants than London; but both Venice and Milan had for four centuries been stationary, if not declining. Under Elizabeth, England rose as rapidly in the scale of European powers as Spain, during the same period, declined. The persecutions in the Netherlands added almost as much to the wealth of Elizabeth's dominions as they detracted from those of Philip II. Weavers and other artisans were encouraged to settle in her cities on condition of taking one English apprentice each; and thus fine manufactures became permanently implanted in the country. Commerce was opened by special treaties with Turkey, Russia, and through the latter country with India, Persia, and Cathay or China. The Russia Company was incorporated by act of Parliament in 1566, the Turkey or Levant Company in 1581, and the far more important East India Company on the last day of 1600.

287. The Dutch Republic was already the chief maritime nation in Europe. Its prosperity had indeed been augmented by immigration from the still oppressed provinces to the southward; so that new towns had to be built or new streets added to the old ones, to accommodate the manufacturers and merchants from Brabant and Flanders. In the latter countries villages, and even towns, were depopulated; foxes, wolves, and wild boars prowled over the land once occupied by a thriving population; and during one year, 1586-7, two hundred persons were killed by wild beasts in the immediate neighborhood of Ghent. As their commercial marine increased, the Dutch planted trading stations in the remotest parts of the world — along the Asiatic coasts from Bassora in the Persian Gulf to Japan, and especially upon the island of Java, where Batavia became the metropolis of their eastern possessions.

RECAPITULATION.

Renewed wars of the League in France. Duke of Guise in possession of Paris. His assassination by order of Henry III. Death of Catherine de' Medici. Mayenne lieutenant-general. Murder of Henry III. and extinction of the Valois. Opposition to Henry IV. who, nevertheless, is victorious at Arques and Ivry, is crowned at Chartres, "buys Paris with a mass," and puts an end to the League. Edict of Nantes guarantees the rights of the Huguenots. War with Spain; victories of the Dutch and English. Peace of Vervins interrupts the long series of Franco-Spanish wars. Establishment of the "Archdukes" in the Spanish Netherlands. Death of Philip II. Superstitions of Rudolph II. Archbishop of Cologne, renouncing his connection with Rome, vainly attempts to hold his province as a secular principality. War with the Turks; the Christians mainly victorious during the first three years; terribly defeated at Keresztes, but favored by the Peace of Sitvatorok. Of the nations of Europe at close of 16th century, France most powerful; England rapidly rising, especially in commercial importance; Spain declining; Holland already the chief maritime power. Desolation of the Flemish provinces; increasing prosperity of the Dutch.

REIGN OF HENRY IV. IN FRANCE.

288. During the unworthy reign of the last of the Valois, France had almost fallen into chaos. Instead of the ancient feudal chiefs, a new class of nobles rivaled and opposed the crown. The heads of the League had been won by fortresses, governments, and money, and often assumed in their own territories powers exceeding those of the king himself. Multitudes of strong castles defied the royal authority. Manufactures had decayed; roads were so bad that merchandise could only be transported by long and circuitous routes, and so haunted by banditti that fraudulent debtors could always elude payment by pretending to have been robbed. Henry IV. and his wise and faithful minister, the Duke of Sully, set themselves to correct the abuses and to restore the prosperity of the country. The king in his own dress and equipage presented an example of moderation, and to avoid the extravagance and frivolous rivalries of a court, the nobles were recommended to live upon their estates. Manufactures were liberally fostered by the government, and the unrivaled fame of the French for the production of fine and curious fabrics dates from the reign of Henry IV. The revenues of the kingdom were doubled during the twelve years following his accession, while the public debt was diminished one-third.

289. By the Pope's dispensation, Henry dissolved his uncongenial marriage with Margaret of Valois, and married Marie de' Medici, daughter of the Grand-duke of Tuscany. A leading motive in his policy was hostility to the House of Austria; and the compactness of his dominion, and the consequent availability of his resources made him a formidable foe to the enfeebled power of Spain. In spite of the treaty of Vervins, which was outwardly observed, large sums of money and whole regiments of recruits passed from France to Holland. A formidable rebellion of the French nobles, fomented by the Duke of Savoy and the king of Spain, broke out during the year of the royal marriage. It was A. D. 1602. proposed to kill the king and make of France an elective monarchy like Germany, each of the great nobles becoming a sovereign prince in his own dominions. The chief mover was Maréchal Biron, the first of the Catholic peers who had attached himself to Henry IV., but whose ambition had not been satisfied by his elevation to a dukedom, a marshal's *bâton*, and the government of Burgundy.

290. Unconscious of the conspiracy at home, Henry declared war against Savoy and intrusted the conquest of La Bresse to the treacherous Biron. The king gained a speedy victory, and before the end of the year Charles Emanuel was compelled to buy peace with the cession of nearly all his territories west of the Alps. Biron, dismayed by the humiliation of his ally, made a full confession of his treason. The king generously pardoned him, and even intrusted him with several diplomatic missions; but Biron renewed his treasonable practices, was convicted and sentenced by the parliament of Paris, and beheaded, July, 1602.

The recall of the Jesuits in 1603, and the king's evident desire to stand well with the Pope, alienated the Huguenots. Their leader, the Duke of Bouillon, even made overtures to Spain. His capital, Sedan, was thereupon seized by the royal forces and occupied during four years. The king, however, either through natural leniency or the fear of offending the German protestant princes, pardoned the duke and reinstated him in all his offices and honors.

291. A favorite scheme of Henry IV., or rather, perhaps, of Sully, was the union of all the nations of Europe into a great Christian commonwealth, where minor differences of faith should be tolerated, all disputes settled by arbitration, and commerce freed from those vexatious restrictions which then paralyzed enterprise in the southern countries. This great confederation was to consist of fifteen states, divided into three groups, viz.: (1) Six Elective Monarchies, comprising the Empire, the States of the Church, Venice, Hungary, Bohemia, and Poland; (2) Six Hereditary Kingdoms—France, Spain, Great Britain, Denmark, Sweden, and Lombardy—the latter to be formed of the two duchies of Savoy and Milan; (3) Three Federal Republics, Switzerland, the Netherlands, and a confederation of Italian states. The Czar of Muscovy was considered as belonging, by his mode of government, rather to Asia than to Europe, but he was to be admitted to the commonwealth on his own application. If this scheme appears too visionary to be even detailed at such length, it was at least more noble than the plan of universal monarchy pursued by Charles V. and Philip II.—a monarchy based upon the suppression of all freedom of thought and enterprise.

292. A preliminary object with Henry was the humiliation of the House of Austria in all its branches. To this end he aided the protestants in Germany and Holland, recommended the Pope to add the two Sicilies to the States of the Church, and renouncing the French claims upon Italy, aimed to deliver the peninsula from all foreign dominion. He also intrigued with the oppressed Moriscoes; but the edict of Philip III., exiling them from Spain, defeated his plan of coöperation in a grand revolt. It is difficult to conceive the distress attending the forced emigration of an entire people. The export of gold from Spain was strictly prohibited, so that the greater part of their property was sacrificed in the removal. Of 130,000 who embarked for Africa, three-fourths perished of hunger and exhaustion; 100,000 sought refuge in France, but were permitted to remain only on condition of their professing the Catholic faith, which they had just rejected in their own country. While waiting for transportation, so many died and were thrown into the sea that the fishes were supposed to be poisoned. Philip III. had given the fatal blow to the prosperity of his dominions. Leagues of fertile fields, once rich in the olive and the vine, lay waste for want of tillage, and Spain never recovered the loss of the persecuted Moriscoes.

293. The Dutch Republic, extending and confirming its power, had, in the meantime, been able to inflict severe blows upon the Spanish dominion. Maurice of Nassau defeated the army of the "Archdukes" before Nieuport and captured from them 100 standards, with all their artillery and baggage. The siege of Ostend by Albert lasted nearly four years, and was attended by all the remarkable incidents of warfare in that amphibious country. A formidable assault of the Spaniards was defeated by the opening of the sluices and the drowning of a multitude of the assailants. The Spaniards were reinforced in 1602 by the celebrated Genoese general, Ambrose Spinola, and 8,000 men; while the Hollanders received from Queen Elizabeth 6,000 men, under Sir Francis Vere.

A. D. 1601–1604.

The great queen died before the siege was concluded, though she had lived to see the close of a rebellion in Ireland, which the Spaniards had fomented to withdraw her attention from the Netherlands. Her death was a severe loss to the protestants of Europe, to whom, in spite of her inconsistencies, she had been a powerful protectress. Her successor, James I., held, if possible, a still more obstinate belief in the divine right of hereditary monarchs, which made him look upon the Dutch as traitors and rebels. The siege of Ostend, which had cost the lives of 100,000 men, ended Sept. 20, 1604, with the surrender of the city. The Hollanders had partly consoled themselves before its fall by capturing Sluys and all the ships in its harbor.

294. A large party in Holland, headed by the Grand Pensionary, Olden Barneveldt, now desired peace, though all were agreed not to treat with Spain except upon a basis of the independence of the United Provinces. A truce of eight months on land was arranged in the spring of 1607, but the Dutch admiral Heemskirk was sent from Amsterdam with a formidable fleet to harass the coasts of Spain and Portugal, and protect Dutch ships returning from the Indies. He gained a great victory in the Bay of Gibraltar and destroyed almost the entire Spanish fleet. Both commanders were slain, but the Dutch fleet was scarcely injured, and was speedily able to intercept the treasure-ships and merchantmen from America. The king of Spain was compelled to beg a truce from the "Beggars of the Sea," but he refused to treat with them except as his subjects, and signed his agreement, "I, the king," without the Great Seal, which was indispensable in all treaties with foreign powers.

295. At length, by the mediation of France and England, a twelve years' truce was signed at Bergen-op-Zoom, ending forty years' war for the independence of the United Provinces. The possession of the Moluccas and the privilege of trade with both Indies was secured to the Dutch. Their home-boundaries were enlarged by the addition of all Dutch Flanders, of several important towns

April, 1609.

on the frontiers of Brabant, and by forts which gave them the command of the Scheldt. Forty years more elapsed before their independence was acknowledged by Spain, but it was virtually secured by the long struggle already so bravely maintained.

296. The emperor Rudolph II. had alienated most of his subjects by his gloomy bigotry. Bohemia was full of discontent; Moravia was in open revolt. Hungary and Austria were already under the government of Matthias, the heir-presumptive of his brother's dominions, who, by his German education, was more acceptable than Rudolph to the vast majority of the people. A revolutionary act signed in April, 1606, by the emperor's three brothers, Matthias, Albert, and Maximilian, and their cousins, Ferdinand and Leopold of Styria, declared Matthias to be the head of the House of Hapsburg in consequence of the alleged insanity of Rudolph. Two years were spent in fruitless negotiations before the brothers appealed to arms. Matthias marched a body of troops into Bohemia, and a treaty was signed near Prague which made him king of Hungary in full sovereignty and immediate possession; while, by the consent of the Bohemian estates, he was entitled King-elect of that country. The parliaments of both countries asserted their religious rights with great boldness, and in spite of long opposition, both sovereigns, Rudolph in Bohemia and Matthias in Hungary, were compelled to sign charters of complete and universal toleration.

297. In Styria and Bavaria, meanwhile, the counter-reformation was proceeding with great energy under Archduke Ferdinand and Duke Maximilian. They were cousins, had been educated together by the Jesuits, and were yet to be more conspicuously associated in the Thirty Years' War — that great contest which filled nearly the first half of the seventeenth century with blood and desolation. The aggression of Maximilian upon Donauwerth — a free imperial city, but anciently claimed by the dukes of Bavaria — led to an *Act of Union* between the chief protestant princes, joined eventually by fifteen cities A. D. 1608. and strengthened by an alliance with France in the Treaty of Halle, 1610. It was retaliated by the *Holy League*, which included the Catholic princes of the Circles of Bavaria and Suabia, and the three archbishop electors, subsequently aided by the Pope and the king of Spain.

298. The death, in 1609, of the Duke of Jüliers, Cleves, and Berg, who had no heir, precipitated the contest between the two religious parties. The emperor bestowed the reversion of the duchies on Christian II. of Saxony, but placed them under the immediate control of his cousin, Leopold of Styria. The Elector of Brandenburg and the Count-palatine of Neuburg, each of whom had married a sister of the deceased duke, took joint possession of the territories with the encouragement and aid of the king of France. The Dutch entered warmly into the affair, hoping to secure the ten remaining provinces of the Netherlands; the kings of England and Denmark declared themselves allies of the protestant princes.

299. The French king and his minister desired above all to wrest the imperial scepter from the House of Austria. Great preparations were made; Henry IV. was ready to march into the Netherlands at the head of 30,000 men. But on the eve of his intended departure,

May, 1610.

he was assassinated by a frantic Jesuit in a street of Paris. His queen, Marie de' Medici, was made regent, in the name and during the minority of her son, Louis XIII. The opposition of the nearest princes of the blood, Condé and his two uncles, was bought off for a time with the ample treasures collected by the murdered king for his wars. The Duke of Sully, though called to the Council-board by the queen-regent, encountered such resistance from the rapacious courtiers who hated his thrifty policy, that he retired in 1611, never to return to court. His remaining thirty years were spent upon his estates, and he lived to see some of his far-reaching plans executed by Richelieu, the famous cardinal and minister of Louis XIII.

300. The treaty of Halle was maintained by the new Council, and the lieutenant of the Archduke Leopold, after holding out several months in hope of profiting by the death of Henry IV., surrendered the city of Juliers, Sept. 4, 1610. The princes of Neuberg and Brandenburg held the disputed territories at first in common — the one holding court at Düsseldorf, the other at Cleves; but dissensions naturally arising from this double government, war broke out in 1621, during which the Spaniards on one side, and the Dutch on the other, made these lands their battle-field. Though two partition-treaties were signed, the question of ownership was not finally set at rest until 1815, when the "Cleve-Duchies" were secured by the Congress of Vienna to the House of Brandenburg, and became the nucleus of West Prussia. The elector-palatine, Frederic IV., died during the same month with the surrender of Juliers, and was succeeded by his minor son, Frederic V., a prince who is celebrated in German history chiefly for his misfortunes. He was educated at Sedan, the capital of the Duke of Bouillon — then, next to Geneva, the main stronghold of Calvinism. The Duke of Zweibräcken, his guardian, became a director of the Protestant Union.

301. In France the establishment of the new government was followed by a complete change of politics and a close alliance with Spain. The young king was married to Anne of Austria, Infanta of Spain, and his eldest sister to Philip, the heir of that monarchy. This alliance of the leading Catholic powers occasioned a closer consolidation of the protestant influence, and thus hastened the impending conflict. The policy of the court was to intimidate the Huguenots, who were too numerous to be won by gifts and pensions. They possessed 200 fortified places, numbered 4,000 of the nobility in their ranks, and could bring into the field an army of 25,000 men.

The queen-regent granted one demand of the Prince of Condé by summoning the States-General at Paris, A. D. 1614. This assembly was marked by the first appearance of Richelieu, the young Bishop of Luçon, as deputy from the clergy of Poitou, Fontenay, and Niort; and his eloquent speech in the interest of his order laid the foundation of his future favor at court. The Third Estate, or commons, having offended the queen, were ignominiously dismissed, and forbidden ever to meet again. Their next assembly, in 1789, was an immediate cause of the great revolution.

302. The councils of Marie de' Medici were controlled by her Italian favorite, Concini, and his wife Leonora. The former bore the title of Maréchal d'Ancre. Perceiving the talents of Richelieu, the marshal caused him to be named secretary of state, thinking thus to secure a useful instrument; but the bishop, as soon as he felt the ground firm beneath his feet, quarreled with Concini and separated from his party. A more dangerous enemy to the marshal was the Sieur de Luines, the king's falconer, a man of dull and insignificant mind, but of great influence with Louis. The king, now sixteen years of age, was beginning to act in resistance to the queen-mother; and the two parties at court were led respectively by the two favorites. Luines obtained a royal order for the arrest of the marshal, and caused him to be murdered on his way to the palace. The king, regarding the scene from a window, cried aloud, "Thank you, good friends! I am now a king!" He dismissed the Council appointed by the queen, and recalled his father's old ministers, except Sully. The queen was exiled to Blois; Leonora d'Ancre was tried for witchcraft and put to death. The new Council, like the old, favored the House of Austria, and its policy hastened the religious war in Germany.

April, 1617.

303. The unhappy disputes of sectaries, which had already so weakened and compromised the Reformation, were renewed in Holland between the Calvinists and the new sect of Arminians. The latter included many of the best minds in the States, among others the noble patriot and Grand Pensionary, Olden Barneveldt, and Hugo Grotius, the celebrated jurist. The worst blot on the record of Maurice of Nassau is his agency in the death of Barneveldt. They belonged to opposite political parties; the aged statesman apprehended danger to his country from the soaring ambition of the young prince. No man, except William of Orange, had done so much for the freedom of Holland as Olden Barneveldt. The Calvinistic Synod of Dort condemned the Arminians without a hearing, and banished or deposed their pastors. Barneveldt and Grotius were arraigned before a council of their enemies and condemned — the one to death, the other to perpetual imprisonment. Barneveldt scorned to ask his life from

M. H.—16.

the son of his old friend; Maurice, who could have saved it, would not interfere; and Barneveldt was beheaded, May 14, 1619.

RECAPITULATION.

Henry IV. remedies the disorders and promotes the prosperity of France; marries Marie de' Medici; is a constant foe to the House of Austria; defeats the Duke of Savoy, and the rebellions of Biron and Bouillon. Great scheme of Henry for the union and pacification of Europe. Final expulsion of the Moriscoes from Spain. Victories of the Dutch; fall of Ostend, capture of Sluys. Death of Elizabeth. Peace of Bergen-op-Zoom secures important benefits to Holland.

Discontent in the dominions of Rudolph II.; Matthias is acknowledged chief of the House of Austria. Counter-reformation in Styria and Bavaria. Protestant "Act of Union," and "Holy League" of German Catholic nobles. War for the Cleve-Duchies involves not only Germany, but Holland, France, England, and Denmark. Assassination of Henry IV.; regency of Marie de' Medici; retirement of Sully. Fall of Jüliers. Accession of Frederic V., elector-palatine. Close alliance of France and Spain. States-General summoned in France; rise of Richelieu. Rival parties in the French court; murder of Concini; banishment of Marie de' Medici. Religious dissensions in Holland; execution of Olden Barneveldt.

The Thirty Years' War.

304. The weak and incompetent Rudolph II. died early in 1612, and his brother Matthias, already crowned king of Hungary and Bohemia, became emperor in his place. The alliance of Holland with the Protestant Union of Germany made the latter far stronger than the Holy League, which was, indeed, paralyzed by divisions in the imperial family and by the withdrawal of the three archbishop electors. Instead of the Jesuits, who had ruled Rudolph II., Cardinal Klesel now controlled the court; while the new emperor contented neither party, but was regarded with increasing distrust by all. The dispute concerning the Cleve-Duchies has already been described. Still more serious disturbances occurred in Bohemia. The imperial line of the House of Hapsburg had so evidently fallen into decay, that the brothers of Matthias resigned all claim to the succession; and their cousin, the able and ambitious Ferdinand of Styria, was crowned in Bohemia, with the consent of the king of Spain.

305. A formidable revolt was organized by Count Thurn, who summarily dismissed the council of King Ferdinand by throwing its three most obnoxious members from a window of the Castle of Prague. A new government of thirty directors was then organized, and a movement was made toward alliance with the protestant party in Austria, Hungary, and Germany. Count Mansfeld was sent to its aid by the young elector-palatine, and laid the foundation of his great military fame by the capture of Pilsen, one of the three towns which alone remained to Ferdinand. The two armies raised by the latter were both defeated by Count Thurn, and the one commanded by the Flemish general Buequoi was pursued into Austria and deprived of all its plunder. The Austrians refused to arm in the emperor's service, or even to permit his reinforcements to pass through their territories.

306. Matthias died suddenly in 1619, and Ferdinand succeeded to all his dominions. In the war which followed his accession, Albert von Wallenstein, the greatest general of the age, first emerged into distinction. He was Bohemian by birth but German by descent, and had been educated at Padua, then one of the most renowned universities of Europe. Here he became imbued with that belief in the mystical science of the stars, which exercised so great an influence over his subsequent career. The army of Thurn, after the death of Matthias, overran Moravia, and, entering Austria, appeared before the walls of Vienna, where Ferdinand II. was surrounded by all the chief estates of his dominions.

The moment was critical; with prompt resolution the city might have been taken, and the supremacy of the House of Hapsburg destroyed. But a detachment from the army of Dampierre succeeded in penetrating the capital with aid to the emperor, while Thurn was recalled by the news that Bucquoi, having conquered Mansfeld, was threatening Prague. The imperial election of Ferdinand had just been accomplished at Frankfort, when news arrived that the Bohemian nation had cast off its allegiance to him and had chosen Frederic, the elector-palatine, to be its king. Against the warnings of his wisest friends, including the whole electoral college, Frederic accepted the dangerous promotion — moved chiefly by the persuasions of his former tutor, Prince Christian of Anhalt, and of his wife, the English princess Elizabeth, who declared that she would rather starve at the table of a king than feast at that of an elector. He was crowned at Prague Nov. 4, 1619.

307. But the friends of Frederic were few, and absorbed in their own affairs. His father-in-law, King James of England, was weak, vacillating, and disinclined to war. Prince Maurice of Nassau, though the most determined foe of the House of Austria, was wholly occupied with the government of Holland. Bethlem Gabor, Waywode of Transylvania, though at first the most active of the protestant allies, soon made a separate truce with the emperor. Vienna was a second time besieged by a Bohemian and Transylvanian army of 80,000 men; but want of supplies compelled them to retire, after 2,000 had died of actual starvation.

Dec., 1619.

308. Frederic, by his lack of energy and dignity, proved his own worst enemy. He allowed his favorite court-chaplain to offend the religious preferences of the Bohemians in the rudest manner; while their army was no less incensed by seeing its own able leaders, counts Thurn and Mansfeld, outranked by Christian of Anhalt and Count Hohenlohe, who had accompanied the king from Heidelberg. On the other hand, Spain, the Jesuits, and the German League, were working actively for Ferdinand II. By French mediation, a treaty was concluded at Ulm between the *League* and the *Union*, which, in the war for Bohemia, gave all the advantage to the former. Peace was concluded between all the German states, but both parties permitted the passage of troops across their territories into Bohemia; and as the "Archdukes" of the Netherlands were not included in the peace, nothing prevented their Spanish forces from invading the Palatinate.

309. In August, 1620, Maximilian of Bavaria, at the head of the army of the League, entered Bohemia, and was joined by Count Bucquoi; their united armies then numbered 32,000 men, who were opposed by scarcely more than 20,000 on the part of Frederic. Next in command to Maximilian was Count Tilly, a ferocious character, whose fame among the German leaders is only second to that of Wallenstein. The Spaniards, under Spinola, were, meanwhile, ravaging the borders of the Rhine; the elector of Saxony, by occupying Lusatia for the emperor, cut off Frederic's hope of relief from that quarter; and the king of Poland sent 8,000 Cossacks to reinforce the imperial army. With firmness and good management, Frederic might even yet have saved his kingdom; but Mansfeld, his best general, was alienated by ill treatment, and the attack of the imperialists upon the forces under the Prince of Anhalt, at Weisse

Nov., 1620. Berg near Prague, resulted in a sudden and complete rout. All was lost; the king and queen could neither trust the Bohemians whom they had offended, nor return to their rightful sovereignty, the Palatinate, which they had so rashly abandoned in grasping at a higher dignity. Forced to flee from Prague, they took refuge in Silesia, and afterward in Holland.

310. Ferdinand II., now established in all his dominions, avenged his insulted dignity with great and wanton severity. Not only were all protestant teachers banished from Bohemia, and all acts of toleration revoked, but the people were insulted by the demolition of the tombs and burning of the bones of the reformers. Thirty thousand families emigrated from the kingdom; but multitudes held fast in secret their reformed faith; and when, after the lapse of 150 years, religious freedom was at length proclaimed, the government was surprised by the number who declared themselves protestants. In Upper and Lower Austria all dissent from the established worship was suppressed by similar means.

311. The two years' war for the Palatinate was ended with its conquest by Tilly, and its transfer, with the electoral title, to Maximilian of Bavaria. The Heidelberg library, then among the richest in Europe for its rare collection of MSS., was partly used instead of straw to stable the horses of Tilly's cavalry; but a part was sent by Maximilian to the Pope, and for 200 years was known among the treasures of the Vatican as the Palatine Library.

During the same years war had been raging between Turkey and Poland. The Poles were defeated with great loss at Jassy, in Moldavia, Sept., 1620; but the young sultan, Othman II., *A. D. 1620-1622.* presuming on this victory to attempt the conquest of Poland, lost the next year, 80,000 men in an unsuccessful battle and a disastrous campaign. He was murdered by his Janizaries at the age of eighteen, after a reign of four years, 1622. His imbecile uncle, Mustapha, was dragged from a dungeon to be placed upon the throne; but he was replaced in a year by Amurath IV., a younger brother of Othman.

312. It is time for a view of the northern kingdoms, which, from their slowly dawning civilization, had hitherto exerted little influence, and formed no part of the States-System of central and southern Europe. Near the close of the fourteenth century, Denmark, Sweden, and Norway, were joined by the Union of Calmar under *A. D. 1397.* the sway of Margaret Waldemar. Each kingdom continued to be governed by its own laws, but all united in the choice of one sovereign, and for the common defense. Eric, the grand-nephew and successor of Margaret, lost his kingdoms after a turbulent reign of 27 years, and ended his life as a pirate. After nearly twenty years' separation, Christian of Oldenburg reünited the three realms, and added to them Schleswig and Holstein, which he had inherited from an *A. D. 1457.* uncle. He was succeeded by his son John, who, though acknowledged in Sweden, never really ruled that country, for its government was administered by native nobles.

313. Christian II., the son of John, married a sister of the emperor Charles V., and made extensive alliances with other European powers, with a view to the conquest of Sweden. He obtained possession of Stockholm (Oct., 1520), and was acknowledged king under the terms of the Union of Calmar; but he treated his now reconciled and obedient subjects with a barbarity which well earned him the title, "The Nero of the North." Eighty or a hundred citizens were beheaded without trial in the market-place at Stockholm; and the city was given up to the rage and covetousness of his soldiery, as if it had been taken by assault. These crimes worked their own retribution by rousing in the people a spirit of revenge, which ultimately drove Christian from his throne.

314. The revolt in Sweden was led by Gustavus Vasa, a young nobleman whose father had been beheaded at Stockholm. He himself had been given, with four others, as hostages for the safe return of Christian to his ships, after a battle which he lost at Bränkirka, in one of his early and vain attempts upon the kingdom. Contrary to his agreement, Christian no sooner found himself in safety than he sailed away with his hostages and kept them as prisoners in Denmark. Gustavus escaped in 1519, disguised as an ox-driver, and hid himself among the peasants of Dalecarlia, wearing their coarse apparel and working with them for daily wages. At length by a secret intelligence among the patriots of Sweden, an army of 5,000 men was raised, and Gustavus was placed at its head. The Hanse-towns, which had been injured by the commercial policy of Christian II., declared for the Swedes and ravaged the Danish islands. Denmark now discarded Christian II., and accepted as its king his uncle, Frederic I. The Union of Calmar was dissolved. Stockholm surrendered to Gustavus Vasa, after a two years' siege, and he was elected king by the Swedish Diet. He favored the Lutheran reformation; and the change of state-religion was quietly effected by the Diet in 1527. Convents were broken up, and the incomes of the bishoprics, which happened to be all vacant but two, were either distributed among the nobles or applied to public uses.

A. D. 1523.

315. The exiled king, Christian II., at length raised an army of nearly 10,000 men in the Netherlands, and invaded Norway in 1531. He was besieged at Opslo by a Danish fleet and a Swedish army; and having consented to be conveyed to Denmark in order to treat in person with his uncle, he was there condemned to perpetual imprisonment, in which state he passed the remaining twenty-six years of his life. Frederic I. was succeeded, in 1534, by his son Christian III., who made good his claim against the Count of Oldenburg with the aid of the king of Sweden. His son, Frederic II., was elected during his father's life-time, and succeeded peaceably to the throne of Denmark and Norway in 1559. His long and prosperous reign of 41 years was celebrated by the progress of arts and sciences, which now first found a congenial home in Denmark. His favorite astronomer, Tycho Brahe, founded an observatory at Uranienborg, which has rendered illustrious service to the science of the stars.

316. Gustavus Vasa, after raising Sweden to great prosperity, died in 1560; and — the kingdom having been made hereditary in his line — was succeeded by his son, Eric IV. This prince being subject to fits of insanity, his three younger brothers, John, Magnus, and Charles, were associated in the government. The first of these obtained the crown and kept Eric in prison, until, at the end of eight years, he caused him to be poisoned. Denmark, at this time, possessed the whole of Norway and the seven southern provinces of Sweden. John, by the treaty of Stettin, recognized the right of Frederic II. to these territories.

A. D. 1569.

317. The Swedish king had married Catherine, heiress of the ancient Polish family of Jagellon, and in 1587 their son Sigismund was elected king of Poland. This vast kingdom possessed no power proportional to its territorial extent; for the yet unsettled conflict between the elective and hereditary principles in its monarchy, the violent feuds of its great nobles, and the lingering traces of its late barbaric condition kept it a continual prey to civil wars. At the death of John III. in 1592, his brother Charles became the rival of Sigismund as a candidate for the Swedish crown. He was supported by strong motives both of civil and religious policy; for the Polish king, like his mother, was under the control of the Jesuits; and, moreover, the Swedes as well as the Poles, required their sovereign to live constantly among them. The dispute of many years resulted in the establishment of Charles IX. as king-elect, and his son Gustavus Adolphus as Crown Prince A. D. 1604. of Sweden. The latter served his apprenticeship in the art of war in a contest with the young Danish king, Christian IV., which began a few months before the death of King Charles. The Swede was to become not only a master in military science, but the inventor of a new system of army organization, which in time superseded the closely serried ranks of the Swiss pikemen and the Spanish lancers.

318. Several causes of complaint had existed between the two kings for years—among the rest, that each bore three crowns upon his shield. Christian IV., at the age of twenty-five, was a successful and powerful monarch. His diligent attention to business, and his personal intelligence in all matters pertaining to the interests of his kingdom, afforded a pleasing contrast to the frivolous character of the kings who, at that time, filled most of the European thrones. Gustavus Adolphus had been no less thoroughly trained to the duties of his station. Becoming king in the autumn of 1611, when not quite seventeen years of age, he chose for his chief minister Axel Oxenstierna, a man of profound wisdom and good judgment, the model of a statesman and diplomatist, and for a long series of years the prime mover in Swedish affairs.

319. The war with the Danes was ended (Jan., 1613) by the mediation of England, but another conflict with Russia had already broken out. The line of Rurie (see Book I, § 93) had become extinct, and a party in the kingdom desired to place a brother of Gustavus upon the vacant throne. Some advantages were gained by the Swedes, but a majority of the Russians succeeded in maintaining the right of Michael Romanoff, ancestor of the present imperial family. By the Peace of Stolbova, the ground where St. Petersburg now stands was A. D. 1617. included in the territory of Sweden. A third war of nine years with Poland now demanded the attention of Gustavus Adolphus. It resulted in a gain to Sweden of some important towns; but of more value were the discipline and experience which enabled the young king to assume his place as the great leader of the protestant armies in the Thirty Years' War.

RECAPITULATION.

Matthias succeeds Rudolph II. as emperor, but the power of the Hapsburgs is soon transferred to the Styrian branch of the family. Ferdinand II. crowned successively in Bohemia, Hungary, and the Empire. Bohemia revolts, and chooses Frederic V., elector-palatine, to be its king. Vienna twice besieged by insurgent armies. By Pacification of Ulm, the German states secure their own peace and leave Bohemia to its fate. Decisive victory of the imperialists at Weisse Berg, near Prague. Frederic loses both kingdom and palatinate, the latter being conferred upon Maximilian of Bavaria. Suppression of religious rights by Ferdinand II. The three Scandinavian kingdoms usually under one crown, from A. D. 1397 to 1523, when Gustavus Vasa becomes king of Sweden, Frederic I. of Denmark and Norway. Reformed religion established in all three kingdoms. Frederic II. of Denmark patronizes astronomical science. Sweden united for a time with Poland under Sigismund II., but his uncle, Charles IX., gains the former kingdom. His son, Gustavus Adolphus becomes a great general by early experience of war and is chosen by the German protestants to be their leader.

AFFAIRS OF FRANCE.

320. A dispute arose, A. D. 1620, between France and Spain concerning the Valtelline territory in northern Italy. This long and narrow valley, watered by the Adda, and reaching from Lake Como to the borders of the Tyrol, was anciently a possession of the dukes of Milan, but had been ceded by the last of the Sforzas to the Swiss Grisons. It was now of great importance to the Spaniards during the wars in Germany, as affording a passage into that country from the Milanese. The people of the district, being Catholics, resented the sway of the protestant Swiss. In July, 1620, they rose against their rulers, massacred all who fell into their power, and called upon the neighboring Spaniards to protect them. The latter sent troops to seize all the fortresses in the valley. The French government demanded their evacuation from the court of Madrid, and a treaty to that effect was signed the following spring, but never executed. The insignificant king, Philip III., died in March, 1621, and was succeeded by his son Philip IV., then sixteen years of age. The death of Paul V., a month or two before, had transferred the papal crown to the head of Gregory XV., who wore it only two years.

321. Richelieu became cardinal in 1622, but his reign in France began two years later with his appointment in the royal Council. In spite of some personal weaknesses of character, he was the ablest statesman whom France has produced. His clear and well defined policy coincided in some points with that of Henry IV. and Sully, especially in his unrelenting hostility to the House of Austria. With this motive, he favored the Protestants of England, Holland, and Germany, though he made war upon those of France. For his injurious treatment of the latter, reason may be found in the second great principle of his policy, namely, the consolidation of royal power and suppression of the feudal aristocracy. The chiefs of the Huguenots, it has been seen, affected to act as sovereign princes in their own dominions; they coined money, held courts, and inflicted penalties without reference to the royal tribunals; and it was not until Richelieu's administration that the long struggle between the king and the nobles, begun in the earliest days of the Capets, ended in the absolute supremacy of the king, or rather, in the present case, of his prime minister. The death-blow of feudal tyranny and private wars was given by the destruction of all castles and fortresses not upon the frontiers, or otherwise needful for the general protection.

322. Among his first measures were a new alliance with Holland, whose twelve years' truce with Spain had but recently expired; a marriage of Henrietta Maria, youngest sister of the king, with Charles Stuart, heir of the English crown; and an interference to wrest the Valtelline from the Spaniards, or rather from the Pope (now Urban VIII., 1623–1644), who held that territory for them. A combined army of Swiss and French entered the valley and quickly drove out the Nov., 1624. papal troops. Genoa, the faithful ally of Spain, was the next object of attack; but at this moment a fresh insurrection of the Huguenots called off the Dutch naval forces in alliance with France to a siege of the Isle of Ré, which guards the harbor of Rochelle.

323. With consummate art, Richelieu disengaged himself from a knot of perplexities. He used the English influence to pacify the Huguenots; he ratified a treaty with Spain by which the affairs of the Valtelline were restored to nearly the condition in which they had been before the invasion of 1620; he consoled the Duke of Savoy, who had coveted the disputed territory, with the hope of a royal title, and conciliated the English, who were reasonably offended by being made tools in matters with which they had no interest, with the promise of a large French army to aid in restoring the elector Frederic to his lost Palatinate.

324. Friendly relations did not long continue between England and France. Charles I. became king by the sudden death of his father in March, 1625; and his marriage with the princess Henrietta Maria was celebrated by proxy at Paris a few weeks later. By the terms of the treaty, the queen was accompanied to England by her own clergy; but these, instead of confining themselves to the duties of their office, destroyed by their intrigues the peace of the court. By their advice and in their company the queen made a pious pilgrimage to Tyburn, where, indeed, some Catholics had suffered martyrdom in the time of Henry VIII., but which was now the place of execution for the lowest criminals. In consequence of this undignified proceeding, all the French attendants of Henrietta Maria were dismissed from the kingdom. The French court apologized for their conduct, and Charles thereupon permitted twelve French priests and a bishop to be attached to his wife's household.

325. But hostile movements had gone too far to be arrested. The Duke of Buckingham, a favorite of Charles I., was sent with a great fleet to capture the forts upon the Isle of Ré, then in the hands of the besiegers. He proved himself no less contemptible as a general than as a man, and the only result of his ill-starred expedition was to hasten the reduction of Rochelle, long contemplated by Richelieu. This remarkable prelate and statesman now discovered the highest qualities of generalship. Across the inlet to the harbor he constructed a mole, which he fortified with strong earthworks and cannon, cutting off all access from the sea, while a besieging army equally prevented the entrance of supplies by land. The starving citizens saw two English fleets approach for their relief, and, after ineffectually cannonading the mole, disappear in the offing. Upon the second of these disappointments, the town surrendered, and the king entered in triumph. The victory Nov. 1, 1628. was used with moderation. Richelieu had previously declared that the time of martyrdom for conscience was past, and that his Majesty waged war, not with Huguenots, but with rebels. As an insurgent city, Rochelle was deprived of its political privileges, but the people were confirmed in the free exercise of their religion. The fall of Montauban in August of the next year, completed the extinction of the Huguenots as a party in the state.

326. Prince Maurice of Nassau died in April, 1625. He was succeeded as Captain General of the United Provinces by his brother Frederic Henry, who was also elected Stadtholder of Holland, Zealand, and West Friesland. About the same time King Christian IV. of Denmark entered into the wars of Germany by accepting an appointment as military chief of the Circle of Lower Saxony, and marching an army from the Elbe to the Weser. He was defeated by Tilly near Hanover, and the first campaign was decidedly in favor of the imperialists. In the spring of 1626, Wallenstein, now Duke of Friedland and a prince of the Empire, marched into the north with an army which he avowedly supported by plunder or by billeting it in free quarters upon the people. Fortunately a jealousy between Wallenstein and Tilly prevented their acting in concert. The former, turning to the east, pursued Count Mansfeld, while the latter captured Münden in Hanover, prevented the junction of the Danish king with the Saxon dukes, and finally defeated him with great loss at Lutter.

327. The next spring, Wallenstein again advanced northward, his freebooting army preceded and accompanied by bands of gypsies, who concealed themselves in the woods and plundered farms and houses as they had opportunity. The king of Denmark was forced to retreat into his own dominions, and even to abandon Schleswig, Holstein, and Jutland to the two imperial armies. Gustavus Adolphus of Sweden, still engaged in his war with Poland, could render little assistance except by preventing that country from sending aid to the imperialists. Wallenstein greatly respected his talents, and tried to draw him into a treaty for the partition of the Danish dominions; Sweden to gain Norway and the

province of Schonen, while either the emperor or Wallenstein himself would receive Denmark, with the control of the Baltic Sea. Gustavus rejected his overtures, and joined Christian IV. in aiding Stralsund when besieged by the imperial forces. The failure of this siege was a check upon the victorious career of Wallenstein, who was forced to withdraw with a loss of nearly half his army. Tilly was at the same time weakened by the detachment of troops to Italy, and Christian IV. was able to drive him successively from Jutland, Holstein, and Schleswig. The treaty of Lubec, May, 1629, restored peace between Denmark and the Empire. Christian abandoned his late allies, and engaged to take no part in German affairs except in his quality as Duke of Holstein.

A. D. 1628.

328. Among the most difficult questions raised by the Reformation in Germany was that which related to ecclesiastical property. Much of this had been bestowed, centuries ago, under conditions of tribute and obedience to the Roman Church. On the other hand, protestant sovereigns, as well as the heirs and descendants of donors, claimed their right to control the disposition of benefices. The imperial Edict of Restitution, enacted by Ferdinand II. in 1629, deprived Protestants of all church property of which they had become possessed since the Peace of Passau. Two of the most important bishoprics so held — those of Halberstadt and Magdeburg — were bestowed upon the emperor's brother, who already held a plurality of sees. In many protestant cities the churches were closed, and even private worship forbidden. So vast were the financial interests involved, that the Edict, if enforced, would have destroyed all commercial security in the Empire.

329. At this juncture the German princes were singularly lacking in spirit and patriotism. The true champion both of civil and religious rights was the king of Sweden, who, with the secret aid of France, now appeared as a principal actor upon the scene. Richelieu, who held the balance of European affairs, gladly saw the imperial power weakened by the religious dissensions in Germany, though his position as cardinal and minister of a Catholic king prevented his making open war in the protestant interests. He had, however, negotiated the truce between Sweden and Poland which set Gustavus Adolphus free to prosecute his designs in the Empire; and he urged upon that sovereign the subsidies and close alliance of the French court. These were at first rejected, but a few months later a treaty was signed at Beerwald in Neumark, binding the two powers for five years to mutual aid and coöperation. The most prudent of the Swedish Council admitted the necessity of the war. Late movements of Wallenstein toward the supreme control of the Baltic, threatened their commerce, while the support rendered to Sigismund of Poland in his claim to the crown of Sweden, and the contemptuous and even violent exclusion of Swedish embassadors from the Congress of Lubec, were flagrant insults to their king.

330. Thus convinced of the justice of his cause, Gustavus "set his house in order like a dying man." Intrusting the government to a Council of Regency, and commending his daughter and heiress, Christina, then but four years old, to the care and fidelity of the estates, he set sail from Sweden, which he was never again to behold, and landed, June 24, on the island of Rugen in Pomerania. The moment was favorable to the invasion. The Diet at Ratisbon had just secured

A. D. 1630.

the dismissal of Wallenstein, whose brutal tyrannies and extortions had exhausted the patience even of his own party, while his ascendency over the emperor enraged the Duke of Bavaria, and his haughty assumption of sovereign state offended all the princes of the League.

Most of his officers quitted the imperial service upon the retirement of their chief, and Tilly, who succeeded him in command, found the army diminished even more in effective force than in numbers. Still the arrival of the Swedes attracted little attention in Vienna, where it was predicted that the "Snow-King" would never dare venture far from his own frozen dominions. But while the courtiers mocked, Gustavus advanced, the fortresses of Pomerania and Mecklenburg falling, one after another, into his possession. In vain the imperial generals laid waste the whole country, even burning towns and villages to prevent their affording shelter and support to the Swedes. The perfect order and discipline of the latter won the hearts of the people, who were surprised to find all their rights respected by the invading army.

331. The electors of Saxony and Brandenburg declined the Swedish king's proposal of coöperation, and even resisted his progress. The former claimed by hereditary right the leadership of the German Protestants— a post which he had not the ability to maintain; while the latter, though a brother-in-law of the Swedish king, was actuated more by jealousy and cowardice than by an enlightened regard to the interests of his people. Thus unsupported by the princes of northern Germany, Gustavus was reluctantly compelled to leave the important city of Magdeburg to its fate. This ancient seat of an archbishopric had become one of the first and firmest strongholds of the Reformation under princes of the House of Brandenburg. Its magistrates had resisted the Edict of Restitution and the investiture of Leopold of Styria, (§§ 316, 328) and in 1629 the walls had sustained a seven months' bombardment by the imperial army. It was now besieged anew by Tilly, and upon its capture thirty thousand citizens were massacred. Hordes of savage Croats and not less brutal Walloons were let loose upon the miserable inhabitants; and their ravages were only interrupted by the smoke and flames, which in a brief time consumed the entire city, except the Cathedral and a few houses in its neighborhood.

332. Both armies being largely reinforced, Tilly with 150,000 men, marched into Saxony, ravaging and plundering with his usual ferocity. When the elector heard that two hundred of his villages were in flames, he was at length willing to ally himself with Gustavus Adolphus, whom he joined with 18,000 men. The battle of Leipzig, which immediately followed, resulted in a brilliant victory to the Swedes, while it revealed the long hidden decline of the Austrian power. Sept. 7, 1631. So complete was the rout of the imperialists, that scarcely two thousand could be rallied for the retreat to Halle; and all their guns remained to the victor. Germany was at the mercy of Gustavus; nothing impeded his march to Vienna, and he might apparently have ended the war by striking directly at the heart of his foe. But he had higher views than conquest, and believed that he could better secure the religious freedom of the Empire by entering the territories of the League, where, in every state, a minority were still struggling for the rights of conscience. Leaving the conquest of Bohemia to the elector of Saxony, he took the road through Franconia to the Rhine. All the important towns and fortresses were taken, in scarcely more time than would have been required for an ordinary tour of pleasure. Many of them gladly opened their gates and welcomed the invader as a deliverer.

333. The Spanish garrison of Mentz surrendered Dec. 13, and that town became the Swedish head-quarters. At Christmas, the "Snow-King" was firmly established on the Rhine, attended by his queen, his chancellor, and a brilliant court of princes and embassadors. But his unexpected approach to the French frontier had alarmed the suspicions of Louis XIII., while Richelieu began to fear the decline of his own influence in the Empire. The elector of Trêves, declining the Swedish protection, admitted a French garrison into Ehrenbreitstein, ceding to that nation a coveted foothold on the Rhine, which was not soon relinquished. Having driven all the Spaniards from the Palatinate, Gustavus returned into Franconia. Nuremberg received him with acclamations of joy as the protector of German liberty. Thence marching to the Danube, he captured Donauwerth, and pursued the imperial army to the Lech, which alone separated him from Bavaria.

The river, though narrow, was deep, rapid, and now swollen by the melting of the winter snows. Tilly occupied a strongly fortified camp on the Bavarian side; the Swedish council of war declared his position too strong to be attacked, but the king, who had personally reconnoitered the whole region, had his own plan of operations, which proved eminently successful. Placing his artillery at a bend of the river where the height of the bank gave him a great advantage over the imperialists, he ordered a tremendous cannonade upon the enemy's camp. Under cover of the smoke and noise, he then caused a bridge to be constructed, while the Bavarians were kept from interfering by the terrible precision with which the Swedish guns swept the opposite bank. Tilly received a mortal wound, and Maximilian, abandoning the defense of his frontier, retired to Ingolstadt.

334. The humiliated emperor was compelled to recall Wallenstein. That general, who had been secretly aiding the Saxon conquest of Bohemia for the sake of forcing this very necessity upon his ungrateful master, now feigned a haughty reluctance, and finally consented to serve only upon conditions which were both injurious and insulting to the emperor. He demanded to be absolute Dictator; no prince of the House of Austria was to be with the army, no appointments made, and no orders given by Ferdinand; all confiscated estates were to be at the disposal of Wallenstein. Revenge and ambition had made him a traitor; and he accepted the imperial commission only as a stepping-stone to sovereignty.

335. The magic of his name drew together a powerful army, and Bohemia was speedily reconquered; but the Swedish king had meanwhile entered Augsburg and received the homage of its citizens, then pressed on and occupied the Bavarian capital. In vain the emperor begged a few regiments to relieve Bavaria and thus avert danger from Austria itself. Wallenstein could not forego the opportunity of revenge upon his bitterest enemy. At last he consented to a formal reconciliation with Maximilian, and adding the Bavarian forces to his own — for he still insisted upon the undivided authority — he followed Gustavus to Nuremberg, and fortified a camp within a few miles of the Swedish lines. Nine weeks the two armies which held in their hands the destinies of Germany, remained facing each other, while hunger and pestilence waged, with both, a more destructive warfare than the sword. At length the Swedish king, failing to draw his enemy into a battle on equal ground, stormed his intrenchments and was repulsed with a loss of several thousands of men. He soon withdrew into Bavaria, and Wallenstein gladly saw the Swedish forces engaged in humbling his rival, while he himself turned to pursue his designs upon Saxony. A revolt of the Austrian peasants opened a way for Gustavus to the imperial capital, but again he sacrificed his own interests to the demands of his Saxon ally.

336. Making a rapid movement to the northward, he collected fresh forces in Franconia, and on the evening of November 15, arrived upon the plain of Lutzen, where Wallenstein was already posted to receive him. The next morning the whole Swedish army, kneeling, joined in the devotions of their king, and then broke forth in singing Luther's hymn, "*Eine feste Burg ist unser Gott.*" The

A. D. 1632.

two greatest generals in Europe were for the first time to meet on equal terms, and every soldier felt that the fate of the Empire hung upon the issue. Three imperial brigades were put to flight by the impetuous valor of the Swedes, but the word and example of Wallenstein were sufficient to rally them and lead them anew to the contest. A colonel of Swedish cavalry having been wounded, the king took command in person, and charging the enemy in advance of his whole army, received a mortal wound. His men, now led by Duke Bernhard of Saxe Weimar, were inspired by a fury of revenge, and after nine hours' obstinate fighting, the troops of Wallenstein were withdrawn. *Te Deums* were indeed chanted as for a victory in all the Spanish and Austrian dominions, but the field, with the imperial artillery, remained to the Swedes.

337. The death of Gustavus Adolphus was a grief to Christendom. Never was king or general more beloved; he hated flattery and demanded absolute sincerity from all with whom he dealt, but he was careful to give every man his due proportion of praise, and never forgot a brave deed done in his service. His death completed the beneficent results of his life, for in the general consternation, the hitherto inert powers of Germany were roused to self-defense, and the united energy of the many was better than the all-absorbing authority of one, however disinterested was his devotion to the common cause. It is possible, too, that a longer career would have revealed lower motives than had yet appeared in the conduct of Gustavus. His failure to restore the Palatinate to Frederic V., his acceptance of sovereign honors at Augsburg, his apparent intention to establish a Swedish kingdom in the heart of the Empire, or even to grasp for himself the imperial crown, awakened anxiety in the lovers of German independence, lest they might have exchanged an Austrian for a foreign despot. As yet, however, no unworthy act had sullied the brightness of his fame. A German poet has celebrated him as the "first and only *just* conqueror that the world has produced."

RECAPITULATION.

War of France for the Valtelline. Accession of Pope Gregory XV., of Philip IV. in Spain, of Frederic Henry of Nassau in Holland. Richelieu prime minister in France; opposes the Hapsburgs; captures Rochelle and Montauban; ends the political existence of the Huguenots; completes the consolidation of the monarchy. Intervention of Denmark in the Thirty Years' War, ended by the Peace of Lubec. Edict of Restitution of confiscated church property. Franco-Swedish intervention. Invasion of Germany by Gustavus Adolphus. Dismissal of Wallenstein. Sack and massacre at Magdeburg by the soldiers of Tilly. Victory of the Swedes at Leipsic. Swedish head-quarters at Mentz. Defeat of Tilly on the Lech, and invasion of Bavaria. Recall of Wallenstein with dictatorial powers. Encampment of both armies at Nuremberg. Battle of Lutzen; victory and death of Gustavus Adolphus.

Thirty Years' War.—*Concluded.*

338. A congress at Heilbronn of the four Circles of Southern Germany with the embassadors of France, England, and Holland, conferred upon

March, 1633.

Count Oxenstiern the same dignity which his master had held as protector of the protestant interests in opposition to the emperor and the League. The unfortunate elector-palatine having died since the battle of Lutzen, his reconquered estates were now secured to his heirs under the guardianship of their uncle, Louis Philip. The bishoprics of Bamberg and Wurtzburg were formed into the duchy of Franconia, and conferred, as a fief of the Swedish crown, upon Duke Bernhard of Weimar. Beside the conquest of these territories, the duke made the important capture of Ratisbon, during the campaign of 1633, thus gaining the command of the Danube.

339. The fall of Wallenstein was soon to follow. His designs upon the crown of Bohemia were more than suspected, and a numerous and powerful party both at court and in the army, demanded his dismissal. Informed by spies of the decision of the imperial Council, Wallenstein assembled his principal officers at Pilsen and obtained their signatures to a paper in which they promised to stand by him to the last drop of their blood. What could not have been effected by open force was, however, accomplished by deception. Ferdinand kept up a friendly correspondence with his doomed victim, even after orders had been distributed through the army releasing officers and soldiers from their obedience, and requiring that he should be brought, alive or dead, into the imperial presence. The Italian general Piccolomini, whom Wallenstein regarded as his best friend, acted under secret orders from the court to incite the soldiery against him and lay snares for his life. The murder was accomplished

Feb., 1634.

at Wallenstein's own quarters in Eger, by some officers of an Irish regiment. His confiscated estates rewarded the more distinguished of his assassins. The emperor, who had twice owed his crown to the man whom he had thus illegally and violently put to death, publicly thanked and praised the instruments of the crime, while he ordered three thousand masses to be sung for the soul of its victim.

340. King Ferdinand of Bohemia assumed the command-in-chief of the army, which, in the summer of 1634, took Donauwerth and threatened Nördlingen. The Swedish general Horn, who had been detached to guard the passes of the Tyrolese Alps, was compelled to rejoin Duke Bernhard, and leave the way open for the advance of the Cardinal Infant, Ferdinand of Spain, with an army from Italy. This warlike prelate was said to be the first Spanish prince since John of Austria who had possessed any military talent. He joined King Ferdinand under the walls of Nördlingen, and a great battle was fought (Aug. 26, 27), which ended in the

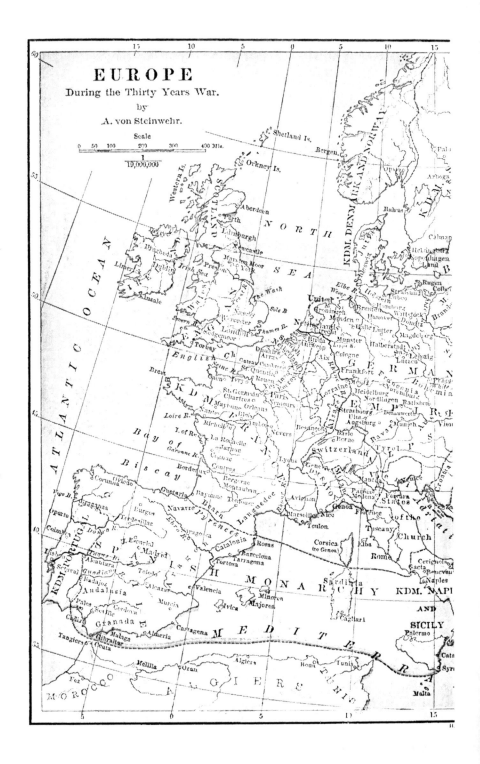

EUROPE

During the Thirty Years War.

by

A. von Steinwehr.

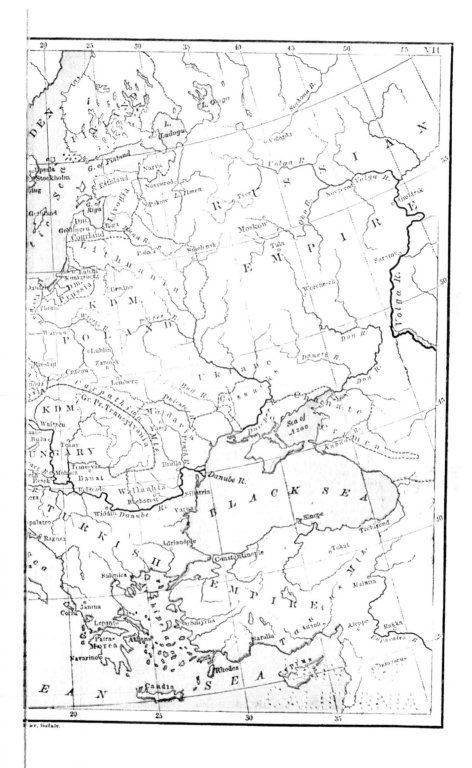

complete and ruinous overthrow of the Swedish army. Horn and three other generals, with 6,000 men, were prisoners; 12,000 lay dead upon the field, while 80 guns, 300 standards, and 4,000 wagons fell into the hands of the victors.

341. The Swedes were now reluctantly compelled to buy the active aid of the French by favoring the annexation of Alsace by Louis XIII. Lorraine had already been forcibly annexed, and a "Parliament of Austrasia" was duly instituted at Metz. The conquered duke, Charles, abdicated in favor of his brother, the cardinal Nicholas Francis, and entering the imperial service, became a valiant and successful general, instead of a faithless and unfortunate sovereign. The French court made a close alliance the same year with Prince Frederic Henry of Nassau for a simultaneous invasion of the Spanish Netherlands from north and south. These provinces were invited to form an independent state, ceding a liberal tract of their territories on either side to the two neighboring nations by whose aid their deliverance from the Spaniards was to be achieved. If they refused this offer, they were to be conquered and divided between Holland and France.

342. Philipsburg on the Rhine had already been wrested by the Spaniards from the French; and in March, 1635, Trèves was likewise seized, its French garrison destroyed, and the elector carried away as prisoner to Antwerp. The Cardinal Infant, failing to surrender him upon the demand of Richelieu, war was declared against Spain by a French herald at Brussels. The elector was already under the ban of the empire for having admitted French troops into Ehrenbreitstein; and he was soon conveyed to Vienna, where he remained in captivity ten years.

343. The elector of Saxony, long wavering, decided after the battle of Nördlingen to make his peace with the emperor. All the German states, with one or two exceptions, acceded in time to the Treaty of Prague, though all joined in condemning the base ingrati- _May, 1635._ tude of John George of Saxony, in defense of whose dominions the king of Sweden had lost his life, but who engaged, by a special article of the treaty, to assist in driving the Swedes out of Germany. The emperor made many concessions with regard to church property and freedom of worship, except in Bohemia, which kingdom was now declared to be hereditary in his family. The Swedes refused to accept the treaty, and their own propositions to the Court of Vienna were disregarded. The Union of Heilbronn was formally dissolved.

344. Germany being thus momentarily pacified, Piccolomini entered the Netherlands with 20,000 men; while the imperial army of the Rhine drove the French not only from that river and the Neckar, but from the lower Moselle and Sarre. Richelieu's operations in the Netherlands and the Milanese were not more successful; and in 1636, France was invaded

M. H.—17.

on four sides by Spanish and imperial troops, though with no great effect.
Bands of Croats and Hungarians ravaged the northern provinces and terrified Paris, where loud complaints began to be heard against the chief minister. The cardinal, however, quickly raised an army which dislodged the imperialists from Corbie and drove them from the country.

345. In Germany, Duke Bernhard of Weimar was performing brilliant feats of arms in the service of France, while the Swedes, under Banner, in spite of one or two reverses, were so far from being expelled that they defeated the faithless elector of Saxony at Dömitz and still more decisively at Wittstock. The emperor Ferdinand II., died at Vienna,

Feb., 1637.

and was succeeded by his son Ferdinand III. More tolerant by nature, and less influenced by the Spaniards and the Jesuits than his father, the new emperor had also been a personal witness of the misery and desolation wrought by the war, and began his reign with an ardent desire for peace. Military movements were, however, prosecuted with unabated zeal, and Banner was compelled not only to raise the siege of Leipzig, but to effect a retreat into Pomerania by a series of adventures and escapes which seem to belong rather to romance than history.

346. The great heroes of the Thirty Years' War — Tilly, Wallenstein, Gustavus Adolphus — had all passed away, and though the conflict continued eleven years longer, with ever-increasing atrocity, its details are more hideous than instructive. The admirable discipline maintained among the Swedes by their king was now dissolved; even the profligate Banner declared that it would be no wonder if the earth should open and swallow them up for their crimes and cruelties. The German armies, on the other hand, lived without a commissariat, and commonly without pay, at the expense of the wretched inhabitants of the countries through which they passed. Each army systematically destroyed the produce of the soil, in order to starve its opponents; the grand weapon of the war in Germany, and toward its last years the exclusive one, was hunger — a means of destruction from which the innocent, women and children, suffered even more than the active combatants.

347. In the latest period of the war — that following the Treaty of Prague — all the leading European states were more or less actively engaged. Duke Bernhard having died at the zenith of his brilliant career, all his conquests on the upper Rhine were absorbed by France. The electoral prince of the Palatinate was aided by his two nearest relatives, the king of England and the Prince of Orange; but his first Dutch army was destroyed by the imperialist general Hatzfeld, and his brother Rupert, afterward unhappily famous in England, remained some years a prisoner in Germany.

348. The home-forces of Spain were for a time absorbed by the revolt of Biscay and Catalonia. The intolerable outrages of a Spanish army quartered in those provinces during the French campaign of 1639-40, incensed the people; bands of half-savage mountaineers, repairing to Barcelona to hire themselves out for labor in the fields, caught the fury, and by a sudden impulse every Castilian or foreigner in the city was murdered. The insurgents sent to all the European powers a statement of their grievances against the Spanish government, and Louis XIII. engaged by formal treaty to provide officers and troops for the inevitable war. A Spanish force of 20,000 men was already on its march to the Catalan frontier, marking its route by fire and massacre, and the rebels soon converted their treaty with France into an act of perpetual union with that kingdom.

349. The liberation of Portugal was a more permanent loss to Spain. This conquered kingdom had only been oppressed, humiliated, and impoverished by its sixty years' subjection to the Spanish crown. Her commerce with the Indies was crippled, her navy destroyed, and her people crushed with taxes which went to build needless palaces for the Spanish kings. On receiving a command to march against the Catalans, the Portuguese nobles and officers resolved rather to imitate those insurgents. The foreign guards of Lisbon and the vice-queen's palace were cut down; the Duke of Bragança, a descendant of the ancient kings of Portugal, was proclaimed sovereign as John IV., and the revolution was complete. The Portuguese colonies, with the single exception of Ceuta in Africa, overpowered their Spanish garrisons; and the *Cortes* assembled in 1641 at Lisbon declared the right of every nation to depose a tyrant, even were he a legitimate monarch and not a usurper like the king of Spain. Thus was founded the dynasty which, in its royal and imperial branches, still rules Portugal and Brazil.

A. D. 1640.

350. The Spaniards were not more fortunate upon the sea. In 1638 their fleet had been destroyed by the French in Guetaria; and in 1639 a great armada — the most powerful they had sent forth since that "invincible" armament which had threatened England — was likewise annihilated by the Dutch. Arras, the capital of Artois, and long the bulwark of the Spanish Netherlands against France, was captured in the same year with Piedmont, 1640.

351. The Swedes had more than retrieved their losses in 1637. The next year they defeated the imperial army at Elsterburg, the Saxons at Chemnitz; captured and destroyed Pirna, and spread terror and desolation throughout Bohemia, where more than a thousand castles, hamlets, and villages were laid in ashes. The campaigns of 1639 and 1640 were sharply contested, and the advantages were more evenly divided. In January, 1641, Banner, by a rapid and masterly movement through the upper Palatinate, appeared suddenly before Ratisbon, where a Diet was

in session. The emperor was very nearly captured, but the city was saved by a thaw which prevented the Swedes from crossing the Danube. Banner died the following May.

352. General Torstenson, who succeeded him in command of the Swedes, was the ablest pupil and imitator of Gustavus Adolphus. He transferred the seat of war to the Austrian territories, which had hitherto escaped the general devastation; captured Glogau, Schweidnitz, Olmütz, and excited terror in Vienna itself. He besieged Leipzig, and defeated the archduke Leopold, who was approaching for its relief, on the very ground which Gustavus Adolphus had, eleven years before, made famous by a decisive victory. The town surrendered three weeks later, and redeemed itself from pillage only by an enormous contribution. A severe winter scarcely impeded the energetic movements of the Swedes; the imperialists were forced from their winter-quarters to defend Freiberg; but scarcely had Torstenson raised his siege of that town, when with a swift and unexpected movement, he penetrated through Bohemia and relieved Olmütz, which was closely pressed by their forces. His fortified camp near that place commanded the whole of Moravia, and his detachments again carried their ravages to the walls of Vienna.

353. The French on the lower Rhine, meanwhile, gained a victory at Kempen which opened to them the whole electorate of Cologne and duchy of Jüliers. In the war for the Catalans, Louis XIII. besieged and captured Perpignan. But the united reign of the king and the cardinal was near its end. Richelieu died in December A. D. 1642. and Louis the following May, 1643. The French people, generally incapable of comprehending the far-reaching plans of the great minister, celebrated his death with bonfires and rejoicings. Though we can not justify the system of deceit which constituted so large a part of the diplomacy of the age, and notably of Richelieu's policy, yet it is evident that the subsequent ascendency of France in European affairs was a direct result of his genius and resolution. With almost his last breath he named Mazarin as his successor, and that Italian cardinal was immediately appointed a member of the royal council. Upon the death of the king, he became the prime minister of the queen regent, Anne of Austria.

354. Louis XIV., now, by his father's death, king of France, was not yet five years old. In his reign of seventy-two years — the longest in European annals — is comprised a most brilliant and eventful epoch, illustrated not less by the variety of talent employed in his service than by his own amazing proficiency in king-craft. His career belongs, however, to the ensuing period of our history. The young Duke d'Enghien, afterward known as the "great Condé," was now giving proof of his consummate genius in his command of the French forces in the Netherlands. He gained a decisive victory over the Spaniards at Rocroi, and soon besieged and captured Thionville, the key to Luxembourg and the strongest place, excepting Metz, in the line of the Moselle.

355. By the victories of Enghien and Turenne in 1644, the French acquired the whole valley of the Rhine from Basle to Coblentz, though they were repulsed with great loss from Freiburg. The next year, Enghien, advancing toward the Danube, gained a brilliant victory over the Bavarian general Von Mercy on the heights of Nördlingen, by which that town and Dinkelsbühl were gained for France. Turenne not only captured many towns in Flanders, but took Trèves, and restored the long-captive elector to his archbishopric. In 1646, Enghien captured Courtrai, Mardyk, and Dunkirk, and only the insanity of the Prince of Orange prevented greater conquests by the combined forces of France and Holland. Turenne, in connection with the Swedes, pushed his operations the same year to the gates of Munich.

356. Sweden had become involved (1644) in a war with Denmark, by the intrigues of the emperor and of the Swedish queen-dowager, who had been excluded from the regency during her daughter's minority. The pretext was found in the demand of the Danish government for a payment of toll by Swedish vessels passing into the Baltic—an imposition from which they had been exempted by special treaty. Denmark was invaded by Torstenson, and the whole peninsula, as well as Schleswig and Holstein, was speedily overrun, while the Danes lost also their province of Schonen and the towns of Helsingborg and Landscrona. A military force sent by the emperor to the relief of his ally, was annihilated or dispersed, with the exception of 2,000 men who accomplished their retreat into Germany.

357. Torstenson, then turning his attention to the latter country, penetrated Bohemia, and gained at Jankowitz, over the imperialists, one of the most decisive victories of the whole war. The young queen, Christina of Sweden, assumed the government on her eighteenth birthday in 1644. Desiring peace, she required her great minister, Oxenstiern, to enter into negotiations with the Danes, and in August, 1645, the treaty of Brömsebro restored tranquillity between the two kingdoms. The southern provinces of the Swedish peninsula, so long held by Denmark, were relinquished, and Swedish vessels were exempted from all tolls in the Sound or Belts.

358. The ancient contest for Naples and the duchy of Milan had been renewed in 1635 by the declaration of war between France and Spain. In 1647, Naples revolted and besought the aid of France in expelling the Spanish viceroy and establishing a republic. The Duke of Guise was offered a position in the new state equivalent to that of the Prince of Orange in Holland; but as a descendant of the French house of Anjou, he doubtless intended to convert his protectorate into a sovereignty; while Cardinal Mazarin desired rather to obtain the Neapolitan crown for Louis XIV. The duke was received at Naples with joy and with cries of "Long live the Republic!" Philip IV., engrossed by his operations against Portugal and Catalonia, and despairing of making good his title to so distant a possession, recalled his fleet; but the inactivity of the French revived his courage. Another armament in 1648 effected a restoration of Spanish authority; and Guise, taken prisoner at Capua, was held four years in captivity in Spain.

Nov., 1647.

359. Already in 1641 movements had been made toward a general peace, and the neighboring towns of Münster and Osnabrück in Westphalia were appointed for the meeting of commissioners from the several nations. More than a year was wasted in disputes concerning minute points of etiquette; but in 1643 the two congresses — one of protestant, the other of Catholic powers — were formally opened. Not only all the great nations of Europe, except England, Poland, and Russia; but the dukes of Savoy, Mantua, Tuscany, Catalonia, the electors and all the princes, temporal or spiritual, of Germany, had their ministers either at Münster or Osnabrück. England was absorbed in civil war, and it was fortunate for the growth of her liberties that the continental sovereigns were prevented from interfering in behalf of the divine right of kings.

360. All the governments were, doubtless, sincere in their desire for peace. Ferdinand III. was at the end of his resources; a large part of the empire was still in arms against him and another large part had declared itself neutral, while his hereditary states were reduced to poverty by their extraordinary exertions. Spain had lost Portugal, Catalonia, and many towns in the Netherlands, and was now reduced to make humiliating concessions to France. This power and Sweden were bent on enriching themselves as much as possible from the crumbling fragments of the empire. Still, so many and conflicting were the claims, that negotiations were protracted more than five years, and peace appeared, at many points in the conferences, utterly unattainable. The ministers felt their own importance increased by the continuance of the discussion, while the generals had an equal professional interest in the prolongation of the war. Disputes concerning the right of precedence between the embassadors of France and Spain, and the title of Excellency borne by the Venetian envoy and claimed by the representatives of the German electors, wasted precious months of the conference at Münster, while that at Osnabrück was wholly suspended during the war between Sweden and Denmark.

361. At length, however, the rebellion at Naples compelled Spain to urge on her negotiations with the United Netherlands; and a peace was signed in which the seven provinces (see § 258) were acknowledged as free and sovereign states. The towns of Dutch Flanders, as well as all the conquests of the Hollanders in Asia,

Jan., 1648.

Africa, and America, were made over to the new Republic. Thus ended the Eighty Years' War of Independence sustained by the northern Netherlands against the power of Spain — a power by far the greatest in Europe when the struggle began, now crippled and reduced, partly by her own suicidal policy, partly by the heroic and persistent efforts of her former subjects.

362. The war still went on between France and Sweden, on the one hand — Spain and the Empire, on the other. Turenne and Wrangel, in command of a Franco-Swedish army, defeated the imperialists near Augsburg and overran Bavaria with all the customary barbarities. Condé gained, at Lens, one of his most brilliant victories over the archduke Leopold; and the Swedish generalissimo, Charles Gustavus, advancing upon Prague, waged an indecisive war with General Königsmark of the imperial army. Thus the Thirty Years' War ended upon the same spot where it had begun; for the emperor, despairing of retrieving his fortunes by a longer contest, consented to a suspension of hostilities, while the conferences at Münster were pressed to a conclusion. The Peace of Westphalia was signed Oct. 24, 1648.

363. In Germany, general amnesty, religious freedom, and the sovereign rights of the several princes in peace and war, were conceded by the emperor. The Upper Palatinate remained to Maximilian of Bavaria; but the "Palatinate of the Rhine," with an eighth electoral vote, was secured to Charles Louis, the son of the deposed elector Frederic V. The Dutch and Swiss republics, hitherto members of the Empire, were recognized as independent states. Sweden received Western Pomerania, Stettin, and three towns on the Oder, several islands and the bishoprics of Bremen and Verden, now secularized into a duchy and a principality. Her sovereign thus became a prince of the Empire, with three votes in the Diet. France was confirmed in possession of all the lands belonging to Metz, Toul, and Verdun, of Alsace, the Sundgau, Breisach, and the prefecture of ten imperial cities, beside the fortress of Pignerol in Piedmont.

364. The Treaty of Westphalia marks an important era in European history, for it was the first attempt to reconstruct the system of states by diplomacy, when their relations had been seriously disturbed. It definitely closed the century and more of religious and consequent civil revolution; it put an end to the international authority of the emperor, while it loosened the bond which had united the German states. Three hundred petty sovereignties existed between the Alps and the Baltic, each with its distinct coinage, its standing army, its custom-houses, and a court which made up in ceremony what it lacked in grandeur. Of the "Roman Empire" there remained only the name, and a system of clumsy formalities which served chiefly to impede and embarrass European diplomacy. All really imperial functions — such as making war or peace, building for-

tresses, raising armies, levying contributions — were transferred to the

A. D. 1654.

Diet, which from an occasional assembly of the princes in person, was soon changed into a permanent organization composed of their envoys with those of the fifty free cities.

365. Pope Innocent X. denounced the treaty as " null, invalid, iniquitous, and void of all power and effect." The great revolution in human thought which this treaty marked and declared, in fact concerned His Holiness more nearly than any other European power, except, perhaps, the emperor. By admitting to full civil rights persons who were aliens and enemies to the Roman Church, it abrogated the whole theory by which the Empire and the papacy had subsisted together for nearly a thousand years. But this theory had been slowly vanishing from among the opinions and motives of men, and the treaty only announced a change already accomplished. The emperor forbade the papal bull to be circulated in his dominions, and the Catholic powers, glad of peace after a generation of conflict, completely disregarded the thunders of the Vatican.

RECAPITULATION.

Union of Heilbronn, Oxenstiern at the head of protestant interests in Germany; Duke Bernhard of Weimar in command of the army. Disgrace and death of Wallenstein. Disaster of the Swedes at Nördlingen. The French occupy Lorraine and Alsace; renew their alliance with Sweden and the United Netherlands. Imprisonment of the elector of Trèves. Treaty of Prague between Saxony and the emperor, joined by most of the German states. Fourfold invasion of France by Spanish and imperial forces. Victories of the Swedes at Dömitz and Wittstock. Accession of Ferdinand III. Last years of the war marked in Germany by increased atrocities, in Europe at large by more active and general coöperation. Spain loses Catalonia and Portugal. Rise in the latter of the Bragança dynasty. Naval disasters of the Spaniards. Devastation of Bohemia by the Swedes. Great victories of Torstenson. The French occupy Cologne and the neighboring territories. Death of Richelieu and Louis XIII.; accession of Louis XIV. under regency of his mother and ministry of Mazarin. War between Sweden and Denmark; repeated discomfitures of the Danes and defeat of the imperialists at Jankowitz. Queen Christina, attaining her majority, concludes the Peace of Brömsebro. Naples revolts and hails the Duke of Guise as protector; is subdued by a Spanish fleet. Congresses of Münster and Osnabrück. End of Eighty Years' War for Independence of the United Netherlands. Continued victories of the French and Swedish armies. Peace of Westphalia closes the Thirty Years' War; puts a period to the Reformation, and changes the Empire into a mere confederation of three hundred states.

QUESTIONS FOR REVIEW.

BOOK III.

1. To what extent was the Atlantic navigated during the Middle Ages? . §§ 2, 3.
2. Describe the enterprises of the Portuguese. . . . . . . 4, 5, 6.
3. What resulted from the opening of a sea-route to India? . . . . . 6, 7.
4. What action was taken by the Popes concerning newly-discovered lands? . 5, 10.

56. Tell the story of the Guises. . . . . §§ 104, 157–159, 163, 189, 191, 192, 196, 201–206,
                                      220, 243, 245, 251, 273–275, 278.

57.   Of Maurice of Saxony. . . . . . 154, 155, 166, 167, 171, 174.

58.   Of Mary I. of England. . . . . 176–178.

59.   Of Philip II. of Spain.   188–190, 193, 205, 211, 216, 222, 225, 226, 239, 245,
                                 249–251, 260–263, 269, 270, 276, 280, 281.

60. Describe the Netherlands, their revolt, and the rise of the Dutch Republic.
      Note p. 193. . . . . 223–240, 256–267, 271, 293–295, 303, 361.

61. Name the successive foreign protectors of the Netherlands. 254, 256, 261, 262, 266, 267.

62. Describe Alexander Farnese, Duke of Parma. . . . 255, 259, 265, 271.

63.   The character and history of Maximilian II. . . 208, 222, 231, 241.

64.   Of Henry III. of France. . . . . . . 242, 243, 246, 247.

65.   Of John of Austria. . . . . . . 181, 211, 214, 215, 253–255.

66. What became of the Spanish Moriscoes? . . . . . . 211, 292.

67. What changes of dynasty in Portugal? . . . . . . 248–250, 349.

68. Describe the relations between England and Spain. 190–193, 205, 216, 234, 269–271, 279.

69.   The reign of Elizabeth Tudor. . . . 193, 216, 217, 222, 286, 293.

70.   The death of Henry II. and subsequent condition of parties in
          France. . . . . 195–197.

71. What changes followed the death of Francis II.? . . . . 201, 202.

72. Give an outline of the religious wars in France. . 202–206, 209, 210, 218–222, 244–247,
                                     251, 252, 272–278.

73. Describe Paul IV. and his successor. . . . . . . 187–189, 198, 199.

74.   Pius V. and Sixtus V. . . . . 208, 216, 268.

75.   Three sons of William, Prince of Orange. . 265, 267, 271, 280, 303, 326, 355.

76.   The character and reign of Henry IV. of France. 219, 244, 247, 251, 275–279,
                                     288–292, 299.

77.   Of Frederic V., Elector-Palatine. . . . . 300, 306–308, 338.

78.   Of Gustavus Adolphus. . . . . 318, 319, 327, 329–333, 335–337.

79.   Of Wallenstein. . . . . . . 306, 326, 327, 330, 334–339.

80. Sketch the history of the northern European kingdoms. . . . 312–319.

81. What part was taken by the Danes in the Thirty Years' War? . 326, 327, 356, 357.

82. Name the most decisive battles of the Thirty Years' War. . 309, 322, 323, 336, 340, 353,
                                      355, 357.

83.   Its most important treaties. . . . . . 327, 329, 338, 343, 359–365.

84. Name the sovereigns belonging to the three branches of the House of
    Hapsburg, from Charles V. to the Peace of Westphalia.

85. Name the English and French monarchs, A. D. 1500–1648.

BOOK IV.

THE MODERN ERA,

From the Peace of Westphalia to the French Revolution,

A. D. 1648–1789.

THE ENGLISH COMMONWEALTH.

1. While the conferences at Münster and Osnabrück were absorbing the attention of continental Europe, England had arrived at the crisis of a revolution occasioned, no less than the Thirty Years' War, by the religious changes of the preceding century. The separation from Rome had appeared, indeed, to exalt and strengthen the royal prerogative. Henry VIII. was the most absolute of English kings. But the movement which began with placing him at the head of the national Church, was far from ending there.

2. Elizabeth, with a temper no less arbitrary, had the prudence to meet the just demands of her people half-way, instead of allowing discontent to gather force. In her successor, James Stuart, "Nature and education had done their utmost to produce a finished specimen of all that a king ought not to be." His undignified person and manner were rendered contemptible by his affectation of the wisdom of Solomon and his demand, as "the Lord's anointed," upon the unlimited reverence and obedience of better men than himself. His son, Charles I., was personally worthy of far greater respect; but he was ignorant of the force of that current of public opinion which had been gaining strength throughout his father's reign, and which, as he rashly attempted to oppose it, carried him away to his destruction.

3. The Petition of Right, presented by both houses of Parliament in 1628, was granted by the king in consideration of a vote of supplies; but though the money was paid, the terms of the petition were violated. Dissolving the Parliament, the king attempted to levy by his own authority the taxes which could only be lawfully imposed by the Commons. His illegal exaction of "tonnage and poundage" was firmly resisted by Hampden and other patriots. The attempt of Charles to impose the rites of the Church of England upon the Scots caused the latter to unite in the "Solemn League and Covenant" and to prepare for open war. Need of money again threw the king upon the Parliament, which he summoned after the long interval of eleven years; but at its first serious reaffirmation of the principles of Hampden, it was dissolved.

4. The Long Parliament which met the following November, adopted bolder measures. The arbitrary and illegal courts of the Star Chamber and of High Commission were abolished, and others of longer standing were reformed. The Earl of Strafford, the king's ablest and most unscrupulous minister, was impeached, condemned, and beheaded. On learning that Charles, who had profited by his extortions, had consented to sign his death-warrant, Strafford exclaimed, "Put not your trust in princes!" "The whole history of the times," says Macaulay, "is a commentary on that bitter text." Archbishop Laud was imprisoned in the Tower. The king now violated a fundamental law * of the kingdom by attempting the arrest of Hampden, Pym, and three other members of the House of Commons. This act broke the last bond of allegiance, and both parties appealed to arms.

5. The king's forces had at first the advantage of military experience over the citizen-soldiery of the Parliament; but their outrages upon private rights cost the king more of the moral support of the nation than their valor and skill could regain. Prince Rupert of the Palatinate — second son of the deposed elector Frederic and the English Princess Elizabeth — had been trained amid the brutalities of the Thirty Years' War, and was leader of the wildest "Cavaliers." The year 1643 was marked by the death of three of the most illustrious patriots: Hampden and Pym on the parliamentary, and Lord Falkland on the royal side. The Parliament entered the League of the Scottish Covenanters, whose army under General Leslie invaded England and joined the forces of Fairfax in besieging York. Rupert hastened to its relief, and in the great battle of Marston Moor, the royalists were decisively overthrown. Subsequent defeats at Newbury and Naseby ruined the hopes of Charles. Rupert surrendered Bristol, and sought a field for his reckless valor beyond the seas. The king put himself in the power of the Scottish leaders, by whom he was surrendered to the English in January, 1647.

A. D. 1644.

6. Serious dissensions had already broken out in the victorious party. Presbyterians and Independents — the civil and the military authorities —

---

* That no subject could be arrested by the king in person.

were ranged in opposition. The latter, under Oliver Cromwell, gained ascendency: the king was forcibly transferred from the control of the Parliament to that of the army, and the House of Commons was intimidated by a guard of soldiers. The king's insincerity of purpose was more than ever apparent; he negotiated with all parties, but kept faith with none. But his enemies were now resolved upon an act which should assert in unequivocal terms the sovereignty of the people. Charles Stuart was impeached and tried for high treason before a court instituted for the purpose. He firmly denied its jurisdiction, and refused to plead his cause before it; but he was sentenced to death, and was beheaded before his palace of Whitehall, Jan. 30, 1649.

7. This act — unprecedented in history — was regarded with very different emotions even by the opponents of the dead king. Irish Catholics and Scottish Covenanters hastened to proclaim Charles II. Prince Rupert was already in the Irish seas with a foreign fleet. All the malcontents in Ireland, of whatever creed or race, enrolled themselves under the banners of the Marquis of Ormond, to oppose the English Commonwealth. Lieutenant-General Cromwell was appointed by the Parliament to deal with the Irish rebellion. By a single act of extreme severity he overawed opposition, and the war, which had raged nine years in that distracted island, was brought to a conclusion in as many months. Cromwell permitted all the disaffected to leave the country, and 45,000 of the most dangerous accordingly enlisted in the armies of France and Spain. By this stroke of wise policy, peace was restored, and Ireland saw a new era of comparative order during the few years that Cromwell and his lieutenants administered her affairs.

8. Charles II. was in every respect a worse man than his father; but his dealings with the Scots showed only the same falsity of character which he had inherited from the victims of Fotheringay and Whitehall. The Marquis of Montrose was, by his urgent entreaties, gathering men and means to do battle for the royal cause, at the same time that Charles was promising adhesion to the Covenant, declaring his complete subserviency to the Scottish Parliament and Kirk, and denying all knowledge or responsibility concerning the movements of Montrose. This brave and loyal servant of a faithless prince was defeated at Kincardine and beheaded at Edinburgh with every circumstance of insult and malice. Charles landed soon after in Scotland, and was crowned at Scone. Cromwell with his army was already in the northern kingdom; he had routed the Scots at Dunbar (Sept. 3, 1650), and of his 10,000 prisoners many were sent to service in the New England plantations. Giving Cromwell the slip, Charles marched with 11,000 men into England, and was proclaimed king at Carlisle and Penrith. Contrary to his hopes, few joined him. He was overtaken by Cromwell at

Jan. 1, 1651.

Worcester, and thoroughly defeated, with the loss or dispersion of his entire army. After wandering six weeks in various disguises, he made his escape to France.

9. The Commonwealth was now established. Order and confidence returned; commerce, long depressed by the monopolies and exactions of the two preceding reigns and the insecurity of civil war, revived. A quarrel with the Dutch concerning the herring fisheries of the Scottish coast led to a war whose field was the ocean and whose prize the commerce of the world. England declared herself Mistress of the Seas; but Holland, by reason of her distant foreign possessions, had a far more numerous and effective marine. "English mariners sought employment in Dutch vessels, while English ships lay rotting at the wharves." The "Navigation Act" passed by the British Parliament in 1652, prohibited any foreign vessel from bringing a cargo into English ports unless it were of the products of the country whence the vessel came. As the products of Holland were few but her ships many, and England her best market, this act was evidently a destructive blow to her carrying trade.

10. After a summer of frequent but indecisive skirmishes among the Orkneys and Hebrides, the Dutch admiral Van Tromp appeared, late in November, off the Naze. He was met by the English under Blake, and a furious combat ended with the retreat of the latter, after great loss, into the Thames. Van Tromp then placed a broom at his mast-head and sailed up and down the Channel, as if to sweep the English from the seas. A four days' battle the next February was indecisive; but in June and July, 1653, Blake and Monk gained great victories over Van Tromp, in the latter of which the Dutch admiral was killed. The war was virtually at an end, though peace was not signed until April, 1654.

A. D. 1652.

11. The remnant of the Long Parliament had by this time forfeited the confidence of the English people, who saw themselves on the verge of anarchy amid the conflicts of rival sects and parties. Cromwell relieved many anxieties when he put an end to its existence by military force. A new assembly of 140 members, called the Little Parliament, was convoked by his own authority. It afterward acquired the nickname "Barebone's Parliament" from one of its most fanatical members. After five months' sitting, it resigned its authority to a council of officers, who requested Cromwell to assume the title and character of "Lord Protector of the Commonwealth of England, Scotland, and Ireland."

Dec., 1653.

12. No man ever lived who appeared to his contemporaries and to succeeding generations under more directly opposite colors than Oliver Cromwell. A late celebrated historian calls him "the greatest prince that ever ruled England," "the greatest prince and soldier of the age."

On the other hand, extreme royalists and lawless republicans have joined the profligate skeptics of Charles II.'s court in branding him with the names of "usurper, traitor, hypocrite, and fanatic;" and until very recently their verdict has doubtless had the predominant influence upon public opinion. Without clearing him from the charge of personal ambition — a trait which is certainly not inconsistent with great virtues and great talents, if, indeed, it is often separated from the latter — we find his usurpation extenuated by the stern necessities of the time and by his unsurpassed ability and disposition to govern well. No contemporary king equaled him in equity of intention; not one — even the "Grand Monarch" himself — excelled him in the efficiency of his administration. England, depressed at home and despised abroad during the reigns of the first two Stuarts, now assumed her true position in the foremost rank of Christian powers, as the protectress of Protestant interests. Every nation prized her friendship and dreaded her enmity. Mazarin courted her alliance by expelling the Stuart princes, the near relations of his king, from France, and by ceding the port of Dunkirk, then nearly the most important on the German Ocean, when it had been taken by the combined French and English forces. Spain eagerly sought the same end, but demurred at Cromwell's conditions, which required her to abolish the Inquisition, and grant to English merchants free trade with her American colonies. The Spanish embassador justly remarked that these two concessions would be equivalent to putting out the two eyes of Philip IV.

13. In his home-rule, Cromwell found it impossible to exercise his new and undefined power within the constitutional limits which he had set to it. The first parliament called under his Protectorate, disputed his authority, reversed his acts of toleration, and left him at its dissolution unprovided with funds to support the army and navy or the necessary expenses of the state. The court of Charles II., now at Cologne, now at Brussels, availed itself of these dissensions to excite seditions in England; and the discovery of their plots led Cromwell to more arbitrary measures. England was divided into ten — afterward eleven — military districts, each governed by a major-general of extreme republican principles. A contribution of one-tenth to the service of the government was levied upon the estates of rich and disaffected royalists; and prisoners taken in a rebellion were transported to the Barbadoes.

14. Cromwell emulated the policy of Elizabeth in fostering the navy. The famous Admiral Blake caused his flag to be respected in the Mediterranean equally by the Pope, the Grand Duke of Tuscany, and the pirates of the African coast. Algiers and Tripoli released their Christian captives at his demand, and Tunis was soon bombarded into submission. Venables and Penn failed in their attempt upon St. Domingo, but they conquered Jamaica, thus gaining for England an important foot-hold in

the West Indies. Blake gained a great victory over the Spaniards off Cadiz, and the next year (1657) destroyed their entire fleet in the harbor of Santa Cruz. Being called home to receive the thanks of Parliament, he died of disease within sight of the English coast. The treasure taken from the Spaniards relieving the immediate necessities of the government, Cromwell dismissed the eleven major-generals and adopted a less arbitrary policy.

15. After long discussion in Parliament, the Protector was desired to assume the royal title and dignity. But this would have offended the army and all extreme republicans, and Cromwell declined it. A new Instrument of Government gave him, however, all the essential rights of sovereignty. He received an oath of allegiance from each member of Parliament, and was publicly invested with the purple robe, the scepter and the sword, according to the usual forms of a royal coronation. An Upper House of Parliament, including only seven of the old nobility, was now organized. The court at Brussels was more active than ever in its plots of assassination; but its desires were accomplished by more natural and peaceful means. On the 3d of September, 1658, the anniversary of his victories of Dunbar and Worcester, the Protector died.

16. His son Richard, whom with his dying breath Oliver had appointed his successor, was recognized by the Parliament. But his gentle and somewhat indolent nature was wholly unfit to deal with those discordant elements of the army and people which his father had held in their respective places with iron hand. A council of military officers dissolved the Parliament. Richard Cromwell retired to his estate in the country. Forty-two members of the Long Parliament assembled and took upon themselves the functions of government. A royalist insurrection was defeated by General Lambert at Chester; but fresh conflicts between the military and civil authorities led soon to the result sought by the insurgents. Charles II. was watching at once with trembling anxiety the revolutions in England and the conferences of the French and Spanish embassadors on an island in the Bidassoa, hoping that the Treaty of the Pyrenees, concluded this year, would lead to a combined action of the two kingdoms for his restoration. The result was better for himself and for England than if his hopes had been fulfilled; for the reëstablishment of Romanism, with the surrender of Jamaica, Dunkirk, and the Channel Islands, would probably have been the price demanded by the contracting powers for their aid. The will of the English people recalled their sovereign without such humiliating concessions. See § 26.

April, 1659.

17. General Monk, who had been governor of Scotland under Cromwell, had an active though at first a secret part in promoting the king's return. Under pretense of an ardent zeal for a republic, he gained absolute control of London. The remnant of the Long Parliament was

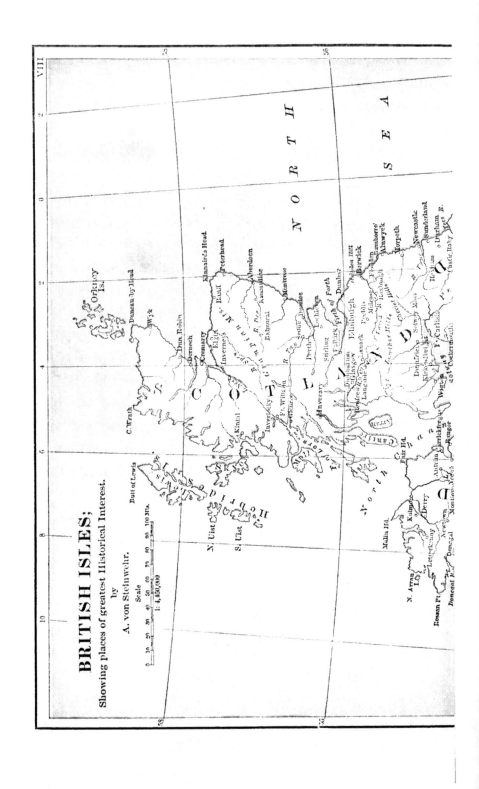

BRITISH ISLES;

Showing places of greatest Historical Interest.

by

A. von Steinwehr.

Scale

1 : 4,400,000

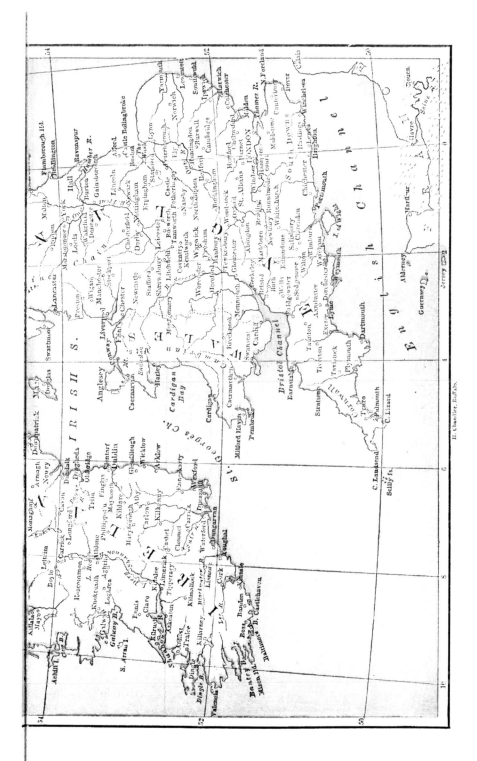

dissolved, and writs were issued for a new election. The Royalists had a majority in the new Houses, which met April 26, 1660. Letters were received from Charles II. promising amnesty and toleration to all his "subjects." In return he was proclaimed king; and such was the fear of exciting discord by long debate, that no limits or conditions were imposed upon his assumption of power. Three weeks later the king, with his train of cavaliers and counselors, arrived

May, 1660.

at London. After twenty years of civil conflict the nation welcomed the return of settled government with transports of joy, and its generous confidence was undiminished by the glaring defects of the king's character. To spare him all temptation to illegal exactions, his yearly revenues were made far more liberal than those of his father.

18. Ignoring the Commonwealth, Charles dated all the Acts of the Restoration in the twelfth year of his reign. A petty revenge was executed upon the lifeless remains of Oliver Cromwell, of General Ireton, his son-in-law, and of Bradshaw, the judge who had pronounced sentence upon Charles I. They were dragged from their tombs in Westminster Abbey and hung upon the gallows at Tyburn. All the regicides — those who had signed the death-warrant of Charles I. — with five others, were excepted from the amnesty. Of twenty-nine persons who were tried as traitors, ten were executed, and the rest imprisoned for life. The illustrious chancellor, Lord Clarendon — a faithful and invaluable friend of Charles in all his adversities, though his virtues drew upon him the ridicule of a dissolute court — honored himself by insisting upon the strict execution of the remaining articles of the Act of Amnesty and Indemnity. The king's promise of religious toleration proved less binding. Not only was the "Solemn League and Covenant" burnt by the hangman, but more than 2,000 clergymen were ejected from their parishes, and subsequent acts against the "Non-conformists" amounted to a bitter persecution. Scotland was gratified by a separate assembly, commonly called the "Drunken Parliament," which sentenced the Marquis of Argyle, the great leader of the Covenanters, to a traitor's death.

19. The shameless profligacy of the court went far to cure the "besotted loyalty" of the nation. To support his wild excesses, Charles became a regular pensioner of Louis XIV., and even sold to him the port of Dunkirk — a sacrifice of national pride which was commonly considered equally disastrous and infinitely more disgraceful than the loss of Calais. The royalist Pepys wrote: "It is strange how every body do nowadays reflect upon Oliver, and commend him, what brave things he did, and made all the neighbour princes fear him, while here a prince, come in with all the love and prayers and good liking of his people, * * * hath lost all so soon, that it is a miracle what way a man could devise to lose so much in so little time."

M. H.—18.

RECAPITULATION.

The Reformation in England undermines the principle of passive obedience to kings. Decline under the first of the Stuarts. Arbitrary exactions of Charles I. lead to the determined resistance of the Long Parliament. His attempted arrest of the five members drives the opposition into armed resistance. Battles of Marston Moor, Newbury, and Naseby are disastrous to the king. Cromwell and the Independents gain chief power; Charles I. is imprisoned, tried for high treason, condemned, and beheaded. Charles II. proclaimed in Scotland and Ireland. The latter country subdued by the massacres of Drogheda and Wexford, and the foreign enlistment of most of the disaffected. Duplicity of Charles II. with the Scots; death of the Marquis of Montrose. Cromwell defeats the Scots at Dunbar, and Charles himself at Worcester. Establishment of the Commonwealth. War with the Dutch. Van Tromp at first victorious, afterward defeated by Blake. Cromwell expels the Long Parliament, calls another, which makes him Protector. Rise of the foreign fame of England under the Protectorate. Blake victorious in the Mediterranean and among the West Indies. Capture of Jamaica. Arbitrary home-rule of Cromwell occasioned by parliamentary opposition and royalist schemes of assassination. He declines the name but accepts the power of king; revives the House of Lords; dies of disease at Whitehall; is succeeded by his son Richard. The abdication of Richard followed by return of Charles II. and restoration of monarchy. Execution of ten regicides and of the Marquis of Argyle. Persecution of Non-conformists. Licentiousness of the court, and venal subserviency of the king to the interests of France.

The Reign of Louis XIV.

20. The only European powers left unpacified by the Treaty of Westphalia were France and Spain. The latter, relieved at length of her eighty years' war with the United Netherlands, was able to renew operations with greater prospect of success; while the former was paralyzed by all the troubles of a minority. The boundless rapacity of Mazarin and his ignorance or disregard of French laws, disgusted the national party; while the arrogance of Condé, who presumed upon his great military services, offended the court. The result was the civil war of the *Fronde*. Its prime mover was the abbé Gondi, afterward Cardinal de Retz; but many great nobles and fine ladies of the court took an active part in the disturbances. The queen-regent and her son withdrew from Paris, and, in the impossibility of levying taxes, were often destitute of the common comforts of life. This early experience of privation, and his resentment against the popular leaders, doubtless gave an impulse to the young king's ambition of absolute power.

21. The domestic war soon became part of the international conflict. Condé sold his services to the king of Spain, and marching from Guienne, defeated the royal army at Bleneau. The same consummate genius which had inspired terror in the enemies of France, exerted itself to waste and consume the forces of the kingdom. A battle in the suburbs of the capital was decided in favor of Condé by the warlike Mademoiselle de Montpensier, daughter of the Duke of Orleans, who with her own hands directed the guns of the Bastile upon the forces of the king. The city opened its gates to the prince; a new government was organized in which the Duke of Orleans became lieutenant-general of the kingdom, and Condé commander-in-chief of its armies. Mazarin retired from office. But De Retz, who had now reconciled himself with the court, soon effected another revolution, which drove Condé from the capital. This time he repaired to Flanders, and became generalissimo of the Spanish forces.

22. The French king and his mother reëntered Paris. Condé was sentenced by the Parliament to a traitor's death; the Duke of Orleans was exiled to Blois; De Retz, whose ambition had by this time overreached itself, was imprisoned and passed the rest of his life in obscurity. Mazarin was recalled, and the Fronde was ended. This civil war, whose details are too tedious to be related at length, is remarkable chiefly as having been the last struggle of the French nobility with the crown. Thenceforth all the privileged orders in the nation made common cause; the nobles were content to revolve as obedient satellites around the king and add their splendor to his court. The same questions had been raised in France and England, to meet directly opposite solutions. In the island kingdom both royalty and aristocracy had been overthrown, though but for a short time, and in the restored monarchy absolutism soon yielded to the just supremacy of law. In France, aristocracy joined with royalty to trample down the hopes and righteous demands of the people.

23. Spain, meanwhile, had profited by the domestic troubles of her enemy. Barcelona was taken after a blockade of thirteen months; and all Catalonia, after a nominal but contested independence of as many years, was reünited to the Spanish dominions. Casale in Italy, and Dunkirk, Ypres, and Gravelines, on the side of the Netherlands, were lost to France. Condé, at the head of the Spanish forces, infused new energy into the war. He was worthily opposed by Turenne, and for six years the two great commanders rivaled each other in feats of generalship. In 1654, England broke her peace with Spain, captured Jamaica, and sent forth fleets to prey upon Spanish-American commerce. The persecution of the Vaudois prevented an alliance of England with France until Mazarin, upon the peremptory demand of Cromwell, had obtained from the duke of Savoy pardon and indemnity for his oppressed subjects. An alliance was then made which threw the whole power of England into the French scale. The Battle of the Dunes resulted in the total defeat of the Spanish governor of the Netherlands, and the capture of Dunkirk, which by the terms of the treaty was made over to England. All Flanders, to the neighborhood of Brussels, soon fell into the power of France; and still more important events in Germany had meanwhile disposed the Spanish government to seek for peace.

24. Ever since the Treaty of Westphalia, the emperor Ferdinand III., though nominally at peace with France, had been indirectly furnishing men and money to the Spaniards. Duke Charles of Lorraine, having been expelled from his duchy by the French, gladly enlisted imperial troops under his own colors, and gained many advantages in Flanders and upon the German borders. To guard against his depredations, the four Rhenish electors, with the bishop of Münster, formed a "Catholic League," for the professed purpose of carrying out the Treaty of Westphalia. A "Protestant League" was formed with the same design in northern Germany. The emperor, intimidated by these coalitions, caused the treaty to be confirmed in 1654, by the Diet at Ratisbon.

25. Ferdinand III. died in 1657, and Mazarin, with all the German princes who were in the interest of France, resolved to prevent the conferring of the imperial crown upon another member of the Austrian family. Mazarin would gladly have obtained it for Louis XIV., but this proving impossible, the French interest was exerted in behalf of the young elector of Bavaria. The eldest son of Ferdinand III. had died before his father, and the second son, Leopold, had been educated only for the Church. He received the electoral votes, however, about sixteen months after his father's death. The French and their allies, unable to defeat his election, imposed upon him the most rigid conditions concerning the wars then in progress; and he solemnly engaged neither to render aid, secret or open, to the enemies of France, nor to interfere in Italy or the Netherlands. The fulfillment of this engagement was insured by the consolidation of the two Leagues above mentioned into one, called the "Rhenish League," under the protection of Louis XIV. The common forces were called "The army of His Most Christian Majesty and of the Allied Electors and Princes."

26. Spain, thus deprived of help from the Empire, sought peace with France. It was accomplished, after long negotiations, by
Nov., 1659.
the Treaty of the Pyrenees, and sealed by a marriage of Louis XIV. with Maria Theresa, the eldest daughter of the king of Spain. An important clause in the contract was the renunciation by the Infanta of all her rights to the Spanish crown, even in case of her brother's death. By the two treaties of Westphalia and the Pyrenees, the supremacy of France in European diplomacy was secured, and Spain resigned the precedence which she had claimed since the reign of Ferdinand and Isabella. Mazarin died in March, 1661, and Louis XIV., whose ambition was becoming impatient of restraint, made, the next day, the important announcement to his council, "For the future, I shall be my own prime minister."

27. He entered at once upon that course of diligent application to business which constituted, perhaps, the main secret of his success. From the beginning to the end of his reign, he spent eight hours each day in the actual labor of governing. The disordered exchequer soon felt the master-hand. The finance minister, Fouquet, who had enormously enriched himself by falsifying the public accounts, was condemned to imprisonment for life. He was succeeded by the celebrated Colbert, a man of stainless honesty and of such marked ability that, though the burden of taxation was diminished, the royal treasury was kept full, even during the most exhausting wars. This was done by introducing strict order and economy into every department of the government, and by a far-reaching and enlightened encouragement of industry which multiplied the sources of wealth, and made the royal demands easier to be borne.

28. The dignity of Louis did not suffer for want of assertion. The Spanish embassador at London having taken precedence of the French, Philip IV. was compelled to make a humble apology, and promise by a special envoy, in the presence of the whole diplomatic body at the French court, never more to infringe the claims of His Most Christian Majesty. Pope Alexander VII. underwent a similar humiliation; for his Corsican guard having insulted the French embassador at Rome, His Holiness was compelled to send messengers over the Alps to beg pardon in the most prostrate terms; to disband his guard and to erect a monument in commemoration of the event. Louis was already preparing a more serious assault upon the Spanish pretensions. Philip IV. having died in 1665, Louis claimed the Spanish Netherlands, with Luxembourg and Franche Comté, in right of his wife. He had already fortified himself by a treaty of commerce and alliance with the Dutch, and by the purchase of Dunkirk from the English (see § 19).

29. A war between his two allies delayed his operations. Charles II. desired to place his nephew, the young Prince of Orange, at the head of the Dutch Republic; but this scheme was firmly opposed by the Grand Pensionary De Witt, and the consequent division of parties nearly proved fatal to the independence of Holland. The war broke out in 1664, though not formally declared until the following year. The Dutch possessions on the Hudson River in America were seized by the English and renamed for the king's brother, the Duke of York and Albany. In June, 1665, the Dutch fleet was totally defeated by the Duke of York in a battle near Lowestoff. The bishop of Münster, an ally and pensioner of England, laid waste the Dutch territories from the eastward, until the German allies of Holland joined the king of France in compelling him to lay down his arms. A severe but indecisive battle was fought four days by the English and Dutch fleets off the North Foreland. In a subsequent action the English were victorious, *June 11-14, 1666.* but their domestic calamities — the Plague and the Great Fire at London — now disposed them to peace. During the progress of negotiations, the Dutch fleet sailed up the Thames and the Medway, destroyed many ships, captured Sheerness and threatened London.

30. The Peace of Breda, July 31, 1667, was effected by three treaties concluded by England with Holland, France, and Denmark. New York and New Jersey were secured to the first-named power, but the other colonial possessions of the Dutch were restored or left undisturbed. Louis XIV. had, meanwhile, astonished Europe by a sudden march into the Spanish Netherlands, where in the course of one summer most of the important places in the Walloon provinces surrendered with little or no resistance. The queen-regent of Spain was blinded by his pacific assurances until within a few days of the actual invasion. In the manifesto which the Grand Monarch then addressed to her in common with all the European rulers, he claimed the Spanish Netherlands not only in right of his queen, Maria Theresa, as the eldest child of Philip IV., but on the ground of a "natural claim" of the French kings to all which had ever belonged to the Frankish monarchy! Franche Comté was conquered the next winter by the Prince of Condé, who had now returned to his allegiance, having been pardoned and restored to his government of ducal Burgundy by the terms of the treaty of the Pyrenees.

31. England, Holland, and Sweden, alarmed by the arrogant pretensions of Louis XIV., now formed the Triple Alliance, with the purpose of setting a limit to his aggressions. Spain, at the last point of exhaustion, was unable to resist the dismemberment of her dominions, and in May, 1668, a definitive treaty was signed at Aix-la-Chapelle by which Louis restored Franche Comté, but retained all his conquests in the Netherlands. The Dutch Republic was now at the height of her glory and prosperity — the protectress of the great power which by her heroic struggle for independence she had most contributed to humble, the successful rival of England in the dominion of the seas, the deliverer of Denmark from the ambitious grasp of Sweden (see ? 46), and able to interpose a barrier to the ambitious career of Louis himself. The Grand Monarch, however, was not likely to forgive the intervention which had cut short his conquest of the entire Spanish dominion in the Low Countries. As the champion of absolute kingly power, he cherished an especial hatred toward the Republic, which afforded a generous asylum to all exiles from civil or religious tyranny.

32. By skillful bribery, Louis gained the neutrality of the emperor and the close adhesion of England, Sweden, and many of the German princes. The "Great Elector," Frederic William of Brandenburg, was the faithful ally of Holland; while the electors of Mentz, Trèves, and Saxony, with the margrave of Baireuth, formed a league for the defense of the Empire. Holland stood almost alone against the world, but Spain, recently delivered from the corrupt and incompetent government of the Jesuit minister Niethard, made an alliance with the States in December, 1671. The Prince of Orange, now twenty-one years of age, was appointed Captain-

General for the first campaign. England and France at nearly the same time declared war against Holland, and equally without honorable reason. The French army of 200,000 men crossed the lower Rhine in three divisions, and in the course of a few weeks had occupied the entire provinces of Guelders, Utrecht, and Overyssel, with part of Holland. The king, at the head of the main division, was attended by Louvois, his minister of war, and Vauban, the famous military engineer.

33. The Dutch were for the moment paralyzed with dismay. "Every man seemed to have received sentence of death." In forlorn hope of securing what remained to them, De Witt offered the most submissive terms, but the invader's reply was so haughty and insulting that it aroused a determination to defend the country to the last breath of its last inhabitant. In the popular fury, the two De Witts—the Grand Pensionary and his brother the admiral—were murdered; and dictatorial powers were conferred upon the young Prince of Orange, with the offices of Stadtholder, Captain-General, and Admiral, for life. The prince proposed in an assembly of the States, that rather than yield to the demands of Louis, they should abandon their country, and embarking on board their fleet, with wives, children, and what movable property they could secure, seek on the other side of the globe new homes among the tropical possessions of the Republic.

34. The tide soon turned in favor of the Dutch, who had at least held their own at sea, in contests with the combined English and French fleets. The progress of the French army was arrested by the opening of the sluices around Amsterdam, which laid that region of country under water, and allowed the Dutch fleet to approach their capital for its defense. The emperor, in spite of his promised neutrality, offered to aid the Republic on certain conditions; and the imperial general Montecuculi joined the elector of Brandenburg with 12,000 men. Turenne, by his masterly maneuvers on the Rhine, prevented their junction with the Prince of Orange, and even pursued the elector in his retreat as far as the Elbe; but the diversion was nevertheless of some advantage to the Dutch. The freezing of the canals enabled Marshal Luxembourg to invade Holland the next winter; but a sudden thaw compelled him to retreat without effecting a conquest.

35. Maestricht and Trèves were taken by the French in 1673; and Louis in person occupied the ten imperial cities in Alsace (see Book III., § 363), which he reduced to absolute subjection, compelling them to renounce the privileges guaranteed by the Treaty of Westphalia. A closer alliance of the Dutch with the Empire and with Spain, and the firm establishment of the allies on the Rhine by the capture of Bonn, compelled the French in the following winter to evacuate Holland, retaining of all their conquests only Grave and Maestricht. By the treaty

of Westminster, Feb., 1674, England made peace with the Republic, and agreed to a mutual restitution of conquests; Sweden alone remained in alliance with France.

36. The campaign of 1674 was, nevertheless, favorable to that country. Franche Comté was reconquered, and the French frontier permanently extended to the Jura. Turenne ravaged the Palatinate with great barbarity, while he held the imperialists in check, and finally wrested Alsace from their grasp. The English colonel Churchill — afterward the famous Duke of Marlborough — served under him in this campaign. The next year was to see three principal actors withdrawn from the military stage: Turenne by a cannon-ball, which ended his life near Salzbach, while he was reconnoitering for a battle which was never to take place; Condé and Montecuculi by the growing infirmities of age and disease.

37. In 1676, the main activity of the war was transferred to the Mediterranean, and in three naval battles near Sicily, the French were completely victorious. In the second of these battles, the brave De Ruyter received his death-wound. The campaign on land was fortunate for the French. In April, 1677, the Prince of Orange sustained a severe defeat at Cassel, while marching to the relief of St. Omer. The prince was the consistent, life-long opponent of Louis XIV., their relative positions in the European States-System being nearly the same with those of Elizabeth of England and Philip of Spain a century before. The English Parliament was warmly in favor of the prince; but Charles II. had just sold himself anew to the king of France for a pension of 200,000 livres, and promised to make no alliance without Louis' consent. He was nevertheless compelled by the Parliament to declare war against France, and to confirm his alliance with the States by the marriage of his niece, Mary of York, with the Prince of Orange.

38. It was agreed to force the French king to accept terms of peace. While negotiations were pending, Louis seized the great city of Ghent, and Ypres; thus gaining the power to dictate his own terms. The Peace of Nimeguen was signed August 14, 1678; Spain and the emperor acceded a few months later. The greatest losses of the war had fallen upon Spain, which was compelled to cede Franche Comté and the region afterward known as French Flanders. Holland lost her settlements in Senegal and Guiana, which had been taken by the French. The Duke of Lorraine was offered the restoration of his dominions only on condition of granting to Louis XIV. four military roads, each half a league in breadth, from France into Germany. Rather than accept these humiliating terms, he exiled himself for life from his paternal estates.

The glory of Louis the Great was now at its height. But the insolence of his pretensions had already excited an enmity throughout Europe which clouded his last days with disappointment and regret.

RECAPITULATION.

Civil war of the *Fronde* during minority of Louis XIV. Prince of Condé enters the service of Spain. With close of the *Fronde* ends the long conflict between royal and feudal power in France. Catalonia is subdued; Spanish army under Condé gains many victories over the French in the Netherlands. Persecution of the Vaudois being discontinued at the demand of Cromwell, the forces of the English Commonwealth, added to those of France, gain the Battle of the Dunes. Dunkirk surrendered to England. The Duke of Lorraine makes war in Spanish interest on the western borders of the Empire. Death of Ferdinand III.; French opposition to Leopold, who nevertheless becomes emperor; his power limited by the Rhenish League. Treaty of the Pyrenees transfers the leadership of European diplomacy from Spain to France. Louis XIV. marries the Spanish Infanta; assumes direct control of affairs upon death of Mazarin. Colbert's thrifty administration. Louis claims Spanish Netherlands and other possessions in right of his wife. Naval war between England and Holland. New Amsterdam becomes New York. Peace of Breda. Louis surprises the Walloon provinces. Triple alliance of England, Sweden, and Holland forces him to accept the Treaty of Aix-la-Chapelle. He bribes the first two powers to aid or permit his vengeance against the Dutch. Murder of the De Witts. Prince of Orange becomes stadtholder and Dictator. Nearly all Europe involved in the war. Brandenburg and afterward England and the Empire take sides with Holland. Alsace and Franche Comté conquered and held by France. Death of Turenne; retirement of Condé and Montecuculi. Increase of French naval power; three victories in the Mediterranean. Prince of Orange defeated at Cassel; he marries the daughter of the Duke of York. Treaty of Nimeguen restores peace and places Louis XIV. at the height of his power.

THE NORTHERN NATIONS.

39. In the north of Europe, important events had meanwhile taken place. Christina of Sweden displayed during the first years of her reign a wisdom, firmness, and manifold ability which astonished her gray-haired counselors. Her influence in favor of peace was felt in the Treaty of Westphalia. Her extraordinary accomplishments won the admiration of the learned foreigners who thronged her court, among others of the French philosopher, Descartes. Unhappily the powers of her mind were not balanced and supported by steadiness of purpose. She wasted her revenues in fantastic entertainments, and bestowed the crown-lands on her favorite courtiers, who in the subsequent reign employed her gifts only to oppose the royal prerogatives. At length she became weary of the cares of state, and naming her cousin, Charles Gustavus, as her successor, abdicated the throne in the twenty-eighth year of her age, and sought freedom in a milder climate. At Innsbruck, A. D. 1654. she abjured her father's faith and was received into the Roman Church. During the thirty-five remaining years of her life, she wandered over a great part of the continent and twice revisited Sweden, but ultimately died at Rome in 1689.

40. Charles X. found his kingdom still exhausted by its efforts in the Thirty Years' War, as well as by the lavish expenditures of Christina; yet his ambition aimed at nothing short of supremacy in northern Europe and the conversion of the Baltic into a mere Swedish lake. The weakness of Denmark and Poland seemed to flatter his hopes. In the latter kingdom—or "Republic," as it was called by the Poles themselves—all real power lay in the hands of the nobles; for the Diet, chosen by and from that class alone, not only elected the king, but made the laws and in one sense executed them, all officers of state being responsible to it and not to the sovereign. When discussions in the Diet failed of peaceable solution, the nobles had a constitutional right to levy armies and settle their differences by force. Sometimes a General Confederation was formed under a military dictatorship, which suspended or absorbed into itself all the regular functions of government.

41. John Casimir (A. D. 1648–1668), a son of Sigismund III. (see Book III., § 317), was destitute of the tact, firmness, and versatility of resources required for the leadership of so turbulent and disorganized a nation. Several provinces threatened to revolt and place themselves under foreign protection; and the vice-chancellor, taking refuge at the Swedish court, urged Charles X. to interfere and deliver the Poles from a dominion which they hated. The great empire of Russia was another formidable neighbor of the Polish king. Alexis, the second of the Romanoffs, had already begun that policy of civilizing his nation and assuming his just place in the European States-System, which was more especially to distinguish his son, Peter the Great. A revolt of the Cossacks of the Ukraine, against the Polish kingdom, to which they had been subjected since A. D. 1386, gave Alexis a pretext for war. United to the Russians by identity of race, language, and religion, the Cossacks claimed the protection of the Czar, who was only too willing to accept their allegiance.

42. Three Russian armies were soon in the field—one, led by the Czar in person, besieged and captured Smolensko and several other towns; a second invaded Lithuania, and a third occupied the entire Ukraine. The next year, two Swedish armies entered Poland, while their fleet blockaded the free city of Dantzic. Charles X. defeated John Casimir
Aug., 1655. and received the surrender of Warsaw. The Polish army and most of the nobility took oaths of allegiance to the Swedish king: Cracow opened its gates, and the province of Lithuania, though chiefly occupied by Russians, acknowledged him as its sovereign. A party in the Senate offered the crown of Poland to the emperor, but a majority in the kingdom inclined to Charles X.

43. At this juncture, the great elector, Frederic William of Brandenburg, having allied himself with John Casimir, marched an army into West Prussia, with a view to protect that duchy from the Swedes. He was defeated by Charles X. in person, and was compelled to acknowledge himself the vassal of Sweden instead of Poland. In subsequent treaties, the embarrassments of the Swedish king enabled the elector to secure the full sovereignty of eastern or ducal Prussia, thus laying the corner-stone of a powerful monarchy. John Casimir, meanwhile, mustered an army of Poles and Tartars for the recapture of Warsaw. It surrendered June 21, 1656; but was recovered, the following month, for the Swedish king and the elector by a three days' battle in its vicinity.

44. If the enemies of Poland had been agreed, the dissolution of that kingdom would have been hastened by more than a century; but the Czar, now jealous of the Swedes, invaded their province of Livonia with 100,000 men, while he sent another army to ravage Ingria, Carelia, and Finland. The emperor Leopold and the king of Denmark, also alarmed or offended by the progress of Charles X., allied themselves with John Casimir to oppose that "Pyrrhus of the North." Cromwell favored Sweden, though he offered no active aid, but A. D. 1657. George Ragotzki, Prince of Transylvania, made a close offensive alliance with Charles X., in the hope of himself obtaining the crown of Poland, or at least the provinces of Red Russia, Podolia, Volhynia, and a large southern portion of that kingdom. The elector of Brandenburg withdrew his contingent force from the Swedish army and made peace with Poland, on being guaranteed his title of Sovereign Duke and the possession of Prussia as an independent state.

45. By a sudden and rapid march, Charles X. appeared with his veterans upon the Danish border, and dispatching his general Wrangel to occupy the duchy of Bremen, he overran the territories of Holstein and Schleswig, almost without encountering resistance. Fredericsodde was taken by siege, Oct. 24; and as soon as a winter of unusual severity, even for those regions, had covered the Baltic with ice, he began a remarkable series of maneuvers among the islands of the Sound by leading cavalry and artillery across the solid surface of the two Belts, capturing Fünen, Langeland, Laaland, Falster, and finally passing over into Zealand. Copenhagen, poorly fortified and taken by surprise, was at his mercy. But France and England now intervened, and mediated the treaty of Roskild, by which Denmark ceded to Sweden March, 1658. some of her most important islands, and abandoned all her offensive alliances.

46. The ambition of Charles X. had grown by indulgence, and he dreamed not only of ruling the whole region of the Baltic, but of marching, like Alaric, with an overwhelming host to Italy, and founding there a new kingdom of the Goths. Early in August he was again in the field, with the pretense that Frederic III. of Denmark had failed to fulfill all the conditions of the treaty of Roskild. The siege of Kronenberg, which he captured Sept. 5, gave the Danes time to strengthen the fortifications of Copenhagen, so that it could hold out until a Dutch fleet arrived to its relief. The Swedes then turned the siege of the

capital into a blockade, but they were themselves besieged by the Dutch and Danish fleets which guarded the sea, while on land the elector of Brandenburg with a combined force of Poles, Austrians, and his own subjects, drove the Swedes from Jutland and captured most of the towns in Swedish Pomerania. Thorn, after eighteen months' siege, surrendered to the Poles, Dec., 1658, and in Prussia only the two towns of Elbing and Marienburg remained to Charles X.

47. The Maritime Powers now interfered to put an end to a war which embarrassed their commerce by closing the ports of the Baltic. But the sudden death of Charles X., Feb., 1660, removed the main cause of disturbance. His son and heir was but four years old. The queen-regent, with her Council of State, immediately entered into negotiations with the hostile powers, and peace was made respectively with Poland, Denmark, and Russia, by the three treaties of Oliva, Copenhagen, and Cardis. Poland continued at war with Russia until 1667, when a truce of thirteen years was agreed upon, and the Cossacks were then permanently divided into the tribes of the Don and the Ukraine — the former under allegiance to the Czar, the latter to the king of Poland. In Denmark the year of the peace was marked by a bloodless revolution, which changed the elective into a hereditary monarchy, and destroyed the excessive power of the nobles. In Sweden, on the other hand, the ancient nobility gained great ascendency during the long minority of Charles XI.

May, July, 1660;
July. 1661.

48. In 1675, war was renewed by the elector of Brandenburg, who was joined by Christian V. of Denmark and aided with a fleet by the Dutch. The Swedes were twice defeated within four days at Rathenow and Fehrbellin ; and sustained several great disasters at sea. The island of Rügen was conquered by Denmark, and Stettin, after six months' siege, surrendered to the elector of Brandenburg. Christian V. was, however, defeated, in 1676, at Halmstadt ; and though the still severer battle of Lunden was indecisive, he was disabled by it from any further attempts that year. The next summer he suffered a disastrous defeat at Landscrona, though his naval force was constantly superior to that of the Swedes. The latter, in 1678, invaded ducal Prussia, but without success ; and so great were their sufferings, that of their army of 16,000 men only 1,500 retraced their way to Riga.

49. The details of this northern war are, however, less important, because Louis XIV., who now assumed to dictate terms to all Europe, interfered, and by treaties signed near Paris, compelled the allies to restore to Sweden all their acquisitions. Though the latter power thus emerged from a disastrous war with no loss of territory, yet her navy was destroyed, her treasury emptied, and her inability to maintain herself without foreign aid rendered clear to the eyes

A. D. 1679.

of Europe. In this state of depression, all classes except the nobility called for a revolution in the government; and in a Diet at Stockholm, the clergy, citizens, and peasants adopted a new constitution conferring absolute and irresponsible power upon the king. A subsequent Diet in 1682 required a strict account from all who had administered the finances during the young king's minority, or who had held leases of crown-lands since the death of Gustavus Adolphus. The prudent measures of Charles XI. during the last years of his reign so far retrieved the resources of his kingdom, that his son, Charles XII., was able for a time to reëstablish the superiority of Sweden in the north.

50. Before describing the remarkable changes which took place in the Russian Empire, we glance for a moment at the relations of Christendom with the Turks. Their "War of Candia" with Venice lasted twenty-four years (A. D. 1645–1669); but its only memorable event was its termination in the surrender of the city of Candia, after a siege of two years and four months. The French made vain attempts to relieve it. The whole island remained nearly two centuries in the undisputed possession of the Turks.

Meanwhile, hostilities broke out afresh, A. D. 1663, between the Empire and the Porte; and Achmet Köproli, the Grand Vizier, invaded Hungary with 200,000 men. In spite of the vigorous exertions of Montecuculi, Neuhäusel and several other fortresses were taken, and Moravia was ravaged by a horde of Tartars who penetrated nearly to Olmütz. In this crisis of peril to all Europe, Sweden, France, the Pope, and the Italian states joined in sending contributions of men and money; and with the extraordinary supplies voted by the imperial Diet, Montecuculi was able to take the field with a formidable army. He routed the Turks in the great battle of St. Gothard, near the frontier of Hungary and Styria; but instead of using this advantage by pushing the war with increased energy, the Court of Vienna hastened to make a twenty years' truce with the invaders. By the treaty of Vasvar, they were permitted to retain all their conquests, and even received a tribute, disguised under the name of a gift, of 200,000 florins.

Aug., 1664.

51. Among the reasons which forced the emperor to this disgraceful treaty, was the enmity of the Hungarians against the House of Austria. The civil oppressions and religious persecutions of the latter gave rise to repeated attempts at revolt, until in 1678, the young Count Tekeli, more fortunate than his predecessors, was able with 12,000 Hungarians to defeat the imperial armies in Upper Hungary, and occupy the whole region of the Carpathian Mountains. He allied himself with the Sultan, who recognized him as king of Hungary in 1682; and the truce of Vasvar having nearly expired, Kara Mustapha, now Grand Vizier, joined him with a large army at Essek and marched upon Vienna. At their ap-

proach, the emperor and his court fled from the capital, followed in a single day by sixty thousand persons.

52. After two months' siege and the loss of 6,000 of its garrison by battle or pestilence, Vienna was saved by the arrival of John Sobieski, king of Poland. This great warrior had already covered himself with glory by his gallant defense of Poland against Cossacks and Tartars; and had been raised in 1676, by the acclamations of his countrymen, to the throne. Increasing his army by German reinforcements, he numbered 83,000 men, when the rockets which betokened his arrival upon the heights of Kahlenberg kindled new hope in the starving citizens of Vienna. The next day the Turks were routed with great slaughter; and their vast encampments, with treasures of money and jewels, as well as horses and materials of war, remained to the victors. They were pursued in their retreat and again defeated by Sobieski and the Duke of Lorraine; and the fortress of Gran, which for nearly a century and a half had been held by the Turks, was wrested from their possession. Kara Mustapha atoned to his enraged sovereign by the loss of his head.

Sept., 1683.

53. The next year the Duke of Lorraine captured Wissegrad, Waitzen, and Pesth, and besieged Buda three months, with a loss of 23,000 men, but without success. Two years later, after a second siege of three months, it was taken by assault and restored to the Hungarians, having been 145 years a Mohammedan city. In 1684, the emperor, the king of Poland, and the Venetians joined the Pope in what was called a Holy League against the Turks; and the Holy War which followed lasted until 1699. Austria in three years regained all Hungary, Transylvania, and Slavonia. In the battle of Mohaez, Aug., 1687, the Turks were defeated upon the field of their former memorable victory. (See Book III., § 122.)

54. By a change in the Hungarian Constitution, the crown of that kingdom was now made hereditary in the House of Austria; and the magnates renounced the valued but mischievous privilege, secured to them by a charter of Andrew II., A. D. 1222, of taking up arms against their sovereign whenever they judged him guilty of having broken his coronation vow. Imperial garrisons were admitted into all the fortresses of the kingdom; Leopold, in return for these concessions, confirmed the ancient privileges of the nation, and granted to all orders and sects of Christians the free exercise of their religion. His son, the archduke Joseph, was crowned king of Hungary in December, 1687.

55. The Czar[*] of Russia — or, as it was still called, Muscovy — joined the League in 1686; but his efforts to conquer the Crimea from the

---

[*] The Czar Alexis had died in 1676; his son Feodor in 1682. Another son, Ivan, under the regency of his sister Sophia, bore the titles of sovereignty until 1689, when Peter the Great, half-brother of Feodor and Ivan, assumed the crown.

Tartars were unavailing. It was reserved for his greater brother, Peter, to capture Azov and secure an entrance to the Black Sea. The Venetians gained brilliant victories over the Turks in southern and central Greece, capturing, among other important but less illustrious places, Corinth and Athens. The Parthenon, the greatest architectural ornament of the latter city — still perfect in its exquisite proportions as in the days of Pericles — was used by the Turks as a powder-magazine. During the siege, a bomb from a Venetian vessel fell into the building, and its explosion scattered the finely sculptured marbles of the central portion to the winds. The conquest of the Morea was completed by the Venetian general Morosini in 1690.

56. The manifold disasters of the Turks in the year 1687, occasioned a mutiny in the army and a riot in the capital, resulting in the deposition and imprisonment of Mahomet IV., and the elevation of his brother Solyman II. to the throne. Their humiliation only deepened during the next two years: Belgrade was taken by the imperialists, and a great part of Bosnia overrun. The Sultan's demands for peace were refused, for the emperor now imagined it possible to annihilate the Turkish power in Europe and recombine the Eastern and Western Empires. In the campaign of 1689, these projects seemed almost on the eve of fulfillment. Several passes of the Balkan and forts on the Danube were taken by the margrave of Baden, who fixed his winter-quarters in Wallachia.

57. The energy and talents of the new Grand Vizier, Mustapha Köproli, son of Achmet, enabled the Turks to recover, in 1690, almost all that they had lost. Belgrade was retaken, Temesvar newly provisioned, and a battle near Essek gained by the Vizier, while a division of the Turkish army entered Transylvania. The next year, however, in the battle of Salankemen, the Turks were defeated, and Köproli slain. Nothing of importance occurred during the next five years, until Mustapha II., becoming Sultan, crossed the Danube at the head of his armies and defeated the imperialists at Bega. John Sobieski died   A. D. 1696.
this year, and the elector Augustus of Saxony, though opposed by a majority of the nobles, received the Polish crown through the combined influence of the Czar, the emperor, the Jesuits, and the Pope. He was succeeded in command of the imperial armies in Hungary by one of the greatest generals of an age especially distinguished by military genius and science.

58. Prince Eugene of Savoy, though born a French noble, had been offended by Louis XIV., and offering his services to the emperor, exacted in later years a bitter revenge. Among his first great exploits was a signal overthrow of the Turks at Zeuta on the Theiss (Sept., 1697), which was among the chief circumstances leading to a termination of the war. The Venetians, meanwhile, had made many conquests in Dalmatia and

Albania; and the Prince of Orange, now king of England as well as stadtholder of Holland, used his influence in favor of peace. Three months' negotiations at Carlowitz, near Peterwardein, resulted in a treaty between the Sultan on one side, and the emperor, the king of Poland,

Jan., 1699.
and the Republic of Venice on the other. The Turks ceded to the House of Austria nearly all their conquests or possessions in Hungary, Transylvania, Sclavonia, and part of Croatia; to Venice several Dalmatian fortresses, the isles of St. Maura and Ægina, and the entire southern peninsula of Greece; to Poland the Ukraine, Podolia, and Kameniek. The agreement with Russia was delayed more than three years, for the Sultan was most unwilling to admit his powerful neighbor to a share in Black Sea navigation. In July, 1702, Azov, with eighty miles of coast, was at length ceded to Peter the Great, who soon made the fortress one of the strongest in Europe.

59. The capture of Azov had been the first success of the young Czar, and it was achieved by foreign aid. But before the signing of the treaty he had put in execution his extraordinary design of exiling himself for a time, that he might become the civilizer of his people by learning the arts and industries of more advanced nations. Traveling in disguise as a subordinate in one of his own embassies, he passed through part of Sweden and Brandenburg, and fixed his residence at length for several months in Holland. Here he labored with his own hands as a ship-carpenter, and adopted the raiment, food, and lodgings of his comrades in the shop and yard, learning by actual experience all the details of their work. Meanwhile he was constantly informed of movements in his distant empire, and often laid down the hatchet or the plane to sign an order for the march of an army or the arrest of a suspected traitor.

60. By the invitation of William III., he passed over into England and established himself near the royal navy yard at Deptford, where he continued his labors in ship-building while receiving instruction in surgery, mathematics, and navigation. After his studies were ended, he paid a visit of ceremony to the emperor Leopold at Vienna, and would have continued his journey into Italy, but news of a revolt of the *Strelitz*, the Russian militia, recalled him to his own dominion. This formidable and turbulent soldiery had more than once attempted the life of Peter in obedience to the orders of his sister Sophia; and the Czar had begun in his boyhood to train a body of infantry after the German tactics to supersede it. The time had now come for its extermination. The ringleaders were already in irons; the barbarous mode of their execution was a warning to those who might have followed their example. The *Strelitz* was forever dissolved, and the princess Sophia, whose enthronement had been the object, if she herself had not been the mover, of the plot, was imprisoned in a convent.

61. Having reëstablished his power by these prompt and decisive measures, Peter began to execute his cherished plans for the civilization of his empire. He invited from other nations generals, artists, and literary men whose talents could aid in the formation of his plans, as well as skilled artisans, whose industries he patronized and sought to establish in his dominion. Arsenals, manufactories, and schools of navigation were established by order of the Czar; maps and charts of various parts of the Empire, and a general survey of mines, were made by competent experts and engineers. Greater difficulty was encountered in introducing European ideas into the domestic habits of the people. The long robes and unkempt beards of the men, the oriental seclusion of the women, gradually gave way to western modes of dressing and living; but a brutal grossness of indulgence still prevailed not less at court than among the common people, and Peter often remarked that though he could civilize his empire he could not reform himself.

RECAPITULATION.

Talents and eccentricities of Christina of Sweden. She abdicates in favor of her cousin, Charles X., who aims at supremacy in the north, and even dreams of founding a Gothic kingdom in the south, of Europe. Aristocratic but unstable character of the Polish constitution. John Casimir threatened by Sweden and Russia. The Czar encourages a revolt of the Ukraine Cossacks. Two Swedish and three Russian armies invade the Polish territories. Charles acknowledged by many as king of Poland. Ducal Prussia ceded to Brandenburg. Russia, Denmark, and the Empire opposed to Sweden. Protector of England and Prince of Transylvania become her allies. Charles X. overruns Denmark, crosses the frozen Belts and captures the islands. Peace of Roskild mediated by France and England. Charles violates its terms; is besieged by Dutch and Danish fleets in harbor of Copenhagen, while his lands are invaded by elector of Brandenburg. Upon his death, Sweden makes peace with Poland, Denmark, and Russia. Power of the nobles overthrown in Denmark, temporarily augmented in Sweden. A new war with Denmark and Brandenburg — disastrous to the Swedes — ended by intervention of Louis XIV. Revolution in Sweden depresses the nobles and makes the royal power absolute.

"War of Candia" ends in subjection of Crete to the Turks. Their conquest in Austrian dominions; defeat at St. Gothard. Truce of Vasvar hastened by disaffection in Hungary. Revolt of Count Tekeli; he seeks alliance of the Turks, who besiege Vienna. It is relieved by Sobieski, who routs and pursues the besiegers. Gran retaken; other fortresses and finally Buda wrested from the Turks. "Holy War" lasts fifteen years. Hungarian crown declared hereditary in the Hapsburg family. Nobles relinquish the right of armed insurrection, and the nation receives a guarantee of civil and religious privileges. Accession of the Sultan Solyman II. Many fortresses on the Danube taken from the Turks. Mustapha Köproli retrieves their losses, but is defeated and slain at Salankemen. Augustus of Saxony becomes king of Poland — Eugene of Savoy imperial general-in-chief. Defeat of the Turks at Zeuta. Treaty of Carlowitz restores Southern Greece to Venice, and most of its southern provinces to Austria. Azov and access to the Black Sea secured by Peter of Russia. Voluntary exile of the Czar for self-education. He introduces science and material civilization into his empire; disbands the *Strelitz* and replaces it with modern infantry.

REIGN OF LOUIS XIV.—*Continued.*

62. Returning to the central and more important figures in the great European picture, we find Louis XIV. still annexing new territories, in spite of the treaty of Nimeguen, or at least by the most artful construction of its terms. The free imperial city of Strasbourg was secured by bribery and then taken by surprise; and the skill of Vauban soon made it a fortress of the first class. So important was it considered as an eastern bulwark of France, that a medal was struck to commemorate the completion of the works, bearing the inscription *Clausa Germanis Gallia.* Twenty other towns were wrested from neighboring princes; and regular "Courts of Reünion" were instituted in France, to ascertain what dependencies might have belonged at any earlier period to these newly annexed dominions. The indignation excited in Germany by this rapacity was only increased by the intrigues of Louis to obtain a promise of the imperial crown at the next election.

A. D. 1681.

63. Under the influence of William of Orange, Sweden, Holland, Spain, and the Empire entered a joint protest against the siege of Luxembourg by the French, and insisted upon a faithful execution of the treaties of Münster and Nimeguen. Warned by this coälition, Louis suspended his aggressions, seizing, however, a pretext for his apparent moderation in the siege of Vienna by the Turks (see §§ 51, 52). He declared that he could not prosecute his personal plans while Christendom itself was threatened by the infidel; but he secretly urged the Sultan not to relax his operations. In the meantime he sent a fleet to bombard Algiers and liberate French and other captives. No sooner had the Turks retreated from Vienna, then Louis marched his troops into the Spanish Netherlands and captured Courtrai and Dixmude. The next spring and summer Oudenarde and Luxembourg were taken, Trèves was dismantled, Mons and even Brussels were threatened. A truce for twenty years was now arranged between France and Holland, and acceded to in a few weeks by the emperor and the king of Spain. It was agreed that Louis should keep Strasbourg and the province of Luxembourg, with all the towns which he had annexed before August, 1681, but should make no farther claim on the imperial territories.

64. In 1683, the queen of France died; and the next year the king privately married Mme. de Maintenon, a woman of remarkable powers of mind, whose influence effected a great change in the life of Louis. Unhappily his reformation of morals was accompanied by an access of bigotry, which led to a renewed persecution of his Huguenot subjects. The king dreamed of expiating his errors and follies by the merit of restoring some thousands of heretics to the communion of the Roman Church; and a succession of edicts soon deprived the protestants of all the civil and domestic privileges secured to them by the wiser policy of Henry IV. and Louis XIII. The great and good Colbert, their patron and protector, was no more. Louvois, the minister of war, sent troops of dragoons to crush resistance in the provinces. This brutal soldiery, quartered in the homes of the defenseless people, reduced them to despair. Many thousands sent in their submission; and the pride of Louis or the flattery of his courtiers declared him as great a conqueror of the souls, as of the bodies and possessions of men.

65. A more decisive and fatal blow was the revocation of the Edict of Nantes, given by Henry IV., and esteemed by the Huguenots as the great charter of their liberties. It was commanded that all protestant churches should be demolished, all ministers exiled, and the children of protestant parents instructed by the parish priest in the Catholic doctrines. These orders were executed with even greater severity than the letter of the Revocation demanded or permitted. The best of the Huguenots were imprisoned in damp and noisome dungeons; those who attempted resistance were shot without mercy. Though the severest penalties were denounced against those who should leave France, hundreds of thousands found means of emigrating; and England, Holland, Germany, Switzerland, even America, gained what France lost — the most valuable source of wealth that any country can possess — an enlightened, industrious, and skillful class of citizens. The great elector, Frederic William of Brandenburg, distinguished himself by his liberality to the refugees — providing them with land and materials for building, and capital for their manufactures. Twenty thousand found refuge in his dominions, and their diligence soon transformed the waste sands about Berlin into a well cultivated garden. Among the exiles were literary men of high reputation; and Marshal Schomberg, who after a short residence in Brandenburg, entered, with a multitude of his compatriots, the service of William of Orange.

66. The greatest opponent of Louis XIV. was not slow to perceive the blunder which that sovereign had committed, nor unwilling to take advantage of it. Through his exertions the League of Augsburg combined the emperor and the chief German states, July, 1686. with the kings of Spain and Sweden as princes of the Empire, in opposition to France. The affairs of Cologne and the Palatinate soon afforded a pretext for hostilities. French gold secured the election of a partisan of Louis to the archbishopric, while the Pope and the League of Augsburg supported the candidature of a Bavarian prince. The Duke of Orleans, brother of Louis XIV., had married the sister of the last elector palatine of the House of Simmern. The duchess at her marriage renounced all feudal rights in the Palatinate, but not her hereditary claim to the movable property or allodial possessions of her family. Louis now claimed as "movables" all the cannon of the electoral fortresses; and his lawyers so interpreted the allodial tenure as to make it include nearly the entire province. The new elector, Philip William of Neuburg, appealed to the emperor; and the alarm excited by these arrogant assumptions, gave new importance to the League of Augsburg.

67. War began in the autumn of 1688, when French troops in two divisions moved from Flanders, and while one under Vauban besieged Philipsburg, the other under Boufflers occupied the electoral territories of Mentz and the Palatinate on the left of the Rhine. The Prince of Orange availed himself of the French movement to prosecute his views in England.

To understand the great revolution in that country, we must briefly resume its history under Charles II. The dismissal of Clarendon in 1667 left the government in the hands of a corrupt ministry, which interposed no obstacle to the king's subserviency to France. Louis XIV. already inscribed in his prospective merit-roll the restoration of England as well as the Huguenots to the Catholic Church. But this prospect was in the highest degree alarming to a majority of the English nation, and the general apprehension secured the passage of the Test Act, requiring all persons in either civil or military office to conform to the rites of the national church and acknowledge the supremacy of the king.

A. D. 1673.

68. The popular excitement was skillfully used by one Titus Oates, who invented or greatly exaggerated the evidences of a "Popish Plot" to kill the king and raise the Duke of York to the throne. Such credence was lent to the wicked fabrications of Oates, that he even dared accuse the queen herself as accessary to the plot. Lord Stafford, a Catholic peer, was executed on the same charge. A bill to exclude the Duke of York, as a papist, from the succession, was passed by the House of Commons, but rejected by the Lords. The duke was sent to "try his hand at governing" Scotland, where the brutal proceedings of Claverhouse against the Covenanters were only exasperating without subduing the resistance of the people to the law prohibiting "conventicles." No great amelioration was wrought by the new Lord High Commissioner, unless the substitution of judicial murder for military execution may be so considered.

69. The wicked and notorious George Jeffreys, Chief Justice of England, now began to distinguish himself in his circuit through the northern and western counties. The king had already violated the ancient privileges of London by making the election of mayor and sheriffs dependent only upon his will. Other towns were forced by Jeffreys to surrender their charters. The indignation aroused by these proceedings led to another real or supposed conspiracy to destroy both the king and the Duke of York.

This "Rye House Plot"— if, indeed, it had any real existence — was the work of obscure persons; but the government — now as credulous and unjust as the people had been in the opposite case of the Popish Plot — accused lords Essex and Russell and Mr. Algernon Sidney of having part in the treason. Essex died in prison, whether by his own hand or by another, has never been proved. Russell and Sidney perished on the scaffold. Both were illegally convicted, in defiance of the clearest demands of the law. No overt act of treason was charged upon either. Sidney was republican by theory — the last of the "Commonwealth-men" who had opposed the protectorate of Cromwell as well as the restoration of Charles — but he was not an assassin nor a patron of assassins. Only one witness could be produced against him; the law required two. A manuscript found among his papers, justifying conspiracy against Caligula and Nero was admitted as evidence. It was never fully proved to have been written by him; but in any case, acts and not opinions are the subjects of judicial inquiry.

70. Charles II. died in February, 1685, and the Duke of York became king without open opposition. James II. was a better man than his brother; but his views both of civil and religious affairs were even more firmly opposed to those of the most enlightened of his subjects. The principle that governments exist for the good of the people, not the people for the government — self-evident as it now appears — was only approaching its triumph in the English Revolution. It was affirmed by the Whig party, then just rising into importance; while the Tories upheld the sacred right of kings, whatever their personal character, to the unalterable allegiance of their people.

71. James began his reign by ordering the release of all persons who had been imprisoned for refusing the oath of supremacy, and commanded his judges to discourage further prosecutions in matters of religion. This act, though apparently just and liberal, was regarded with distrust by the mass of the nation, who saw in it a first step toward the introduction of popery. The general discontent favored a concerted invasion of England and Scotland in the interest of a rival claimant to the crown. The banished Earl of Argyle landed in the western Highlands; and the Duke of Monmouth, a son of Charles II., invading England, was proclaimed king at Taunton. Both movements failed. Argyle, deserted by his followers, was captured and put to death at Edinburgh; Monmouth, though joined by several thousands of Whigs, was defeated in battle at Sedgemoor, and beheaded at London. The revenge of the court was gratified by a series of brutal massacres perpetrated by Colonel Kirke in the western counties; and by the not less barbarous proceedings of Jeffreys under forms of law. The chief justice boasted that he had hanged more persons for high treason than all English judges since the Norman Conquest.

72. Presuming upon his success, the king increased his standing army, nullified the Test Act by his own authority, and received a nuncio from the Pope with ceremonious homage. The primate, Dr. Sancroft, and six other bishops venturing to remonstrate, were imprisoned in the Tower. The people, though alarmed, waited in patience; for the king was growing old, and his eldest daughter, the heiress-apparent, was the wife of the Prince of Orange, the great opponent of absolutism in civil and religious affairs. Many years before his accession, James had contracted a second marriage with an Italian princess, Mary of Modena. In June, 1688, his first son was born. This event hastened the revolution. Despairing of a return of just government by constitutional means, many men of rank and influence sent an invitation to the Prince of Orange to lead an army into England.

73. It was accepted, and William landed in Torbay. The common people flocked about him from the first; and soon officers of the army and the government, with their dependents, began to arrive in his camp. The king, whose late repentance had failed to retrieve his errors, sent his wife and son to France, and then himself fled from the capital, throwing the Great Seal into the Thames, and leaving England without a government. The Prince of Orange summoned a convention of the Estates of the realm according to the usual parliamentary forms. This body having recognized the flight of James II. as an abdication, proceeded to "secure the religion, laws, and liberties" of England by a Declaration of Rights, and then offered the crown to William and Mary in joint sovereignty. Their reign began Feb. 13, 1689, the two preceding months being called an Interregnum.

Nov., 1688.

74. Scotland followed the example of England, though several clans of Highlanders made armed resistance. They defeated General Mackay in the pass of Killiecrankie; but their leader, Graham of Claverhouse, now better known as Viscount Dundee, was slain, and the victory was without effect. In Ireland the contest was conducted by James II. in person, with forces furnished by his cousin, the king of France. But the heroic defense of Londonderry, his defeat at Newton Butler, and the still more decisive battle of the Boyne gained by William III., wrecked the hopes of the Stuarts. James, once more a fugitive, became a pensioner for the rest of his days, on the generosity of Louis XIV. So altered were the relations of European powers, that the king of Spain, the emperor, and even the Pope, joined in congratulating William on his accession to the throne; for this event, by turning the last remaining ally of Louis into an enemy, imposed a check upon that extravagant ambition which was dreaded by all Europe alike.

July, 1690.

75. Unable to defend his conquests beyond the Rhine, the French king had commanded his generals to burn all the towns and villages which they could not garrison. By this brutal order 100,000 human beings were made homeless, and rich and thriving cities, not less than farms, orchards, and vineyards, were changed into a blackened and desolate wilderness. The emperor Leopold, in declaring war against Louis, denounced him as the enemy of Christendom. England, Holland, Spain, and Savoy now joined in the Grand Alliance with the emperor and the German states. The war which followed can not be related in detail. The greatest generals on the side of France under the king himself, were the Duke of Luxembourg, a pupil of Condé, Catinat, who rather resembled Turenne in the caution and scientific complexity of his movements, and Vauban who still occupies a first rank among military engineers. On the other side were the consummate tactics of William of Orange, Eugene of Savoy, the Earl of Marlborough, and the Dutch engineer, Cohorn. The Duke of Lorraine, the emperor's best general, died in 1690, and was succeeded in the chief command by the Bavarian elector, Maximilian Emanuel.

A. D. 1690.

76. In June, 1690, Luxembourg gained a great and decisive victory at Fleurus, over the Prince of Waldeck. The next year was marked by the death of the French war-minister, Louvois. Though his insolence had been almost as intolerable to his master as his inhuman atrocities to the conquered peoples, the loss of his great abilities was severely felt. In 1692, by extraordinary efforts, Louis XIV. had under his control the largest military and naval forces that France had ever raised. His first object was the restoration of James II. to the throne of England; and 30,000 British exiles were assembled at Havre, La Hogue, and Cherbourg in readiness to embark for their native land. A great victory gained by Admiral Russell over the French fleet annihilated their hopes. As James II. watched the combat from the heights near La Hogue, his pride as an English admiral is said to have surmounted his disappointment as a banished king, and he expressed his delight in the skill and bravery of the forces of William.

77. The king of France was more fortunate on land. Namur was taken after ten days' siege, though king William was approaching with a large army to its relief. In the battle of Steinkirk, which soon followed, both sides suffered enormous losses, but the chief advantage remained with the French. The next year, the two kings were at the head of their respective armies near Louvain. Louis had more than double the numbers of his opponent, and the whole Spanish Netherlands seemed within his grasp. But fearful of risking his reputation, he withdrew and disbanded part of his forces, thus exposing himself to the derision not only of the enemy but of his own officers; which the glory-loving king felt so keenly that he never more appeared in the field. In Piedmont, however, Marshal Catinat gained the great battle of Mar-

saglia, and in Catalonia the Duke of Noailles captured Rosas; while Admiral Tourville in the Bay of Lagos defeated the English squadron of Rooke, who was convoying an English and Dutch merchant fleet toward Smyrna.

78. In spite of these successes, the king of France was desirous of peace. "The people were perishing to the sound of *Te Deums*." The peasantry had been largely drafted into the armies, and the lands lay uncultivated. Taxes upon industry dried up the very sources of revenue, while the kingdom was burdened with an enormous debt. A still stronger motive for peace was found in Louis' views concerning Spain, whose childless king, Charles II., was evidently near his death. An understanding had long before existed between Louis and the emperor Leopold — who, by a singular coincidence,* sustained precisely the same relation to the Spanish royal family — respecting a partition of King Charles' dominions in the event of his death. But Louis could not hope for a realization of this scheme, if the fatal moment should arrive while all Europe was combined in arms against him. He therefore sought the mediation of the Pope — now Innocent XII. — and of the kings of Sweden and Denmark; and offered ample concessions as the price of peace. The emperor and the king of England, well aware of his exhaustion, opposed and neutralized all his efforts, and the war went on four years longer.

79. Few of its events deserve to be recorded. French privateers preyed upon Dutch and English commerce; and the French armies renewed their devastations in the valley of the Rhine. Namur was retaken by King William; and, as it was the first of Louis' conquests that had been wrested from him by force, great encouragement was felt by the allies. The Duke of Savoy was the first to desert the Grand Alliance, and reunite himself with France. The emperor was most averse to peace; but on the intimation that England and Holland would make a separate treaty with Louis, he consented at last to negotiate. The ministers of all the powers of Europe met in May, 1697, at Ryswick, a little village near the Hague; and in the following September, the French embassadors concluded three distinct treaties with England,

July, 1695.

---

* For a table of this family connection, see Appendix. Each monarch was a grandson, by his mother's side, of Philip III. of Spain; each had married a daughter of Philip IV. and was therefore a brother-in-law of Charles II. The mother and the wife of Louis XIV. were the eldest of their respective families; but each, on the other hand, had solemnly renounced her claim to the Spanish dominion. Louis insisted that the Low Countries belonged of right to the eldest child, whether son or daughter; and this theory had led to the War of Devolution described in §§ 28, 30.

The electoral prince of Bavaria, a grandson of Leopold and his Spanish wife, was held by many to have the best right to the Spanish crown on strictly hereditary principles, the renunciation by the two Infantas being considered binding. But, having been born in 1693, the Bavarian prince was too young to have a personal share in the dispute.

Holland, and Spain. By the first, Louis bound himself to acknowledge William III. as rightful king of England, and to render no further aid to James Stuart or his family. Thus forever withdrawn from French influence, England became in the European system the chief counterpoise to France. Spain received back all the towns taken by the French in Catalonia, and most of those in the Netherlands of which Louis had obtained possession in various ways since the treaty of Nimeguen. The following month a treaty was also concluded with the emperor on the basis of those of Nimeguen and Westphalia. The Duke of Lorraine — Leopold, son of Charles V. (see §§ 24, 38, 75) — was restored to his paternal dominions, but Alsace remained to France. Joseph Clement of Bavaria was confirmed in the electorate of Cologne; and the Duchess of Orleans resigned all her claims in the Palatinate upon receiving a sum of money from the new elector.

80. All Europe, during the next three years, watched the declining health of the king of Spain. That kingdom seemed in fact almost as near its dissolution as the king; for earthquakes, hurricanes, inundations, and famine were added to the more avoidable sources of misery in a bankrupt treasury and the general neglect of public discipline. To disarm the opposition of all Europe to the combination of two such dominions as those of Spain and the Empire in one person, Leopold assigned his Spanish claims to his second son, the archduke Charles, while Louis for a similar reason proposed as his candidate his grandson, Philip of Anjou, second son of the Dauphin.

81. Since the emperor, disregarding his former compact, assumed to dispose of the whole dominion of Spain at home and abroad — not less as the head of the House of Austria, than as the grandson of a Spanish king — Louis sought an ally in his late most bitter enemy, the king of England. To prevent the absorption by Louis of the entire patrimony of Charles II., and the consequent enormous increase of French power, William III. entered into a secret treaty of partition, concluded at the Hague between England, Holland, and France, by which the Bavarian prince was to receive the kingdom of Spain, with its possessions in the Low Countries and in America; only its Italian dependencies being divided between the Dauphin and the archduke Charles. No territorial advantage was sought by either England or Holland, their action being purely defensive. This treaty coming to the knowledge of Charles II., he was naturally incensed, and retaliated by a will in which he made the Prince of Bavaria his sole heir. The little prince died suddenly, however, in 1699; and both the will and the treaty were rendered void.

82. A new partition was arranged in 1700 by William and Louis, assigning to the Dauphin Lorraine and all the Spanish possessions in Italy, except Milan ; while Spain itself was allotted to the archduke Charles on condition of its being forever kept separate from the Empire. The Duke of Lorraine was to have Milan in exchange for his hereditary duchy. If the emperor rejected this arrangement, Spain was destined for a third party, supposed to be the Duke of Savoy. The unseemly dispute was carried on in the very court of Madrid, where the envoys of the several conflicting powers obtained ascendency by turns over the feeble and vacillating mind of Charles II. The French interest prevailed at length, and the king made a new will, bequeathing his undivided dominions to the Duke of Anjou. A month later he died, in the 39th year of his age and the 37th of his reign.

RECAPITULATION.

Strasbourg and many other towns annexed by Louis XIV. after the peace of Nimeguen. A fresh coalition of the Treaty Powers compels a truce. Revocation of the Edict of Nantes; *dragonnades;* emigration of nearly half a million Huguenots to protestant countries. League of Augsburg unites the German states against Louis.

Discontent in England with the French policy of Charles II. Popish and Rye House Plots lead to the execution of Stafford, Russell, and Sidney. Accession of James II. Rise of the " Whigs " and " Tories." Failure of Monmouth's rebellion. Birth of a Prince of Wales disappoints the Whigs, who invite the Prince of Orange into England. James deserts his capital ; William and Mary are proclaimed, upon their acceptance of the Declaration of Rights. James is defeated in Ireland — most signally in the battle of the Boyne. Grand Alliance of all Europe against Louis XIV. The allies are defeated at Fleurus ; victorious in a naval battle off La Hogue; defeated at Steinkirk. Namur taken by Louis XIV.; recaptured after three years by William III. Louis seeks peace in order to secure the inheritance of Spain. Treaty of Ryswick, A. D. 1697. Treaty for partition of the Spanish possessions signed by the kings of France and England. Death of the Prince of Bavaria occasions a new Partition Treaty. The king of Spain bequeaths his dominions to a grandson of Louis XIV.

WAR OF THE SPANISH SUCCESSION.

83. Less than three months from the death of Charles II., Philip V. was welcomed with acclamations to his capital of Madrid ; and most of the European powers hastened to acknowledge him. The emperor's interference was delayed by symptoms of a Hungarian insurrection, and by disturbances in northern Germany occasioned by the creation of a ninth electorate — that of Hanover. All seemed to favor the interests of Louis XIV., and by a conciliatory policy he might perhaps have secured the advantages which he had gained. But he gave needless offense to England and the Spanish nation, and alarmed the Dutch by expelling their garrisons from several towns in the Netherlands which had been guaranteed to them as a frontier on the side of France. Thus several nations were ready to combine against him when the favorable moment should arrive. The emperor listened to the urgent advice of Eugene of

Savoy, who represented that the Empire could never be safe while the French held entrances to it through northern Italy and Belgium.

84. By the Treaty of the Crown, executed at Vienna, Leopold gained a powerful ally without cost. Frederic III., elector of Brandenburg, coveted the title of king. The emperor engaged to recognize his royal dignity, in consideration of certain aids to be rendered in the field, the Diet, and the electoral Council; and the elector, hastening to Königsberg, assumed with great ceremony the crown and title of "King of Prussia." The new kingdom, from the necessity of its position, assumed from the first that military character which it still retains. Owing its rise to the energetic war-policy of the Great Elector — father of the first king — it was raised by a progressive military organization during the next two reigns to a rank among the "Great Powers" of Europe. Prince Eugene, having massed his forces near Trent, descended in May, 1701, upon the plain of Lombardy. Catinat was defeated, and the imperialists occupied the whole country between the Adige and the Adda. Villeroy, succeeding to the command of the French forces, was still more signally worsted at Chiari and Cremona.

Nov., 1700.

85. A second Grand Alliance of the emperor with the kings of England and Prussia, the States-General, and the elector palatine, avowed its determination to secure the reasonable claims of the House of Austria, as well as the colonies and commerce of Holland and England, against French aggression. As before, William of Orange was the soul of the movement. To his rupture of the Partition Treaty, Louis XIV. now added a more flagrant insult to that prince, by recognizing James Stuart, upon the death of his father, the late king James II., as king of England, Scotland, and Ireland. This act aroused the slumbering loyalty of the English Parliament, which immediately voted liberal supplies for the war, with the petition that "no peace shall be made with France, until his Majesty and the nation have made reparation for the great indignity offered by the French king." An "Act for adjuring the pretended Prince of Wales" passed a few months later.

86. The death of William in March for a moment disconcerted the allies. His sister-in-law and successor, Queen Anne, however, declared her intention to pursue the same policy which he had begun; and the Earl of Marlborough proceeded with an army to Holland. By a peaceful revolution, the United Provinces — or rather the five, exclusive of Friesland and Groningen — abolished the office of Stadtholder, which had been borne by William until his death, and resumed the more purely republican government, supported by the De Witts. Heinsius, Grand Pensionary of Holland — a firm adherent to the policy of the Prince of Orange — had the chief voice in the affairs of the United Netherlands, and with Marlborough and Prince Eugene

A. D. 1702.

constituted what was called the **Triumvirate** of the **Second Grand Alliance**.

87. England, Holland, and the Empire declared war against France and Spain in May, 1702. The elector of Bavaria and his brother, the archbishop of Cologne, whose investiture had been so strenuously opposed by Louis XIV. in 1688, were nevertheless allies of France; and the territory of Cologne was the first object of attack by the English and Dutch. Kaiserswerth, Venloo, Stephanswerth, Ruremond, and finally Liège, were successively captured during the campaign of 1702. The king of the Romans meanwhile commanded on the Upper Rhine, where Prince Louis of Baden, his associate in command, took Landau in September. Prince Eugene, as before, conducted the campaign in Piedmont, where Philip V. appeared for a few months at the head of the French and Spanish forces. On the sea, the allied fleet succeeded in sinking or capturing the entire Spanish West India squadron, laden with gold and silver.

88. The next year, Marlborough, now duke, completed the conquest of the electorate of Cologne, while the allies captured Limburg, and Guelders. The French party was more successful in Germany, where the elector of Bavaria not only repulsed a two-fold invasion of his dominions, but seized Ratisbon and with Marshal Villars defeated the imperialists at Hochstädt. An insurrection in Hungary under Prince Ragotzki diverted the Austrian forces, and Vienna might have fallen into the hands of the elector, had he not delayed his attack until the season was too far advanced. The French on the Rhine had meanwhile taken Breisach, defeated the emperor's army at Spirebach and recaptured Landau. The Duke of Savoy, offended by not receiving the command of the French and Spanish forces, now deserted the cause of his son-in-law, the king of Spain, and joined the Grand Alliance, thus cutting off the communication between France and Italy. Pedro II. of Portugal, also — led by the admiral of Castile, who found himself slighted by Philip V. — entered into a perpetual alliance with England and the United Netherlands. These accessions emboldened the allies to extend their plans, and not only push the Austrian claims in Italy and the Netherlands, but substitute the archduke Charles for Philip of Bourbon upon the throne of Spain.

89. In 1704, Marlborough was in Germany. His army having joined that of Louis of Baden near Ulm, he took the heights of Schellenberg by storm, and thus gained an important control of the Danube. A junction was now effected with Prince Eugene, and in the great battle of Blenheim near Hochstädt, the allies gained a decisive victory over the French and Bavarians. A great mass of infantry who had taken no part in the action, surrendered themselves prisoners, and the French were compelled to evacuate Germany. They were pursued across the Rhine;

and Marlborough, after taking Trèves and several other towns, fixed his advanced posts upon the Sarre. All the Bavarian fortresses were surrendered to the emperor, except Munich, which was dismantled, but continued to be the residence of the electress; while the elector retained only his appointment as governor-general of the Spanish Netherlands.

90. In Italy, fortune favored the French, who regained their communication with the Milanese by reconquering the northern part of Piedmont. Meanwhile, Charles III., the Austrian candidate for the Spanish crown, landed in Portugal with a Dutch and English army; but his progress was checked by the Duke of Berwick, a son of James II., who was in the French service. The English fleet of Admiral Rooke gained possession, almost by accident, of the fortress of Gibraltar. It had been but slightly garrisoned by the Spaniards, who presumed upon its enormous natural strength. A party of English sailors, availing themselves of a holiday, when the eastern side had been left unguarded, scaled that precipitous height, while another party stormed the South Mole; and Rooke occupied the fortress in the name of the queen of England. The campaign closed favorably to the allies. Louis XIV., expelled from Germany, had lost the alliance of Bavaria; the key to the Mediterranean was in the hands of the English; and France herself was threatened with invasion by the allied army on the Moselle.

91. The next year was marked by the death of the emperor Leopold and the accession of his son, Joseph I., a prince of more energetic and decisive character. The Hungarians under A. D. 1706. Ragotzki were still in revolt; and in spite of all Joseph's concessions, demanded a return to their former elective constitutions. A rebellion in Bavaria was suppressed by force, and the emperor resolved to blot out that electorate from the map of Germany. Its territories were divided among several princes, the Upper Palatinate being restored to the elector-palatine, from whose dominions it had been separated since the Thirty Years' War. The main actions of 1705 were in Italy and Spain. Prince Eugene was defeated at Cassano by the Duke of Vendôme; but on the other hand, the French were compelled to raise the siege of Gibraltar, and the Earl of Peterboro', having captured Barcelona, secured the allegiance of Catalonia and a great part of Valencia for Charles III. The archduke was present at the surrender, and was hailed with acclamations as king of Spain.

92. The next year Aragon also proclaimed him; and from the western border, the allies marched upon Madrid, which, deserted by Philip and his court, fell easily into their hands. The people, however, preferring the French to the Austrian succession, rose against their invaders, expelled the garrisons, and forced the two allied armies, now united, to retire into Valencia. Alicant and Cartagena were taken by the English, but

the latter was recaptured by the Duke of Berwick. The same year,
Prince Eugene, having joined his cousin, the Duke of
Savoy, gained a brilliant victory over the French before
Turin. Charles III. was proclaimed in Milan, and all Lombardy submitted to the imperialists. Marlborough in the Netherlands had gained in May the no less brilliant and decisive victory of Ramillies, by which Brabant and the greater part of Flanders were conquered for the allies; and had taken Menin, Dendermonde, and Ath.

Sept., 1706.

93. Humiliated by these reverses, Louis XIV. offered to abandon Spain and the Indies to Charles III. and the Spanish Netherlands to Holland, on condition of the Italian possessions being secured to Philip of Anjou. The allies refusing to accept less than the whole Spanish inheritance, the war went on, and in the spring of 1707, fortune began to favor the French. In the fatal battle of Almanza, the allies lost all their infantry, with their standards, baggage, and artillery. Valencia and Aragon submitted to Philip V.; Lerida and Ciudad Rodrigo, on the frontiers of Catalonia and Portugal, respectively, were recaptured. The allies were scarcely more successful in northern Italy or in their invasion of France. Toulon was blockaded by the united forces of Prince Eugene and the Duke of Savoy, on the land, and by the fleet of Sir Cloudesley Shovel on the sea, but the approach of a French army compelled the raising of the siege. In southern Italy, however, the whole kingdom of Naples was gained for Charles III. by a small imperial army under Marshal Daun.

94. The union of England and Scotland this year excited some discontent in the latter kingdom, of which Louis XIV. attempted to avail himself by sending a fleet and 5,000 men to escort the Pretender, James III., to the Firth of Forth. His design was frustrated by Admiral Byng; and it is only worthy of mention as the first of a series of similar attempts, some of which were more formidable, but all equally in vain. Loyalty to the Stuarts naturally lingered longer in Scotland, their ancient home, than in England, their recently acquired dominion.

In the Netherlands, this year, the French gained possession of Ghent and Bruges; but the armies of Marlborough and Prince Eugene won a brilliant victory at Oudenarde over the dukes of Burgundy and Vendôme, captured Lille by a long and difficult siege, rescued Brussels from the elector of Bavaria, and reconquered the two revolted cities, thus regaining all Spanish Flanders, and occupying part of that which had belonged to France. In the Mediterranean, Admiral Leake received the submission to Charles III. of the island of Sardinia, and established a British garrison at Port Mahon. Majorca and Iviça had already declared for the archduke.

A. D. 1708.

95. The exhaustion and ruin of France at the end of 1708, were ag-

gravated by a winter of extraordinary severity, which destroyed vineyards, orchards, and the grain already sown, and produced for the ensuing season a terrible famine. Whole families of the poor were found frozen to death in their wretched hovels; the rapid current of the Rhone was arrested, and the Mediterranean seemed almost transformed into a polar sea. The misery of the people produced a universal outcry against the war, and Louis was compelled to offer still more humiliating terms than before, as the price of peace. But his sincerity was doubted, and the allies demanded that he should himself aid in expelling the Duke of Anjou from Spain. The pride of the French, even in the depth of their distress, revolted at this indignity, and they resolved to continue the war.

96. In the next campaign, Marlborough and Eugene captured Tournay, and by a dearly-bought victory at Malplaquet obtained the surrender of Mons. The Pope recognized Charles III. as king of Spain. In 1710 Louis renewed his former proposals of peace, and even offered a million livres a month to aid the allies in expelling Philip from the peninsula. Their haughty rejoinder required him to use his own armies for that purpose. The old king exclaimed, "If I must needs fight, I will war against my enemies, not my children!" His determination was justified by two brilliant victories, gained by his armies at Brihuega and Villa Viciosa, which confirmed the power of Philip V. in Spain.

97. England by this time was weary of a war in which she bore the chief burdens and reaped few advantages. A Tory ministry succeeded the party of which Marlborough was a leading member; and in 1711 the early and unexpected death of the emperor Joseph changed the whole interest of Europe in the War of the Spanish Succession. The archduke Charles was the foremost candidate for the imperial crown, and if he should also obtain that of Spain and the Indies, Europe would again be threatened with a universal monarchy, the dread of which had armed all the nations against Louis XIV. Preliminary articles between England and France were signed at London in October, 1711. In December, the archduke was crowned at Frankfort as the Emperor Charles VI. Notwithstanding the discontent of the allies at the desertion of their cause by England, the new ministry succeeded in obtaining the dismissal of Marlborough from all his appointments, and the chief supporter of the war-policy thus lost his influence in public affairs.

98. A congress for the conclusion of peace was opened at Utrecht in January, 1712. Eighty ministers on the part of the allies conferred with three representatives of the French king. During the progress of negotiations, a series of domestic calamities befell Louis XIV., which complicated the tasks of the diplomatists. By the death of his eldest son in 1711, the title of Dauphin and successor to the throne had descended to

the Duke of Burgundy, a prince of the greatest promise, whose talents and virtues had been strengthened and improved by the wise instructions of Fénélon. In February, 1712, the young Dauphin suddenly died of a fever which had robbed him, a few days before, of his wife, and which now attacked their two little children. The elder of these, the Duke of Bretagne, died; but the younger, only two years of age, his infant constitution weakened by the disease, survived; and his feeble life was the only barrier — except, indeed, an oath of renunciation, which experience showed could be too easily disregarded — between Philip V. of Spain and the throne of France. Upon the demand of England, the Spanish king ceded his French claims to his younger brother, the Duke of Berri.

99. The emperor refused to join in the conference at Utrecht, and continued the war, though it brought him only disaster. At length he consented to a separate treaty with France; and Prince Eugene met Marshal Villars, his former opponent in arms, for a conference at Rastadt, in which military directness took the place of the slow and ceremonious action of the diplomatists. The Peace of Rastadt restored the entire right bank of the Rhine to the Empire. All the Spanish possessions in Italy — the kingdom of Naples, Sardinia, Milan, and the fortresses on the Tuscan coast — with all the Spanish Netherlands, except certain frontier towns which were secured to the Dutch, were ceded to Charles VI. In a subsequent Barrier Treaty between the emperor and the States, it was agreed that a standing army should be maintained in the "Austrian Netherlands," as they are now to be called; three-fifths of the men being in the imperial, and two-fifths in the Dutch service. The electors of Cologne and Bavaria were restored to their estates, on consenting to acknowledge the new electorate of Hanover.

March, 1714.

100. The terms of the Treaty of Utrecht, which regulated almost all the boundary lines in Europe, can only be generally indicated. The succession of the elector of Hanover * to the English crown after the death of Queen Anne, was acknowledged by the king of France, who engaged also to dismantle Dunkirk, and to cede to England the whole tract in North America including Nova Scotia, Newfoundland, and Hudson's Bay. Louis recognized the royal title of the king of Prussia, and ceded to him, as representative of the House of Orange, the principality of Neuchâtel in Switzerland, while Frederic I. relinquished his claims to the principality of Orange. The Duke of Savoy received back his territories, which were divided from those of France by the water-shed of the Alps. He was invested by Spain with the island-kingdom of Sicily, and the ultimate succession to the Spanish crown in case of the failure of the line of Philip V. The duke was crowned at Palermo, November, 1713. Philip

---

* See Appendix — for the derivation of the Hanoverian from the Stuart dynasty.

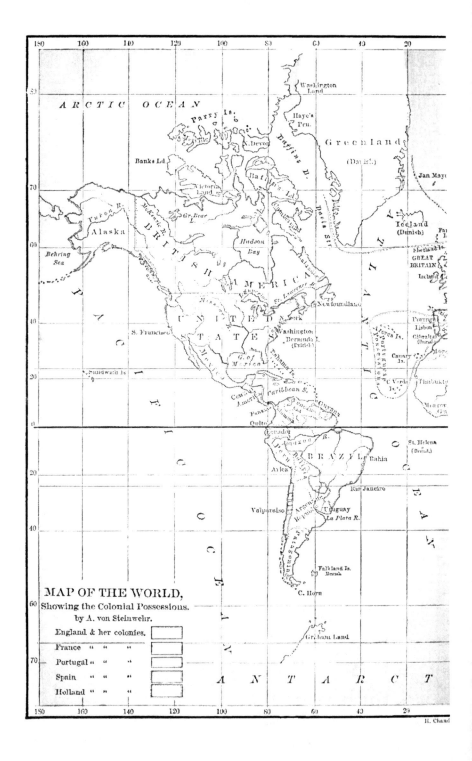

MAP OF THE WORLD,
Showing the Colonial Possessions.
by A. von Steinwehr.

England & her colonies.
France   "   "   "
Portugal "   "   "
Spain   "   "   "
Holland   "   "   "

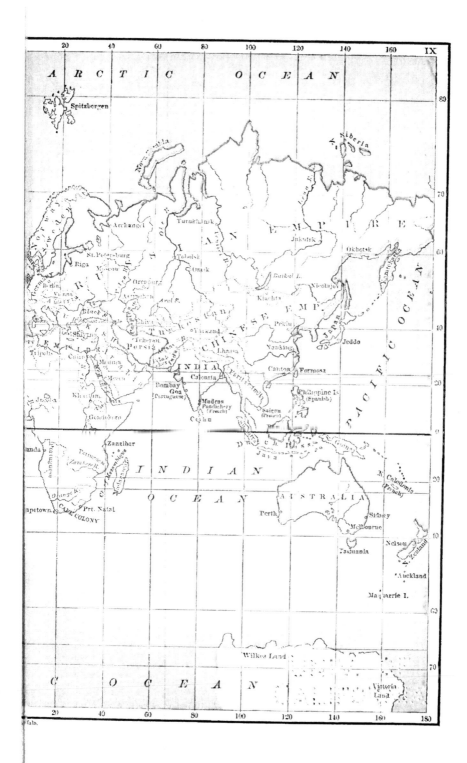

V. was formally recognized by the other powers, as king of Spain. He ceded Gibraltar and Minorca to England on the condition that neither Moors nor Jews should be tolerated in either; recognized the Hanoverian succession, and assigned to England a monopoly of the slave-trade with the Spanish colonies for thirty years. Spain and Portugal resumed their former boundaries. The remaining articles of the treaty related chiefly to commercial and colonial matters, and though important to the nations concerned, were too minute to be detailed here.

101. Two of the high contracting parties to the Peace of Utrecht died soon after its completion. Anne was succeeded upon the English throne, in 1714, by George Lewis, elector of Hanover, a prince whose ruling motive was hatred of France, and who immediately recalled the Whig ministry and reinstated Marlborough as captain-general of the armies. Louis XIV. died, Sept. 1, 1715, after a reign of 72 years, which had formed a most memorable era in European history. His great talents and his rich inheritance would have given him, in any case, a leading power among the nations; but his immoderate desire of conquest made him the scourge rather than the benefactor of Europe. His treasury — which in the earlier years of his active reign had been always well filled by his own thrift and the able management of his ministers — was long ago drained by ruinous wars, and he resorted to the most oppressive measures to wring further supplies from a starving and exhausted people. Conscious of his failures, and of the worthlessness of that "glory" which had been the Idol of his youth, the king sought refuge in an abject superstition which inflicted a last injury upon his realm. He committed the keeping of his conscience to the Jesuit Le Tellier, who engaged him in a bitter persecution of the Jansenists — the steadfast opponents of the moral and political, no less than the doctrinal system of the Jesuits.

102. If Louis' life had been prolonged, his evasion of several articles of the Treaty of Utrecht — especially the aid which he rendered to James Stuart in his invasion of Scotland in 1715 — would probably have again broken the peace of Europe. But a fever ended his days, and the admonition which he addressed to his great-grandson from his death-bed, contained a condemnation of his life-long policy: "Live at peace with your neighbors; do not imitate me in my fondness for war, nor in my exorbitant expenditure. . . Endeavor to relieve the people at the earliest possible moment, and thus accomplish what, unfortunately, I myself am unable to do." It would be unjust, however, to omit the more favorable view of the reign of Louis XIV. He encouraged and rewarded the industries of his people. The wise economy of Colbert fostered the colonial system, and while stimulating agriculture, manufactures, and commerce, did not neglect the moral and intellectual interests of the nation. The French Academy, founded by Richelieu, became a great institution of the state. Four other academies, established during this reign — those of Inscriptions and *Belles Lettres*, of Sciences, of Architecture, and of Painting and Sculpture — have been distinguished ever since by the zeal, industry, and learning of their members.

103. Colbert first connected the Mediterranean with the Atlantic by the Canal of Languedoc, enlarged and improved several harbors, formed great marine arsenals at Toulon, Brest, Havre, and Dunkirk, and augmented the naval power of France by his unremitting attention to the fleet. According to the notions of the time, he thought to promote commerce by the formation of great monopolies, such as the trading companies of the East and West Indies, the North and the Levant.

The "Age of Louis XIV." is remarkable as a great literary era. The dramas of Corneille, Racine, and Molière, the letters and "Thoughts" of Pascal, the sermons of Bossuet, Bourdaloue, Fénélon, and Massillon, are masterpieces in their several departments of literature. The court of Louis was the model to all Europe of elegance and refinement; and though deficient in the substantial virtues — more especially during the first half of his reign — it has never been surpassed in the charms of graceful conversation, or of that delicate and chivalrous courtesy of which the king himself was the most illustrious example. It was at this period that French taste, manners, and modes of living and thinking gained their ascendency in Europe.

RECAPITULATION.

Philip of Bourbon receives the Spanish crown by the will of the late king and with the consent of the people. War of the Spanish Succession begun by victories of Prince Eugene over the French in Lombardy. Second Grand Alliance organized by William III. of England. James Stuart acknowledged as king by France, but abjured by England. Queen Anne continues the war-policy of William III. Marlborough, Heinsius, and Eugene of Savoy are the Triumvirate of the Grand Alliance. Victories of Marlborough on the lower Rhine. Rebellion of Ragotzki in Hungary. Savoy and Portugal join the Grand Alliance, which now aims to wrest Spain itself, as well as its foreign dependencies, from the French. Victories of the allies at Schellenberg and Blenheim. Elector of Bavaria loses all his fortresses and most of his territories. Gibraltar taken by the English. Emperor Joseph I. succeeds Leopold. Charles III. proclaimed King in Catalonia, Valencia, Aragon, and Lombardy; the next two years in Naples and Sardinia. Victories of Marlborough at Ramillies and of Eugene at Turin. Victory of the French at Almanza, and reconquest of Valencia and Aragon. Act of Union between England and Scotland; ineffectual invasion by James III. Victory of the allies at Oudenarde and capture of Lille, Ghent, and Bruges. Misery of the French people; unavailing concessions of Louis for the sake of peace. The allies, victorious at Malplaquet, capture Tournay and Mons. Fall of Marlborough's party detaches England from the alliance. Death of the emperor Joseph and of the son and grandson of Louis XIV. alters the conditions of the Spanish succession. Treaties of peace, negotiated at Utrecht and Rastadt, convert the Spanish into the Austrian Netherlands; recognize the Hanoverian succession in England and that of the Bourbons in Spain; acknowledge the elector of Brandenburg as King of Prussia and Prince of Neuchatel; confirm England in the possession of Gibraltar and Minorca, and a vast region of North America; secure Sicily (afterward exchanged for Sardinia) to the Duke of Savoy.

Death of Anne of England and of Louis of France. Bigotry of Louis XIV. in his later years; ascendency of French taste in Europe, owing to the material and intellectual activity of his reign.

CHARLES XII. AND PETER THE GREAT.

104. The first twenty-one years of the eighteenth century were occupied by the great Northern War, in which the two chief actors were Charles XII. of Sweden and Peter I. of Russia. The accession of Charles in 1697, when only fifteen years of age, inspired his neighbors with the hope of wresting from Sweden her possessions east and south of the Baltic.* The mover of the conspiracy was Augustus II. of Poland and I. of Saxony; but hostilities were actually begun by his ally, Frederic IV. of Denmark, who, in March, 1700, invaded the territories of the Duke of Holstein-Gottorp, a brother-in-law and intimate friend of Charles. The young king of Sweden displayed at this crisis a firmness and energy which surprised both his enemies and his counselors. He reassured his senate by the spirited declaration: "I have resolved never to wage an unjust war, nor ever to close a just one except by the destruction of my enemies." The sentiment was doubtless sincere, but it was doubly contradicted by events. He allied himself with Holland and England — now known by preëminence as the Maritime Powers — and their fleet combined with his own covered his descent upon Denmark. Frederic IV. was compelled to treat for the preservation of his capital. By the Peace of Travendal, he renewed his ancient treaties with the Duke of Holstein, and engaged to pay a large indemnity for the losses he had inflicted.

105. His first war being thus ended without a blow, Charles was at liberty to meet the Czar, who, with 80,000 men drawn from his provinces in Asia and Europe, had commenced the siege of Narva. The Swedish army of scarcely one-tenth the number of the Russians, forced a defile hitherto deemed impregnable, and inflicted a severe and total defeat upon the besieging host. Peter had fled before Nov., 1700. the battle, but he learned from it a useful lesson; and strove with untiring energy to bring his vast, undisciplined masses of troops into a condition to meet the more civilized armies of Europe. To this end he sent nearly 20,000 men to serve under the king of Poland, who had to sustain the next attack. In 1701, Charles defeated the Saxon troops near Riga and occupied all Courland. The Maritime Powers, now on the eve of the War of the Spanish Succession, and desiring peace in northern Europe, attempted to mediate; but Charles refused to treat until he had more signally avenged the perfidy of Augustus. He marched in May, 1702,

* These were Finland, Carelia, Ingria, Esthonia, and Livonia; most of Pomerania; the fortresses of Stettin, Wismar, and Stralsund; the duchies of Bremen and Verden.

upon Warsaw and entered it without opposition, while the king fled to Cracow; and in July the combined army of Poles and Saxons suffered a decisive defeat at Clissow between the two capitals. The next year Charles again defeated the Saxons at Pultusk, and captured Thorn, whose fortifications he demolished.

106. As usual, a strong party of the Polish nobility was opposed to the king; and with it, though indecisively, acted the Primate Radziejowski. In a diet called by this prelate at Warsaw, Augustus was declared to have forfeited his crown by attempting to purchase peace with the cession of some Polish provinces to Sweden. The desire of this party was to raise James Sobieski to the throne, but Augustus had anticipated their movement by imprisoning that prince with his younger brother. The Swedish influence was exerted in favor of Count Stanislaus Leczinska, who in July, 1704, was proclaimed King of Poland. He was crowned, under a guard of Swedish soldiers, the following October, and soon signed a treaty of peace and alliance with Charles XII. Augustus retired to Dresden, his ancient Saxon capital, whither he was followed in 1706, by the king of Sweden and 20,000 men. Unable to resist, he signed the treaty of Altranstadt, by which he renounced the crown of Poland for himself and his descendants, abandoned his alliance with Russia, and released the princes Sobieski from their captivity.

107. During the interval since his defeat at Narva, the Czar had been busily improving his army and navy, and had taken possession of the provinces of Ingria and Carelia, which had been lost to his empire in 1617. The foundations of his new capital, St. Petersburg, were laid upon an island in the Neva which, by treaties still in force, belonged to Sweden; but the Czar's confidence in himself and presentiment of his adversary's failure, were justified by the results. For the protection of the new city, the fortress of Cronstadt was founded near the head of the Gulf of Riga. During 1704, Dorpat and Narva were captured, Lithuania and Courland occupied; though in the latter province the Russian general was defeated by the Swedes at Gemauers. Learning at Narva of the Peace of Altranstadt, Peter hastened into Poland, hoping to retain the alliance of the nobles, without whose knowledge or consent that treaty had been concluded. A diet at Lublin, July, 1707, declared the throne vacant since the abdication of Augustus, and summoned the electors to the choice of a king. Charles marched from Saxony to defeat this movement; but the Czar, now too wise to meet him in regular battle, harassed and fatigued him by long and fruitless marches, and effectually disconcerted his plans.

May, 1703.

108. In 1708, the Swedish king invaded Russia, probably intending to march upon Moscow. But he found the country destitute of forage for man or beast, the roads well guarded, and the enemy's cavalry constantly ready to harass his columns, though they could never be brought to a general engagement. Without waiting for his reinforcements which were on the way, Charles suddenly marched toward the Ukraine, where Mazeppa, the aged Hetman of the Cossacks, was plotting with his aid to become independent of the Czar. Peter, marching to meet the Swedish reinforcements, defeated General Löwenhaupt at Liesna, destroyed half his men and captured his entire convoy; while Charles, to his disappointment, found Mazeppa, not at the head of the army of 30,000 which he had promised, but a suppliant fugitive, with only a few personal attendants.

109. The Swedes, worn out by their march through forests and marshes, were ragged and many of them shoeless, but their king, disdaining retreat by a shorter route into Poland, insisted on laying siege to Pultawa. Here he was overtaken by 60,000 Russians under their best generals, the Czar himself serving, according to his custom, in a subordinate rank. With only one-third the number, Charles resolved to give battle, though a wound in his foot compelled him to devolve the chief command upon his general Rhenskiöld. He was present in a litter, but the movements of his men lacked the precision which he was accustomed to give them. They fought with great valor, but were overpowered by superior numbers, and nearly half were left dead upon the field. The king escaped with difficulty. Rhenskiöld with the most distinguished officers were prisoners.

110. The battle of Pultawa ended the Swedish superiority in northern Europe, while it marked the rise of Russia as a great European power. Leaving Löwenhaupt in command of the shattered remnant of his forces, the king crossed the Dnieper and sought refuge with the Turkish commandant of Bender. Löwenhaupt capitulated, and Sweden was left without king or army, at the mercy of her foes. The treaties of Travendal and Altranstadt were speedily broken. Augustus II. resumed the crown of Poland, which was abandoned by Stanislaus, and renewed his connections with Russia and Denmark. Frederic IV. invaded Sweden and captured Helsingborg, but was thwarted in his further designs by the good conduct of General Stenbock. At the same time the Swedish-German provinces were attacked by a combined force of Saxons, Poles, and Russians. The emperor and the Maritime Powers then interfered, and by the Treaty of the Hague secured at least a brief neutrality to those provinces, as well as to Schleswig and Jutland.

111. Through the instigation of Charles XII., the Sultan Achmet had meantime been moved to declare war against the Czar. Encouraged by the flattering promises of the Hospodar of Moldavia, Peter invaded that province in the spring of 1711. But the promises were unfulfilled, and the Czar found himself surrounded by a Turkish army more numerous than his own, cut off from supplies, and unable either to advance or retreat. In this desperate case, relief was only obtained through the tact and resolution of the Czarina Catherine.* Sending all her jewels as a present to the Grand Vizier who was in command of the Turks, she induced him to listen to terms of peace. Peter surrendered Azov, and engaged to withdraw his army from Poland, whereupon he was permitted to recross the Pruth without molestation.

112. Charles XII. was no longer a welcome guest in the Turkish dominions; while the progress of the Czar in Finland and the Baltic provinces urgently demanded his presence. He waited, however, to be forcibly dislodged by the Janizaries from his camp at Varnitz, and conveyed as a prisoner to Adrianople, before he accepted the Turkish escort to the frontier and the emperor's safe-conduct for his passage through Germany. His face being once turned homeward, his characteristic impatience led

Nov., 1714.   him to make the journey of 1,100 miles on horseback in less than seventeen days. Arriving at Stralsund, he immediately renewed hostilities with Frederic William I. of Prussia for the possession of Pomerania. But the alliance against him now included Russia, Poland, Denmark, and England; Wismar and Stralsund, besieged by their united forces, surrendered; and Sweden was thus driven from her last remaining possession south of the Baltic. Having humbled their common enemy, the allies began to distrust each other, and preliminaries of peace between Sweden and Russia were already signed, when in December, 1718, Charles met his death in the siege of Frederickshall in Norway.

113. His nephew, the young duke of Holstein-Gottorp, was the rightful heir, but a revolution made the Swedish crown elective, and elevated Ulrica Eleanora, the second sister of Charles, to the throne. Her husband, Frederic of Hesse Cassel, was already in command of the army and became really the head of the state. The peace with Russia was broken off, but treaties were made successively with England, Poland, Prussia, and Denmark. The latter kingdom was confirmed in the possession of Schleswig. Prussia received Stettin and the district between the Oder and Peene, with the islands of Usedom and Wollin; Hanover retained the duchies of Bremen and Verden. The war with Russia continued three years longer by sea and land; but at length, through the mediation of France, the Peace of Nystadt was concluded in September, 1721. Russia restored Finland but retained the other provinces east of the Baltic. The Czar wrote to his embassador in Paris: "Apprenticeships usually end

---

*This extraordinary woman had been an Esthonian peasant. Taken prisoner by the Russians in the siege of Marienburg, she had won the admiration of the Czar by her native talents, and had recently been raised to the throne.

in seven years; ours has lasted thrice as long; but, thank God, it is at length brought to the desired termination." In the twenty-one years which he had spent in learning—chiefly from his adversaries—the arts of conquering and governing, Peter had reörganized an army and created a navy, had built a city of palaces among the marshes of the Neva, and had raised himself by his personal energy and industry to be one of the greatest monarchs in Europe. The Senate and Synod conferred upon him the title of "Emperor of all the Russias;" and the nobles and people of the capital hailed him as the Father of his country, Peter the Great.

RECAPITULATION.

Accession of Charles XII. of Sweden. His dominions attacked or menaced by Denmark, Poland, and Russia. The first is humbled by the Peace of Travendal; the Czar with vastly superior numbers is defeated at Narva; the king of Poland at Riga, Clissow, and Pultusk. By Treaty of Altranstadt, Augustus resigns the Polish crown, which the Swedes bestow upon Stanislaus Leczinski. Peter of Russia seizes the Baltic provinces, and lays the foundation of St. Petersburg; protects Moscow by devastating the country; defeats the Swedes at Liesna and Pultawa. Charles takes refuge with the Turks; the remnant of his army is surrendered. Sweden is attacked by Danes, Saxons, Poles, and Russians. The Sultan declares war upon the Czar, who obtains peace by the surrender of Azov. Charles, returning to his kingdom, is killed before Fredericshall; is succeeded by his sister, who resigns public affairs to her husband, Frederic of Hesse Cassel. Cessation of the Northern War completed by the Treaty of Nystadt, which recognizes the rank of Russia among the Great Powers of Europe.

EUROPEAN COLONIES.

114. It is time for a view of those foreign settlements which had extended the fame and power of several European nations to the remotest regions of the globe. Their purposes were four: mining, agriculture, commerce, and increase of dominion; and though these may have been to a certain degree combined, yet in general it may be said, that, while America became the seat of extensive mining and agricultural colonies, western Africa and the East Indies—owing to the noxious climate of all, and the dense population and powerful Mogul government of Hindustan —admitted little more than the forts and factories of European traders. The colonial system of all the European states was narrowly restrictive. The colonies existed for the advantage of the parent state, never for their own. But this policy was carried to its extreme by Spain.

115. Three Spanish viceroys governed her possessions in the New World. The Royal Court of the Indies appointed all officers, civil, military, or ecclesiastical, almost uniformly from natives of the mother country. These must prove their descent from "old Christians," *i. e.*, from families untainted with Jewish or Mohammedan blood, and never censured by the Inquisition. Long residence in America, being supposed to weaken their affection for Spain, was held as sufficient reason for distrust and exclusion from office. Hence the officers of government, having no community of interest with the colonists, were in haste to make their own fortunes, often by means of extortion and oppression.

116. To prevent any sort of independence, those branches of agriculture and manufactures which supply the common wants of life, were expressly forbidden to the colonists. Their clothes, furniture, tools, even a considerable part of their food, were brought from Spain, and only by Spanish ships, for the colonists were not permitted vessels of their own. Intercolonial trade was either forbidden or so jealously restricted that its motives were destroyed. The only exception was the commerce with the Philippine Islands, the sole Spanish possession in Asia, which had been settled by a colony from Mexico. By their A. D. 1564. active trade with the Chinese, the Philippines were supplied with Asiatic fabrics, and these were permitted to be carried, though only by one or two ships yearly, to the port of Acapulco.

117. Beside the precious metals, of which an annual average value of $20,000,000 was for three hundred years regularly entered at the Spanish ports, the most important products of the colonies were the cochineal of Central America, the indigo of Guatemala, the chocolate of that province and Caraccas, the sugar of Hayti, the tobacco of Cuba, the quinine of Peru, and hides from the herds of cattle roaming on the vast plains south of the La Plata. Commerce with the three American viceroyalties was carried on by a fleet sent once in each year to the ports of Cartagena, Porto Bello and Vera Cruz. The annual fair of forty days at Porto Bello witnessed the most lucrative trade in the world. At the season when the galleons were expected, this squalid negro village — whose atmosphere was almost fatal to Europeans, from its excess of heat, moisture, and vegetable decay — was suddenly transformed into a busy mercantile exchange, crowded with merchants and wares from the whole western portion of South America. A few commercial houses in Seville had not only control but entire possession of the American market; the colonists, deprived of all share in the enterprise, were compelled to buy at the most enormous prices, or forego the opportunity to dispose of their products.

118. When the colonies were founded, Spain was able to supply their wants from her own manufactures, and thus greatly increase her wealth. This state of things altered when Philip III. expelled nearly a million of his most industrious subjects from the kingdom (see Book III., § 292); the Spanish merchants, unable longer to keep up the exchange with the colonists, eluded the law by sending foreign goods under their own names, and the treasures received in return went to reward and improve the skill of English, French, and Dutch artisans. Spain, possessing lands greater than all Europe and unsurpassed by any in the world in the value of their products, became destitute of either money or industry. Upon the extinction of the Austrian line in Charles II., the attempts of foreign nations to control the succession to the throne brought back a portion of the gold and silver which had been diverted into other lands, and occasioned some revival of prosperity. Philip V. opened the American trade to France, and, under stringent limitations, to England. The limitations were evaded, and the superior enterprise of the English merchants gave them almost the control of the South American markets.

119. Nearly a hundred years before, the jealous attempts of the Spaniards to prevent the approach of foreigners to their colonies had caused the West Indian seas to swarm with buccaneers. A pirate-state was formed on Tortuga; and similar settlements on the western portion of Hayti or St. Domingo were recognized as French possessions in 1664. Ten or a dozen of the smaller islands were purchased by Colbert, and systematic efforts were made to encourage the culture of sugar, cotton, and coffee. The slave trade with the African coast found its most profitable markets in the mining and agricultural colonies of the New World. Begun by the Portuguese as early as 1440, it had been introduced into the West Indies by the good Las Casas, in pity for the feeble and overworked Indians.

. The frightful inhumanity of the traffic was not yet apparent to Christian nations; and England, Holland, and France competed with Portugal for a share in its profits. Queen Anne, after the Treaty of Utrecht, retained one-fourth of the monopoly for her own private account, and thus became the greatest slave-merchant in the world. Spain, for some reason, never engaged directly in this trade; but contracted with foreigners for the requisite supply. The system of *ripartimientos* (see Book III., § 12) was greatly mitigated by ordinances of Charles V., who raised the natives of his Spanish possessions from the rank of slaves to that of subjects. They were governed in their own villages by *caziques* or chiefs, descended, in many instances, from their former monarchs; and though certain labors were exacted from them, they were rewarded and made as little oppressive as possible. One inferior race was relieved at the expense of another.

120. The annexation of Portugal to Spain made her colonial possessions the prey of English and Dutch attacks, and led to the downfall of the Portuguese empire in Asia. The Dutch $^{\text{A. D. 1580-1640.}}$ were ultimately driven from Brazil; but in India only Goa and Diu remained to Portugal, while Ormuz was reconquered by the Persians. Jesuit missionaries opened the way to Portuguese commerce with China and Japan. St. Francis Xavier, one of Loyola's first converts — canonized after his death as patron and protector of the East Indies — was among the pioneers. Macao, in China, was presented to the Portuguese

as a trading station and continued in their possession until it was opened
to all nations; but their residence in Japan was ended, in
less than a hundred years from its beginning, by a massacre
of Christians and expulsion of all foreigners. Fortunately for Brazil, her
great gold mines were not discovered until 1696, when the rich agricultural resources of the country had been in some slight degree developed.
The lands along the coast were granted in fief to great families, forming
distinct *captaincies* subject only to the crown.

121. In North America, the rival pretensions of France, England, and
Spain, had given way to an actual division, by which France claimed the
entire basins of the St. Lawrence and Mississippi in right of exploration;
England occupied a strip of Atlantic coast scarcely a hundred miles in
width, extending from the Penobscot to the limits of Florida; and Spain,
in spite of the exclusive grant of Pope Alexander VI., was forced to
content herself with what remained. At the opening of the eighteenth
century, the English dominions were more populous and flourishing,
though far less extensive, than those of the French. Relying less upon
the patronage of the great than upon their own resolute industry; freely
choosing the toils and perils of the wilderness in exchange for the restrictions — in many cases, the persecutions — which they had suffered in
Europe, the English colonists in less than a hundred years had established
twelve states whose permanence was no longer doubtful.

122. The origin of these colonies is too familiar to need detailed narration. Under the London Company, chartered by James I., in 1606,
for "planting and ruling" part of his American dominions, the first permanent English settlement was made at Jamestown in Virginia. The hero of the enterprise was Captain John Smith,
whose native genius had been developed by a series of remarkable adventures against the Spaniards in Holland and the Turks in Hungary
and Africa; and whose resolution alone saved the colony from destruction by the faults and follies of the first settlers. A settlement of different character was planted by a hundred English Puritans on the rockbound coast of Cape Cod Bay, under the auspices of the Plymouth
Company, from whose seat in England the first town derived its name.
The new state had a firm foundation in the virtue and intelligence of
its citizens.

By fresh immigrations, English colonies spread northward along the
coast, where are now the busy manufacturing towns of Massachusetts and
New Hampshire. Settlements were made in Connecticut by detachments
from Massachusetts Bay. It is perhaps no just cause for wonder that the
fathers of New England had not learned universal tolerance in the school
of persecution. The Providence Plantation, germ of the state of Rhode
Island, owed its existence to the expulsion of Roger Williams, minister

A. D. 1637.

A. D. 1607.

of the church at Salem, from the Massachusetts Bay Colony, for the utterance of more liberal sentiments than were then prevalent. The charter obtained by Williams in 1644 provided that no person should be in any way "molested, punished, disquieted, or called in question, for any difference of opinion in matters of religion;" the first example in Europe or America of a civil government formally and legally abdicating its claim to control the spiritual affairs of men.

123. Nearly equal freedom was enjoyed under the charter of Maryland, obtained by Lord Baltimore in 1632, which protected all forms of Christianity within the limits of that colony. The two Carolinas were peopled under a patent granted by Charles II., soon after his restoration, to the Earl of Clarendon and seven other lords and baronets, in recognition of their loyal and faithful service. Desirous of concentrating the wisdom of all ages into the management of the infant state, Lord Shaftesbury, one of the proprietors, with the aid of John Locke, the philosopher, drew up a "Grand Model" of government, by which he proposed to transplant the cumbrous ceremonials of the old world into the woods and wildernesses of the new. But while waiting for the "Model," the farmers and artisans of Albemarle had improvised a form of government suited to their immediate necessities, and which continued in force long after the elegant and elaborate code had been abandoned.

124. Early in the seventeenth century the Dutch claimed the lands between Chesapeake Bay and Connecticut River, in right of the explorations of Henry Hudson, then in their service, during his search for a north-west passage to India. The Dutch West India Company undertook the colonization of New Netherlands; a lucrative fur-trade with the Indians drew many adventurers, and the trading post on the island of Manhattan grew into a thriving town, where now stands the greatest city of the western world. A settlement of Swedes on the lower Delaware was conquered and absorbed into New Netherlands. But in 1664, Charles II. of England, always willing to make war upon Holland at the bidding of France, granted all the lands of the Dutch colony to his brother, the Duke of York. The government of the West India Company had become obnoxious to many of the colonists, especially to the English, who were numerous, and when the English squadron appeared in the harbor a majority of the people clamored for surrender.

Stuyvesant, the governor, was forced to yield. "New Amsterdam" and the colony in general, became New York, and Fort Orange on the Hudson was named Fort Albany from the duke's Scottish title. The lands between the Hudson and the Delaware were conferred upon Berkeley and Carteret, two of the proprietors of Carolina, and received the name New Jersey. Seventeen years later a large   A. D. 1681. tract west of the Delaware was bestowed by King Charles II. upon William Penn, a celebrated English Quaker, who desired to found an asylum of perfect civil and religious freedom. His justice and benevolence toward the Indians preserved his colony from the perils which beset the others, and his new city of Philadelphia enjoyed unbroken peace and prosperity.

125. The English colonies had their share in every war of the mother country with France; and this was aggravated by the neighborhood of the native tribes, ever ready to be stirred by French emissaries to acts of savage atrocity. Two great Indian families — the Huron-Iroquois and the Algonquin — occupied the region north of the Carolinas and east of the Mississippi. Of these the Iroquois proper, or Five Nations of central New York, were superior to all others in intelligence and political organization. Perfectly understanding the advantages of their position at the entrance to the great lakes and at the head of streams flowing to the Atlantic and the Mississippi, they made themselves feared by every tribe in their vast hunting grounds. "Patient and politic as they were ferocious, they were not only conquerors of their own race, but the powerful allies and the dreaded foes of the French and English colonies, flattered and caressed by both, yet too sagacious to give themselves without reserve to either."

126. The Algonquins were most numerous in New England, where they displayed all the worst traits of savage character in their fierce and treacherous assaults upon the feeble colonies. It is to be observed, however, that two radically different lines of policy toward the Indians were pursued by the English and French. To the latter, their savage allies bore an essential part in the scheme of colonization. To the former — especially the earliest settlers of New England — the dark, revengeful faces that appeared in the gloom of the forests, were those of demons rather than of men; and though they might sometimes be conciliated from fear, they were seldom admitted, as by the French, to the rank of allies and companions.

127. The first colony within the present limits of the United States was planted, as we have seen, by the far-seeing policy of Coligny, who availed himself of a lull in the storm of persecution to obtain royal orders for a settlement of Huguenots in a region which they named Carolina. Though this generous design failed, its memory survived, and the revival of persecution under Louis XIV., though a calamity to France, conferred an inestimable boon upon America. The Revocation of the Edict of Nantes drove to the new world thousands of refugees, who brought to their homes in the wilderness all that was best in the refined French society of that Augustan age. Their perfect and genial courtesy — not less than their financial thrift and enterprise — and that moral elevation which had been proved by the renunciation of

all worldly advantages for conscience' sake, added precious elements to colonial life.

New Rochelle in New York perpetuated the name of the Huguenot capital in France; Massachusetts, Maryland, and Virginia, offered a cordial welcome with lands and citizenship; but it was in the Carolinas, whose climate resembled that of their native Languedoc, that the greatest number of the exiles found a congenial home. Here they introduced the vine, olive, and mulberry, and the manufacture of silk. No citizens had a more important influence in shaping the character of the future Republic; none were more steadfast in their devotion to rightful liberty. Laurens, Marion, Jay, and Faneuil are but few of many Huguenot names celebrated in our Revolutionary annals.

128. The long and romantic tale of French exploration in America can only be sketched in faintest outlines. A leading policy with the French was to make themselves necessary to the Indians in three distinct characters as soldiers, traders, and priests. Fighting their battles with the novel and terrible fire-arms, and thus giving them at least a temporary superiority over their most dreaded foes; supplying their wants from European factories, and gaining their confidence by the self-denying and devoted lives of missionaries who taught them a holier faith — the handful of Frenchmen were reinforced for exploration and conquest by thousands of savage allies, whose brutal manners they endured and whose nauseous fare they partook with brotherly good nature. Jesuits were among the foremost " Pioneers of France in the New World " The " mission " was the outpost of French civilization; the cross and the lilies of the Bourbons were planted together in the depths of primeval forests, on the banks of the Mississippi and the Great Lakes. In this way the rocky coast of Maine, the lakes of Central New York, the straits and northernmost peninsula of Michigan, the prairies of Illinois, Indiana, and Texas, the frozen solitudes near Hudson's Bay, were all claimed for France.

129. Among the first and greatest heroes of exploration was Samuel de Champlain, the founder of Quebec. Joining a war-party of Algonquins at Montreal, he traversed the beautiful lake which still bears his name, and in a battle on its shore gave to the A. D. 1609. astonished Iroquois their first experience of white men and gunpowder. On another occasion he ascended the Ottawa, and crossed from its upper waters to Lake Huron, gaining every-where accessions of Indian allies. Again, crossing Lake Ontario, he led an attack upon a fortified village of the Iroquois. Twenty-seven years of unwearied toil and hardship were devoted to the Canadian colony, and Champlain is truly entitled the Father of New France.

130. Still more remarkable were the adventures of Robert de la Salle, discoverer of the Mississippi. While the Jesuits desired to establish a new Paraguay among the North American savages, La Salle aspired to a great feudal sovereignty over the tribes of the interior, to be enriched by the fur-trade of the North-west, while it maintained the ascendency of the French crown from the Great Lakes to the Mexican Gulf. Having planted several forts and trading factories on the lakes and the upper branches of the great river, he explored the latter to its mouth, and where it enters the Gulf, solemnly proclaimed the "most high, mighty, invincible, and victorious prince, Louis the Great, King of France and Navarre" to be sovereign of all the countries from which that vast volume of waters is derived. Pleased with this accession of dominion, the Grand Monarch fitted out a colony for "Louisiana" under the direction of La Salle. But the enterprise was one series of disasters. Passing by mistake the mouth of the Mississippi, the emigrants were landed on the coast of Texas, and the naval commander, always hostile if not treacherous, sailed for France. Unable to remove his colony, La Salle set out for Canada to obtain supplies. He was murdered on the way, and the settlement became a prey to the Spaniards. The colonization of Louisiana was reserved until another reign.

131. During "King William's War," the French and English colonies preyed upon each other with a ferocity hardly surpassed by their savage allies; but the midnight massacres of women and children need not be related. The French project for the capture of New York failed, equally with a combined expedition of the English colonists against Quebec and Montreal. The English conquered Acadia, now Nova Scotia, but the shores of Hudson's Bay were preserved to the French by the bravery of two brothers — Sainte Helene and D'Iberville. The Peace of Ryswick restored to France the whole north-eastern coast of America from Maine to Hudson Straits, with the exception of the eastern half of Newfoundland.

A. D. 1689–1697.

132. The establishment of the British Empire in India belongs to the eighteenth century, though the three presidencies of Bombay, Madras, and Calcutta were organized before 1700. The Dutch had exclusive possession of the Spice Islands, beside Java, Celebes, Sumatra, Malacca, a great part of Ceylon, and two posts on the mainland of Hindustan. Their agricultural colony at the Cape of Good Hope was of great importance to the preservation of their Indian possessions. One of their most flourishing colonies was that of Surinam or Dutch Guiana, and several rocky islets of the West Indies, which had been neglected as worthless by the Spaniards, became valuable trading posts to the Hollanders. Though the Dutch had been first by sword and pen to assert the freedom of the seas, their colonies were governed by a system of commercial monopolies almost as narrow and exclusive as that of Spain. Two great trading companies for the East and West Indies were intrusted with the civil, military, and ecclesiastical management of all their settlements, and this mode of government was sometimes, as in the New Netherlands (§ 124), galling to the independent spirit of the people.

RECAPITULATION.

Restrictive policy of European nations toward their colonies. Spanish viceroyalties in America trade exclusively with the Philippines and with Spain. Annual fairs at Cartagena, Porto Bello, and Vera Cruz. Decay of Spanish industry. Slight relaxation of colonial monopoly under the Bourbons. French corsairs gain part of St. Domingo. Negroes imported to relieve the West Indians. Portugal, being annexed to Spain, loses nearly all her foreign possessions except Brazil. Her Jesuit missions overthrown in Japan. Captaincies in Brazil.

North America divided among France, England, and Spain. Virginia colonized by the London, New England by the Plymouth Company. Religious liberty established in Rhode Island, Maryland, and Pennsylvania. Model constitution of the Carolinas. Dutch settlements on the Hudson River grow into the province of New Netherlands. Conquered by the English, it becomes New York. Danger to the colonies from the native savages, of whom the Iroquois were most highly organized — the Algonquins most treacherous. Early failure of Huguenot settlements in Carolina; benefit to English colonies from immigration consequent on the Revocation of the Edict of Nantes. Friendly alliance between French and Indians. Self-sacrifice of the Jesuits. Explorations of Champlain and La Salle. Sufferings of the colonies in King William's War. Beginning of English dominion in India. Island possessions of the Dutch; their colonies in Africa and South America; oppressive policy of the East and West India Companies.

REIGN OF LOUIS XV.

133. Louis XV., like his predecessor, came to the French throne at the age of five years. The regency was seized by the Duke of Orleans, nephew of Louis XIV. —a bad man, who A. D. 1715. had even been accused of accomplishing the deaths of the father, mother, and brother of the king. (See § 98.) It is probable, however, that the improvement of his own chance of the succession through these events was the only ground for the suspicion. His rivalry with the king of Spain for the French crown, in the not improbable event of the death of Louis XV., led him to cultivate the friendship of England, whose sovereign had a similar interest in upholding the faith of treaties against absolute hereditary principles. Strict legitimists, on the other hand, asserted that no act of Parliament could justly exclude James Stuart from the English throne ; and that neither oath nor treaty could abrogate the "divine right" of Philip V. to that of France. A Triple Alliance of England, Holland, and France, renewed the provisions Jan., 1717. of the Treaty of Utrecht, and confirmed the Duke of Orleans in the regency in opposition to the pretensions of the king of Spain. It became the Quadruple Alliance by the accession of the emperor the following year.

134. By the Peace of Passarowitz, Charles VI. had just concluded a war with the Turks, in which Eugene of Savoy had gained some of the last and greatest of his victories in the field. The fortresses of Belgrade and Temesvar were secured to Austria, but the Turks retained all southern Greece, which they had previously conquered from the Venetians. The war between the two ancient rivals, Philip V. and the emperor, resulted in the conquest of Sardinia by the Spaniards and of Sicily by the imperialists. The Duke of Savoy resigned the latter island for the title of King of Sardinia, which was borne by his house until 1861, when it was merged in the greater sovereignty of Italy.

135. The queen of Spain, Elizabeth of Parma, was conciliated by the betrothal of her daughter, then but three years of age, to the king of France. Being the second wife of Philip V., the ruling motive of this able and ambitious woman was a desire to make some royal provision for her own sons. She was descended from the nearly extinct family of the Medici; and the imperial fiefs of Tuscany, Parma, and Piacenza were promised to her son Don Carlos. This young prince married one daughter of the regent Orleans, while his half-brother, the heir to the Spanish crown, espoused the other. The short-lived cordiality between France and Spain greatly increased the influence of the Jesuits in the former kingdom. Philip V. was not less bigoted than his predecessors of the same name though of a different family, and during his reign 2,346 persons were burned at the stake for their religious opinions.

136. One fatal legacy of Louis XIV. to France was a debt of $400,-000,000, the yearly interest upon which amounted to nearly nine times the surplus revenues of the state. The regent, who, in spite of his profligacy, was a man of brilliant talents, attempted to grasp the yet unrealized wealth of the American dominion as a relief from present embarrassments. With his favor, John Law, a Scottish banker, proposed the famous Mississippi Scheme. The public credit was to be retrieved by an enormous issue of paper money secured by shares in the Mississippi Company, and based upon a monopoly of trade with Louisiana and Canada. For a year speculation raged high in France. The very vastness of the enterprise and the unknown extent of its basis appealed to the popular imagination. The days were not long enough to satisfy the eager throng of purchasers of the company's stock; princes, bishops, scholars, and ladies of noble rank embarked their fortunes. Paper money of large denominations was preferred to gold, if only for the speed with which it could be counted. The public debt disappeared, its bonds having been exchanged by their holders for the shares of the company.

137. The transient excitement gave a great impulse to colonization; and eight hundred emigrants planted the title of the regent in the city of *New Orleans* on the banks of the Mississippi. Law himself received vast territories in Arkansas, and lavished immense wealth in transporting thither French and German settlers and

A. D. 1718.

negro slaves. But the bubble burst. In May, 1720, the notes of Law's bank were found to be irredeemable in specie. The stock of the Mississippi Company had a thousand-fold outrun the available value of its possessions, and men who had dreamed themselves rich awoke to poverty. It is possible that ignorance of the true nature of money bore a larger part than deliberate fraud in this remarkable scheme; but the ill-judged attempt to restore the public credit was almost as disastrous to the nation as the wars which had indirectly occasioned it. During the same year, 1720, a similar delusion, known as the "South Sea Bubble," prevailed in England, with nearly the same results.

138. In February, 1723, Louis XV. was declared of age, and Orleans resigned the regency. As president of the Council of State he might have continued to control France, but near the end of the same year he died and was succeeded by the Duke of Bourbon. In renewed anticipation of the death of Louis XV., the king of Spain surprised all Europe by abdicating his crown in favor of his eldest son, Don Louis. His design was, of course, to clear his way to the throne of France; but when, contrary to all expectation, the French king recovered and the younger Louis suddenly died, Philip V. resumed the Spanish crown. His daughter was, a few months later, sent back from Paris to Madrid, and Louis XV. married Maria Leczinska, daughter of the exiled king, Stanislaus of Poland.

139. The tangled web of European diplomacy at this period is hardly worth the trouble of unraveling. Many an intricate plot came to no result, being thwarted by some other scheme still more cunningly contrived; and the multitudes of conflicting interests only fatigue the attention, while they afford no satisfaction to the mind. The only question of permanent importance was that of the Austrian succession. The emperor, having no sons, desired to secure his hereditary possessions to his daughter Maria Theresa — though by the will of his father they had been destined in such a case to the daughters of his elder brother, Joseph. The Pragmatic Sanction, by which in 1713, Charles VI. had declared his own will concerning his inheritance, had been confirmed by the Estates of Austria, Silesia, Bohemia, Hungary, and the Netherlands; and the great object of imperial diplomacy was to obtain the guarantee of foreign powers. The Treaty of Vienna secured the adhesion of Spain; and it was commonly believed that a secret article provided for a marriage between Don Carlos and the imperial princess, and the ultimate reunion of the great dominions of Charles V.   April, 1725.

140. A counter-alliance, known as the League of Herrnhausen, united France, England, Prussia, Holland, Sweden, and Denmark in opposition to the League of Vienna. The latter was joined by the empress Catherine of Russia, and eventually by the king of Prussia, who deserted the

M. H.—21.

Hanoverian alliance for that of the emperor. Only the profound and peaceful policy of Cardinal Fleury—prime-minister of France since 1726—prevented the outbreak of another general war. The death of the empress Catharine, and the quiet accession of George II. in England,

A. D. 1727.

contributed to the same result. Spain was the only great power which had lately encouraged the attempts of James Stuart to regain the English throne; and by the Treaty of Seville in 1729, Spain made peace with England, France, and Holland. The second Treaty of Vienna, in 1731, reconciled the last two nations with the emperor, and Spain also acceded within a month. A Family Convention, by which the Grand Duke of Tuscany named Carlos of Spain as his heir, completed the pacification of Europe.

141. The next general disturbance arose from the War of the Polish Succession, which followed the death of Augustus II. in 1733. Frederic Augustus, son of that monarch and his successor in the Saxon electorate, was supported by Russia and by the emperor Charles VI., whose niece he had married, but whose influence he gained only by renouncing the claims of his family to the Austrian succession and giving his solemn guarantee to the Pragmatic Sanction. The king of France, on the other hand, determined to restore his father-in-law, Stanislaus Leczinski. The defects of the Polish constitution placed the country at the disposal of foreign powers. A pretense was indeed made of respecting the freedom of the election, but not only was money used lavishly in securing votes, but a Russian army was quartered in Poland itself and an Austrian in Silesia.

142. Stanislaus, as a native of the country, was the more popular candidate, and was actually elected by a large majority; but a small number of electors crossed the Vistula to Praga and gave their votes to the Saxon prince, who was immediately proclaimed as Augustus III. and recognized by the Russian and Austrian courts. Unsupported by either his French or Polish adherents, Stanislaus became a second time a fugitive from Warsaw. Dantzic, where he first took refuge, was besieged and taken by the Russians in 1734, and the king, in the disguise of a peasant, fled to the court of Frederic William of Prussia. That sovereign protected him personally, while sending 10,000 men to join the Austrians in opposing his cause. The unhappy people of Poland suffered all the injury of a strife in which they had no voice; for the Polish succession was in fact only a pretext of which the powers of Europe availed themselves to fight out their own quarrels.

143. France had already begun the war by seizing Lorraine in 1733; while Marshal Villars, with a French and Piedmontese army, conquered the duchy of Milan. Berwick, in command of the army of the Rhine, took Kehl, Trèves, and Trarbach, and besieged Philipsburg, where he was

killed in June, 1734. Villars died a few days later at Turin. They were the last of the great generals of Louis XIV. The Spanish troops meanwhile effected an easy conquest of Naples, where the Austrian rule was universally detested. The defeat of the imperial troops at Bitonto, May, 1734, completed the acquisition of the mainland, and Sicily was reduced in a few months. Don Carlos, as Charles III., was crowned at Palermo, and thus began the reign of the Spanish Bourbons in Italy. The mild disposition of the young king, and the wisdom of his minister, Bernardo Tanucci — formerly a professor of law at Pisa — made the commencement of this dynasty far more beneficent than its later years.

144. Austria having lost her last possession in Italy, all parties began to incline toward peace. Hostilities ceased in 1735; but the Third Treaty of Vienna was not signed until 1738. King Stanislaus resigned the troublesome sovereignty of Poland for the duchies of Lorraine and Bar, which had already been acquired by France. They were considered as the dowry of his daughter, and reverted on his death to the French crown. The former Duke of Lorraine, Francis Stephen, was indemnified by the Grand-duchy of Tuscany, and the French court withdrew its protest against his marriage with the imperial princess, Maria Theresa. A small portion of his former possession was secured to him that he might continue to be a prince of the Empire, and have a better prospect of election to the imperial crown upon the death of his father-in-law, Charles VI. The last of the Medici died before the treaty was concluded, and Francis became Grand-duke of Tuscany. Charles III. was acknowledged as King of the Two Sicilies, and resigned to the emperor his fiefs in northern Italy.

145. The year before this treaty, Charles VI. had declared war against the Turks, in pursuance of his alliance with Russia. The Ottoman Empire was so far gone in its decline, that it continued to exist chiefly through the mutual jealousies of the European powers, neither of which would permit the others to be aggrandized by the absorption of the Turkish provinces.

Peter the Great had died in 1725. His eldest son, Alexis, who had joined the Old Russian party in opposition to his father's favorite reforms, had, seven years before, been convicted of conspiracy and put to death, leaving only a son three, and a daughter four years of age. By the aid of the New Russian party, the empress Catharine, who had been crowned at Moscow during the life of her husband, ascended the throne. On her death in 1727, Peter II., the son of Alexis, became Czar under the control of Menschikoff, whose daughter he married. The insolence of the prime minister became so unbearable that he was banished in a few months to Siberia — that vast and frozen region which served the Russian government as a prison for political offenders.

146. Peter was succeeded in 1730 by Anna Ivanowna, duchess of Courland, a niece of Peter the Great. She made peace with Kouli Khan,
afterward better known as Nadir Shah, of Persia, by restoring the greater
part of her uncle's conquests in that country; and in 1735 began a war,
first against the Tartars of the Crimea, and then against the Turkish
Empire itself. Münnich, her general-in-chief, is considered as the founder
of the Russian military system. By his masterly tactics, Azov was reconquered and many victories were gained. The Austrian allies were not
so fortunate. They suffered a disastrous defeat at Krotzka, and were
driven from Servia, Bosnia, and Wallachia. By the Peace
A. D. 1739.   of Belgrade, that important fortress, with Sabatz and Or-
sova, was surrendered to the Turks. Russia soon made a treaty by which
she retained Azov, and enlarged her boundaries in the Ukraine, but
agreed to keep no fleet in the southern seas.

147. During this year a colonial war broke out between Spain and
England — the beginning of a long rivalry between the so-called Latin
and Saxon races for the possession of the American continent. The
boundaries of Carolina and Florida — the privilege of supplying the
Spanish colonies with African slaves, and the right, claimed by the
Spaniards, of searching English vessels for contraband goods, were among
the points in dispute. Philip V. had fortified himself in 1735 by a
Family Compact with Louis XV., who engaged to procure the restoration of Gibraltar to Spain, and to harass English commerce by means of
a swarm of privateers as well as by his national fleet. Prizes amounting
to more than a million of dollars were taken by the Spaniards during
the first three months, but the capture of Porto Bello by Admiral Ver-
non, and the subsequent depredations of Anson in his cruise round the
globe went far toward turning the balance.

148. The death of the emperor Charles VI. in 1740, converted this
maritime war of two nations into a general conflict, known as the War
of the Austrian Succession. The archduchess Maria Theresa, now in her
twenty-fourth year, assumed the crowns of Hungary and Bohemia, and
received assurances of friendship from England, Russia, Prussia, and the
United Netherlands. France dissembled; the elector of Bavaria claimed
the Austrian provinces in his own right as descended from Ferdinand
II. and in that of his wife, a daughter of Joseph I. The queen of Poland
was the eldest daughter of the latter emperor; and though her husband
had guaranteed the Pragmatic Sanction, he joined the secret alliance at
Nymphenburg, of France, Bavaria, and Spain. The kings of Prussia and
Sardinia and the electors of Cologne and the Palatinate acceded to this
league, which destined the imperial crown for Charles Albert of Bavaria,
while it apportioned the Austrian possessions in Germany and Italy
among the various contracting parties. To this powerful coalition Maria

Theresa could only oppose the alliance of England, which was ineffective for several years; while her own army was feeble and her treasury drained. The empress Elizabeth of Russia was friendly but absorbed at home by a Swedish invasion* which had been instigated by the French.

149. The first blow was struck by Frederic II. of Prussia who overran and conquered the province of Silesia in less than four months. The important battle of Mollwitz, in which the Prussian infantry defeated the Austrian by the unprecedented quickness and precision of its fire, demonstrated the superiority of the military system organized by Frederic William I. The elector of Bavaria marched into Upper Austria where he occupied Linz without a blow and received the homage of the Estates as Archduke; then turning to Bohemia captured Prague with the aid of the Saxons and was crowned as King. Maria Theresa took refuge in Hungary, where, presenting her infant son — afterward the emperor Joseph II. — to the assembled magnates, she besought their aid. The brave princes, though they had little reason to serve a dynasty which had overthrown their ancient constitution and avenged their fathers' resistance with the ax, could not resist the appeal of this royal woman and child in their distress. The hall resounded with their shout, "Let us die for our king, Maria Theresa!" Magyars, Croats, Pandours sprang to arms, and 100,000 men were soon on foot. They were joined by the Tyroleans, who rose almost to a man; and during the respite afforded by Charles Albert's absence in Bohemia, the whole force was thoroughly armed and drilled.

150. The electors met at Frankfort, Jan., 1742, and gave their unanimous vote to the Bavarian prince, who received the imperial crown under the name of Charles VII. But the new levies of the queen of Hungary were already in the field. One division under General Khevenhüller reconquered Upper Austria, invaded Bavaria, and captured Munich; while a second, under the Grand-duke of Tuscany, the queen's husband, entered Bohemia. The long and hard-fought battle of Czaslau was gained by the king of Prussia, but at this point Frederic, who distrusted his allies, and had, moreover, accomplished his only personal object in the war, suspended hostilities, and concluded, the following month, a treaty with Austria. Silesia, with the county of Glatz, was the price of his neutrality.

151. The French, thus deprived of their best ally, were besieged in Prague; and though they managed to evacuate the city and escape, the sufferings of the autumn and winter reduced the 60,000 men commanded

---

* This northern war ended in the surrender by Sweden of all her provinces east of the Gulf of Bothnia, which were added to the Russian Empire.

by Belleisle to 12,000 before his arrival in France. The death of Cardinal Fleury left the French government in great disorder. Imitating the words of his predecessor on the death of Mazarin, Louis XV. declared himself prime minister, but he had neither the talents nor the industry to make good his promises; and the slackness of the French military movements soon betrayed the want of a common and efficient head of the several departments of government.

152. The emperor Charles VII. saw himself deserted by the French, and disastrously defeated by the Austrians, while his capital was once more in possession of his foes. In these humiliating circumstances, he consented to abandon Bavaria on condition that the remnant of his army might be quartered unmolested in some neutral state of the Empire. The queen of Hungary received the allegiance of the Bavarian estates. At the same time great enthusiasm began to be felt in England for the cause of Maria Theresa. Walpole, after being at the head of affairs for more than twenty years, was compelled to resign, and with the elevation of Lord Carteret, measures were taken for a more vigorous prosecution of the war.

153. An army of 40,000 men, joined a few months later by King George II. in person, entered Germany in the spring of 1743, and gained in June the battle of Dettingen. The king of Sardinia, who had already withdrawn from the League of Nymphenburg, now made a close alliance with the queen of Hungary, engaging to keep 45,000 men in the field on condition of an annual subsidy from England and some accessions of territory in northern Italy. The French and Spanish Bourbons at the same time made a second Family Compact providing for war against England and Sardinia. The "Young Pretender," grandson of James II., was furnished with a French fleet and army for what proved the last invasion of the British dominions by any member of his family. It was delayed until 1745. In the absence of the king and the Duke of Cumberland, the Pretender advanced within four days' march of London; but his fortunes were ruined by the battle of Culloden, and the Hanoverian dynasty has ever since reigned in peace.

154. The events of the intervening two years, though crowded and sufficiently exciting, produced too little lasting effect to require much detail. Louis XV. took the field in March, 1743, with an army of 80,000 men commanded by the Duke of Noailles and Count Maurice of Saxony, better known to history as Marshal Saxe. Many towns in the Netherlands were taken, and as Alsace was now threatened by the Austrians, the king hastened with a chosen body of troops to its rescue. A severe illness at Metz nearly put an end to his life; and the Parisians, in their impulse of joy at his recovery, gave him the title of Well-beloved — a description which few sovereigns have so little deserved.

155. The Union of Frankfort between the emperor, the kings of Prussia and Sweden, and the elector palatine, led almost immediately to the second Silesian War. Frederic II. invaded Bohemia and captured Prague; but he was expelled from that kingdom and even from Silesia in a few months by a combined force of Austrians and Saxons. Silesia was recovered the following spring. The emperor, meanwhile, took advantage of the engagement of the Austrian troops in this war to recover his hereditary dominion and reëstablish himself at Munich. The Austrian army in Italy, which in 1743 had advanced almost to the kingdom of Naples, was this year driven northward nearly to the Po.

156. A new Fourfold Alliance, Jan., 1745, drew more closely the interests of Maria Theresa, the elector of Saxony, the Dutch Republic, and Great Britain; but the death of Charles VII., the same month, suddenly altered the state of affairs. His son, Maximilian Joseph, being but seventeen years of age, could hardly hope to receive the imperial crown. He made a treaty with the queen of Hungary by which he renounced all his claims to her hereditary estates and promised his electoral vote to her husband, Francis of Lorraine, upon their retrospective acknowledgment of his father's imperial title and guarantee of his own undisturbed possession of Bavaria.

157. The king of Prussia gained this year two signal victories over the Austrians at Hohenfriedberg and at Sorr. Then turning against the Saxons, he conquered Lusatia and marched upon Dresden. His general, Prince Leopold of Dessau, also entered Saxony, captured Leipzig and Meissen, and defeated the army of General Rutowski at Kesselsdorf. Prince Charles of Lorraine was obliged to retreat; Dresden surrendered without conditions; and Saxony was at the mercy of Frederic. At this point the king of Prussia was willing to make peace; and two treaties were signed at Dresden——one with the sovereign *Dec., 1745.* of Poland and Saxony, the other with the queen of Hungary. The former paid a large ransom and received back his Saxon dominions. The latter ceded Silesia; and Frederic in return acknowledged the Grand-duke of Tuscany as Emperor of the Romans. Notwithstanding the protests of the electors of Brandenburg and the Palatinate, Francis I. had already been elected and crowned at Frankfort, and thus became the founder of the new imperial House of Austria——that of Hapsburg-Lorraine.

158. The war went on between the Austrians and the French, and the latter, under Marshal Saxe, gained many victories in the Netherlands. Among the most brilliant was that of Fontenay, in which the king and the Dauphin were present, and the Duke of Cumberland was completely defeated. As a consequence of their victory, Tournay, Ghent, Bruges, Oudenarde, Nieuport, and Ath fell into the hands of the French. Their allies in Italy were equally successful this year. A new alliance of the three Bourbon courts with Genoa was formed in May, and their combined forces not only took Tortona, Piacenza, Parma, and Pavia, but defeated the king of Sardinia at Bassignano and received the surrender of Alessandria, Asti, and Casale. Don Philip of Spain, brother of the king of Naples, entered Milan in triumph. The next spring, however, the Austrian troops released from Germany by the Peace of Dresden, gained a decisive victory near Piacenza, which was followed by a retreat of the French and Spaniards beyond the Alps.

159. The sudden death of Philip V. severed Spain from the alliance. Ferdinand VI. did not share his step-mother's ambition for Italian conquest, and he withdrew his armies with such precipitation, that all northern Italy fell at once into the possession of the Austrians. The city of Genoa was treated with inhuman cruelty by the conquerors, who even attempted to harness the people in the streets to their heavy artillery. A revolt succeeded, in which the Austrians were expelled with a loss of 5,000 men.

In the Netherlands, the campaign of 1746 was no less fortunate to the French than that of the preceding year. Brussels, Antwerp, Mons, Namur, and other places were taken, and Saxe gained an important victory over Prince Charles of Lorraine at Raucoux. In 1747 an attempt was made to divide the allies by an invasion of Holland. Many important places were taken by the French forces under Count Lowendahl. In consequence of this attack, the Republican party in the United Provinces was defeated, and the hereditary stadtholder restored. This was William IV. of Nassau-Dietz, a son-in-law of the king of England.

160. While victorious on land, the French suffered many disasters by sea. Their colonies had an important part in the war. Louisbourg and the whole island of Cape Breton were captured in 1745 by the people of New England and effectually resisted all attempts to regain them. On the other side of the globe, however, the French made the important acquisition of Madras. The year 1748 was marked by extraordinary efforts of the allies to retrieve their losses. England, Holland, Austria, and Sardinia engaged to arm 280,000 men; and Russia, joining the alliance, invaded Germany for the second time in history. These gigantic movements resulted, however, in peace rather than war. France and Spain were exhausted; England and the Dutch States had sustained great burdens and received but a small share of the profits of the contest.

Oct., 1748. After some months of negotiation, the Treaty of Aix-la-Chapelle was signed by the ministers of France, England, and Holland, and a few days later by those of Spain, Genoa, Sardinia, and Austria. All conquests were restored. The Treaty of Madrid, two years later, restored the commercial relations of England and Spain to a friendly footing.

161. The eight years' War of the Austrian Succession left Austria still a power of the first rank, though deprived of Silesia and the Italian duchies. France, its chief promoter, in spite of the brilliant victories won by foreigners in her service, gained absolutely nothing, while the addition of $250,000,000 to her debt was among the chief causes which hastened the terrible catastrophe of the Revolution. She had lost, moreover, her cherished position as the arbitress of European affairs. The gay and frivolous courtiers who surrounded Louis XV. already congratulated each other that the world would last *their* day; and a current motto of the time was, "After us, the deluge!"

162. England, by subsidizing all her allies, had greatly increased her influence in continental politics. The same series of events which had undermined the specious prosperity of France, had elevated Prussia, through the energy and military genius of her king, to a foremost rank among the European powers; and the period of his reign is frequently mentioned even in universal history as the Age of Frederic the Great.

RECAPITULATION.

Regency of the Duke of Orleans during minority of Louis XV. Quadruple Alliance of England, Holland, France, and the Empire. Peace of Passarowitz with the Turks, who retain the Morea, but surrender Temesvar and Belgrade. Duke of Savoy becomes king of Sardinia. Close alliance between France and Spain; ambition of Elizabeth of Parma to establish her sons in Italy. Failure of the Mississippi Scheme. Pragmatic Sanction of Emperor Charles VI. aims to secure his inherited dominions to his daughter. League of Vienna supports, while that of Herrnhausen opposes the Sanction. War averted by pacific policy of Fleury; general cordiality restored by Second Treaty of Vienna. In War of the Polish Succession the elector of Saxony is the candidate favored by Russia and Austria, Stanislaus Leczinski by France. Duchies of Lorraine and Milan taken by the French; the former bestowed on the exiled king Stanislaus. Kingdom of Naples transferred from the Hapsburgs to the Spanish Bourbons. Peter the Great succeeded on the Russian throne in turn by his wife, his grandson, and his niece. War of Anna with the Turks; Azov retaken by Münnich.

Colonial war between Spain and England expands, upon the death of the emperor, into the general war of the Austrian Succession. England and Russia favor Maria Theresa; the kings of France, Spain, Sardinia, Prussia, with the electors of Cologne, Bavaria, and the Palatinate, are leagued in opposition. Silesia conquered by Frederic II. of Prussia. Most of the Hapsburg dominions preserved to Maria Theresa by the loyalty of Hungary and the Tyrol. Elector Charles of Bavaria becomes emperor. Bavaria itself submits to Maria Theresa. The king of Sardinia joins her party, and the king of England comes in person to her aid. Last invasion of England by the Stuarts defeated at Culloden. Second Silesian War. Frederic II. conquers Saxony and dictates a peace at Dresden. The emperor recovers Bavaria; dies and is succeeded in that electorate by his son, in the empire by Francis I. Continued victories of the French in Hainault and Flanders — of their allies in northern Italy. Death of Philip V. and recall of the Spanish troops. Austria regains Milan and Genoa, but the latter is freed by insurrection. The French invade Dutch Flanders; William IV. becomes stadtholder of the United Provinces. Treaty of Aix-la-Chapelle lessens the territories, without lowering the rank, of Austria; confirms the rising importance of England and Prussia, and the decline of France.

The Seven Years' War.

163. After the desolating storm of war, Europe enjoyed seven years' repose, which may be regarded as one of the most prosperous periods of her history. Commerce flourished; the minor arts of life were brought to a degree of elegance and refinement seldom before attained. Unhappily the causes of discord still existed; and the ancient rivalries of France and England soon broke forth in a strife which surrounded the globe. The boundaries of the French and English provinces in North America had been left undefined by the treaties of Utrecht and Aix-la-Chapelle, and though commissioners from both nations were employed five years at Paris in discussing the conflicting interests, their labors were of no effect. France claimed the Ohio Valley as part of Louisiana — England, as part of Virginia; and the former power attempted to unite her possessions by a chain of forts extending from the St. Lawrence to the Mississippi.

164. Border warfare between the colonists of the two nations, secretly incited by their respective governments, was a natural result. Naval hostilities began with combats of privateers and mutual depredations upon commerce. As before, the quarrel of two nations became part of a general European war; and disputes concerning American possessions were fought out upon the plains of Germany. Hence, what is known to American history as the "French and Indian War," from the employment of native savages by the agents and generals of France, is named in European annals the Seven Years' War, and its foremost figures are the empress-queen of Austria and Hungary and Frederic the Great.

165. The treaty of Aix-la-Chapelle had never pacified the mind of Maria Theresa in view of the loss of Silesia; and her resentment toward her best ally, Great Britain, which had counseled her to yield that province, was hardly less than toward Frederic, who had availed himself of her humiliation and distress to seize it by force. Her great minister, Kaunitz, had long ago confided to her a scheme for ultimately uniting France and Austria against Prussia. To further this secret design, Kaunitz himself spent five years as Austrian embassador at Paris. He learned that the foreign affairs of that court were ultimately decided by the king and his unworthy favorite, the marchioness of Pompadour, without reference to the Cabinet. To gain this all-controlling influence to her side, the proud and stainless empress condescended to write a flattering letter to the marchioness, and the alliance of Louis was gained.

166. The next steps were to break with the king of Prussia by violating the terms of the late treaty, and to renew an alliance already existing with the Czarina Elizabeth. Frederic, in view of the coming contest, allied himself with England, Jan., 1756; and in the following May two treaties between France and Austria were signed, by one of which Maria Theresa bound herself to neutrality in the war with England; by the other each party promised to furnish 24,000 men in case of attack upon the other, with the single exception of aggressions of England upon France. Hostilities began with the descent of a French fleet upon Minorca, which, in the absence of any sufficient English force for its defense, was speedily captured. Admiral Byng, who had been dispatched too late with a small squadron to its relief, made June, 1756. no effective movement against the French; and such were the excitement and regret felt in England at its loss, that Byng was sentenced to death by court-martial and shot. During the contest for Minorca, war was first formally declared by the French and English governments.

167. Frederic of Prussia, finding that Austria, France, Russia, Sweden, and Saxony were leaguing themselves for the annihilation of his kingdom and the division of its spoils, resolved to anticipate their movement by an invasion of Saxony. His army moved in three divisions, of which the king himself led one. At Dresden he seized the government papers, and caused the secret dispatches of the allies, proving their designs against him, to be published in justification of his conduct. Desiring, if possible, to join the Saxon forces to his own, he avoided a battle, but blockaded their army of 17,000 men in its strongly fortified camp near Pirna. Then turning toward Bohemia, he met the Austrians who were marching to the relief of Saxony. The battle of Lowositz resulted in his favor, and on his return to Pirna he received the surrender of the entire Saxon army. The officers were paroled, but most of the common soldiers entered the service of Prussia.

168. Frederic remained in possession of Saxony; but the armies of the League were now in motion, and the Diet of the Empire pronounced its sentence against him as a disturber of the public peace. The northern German states protested against this decision, and their sovereigns preferred hiring out their subjects to serve in the armies of England, to furnishing the contingents required by the emperor. Nevertheless the allied armies numbered more than 400,000 men, while the combined Prussian and Hanoverian troops fell short of half that number. The latter were commanded by the Duke of Cumberland, eldest surviving son of the king of England.

169. Three French armies entered Germany in April, 1757 — that of the Upper Rhine being commanded by the Duke of Richelieu, that of the Main by the Prince of Soubise, and that of the Lower Rhine by Marshal d'Estrées. The latter gained a victory over the Duke of Cumberland at Hastembeck; but was soon superseded by the Duke of Richelieu, who had acquired a brilliant reputation by the conquest of Minorca and was the most popular general of the day. Aiming to secure the neutrality of Hanover, he overran that electorate and Brunswick, where, under the mediation of Denmark, he entered into the convention of Kloster Seven with the English prince. This was soon annulled, but the king of England was so offended by the suspension of hostilities, that he never again intrusted his son with a military command.

170. Frederic the Great, meanwhile, had invaded Bohemia, and gained a long contested and dearly bought victory over Prince Charles of Lorraine, brother of the emperor, near Prague. Each army lost a marshal; but the entire Austrian camp and treasure remained to the victor. Charles, with a force nearly equal to that of Frederic, was blockaded in Prague; and the Prussian king even ventured to march with the greater part of his army to oppose Marshal Daun, who was approaching to relieve the Austrians. Being greatly outnumbered, Frederic sustained his first defeat at Kolin, and was compelled not only to raise the siege of Prague, but to retire into Silesia. It was a period of extreme depression in Prussian affairs. The French occupied Westphalia; an imperial army was in Thuringia; 100,000 Russians under Marshal Apraxin invaded Prussia and gained a victory at Gross Jägerndorf, while a Russian fleet captured Memel. The Hanoverian allies were dispersed; the Swedes were invading Pomerania; Brandenburg lay open to the Austrians, who in October actually seized Berlin and levied contributions upon its citizens, though they held the place only a few hours.

171. Frederic, in a momentary despair, even meditated suicide; but he took more manly counsel, and roused himself to collect the forces which were still on his side. Though Russia was in arms against him, the heir of that empire was his enthusiastic friend and admirer. The Duke of Richelieu inherited the anti-Austrian policy of his great-uncle the Cardinal, and opposed extreme measures against Prussia; finally the national enmities between the French and German troops lessened their efficiency. Under these slight encouragements, Frederic mustered the remnant of his forces, and gained at Rossbach near Weissenfels one of his most remarkable victories over the French and imperial armies. A month later he defeated Charles of Lorraine at Leuthen, and with his army of 33,000 men, killed, captured, or utterly dispersed, 40,000 Austrians. Silesia was the prize of this victory. Prince Charles resigned his command and became governor of the Austrian Netherlands.

Nov., 1757.

172. A change in the British government was now added to the circumstances which favored Frederic's interests. William Pitt, becoming premier, infused new energy into the war-policy of the kingdom. The Convention of Kloster Seven was repudiated, and preparations were made for settling the various disputes with France once for all on continental fields. A subsidy of £3,000,000 was paid to the king of Prussia, and he was requested to name the commander of the British forces in Germany.

Ferdinand of Brunswick, brother of the reigning duke, was appointed; and having reässembled his army, he announced to Richelieu that hostilities were renewed on the part of Hanover and Great Britain.

173. Living by plunder, the French soldiers had wholly lost their efficiency. In a few months they were driven from Hanover, Brunswick, East Friesland, and Hesse, with great loss of lives. Count Clermont, who had succeeded Richelieu, was defeated at Krefeld; Ruremond and Düsseldorf were taken by the Hanoverians, whose scouting parties penetrated even to Brussels. The French retrieved some of their losses by a victory near Cassel, but little more was accomplished this year. Frederic—though his masterly generalship was never more clearly displayed—had fewer successes than usual, owing to the perplexing multitude of his foes. A half-civilized Russian horde—the regular forces being surrounded and followed by wild troops of Cossacks and Calmuck Tartars—invaded Pomerania and burned the town of Cüstrin during a siege, though the fortress still held out. The battle of Zorndorf, one of the bloodiest in the war, resulted in victory to Prussia. The Russians lost 19,000 men killed and 103 cannon.

174. Hastening into Lusatia to the relief of his brother, Frederic was surprised by Daun at Hochkirchen, and defeated with a loss of his artillery and 9,000 men. France, England, and Prussia now signified their willingness to make peace; but Maria Theresa, whose finances were more prosperous than those of Frederic, and whose resentment was unappeased, refused to listen. The Duke of Choiseul, lately placed at the head of the French ministry, failing in his mere pacific overtures, made a new treaty with Austria less favorable to that power, and the war was less vigorously prosecuted by the French. They, however, repulsed an attack of Prince Ferdinand upon their winter-quarters at Bergen, and captured Münster the following July. They were defeated by the British infantry at Minden, and were compelled to withdraw from Hesse.

175. The Russians seized Frankfort on the Oder, and with the aid of an Austrian corps, defeated Frederic at Kunersdorf with great loss. He himself acknowledged that his kingdom must have been sacrificed if they had pursued their advantage. But Soltikoff, their general, was jealous of the Austrians, and withdrew without reaping the fruit of his victory. Frederic reëntered Saxony and drove out the imperial army which had captured Leipzig, Torgau, and Wittenberg. Dresden alone was held by Marshal Daun.

Meanwhile a projected invasion of England by a French armament, under Charles Edward Stuart, was thwarted by the vigilant activity of the British navy. Admiral Rodney bombarded Havre and destroyed part of the magazines and transports which lay there ready for the expedition, while Dunkirk, Brest, and Toulon were all blockaded by English fleets.

A French squadron managed to escape from Toulon and slip through the Straits of Gibraltar, but it was pursued and defeated by Admiral Boscawen off Cape Lagos in Portugal. A larger fleet which sailed from Brest, during an easterly gale which drove the blockading squadron off the coast, was encountered and dispersed by Admiral Hawke. Four frigates escaping from Dunkirk menaced the Scottish coast, and entering the Irish Sea, landed a force at Carrickfergus which plundered the town; but after leaving the bay the ships were all captured.

176. In 1759, Russia, Sweden, and Denmark formed an alliance for mutual defense and to maintain the commercial neutrality of the Baltic. The French, in 1760, occupied Hanover and Hesse, defeated the hereditary Prince of Brunswick at Corbach and Kloster, and maintained their possession of the electorate during the winter. The Prussians were defeated at Landshut with a loss of more than 10,000 men, killed, wounded, and prisoners. Never was Frederic's position more alarming. An overwhelming force of Russians was on the march, while three Austrian armies were moving to surround him near Liegnitz. He managed, however, to hold Daun in check while he totally defeated Laudon, and ultimately drove the Austrians from Silesia. The Russians occupied Berlin three days, destroyed its foundries and arsenals, and imposed heavy contributions upon the citizens. Frederic resolved to risk all for the recovery of Saxony. To this end he stormed the fortified position of Daun at Torgau, and with far inferior forces, gained a complete victory.

177. In America the first two years of the war were favorable to the French. The English fort at Oswego was captured, with a great quantity of vessels and stores, in 1756, and Fort William Henry on Lake George, the following year. Cape Breton Island, which had been restored to the French by the Peace of Aix-la-Chapelle (see § 160), was reconquered in 1758 by the English, who also captured, the same year, several French forts on the lakes and the Ohio River, and, in Africa, Fort Louis on the Senegal and the island of Goree. The next year a small British force under General Wolfe scaled the precipitous Heights of Abraham, and by a short, sharp, and decisive battle gained the fortress of Quebec, the strongest, in its natural position, on the American continent. The French commander, the Marquis of Montcalm, was mortally wounded, and Wolfe also lost his life in the engagement. Montreal and all Canada were shortly surrendered to Great Britain.

178. The death of Ferdinand VI. in 1759, changed the jealously guarded neutrality of Spain into an alliance with the French. As the crowns of Spain and the Two Sicilies were never to be united, Charles III. in assuming the former, resigned the latter to his third son, who became Ferdinand IV., though first of the name in Sicily. A third Family Compact between the courts of Madrid and Paris engaged Spain to declare war against England in May, 1762, unless peace should be concluded before that date. Unable to attack the English by sea, but trusting to their own ancient superiority on land, the Spaniards marched an army to the borders of Portugal, and required its king to renounce the British alliance for that of the Bourbons. Joseph I. replied by a declaration of war against France and Spain, and an appeal to England for aid. It was granted, and the Spaniards, after capturing Miranda, Bragança, and several other Portuguese towns, were driven from the kingdom by a German and English force under the Count of Lippe-Schaumburg and generals Burgoyne and Lee. The allies then invaded Spain and took several towns by way of reprisals. The English fleet captured Havana in Cuba, Manilla, and the Philippine Isles, and an immense amount of treasure and merchandise.

A. D. 1762.

179. The death of the English king in October, 1760, and the accession of his grandson, George III., had an indirect influence in favor of peace. The first two kings of the House of Brunswick had regarded themselves chiefly as electors of Hanover; they spoke German, thought of England as a foreign country, and were always longing for their native land. George III., on the contrary, had been educated in England, and declared in his first speech to Parliament that he "gloried in the name of Briton." In the continental war England had little concern, though the electorate of Hanover was vitally interested. The war-party prevailed, however, so long as Mr. Pitt was in power; and for many months afterward the war went on, in spite of negotiations.

180. Prince Ferdinand was defeated at Gränsberg and driven out of Hesse, but the French were in their turn repulsed from their position at Wellinghausen. The Russians besieged and captured Colberg, and the Austrians took Schweidnitz by surprise, making prisoners of its garrison of 3,600 men, and gaining a stronghold in Silesia. Upon the retirement of Pitt from the English ministry, Frederic found himself again in an almost hopeless situation. Pitt had been his firm friend; Bute, the new premier, was his equally determined enemy. The new ministry not only withdrew his subsidies, but proposed to abandon him altogether for the sake of peace with Austria. Fortunately for Frederic, the empress-queen was at that moment so confident of recovering Silesia, that she rejected the English propositions with disdain. The death of the Czarina, and the accession of her nephew, Peter III., unexpectedly turned the scale. On the day of Elizabeth's decease, the young Czar wrote to the Prussian king, for whom, as we have said, he cherished a romantic admiration, requesting a renewal of their friendship. He ordered his generals to cease from hostilities with Prussia and engaged to restore their conquests. An alliance was made the following May, by which each power promised to aid the other with 15,000 men

Jan., 1762.

in case of need. Sweden likewise made peace with Frederic. The treaty of Hamburg was negotiated by his sister, the Swedish queen.

181. The reign of Peter III. was short, for in July, 1762, his wife by a wicked conspiracy with the five brothers Orloff, deposed him and reigned in his stead as Catherine II. Herself the daughter of a Prussian general, she maintained the peace to which her husband had agreed, though she recalled the Russian troops which were preparing to serve in the armies of Frederic. Their presence, however, aided him to gain one more victory over the Austrians at Burkersdorf, and being now able to concentrate his forces, he recaptured the important town of Schweidnitz with 9,000 prisoners of war. His brother, Prince Henry, was no less fortunate in Saxony, where the campaign of 1762 closed with a great victory over the Austrian and imperial armies at Freiberg. Austria consented to a truce, and to compel the Empire to accede to it, Frederic overran Franconia, Suabia, and Bavaria, even to the very gates of Ratisbon. The princes thus attacked withdrew their forces from the imperial army, which was compelled to treat for a suspension of hostilities.

182. By the Peace of Hubertsburg, Feb. 15, 1763, Maria Theresa resigned her claim to Silesia and all other territories in dispute between herself and the king of Prussia. Frederic promised his vote to the archduke Joseph, her eldest son, at the next imperial election, and engaged to restore the Saxon electorate with all its archives to the king of Poland. Thus, so far as Germany was concerned, seven years of exhausting war, and the sacrifice of 886,000 human lives, had made no change in the boundaries of the contending powers. The heroic struggle maintained by Frederic the Great against such tremendous odds, heightened not only his military fame, but the political importance of his kingdom. This war, unlike that of the Austrian Succession, had been essentially a defensive one on his part; and his character, at this period, presented nobler traits than had appeared in the earlier years of his reign.

183. During the same month with the treaty of Hubertsburg, a definitive peace was signed at Paris between France and Spain on the one hand, England and Portugal on the other. In America, all the French possessions east of the Mississippi, except the little islands of St. Pierre and Miquelon, were ceded to England, together with Grenada, Dominica, St. Vincent, and Tobago in the West Indies. In Africa, the Senegal country; in Asia, the French settlements made within fourteen years; in Europe, all the French conquests in Hanover and the island of Minorca were likewise surrendered to Great Britain. England restored Belle Isle on the coast of France, and St. Lucia in the West Indies. Spain exchanged the Floridas for the English conquests in Cuba and the Philippine Islands, and was indemnified for her losses through the Family Compact by the cession of all that remained to France of Louisiana.

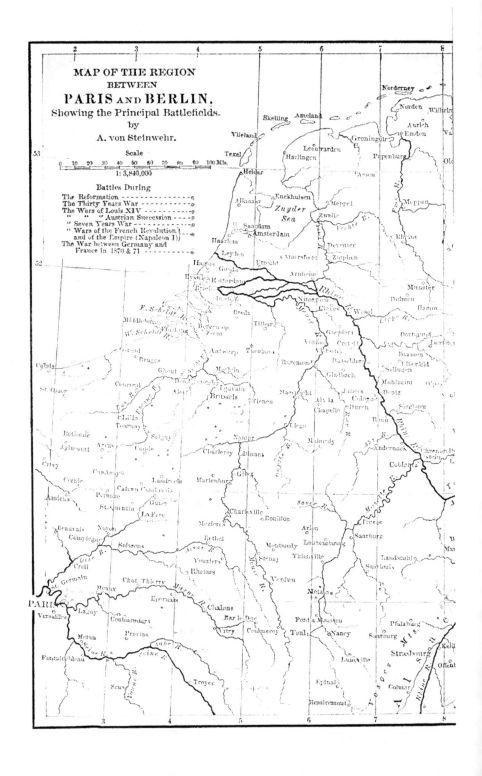

MAP OF THE REGION
BETWEEN
PARIS AND BERLIN.
Showing the Principal Battlefields.
by
A. von Steinwehr.

Scale

0 10 20 30 40 50 60 70 80 90 100 Mls.

1: 3,840,000

Battles During

The Reformation - - - - - - - - - - ○
The Thirty Years War - - - - - - - - ○
The Wars of Louis XIV - - - - - - - ○
" " Austrian Succession - - - ○
" Seven Years War - - - - - - - - - ○
" Wars of the French Revolution
and of the Empire (Napoleon I) - - -
The War between Germany and
France in 1870 & 71 - - - - - - - ○

RECAPITULATION.

Seven years' peace and prosperity in Europe followed by the Seven Years' War. Rival claims of France and England in America, and resentment of Maria Theresa for the loss of Silesia, are disturbing causes. France and Russia—ultimately Sweden and Saxony also—are allies of Austria; Great Britain, of Prussia. Minorca captured by the French. Frederic II. invades Saxony, takes Dresden, defeats the Austrians at Lowositz, captures a whole Saxon army and enlists prisoners in his own ranks; is placed under the ban of the Empire. The French gain a victory at Hastembeck; occupy Hanover; make a truce at Kloster Seven with the Duke of Cumberland. Victory of Frederic at Prague; he is defeated at Kolin, but in spite of great disadvantages, victorious again at Rossbach and Leuthen, and regains Silesia. Under Pitt's ministry, England takes an efficient part in the war. The French are driven from Hanover, Hesse, etc.; defeated at Krefeld, but victorious at Cassel. Russians invade Pomerania, but are ruinously defeated at Zorndorf. Disasters of Frederic at Hochkirchen and Kunersdorf, only partly balanced by the English victory at Minden. Renewed occupation of Hanover by the French. Blockade of French ports by the British navy prevents invasion of England by the Young Pretender. Frederic, though defeated at Landshut, gains great victories at Liegnitz and Torgau. Berlin occupied and despoiled by the Russians. In America the French are at first successful, but ultimately lose not only their forts on the Ohio, but Quebec, Montreal, and all Canada. Deaths of Ferdinand VI. of Spain, George II. of England, and Elizabeth of Russia. Spain becomes a close ally of France; Russia of Prussia. Portugal maintains her independence only by British aid. Victory of Frederic II. at Burkersdorf and recapture of Schweidnitz. Treaty of Hubertsburg ends the war between Austria and Prussia; that of Paris, between England, France, and Spain. No territorial changes in Europe. In America, Florida and Canada acquired by England, Louisiana by Spain.

AFFAIRS OF RUSSIA.

184. The reign of Catherine the Great, and her conspiracies with Austria and Prussia for the partition of Poland, are the prominent features in the history of eastern Europe during the remainder of the eighteenth century. That singular woman possessed talents only equaled by her crimes, and if her personal errors could be forgotten, the wonderful success of her administration would fully justify the title by which she is known in history. Many of the well-meant reforms which had contributed to the downfall of her husband were safely accomplished in her reign. The funds of Church-sinecures were applied to secular uses; the army and civil service were reorganized to the highest efficiency; the whole empire was divided into its present "governments" for convenience of administration. The unfortunate Peter III. was refused the permission he humbly sought, to retire to his duchy of Holstein-Gottorp; and was strangled in his prison by Alexis Orloff, probably with the consent of the empress. Ivan VI., the true heir to the throne, had been deposed by Elizabeth in 1741 and kept twenty-three years in a loathsome captivity which had reduced him to idiocy. He also was put to death by the orders of Catherine, who artfully engaged her former favorite Mirowitch in an attempt to release him. The conspiracy was made a pretext for the death of both, and the execution of Mirowitch, while

M. H.—22.

eagerly and confidently expecting the promised pardon, concealed the Czarina's share in the plot.

185. The condition of the neighboring nations, Sweden, Poland, and Turkey, encouraged Catherine's ambition to become the head of the Northern States-System. The poverty of Sweden had long subjected her to the control of foreign courts. The whimsically named parties of the " Hats " and the " Caps," favored, respectively, the French and the Anglo-Russian influence. It was reserved for Gustavus III.—a grand-nephew of Frederic the Great, whom he resembled in genius and elevation of mind—to put an end to both factions and restore justice and order by an increase of the royal authority. This independence of Sweden was extremely distasteful to Russia, and led ultimately to a war, whose details we shall be compelled to omit. It was ended by the Peace of Werela and a subsequent treaty of alliance and friendship at Drottningholm, which maintained the most cordial relations between the two powers during the great revolutions in southern and central Europe.

186. The death of Augustus III. in 1763 left Poland in that condition of anarchy to which its wretched constitution made it at all times liable. Of the two factions which fought for the disposal of the crown, one was supported by Russia, the other by France. Catherine, allying herself with Frederic the Great, was able to secure the election of Stanislaus Poniatowski, whose weak and pliable character promised to make him a useful tool of the Russian interests.

A description of Poland a few years before its extinction, will sufficiently reveal the causes of that event. Two-thirds of the nation were serfs, whose ignorance and squalid misery held them in a condition scarcely different from that of the brutes. They were incapable of possessing property; if a crop failed, thousands died of starvation. The remaining third consisted of three orders of nobility, with clergy, lawyers, citizens, and Jews. Of the magnates, or highest nobles, there were not more than 120, of whom four or five were the heads of powerful factions. The middle class of nobles numbered 20,000 or 30,000 persons, and the lower nobility more than a million. These were an idle, ignorant, and often beggarly class of people, shut out by their pride of birth from the thrift and comfort which might have been gained by industry; yet the most insignificant of them could nullify the proceedings of a whole diet by his single veto.

187. The citizens chiefly consisted of 40,000 or 50,000 artisans, who, scattered in wretched villages, were almost as absolutely subject to the oppressions of the nobles as the serfs themselves. Taxation fell only on Jews, artisans, and clergy; but the finances were wholly destitute of system. The heads of all the departments of government were responsible to the Diet and not to the king. To aggravate all these elements of weakness, the nobles clung to their ancient and constitutional privilege of forming armed confederations against the king whenever they were dissatisfied with his policy. So evident was the tendency to dissolution in so loosely constituted a state, that John Casimir, the last of the Vasa dynasty, clearly predicted, in 1661, the dismemberment of the kingdom by Russia, Austria, and the House of Brandenburg.

188. The first interference of Catherine was in the apparently just and liberal demand for toleration of dissidents from the Roman Church. Many of the nobility were Calvinists, and during the century of the Reformation, Poland had numbered a million of Protestants, who enjoyed equal civil rights with their Catholic fellow-citizens. But a period of intolerance had succeeded; Protestant places of worship were demolished, and under the influence of the Jesuits, a bloody persecution had occurred in 1724. The Poles could not fail to perceive the motive of the Czarina's intervention, especially when her further demand of political equality for dissenters had been followed by the entrance of a Russian army into the country. In an impulse of national independence, the Diet of 1765 renewed all the intolerant edicts against heretics. Stanislaus was forced to submit; and Catherine, enraged at his evasion of her commands, secured as her instrument of revenge, Prince Charles Radzivil, the chief of his opponents, and formerly the enemy of all Russian influence in the kingdom.

189. Through his efforts, with a liberal distribution of Russian gold, 178 distinct confederations were formed among the nobles. These were ultimately united into one of 80,000 members, which assumed, according to custom, dictatorial powers. Its business was delegated to two committees, one of sixty and one of fourteen members, the latter having power to pass resolutions of binding force upon the nation by a majority of votes. Eight men were thus entrusted with the fate of Poland. But the committees were soon found to be under the absolute control of Prince Repnin, the Russian minister, who arranged with the king, the Primate, the Grand Treasurer, and Prince Radzivil all the business that was to be brought before them. A conviction grew strong in the nation at large that Stanislaus had sold himself and the kingdom to Russia, and that his late semblance of independent action had only been part of the plot to deceive his subjects. A counter-federation was formed at Bar, with the aid and instigation of France, to dethrone the king and expel the Russians. Their armed force was defeated, A. D. 1768. and Cracow taken by the Russian general Suwarof, who thus began a long and celebrated military career.

190. A declaration of war by Turkey partly interrupted the movements of the Czarina against Poland. The Tartars of the Crimea overran her southern provinces and committed frightful devastations. The campaign

of Prince Galitzin on the Dniester in 1769 had little success; but the next year Romanzoff assumed the command and became in fact the hero of the war. He conquered Moldavia and Wallachia, while the fleet of Alexis Orloff gained a great victory over the Turks off Scio, and burned their ships in the Gulf of Smyrna. Among the vast projects of Catherine was the erection of a new Greek Empire on the ruins of the Ottoman. Her premature efforts for the liberation of the Greeks resulted only in misfortune; for as soon as her other plans required the withdrawal of her forces from the Mediterranean, the insurgents were left unprotected to the vengeance of the Turks, and the Morea became the scene of terrible barbarities.

191. Fearing that both Poland and Turkey would be destroyed by the ever-increasing power of Russia, other nations combined to preserve the European balance or at least to obtain part of the spoils. Joseph II., emperor since the death of his father in 1765, had several interviews with Frederic II. to concert plans for checking Russian aggrandizement. In the summer of 1770, Austrian troops took possession of the county of Zip and overran Gallicia even beyond Cracow. These territories were declared reünited to Hungary and were placed under Austrian governors. In the anarchy and terror that prevailed, the peasantry ceased from the cultivation of the soil, and herded together in the towns, where pestilence soon broke out in consequence of famine. The king of Prussia, under pretense of forming a cordon of defense against the plague, marched an army into Polish Prussia.

192. Russia, still involved in the Turkish war, could not resist these appropriations of part of her coveted prize. After long and intricate diplomacy, Russia and Prussia came to an agreement in the convention of St. Petersburg, and the empress-queen was invited to share the spoils of the doomed kingdom. Maria Theresa long resisted the nefarious scheme, but her counsels were overruled by her son, the Emperor, and Kaunitz, her long-trusted minister. When at length she put her hand to the document it was in these words: "*Placet*, because so many great and learned men will it; but when I am dead, the consequences will appear of this violation of all that has been hitherto held just and sacred." The triple treaty between Russia, Austria, and Prussia, providing for the appropriation of one-third part of Poland, was signed at St. Petersburg in August, 1772. Polish Livonia was assigned to Russia, together with the countries between the upper waters of the Dwina and Dnieper. Austria had the palatinate of Gallicia with Lodomiria. To Frederic II. were assigned Polish Prussia except Dantzic and Thorn, and a considerable portion of Great Poland. The maritime district was of especial value as connecting the kingdom of Prussia with Brandenburg, and though the territory acquired by Frederic was smaller

Feb., 1772.

and less populous than the share of either of his allies, its value was enhanced by the industry and wealth of the people.

193. The Confederates of Bar had already been driven from their last stronghold, and the three powers took possession without difficulty of their respective shares in the spoils. Stanislaus was compelled to summon a diet to confirm their usurpations; and an army of 30,000 men from the three nations marched into the territories still left to Poland, in order to overawe resistance. Those nobles whose estates had been seized were expressly excluded from the assembly. Only 111 members met at Warsaw, and in a series of balls and banquets of unexampled extravagance seemed to celebrate the ruin of their country with the insane frivolity of despair. The Diet continued in session nearly two years, in which time seven treaties were signed: three A. D. 1773-75. with Russia, two with Austria, and two with Prussia. A new constitution guaranteed by Russia was adopted by the Poles; but as the crown continued elective and the king was rendered still more helpless than before, the ruin of the country was only accelerated. The successive partitions of Poland have ever been regarded as among the greatest of political crimes. True, the vicious constitution of the government, and its blind adherence to the worst institutions of the Middle Ages, centuries after other European nations had developed more rational and stable systems, might in any case have ensured its destruction. But the sovereigns who enriched themselves by its ruin might as easily and more justly have made their power manifest by the introduction of a better order of things.

194. The Russo-Turkish war was ended in July, 1774, by the Peace of Kutchuk-Kainardji. The Sultan was glad to purchase the restoration of Moldavia, Wallachia, Georgia, Mingrelia, and some other territories by acknowledging the political independence of the Tartars north of the Black Sea, who were to elect their own sovereign from the family of Zenghis Khan, while they continued to acknowledge the religious supremacy of the Sultan as successor of the Prophet. Russia was also confirmed in the free navigation of the Black Sea and all Turkish waters for purposes of commerce. The dominion of the Black Sea and its shores never ceased to be a leading aim of Catherine's policy, and in the years following the treaty of Kainardji, frequent disputes arose concerning the independence of the Tartars. In 1783 the Crimea and Cuban or Little Tartary were formally annexed by Russia, and when the people rose in resistance, a terrible massacre ensued in which 30,000 perished.

195. Paul Potemkin, the all-powerful favorite of Catherine, was the prime mover in Crimean affairs. He founded the new capital, Cherson, for the provinces of Taurida and Caucasia; and in 1787 the Czarina herself visited the newly-acquired territories at once to do honor to Potemkin and to receive the homage of her Tartar subjects. Embarking at Kiev, she descended the Dnieper with a sumptuous flotilla of twenty-two vessels. She was joined by the exiled king Stanislaus of Poland, the victim of her wiles, and by the emperor Joseph II., who accompanied her in disguise and discussed their common plans for the spoliation of Turkey. To give the new dominions an air of prosperity, Potemkin had caused temporary villages to be erected along the route, and peopled with inhabitants brought from a distance and dressed in holiday attire. Herds of cattle grazed in the intervening pastures; but as soon as the gay procession had passed, hamlets, people, and herds vanished like a scene in a play. No sooner had the Czarina returned to St. Petersburg than her embassadors at the Porte were seized and confined in the Seven Towers, and war was declared by Turkey against Russia.

196. It was opened by an attack of the Turks upon Kinburn in September, 1787. They were repulsed, and the next June their entire fleet was destroyed in a battle near Oczakoff. This place was reduced by Potemkin in a six months' siege, and finally taken by storm with terrible carnage. The emperor Joseph declared war against the Porte, but his movements were ineffective, and he soon retired to Vienna. Sweden, the ancient ally of the Turks, began a war with the Czarina and prevented the sailing of Russian fleets for the Mediterranean. Christian VII. of Denmark, in fulfillment of treaties of friendship with Russia, sent an army to invade Sweden; but England, Holland, and Prussia now interfered and compelled him to remain neutral. Frederic the Great had died in 1786; his successor, Frederic William II., having thus withdrawn from his father's alliance with the Czarina, entered into the war as an ally of the Turks. All these powerful interventions did not avert the loss of many fortresses by the Sultan; and they rendered peace more difficult because of the offense given to the Russian empress by the attempt of foreign nations to dictate terms. The death of Joseph II. and the discontents in Hungary and the Netherlands rendered peace a necessity, however, to Austria. Her war with Prussia was closed by the convention of Reichenbach, June, 1790; and that with Turkey by the treaty of Sistova, August, 1791.

197. The war between Russia and the Porte was now at an end. The campaign of 1790 had been signalized by several Russian victories by sea and land; especially by the storm and capture of Ismail by Suwarof, and the destruction of the Turkish fleet near Sevastopol. The summer of 1791 was not less disastrous to the Turks. But Prussia and Great Britain were now in arms to enforce peace upon Russia, and the last obstacle was removed by the sudden death of Potemkin, who had prolonged the war in the hope of conquering for himself an independent sovereignty. In January, 1792, the Peace of Jassy was signed, the Dniester being

mutually recognized as the boundary line between the Russian and Turkish empires.

The portentous movements in France since 1789 disposed all European powers to suspend hostilities. But before entering upon that subject, we return to mark a series of events still more nearly concerning ourselves: the rupture between Great Britain and her colonies west of the Atlantic.

RECAPITULATION.

Catherine the Great reforms the internal administration of Russia, and becomes arbitress of the States-System of northern Europe. Revolution effected in Sweden by Gustavus III. makes the royal power absolute. Constitution of Poland is a sort of organized anarchy. Catherine secures the election of Stanislaus Poniatowski; finds a pretext of intervention in behalf of religious dissenters; by conspiracy with Radzivil places all power over Poland in the hands of her minister, Repnin; is opposed by the Confederation of Bar. Turkey declares war in the interest of Poland. Russians gain many victories by land and sea; incite the Greeks to a fruitless revolt against the Turks. Invasion of Polish provinces by Austria and Prussia. Convention of St. Petersburg arranges the partition of one-third part of Poland, whose king and diet are forced to confirm the wrong by treaties of Cession. Russo-Turkish War is ended by Peace of Kutchuk-Kainardji. Continued aggressions of Russia north of the Black Sea. Annexation of "Taurida" and "Caucasia;" triumphal progress of Catherine followed by renewed war with Turkey. Austria and Denmark take sides with Russia; Sweden, England, Prussia and the United Netherlands, more or less actively with the Turks. Austria concludes a peace at Reichenbach and Sistova; Russia at Jassy.

WAR OF AMERICAN INDEPENDENCE.

198. By the Treaties of 1763, it will be remembered that France had relinquished her last continental possession in North America, though the cession of Louisiana to Spain was not actually accomplished until six years later. All Europe was filled with jealous apprehension by the increased power of Great Britain; and when the blind and narrow policy of the home-government — a policy which every intelligent Englishman now condemns — had driven the American colonies to revolt, several nations seized the opportunity to injure their dreaded rival by aiding the insurgents. The details of the war must be sought in American histories; it can only be sketched here in outline, and chiefly with regard to the complications in Europe which grew from it.

199. The colonies planted by the English in America now extended from the St. John River to the St. Lawrence. The settlements north and south of these limits had been acquired by conquest or negotiation from France and Spain; and their people had been less trained in principles of civil freedom than were those who had been engaged either personally or by sympathy in the two great English revolutions. The French inhabitants of Canada accordingly remained subject to Great Britain rather than assume an active part in the rebellion. The colony of New York, on the other hand, had not only been more than a century in English possession, but it had derived from its parent Republic the impulse of the great war against Spanish despotism which was raging at the time of its birth; and it was first to join with New England in resistance to the oppressions of the British parliament.

200. These oppressions took the double form of direct taxation and of restrictions upon trade. To the first the colonists opposed the argument that they were not represented in the British government, and should not be burdened with its support; to the second, that as they and their ancestors had sustained the toil and peril of founding states in the wilderness, they might fairly claim the free and full advantage of all the facilities that nature had bestowed upon them, unfettered by artificial and arbitrary restraints. The Stamp Act, passed by Parliament in 1765, brought this resistance to a head. The act was repealed, upon a change of ministry the next year, but the odious principle was reasserted. In 1767 fresh duties were imposed, but so strong was the resistance which they encountered, that they were remitted in 1770 upon all articles excepting tea; and this was ordered to be conveyed directly from India to America that its price might be lower in the colonies than even in the mother country. But the oppressive principle remained the same; and it was not for mere pecuniary interests that the colonists were contending. Cargoes of tea were seized in the harbors of Boston, New York, and Annapolis, and either returned whence they came or discharged into the water.

201. The British government became more peremptory; the port of Boston was closed, the charter of Massachusetts abolished; and rebels in all the colonies were ordered to be sent to London for trial. The first general Congress of all the Colonies met at Philadelphia to concert measures of resistance. Addresses were voted, to Dec., 1774. the people of Canada, to those of Great Britain, and to the king; all breathing unalterable loyalty, but remonstrating against what were termed oppressive and cruel acts. A levy of militia was recommended to the colonies. Reinforcements arrived for the British army quartered in Boston under General Gage; and the first serious collision occurred at Lexington, Massachusetts, April 19, 1775, when a few farmers and villagers drove a whole English regiment with its cannon back to its quarters.

202. In the subsequent battle of Bunker's Hill, the British forced the American position, but with a loss of half the attacking party. George Washington soon afterward assumed command of the colonial armies, and with fewer than 15,000 men, poorly equipped, proceeded to blockade Gage in Boston. The next spring the royalists evacuated that city and sailed to Halifax. So far the regular British troops have appeared at a disadvantage in comparison with the hasty levies of the colonies. By treaties with several German princes nearly 18,000 mercenaries were procured for service in America. This employment of foreigners to crush their just resistance, was felt by the colonists as an intolerable insult; and the Congress at Philadelphia agreed upon a Declaration of Independence. Reviewing in a manly and dignified tone, July, 1776. the injuries which the American people had suffered from King George III., it proceeded from the premise that "governments derive their just powers from the consent of the governed," to the conclusion that "these colonies are, and of right ought to be, independent States."

203. The British force in America was now increased to 55,000 men, while the army of Washington, reduced by sickness and desertion, mustered at one time only 3,000 and these without uniform or suitable arms. A severe defeat on Long Island led to the abandonment of New York. Nevertheless by a brilliant winter campaign in 1776 and '77, Washington suddenly reconquered a great part of New Jersey. The European enemies of Great Britain were preparing to take part in the contest. A strong party in France overruled the natural scruples of the king; money and war-materials were placed at the disposal of the "rebels," and French privateers under American colors began to prey upon English commerce. Franklin and Lee, the envoys of Congress, were received with great enthusiasm at Versailles, and several noblemen, among whom the Marquis de Lafayette, the Count de Ségur, and the Viscount de Noailles were most celebrated, enlisted in the service of the Republic.

204. Still the balance in America was in favor of the British. They possessed New York, and holding the line of the Hudson, hoped by a junction with the powerful army under Burgoyne, who was advancing from Canada, to sever the eastern from the southern states. General Howe gained a victory at Brandywine, Sept. 11, captured Philadelphia the 26th, and again defeated Washington at Germantown, A. D. 1777. Oct. 24. The more important scheme of the English generals was thwarted, however, by the defeat and capture of Burgoyne's entire army at Saratoga, Oct. 16. France now made an open alliance of friendship and commerce with the United States, followed by a declaration of war against Great Britain. The naval contest soon spread to every quarter of the globe where either nation had possessions; the French forts and factories in India were attacked as soon as the news of war arrived. Several surrendered without resistance; Pondicherry was reduced by a siege of seventy days and its fortifications were demolished. France lost her power in India, but gained in Africa, about the same time, the English factories at Senegal. Several of the West Indies were captured by the fleet of D'Estaing.

205. In 1779 Spain declared war against England, and great preparations were made for an invasion, such as had not been dreamed of since the days of Philip's Armada. But for some unknown cause the French and Spanish admirals raised the blockade of Plymouth; and the army of 60,000 men which had assembled on the opposite French coast was withdrawn. The chief object of the Spaniards was to regain Gibraltar, which they besieged at the beginning of the war. The garrison, however, was reinforced and revictualed by Admiral Rodney, who on his way from England had captured a Spanish fleet carrying stores to Cadiz; and the fortress was valiantly defended three years by General Elliot against the most ingenious and persistent assaults. In the southern colonies of America, the English had also the advantage. A great part of Georgia had been conquered in 1778; and a combined attack upon Savannah by the American general Lincoln and the Count d'Estaing was repulsed with great loss in October, 1779. The next year the British captured Charleston and defeated General Gates at Camden; but most of their forts on the Mississippi were at the same time taken by the Spaniards.

A. D. 1779–1783.

206. The discovery of a secret commercial treaty between Holland and the United States, by which the independence of the latter was fully recognized, led Great Britain, in 1780, to declare war against the Dutch. The same year Catherine the Great of Russia declared an Armed Neutrality, which was acceded to by Denmark, Sweden, Prussia, Austria, Portugal, and the United Netherlands. The object of this combination was to protect the rights of neutral flags, and its principles were of great importance during the continuance of the war, especially to the northern nations whose territories abounded with timber, tar, hemp, and other materials for the construction and rigging of ships.

207. Several of the Dutch West India Islands now fell into the hands of the English, who also captured in 1781 a rich merchant fleet of thirty vessels; but these were retaken by a French squadron and conveyed to Brest. A British fleet reduced Demerara and Essequibo; but another squadron designed for the reduction of the Cape of Good Hope was defeated off the Cape de Verde Islands by the French under the Bailli de Suffren. In America the campaign of 1781 was disastrous to the English. Tobago and St. Eustatia with the small adjacent islands were taken by the French. Lord Cornwallis, on the mainland, after gaining a victory at Guilford, North Carolina, and capturing Gloucester and Yorktown, was besieged in the latter place by the French fleet and the American army, and forced to surrender with all his troops.

Oct., 1781.

During the summer the Spaniards had completed the recovery of Florida by the capture of Pensacola, while in Europe they were retaking the important island of Minorca. If the French and Spanish fleets in the West Indies could have effected their desired junction, the entire British possessions in that region would probably have been lost. This was prevented by Admiral Rodney, whose new naval tactics had already given fresh luster to the British flag, and who gained a brilliant victory over the Count de Grasse near Martinique and Guadaloupe, April 12, 1782.

208. A change of ministry in England, consequent upon the events of 1781, soon led to peace. The French court, always divided on the subject of the war, was now alarmed by the unexpected display of power on the part of the American colonies, and apprehended their ultimately combining with Great Britain to the detriment of France. Secret communications of the French government to its agent in Philadelphia, proposing to divide and thus weaken the several states, were intercepted, and induced the Americans to enter into preliminaries with Great Britain on their own account. A definitive treaty of peace between these two chief parties to the war, as well as between England, France, and Spain, was signed at Paris, Sept. 3, 1783. The thirteen United States were acknowledged as independent and sovereign over all the lands between the Atlantic and the Mississippi, the St. Croix and the St. John. France and England restored their respective conquests, except Tobago and the forts on the Senegal, which were retained by the former country. Spain kept Minorca and Florida, but could not purchase Gibraltar, though she offered Oran and Porto Rico in exchange.

209. The release of her American colonies abated nothing from the prosperity of England, whatever it may have cost her pride. Freed from absurd restrictions upon their industry, the States became of far greater commercial value to the mother country than the colonies had been, while the relief from the necessity of supporting an expensive military establishment at so great a distance from home, was sensibly felt by the overtaxed English people.

210. To America the close of the war brought only a change of perils. No governments existed except by the colonial charters, which were manifestly inadequate to the new situation. The thirteen states were as tenacious of their mutual and several independence as of their separation from Great Britain. All were burdened with debts far beyond their resources; and the people who had so violently resented the moderate though unjust impositions of the Parliament, were scarcely more willing to tax themselves to the amount of millions. To the unthinking, their hard-bought independence signified freedom from all restraint. It was a momentous crisis in the history of popular freedom, now to be put on its most signal trial before the world. After four years of threatened anarchy, delegates from eleven states met at   May, 1787. Philadelphia to frame a plan of government for the whole country. The representatives from New Hampshire appeared two months later, but Rhode Island was never represented at all.

211. The constitution then agreed upon and ratified within a year by most of the states, has been esteemed by competent judges among the best models of government ever devised. All the guarantees of personal liberty won by the English people in successive contests with the Crown, were adopted into the American constitution. The several states were left independent in all affairs where their interests could not conflict; but matters of war or peace, postal service, coinage, and duties were intrusted to the general government. The President, elected once in four years, was, by virtue of his office, commander-in-chief of the army and navy, and had a limited veto upon acts of Congress. At the first constitutional election, General Washington received the unanimous votes of his countrymen, and rendered not less illustrious service in the maintenance of peace and order than he had previously rendered in the establishment of liberty. Amid all the conflicts of opinion that have filled the revolutionary age that has succeeded him, history records but one estimate of Washington: "Whatever was the difficulty, the trial, the temptation, or the danger, there stood the soldier and the citizen, eternally the same, without fear and without reproach; and there was the man who was not only at all times virtuous, but at all times wise."

RECAPITULATION.

Jealousy toward England engages several nations in aiding the American Revolution. The colonies resist taxation; retaliatory measures of Great Britain. War opens with the battle of Lexington. British army is blockaded in Boston. Battle of Bunker Hill proves the resolution of the colonists. Boston is evacuated. German mercenaries employed by the British. Congress at Philadelphia declares the colonies independent. Americans defeated on Long Island. Howe takes New York. Washington gains victories in New Jersey; is defeated at Brandywine and in a suburb of Philadelphia. British army of Burgoyne captured at Saratoga; France and subsequently Spain and Holland make alliances with the United States. Gibraltar is successfully defended by Elliot against a three years' siege. The British are victorious in Georgia and South Carolina. Armed Neutrality of most of the European powers not directly engaged in the war. Surrender of Cornwallis at Yorktown virtually ends the contest. By Treaty of Paris, Great Britain acknowledges the independence of the United States. Florida is ceded to Spain. American constitution drawn up by Convention at Philadelphia. Washington the first President.

REVOLUTIONS IN OPINION.

212. Among many signs of change which marked the latter half of the eighteenth century in Europe, one of the first and most significant was the expulsion and temporary suppression of the Jesuits. Its chief mover was Carvalho, Marquis of Pombal, chief minister of Portugal, and one of the most remarkable statesmen of his age, who with some justice attributed the decline of his country to the grasping ambition of the Order. All the gold and diamonds of Brazil had indeed been insufficient to save the nation from bankruptcy under the bigoted and prodigal reign of John V. (1706–1750.) One-tenth of the people were immured in convents, while every form of industry was in foreign hands. By a treaty with Spain, Portugal acquired the Seven Missions of Paraguay, whose people were ruled by the Jesuits (see Book III., § 186.) The treaty provided for the removal of the natives to Spanish soil; but the commissioners of both nations who were appointed to superintend the migration were successfully resisted by the people themselves under the orders of their teachers. Before the latter could be brought to terms, the great earthquake of 1755 destroyed a considerable part of Lisbon, and buried many thousands of its people. The Jesuits did not fail to represent this terrible catastrophe as a token of Heaven's wrath against the minister, but Carvalho was undaunted. After quelling with prompt severity the pillage and disorder which had followed the earthquake, and organizing the most liberal efforts for the relief of the sufferers, he proceeded with new vigor to the execution of his chosen policy. An attempt upon the life of King Joseph I. afforded a new pretext for severity, and in September, 1759, all the Jesuits in the kingdom were shipped for the Pope's dominions.

213. Other governments soon followed the lead of Portugal. The extensive commercial operations of the Jesuits excited many jealousies. One of their banking establishments becoming insolvent, its French creditors obtained a judgment against the whole Order. They were accused of many crimes, but the one which included all others was their allegiance to a foreign government. In 1764, after several years of contest, the Order was suppressed in France. Spain, Naples, Austria, and the minor states of Italy in turn broke up their establishments and expelled them from their territories. In all the Spanish dominions, the Jesuits were ordered to be seized on the same day and shipped to the States of the Church, to which, by their own declaration, their obedience was due. But the Pope refused to receive them, and even belied his chosen name (Clement XIII.) by ordering his cannon to be fired upon the ships which brought so unwelcome an immigration. The harshness of these proceedings moved the displeasure of non-Catholic governments, and it was only in Protestant countries that the fugitives found personal security. A new Pope, Clement XIV., moved by the urgency of all the Catholic sovereigns, dissolved the Order as a disturber of the peace of Christendom.

214. The spirit out of which the Society of Loyola sprang, was perhaps extinct in Europe. The House of Hapsburg, for two centuries the powerful patron and protector of the Jesuits, had now at its head their most determined enemy. The emperor Joseph II. had contracted so strong a dislike for the severe instructors of his youth, that he thwarted their designs on every possible occasion. Protestant and Greek Christians were treated with an indulgence which was partly due to a just liberality,

A. D. 1750.

A. D. 1773.

partly to a desire to foster the industrial interests of his states. Seven hundred convents were dissolved; and 36,000 monks and nuns, thus restored to the world, were pensioned from their funds. The papal nuncios were informed that they would be received merely as political embassadors. Pope Pius VI. himself, who visited Vienna in the hope of conciliating the emperor, was not even heard upon matters of business, while Kaunitz, the all-powerful minister, treated him with studied personal neglect.

215. The restless disposition of the emperor engaged him in long and frequent journeys. Rome, Paris, St. Petersburg, and the Crimea, as well as Holland and his own provinces in the Netherlands, were visited in turn. He cultivated an especial friendship for Catherine II. of Russia with whom he discussed a project for reviving the two empires of the East and the West. She was to conquer Constantinople and all the shores of the Black Sea, while he seized Italy, and became in fact, as well as by title, Emperor of the Romans. Meanwhile the Hungarians were driven into insurrection by the enforced use of the German language in their courts of law, and the violation of many ancient customs. Upon the death of Maria Theresa in 1780, her son was not even crowned in their capital, but caused the sacred diadem of St. Stephen, for eight hundred years the object of their reverence, to be carried to Vienna and deposited permanently in his treasury.

216. In his foreign dealings Joseph was equally arbitrary. He ordered the Dutch to withdraw their garrisons from the barrier towns in the Austrian Netherlands (see ? 99), and caused the fortresses to be demolished. War was only prevented by the armed intervention of France, which secured the Treaty of Fontainebleau. During the long minority of William V. the republican or patriotic party had gained strength in Holland, and it was now reinforced by a close alliance with France. The Orange party, on the other hand, which upheld the hereditary dignities of Stadtholder, High Admiral, and Captain-General, was supported by England and Prussia. In the latter kingdom, Frederic the Great was succeeded (Aug., 1786) by his nephew, Frederic William II., whose sister was wife of the Prince of Orange. When the patriot party even expelled the Stadtholder from the fortress of the Hague, and treated the princess like a prisoner, on her attempt to enter the city, the new king of Prussia invaded Holland with 30,000 men; another revolution was effected and the Stadtholder was restored. Some of the extreme republicans, being excepted from the general amnesty, found a congenial field for their activity in France. The alliance with that nation was exchanged by the States for closer treaties of mutual defense with England and Prussia. The Triple Alliance, concluded at Loo in June, 1788, obtained, during the remarkable events of the next few years, an important influence in the affairs of Europe.

Nov., 1785.

217. The reformatory policy of the emperor occasioned great discontent in the Austrian Netherlands. Himself set free by philosophy from many superstitions of former ages, he desired the enlightenment of his people, but his efforts to make them prosperous in spite of themselves were not crowned with success. Their bigotry was alarmed by the suppression of convents, their patriotism by the abrogation of their ancient charters. A secret society in opposition to the emperor, formed in 1787, soon numbered seventy thousand members. Encouraged by the outbreak of the French Revolution, they met openly at Breda and demanded the restoration of their ancient rights, appealing in case of the emperor's refusal, "to God and their swords." Imperial troops were expelled from Ghent and from all Flanders. A Declaration of Independence, and an Act of Union of the Belgian United Provinces were published at Brussels in January, 1790.

218. At this point Joseph II. died and was succeeded both in the imperial and hereditary crowns by his brother Leopold II., who for twenty-five years had ruled the Grand-duchy of Tuscany with equal liberality and greater moderation than had marked the policy of the elder prince. He restored, and even increased the liberties of the Netherlands, his armies at the same time overawed or defeated the revolutionary forces, and the Belgian Republic was dissolved, after an existence of scarcely a year.

But the age of revolutions was only begun. Before the storm passed, every country in Europe was to undergo changes, though France was the scene of the most violent transformation. The oppressions of a thousand years were sure to be avenged whenever the masses of the people should acquire intelligence and a consciousness of their power. The latter half of the eighteenth century was marked by the multiplication of clubs and secret societies in every country in Europe, as well as by the universal diffusion of light periodical literature, instilling into the common people that skeptical philosophy which had already, in the minds of the higher classes, undermined all principles of civil or religious obedience. The success of popular revolution in America seemed to justify the leveling of all thrones and distinctions of rank — the more, because few took account of the severe moral training which had prepared the American colonists for their unique and heroic task.

219. Most of the governments in western and central Europe had, indeed, outlasted their vital power. Spain, since the suppression of the Cortes, was enslaved by the Inquisition; France, for nearly two centuries destitute of a national legislature, had become a mere autocracy, against which the parliaments made but a feeble and formal protest; Holland was rent by the Orange and republican factions; the Empire was stifled in obsolete and unmeaning forms; all the Austrian states were distracted by the well-meant but ill-considered innovations of Joseph II.; Prussia, lately powerful under two sovereigns of remarkable ability, had no constitution which could secure a continuance of its greatness; Poland and Turkey were in hopeless anarchy. In every country the intelligence of the best people was in advance of the national government; and the institutions which had served the needs of the middle ages were no longer adequate to the multiplied demands of the modern era.

220. The crisis was favorable to the ascendency of that brilliant company of French philosophers who aimed to supersede all former writings by their *Encyclopædia.** Contradicting the system of Descartes, who assumed the soul of man as the starting point in all investigations, they reasoned from a physical basis, and regarded thought, sentiment, and worship as mere phenomena of matter. Their speculations might have been almost as harmless as those of the mediæval Schoolmen, if they had not been recommended by the clear and popular style of most of the writers; or if they had been opposed by any thing better than the hollow show of a state-religion, which served chiefly as the cloak of the worst of despotisms. Not content with attacking tyranny and priestcraft, several favorite writers of the day assaulted the moral foundations on which the very existence of human society depends. Thus all things seemed tottering on the verge of chaos, and the revolt against authority was soon extended from speculation to action.

221. In France the political causes of revolution were especially numerous and powerful. At the death of Louis XV., the finances were in hopeless ruin. To advance his private fortune, the king had speculated in national securities and thus in the distresses of his people. So well was this understood, that the multitude, who in one generous impulse had styled him the "Well-beloved," now bestowed upon his successor the title of "Louis the Desired." Louis XVI. was in his twentieth year

A. D. 1774.   when the death of his grandfather raised him to the tottering throne of France. His intentions were good, but he lacked that energy, both of intellect and of will, which alone could have saved the nation.

222. The war with Great Britain consequent upon the recognition by France of the independence of the United States, not only drained the treasury, but excited among the chivalrous youth of the nation an enthusiasm for popular freedom, most dangerous to the traditions of the Bourbons. A series of ministers undertook the difficult or rather impossible task of retrieving the finances. The Swiss Necker persuaded the

*Chief of the *Encyclopædists* were Condillac, D'Alembert, Diderot, Helvetius, and Baron d'Holbach, whose house was considered as the head-quarters of the atheistical philosophy. Voltaire was a leading spirit, and may be regarded perhaps as the representative Frenchman of the eighteenth century, not only for his intellectual brilliancy but for his conceited antagonism to all authority, human and divine.

king to publish the treasury account. It was the first time that the nation at large had been intrusted with the balance-sheet of public revenue and expense; and an immense loan was negotiated during the excitement caused by the sudden revival of confidence. Necker was compelled, however, to resign in 1781, and after several changes the finances fell into the hands of Calonne, a plausible but reckless character, whose mismanagement soon compelled the king to choose between reform and bankruptcy. The former could only be accomplished by the States-General; but so unsteady were the foundations of government, that the court naturally feared this appeal to the people.

223. As a compromise, an Assembly of Notables—*i. e.*, nobles, clergy, and a few municipal magistrates—was convened, Jan., 1787, at Versailles. After long and stormy discussions, they refused to pass a proposed self-denying ordinance taxing all land in the kingdom, including the hitherto exempt estates of nobles and clergy and even the royal domains. At the end of four months' session, the assembly was dissolved, and the king was left as before, with only the parliaments and his own arbitrary edicts as means of raising money. The clergy, being convoked in the vain hope of extorting a loan from them, only joined the parliaments in demanding an early meeting of the States-General. Necker, again in charge of the finances, reässembled the Notables to deliberate concerning the manner in which the popular assembly should be composed.

224. It was decided, against great opposition, to summon more than a thousand persons, of whom at least half should be deputies of the Third Estate. A still more important question concerned the voting by orders or by individuals; if the latter method were chosen, the commons had the advantage, and the nobles and clergy naturally insisted on their ancient privileges. But the day had gone by when a noble could say, as did a member of the States-General of 1614: "The relation between ourselves and the Third Estate, is precisely that of master and valet." The great assembly was opened by the king at Versailles. The commons attempted to decide the still open question by inviting the nobles and clergy to join them in the hall allotted for their debates. The invitation being refused, they assumed the exclusive title of The National Assembly. Subsequently the great body of the clergy and forty-seven nobles acceded to the request. But the question of precedence was already settled, and the Revolution was begun.

May 5, 1789.

RECAPITULATION.

Expulsion of the Jesuits from Portugal under the ministry of Pombal. Similar policy of all the Catholic governments. Clement XIV. abolishes the Order. Liberal innovations of the emperor Joseph II.; he violates the charters of Hungary and the Netherlands, and his treaty with the Dutch. The Belgian United Provinces declare themselves independent. Accession of Leopold II. Causes of the Revolution: Growth of skeptical philosophy;

increased number and influence of clubs and newspapers; example of American independence; decline of most of the European governments; ruined finances of France. Convocation of the Notables, and of the States-General — the latter for the first time in 175 years.

QUESTIONS FOR REVIEW.

Book IV.

1. What causes led to the rise of the English Commonwealth? . . . . ¶¶ 1-7.
2.   To the Revolution of A. D. 1688? . . . . 67-74.
3. Name the Stuarts who reigned in England. . . . . . . 2, 18, 70, 73, 86.
4. What sovereigns of England were also electors of Hanover? . . 101, 153, 179.
5. Tell the story of the Fronde. . . . . 20-22.
6. Describe the causes and effects of the Treaty of the Pyrenees. . . . . 23-26.
7.   The character and policy of Louis XIV. . . . 27, 62, 64-66, 101-103.
8.   His wars. . . . . 30, 32-38, 63, 67, 75-79, 87-96.
9. Name the cardinal-ministers of France. . . Book III., 35; Book IV., 20, 25, 140.
10. What circumstances led to the War of the Spanish Succession? . . . 78-85.
11. Describe the Treaty of Utrecht and the circumstances which led to it. . . 97-100.
12. Sketch the character and career of Peter I. of Russia. . . 55, 59-61, 107, 109, 111, 113.
13.   Of Charles XII. of Sweden. . . . . . 104, 105, 108-110, 112.
14. Name other Swedish sovereigns of this period. . . . 39, 40, 42-47, 49, 113, 185.
15. What Turkish wars during the period? . . . . . . 50-53, 56-58, 190, 196.
16. Sketch the constitution and history of Poland. . . 40-44, 47, 52, 105, 107, 110, 111, 186-189, 191-193.
17. What can be told of Hungary? . . . . 51, 54.
18. Describe the Spanish colonial system and its results in America. . . 114-119.
19.   The Portuguese settlements. . . . . 120.
20.   The English in North America. . . . . . . 121-124.
21.   The Northern Indians. . . . . 125, 126.
22. Give some account of French explorations. . . . . . . 127-131, 137.
23.   Of the wars of the French and English colonies. . . 163, 164, 177.
24.   Of Dutch colonization. . . . . 9, 33, 124, 132.
25. Tell the history of the Dutch Republic during this period. 9, 10, 31-35, 37, 38, 63, 75, 140, 159, 160, 206, 216.
26. Describe the character and reign of Louis XV. . . . . 133, 151, 154, 161.
27.   Of Frederic the Great. . . . . 119, 155, 157, 166-175, 180-182.
28.   The War of the Austrian Succession. . . . . . 148-160.
29.   The Seven Years' War. . . . . . . 165-176, 178-183.
30.   The War of American Independence. . . . . . 198-207.
31.   The establishment of the Federal government. . . . . . 210.
32.   The character of Catherine II. of Russia. . . 181, 184, 188, 194, 195.
33.   Of the emperor Joseph II. . . . . . . 214-217.
34. Sketch the history of the Jesuits. . . Book III., 184-186; IV. 120, 128, 135, 212, 213.
35. Name some of the causes of the French Revolution. . . . . . 218-223.
36. How many kingdoms were ruled by Bourbons? . . . . . . 100, 143.
37. Name the kings of this family in France. . . Book III., 26; Book IV. 133, 220.
38.   The German emperors during this period. 25, 91, 97 (see 139, 148), 150, 156, 157, 214.

BOOK V.

THE AGE OF REVOLUTIONS.
A. D. 1789-1873.

THE FRENCH REVOLUTION.

1. The perilous crisis in France was aggravated at once by dissensions in the royal family, and by famine arising from the failure of a harvest as well as from the disordered and ruined finances. Thousands of half-starved wretches crowded in from the provinces and formed a camp on the heights of Montmartre, overlooking Paris. The Duke of Orleans was animated by a jealous spite against the king, and joined the rebellion, probably with some vague hope of raising himself to the throne. His residence, the Palais Royal, was a rallying point for sedition; here a proscription list was drawn up, in which the queen, the king's brother, and several others were condemned to death. The queen — Marie Antoinette, a sister of the emperors Joseph II. and Leopold II. — added to the imperious temper of the Hapsburgs a thoughtless frivolity, which led her too often to violate the customs and shock the prejudices of the court. In the present crisis she persuaded the king to dismiss Necker, and to concentrate near the capital an army of 40,000 men, partly German and Swiss mercenaries.

2. Upon the news of Necker's retirement the mob burst into open riot. They promenaded the streets with a bust of the favorite minister at their head, and being attacked by the royal cavalry, in the Place Louis XV. — soon afterward called *Place de la Revolution* — shed the first blood in the long and terrible conflict. A civic militia, now mustered, outnumbered the king's troops. Arming itself with muskets and cannon at the Hotel des Invalides, this National Guard proceeded to attack the Bastile. The fortress, though bravely defended, capitulated after five hours' cannonade. Contrary to the terms of surrender, its governor De Launay and his second in command were basely murdered, and their heads were borne upon pikes in triumphal procession through the city. The stronghold of centuries of despotism was leveled with the ground. The king weakly visited the city in token of his acceptance of a revolution which he had been unable to prevent. He was received by the astronomer Bailly, president of the National Assembly and now bearing the new title of Mayor of Paris. In presenting the keys, Bailly remarked with more sincerity than courtesy: "These, Sire, are the keys that were offered to Henry IV., the conqueror of his people; to-day it is the people who have reconquered their king." Necker was recalled and the Marquis de Lafayette received a royal commission as commandant of the National Guard.

3. Many nobles and princes of the blood, perceiving the strength of the popular movement and the weakness of the court, now emigrated, leaving the king to his fate. The national representatives, charging themselves with the preparation of a new constitution for France, assumed the name of *Constituent Assembly.* They numbered the best and ablest men in France, many of whom deplored and earnestly sought to alleviate the miseries of their countrymen. On the President's *right* sat the conservatives, who desired no changes in the form of government. In the *center* were moderate reformers, who preferred a constitutional monarchy like that of England. On the *left* were extreme liberals; but even of these no man yet pronounced the word *Republic.* Among the ablest and by far the most remarkable of the popular leaders at this time, was the Count de Mirabeau, a man of brilliant talents and irresistible eloquence, but of no moral principles — who had squandered fortune and credit in the wildest dissipation, and was ready to serve either despotism or democracy, if either would pay the price which his necessities demanded.

4. The disorders of Paris spread into the provinces, especially to those of the south-east of France, where the peasantry, rising against the proprietors of lands, plundered and even murdered those whom they regarded as hereditary foes. The National Assembly, moved by the proposition of a duke and a viscount, resolved upon a thorough remedy for these disorders, by abolishing those exclusive privileges which lay at the root of the popular discontent. The generous enthusiasm ran through the assembly, and all the privileged orders vied with each other in devising sacrifices for the public good. The ancient feudal constitution of France, so far, at least, as laws could repeal it, disappeared at a blow. Serfdom was abolished; all restrictions upon hunting and fishing were removed; civil and military appointments were thrown open to all ranks. Church rates were annulled — the clergy to be maintained by a general tax, thus relieving the rich at the expense of the poor. The Abbé Sieyès, who had in vain attempted to expose this

Aug. 4, 1789.

blunder, exclaimed, "Alas, my countrymen! they want to be free and know not how to be just!" To commemorate the death-blow of centuries of abuse, a medal was struck representing Louis XVI. as the restorer of French liberty, and the king himself presided at a Te Deum to celebrate the happy event.

5. The main principles of the new constitution were embodied in a Declaration of the Rights of Man, which, by the express motion of Lafayette, included the right to resist oppression. Those who hoped to see a fair fabric of constitutional freedom grow from the labors of the Assembly were, however, doomed to disappointment. A bread riot arose in Paris, conducted chiefly by women — who rousing each other to fury as their numbers increased, upon some unknown impulse took the road to Versailles. Lafayette followed with a division of the National Guard, and for some hours held them in check. They encamped for the night around huge fires which they kindled in the streets of the town. But next morning the tumult broke out afresh; the mob entered the palace, killed the guards at the doors of the queen's apartments, and would probably have massacred the royal family but for the firm and loyal conduct of Lafayette. He persuaded the king to remove with his family to Paris, and take up his abode at the palace of the Tuileries, which had been unoccupied for a century.

6. The Assembly also removed to Paris and now sat without distinction of rank — nobles, priests, and commons occupying the same benches. But its independence was gone, for power was usurped by the Jacobin Club, which superseded the late meetings in the Palais Royal, and assumed inquisitorial powers. At first this noted Club included many persons of character and distinction; but its violent proceedings soon repelled the more reasonable and moderate members. Its principles were diffused by its Journal and Almanacs; no fewer than 2,400 similar societies were planted throughout France and became the terror of Europe. For a year, however, the Assembly carried on its work of innovation with comparative order and tranquillity. All sects and creeds were declared equal before the law; every citizen was admitted to vote for his representative in the legislative assembly; inheritance by primogeniture and all titles of nobility were abolished. The old provincial boundaries were obliterated, and the country redivided into eighty-three departments. The parliaments were virtually abolished. Church lands and other property were confiscated, together with nearly all the royal domains. Monasteries were broken up, and monastic vows annulled. All ecclesiastical dignities were suppressed, except the offices of bishop and curé; and these were conferred by the people, no longer by the king or patron. The Pope refused his sanction to these innovations; but all the French clergy were required to take the oath of obedience on penalty of depri-

vation. Only four bishops consented to swear; the rest, with 50,000 curés and vicars were subjected to penalties as non-jurors.

7. The anniversary of the destruction of the Bastile was celebrated by a *fête* of several days, during which the king, in the presence of the assembly, the clergy, and the army, took an oath to support the new constitution. The queen raised her little son, the Dauphin, in her arms, in pledge of his fidelity. In that moment of enthusiasm all wrongs were forgotten; but unhappily the day of hope and confidence "had no morrow." Mirabeau became president of the National Assembly, and at the same time secretly pledged his immense influence to the support of the king. His death in April, 1791, was lamented by all who desired a settled order of government. The king, wearied of the constraint in which he was held, attempted an escape with his family to the army at Montmédy. They were apprehended at Varennes, and escorted with brutal insults back to Paris. Louis was suspended from his kingly functions, and a guard of citizen soldiery was stationed in the palace.

July, 1790.

8. By this time nearly all the European powers were preparing to interfere for the suppression of popular violence in France. The emperor and the Spanish and Italian Bourbons were moved by claims of kindred to protect the royal family. Catherine of Russia hastened to make peace with Turkey, hoping, indeed, to further her own designs upon Poland by engaging the forces of Austria and Prussia in the rescue of France. The divided jurisdiction of the border provinces between France and Germany called for immediate action on the part of the emperor and the Diet. By the famous Act of Aug. 4, 1789 (see § 4), several German princes were deprived of their feudal claims in Franche Comté, Alsace, and Lorraine, while the archbishop-electors of Trèves and Mentz, by the civil constitution imposed upon the clergy, lost their metropolitan rights over Spires, Strasbourg, Metz, Toul, and Verdun. At the conference held at Pilnitz in Saxony, the emperor and the king of Prussia united in an appeal to the other European powers for the reëstablishment of Louis XVI. in his former authority. Troops were consequently assembled by Austria, Prussia, Sardinia, and Spain. The Count of Provence, having fled from France, assumed command of the emigrant forces and established at Coblentz a little court which became the head-quarters of the refugees. The movements of the Coälition were delayed by the death of the emperor Leopold, and the assassination of the king of Sweden, who had been preparing to lead his own army in person. Both events occurred in March, 1792.

Aug., 1791.

9. Meanwhile the Constituent Assembly, having completed its labors, presented the new constitution to the king, who, now restored to his royal functions, confirmed it by an oath, Sept. 14, 1791. The best and

most permanent part of their work was the abolition of feudalism and the arbitrary features of the government; the removal of fetters upon industry and worship; the establishment of juries and the English mode of administering justice. But they had provided no checks upon the despotism of the mob, which was the most imminent peril of France. By a self-denying ordinance moved by Robespierre, the Constituent Assembly declared all its members ineligible to the legislative body which was to succeed it. But France had sent to the first assembly all her best men, who had moreover gained, by two years' experience, some skill in the difficult and dangerous navigation of the ship of state. The second assembly proved inferior in talents and authority. Its ablest men were comprised in the Girondist party, which gained ascendency upon the first actively hostile movement on the part of Austria. The king was then compelled to accept a ministry composed entirely of Girondists, and to declare war against his nephew, Francis II., who had succeeded his father, Leopold, as king of Hungary and Bohemia, though not yet elected to the imperial crown.

10. The confiscations of ecclesiastical and royal property had filled the treasury of the Convention, and three effective armies were promptly marched to the northern and eastern frontier. Their first operations were unsuccessful. Two strong detachments were routed by the Austrians near Lisle and Valenciennes. The Girondists were now forced to make further bids for the favor of the mob by decreeing the banishment of all non-juring priests, the dismissal of the king's guard, and the formation of a federal army to be encamped near Paris. Lafayette, disgusted and alarmed by these movements, wrote from his camp on the Belgian frontier to the Legislative Assembly, demanding the suppression of the Jacobin faction and the clubs which had sprung from it. But his efforts only hastened the tragedy which was to follow.

11. The king had dismissed his Girondist ministry on June 13, 1792. One week later 20,000 rioters, armed with scythes, clubs, axes, and pikes, marched through the hall of the Legislative Assembly, where their leader, a brewer named Santerre, addressed the members in a violent harangue. Thence they thronged into the Tuileries, menacing the royal family with insolent language, but departing, after some hours, without actual bloodshed. The "federal army" was now mustering throughout France under the orders of the Jacobins. Prisons were emptied, and the vilest wretches, assuming the national livery, marched toward Paris, singing the revolutionary song just written by Rouget de l'Isle and named from the place of its publication, the *Marseillaise.* The passions of the mob were still further inflamed by the massing of 80,000 foreign soldiers upon the northern frontier, and they burst into ungovernable fury when the Duke of Brunswick, commander-in-chief of the allied forces, published

a manifesto, requiring the French nation to submit at once to its lawful sovereign, and threatening to level Paris itself with the earth in case of the least violence to the royal family. Not less offensive was the duke's promise, in case of prompt obedience to these orders, to obtain from Louis XVI. a free pardon for the crimes of his rebellious subjects.

12. The guards of the Tuileries were now doubled in preparation for the hourly expected attack; but Mandat, their commandant, was summoned before the Commune, or Municipal Council, and summarily put to death. The cannon of the National Guard were turned upon the palace which they had been placed to defend. As the dense mass of insurgents rolled onward toward the gates, the king with his family took refuge with the Legislative Assembly. They never returned to the Tuileries. The Swiss Guards fought bravely, even when deserted by the sovereign whom they served, but the greater number were slain. The royal family were imprisoned in the Temple, a gloomy building which had once belonged to the Knights of the Order of that name. The *guillotine* * was set up beneath the windows of the palace, and among its first victims was a member of the queen's household.

Aug. 10, 1792.

13. The Reign of Terror had begun. Three thousand persons were seized by night in their own houses and hurried away to prison. Twenty-four priests, who had refused the civic oath, were the first victims of the September massacres. Two hundred more were slaughtered in the Church of the Carmelites. The same terrible scenes went on five days in the prisons of Paris—women, children, paupers, and lunatics were put to death for no cause, except a blind rage for blood on the part of the mob. The frenzy spread to Meaux, Rheims, Lyons, and Orleans, until all the prisons and asylums were emptied of their wretched inmates.

14. The chief directors of the massacres at Paris were Danton, Robespierre, and Marat, the latter a bloodthirsty wretch whose malignity amounted to madness. Danton was well fitted by his enormous stature and the deafening loudness of his voice to be the leader of a mob; by the singular inconsistency of the times he bore the title, Minister of *Justice*. Robespierre was small and of insignificant appearance, nor did the qualities of his mind compensate his personal defects. His intense and unscrupulous ambition made him, however, for two years the tyrant and leader of the Revolution. In the September massacres, he had the art, by working through others, to avoid all apparent participation.

15. In the meantime, the grand army of the Coälition now numbering

*This famous instrument of public execution derived its name from Dr. Guillotin, a member of the Legislative Assembly, who invented it from motives of humanity. Its constant and murderous employment during the Revolution dragged the name of the merciful physician into unenviable fame.

110,000 men, had crossed the borders, captured Longwy and Verdun by short sieges, and threatened Paris. They were opposed by Dumouriez in the defiles of the Forest of Argonne. Though no great battles were fought, the Duke of Brunswick, disappointed of the supplies of provisions which he had hoped to draw from a friendly peasantry, was compelled to recross the Rhine with a loss of 30,000 men. Elsewhere the republican armies were victorious; and Dumouriez, after a hard-fought battle at Jemappes received the submission of the entire Austrian Netherlands. This result was largely due, however, to the revolutionary spirit of the people, who under French influence, immediately abjured their allegiance to the Hapsburgs, and again proclaimed the Belgian Republic. (See Book IV., §§ 217, 218.)

Nov., 1792.

16. The Legislative Assembly at Paris, after sitting less than a year, merged into the National Convention, which began its sessions, Sept. 22. At its first meeting, royalty was abolished and a Republic proclaimed. The Girondists, now the more moderate or conservative party, had the advantage both in numbers and intelligence; but the "Mountain," as the Jacobin delegates began to be called, exerted greater force through the audacity of its members and the support of the mob. Amid the excitement consequent upon the victories of Dumouriez, it was resolved that every French general should proclaim the sovereignty of the people and the overthrow of monarchy in whatever country he should invade, and should treat as enemies any people which should refuse "liberty, fraternity, and equality." In defiance of the treaties of Münster and Fontainebleau, the Scheldt was declared open, and war-ships of the Republic forced a passage up that river to bombard Antwerp. The Convention thus asserted itself the arbiter of international law, even setting aside treaties which former French governments had confirmed.

17. After long and fierce discussion between the Mountain and the Gironde, it was decreed that "Louis Capet" should be brought to trial before the Convention, and on the 10th of December his accusation was read. The main articles charged him with having invited foreign powers to invade France, with having occasioned the loss of Longwy and Verdun by neglect of the army, and with having provoked the insurrection of the 10th of August in order to sacrifice the lives of his people. The innocence of the king was ably set forth by three lawyers, who risked their lives in his defense; but neither reason nor eloquence could be heard in the whirlwind of passion. Louis was almost unanimously declared guilty; the mode of punishment was yet to be determined. Each deputy rose as his name was called, and gave his vote for death, exile, or imprisonment. The Duke of Orleans, who, under the name of Philip Égalité, sat as a member of the Convention, covered himself with infamy by voting immediate death. A bare majority agreed in the same verdict; the Giron-

dists, who desired to save the life of the king, were equally lacking in courage and effective organization.

On the morning of Jan. 21, Louis, accompanied by his faithful friend and confessor, the Abbé Edgeworth, was escorted to the guillotine in the Place de la Revolution. The crowd received the melancholy procession in unbroken silence, save when a few women cried for "mercy." Upon the scaffold the king attempted to address the people, but his voice was drowned by the beating of drums. When the fatal knife had fallen, the executioner held up the dissevered head, crying, "Long live the Republic!" Louis XVI. had reigned nearly nineteen years. His brother, the Count of Provence, assumed the title of Regent for his nephew, Louis XVII., who was still imprisoned in the Temple.

18. The horror and resentment of the European courts led to the dismissal of French embassadors and vigorous preparations for war. Great Britain made alliances with Russia, Prussia, the Empire, Sardinia, the Two Sicilies, and Portugal; no states remained friendly to France except Sweden, Denmark, and Switzerland. On the other hand, the Convention ordered a levy of 500,000 men, and declared war against the *rulers* of England, Holland, and Spain, carefully distinguishing between governments and peoples. The confiscated treasures of Church and State, which had been accumulating for centuries, poured into the coffers of the Republic greater wealth than even Louis XIV. had been able to command. The war thus begun was to continue, almost without respite, for more than twenty years, and to tax the physical and mental energies of Europe more severely than any other conflict known to history. Yet so completely did each party underrate the resources of the other, that William Pitt, then the ruling spirit in England, expected to see the war ended in one or two campaigns.

19. After his conquest of the Austrian Netherlands, Dumouriez had returned to Paris, hoping to save the life of the king, defeat the Jacobins, and establish a constitutional monarchy. These hopes failing, he resumed his command, and invading Holland seized Breda, Klundert, and Gertruydenberg. He was followed, however, by spies of the Jacobins, who knew his enmity to their proceedings, and upon whose report the Convention sent orders for his arrest. Dumouriez, on the contrary, arrested the commissioners and handed them over to the Austrians. His army refused to march with him to Paris, and the disappointed general took refuge in the Austrian camp. He never again appeared in the civil or military service of France.

20. Meanwhile the deadly strife between the Gironde and the Mountain led to the establishment of a Revolutionary Tribunal

A. D. 1793.

to decide without appeal upon all crimes against "liberty, equality, and the indivisibility of the Republic." A Committee of

Public Safety was invested with dictatorial powers. The Gironde was doomed to fall by the same mob violence which it had itself conjured up against the priests, the nobles, and the throne. In the country at large, a vast majority desired the return of order and justice. If the "French people," so often apostrophized and so seldom consulted, had been really predominant, a rational and beneficent government might have arisen upon the ruins of old despotism. The supremacy of the Parisian rabble was the downfall of all reasonable hope from the revolution. On June 2, eighty thousand armed men surrounded and overawed the Convention, demanding the arrest of the Girondist members. Thirty-two were imprisoned, and seventy-three more who protested against this violence, were expelled. Many of these escaped to the provinces and took part in a counter-revolution which had already begun.

21. About this time, Charlotte Corday, a young woman of genius and exalted character, a warm partisan of the Gironde, hastened from Caen to Paris, obtained admission to the house of Marat, and stabbed him to the heart. Making no attempt to escape, she bravely met her death by the sentence of the Revolutionary Tribunal. Blasphemous honors were paid to the memory of Marat. His heart, deposited in an agate vase, was placed upon an altar, and surrounded with flowers and the smoke of incense. Maddened by the increase of the forces of the Coälition, both upon the northern and southern frontiers, and strengthened by the accession of Robespierre to the Committee of Safety, the Parisian government proceeded to still more ferocious violence. A levy *en masse* of all the citizens was ordered. A "Law of the Suspected" destroyed the last vestige of personal security, and crowded the prisons throughout France with more than 200,000 victims. General Custine was guillotined for the loss of a battle and of the town of Valenciennes.

22. The captive queen, Marie Antoinette, was tried, condemned, and beheaded upon charges which, so far as they concerned her character, were not less false than vile and malignant. The Girondists were the next victims. Madame Roland exclaimed upon the scaffold, "O, Liberty! what crimes are committed in thy name!" Those who had escaped into the provinces were hunted to death like wild beasts. The Duke of Orleans was guillotined amid the curses of the mob. In its zeal for innovation, the Convention abolished the names of months and days of the week, and decreed that every tenth day only should be a period of rest. The French era was dated from Sept. 22, 1792. Little remained of the ancient order except the rites of Christian worship, and these were abolished with insolent and brutal profanity. A woman personating Reason was enthroned at Notre Dame, and worshiped by the members of the Convention and the Commune.

23. A counter-revolution had meanwhile broken out in La Vendée, a country noted for the simple and loyal character of its people. The republican generals were several times defeated; but in the autumn of 1793 the tide turned against the insurgents, who thenceforth confined their enterprises to a sort of brigandage among the marshes of the lower Loire. A wretch named Carrier was intrusted by the Convention with the work of vengeance, and so constant were his "drownings" at Nantes that the waters of the river were poisoned, and the fishes became unfit for food. No fewer than 15,000 persons were destroyed by his orders during the last three months of 1793. At Lyons the Girondists joined the royalists and defeated the army of the Convention. The city was reduced by famine; and it was then ordered that its name should be blotted out and that the poorer dwellings, which alone were permitted to stand, should be known henceforth as the "Free Commune."

24. Toulon, having revolted against the Republic, received an English fleet into its harbor and an allied garrison of 16,000 men into its forts. It was besieged by a republican army, and the Convention decreed that the city should be taken or the general guillotined. It was captured, through the alertness and skill of Napoleon Bonaparte; then an obscure young captain of artillery; and the garrison in its departure carried several thousands of royalist refugees.

RECAPITULATION.

Famine in France, plots of the Duke of Orleans, and indiscretions of the queen hasten the Revolution. Necker dismissed, and the first blood shed in a riot. The Bastile destroyed; the king accepts the revolution, and recalls Necker. Emigration of the nobles. Constituent Assembly abolishes all feudal customs and makes Declaration of Rights. Rioters storm Versailles. The king and Assembly remove to Paris. Supremacy of the Jacobins. Great numbers of the clergy refuse the civic oath. Fête of the Federation; flight of the royal family, their return. Conference at Pilnitz; Europe arms in defense of monarchy. New Constitution accepted by the king. Close of Constituent and opening of Legislative Assembly; Girondists in ascendency. War declared against Austria. Defeat of the French. Muster of federals under Jacobin control. Irritating manifesto of the Duke of Brunswick. Attack upon the Tuileries, murder of the Swiss guards. Imprisonment of the king and his family in the Temple. Reign of Terror begun by September Massacres. Invasion of France by the allies. Victories of Dumouriez. Proclamation of French and Belgian Republics. National Convention declares itself the liberator of all nations. Trial and execution of Louis XVI. Coalition of all Europe against France. Defection of Dumouriez. Revolutionary Tribunal and Committee of Public Safety at Paris. Overthrow of the Gironde. Assassination of Marat. Levy in mass, and law of the suspected. Execution of the queen. Christianity abjured and Worship of Reason proclaimed. Royalist insurrections in La Vendée, Lyons, and Toulon. Rise of Napoleon Bonaparte.

THE FRENCH REVOLUTION.—*Continued.*

25. In Paris the Terrorists soon became divided among themselves. The ultra-democrats — called Hébertists from their leader — desired still wilder excesses of profanation and havoc. By reaction a "party of Clemency" had sprung up, to which even Danton belonged. Between the two stood Robespierre and others who called themselves the "party of Justice," desiring terror still, but under regular forms. Robespierre allied himself for a time with the party of Clemency, that he might crush the Hébertists, who were in fact guillotined in March, 1794, to the number of nineteen—their leader, after all his insolent bravado, meeting death like a coward. Danton and fourteen of his party were next arrested and guillotined after a show of trial. Robespierre for three months reigned supreme; and to prove that he was not to be accused of mercy or moderation, the butchery of the guillotine went on more constantly and atrociously than ever. But he had never been an atheist, and among his first acts was the obtaining of a decree from the Convention affirming the existence of God and the immortality of the soul.

26. At the height of his power Robespierre received intimations which alarmed him. He succeeded, nevertheless, in gaining absolute control of the Revolutionary Tribunal, whose powers were enormously increased, so that the lives of the whole French nation were at his disposal. Fourteen hundred heads fell beneath the guillotine in less than seven weeks. A secret proscription-list was discovered, containing the most illustrious names in the Convention. But the confederacy against Robespierre gathered strength, and on the 27th of July, suddenly declared itself. Vainly striving to obtain a hearing, he was carried out together with four of his associates amid tumultuous cries of "Down with the tyrant!" The Commune armed in his defense, broke open his prison and carried him in triumph to the Hotel de Ville. The troops of the Convention surrounded the building; the prisoners surrendered, and at sunrise the next morning were led out to execution. As the head of Robespierre fell, the shouts of the multitude proclaimed that the Reign of Terror was ended. Eighty of his accomplices, including the infamous Carrier, followed him to the guillotine.

27. A counter-movement thus began, which destroyed the Jacobin Club and the influence of the Commune. The seventy-three deputies who had protested against the imprisonment of the Girondists were readmitted to the Convention; 10,000 of the "suspected" were released from the dungeons of Paris alone; decrees for the banishment of priests and nobles, and for the death of English and Hanoverian prisoners, were repealed; divine worship was restored. The reckless conduct of the revolutionary government, followed by the hardships of a severe winter, had produced so frightful a scarcity, that each inhabitant of Paris had to be put upon a fixed allowance of bread. The rich being proscribed, the poor were without employment. Assignats—the paper money of the time—had fallen so low, that 24,000 francs were paid for a load of fire-wood, and 6,000 for a single fare in a hackney coach. In the provinces, especially in the south, the counter-revolution was even more violent, and the

Jacobins became in turn the victims of the " White Terror "—a system
of wholesale massacres — so called to distinguish it from the "Red Terror" of which they had been authors. Scarcely a town of southern
France was without its band of assassins, led, in most cases, by an exiled
royalist or Girondist, who avenged his own wrongs by fresh barbarities.

28. During the year 1794, France had thirteen armies in the field,
numbering between 600,000 and 700,000 men. On the side of the Netherlands and Germany, the allies were posted in lines extending with little
interruption from Ypres through Trèves, Mentz, and Heidelberg, to Basle.
Most of them were subsidized by England, whose commercial interest
affected by the war was greater, though her political concern was less
than that of any other power. The king of Prussia was absorbed in his
designs upon Poland, and a strong party in Austria, including the chief
minister, preferred a share of Polish spoils or the prosecution of the
emperor's claims upon Bavaria, to war with France. Francis II. accordingly withdrew to Vienna and abandoned the Austrian Netherlands. To
keep up appearances with the allies, the imperial armies were left in the
field, with orders to dissemble and even suffer themselves to be defeated,
rather than waste their forces. They were in fact beaten by inferior
numbers at Fleurus, and the Belgian towns without delay opened their
gates to the French.

29. The republican party in Holland welcomed the French, who by
a series of easy victories obtained possession of the whole country. The
Prince of Orange took refuge in England, and the States-General, abolishing the stadtholderate, proclaimed the Batavian Republic in close alliance
with that of France. The following April peace was signed
A. D. 1795.   at Basle between Prussia and the French, the latter retaining the provinces on the left bank of the Rhine. The fickle, selfish, and
short-sighted policy of Frederic William II. was a chief cause of his
subsequent calamities. Most ardent in promoting the Coälition, he was
now the first to desert it. Instead of performing his allotted part in the
military service, he had spent the English subsidies in obtaining larger
shares of Poland; while by opening a way for the French into the heart
of the Empire he was preparing for the despoiling of his own kingdom
ten or twelve years later.

30. By their operations in the south-east, the French had grasped
the keys of Italy, in capturing Mont Cenis and the passes of the Maritime Alps. Alarmed by their advance, the Grand-duke of Tuscany abandoned his brother the emperor, revoked his adherence to the Coälition,
and signed a treaty of neutrality with the French. The latter had been
less successful on the sea. Corsica had revolted and placed itself under
the government of Great Britain. Lord Howe had gained a great victory
off Ushant over a French fleet of superior force to his own; and in the

West Indies, Martinique, St. Lucie, Guadaloupe, and St. Domingo were successively captured by the English.

31. The year 1795 was mainly spent in negotiations. The Diet at Ratisbon expressed a desire for peace, and when this failed to be negotiated several princes of the Empire made separate treaties with France by the mediation of Prussia. The death, in his loathsome dungeon, of the young king Louis XVII. opened the way June, 1795. for peace between the king of Spain and the French Republic, for so long as the young prince lived, the honor of his kinsman demanded his liberation as the first condition of any treaty. By a peace signed in July, Spain recognized both the French and the Batavian Republic. The worthless favorite, Godoy, who ruled the court of Madrid, received the title Prince of the Peace, for his share in the treaty which diffused unbounded joy throughout the country.

32. A fresh insurrection in La Vendée, led by generals Stofflet and Charette, was aided by the descent of an English squadron bearing 3,000 French emigrants. The latter proclaimed Louis XVIII. and established themselves on the island or peninsula of Quiberon; but they were reduced by General Hoche, who ordered all the survivors to be shot. Charette retaliated by the massacre of more than a thousand republicans who were in his power. The insurgents on the mainland were not more fortunate. In February and March, 1796, their two generals were captured, and their execution ended the Vendean war which had cost the lives of 100,000 Frenchmen.

33. A new revolution at Paris had now overthrown the Constitution of 1793, and restored to the middle class its natural importance in the government. The legislative power was vested in two Councils, the one consisting of five hundred members, the other of 250. The latter, composed of men over forty years of age, was called the Council of the Ancients. The former alone could propose laws, but the consent of the latter was essential to their enactment. The executive power was intrusted to a Directory of five persons who were chosen by the Ancients from a list of ten presented by the Five Hundred. The new constitution was not established without armed resistance, led by the royalists and persons formerly of rank, who, after the fall of Robespierre, had returned in great numbers to Paris. Between 25,000 and 30,000 persons attacked the Tuileries where the Convention was sitting, but the prompt and decisive measures of General Bonaparte, who had posted his cannon around the palace, gained a victory for the government. General amnesty, except to emigrants and their families, was now proclaimed; Belgium was annexed to France; and the Convention closed its tragical history of three years and two months by declaring itself dissolved.

34. The Directory began its administration with a treasury absolutely empty, a paper currency so reduced that it was not worth the expense of printing it, and a starving mob to be maintained at the charge of the government. Each poor inhabitant of Paris had to subsist upon two ounces of bread and a handful of rice each day, and even this wretched pittance often failed. The army was without clothes or rations; roads, bridges, and canals had fallen into ruin during the reign of assassination which called itself a government, while bands of robbers scoured the country in every direction, plundering and murdering without check. Under the more just and orderly management of the Directory, civilization revived, public confidence was restored, commerce began to flourish, and abundance took the place of scarcity. The advantages arising from the abolition of the old restraints upon industry were now first perceived.

Oct., 1795.

35. But, not contented with prosperity at home, the Republic began with energy to direct its movements abroad, and the Revolution became aggressive, aiming to overthrow or radically reform all existing governments. Thus the war became universal. Holland, by her subserviency to France, was already involved in a war with Great Britain, by which she had lost colonies on both sides of the world. Demerara, Berbice, and Essequibo in the West, Ceylon, Malacca, the Spice Islands, Cochin, and other settlements in the East Indies, as well as the Cape of Good Hope in Africa, were the prizes of the English. The French operations on the Rhine during 1795 resulted mainly in disaster. In their lines around Mentz they were attacked by the Austrian general Clairfait, and ruinously defeated, with the loss of all their artillery, ammunition, and baggage. This was partly owing to the treachery of Pichegru, the French general, who, like Dumouriez, had dreamed of playing the part of Monk in England, and restoring the Bourbons to their throne. His indecisive movements, however, only lost him the confidence of the Directory, and he retired from the army. In 1797 he was imprisoned in the Temple, and, a few months later, was transported in an iron cage to Cayenne.

36. For the campaign of 1796, three French armies were voted by the Directory; two in Germany under generals Moreau and Jourdan, and one in Italy under Bonaparte. The Italian campaign, conducted in his twenty-seventh year, was the opening act in the surprising military career of Bonaparte. He found his army of 35,000 men at Nice, in a wretched state of disorder and inefficiency through the neglect of the government. But he soon infused into them his own energetic spirit, firing their imaginations with promises of wealth in Italy and applause in France, and without delay marched toward Genoa. The Austrian army was at Tortona and Alessandria, the Sardinian at Ceva. A strong detachment of the former was defeated at Montenotte, and by capturing the fortress of Cherasco, Bonaparte separated the Sardinians from their allies. The old and feeble king, Victor Amadeus, renounced the Coälition and made peace with France, ceding to the Republic the duchy of Savoy and the county of Nice, and expelling all French emigrants from his dominions, including even his own daughters, who were married to the two brothers of Louis XVI. The strongest fortresses of his kingdom were placed as securities in the hands of the French, until the conclusion of a general peace.

37. Bonaparte next defeated the Austrians by a furious battle at Lodi which gained him all Lombardy except the city and fortress of Mantua. Fixing his head-quarters at Milan he proceeded May, 1796. to sell peace to the minor princes of Italy at the price of heavy contributions. Not only money and war-materials were exacted, but inestimable works of art, with which Paris was afterward adorned. The great object with the French was now the reduction of Mantua, the strongest place in Italy, and the key to all further operations against Austria. It was besieged seven months, and the strenuous efforts of the imperial generals to relieve it showed their sense of its importance. Marshal Wurmser with 70,000 men, twice advanced from the Tyrol for that purpose; but he was defeated at Brescia and Castiglione, at Roveredo, and Bassano. Alvinzi, with almost equal numbers, was not more successful; he was routed by a three days' battle at Arcole, and still more signally at Rivoli, where the triumph of the French was won against tremendous odds by the perfection of military science. Mantua surrendered, and the way was open into Austria.

38. But first, by a sudden and rapid movement, Bonaparte overran the States of the Church. He had received orders from the Directory to overthrow the papal government; but either feeling or policy led him to disregard his instructions, and sign the Peace of Tolentino, by which a third part of the dominions of the Pope were ceded to France, beside a contribution of 15,000,000 francs. During less than a year in Italy, Bonaparte had conquered Piedmont and Lombardy, destroyed or captured four Austrian armies, detached the kings of Sardinia and Naples, the dukes of Parma, Modena, and Tuscany from the Coälition, laid Venice and Genoa under heavy contribution, and added to the French dominion Avignon and the Venaissin, Nice and Savoy, and the territories of Bologna, Ferrara, and the Romagna. The spoils of war had not only supported its expense, but had enriched both officers and soldiers, and enabled their general to remit six millions of dollars to France.

39. Leaving Italy, he now led his army through the narrow defiles of the Tyrolese Alps into the Austrian territories. The archduke Charles, one of the greatest generals of the time, awaited him in Friuli, but was defeated in a series of sharp engagements and driven beyond the Save. Bonaparte advanced within a few days' march of Vienna, when he con-

M. H.—24.

sented to the proposal of the court for a suspension of hostilities. Meanwhile the Venetians had risen against the French, upon a false report of the defeat of Bonaparte in the Tyrol. Four hundred sick soldiers in hospital at Verona, as well as many others, were massacred. Bonaparte instantly declared war against the Venetian Republic, and sent a force to occupy its arsenal and forts. He then demanded the overthrow of the aristocratic government, the arrest and trial of the principal magistrates, the release of all political prisoners, and a total suppression of the fleet and army. The French party prevailed. The Council of Ten abdicated its sovereignty and acknowledged that of the people. A riot which broke out in the city served as a pretext for the introduction of French troops, which seized the fleet and with its aid conquered the Ionian Isles for France.

40. A strong party in the French Directory desired a continuance of the war. Bonaparte, on the contrary, was strenuous in favor of peace. He was intrusted with the whole conduct of the negotiations with Austria, and, Oct. 17, 1797, signed the peace of Campo Formio, so called from the ruined castle near Udine where it was concluded. In this treaty, Francis II. deserted the interests of the Empire, and acted only as sovereign of Hungary, Bohemia, and Austria. He promised to withdraw the imperial troops from the fortresses on the Rhine, and in case the Diet refused peace on these terms, to contribute only his contingent as archduke of Austria. The Austrian Netherlands were ceded to France, and their former sovereign received in exchange the whole Venetian territory, ceding a tract on its western border to the Cisalpine Republic, which had lately been formed of Milan, Modena, Ferrara, Bologna, and Romagna, with all their dependencies, and which the emperor by this treaty formally acknowledged. The republic of Venice, which thus disappeared from the family of states, was the oldest government in Europe, having lasted, from its foundation to its fall, 1345 years. On the other side of the peninsula, Genoa and some surrounding territories were formed into a Ligurian Republic.

41. Although Bonaparte had spared the Pope, the Directory had not abandoned its views, and the less, because the States of the Church were known to be swarming with malcontents who would readily join in a revolution. General Berthier, who had succeeded to the command of the army in Italy, marched to Rome, was welcomed by the people as a deliverer and proclaimed the restoration of the Roman Republic. Pius VI. made no resistance, though his personal property was inventoried and publicly sold, even to the rings upon his hands. He refused a pension from his captors, and was conveyed like a prisoner to a convent at Siena. A year later he was carried away to the fortress of Briançon in the high Alps, a region of almost perpetual frost, to which French soldiers were

sent for punishment. With a change in the Parisian government, this unprovoked severity was discontinued, and the aged pontiff was permitted to die in the milder climate of Valence. Rome Aug., 1799. was delivered over to a pillage unsurpassed in former days by Goths, Vandals, or Normans. Priestly robes were burned for the gold in their embroidery, palaces and churches were ransacked, and their treasures of art carried away or destroyed. The people, disappointed in the friends who had won them by the pleasant-sounding names of liberty and brotherhood, rose against the usurpers, but their efforts were put down with slaughter. Berthier, disgusted by the violation of his own engagements to respect private property, demanded to be recalled, and Masséna, who was sent to relieve him, was so notorious a freebooter, that the army itself mutinied and refused to receive him.

42. Switzerland, hitherto neutral, now drew the covetous eyes of the Directory, especially as occupying some military roads from France into northern Italy. In the Pays de Vaud, where the French language and ideas were most prevalent, revolutionary doctrines had made great progress, and several fruitless insurrections against the assumed sovereignty of Berne, had already occurred. Talleyrand, Minister of Foreign Affairs to the Directory, discovered a pretext for interference in some old treaties of Charles IX. and his brother, by which France guaranteed the independence of the Vaudois. A French force from Italy advanced without serious resistance into Switzerland, and proclaimed at Lausanne the freedom of the Pays de Vaud. The Forest Cantons made brave and obstinate resistance, and in several battles inflicted heavy loss upon the invaders; but at length they were overpowered by superior numbers, and a terrible massacre was the punishment of their efforts. The ancient confederation gave way to the "Helvetic Republic, one and indivisible," which by a treaty of peace and alliance, became the humble vassal of the French, and secured to them two military roads—one into southern Germany, and one over the Simplon into Italy.

43. Thus ended, so far as the European continent was concerned, the first war of the French Revolution. France had begun to surround herself with a cluster of republics constituted after her own model, and had renewed with Spain and Austria—the nations most firmly devoted to ancient principles of government—the cordial alliances formed by those powers with a sovereign whom the revolution had destroyed. The Treaty of San Ildefonso (Aug., 1796) was based upon the Family Compact of 1761. It placed the resources of Spain at the disposal of France, and especially engaged the former power in the war against England. Godoy became a pensioner of the Directory, and through the ascendency of this insolent and rapacious courtier, France acquired a sovereign control of Spanish affairs. Portugal was withdrawn by Spanish influence from the Coalition.

England alone remained at war, and an invasion of the British Isles was planned by the Directory, to be commanded by Bonaparte. It was resolved, however, to substitute the conquest of Egypt for that of England, thus securing a base of operations either against the British Empire in India or for intervention in the affairs of Turkey. A French conquest of Egypt had indeed been proposed as early as the reign of Louis XIV., and again in 1781, when Turkey seemed likely to fall under the attacks of Catherine II., and France desired to share in the spoils.

44. In May, 1798, the forces of the Egyptian Expedition — an army of nearly 40,000 men, convoyed by a fleet, and accompanied by a scientific commission of artists and *savants* — was gathered in the harbor of Toulon. Beside Bonaparte, who was in chief command, many other generals yet to attain high distinction — Berthier, Kleber, Murat, Junot, Desaix, Davoust, Lannes, and others — were included in the corps. A first object was the capture of Malta, still, after nearly 300 years, held by the Knights of St. John of Jerusalem. Last of the military orders which had sprung from the Crusades, the Knights had long outlived the valiant spirit of their predecessors; their Grand Master, unworthy heir of La Valette (Book III., § 212), was in secret correspondence with the French. The defense was merely nominal, and upon the surrender, ships, cannon, and stores, with the treasures of the churches, fell into the hands of the victors.

45. Leaving a strong garrison in Malta, Bonaparte sailed for Egypt, where finding the Mamelukes unprepared, he easily took possession of Alexandria and pursued his march toward Cairo. In the great plain of the Pyramids opposite that city, an army of 30,000 Mamelukes and Arabs was drawn up to receive him; and the furious combat which followed, was among the most remarkable of his battles. The desperate valor of the soldiers of fate gave way at last before the resolute spirit of Bonaparte which animated all his men. The next day the French took possession of Cairo. The English admiral Nelson, who had vainly sought to encounter the French fleet on its way to Egypt, now came up with it at its moorings in the Bay of Aboukir. The battle of the Nile, Aug. 1 and 2, resulted in a decisive victory of the English, and an almost total destruction or capture of the French vessels. The consequences of this disaster were far more important than the cutting off of Bonaparte's retreat. In Europe it awakened fresh hopes among the enemies and unwilling subjects of the Directory. The Sultan, who was not deceived by the assurances of friendly intentions, and was naturally incensed that France, the earliest ally of his dynasty, should be watching to partake his spoils, sent magnificent gifts to Nelson and hastened to make a treaty with Russia, hitherto his bitterest enemy.

46. A second coalition was formed, consisting of Russia, Turkey, Great

July, 1798.

Britain, Austria, and the Two Sicilies. Ferdinand IV. of the latter kingdom, without awaiting the signing of the treaties, marched 40,000 men into the States of the Church, in three columns, of which the central one, led by General Mack, moved directly upon Rome. The French evacuated the city, leaving a garrison in the Castle of St. Angelo; and the Neapolitan king was welcomed with acclamations. Mack was defeated, however, with great loss in several battles, the French reöccupied Rome, and King Ferdinand was not only pursued into his own territories, but compelled to embark upon the English fleet for Palermo. The French advanced upon Naples, which for several days was defended only by *lazzaroni* and peasants. This irregular force was won over to the French cause by a miracle. The blood of St. Januarius, which is still preserved in a vial as the most precious possession of the Neapolitans, had refused to liquefy at the departure of the king; but a prince who favored the French having threatened to kill the archbishop in case of further delay, the miracle was duly performed in favor of the General Championnet. The people were satisfied; monarchy was abolished, and the Parthenopean Republic was proclaimed.

Nov., 1798.

47. In March, 1799, the Directory declared war against Austria and Tuscany. Masséna was first in the field and gained several advantages, but the archduke Charles defeated Jourdan — who had assumed for his command the name of "Army of the Danube" — and by the two battles of Ostrach and Stockach, drove him even to the French side of the Rhine. The armies in Italy had been ordered to coöperate by advancing through the Engadine, but their dearly bought captures of Martinsbrück and Münsterthal were rendered useless by Jourdan's retreat. A congress of diplomats at Rastadt was abruptly terminated by the recall of the imperial minister and the announcement that the emperor annulled all previous proceedings. The French ministers were assassinated as they were quitting the town — an outrage upon the laws of civilized nations, which was only too clearly chargeable upon the imperial court.

April, 1799.

48. In Italy, meanwhile, Gauthier had overrun Tuscany, and the grand-duke had retired to Venice. The main French army under Schérer was repulsed after several days' obstinate and continuous fighting at Verona, and still more severely defeated at Magnano. In less than a fortnight Schérer lost half his army and was succeeded by Moreau. The Russian general Suwarof now assumed command of the allied forces, defeated Moreau at Cassano and entered Milan. Moreau would doubtless have been crushed by overwhelming numbers had not the Aulic Council at Vienna, with its usual dignified dullness, interfered for his relief. Suwarof was ordered to besiege Mantua, Peschiera, and other places which were deemed essential to the preservation of what he had already

gained; and Moreau, with consummate skill, effected his retreat to Coni, where he strongly posted himself in communication with Genoa and with France. Macdonald now marched from Naples with his victorious army, which was joined at Florence by that of Gauthier, and might have placed the French in northern Italy upon an equal footing with the allies, had he united at once with Moreau. Desiring, however, to make an independent display of his ability, he marched to meet Suwarof near the Trebia, and suffered in a three days' battle one of the most disastrous overthrows ever experienced by an officer of the Republic. All the conquests of Bonaparte were lost. The allies entered Turin, and occupied Pignerol, Susa, and other strong points, while the Cossacks even penetrated through the mountains into Dauphiny. Joubert, arriving to supersede Moreau, was defeated and slain at Novi; by another disaster Tortona was lost to the French, and the Cisalpine Republic submitted to Francis II.

A. D. 1799.

49. About the same time a fresh Russian army under Korsakoff arrived in Switzerland, whither Suwarof proceeded in order to coöperate with it. But before his arrival Korsakoff had been attacked and routed by Masséna, while another French army, led by Soult, defeated the Austrians under Hotze. The defeated Russians took refuge in Zürich, where, on the 26th of September, a terrible massacre was perpetrated by the French. Among the victims was the philosopher Lavater, shot and dangerously, if not mortally wounded, by a French officer who had lately been his guest. Suwarof, meanwhile, was advancing from Italy by the St. Gothard, when he found himself surrounded by the French, and for the first time learned the disaster which had befallen Korsakoff. He was defeated in the attempt to cut his way through Masséna's lines, and was compelled to retreat into the Grison territory, whence with the remnants of the two armies he returned to Russia.

50. A formidable demonstration of the allies in southern Italy meanwhile effected a counter-revolution, and Ferdinand IV. returned to his throne. A combined force of Russians, Turks, and Neapolitans, then marched upon Rome, and that city capitulated, Sept. 27. A descent of the allies upon the Batavian Republic was less successful; and the Czar, disgusted by a series of failures, abandoned the Coälition.

Meanwhile, Bonaparte, cut off from France by the destruction of his fleet, had fixed himself the more firmly in Egypt, conciliating the people by professing a belief in their prophet, and contenting his army by introducing into Cairo all the luxuries and amusements of Paris. The learned men pursued their researches among the palaces and tombs of the Pharaohs, while the soldiers found their diversion in French newspapers printed in the camp, as well as in cafés, lyceums, and gaming-tables. The active mind of the general struck out a new and extraordinary plan — to conquer Syria and Asia Minor, capture Constantinople, attack Austria in the rear, and thus march to Paris. With 12,000 men and his best generals he left Egypt in February, 1799. Gaza was taken at the first assault; Jaffa resisted and was punished by a general massacre. At Acre his progress was staid by 1,000 Turks and fewer than 300 English marines under Sir Sidney Smith. They withstood a siege of sixty days, and the plague breaking out, Bonaparte was compelled to retire with a loss of one-third of his army. During his absence from Egypt, Desaix had advanced to the Cataracts of the Nile, the farthest station of the Roman legions. A Turkish army which arrived shortly after the retreat from Syria, was wholly destroyed at Aboukir, by one of the most brilliant and complete of Napoleon's victories.

51. Learning the French disasters in Italy, and the exhausted state of the government at home, Bonaparte sailed for France, accompanied only by five generals who were devoted to his interests.   Aug., 1799. The universal dissatisfaction felt with the existing state of affairs opened a way to his ambition, and with the Abbé Sieyès, the most active member of the new Directory, he planned a virtual overthrow of the Republic. The Council of Five Hundred was dispersed by military force; and a minority of its members, reassembling, voted to abolish the Directory and intrust the executive power to three Consuls — Bonaparte, Sieyès, and Roger Ducos. A committee of fifty was chosen equally from the two legislative bodies, to propose changes in the constitution. The "Constitution of the Year VIII" overthrew popular sovereignty by destroying municipal governments, and committing to the Consuls the sole right of originating laws. The Senate of eighty members was chosen for life by the Consuls, the Tribunate of one hundred and the legislature of three hundred members for a limited period by the Senate, from a body called Notables of France, which was elected only at third remove * by the people. The second and third Consuls were merely counselors, all real power and responsibility being vested in the first. Thus, under the name of a Republic, France was again an autocracy.

RECAPITULATION.

By overthrow of Danton and the Hebertists, Robespierre becomes absolute; restores worship of the Supreme Being, but increases the slaughter of the guillotine. His fall and execution end the Reign of Terror. Dissolution of the Jacobin Club; massacres of "Red Republicans" in the south of France; starvation in Paris. In the campaign of 1794, France conquers the Austrian Netherlands, and the Prussian provinces west of the Rhine; makes Holland a dependency, by the Treaty of Basle detaches Prussia from the Coalition; is victorious in Italy, but defeated upon the sea. Death of Louis XVII., and peace with

---

* The whole mass of citizens voted for "Notables of the Communes;" these elected one-tenth of their own number as "Notables of the Departments," of whom one-tenth were likewise chosen as "Notables of France."

Spain. End of the Convention; establishment of the Directory, Council of Ancients and the Five Hundred. Revival of prosperity at home and aggressions abroad. First Italian campaign of Bonaparte; conquest of Piedmont and Lombardy, departure of five Italian sovereigns from the Coalition. Mantua taken by destruction of four Austrian armies; Papal states despoiled by Peace of Tolentino. Invasion of Carinthia and Styria, overthrow of Venice, whose territories are ceded to Austria in exchange for the Netherlands; Peace of Campo Formio. Cisalpine and Ligurian Republics dependent upon France. Pillage of Rome and overthrow of the papal government. The Swiss Confederation gives way to the Helvetic Republic one and indivisible. Spain under Godoy becomes subservient to France. Bonaparte sails for Egypt, captures and garrisons Malta, occupies Alexandria, gains Battle of the Pyramids and takes Cairo; loses his fleet in Battle of the Nile; attempts the conquest of Syria, fails, defeats the Turks at Aboukir, leaves Kleber in command and returns to France. New Coalition against the French Republic. Revolution in Naples, Parthenopean Republic proclaimed. Defeat of Jourdan in Germany and of Schérer in Italy; close of Congress at Rastadt. Suwarof defeats Macdonald on the Trebia and Joubert at Novi. Defeat of the allies in Switzerland, of Suwarof in the pass of St. Gothard. Overthrow of the Parthenopean and Roman Republics. Failure of the allies in Holland; the Czar deserts the Coalition. Bonaparte overthrows the Directory and becomes First Consul.

THE CONSULATE AND THE EMPIRE.

52. Bonaparte, being intrusted with almost absolute power, dismissed his provisional colleagues, and appointed in their places Cambacères and Lebrun, men distinguished not more by talents and acquirements than by pliability of character. The First Consul established a court at the Tuileries, and his great administrative talents soon restored confidence. Forced loans were abolished; thousands of non-juring priests were released from prison; the churches were opened and the observance of the Sabbath restored. Strongly desirous of peace, the First Consul addressed conciliatory letters to the sovereigns of England and Austria; but both powers refused to treat except upon the restoration of the Bourbons. War being renewed, Bonaparte himself undertook the campaign in Italy, where only Genoa and the Riviera now remained to the French. Forcing a passage across the Grand St. Bernard — most difficult and dangerous of the Alpine routes — he descended into Piedmont in the rear of the Austrian lines, and being joined by columns which had crossed Monts Cenis and St. Gothard, moved swiftly upon Milan. That city surrendered without opposition; but, on the other side, Genoa, which had withstood a two months' siege by the British fleet, capitulated three days later.

The Austrian general Melas, finding his communications severed by the sudden and decisive movements of the French, gave battle at Marengo. June, 1800. The fighting was long and obstinate, but at length Bonaparte was victorious. Melas, a veteran of eighty years, lost his presence of mind, and by the convention of Alessandria abandoned twelve great fortresses, including those of Milan, Turin, and Genoa, with all northern Italy as far as the Mincio to the French. The Cisalpine Republic was restored, and after a brilliant campaign of five weeks,

Bonaparte returned to Paris more powerful and secure of popular favor than ever.

53. The campaign of Moreau in Germany was almost equally successful. The Austrians by a series of defeats, were driven from Wirtemberg and Bavaria, and the French had occupied Munich, when news of the agreement between Bonaparte and Melas led to a cessation of hostilities. Efforts toward a permanent and general peace were, however, unavailing, and late in November the war was renewed. The archduke John of Austria, attempting to approach Munich through the forest of Hohenlinden, was fiercely attacked by Moreau, and sustained a ruinous defeat; 15,000 imperialists were either killed, wounded, or prisoners, while a hundred cannon remained in the hands of the victors. The archduke Charles, whose inclination for peace had occasioned his removal from command, was now reinstated; and among his first acts was the arrangement of a truce which was shortly followed by the Peace of Lunéville. Austria recognized the independence of the [Feb., 1801.] Batavian, Helvetic, Ligurian, and Cisalpine Republics, and added to the latter the duchy of Modena. By a subsequent treaty with Spain, Tuscany was erected into a kingdom of Etruria and conferred upon a son-in-law of Charles IV., while France, by this concession in Italy, bought back the vast territory of Louisiana in North America.

54. England, still fiercely active in the war, had conquered Malta in September, 1800, and resolved to wrest Egypt from the French. Kleber had been assassinated by a Turk, on the same day that his former comrade, Desaix, expired on the battle-field of Marengo. His successor, Menou, was defeated by the British general Abercrombie in the battle of Canopus, and was at length compelled to surrender [Aug., 1801.] Alexandria, and consent to the transportation of his army on English vessels to France. Separate treaties of peace were made by the French government with the kingdom of Naples, with Portugal, and with Turkey. The Coalition was already weakened by the defection of Paul I. of Russia and his reässertion of the Armed Neutrality of 1780. The offensive conduct of both English and French officers in seizing and searching neutral vessels, had offended the northern nations of Europe as well as the United States of America, whose commerce with Great Britain was already lucrative and extensive. The Czar, who had constituted himself the Grand Master of the Knights of St. John, was moreover incensed by the English retention of Malta; and in December, 1800, he entered into a Quadruple Alliance of Russia, Sweden, Denmark, and Prussia to maintain the rights of neutrals.

55. Denmark was the only sufferer by the new Coalition. Admiral Nelson, now Baron Nelson of the Nile, passed the Sound and defeated the Danish fleet before Copenhagen, notwithstanding its brave and resolute resistance. The Swedish port of Carlscrona was similarly threatened, when the assassination of Paul I. suddenly changed the balance of affairs. His successor, Alexander I., agreed with England upon a new maritime code, to which the other northern powers acceded. In October, 1801, Russia made treaties of peace and alliance with Spain and France. At last a change of ministry in England favored peace, and after long ne-

March, 1802.   gotiations the Treaty of Amiens was signed by the com- missioners of that power with those of France, Spain, and the Batavian Republic. England restored all her conquests except Ceylon and Trinidad; and evacuated all ports and islands in the Mediterranean. Malta was guaranteed by all the European powers to the Knights of St. John. Egypt again submitted to the Turkish dominion. The Ionian Islands were recognized as an independent republic, under the joint protection of Turkey and Russia. The results of these negotiations added immensely to the fame of Bonaparte, and in August, 1802, he was elected First Consul for life.

56. The power thus established was used for the promotion of enlightenment and social order, long interrupted by the storms of revolution. A commission of the ablest lawyers was intrusted with the preparation of a civil code — the first since St. Louis — evolving a clear and equitable system of laws from the perplexing mass of local customs and traditions.* Great public works were vigorously carried on — among others, a magnificent military road across the Simplon from France into Italy. Every department of public and private industry received an impulse from the energetic genius of Bonaparte, while institutions of learning were the especial objects of his munificence. By his Concordat with Pope Pius VII., the rites of the Roman Church were reëstablished as the religion of the state, though equal freedom was guaranteed to Protestant worship. All former sees were suppressed; ten new archbishoprics and fifty bishoprics were created, the incumbents of which were to be appointed by the First Consul. By an Act of Amnesty 150,000 emigrants were permitted to return, and such of their confiscated estates as still remained in the possession of the government, were restored to them.

57. The French colony of St. Domingo had formed itself into a negro republic, with Toussaint l'Ouverture, once a slave, at its head. A force was now sent for its reduction under General Leclerc, a brother-in-law of Bonaparte. After several months' desperate fighting, Toussaint was captured and conveyed to a dungeon in France; but his followers, aided

---

* Voltaire, in the previous century, had remarked that a traveler through France changed laws oftener than he changed horses, and that an advocate might be profoundly learned in one city and an ignoramus in the next. Roman laws, provincial customs, and local usages were endlessly modified by royal edicts, ordonnances, and arrêts of parliaments, making at least 300 distinct and often conflicting systems.

by the ravages of yellow fever, which destroyed more than two-thirds of the invaders, held out until a renewal of the war between France and England brought a fleet of the latter to their assistance. The French were expelled, and the independence of the republic, under its ancient name of Hayti, was proclaimed.

58. The execution of the Treaty of Lunéville laid the Empire at the feet of Bonaparte. Of all the free imperial cities, only six remained. In the process of indemnifying temporal princes out of the territories of the Church, two of the ecclesiastical electorates disappeared, and the third was transferred with the primacy to Ratisbon. The number of electors was more than made good by the elevation of one Catholic and three Protestant princes to that dignity. The archbishopric of Salzburg was made an electorate and conferred upon the emperor's brother, Ferdinand, in exchange for his grand-duchy of Tuscany. In defiance of promises, Bonaparte annexed to France all that part of Piedmont which had not been absorbed into the Cisalpine Republic, with the duchies of Parma, Piacenza, and Guastalla, the canton of Valais, and the cities of Geneva and Basle. Nineteen Swiss cantons, under the Act of Mediation, resumed a federal government. The Batavian Republic received a new constitution corresponding nearly to the Consulate in France, the Grand Pensionary enjoying even greater authority than had been conferred upon the stadtholders.

59. The Peace of Amiens was not of long duration. England violated the terms of the treaty by refusing to quit Malta, and by maintaining an army in Egypt more than a year after its evacuation by the French. These and other provocations had long indicated a rupture, when George III. suddenly ordered the seizure of all French vessels in English harbors, and followed this act by a declaration of war. Bonaparte retaliated by the arrest of all British travelers in France, and a French army immediately took possession of the electorate of Hanover. The First Consul hastened to sell Louisiana to the United States with a view both to augment his resources in the war, and to keep that distant possession from falling into English hands.* Spain and Portugal purchased the privilege of neutrality with enormous subsidies. Great preparations were made by Bonaparte for an invasion of England, a vast army was assembled on the coast, and a fleet of transports was distributed in the various ports from the Seine to the Texel.

60. The popularity of the First Consul was only increased by a nefarious plot for his assassination, formed by royalist refugees in London and believed by many to have the sanction of the British government. The

---

*Congress agreed to pay $11,250,000 and to assume the debts of the French government to American citizens, to an amount not exceeding $3,750,000.

Count of Artois boasted that he maintained sixty assassins in Paris. The brave and able general, Moreau, though he had cause of complaint against Bonaparte, refused to take part in the conspiracy. He was tried, nevertheless, and sentenced to two years' imprisonment, which Bonaparte commuted to exile in America. Eleven of the chief conspirators were put to death. The provocation was great, but it could not excuse the murder of the Duke of Enghien, a member of the House of Bourbon, who was seized on neutral territory near the French frontier, brought by order of Bonaparte to the castle of Vincennes, and shot after a mere mockery of trial for complicity in the plot.

61. The chief result of the conspiracy was the more speedy transformation of the Consulate into the Empire. The country was insecure, so long as one man's death involved the overthrow of the government. By decree of the Senate, ratified by the Legislative Chamber, Napoleon Bonaparte was declared Emperor of the French, and the throne was made hereditary in his family. Cambacères became Arch Chancellor, Lebrun Arch Treasurer, Prince Joseph Bonaparte Grand Elector, and Prince Louis Constable. Eighteen of Napoleon's most illustrious generals were named Marshals of the Empire. Pope Pius VII. made the journey to

Dec. 2, 1804.

Paris, in order to bless the coronation of the new Cæsar, who had fixed the seat of his universal monarchy on the Seine instead of the Tiber. It was, in truth, a second, though brief revival of the Western Empire, against which the obsolete pretensions of the Hapsburgs availed no more than had those of the Byzantine Cæsars against the first Frankish emperor.* The Cisalpine Republic was transformed into the kingdom of Italy; Napoleon received its crown in the Cathedral of Milan, May, 1805, and appointed his step-son, Eugene Beauharnais, to act as his viceroy. The Ligurian Republic was annexed to France.

62. A third Coälition against France was now concerted by the resolute energy of William Pitt. The Czar entered heartily into the scheme. Austria acceded in August, 1805. Prussia claimed to be neutral, and ultimately became the chief victim of the war. Hostilities began in September, when General Mack, with an Austrian army of 80,000, advanced upon Munich. Napoleon, abandoning the invasion of England (§ 59), rapidly moved the forces which he had gathered for that enterprise, from the Channel to the Rhine, and, contrary to the expectation of the Austrians, undertook in person the German campaign. By a series of brilliant maneuvers, he gained the rear of his opponent at Ulm, cut-

---

* Napoleon constantly maintained the parallel between himself and Charlemagne, by assuming the iron crown of the Lombards at Milan, by conferring upon his son the title King of Rome, and, in annexing the papal states to his dominion, by "revoking the donations of his predecessors, the Frankish emperors."

ting him off both from Vienna and from his Russian allies. Mack was compelled to surrender the 30,000 men who remained with him, with all their colors, magazines, and artillery. A division of nearly 20,000 which had escaped from Ulm before the capitulation, was surrounded and captured at Nördlingen. The French army pushed forward and entered Vienna, Nov. 13. Frederic William III. of Prussia was now forced or persuaded by Alexander I. to join the Coalition. During a visit of the Czar at Berlin, the two sovereigns, at the tomb of Frederic the Great, swore eternal friendship for each other and enmity to Napoleon. Yet a month had hardly elapsed when the king tore the treaty he had signed, and sent to congratulate the French conqueror upon his victory at Austerlitz. Napoleon coldly replied, "This compliment was intended for another, but Fortune has changed the address."

Oct., 1805.

63. The archduke Charles, commanding in Italy, heard of Mack's critical position and hastened to his relief, but arrived too late. Napoleon, crossing the Danube, gained one of his greatest victories over the Austro-Russian armies at Austerlitz in Moravia. Ten thousand of his enemies lay dead upon the field, while 120 cannon and 20,000 prisoners remained in his hands. The allies were still superior in numbers; for beside the 80,000 men of the archdukes Charles and John, the unworn levies of the Hungarian barons were approaching; but the defeated sovereigns gave up the game in despair, and the Czar began his homeward march. By the Peace of Presburg, the Hapsburgs renounced not only their last foot-hold in Italy — Venice being annexed to the kingdom of Napoleon — but the most ancient patrimony of their house, the Tyrol and Vorarlberg, which were added to the dominion of the elector, now king, of Bavaria. The royal titles of the electors of Bavaria and Wirtemberg, allies of the French, were recognized by the treaty. By a disastrous campaign of only two months, Austria had lost three millions of subjects and a revenue of nearly 14,000,000 florins.

64. The marvelous success of Napoleon on land was balanced by the naval battle off Cape Trafalgar, in which Nelson destroyed the French and Spanish fleets, and secured to England the undisputed dominion of the seas. But this victory was dearly bought with the life of the great admiral. A no less serious check to the prosecution of the war was the death of Mr. Pitt in January, 1806. He had been the soul of the war-policy of Great Britain, and the elevation of his rival, Mr. Fox, to the ministry was followed by negotiations for peace. But Fox died a few months later, and the war went on. Prussia was forced to take an active part in hostilities, by the dictate of Napoleon, who required Frederic William to occupy the German territories of George III., and to close all Prussian ports against English vessels.

65. The kingdom of Naples having violated its neutrality, was invaded by the French army under Masséna, just as the Russian and English troops were withdrawn in consequence of the battle of Austerlitz. King Ferdinand fled to Sicily; but his queen,* with a spirit worthy of her empress-mother, remained at Naples and raised an army of lazzaroni and brigands which she reinforced by convicts from the jails. The better class of Neapolitans, however, hailed the French as deliverers from this disorderly and dangerous rabble, and Masséna was able to enter the capital without resistance. Joseph Bonaparte, who had accompanied the army, was proclaimed King of the Two Sicilies, though in a certain dependence upon the imperial crown of France. His army was defeated at Maïda by the English general Stuart, and a general rising of the peasantry incited by the agents of Queen Caroline, still further threatened the new dominion; but Masséna, having captured Gaëta, put down the insurrection and restored order.

July, 1806.

66. Proceeding to the organization of his vast dominions, Napoleon endowed his sisters with Italian principalities and his brothers with kingdoms (see ¾ 72). His favorite generals were rewarded by the investiture of newly created "fiefs of the Empire;" Berthier became Prince of Neuchâtel; Talleyrand of Benevento; Bernadotte of Ponte Corvo. The most decisive act in his foreign policy was the overthrow of the Roman Empire, 1,836 years from its establishment by Cæsar Augustus, and 1,006 from its revival under Charlemagne. Sixteen German princes, including the kings of Bavaria and Wirtemberg, the grand dukes of Baden and Hesse Darmstadt, and the Primate, declared themselves separated from the Empire and formed the Confederation of the Rhine in strict alliance with France. The French embassador at Ratisbon thereupon notified the Diet that his master, having accepted the protectorate of the Confederation, "no longer recognized the existence of the Empire." Francis II., the one hundred and twentieth of the Cæsars, hastened to resign his shadowy dignity. In a declaration on Aug. 6th, he stated that, finding it impossible to fulfill the obligations which he had assumed with the imperial crown, he considered the bonds which attached him to the Germanic body as dissolved, released its members from their allegiance, and retired to the government of his hereditary dominions. He had already assumed the title still borne by his house — Hereditary Emperor of *Austria*.

Aug. 1, 1806.

67. The accession of so numerous and powerful a clientage was of immense importance to Napoleon, for it placed at his immediate disposal an army of 70,000 men — a number which by the enlargement of the Confed-

* Maria Caroline, queen of Naples, was a sister of the emperors Joseph II and Leopold II., and of the unfortunate queen Marie Antoinette of France.

eration was afterward increased to 120,000. The Confederates had kept their movements secret from the king of Prussia, though his brother-in-law, the Prince of Orange, was thereby made a vassal of Murat, the new grand-duke of Berg. At the same time it became known that Napoleon was proposing to restore Hanover to the king of England. This province had been forced upon Frederic William in order to plunge him into a war with Great Britain, and had been regarded as the badge of his humiliation; that it should now be wrested from him to suit the further convenience of the conqueror, was a mark of contempt too obvious to be endured. A strong war-party arose at the court of Berlin, in which the queen was the chief mover, but which included the leading statesmen and generals. Unhappily, Prussia had forfeited the confidence of all Europe for the sake of peace with France, and had to brave the entire force of Napoleon with no other immediate aid than that of the elector of Saxony.

68. Most of the Prussian generals were old men; their leader, the Duke of Brunswick, had won his spurs in the Seven Years' War, as comrade in arms of Frederic the Great. Napoleon began the campaign with his customary energy, and surprised the duke by the same maneuver which he had already practiced upon the Austrians, Melas at Marengo, and Mack at Ulm. While the Prussian general vainly thought to find the French forces dispersed in Franconia, they were turning his left wing and cutting him off from communication with the Russians. Bernadotte gained a victory at Schleitz and Lannes at Saalfeld over detached corps of the Prussians, but it was not until a large French force was marching upon Leipzig directly in his rear, that the duke perceived the true condition of affairs. He then attempted a retreat, accompanied by the king, the Prince of Orange, and many of the most distinguished generals, leaving Prince Hohenlohe with part of the army at Jena, where he was defeated by Napoleon in person. On the same day the retreating army was defeated still more signally at Auerstadt by Marshal Davoust. A panic seized the troops; 14,000 surrendered at Erfurt to Murat and Ney, and in the north the strong and well provisioned fortresses of Stettin, Custrin, even Magdeburg with a garrison of 20,000 men, were given up to inferior numbers of French. Blucher was overtaken at Lubec and surrendered himself with his entire division of 20,000 men.

Oct. 14, 1806.

69. The elector of Saxony hastened to desert his ally and make peace with Napoleon, from whom he accepted the title of King and a place in the Rhenish Confederation. The French emperor entered Berlin as a conqueror, less than a year from the day when he similarly occupied Vienna. The sword and insignia of Frederic the Great were sent as trophies to Paris. The Duke of Brunswick, fatally wounded at Auerstadt, wrote to the conqueror begging mercy for his subjects. He was answered with bitter reproaches. During his flight from his capital he died in the arms of his son, who swore to avenge him.

70. From the royal palace at Berlin, Napoleon issued his famous Decree declaring the British Isles in a state of blockade, confiscating all English merchandise, and prohibiting all commerce and correspondence with that country. The court at London responded by an Order in Council, declaring the blockade of all ports in Europe from which the British flag was excluded, and claiming the right to seize and search all vessels bound for such ports. The "Milan Decree" of Napoleon (Dec. 17, 1807) retaliated by declaring all vessels submitting to the English regulations to be lawful prizes. All these and several subsequent decrees were in pursuance of the Continental System by which Napoleon hoped to ruin the commerce of England and thus strike a mortal blow at the prosperity of his chief enemy. The paralyzing effects of his policy were, however, most severely felt by the continental states; and it is a singular fact that in spite of the decrees, contracts for the clothing of French soldiers had actually to be made in England, the Hanse towns being unable to execute them.

Nov., 1806.

71. The Prussian Poles were easily roused by French emissaries to rebel against their late masters, but the patriot Kosciusko, who had accepted the protection of the Czar and felt that his countrymen had nothing to gain by a change of tyrants, disavowed and discouraged the enterprise. The Russian armies appeared on the field in November, 1806, and inflicted great losses upon the French, though no decisive victory was gained by either side until February. After a few weeks in winter-quarters, both armies resumed operations, and one of the most tremendous of Napoleon's battles was fought at Eylau, Feb. 8. The field remained to the French, but so terrible was their loss of men, that Napoleon, falling back on the Vistula, made propositions for peace. It was refused by the king of Prussia, who was reassured by a new convention with Russia and Great Britain, and a subsidy of $5,000,000 from the latter. The French were, however, victorious at Friedland, May 14, and the surrender of Dantzic on the 24th of the same month, restored to active service 30,000 of their troops who had been engaged in its siege. Königsberg fell into their hands, and the Czar was now the one to offer terms of peace.

A. D. 1807.

72. The two emperors met on a raft moored in the Niemen at Tilsit, and their conference came to a more speedy conclusion than is customary with diplomatic dealings. The Czar seems to have conceived a sudden and romantic admiration for Napoleon, not unlike that of his predecessor, Peter III., for the military genius of Frederic the Great. He assured the French emperor that he fully shared his dislike for England, and

EUROPE

during the
Reign of Napoleon I.
by
A. von Steinwehr.

Scale

0   50   100   200   300   400 Mls.

$\frac{1}{19,000,000}$

KDM. - KINGDOM ,
G. D. - Grand Duchy.

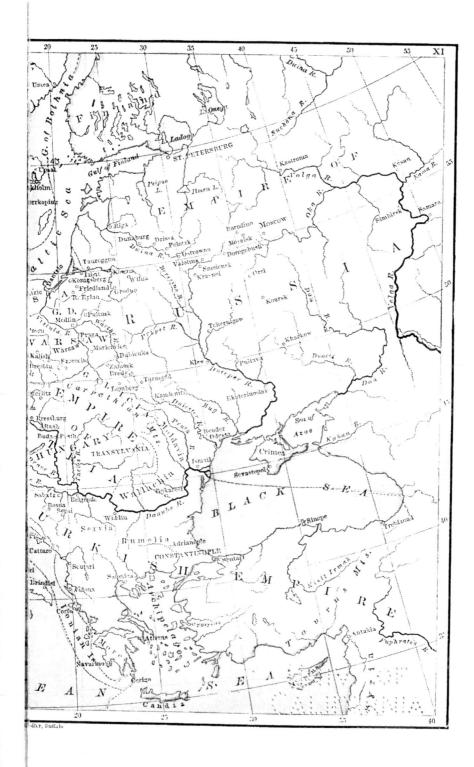

was ready to concert measures for diminishing her power; whereupon Napoleon declared that, if that were the case, peace was already made. Alexander recognized the three brothers of the French emperor—Joseph as king of the Two Sicilies, Louis of Holland, and Jerome of a new kingdom of Westphalia which was formed of the spoils of Prussia and Brunswick. Prussian Poland, under the name of Grand-duchy of Warsaw, was ceded to the king of Saxony. It had been proposed in the French cabinet to blot out Prussia from the map of Europe; at the intercession of the Czar, Frederic William was permitted to retain his crown and somewhat more than half his dominions.

The details of the scheme by which the emperors of the East and the West divided the world between them can not here be recorded. Russia was to have the Turkish dominion, except Constantinople, with whatever more she could conquer on the side of Asia; and was to become the head of a new League in northern Europe which aimed to reduce the maritime supremacy of Great Britain. A Bonaparte was to become king of Spain and Portugal. The trade of the Mediterranean was limited to the two contracting powers with their dependents. The general result of the northern war and the Peace of Tilsit was to make Napoleon more absolutely than ever the master of Europe. Russia, the only power which could cope with him on land, was changed, for a time, from a foe into an ally.

73. England and Sweden were still at war with France. Denmark, though hitherto neutral, was forced into the war by the extraordinary action of the British government in sending a fleet to bombard Copenhagen. The town, after three days' cannonade, was forced to surrender with the entire Danish fleet, artillery, and naval stores. It was two months after this high-handed violation of her peace and neutrality, that England declared war against Denmark. The Danish West Indies were the immediate sufferers, their colonies of St. Nov., 1807. Thomas and St. Croix falling at once into the hands of the English. The Czar's offer of mediation being rejected, Russia and Austria entered with France into a league against Great Britain, which thus became in her turn the object of a Coälition embracing all Europe except Sweden and Turkey. All the ports of Russia, Prussia, Denmark, Germany, Holland, France, Italy, and Dalmatia were closed to the commerce of England, and her trade with Hamburg was conducted by way of Constantinople. The details of the war between Sweden and Russia need not be related. It was virtually closed by the forced abdication of Gustavus IV., and the accession of his uncle, Charles XIII., who soon made peace with the allied powers. Finland, with the Aland Isles and part of West Bothnia, was ceded to Russia.

M. H.—25.

RECAPITULATION.

As First Consul, Bonaparte restores order and security at Paris. Gains a great victory at Marengo, reconquers Italy, restores the Cisalpine Republic and becomes its president; while Moreau in Germany wins the battle of Hohenlinden. By Peace of Lunéville with Austria, four republics are recognized, the kingdom of Etruria established, Louisiana regained by France. England, still at war, wrests Malta and Egypt from the French; Naples, Portugal, and Turkey make peace with France. The Czar proclaims armed neutrality; forms a coalition of northern powers to maintain it. Nelson defeats the Danes before Copenhagen and threatens the Swedes. Murder of Paul I. of Russia; Alexander makes peace with England. Peace of Amiens. Concordat with Pius VII. restores Romanism as the state-religion of France. Captivity of Toussaint l'Ouverture; independence of Hayti established with English aid. Terms of the Peace being violated, Napoleon prepares for invasion of England; sells Louisiana to United States; retaliates plots against his life by execution of the Duke of Enghien; assumes an imperial crown; in campaign against Austria forces the capitulation of Mack at Ulm; defeats the Austro-Russian army at Austerlitz, and dictates the Peace of Presburg. Nelson gains a great naval victory at Trafalgar. The French conquer Naples. Francis of Lorraine abdicates his title as Emperor of the Romans. Confederate princes place themselves under Napoleon's protection. Defeat of Prussian armies at Jena and Auerstadt; surrender of Stettin, Custrin, and Magdeburg. Napoleon occupies Berlin, whence he issues a Decree enforcing his Continental System of commercial hostility to England. Grand-duchy of Warsaw formed from Prussian Poland. Napoleon victorious at Eylau and Friedland; receives surrender of Dantzic and Königsberg. Peace of Tilsit concluded by Napoleon and the Czar. Bombardment of Copenhagen by the English, forces Denmark into the war by which she loses her West Indian possessions.

THE PENINSULAR WAR.

74. In southern Europe, Napoleon's continental blockade was completed by the subjugation of Portugal, the old and steadfast commercial ally of Great Britain. It was accomplished by General Junot with an army of 30,000 men. The insane queen, Maria I., and the Prince Regent, her son, sailed to Brazil, accompanied by most of the rank and wealth of the kingdom; and the new empire of the Braganças was established at Rio Janeiro, Jan., 1808. A few weeks later the Pope's temporal power was overthrown by the occupation of Rome by French troops. General Miollis was directed to assume the temporary government of the States of the Church. Pius VII. responded by a brief of excommunication against Napoleon; but this harmless manifesto was only followed by the annexation of the richest provinces of the Church to the kingdom of Italy. (See note, p. 380.)

75. Spain was the next victim. A violent dissension existed between Prince Ferdinand, the heir of that kingdom, on one side, and his father, mother, and the unworthy favorite Godoy, on the other. This quarrel was made the occasion of ruin to all. Under various pretenses the northern provinces of Spain were occupied by a French army of 100,000 men. The king, having in vain attempted to reach the coast and embark for his American dominions, abdicated in favor of his son, who assumed the title of Ferdinand VII. and was welcomed to Madrid by the joyful acclamations of the people. Charles IV., however, was no sooner relieved from immediate danger than he regretted the loss of his crown, and besought the aid of Napoleon to regain it. The whole royal family were drawn by various motives to Bayonne, where, after a personal interview with their conqueror, both father and son resigned their sovereign rights to their "dearly beloved friend and ally, the Emperor of the French." Ferdinand had previously refused the kingdom of Etruria as the price of his inheritance. He was imprisoned with his brother Carlos in the castle of Valençai. His father sold Spain and the Indies for the castle of Chambord and a yearly pension of 7,500,000 francs.

76. The crown of Spain was bestowed upon Joseph Bonaparte, who resigned that of the Two Sicilies to his brother-in-law, Murat. The Spanish people, thus bartered away like a flock of A. D. 1808. sheep, were filled with indignation. Though a formal assent to the accession of Joseph was extorted from the Council of Castile, Juntas in opposition to his government were formed in the principal towns; and that of Seville declared war upon Napoleon, in the name of Ferdinand VII. The Peninsular War began with the seizure of six French war-vessels in the harbor of Cadiz, and a disastrous defeat of Marshal Moncey in his advance upon Valencia. The Spaniards were subsequently defeated at Medina del Rio Seco, but more than retrieved that loss by the victory of Baylen in Andalusia. General Dupont and 20,000 French became prisoners of war. The heroic defense of Saragossa equally proved the Spanish spirit. Though but slightly fortified, the city sustained a two months' siege and many desperate assaults. The French forces, fearfully reduced by their hardships, were at length compelled to retreat without their guns.

77. Portugal followed the Spanish example and organized an insurrection. The British government sent Sir Arthur Wellesley — afterward Duke of Wellington — with an army to her aid. In the battle of Vimeira, Junot was decisively defeated, and by the Convention of Cintra barely obtained permission to evacuate the country with his surviving troops. A Russian squadron in the Tagus was surrendered about the same time, and the English took possession of Lisbon. In order to concentrate his forces in the south, Napoleon now drew closer his alliance with the Czar in a congress at Erfurt, where, beside the two emperors, a crowd of inferior sovereigns were in attendance. Alexander consented to all the changes in Italy and the Spanish peninsula, in return for Napoleon's agreement to his annexation of Moldavia, Wallachia, and Finland. A joint request for peace was addressed to the king of Great Britain, but was refused on the ground that the Spanish nation was not recognized as a party to the transactions at Erfurt.

78. In November, 1808, Napoleon put himself at the head of his armies in Spain, and a series of brilliant victories cleared his way to the capital, which he entered Dec. 4. By an imperial decree he abolished the Inquisition, reduced the number of convents to one-third, and annulled all feudal rights and provincial barriers. Sir John Moore, at the head of the British forces, commenced a most difficult retreat into Galicia; and Napoleon, being at the same time recalled into Germany, left the pursuit to Soult. The marshal only overtook the British at Corunna, where in spite of his superior numbers, he sustained a severe defeat. But Moore was struck by a cannon-ball in the very moment of his victory; and his followers having buried him "at dead of night," hastily embarked for England. Galicia submitted to the French; but these had been so disabled by their losses as to remain comparatively inactive for several months.

79. Austria, always restive under the humiliating conditions of the Peace of Presburg, had been silently mustering her forces until their numbers were more than double those of Napoleon. England promised aid to the amount of four millions sterling. The moment when the best troops of Napoleon were absorbed in the Spanish campaign seemed favorable for the attempt, but Francis little appreciated his adversary's power of swift and decisive action. Learning at Paris, April 13, of the invasion of Bavaria by the archduke Charles, Napoleon proceeded at once to Stuttgardt and Carlsruhe, organized the forces of Wirtemberg and Baden, and by the 18th had fixed his headquarters at Ingolstadt. By five battles fought in as many successive days, he forced the Austrians to draw off their shattered columns toward Bohemia, leaving the road to Vienna open to his advance. That city capitulated, May 12.

A. D. 1809.

80. At the first outbreak of the war, the Tyrolese had risen against their new masters, the Bavarians, and had either killed or imprisoned 8,000 French soldiers between Innsbrück and Brixen. The Bavarians were driven from the Tyrol, except the fortress of Kufstein on their own border, which was besieged. The advance of Marshal Lefèvre turned the scale. He defeated the Austrians at Mörgel and captured Schwatz and Innsbrück. Even after the Austrian troops were withdrawn, the brave and loyal Tyrolese maintained the conflict until the innermost recesses of their mountains had been ransacked by the French troops. Their leader, Andrew Hofer, was at length taken, tried by court-martial and shot at Mantua, Feb., 1810.

81. The efforts of the Austrians on the side of Poland were equally unsuccessful. In Italy the archduke John was effectually opposed by the Viceroy Eugene Beauharnais; his defeat on the Piave was followed by the loss of Gortz and Laybach, and being pursued even into Hungary he suffered another overthrow near Raab. The archduke Charles in command of the main army, had meanwhile taken up his position on the Marchfield near Vienna, where the fortunes of Austria and Germany had more than once before been decided. Here a two days' battle was fought with great loss on both sides and no decisive victory on either; but Napoleon was at length compelled to order a retreat. The battles are usually named from the two villages, Aspern and Essling, near which they occurred. A few weeks later the decisive battle of Wagram resulted in victory to the French. The archduke Charles retired into Moravia and was again defeated at Znaym, July 11.

May, 1809.

82. The terms of the Peace of Schönbrunn which followed, were even more humiliating to Austria, after all her efforts and sacrifices, than those of the treaty of Presburg. The countries about the head of the Adriatic, under the name of Illyrian Provinces, became members of the French Empire. The greater part of Austrian Poland was divided between the Czar and the king of Saxony; Salzburg with its territories was ceded to Bavaria. Francis II. renounced his alliance with England, and engaged to uphold the Continental System of hostility to her commerce. The deposition and imprisonment of Pope Pius VII. had been accomplished during the Austrian war. Refusing a liberal endowment and the possession of the Vatican — where he might reign as the spiritual head of Catholic Christendom without the distraction of worldly interests — the Pope shut himself up in the Quirinal with his Swiss Guards; but his palace was surrounded at midnight by the French soldiery, and he was conveyed as a prisoner first to Grenoble and finally to Fontainebleau. Rome was declared the second city of the Empire.

83. Shortly after the Peace of Schönbrunn, Napoleon resolved upon the dissolution of his marriage with Josephine, the faithful and beloved companion of his rising fortunes, and the formation of a new alliance with one of the ancient dynasties of Europe. The empress gave her unwilling consent to what was pronounced a state necessity, and the divorce was ratified by the civil and ecclesiastical authorities at Paris. Napoleon then demanded from the Austrian emperor the hand of his daughter, Maria Louisa. However averse he may have been to the match, Francis dared not refuse; the marriage was celebrated at Vienna, March 11, and at Paris April 2, 1810. It was perhaps the turning point in the career of Napoleon — the moment when his star reached its zenith and began to decline. The man who by mere force of genius had raised himself from a penniless charity student at Brienne to be master of all the crowned heads in Europe, had nothing to gain by connection with a family which, now at least, had nothing but antiquity to recommend it; while by the people of France he was regarded as having abjured the principle on which his greatness rested.

84. The just and liberal policy of King Louis of Holland, especially his resistance to the Continental System in favor of the commercial interests of his people — bitterly displeased his brother, who sent an army to occupy the country. Louis abdicated and retired into Austria. Holland, with the Hanse Towns and an important district on the North Sea, was annexed to France. The electorate of Hanover was already added to the kingdom of Westphalia, and the Valais in Switzerland was incorporated with France in order to secure the road over the Simplon in the undisturbed possession of that power.

85. The Peninsular War was still in progress. Saragossa surrendered to the French, Feb., 1809, after a resistance unsurpassed in heroism even by that of the Numantines against the Romans. Monks and even women had taken part in the defense; and 40,000 dead bodies lying in the streets bore silent witness to the courage which had yielded only to necessity. The great battle of Talavera resulted, after an obstinate and long continued struggle, in the defeat of the French by the combined forces of British, Spaniards, and Portuguese. Wellington, however, was compelled to retire even north of the Tagus, while his allies were repeatedly worsted by the French. Gerona, the bulwark of Catalonia, was reduced by famine after six months' siege and many assaults. Foreseeing a concentration of all Napoleon's forces in the peninsula, Wellington proceeded to fortify himself in the famous lines of Torres Vedras, where by defending Lisbon to the last he secured at once the free entrance of supplies and an unobstructed retreat in case of need. The three lines were made impregnable with forts, batteries, and redoubts, while the surrounding country was stripped of all that could afford subsistence to an enemy.

86. Napoleon, meanwhile, once more at peace with all the rest of the continent, had collected from his subject nations an army of more than 300,000 men for the recovery of Portugal, and the reëstablishment of his power in the peninsula. Masséna opened the campaign by the siege and capture of Ciudad Rodrigo, soon followed by that of Almeida, a frontier fortress of great strength. Wellington retired within his lines, and Masséna placed his army in winter-quarters at Santarem. In the spring of 1811 the British besieged Almeida and Badajoz, and defeated Masséna at Fuentes de Onor. A still more disastrous defeat was suffered by Soult at Albuera; but his object was nevertheless attained, for learning that he was to be reinforced, Wellington abandoned the siege of Badajoz. Already in the preceding year, King Joseph had captured Cordova, Seville, Granada, and Malaga, and the Spanish government had taken refuge in Cadiz, which was closely invested by the French.

87. Wellington opened the campaign of 1812 by the reduction of the two strong fortresses of Ciudad Rodrigo and Badajoz. Then penetrating to the interior of Spain he gained a great victory at Salamanca. The

French were forced to evacuate New Castile and Andalusia and to raise the siege of Cadiz with the abandonment of all their artillery. Madrid was occupied by the English, but was soon abandoned. The national pride of the Spaniards, which sustained them against the power of Napoleon, made them almost equally jealous of their English allies, and seriously abated their success.

88. Russia was now the only continental power which could resist Napoleon, and Russia had many causes of complaint — her commerce ruined by the system of blockades, her peace threatened by the aggrandizement of the duchy of Warsaw, and her sovereign insulted by the annexation of Oldenburg, a possession of the Romanoffs, to the French empire. The threatened establishment of a French maritime arsenal at Lubec, the continued occupation of the Prussian fortresses and concentration of French troops between the Oder and the Vistula, together with the attempt to combine Denmark, Sweden, and the duchy of Warsaw in a Northern Confederation under Napoleon's protection — all indicated a design to violate the treaty of Tilsit as soon as it should suit the convenience of the French emperor to dispense with it. The Czar prepared for resistance by placing an army of 90,000 men upon his frontiers; at the same time excluding or limiting the introduction of French merchandise, while he admitted products of the British colonies. He closed a three years' war with the Turks by the treaty of Bucharest, May, 1812. in which the Porte ceded Bessarabia, Ismail and Kilia, one-third of Moldavia, and the fortresses of Chotzim and Bender.

89. War with Napoleon was hastened by the influence of Sweden. Charles XIII. having no son, the four Estates of that kingdom had, in 1810, elected Charles John Bernadotte (§ 66) to be crown-prince and ultimately sovereign. The choice had been made in the hope of gaining the good-will of Napoleon; but Bernadotte's sincere disapproval of the Continental System, and the admission of English goods into Pomerania soon led to hostilities between Sweden and France. Swedish ships in German harbors were seized, and their crews sent in irons to Antwerp. Davoust, commanding the French in northern Germany, occupied Pomerania, imprisoned the Swedish civil officers at Hamburg, and filled their places with French. Bernadotte, ruling Sweden during the illness of his adoptive father, appealed for aid to the Czar. It was granted, and the war which followed was on a grander scale than any that had preceded it. Austria and Prussia allied themselves with Napoleon; Russia and Sweden with Great Britain.

90. On the 29th of May, Napoleon left Dresden — where he had met the emperor Francis and a throng of German princes, and had displayed his magnificence by a series of gorgeous entertainments, while he completed his preparations for the campaign. On the frontier of Russia he

first declared war against the Czar. His army of nearly half a million of men crossed the Niemen in five columns, followed by a train of 1,200 cannon. Napoleon himself with half his force sought to gain the watershed between the Dwina and Dnieper, whence by a decisive battle he might command the road either to St. Petersburg or Moscow. His movements were delayed by a terrible storm which, sweeping over Lithuania, impeded the march of King Jerome and Prince Eugene. In the hurricane, inundations, and the excessive cold which followed, many horses perished, and the movements of artillery were seriously embarrassed.

91. The Russians, retreating before superior forces, burned their magazines, and the French already suffered for want of food. Smolensko was taken after a furious assault which lasted an entire day, but it was dearly purchased with the lives of 12,000 men, for it was only a heap of smoking ruins. Pursuing the same policy, the Russians burned and abandoned Dorogobourg, Viazma, and Gjatsk. Before reaching Moscow, Napoleon found the army of Kutusoff strongly posted at Borodino, and by a severe and terrible contest won another costly victory. Of the 80,000 killed or wounded men who lay upon the field, more than half were Russians; Kutusoff, with his remaining troops, retreated upon Moscow. Unable to defend that ancient capital, he passed through its streets to the great eastern plain, followed by all the inhabitants who were able to remove. The French, following, entered the gates without opposition, and Napoleon took up his abode in the Kremlin or fortress. But in the night innumerable fires broke out in all parts of the city. Trains had been laid from house to house and heaps of combustible materials were fired by men left behind for the purpose. For five days the city was an ocean of flames. Returning to the Kremlin after the conflagration had subsided, Napoleon attempted to negotiate with his former partner in the treaty of Tilsit. He had fancied that from that ancient palace of the Czars he might again dictate terms to Europe; but the act of the governor had shown the futility of the dream.

92. Alexander adhered to his former declaration that he would treat with no enemy on Russian soil. A terrible winter was coming on; and

Oct. 19, 1812. vanquished both by frost and flame, Napoleon was compelled to retreat. The roads were already obstructed by snow, and troops of Cossacks were ready to seize stragglers from the main body. In one terrible night (Nov. 6-7), thousands of men and nearly all the horses perished with cold. The line of retreat was strewn with corpses like a continuous battle-field. In crossing the river Beresina, a bridge became clogged with carriages and men. The Russian general Witgenstein came up and directed a terrible cannonade upon the crowded mass. The hideous carnage which followed may be imagined but can not be described. Those were happiest who found a speedy grave beneath the icy waters. But a small fragment remained of the grand army which had undertaken the conquest of Russia, and that consisted of charred, maimed, and shattered specimens of humanity, victims of the most disastrous retreat since that of Xerxes.

93. Leaving Murat in chief command, Napoleon hastened to Paris, where a false report of his death had led to a dangerous insurrection. The presence of the emperor restored order, and by extraordinary conscriptions he was soon at the head of nearly half a million of men, but the immense destruction of horses in the Russian campaign rendered his remarkable victories of 1813 ineffective. As a natural result of his misfortunes, many of his German allies deserted him. The Confederation of the Rhine was dissolved. Frederic William of Prussia allied himself with the Czar, and welcomed a Russian army in Berlin. Austria and Saxony for a few months maintained an armed neutrality. The people of Hamburg rose against the French garrison, and opened their gates to the Russians, their harbor to the English.

94. The campaign of 1813 embraced the whole continent of Europe. The left of the French army rested on Hamburg and Lubec, its right on Venice and Verona. The main action took place in the northern portion of the line and chiefly in the Saxon territory. The first general encounter was upon the plain of Lutzen, rendered famous nearly two hundred years before by the victory and death of Gustavus Adolphus. The Russian and Prussian monarchs commanded in person; they were defeated, and the Saxon capital remained in the hands of the French. A more decisive victory was gained by Napoleon in a two days' battle at Bautzen. Hamburg was retaken by Davoust with a corps of French and Danes. In revenge for the expulsion of the garrison, 8,000 houses were destroyed and 48,000 people rendered homeless.

95. Napoleon now consented to a truce of eight weeks, to afford time for negotiations. A Peace Congress assembled at Prague; but the allies were insincere, and the time was spent in perfecting the Fifth Coalition of European powers against Napoleon. England was most active in the use of money and influence. Austria gave in her adhesion, increasing the allied armies to a marked superiority over their opponents. Napoleon meanwhile concluded a treaty with the Danes. War was renewed Aug. 10; and in the great battle of Dresden, Napoleon was again victorious. Throughout the campaign, however, the advantages gained where he commanded in person were balanced by the almost uniform defeat of his generals. Oudinot lost a battle at Grossbeeren, Macdonald at Katzbach; a French division pursuing the allies after their defeat at Dresden, was cut off from the main body and 20,000 men were either killed or captured. Ney in his march upon Berlin was defeated by Bernadotte with great loss.

96. Bavaria joined the Coälition Oct. 1. Napoleon, outnumbered and partly surrounded by the allies — who, reinforced by 60,000 Russians, had advanced again into Saxony — resolved to stake all upon a great battle, which was fought accordingly at Leipzig, Oct. 16–18. On the first day the French had generally the advantage; but at night Napoleon, conscious of the tremendous odds against him, renewed proposals for peace. They were rejected, and after a day's respite the battle recommenced, this time with still greater superiority of numbers on the part of the allies. The French were driven from their positions, and at night began a retreat, which but for the milder season would have been as disastrous as that from Moscow. The Bavarians under Wrede tried in vain to intercept their march, but were routed at Hanau.

97. The vast empire built up by the genius of Napoleon rapidly fell to pieces. French garrisons were expelled from towns on the Elbe, the Vistula, the Oder, and the Baltic. Hanover was reöccupied by the king of England; Holland proclaimed the Prince of Orange as sovereign of the Netherlands under the name of William I. Jerome Bonaparte abandoned his kingdom of Westphalia, and the sovereigns of Hesse, Oldenburg, and Brunswick resumed their hereditary dominions. The Danes made a treaty with Great Britain and Sweden, ceding Norway to the latter power, and receiving in exchange Swedish Pomerania and the Isle of Rügen. They entered the Coälition and accepted a liberal subsidy from Great Britain for the maintenance of 10,000 troops. The Austrians had meanwhile recovered Illyria, Carinthia, and Dalmatia; and the opening of the Tyrol to the allies had driven Eugene beyond the Mincio. Murat, believing his brother-in-law irretrievably ruined, accepted the promises of the allies and declared war against Napoleon. Eugene was offered the crown of Lombardy on similar terms, but he remained faithful to his emperor.

98. In Spain, some of the best French troops having been withdrawn, Wellington gained the great battle of Vittoria, which decided the fate of the peninsula. Joseph Bonaparte retired into France. Nearly a week of severe fighting in the passes of the Pyrenees resulted in the expulsion of Soult from the Spanish territory. San Sebastian was taken by storm, Pampeluna by siege, and even Bayonne was invested by a force of English and Portuguese. Napoleon released Ferdinand VII. from his captivity of six years, and solemnly recognized his dignity as King of Spain and the Indies. The Pope was likewise released from Fontainebleau, and resumed his sovereignty over the States of the Church.

99. In the campaign of 1814, the allies prepared to converge their columns from the north, east, and south, upon Paris. Schwartzenberg, with the grand army of Austria, crossed the Rhine at Basle; Blucher, with that of Silesia, between Mannheim and Coblentz; while the Russians approached through the Netherlands. Before the end of January nearly one-third of France was actually occupied by the allies. In this desperate condition, the wonderful resources of Napoleon's genius appeared more inexhaustible than at the height of his good fortune. Though defeated by Blucher at Brienne, he persevered in assaulting that general until by successive victories he drove him back upon Bülow's advancing columns. Then turning upon Schwartzenberg, he defeated him at Montereau so decisively that the Austrian made proposals for a peace. Blucher again advanced and gained a victory at Laon. Leaving Marmont and Mortier to hold him in check, Napoleon attacked Schwartzenberg at Arcis-sur-Aube; but the battle, though the most fiercely contested of the whole campaign, had no decisive result.

100. Napoleon then determined to get into the rear of the Austrians, and carry the war into Germany. Learning his design, the allies resolved to take advantage of it by hastening their march upon Paris. The emperor was at St. Dizier when he discovered the snare into which he had fallen. Traveling with extraordinary swiftness in advance of his army, he arrived at Fontainebleau late at night, only to find that the battle which deprived him of a throne had been fought that very day on the heights of Montmartre, Belleville, and Romainville. The empress-regent and her son had retired to Rambouillet. Marmont and Mortier with the National Guards and 8,000 regular troops had defended the capital to the last extremity, until, further efforts proving hopeless, they had been authorized by Joseph Bonaparte to agree with Schwartzenberg upon terms of capitulation.

101. The Czar and the king of Prussia entered Paris, March 31, followed by their victorious armies. After a conference with the principal officers of the government, they issued a proclamation declaring that they would no longer treat with Napoleon Bonaparte nor with any member of his family. The next day the Senate pronounced his deposition from the throne. Finding armed resistance impossible, Napoleon signed an abdication in favor of his son. This was rejected by the allies, who exulted in having their great enemy absolutely at their disposal; and he was compelled to follow it by an unconditional surrender of the crowns of France and Italy, accepting as a nominal exchange the sovereignty of the Island of Elba and a pension of two millions of francs. The war in the south was already ended by the victories of the British at Orthez and Toulouse. Bordeaux had proclaimed Louis XVIII., and Wellington was marching northward with his victorious army. The Count of Artois, appointed by his brother Lieutenant-General of the kingdom, signed a convention with the allied sovereigns at Paris. On the 20th of April, Napoleon took leave of his guard at Fontainebleau, and departed for Elba.

102. The allied sovereigns in possession of France proceeded to settle its government and boundaries to their own satisfaction. The Czar, to his lasting honor, became the guarantee of a liberal constitution; and it was only after signing this document that Louis XVIII., having arrived from England, was permitted to make his public entry into Paris. The throng of royalists who had returned under the protection of the allied armies, received him of course with acclamations, but it was noticed that the people in the streets regarded the royal cortège with ominous silence. The charter which the king granted to his people was dated in the nineteenth year of his reign! It conceded many invaluable rights — freedom of person, security of property, unobstructed exercise of religion, and liberty of the press — but its refusal to recognize the eventful history of the Republic and the Empire was worse than a silly affectation; it went far to prove, to the great discontent of the people, that the Bourbons during their long exile had "learned nothing and forgotten nothing."

103. By the Peace of Paris, May 30, France was reduced to her limits at the beginning of 1792, with a few slight additions; independence was restored to Germany; Holland was increased by the annexation of Belgium, and the Prince of Orange became King of the Netherlands. Upon learning of Napoleon's abdication, Eugene Beauharnais surrendered the fortresses of northern Italy into the hands of the Austrians. On the 2d of October all the European sovereigns assembled either in person or by embassadors at Vienna to rearrange the affairs of the continent. But there is the less need to record their decisions, as their conferences were interrupted by a most unwelcome event.

104. Napoleon had quitted Elba, Feb. 26, and having landed at Cannes, was marching toward Paris, joined every-where by companies of his old soldiers, whose idolatrous affection for his person quickly effaced their allegiance to Louis. The presence of Napoleon upon a battle-field had been estimated by his opponents as equal to an additional force of 40,000 or even 100,000 men. Never had his personal ascendency been so manifest as when he stood alone and unarmed in the presence of royal brigades sent to arrest his progress. Whole battalions passed over to his side as soon as officers and men caught sight of his familiar face and figure. The Count of Artois fled almost unattended, his whole army serving to swell the triumphal escort of the emperor. The king quitted his capital, and Napoleon, entering the same evening, was reëstablished
March, 1815. in the Tuileries amid the joy and congratulations of all the dignitaries of the Empire. Most of the Bourbons took refuge in England, but Louis XVIII. resided in Belgium during the "Hundred Days" that comprised the brief and eventful second reign of Napoleon.

105. The emperor sought the approval and support of the liberal party by an "Act additional to the Constitutions of the Empire," in which he

granted even greater securities for popular freedom than had been conceded by the charter of 1814. Laboring night and day at the organization of his army, he was surrounded on the 1st of June by a magnificent
array of 367,000 men, including the National Guard. A few weeks more,
he afterward remarked, would have placed around France "a wall of
brass which no earthly power would have been able to break through."
But the Belgian frontier was already threatened by the English and
Prussian armies under Wellington and Blucher. Marching northward
with his usual promptitude, Napoleon attempted to divide his enemies—
himself attacking Blucher, while he ordered Ney to keep the British
engaged and prevent their rendering aid to their allies. Blucher was in
fact driven back from Ligny with tremendous loss; but Ney was at the
same time repulsed from Quatre Bras.

106. The general and decisive conflict took place at Waterloo on the
18th of June. The splendid valor of the French was never more signally
displayed; all depended upon their capture of the two positions of Hou-
goumont and la Haye Sainte, before Blucher, who was contesting with
Grouchy the defile of St. Lambert, could come to the aid of Wellington.
English steadfastness won the day. Late in the afternoon the Prussians
began to arrive; the imperial Guard, the last reserve of Napoleon, was
brought into action, surrounded and overpowered by the British. Seeing
this disaster, the French broke and fled. Napoleon, exclaiming "All is
lost!" commenced his flight toward Paris. Here he signed a second act
of abdication, but proclaimed his son as Emperor of the French. Lafayette, who for a quarter of a century had held himself aloof from public
affairs, was now a member of the legislature and insisted on unconditional abdication. He was also one of an embassy sent to the allied
sovereigns to treat for peace. They refused all negotiations until " Bonaparte " should be placed in their custody as a guarantee against his ever
again disturbing the peace of Europe.

107. On the 6th of July the allies again entered Paris and on the 8th
Louis XVIII. was reinstated. Napoleon designed to take refuge in the
United States, but finding it impossible to elude the vigilance of the
English who blockaded the coast, he resolved to throw himself on their
generosity. In a letter to the Prince Regent (afterward George IV.) he
compared himself to Themistocles seeking the protection of Admetus.
The "first gentleman of Europe" appears at a disadvantage compared
with the Molossian chief. The humiliated emperor was not even permitted to land in England, but after being kept several weeks on board
ship, he was conveyed to the prison rock of St. Helena, where he lingered
out six years of captivity in a noxious climate, and died May 5, 1821.
Twenty years later a more generous spirit animated the British government. The remains of Napoleon were permitted to be conveyed by a

guard of honor to Paris, where they rest under the dome of an institution which his munificence had fostered.

108. The faults and crimes of this remarkable man are too evident to need enumeration. He drained the life-blood of France by reckless conscriptions; he overthrew the liberty of the press and of opinion; he involved his empire in two ruinous wars by a tyrannical commercial policy arising from his resentment against England; he heartlessly pursued his own ends at the expense of the life, liberty, and happiness of others—both individuals and nations. Yet it may be questioned whether he was more selfish, or only more able, than the hereditary sovereigns, into whose feebly ceremonious courts his energetic movements struck terror and confusion. He found Europe encumbered with lifeless forms, the remains of institutions of former ages; his mission seems to have been to clear the ground for new and better growths. If his fall was owing to his errors, his extraordinary success was not less the natural result of profound knowledge, untiring industry, and irresistible will.

Napoleon was the heir of the Revolution, but he knew how to avail himself of its opportunities without sharing its godless and cruel fanaticism. Nor is it just to charge the twenty years' war in which he was the leading actor wholly to his unscrupulous ambition. With the two exceptions of the Peninsular and the Russian war, brought about by his Continental System, the remaining conflicts may be more justly attributed to the allies, especially to Great Britain, who refused all overtures for peace, or violated a treaty as soon as it had been made. It is doubtless true, however, that the Napoleonic style of government could never have long coexisted in peace with the old European system, which the Revolution had overthrown and which the four Great Powers were determined to build up; war may therefore be charged upon their irreconcilable differences of character rather than upon any man's will.

RECAPITULATION.

Enforcement of the Continental System in southern Europe leads to the Peninsular War, in which Portugal and finally Spain become dependencies of Napoleon. Empire of Brazil is founded by the exiled Bragança's. Dissensions between Charles IV. and his son lead to abdication of the Spanish crown, which is conferred upon Joseph Bonaparte, Murat becoming King of the Two Sicilies. Victories of the Spaniards at Valencia and Baylen; defense of Saragossa. Junot defeated in Portugal; Lisbon taken by the English. In the Congress of Erfurt the Czar confirms his alliance with Napoleon. The latter gains victories at Spain and dictates laws at Madrid. Victory and death of Sir John Moore at Corunna. Austria begins a war by invading Bavaria; is many times defeated, but most decisively at Eckmühl, and Vienna is surrendered to Napoleon. Andrew Hofer leads a revolt of the Tyrol against Bavaria; it is subdued by the French. Severe but indecisive battles of Aspern and Essling followed by great victory of Napoleon at Wagram. By peace of Schönbrunn, Austria resigns her Adriatic provinces and her share in the spoils of Poland. Deposition of Pius VII.; annexation of papal states to the French Empire. Marriage of Napoleon with Maria Louisa of Austria. Abdication of King Louis of Holland; annexation of that and other territories to France.

Surrender of Saragossa; victory of Wellington at Talavera; his fortifications at Torres Vedras. Capture of fortresses by Masséna; defeat of the French at Fuentes de Onor and Albuera. In campaign of 1812, Wellington takes Ciudad Rodrigo and Badajoz; gains a great victory at Salamanca; drives the French from Cadiz.

Aggressions of France upon Russia, retaliatory edicts of the Czar and resistance of Sweden to the Continental System, lead to invasion of Russia by Napoleon. Smolensko and other cities burned and abandoned by the Russians. Victory of Napoleon at Borodino; his occupation of Moscow. It is burned, and the French in retreating are overwhelmed with disasters. In campaign of 1813, all Europe forms a Fifth Coalition against Napoleon, who is victorious at Lutzen, Bautzen, and Dresden, but his generals suffer many reverses and he is finally defeated at Leipzig. Loss of dependencies of the Empire. Victory of Wellington in Spain leads to restoration of Ferdinand VII. In 1814, France becomes the field of war. Able but desperate resistance by the emperor. Capitulation of Paris. Napoleon abdicates and retires to Elba. Restoration of Louis XVIII, who grants a charter of liberties. Holland and Belgium united under sovereignty of the Prince of Orange. Return of Napoleon from Elba; flight of the Bourbons; the Hundred Days' reign of Napoleon; his campaign in Belgium; final defeat at Waterloo; second abdication; imprisonment and death on St. Helena.

WAR OF THE UNITED STATES WITH ENGLAND.

109. Though the absorbing interest of the period just narrated centers in the movements of Napoleon, important events had meanwhile occurred west of the Atlantic. The United States had long been justly offended by the maritime policy of Great Britain, whose officers claimed the right to board and search all vessels and impress American seamen into their own service, on the plea that no British subject could ever become an alien. The tendency of Napoleon's Continental System and of the English Orders in Council was to annihilate neutral commerce. The retaliatory acts of Presidents Jefferson and Madison were doubtless more injurious to the United States than to the European powers; but they were part of a series of events which led to a declaration of war against England in June, 1812. The American coast was then almost unfortified, and a navy could scarcely be said to exist; the main action upon the sea was therefore carried on by privateers, which, during the two and a half years of the war, captured more than 1,500 British merchantmen. The details of the conflict must be sought in American history; we have room but for the briefest outline.

110. Repeated attempts to persuade or force the Canadas to throw off their allegiance to Great Britain were unavailing; and in August, 1812, General Hull's surrender of Detroit threw open the whole territory of Michigan to a Canadian and Indian army. During the same summer, however, our infant navy had several victorious encounters with English war-vessels on equal terms, which went far to disprove the boasted supremacy of Great Britain on the sea. The next year Ogdensburgh was taken by the British, but the Americans captured York, the capital of Upper Canada, gained the entire control of Lake Ontario, and drove their opponents from Niagara River. Still more brilliant was the success of

Commodore Perry on Lake Erie. Creating a squadron from the forests on its shores, he conquered the English fleet, and obtained the mastery of the upper lakes. Following up this victory, General Harrison recovered all that General Hull had lost, and imposed peace on the Indians of the North-west.

111. In 1814, decisive victories were gained by the Americans at Chippewa, at Niagara Falls, and at Plattsburg, where battles were fought at the same time on land and on the waters of Lake Champlain. All the cities of the Atlantic coast were meanwhile blockaded by British vessels. A strong force occupied the Chesapeake and levied contributions from the towns upon its shores; while General Ross with 5,000 men marching upon Washington, burned the Capitol, the President's house and other public buildings. An attack upon Baltimore was unsuccessful. The last act of the war was the Battle of New Orleans, in which the American general Jackson gained a decisive victory. But before it was fought, the triumph of the allies in Europe had removed the direct causes of the American war; and soon after the battle, news arrived of a peace concluded at Ghent by the commissioners of Great Britain and the United States. Happily exempted by distance from taking part in European strife, the American Republic enjoyed thirty years of undisturbed tranquillity — a period marked by an unexampled increase of material prosperity and advance in civilization.

112. By the second treaty of Paris, France was reduced to her limits in 1790, and was rendered incapable of again disturbing the peace of Europe, by the quartering of a foreign army of 150,000 men upon her borders. This army was maintained by the conquered people, who were also compelled to pay the allies seven hundred millions of francs toward their expenses in the war, beside a still larger sum for injuries wrought by French troops in other countries. The pictures and statues brought from German and Italian cities for the decoration of Paris, were returned to their rightful owners. A second Congress at Vienna undertook the difficult task of restoring the balance of power so long disturbed by the irresistible ascendency of Napoleon. It was indeed impossible to reëstablish boundaries and political relations as they had been before the revolution; but the sincere desire of the sovereigns for peace, aided by the patient ingenuity of the diplomats, resulted in a new order of things which lasted with little interruption until 1848. To secure the continuance of concord and amity, the Czar persuaded the Austrian and Prussian sovereigns to join him in a Holy Alliance, binding themselves "to remain united in the bonds of true and indissoluble brotherly love; to govern their subjects as parents; to maintain religion, peace, and justice."

113. Thirty-nine sovereigns and cities, with Austria and Prussia at

their head, formed a German Confederation whose capital was Frankfort on the Main. Austria received back her lost provinces and was confirmed in possession of those which she had gained by the treaty of Campo Formio. These were erected into a Lombardo-Venetian kingdom, while Tuscany, Modena, Parma, and Piacenza were secured to younger branches of the Hapsburgs. The empress, Maria Louisa, not choosing to share the exile of her husband, was endowed with the duchies of Parma, Piacenza, and Guastalla. Her son spent most of his short life near the imperial court of Vienna, and died in 1832.

114. Prussia resumed her place among the Five Great Powers, being indemnified for her losses by nearly half the Saxon kingdom, the duchies of Posen, Cleves, and Berg, and the left bank of the Rhine to the Saar. England and Russia emerged from the conflict with a great increase of power and fame. The former, indeed, had nearly quadrupled her national debt, of which the annual interest, now amounting to $140,000,000, involved an inconceivable burden of taxation and misery; but her dominion of the sea, so far as any European rival was concerned, was established beyond dispute. Russia, on the other hand, by wars with Sweden, Turkey, and Persia, had vastly increased her territories on the Baltic, the Danube, and the Caspian; while Poland, reconstituted as a kingdom, was now added to the dominions of the Czar. A subsequent Congress at Aix-la-Chapelle, in providing for the withdrawal of the army of occupation from France, restored that nation to Nov., 1818. her rank among the Five Great Powers. The supremacy of the Five in the States System was more distinctly marked than ever, each being charged with the duty of maintaining the existing balance by war, if diplomacy should fail; while minor powers might indeed protest against any disturbance of the equilibrium, but were not required to arm for its preservation.

115. Hereditary monarchy was restored in all countries of any extent except Switzerland. That confederacy, by the addition of Geneva, Valais, and Neuchâtel, now attained its present number of twenty-two Cantons. Of the five leading nations only England and France possessed representative constitutions; Russia, Austria, and Prussia were governed by the arbitrary will of their sovereigns; and the struggle between absolutism and popular rights occasioned a great intellectual ferment throughout Europe until it resulted in the revolutions of 1848. In France, Talleyrand, the profound and dexterous diplomatist, who had been minister of foreign affairs under four governments, was succeeded, Sept., 1815, by the Duke of Richelieu, a royalist of the most extreme and uncompromising type. The nation seemed to have undergone one of those violent reactions, both religious and political, of which its history affords so many examples. In Nismes, Avignon, and Toulouse the sanguinary scenes of

M. H.—26.

the Revolution were revived in the massacre of Protestants, Republicans, and Bonapartists.

116. The collateral branches of the Bourbons were restored to their thrones in Spain and Italy. Ferdinand VII. reëstablished the Spanish Inquisition and all the suppressed convents. The Spanish colonies in America, encouraged partly by the example of the United States, partly by the absorption of the mother country in the wars of Napoleon and the anarchy which followed his fall, commenced in 1810 a revolution which resulted in the independence of Colombia and the Argentine Republic. Chili, Peru, and Bolivia gained their independence a few years later.* In Mexico the popular chieftain, Iturbide, proclaimed himself Emperor in 1822, but he was dethroned the next year, and the Republic of Mexico was established in alliance with that of Colombia. The exhausted treasury of Spain was taxed with vain attempts to recover these lost provinces; and the unpaid soldiers, uniting with great numbers of discontented citizens, organized a revolution which overthrew the Inquisition and the convents, and restored the liberal constitution of 1812.

Dec., 1819.

117. The Holy Alliance interfered and required the restoration of absolute monarchy. The Cortes refusing, Spain was invaded by a French army of 100,000 men, commanded by the Duke of Angoulême. The Liberals were every-where defeated; the French traversed the peninsula to Cadiz, which was taken by assault; and King Ferdinand VII., who had been detained in captivity by the Cortes, was reëstablished at Madrid in 1823. The French generals exerted their influence in favor of moderation, but their counsels could not abate the revengeful spirit of the king, and despotism in its most odious form was again fastened upon Spain.

118. Portugal, offended by the continued residence of the Regent — now King John VI. — in Brazil, revolted in 1820, and established a government even more liberal than that of the revolutionists in Spain. But the king was the next year driven from Brazil by a revolution, and leaving his eldest son, Pedro, as Regent of that country, returned to Lisbon. His younger son, Miguel, rebelled, both during the life and after the death of John, in 1826, and was even declared King by the Cortes; but he was subdued by an English fleet, and Maria da Gloria, daughter of Pedro of Brazil, reigned undisturbed from 1834 till 1853. Brazil, in

---

* The hero of these revolutions was Simon Bolivar, a Spanish native of Caraccas. While pursuing his studies in Europe, he witnessed the two coronations and part of the extraordinary career of Napoleon. The memoirs of Washington and Franklin excited his emulation; and upon the Sacred Mount at Rome he vowed to become the liberator of his country. He failed to unite all South America in one great Federal Republic, and died — perhaps by poison — in December, 1830, at the age of 47.

1822, constituted itself an independent empire with Pedro I. at its head; and in 1825 it was recognized as such by John VI.

119. In Italy the arbitrary rule of the Hapsburgs and the Neapolitan Bourbons was threatened by several secret political societies, among which the most widely extended was that of the *Carbonari*, numbering half a million of members in Italy alone. Encouraged by the Spanish revolution of 1820, the Carbonari marched upon Naples, and the king, Ferdinand IV., without an effort at resistance, conceded all that they asked— replaced his ministers by liberals and proclaimed the Spanish constitution of 1812. Army, people, court, and July, 1820. even the Crown Prince assumed the colors of the Carbonari. In Sicily a strong party of counter-revolutionists demanded the independence of the island-kingdom. A fierce battle was fought by the two factions, and Palermo, for two days in the hands of the mob, was given up to murder and pillage. It was retaken by the army of the revolutionary government at Naples; but the next year the Carbonari were put down by the intervention of the Holy Alliance and the march of 60,000 Austrians into the Neapolitan territories.

120. A similar insurrection in Piedmont compelled King Victor Emmanuel I. to abdicate in favor of his brother Charles Felix. In Lombardy, the severity of the Austrian police prevented any outbreak of the malcontents; but many popular leaders were imprisoned, among whom Silvio Pellico is best known through his own narrative of his captivity. The same discontents which were produced in Italy by the severity of the Austrian government, were encouraged elsewhere by its weakness. Its treasury was bankrupt, and its debt every year greater, even in time of peace. At the same time, in Hungary and Bohemia, a renewed study of national antiquities and literature intensified the desire for independence. At the crowning of the archduke Ferdinand as King of Hungary in 1830, the Diet made a formal demand for the use of the Magyar language instead of Latin in its debates, and the exclusive appointment of Magyars to command Hungarian regiments. The Diet was consequently dissolved; when it reassembled in 1832, Louis Kossuth was one of its members.

121. In Germany the revolutionary spirit was kept alive only among the youth, and chiefly by students in the universities, whose imaginations, fired by the new romantic school of poetry, impelled them to great deeds for the glory and unity of the Fatherland. A harmless overflow of youthful eloquence and enthusiasm upon the third centennial of the Reformation, which happened also to be the anniversary of the last battle of Leipzig, attracted the attention of the Prussian and Austrian ministers, and thence of the Czar, who, the next year, formally denounced the German Student-society to the congress of sovereigns at Aix-la-Chapelle.

Kotzebue, a celebrated dramatist and Russian Consul-general in Germany, having ridiculed the demonstration through the press, was murdered at Mannheim by a student of Jena in 1819. This crime only confirmed the belief of the German statesmen in the existence of a dangerous conspiracy; and at their congress at Carlsbad, they adopted resolutions limiting the freedom of the Universities, and appointing a commission for discovering and punishing the supposed plotters. The commission spent ten years in its researches and filled the prisons with students, but failed to discover an organization which probably never existed.

122. A few changes among the European sovereigns may here be noted. George III., the aged king of England, had spent the last ten years of his long reign in a melancholy state of blindness, deafness, and almost continual insanity; his son, as Prince Regent, being the recognized head of the government. The latter prince succeeded in 1820 to the title of King George IV. Bernadotte, Crown Prince of Sweden by adoption, had received, two years earlier, the full sovereignty with the name of Charles XIV. Pope Pius VII. ended his troubled and eventful reign in 1823, and was succeeded by Leo XII., whose severe rule repressed for a time the activity of the Carbonari in the States of the Church. The next year Louis XVIII. died at Paris, and his brother the Count of Artois received the crown of the Bourbons. The royal dignity having been so severely shaken by the storms of revolution, the most sacred and imposing of its ancient forms were revived in the new coronation. A drop or two of the holy oil which had served for the consecration of Clovis, was opportunely discovered at Rheims, and Charles X. was seven times anointed with the precious fluid.

123. Unhappily for the well-meaning but narrow-minded prince, no magic could recreate the vanished superstition of his people. Every election returned a still larger majority of liberal deputies. The people were incensed by restrictions upon the freedom of the press; the army was alienated by the dismissal of 150 officers of Napoleon and the disbanding of the National Guard; and finally the appointment in 1829 of an ultra-royalist ministry — with Prince Jules de Polignac at its head, and for war-minister General Bourmont, who had deserted to the allies just before the battle of Waterloo — completed the general discontent. Bourmont's brilliant and permanent conquest of Algiers failed to awaken enthusiasm. The final stroke of misgovernment was dealt in the Ordinances of St. Cloud, which suppressed several liberal journals, limited the right of suffrage, and dissolved the new Chamber of Deputies before it had met. The force commanded by General Marmont was insufficient to suppress the riot which ensued. The National Guard reappeared in uniform with the veteran Lafayette at its head. The tricolor replaced the white flag of the Bourbons on the Hotel de Ville; the streets were bar-

ricaded, and citizens at their own windows took an active part in the combat. Symptoms of disaffection appeared in the army itself, several regiments were removed, and the mob took possession of the Tuileries. The king at St. Cloud too late decided to dismiss the unpopular ministry and revoke the Ordinances. A municipal commission, organized July 31, announced to the royal messenger that the throne had fallen.

124. The Duke of Orleans — head of the younger branch of the House of Bourbon — had lived in retirement since the Restoration, choosing to maintain merely the style of an opulent citizen. His sons — to the great scandal of the king — attended the public colleges. These circumstances enhanced his popularity; he was invited by the peers and deputies to Paris, and many voices already hailed him as the "Citizen King." For a few days Louis Philippe dissembled — accepted at once from the government at St. Cloud and from that at Paris the title of Lieutenant-General of the kingdom, and received from Charles X. his abdication in favor of his grandson the Duke of Bordeaux. A. D. 1830. The Chamber of Deputies, Aug. 3–7, declared the throne vacant by the abdication of the Elder Line of the House of Bourbon, and proceeded to elect Louis Philippe as "King of the French." The new title indicated the fall of absolutism, and the establishment of the opposite principle which makes the will of the people the source of power.

125. Charles X. fled to Rambouillet and thence to Great Britain, where the palace of Holyrood in Edinburgh was assigned for his residence. Before his arrival the crown of England had again been transferred by death, this time to William IV., who succeeded his brother, George IV., in June, 1830. Five years earlier the Czar Alexander had died, and his younger brother, Nicholas, was now Emperor of all the Russias.

126. The French Revolution of 1830 was shortly followed by the independence of Belgium. The people of the southern Netherlands had never been cordial in their obedience to the House of Orange, nor in their union with the Dutch, from whom they differed in religion, language, and customs. A riot broke out in the college at Louvain, and the result of the "July Days" in Paris only encouraged a spirit of insurrection in other Belgian cities. The Dutch troops were every-where expelled; a provisional government was established in Brussels: the House of Orange-Nassau was declared to have forfeited its claims upon Belgium. The Five Great Powers, by their representatives in London, recognized the independence of the southern Dec., 1830. kingdom and arranged the terms of its separation from Holland. The latter retained Luxembourg, but was otherwise confined within its limits in 1790. A Belgian Congress at Brussels (June, 1831) adopted a new constitution and conferred the crown upon Prince Leopold of Saxe Coburg. The siege of Antwerp by a French army compelled the king of Holland to withdraw his forces from the Scheldt, leaving the navigation of that river open to the Belgians.

127. Less fortunate was the revolt of the Poles in Nov., 1830. The harshness of the grand-duke Constantine, viceroy for his brother the Czar, had worn out the patience of the people. They were joined by the Polish regiments in the Russian army; and many princes and magnates took part in the rebellion. Prince Adam Czartoryski, a descendant of the ancient Lithuanian dukes, was to be king of Poland in case of success; and to gain the favor of foreign nations it was resolved to establish a constitutional and hereditary monarchy. The details of the heroic struggle can not here be related. The overwhelming force of the Czar prevailed, and Poland became a mere province of Russia. The university of Warsaw was suppressed; the national archives, libraries, and scientific collections were removed to St. Petersburg; the soldiers were enrolled in Russian regiments. Eighty thousand Poles were in one year exiled to the frozen deserts of Siberia; children were torn from their parents and carried away to military colonies. Religious persecution was added to the pain of national extinction; for the Greco-Russian Church was made preëminent in the conquered country.

128. The two years following the French and Belgian revolutions were marked by fresh efforts and triumphs of the Liberals in Spain, Italy, and Germany, but in no case with any permanent result. Francis I. of the Two Sicilies, who had succeeded his father Ferdinand in 1825, died in 1830, leaving his throne to his son Ferdinand V. of Naples, but II. of Sicily. The crown of Sardinia devolved in 1831 upon Charles Albert, Prince of Carignano, and the same year Pope Pius VIII. was succeeded in the chair of St. Peter by Gregory XVI. The two sons of the ex-king Louis of Holland joined the insurgents in the papal states. The elder of these brothers died during the riots at Forli, leaving the younger, Louis Napoleon, to represent — after the death of the Duke of Reichstadt — the Bonapartist interests in France. He escaped in disguise from Italy and spent the next five years with his mother, Queen Hortense, at her castle in Switzerland. Perceiving the unpopularity of Louis Philippe, he intrigued with the French troops at Strasbourg and suddenly appearing among them in 1836, announced himself their Emperor! The rash attempt only covered him with ridicule. Stripped of his imperial ornaments, he was locked up in the guard-room to await the royal commands. Louis Philippe allowed him to depart unmolested for the United States. Making a similar descent upon Boulogne, four years later, he was captured and imprisoned in the fortress of Ham.

RECAPITULATION.

Conflicting maritime interests lead to War of 1812 between Great Britain and the United States. American naval victories on the Atlantic and the Lakes. Blockade of the coast. Washington burned; Baltimore attacked; New Orleans victoriously defended by General Jackson. Peace of Ghent.

Humiliation of France after the campaign of Waterloo. Balance of power secured by the Holy Alliance. New German Confederacy takes place of the Empire and the Confederation of the Rhine. Addition of territories to Austria and Prussia; aggrandizement of Russia and Great Britain; restoration of France. Absolutism of three of the five "Great Powers." Reënthronement of the Bourbons in Spain and Italy. Independence of all Spanish colonies on the American continent accomplished, A. D. 1810-1821. Insurrections in Spain; absolutism restored by intervention of France. Separation of Portugal from Brazil. Usurpation by Don Miguel; accession of Maria da Gloria. Rule of the *Carbonari* at Naples ended by Austrian interference. Discontent with Austrian supremacy in Italy, Hungary, and Bohemia. Liberalism in German universities. Assassination of Kotzebue. Severity of the Commission of Inquiry.

Accession of Charles XIV. in Sweden; George IV. in England; Pope Leo XII.; and Charles X. in France. Despotic acts of the latter lead to his dethronement in the Three Days' Revolution, 1830; Louis Philippe becomes King of the French; Leopold I. of Belgium; Poland a province of Russia. Revolutions of 1830 usually followed by triumph of absolutism. Vain attempts of Louis Napoleon Bonaparte at Strasbourg and Boulogne; his captivity at Ham.

THE GREEK REVOLUTION.

129. We have reserved for a more connected narrative the twelve years' conflict which resulted in the independence of the Greeks. For nearly four hundred years that brave people had borne the yoke of servitude to a race alien in religion and inferior in civilization to themselves. Turkish officials, hardly less violent and rapacious than the highwaymen whose robberies they permitted and whose spoils they shared, ruled the land. But the Ottoman Empire was apparently tottering to its fall. The Turks in Europe numbered scarcely two millions, while their Christian subjects of various nationalities exceeded eleven millions. If these had been able to combine they might have thrown off the foreign dominion; but differences of race and language prevented a concentration of their forces. Of the four distinct races inhabiting Turkey in Europe, the Sclavonians of Bulgaria, Servia, Bosnia, the Herzegovina, and Montenegro were by far the most numerous. The Roumanians of Moldavia and Wallachia numbered four millions; the Albanians, inhabiting ancient Epirus, only a million and a half. It was reserved for the Greeks, the least numerous of all, first to achieve their independence.

130. Zeal for their Church had done much to preserve the separate nationality of the Greeks. The Mainotes of the Peloponnesus, and the mountaineers of the Thessalian border had never submitted to the Turks, but continued to bear arms in their own defense. Beside these, multitudes of the more adventurous had betaken themselves to a wild sort of outlawry, and under the name of Klephts or Robbers, waged a predatory warfare upon the Turkish villages, easily escaping to their eyries among the mountains whenever they were pursued. The close of the eighteenth century was marked by a great revival of Hellenic genius. The fires of patriotism were rekindled in every Greek heart by increased acquaintance with the history of the ancient heroes; and a secret society, called the Heteria, united all Hellenes, however separated by distance, in a resolution to strike off the hated yoke of the oppressor. Catherine II. had availed herself of the dawn of this enthusiasm in order to further her own plans against the Porte; but when at her call the whole Hellenic race had sprung to arms for the recovery of their liberty, the crafty empress abandoned them to the vengeance of the Turks, and the sedition was quenched in blood. Alexander I., in his zeal for the restoration of absolutism, had no sympathy to spare to oppressed members of his own Church. The Holy Alliance in its successive congresses at Laybach and Verona condemned all revolutionary movements, alike in Greece, Italy, and Spain, and uttered the cruel command, " Let the Greek rebels obey their lawful sovereign." * The beginning of the struggle was therefore left to the unaided valor of the oppressed people.

131. The first blow was struck by Prince Alexander Ypsilanti, leader of the Heteria, who in March, 1821, proclaimed that all the Greeks renounced their allegiance to the Turks. The people of the peninsula and the islands sprang to arms at his call. But the first movements were disastrous. The news of the revolt was followed in Constantinople by a general massacre of the Greek inhabitants of the capital. The venerable patriarch Gregorios, with three bishops and eight priests, was hanged in his robes before the gate of the church in which he had just been officiating. The Sacred Band — a regiment of students who bore upon their shields the Spartan motto, " Either this or on this"— lost four hundred of its members at the fatal battle of Dragaschan, June 19, 1821. About the same time a small number of Klephts withstood an overwhelming Turkish force near Thermopylæ. All but eighteen at length perceived the hopelessness of the contest and retired to their mountains; but this handful stood their ground, killing many times their own number, until all were either killed or taken. Several towns in southern Greece were besieged and taken by the insurgents, the most important being Tripolitza, the Turkish capital of Morea.

132. In January, 1822, the first national congress of new Hellas proclaimed at Epidaurus the national independence, and adopted a provis-

---

* " As if," says Prof. Felton, " at any moment of the four centuries of their enslavement there was a single element of legal sovereignty in the oppressive rule of the Turks; a single moment when the Christian victims had not a right to use every means within their reach to reclaim the freedom theirs by inheritance and ravished from them by overpowering wrong."

ional constitution. Alexander Mavrocordatos was the first president. In the following spring Scio became the chief object of the vengeance of the Turks. To avenge an insurrection, men, women, and children were subjected to indiscriminate massacre. More than 40,000 perished; thousands of the most accomplished were carried away to the slave-markets of Smyrna and Constantinople. The grief and indignation of the Greeks soon found vent in action; in an encounter with their fire-ships the author of the massacre and 2,000 of his followers were slain.

The next year was signalized by the gallant attack of Marco Bozzaris and his Suliote band upon a Turkish camp. Bozzaris fell, but the fame of his valor contributed greatly to awaken sympathy in Europe and America. Though governments were still indifferent, and those embraced in the Holy Alliance even expelled the wretched Greek fugitives from their borders, the people sent supplies of money, arms, and men to aid in the combat for freedom. Classical enthusiasm quickened the zeal of the educated classes; and so, at last, the ancient orators achieved against the Moslem what they had in vain attempted against the Macedonian tyrant. Foremost of the *Philhellenes* was Lord Byron, who resolved to devote his fortune and talents to a great cause. His death at Missolonghi, April, 1824, filled all Greece with sorrow.

133. The Sultan, unable to reduce the Greeks with his own forces, called in Mehemet Ali, the almost independent Viceroy of Egypt, whom he won to his service by an offer of making Mehemet's step-son, Ibrahim, Pacha of the Morea. That peninsula became the scene of a frightful series of ravages; men were slaughtered, women and children sent as slaves to Egypt. Missolonghi was besieged five months and taken in spite of its heroic defense. The next year Athens fell, and hope seemed to expire. But changes had meanwhile occurred in several European courts. The Holy Alliance had been shaken by the death of Alexander I.; his brother Nicholas was more zealous in protecting his co-religionists, and perhaps more ambitious of conquest from the Turks. France and England, alarmed by the aggrandizement of the able and ambitious Mehemet, joined with Russia in a plan for intervention. July, 1827. The Sultan refused even to receive their communication, and the three powers immediately increased and combined their naval forces in the Mediterranean. On the 20th of October the allied fleet encountered that of the Turks and Egyptians in the Bay of Navarino, and after a severe engagement of four hours, won a decisive victory.

This timely and unexpected aid revived the spirit of the Greeks. Their newly elected president, Capo d'Istrias, was now on a visit to the capitals of the three allies, where he was able to negotiate a loan which relieved the most urgent necessities of his government. The next year the Czar declared war against the Sultan, and his invasion of the provinces on the Danube forced that sovereign to accept terms of accommodation, and by the treaty of Adrianople to acknowledge the independence of the Greeks.

134. To secure the permanency of a deliverance so hardly won, it was resolved to give Greece a ruler from one of the reigning families of Europe. Among many candidates, the choice fell at last upon Otho, second son of the king of Bavaria, who was welcomed at Nauplia, Feb., 1833, by the joyful acclamations of the people. Two years later the seat of government was fixed at Athens. The purpose of the allies had doubtless been to invest Otho with an arbitrary sovereignty; but in 1843 a peaceful revolution resulted in the convoking of a representative assembly to which the king conceded its just share in the government. In 1863, the Bavarian dynasty was expelled and Prince George of Denmark became King of Hellas. The next year Great Britain abandoned her fifty years' protectorate — which had really amounted to a sovereignty — of the Ionian Islands, and they were added to the dominion of Greece.

135. Mehemet Ali had been rewarded for his services in the Greek revolution by the sovereignty of Crete. His ambition still unsatisfied, he sent his son Ibrahim, in 1831, to attempt the conquest of Syria. The rapid progress of the invader alarmed the Sultan Mahmoud, who hastened to ally himself with Russia, and subsequently with England and France. His forces were defeated, 1839, at Nisibis on the Euphrates, and a few days later the Sultan died. His son and successor, Abdul Medjid, was but seventeen years of age; and the French government desired to place upon the throne the more able and experienced Mehemet, or at least to make him the independent sovereign of Syria and Egypt. England united with Russia, Austria, and Prussia to oppose this arrangement. The allied forces defeated Ibrahim at Kaleb Medina, and captured Acre for the Turks. By the Treaty of London, 1840, Crete and Syria were restored to the Porte; and English influence, ably represented by Sir Stratford Canning — afterward Lord Stratford de Redcliffe — for many years controlled the counsels of the Sultan.

136. Meanwhile important revolutions were preparing in western Europe. Louis Philippe had a difficult if not an impossible part to play. Legitimists denounced him as a usurper, Republicans as a tyrant, Bonapartists as ruling in defiance of the will of the people. But his prudent management, strengthened by close alliances with England, Spain, and Portugal, secured several years of peace and prosperity. The responsibility of ministers for all the acts of the government, and the ultimate supremacy of the people as represented in parliament, were as firmly established in France as in England. The attempt of the Duchess of Berri to excite rebellions in the western provinces in favor of her son rather increased than diminished the popularity of the king. M. Theirs, at the head of the ministry, managed to absorb the attention of the dangerous classes in the pursuit of glory abroad, by making war against the wandering Kabyles who still claimed the interior of Algeria. The severest shock that the new dynasty had yet sustained was the death of the king's eldest son, the Duke of Orleans. The next heir was less than four years old, and the prospect of a long minority in the present unsettled state of affairs was disastrous. The intervention of the king in Spanish affairs added the displeasure of foreign courts to the discontent of his own people.

137. Ferdinand VII. had died in 1833, leaving two little daughters, the eldest of whom was scarcely three years of age. By a Pragmatic Sanction in 1830, he had annulled the law which excluded women from the throne of Spain; but during the mental feebleness which attended his last days, his brother Don Carlos had either forged or extorted from him a revocation of that Sanction, and proceeded, upon Ferdinand's death, to assert his own claim to the crown. Spain was thus divided between two parties, the Carlists or "serviles," and the Christinos or liberals, who supported the regency of the queen-mother, Christina of Naples. England and France favored the Pragmatic Sanction, while the northern powers with the Pope refused to recognize it. The Christinos ultimately prevailed, and the young queen, Isabella II., was duly acknowledged. Don Carlos, however, maintained for six years a formidable force of adherents, and in 1837 even attempted the capture of Madrid. He was defeated by the queen's general, Espartero; and in 1840 the Carlists in the Biscayan provinces were wholly suppressed.

138. The destiny of Spain seemed to hang upon the marriage of the queen. Her union with the Count of Montemolin, the son and heir of Don Carlos, would have united all claims to the crown and restored peace to the country; but France and England opposed the alliance. Louis Philippe desired to strengthen his dynasty by a connection with that of Spain. He selected for the husband of Isabella, her cousin, the half-idiotic Francisco of Assis, while he married his son, the Duke of Montpensier, to her sister Maria Louisa, who from her more robust health had every prospect of outliving the queen. This deeply laid scheme did not however confirm the power of the French king, but rather undermined it, by alienating the confidence of his allies.

139. The scarcity of the years 1846 and 1847 aggravated the uneasiness in France. The Liberal party began to make its power felt in reform banquets, at one of which near Paris in 1847, the king's health was omitted, but the "sovereignty of the people" was received with shouts of applause. Guizot, who had long before succeeded Thiers at the head of the ministry, represented high monarchical principles; and Thiers, by way of political opposition, encouraged the popular discontent. A grand

reform banquet had been announced for Feb. 22, 1848; and it was expected that 100,000 people would be present in the Champs Elysées. The government prepared to prevent the meeting by force; the guns of the forts were pointed inward upon the city; and an army of nearly 60,000 men was massed in the neighborhood. A mob now appeared in the streets, composed of those squalid, hideous, half-human inhabitants of the Parisian cellars, who are never seen except in times of revolution, and then constitute its worst elements. They erected barricades, and uttered the cry, terrible in the ears of despots, and unheard for forty-four years in France, "Long live the *Republic!*"

140. The king and his sons escaped from Paris and found a refuge in England. The widowed Duchess of Orleans, leading her little son, the heir to the crown, presented herself calm and undaunted before the tumultuous assembly of the two Chambers. She reminded the deputies of her husband, whom all men had trusted, and promised that her son should fulfill the promises which his grandfather had broken. A voice from the tribune declared as in the case of Charles X., "It is too late,"

Feb., 1848.

and a Republic was proclaimed. A provisional government was formed, consisting of Lamartine, Dupont de l'Eure, Arago, Ledru-Rollin, Marie, Garnier-Pagés, and Crémieux. The eloquence of Lamartine was exerted with marked effect in the preservation of order. The mob, however, took possession of the Tuileries, made a bonfire of the throne, planted "trees of Liberty" in all public places, and clamored for a Red Republic under Ledru-Rollin. But the better class of the people, instructed by experience, firmly opposed these irregularities; 100,000 National Guards declared for the provisional government, and shouted, "Down with Communism!" Some of the most violent Socialists were sentenced to exile or imprisonment.

141. Among the first and least considerate acts of the provisional government had been the establishment of national workshops, where all who applied found employment and wages. Private manufactures were ruined; for the state, supported by taxation, could easily outbid the wages which they were able to pay; and the public workmen, soon numbering 100,000, became a dangerous political institution. The attempt to abate this peril by dismissing a great number of men, led to a terrible four days' battle in the streets of Paris. General Cavaignac was appointed Dictator with unlimited powers; but as soon as order was restored by a victory of the National Guards, he resigned that office and was named President of the Council. For the new Assembly, Louis Napoleon Bonaparte — who had escaped in 1846 from his imprisonment at Ham — was elected as a member from Paris as well as from four provincial departments. The new constitution requiring a President chosen for a term of four years, he received an overwhelming majority

of votes. He took the prescribed oaths, Dec. 20, 1848, and the Provisional Government was superseded by the Second French Republic.

142. Before describing the revolutions of 1848 in other countries of Europe, we briefly state the changes of sovereigns during the preceding twelve years. William IV. died at London, 1837, and the crown of the United Kingdom devolved upon Victoria, daughter of his brother, the Duke of Kent. That of Hanover being limited to the male line, descended to a younger brother, the Duke of Cumberland.* Frederic William III. of Prussia closed his long and humiliating reign in 1840. His son, Frederic William IV., summoned a Diet, and made some other concessions to the demands of his people. In Sweden the beneficent rule of Charles XIV. (Bernadotte) was followed by the accession of his son Oscar in 1844. Pope Gregory XVI. died, 1846, and Cardinal Mastai Ferretti, having received the votes of the conclave, assumed the tiara with the name of Pius IX.

143. The "Schleswig-Holstein question" already began to agitate the northern countries. If the only son of Christian VIII. of Denmark should die without heirs, the crown of that kingdom would devolve upon the dowager-landgravine of Hesse. The two duchies, however, by their ancient constitutions, could not be inherited by a woman; and a strong German party claimed them for Duke Christian of Augustenburg, head of a collateral branch of the Danish house. Holstein was a member of the German Confederation, and its affairs were therefore within the jurisdiction of the Diet at Frankfort. Schleswig, on the contrary, had belonged, more than eight hundred years, to Denmark, but the desire of a great proportion of its people for union with Holstein and admission into the Confederacy, awakened a strong interest in Germany. King Christian opposed the German party by issuing letters-patent extending the Danish law of female succession to his ducal dominions. His death, Jan., 1848, was shortly followed by a revolt of the two duchies, aided by Prussia and Hanover with the approval of the Frankfort Diet.

144. The news of the events at Paris set all Europe in a blaze. The long smoldering conflict between absolute and popular principles of government became open and violent. All the races subject to Austria—Magyar, Slavonian, and Italian—rose in revolt, and the emperor was forced to yield the general demand by dismissing Prince Metternich and granting a free press, a national guard, and liberal constitutions to the several members of the empire. Similar insurrections in Prussia, Hanover, Saxony, Wirtemberg and several smaller states were met by similar con-

---

*This king, Ernest Augustus, was one of the most extreme of absolutists. On his arrival in Hanover he refused to receive the congratulations of the Chamber of Deputies, annulled the representative constitution, and ejected some of the best professors in the University of Göttingen for their liberal opinions.

cessions. King Louis of Bavaria, who in many ways had forfeited the confidence of his subjects, resigned the crown to his son Maximilian II. A party in Baden and other states, aided by "free bands" in Switzerland, desired a Republic. Switzerland herself had lately passed through a crisis of opposition between the Jesuit or reactionary party and the Liberals. Seven Catholic cantons formed a separate League and appealed to arms, but they were defeated by a Federal force under General Dufour; and ultimately the Jesuits were expelled, the convents broken up and the "Sonderbund" dissolved. Warned by this peril, the Swiss increased the strength of their federal government by adopting a new constitution, modeled, with slight variations, upon that of the United States.

A. D. 1846.

145. In Germany the Republican project made little impression. A National Parliament at Frankfort, after declaring the "fundamental rights of the German people," resolved to reünite the several states under an imperial head, and ultimately offered the sovereignty to the king of Prussia. Events had long been pointing toward Prussian leadership in German affairs, since in 1819 a *Zollverein* or Customs-union, founded by Frederic William III., had begun to combine the commercial relations of the different states in a uniform system. In spite of the urgent request of the Prussian Estates, Frederic William IV. refused the imperial crown, and the consummation, then doubtless desired by a majority of the German people, was delayed nearly a quarter of a century. Willing, however, to make his power felt, the king not only renewed his war against Denmark, interrupted a few months by the truce of Malmö, but sent armies to put down democratic risings in Saxony, Baden, and Wirtemberg. He proposed also to satisfy the demand for German unity by a new imperial constitution similar to that of Frankfort, but placing the three kings of Prussia, Hanover, and Saxony at its head. The last two sovereigns, however, soon departed from the agreement, and the bond of union among the German states remained for some years slighter than ever. The Schleswig-Holstein question — after several battles and sieges which we have not room to recount — was at least temporarily disposed of by a marriage of Prince Christian of Schleswig-Holstein-Glucksburg with a Princess of Hesse, and a treaty signed at London, in 1852, by most of the great powers of Europe providing for the union of the whole Danish dominion in their family.

April, 1849.

146. The power of the Hapsburgs had meanwhile been shaken to its foundations. In March, 1848, a Hungarian deputation with Kossuth at their head arrived at Vienna, bearing a demand for the complete separation of their country from Austria in all matters of war, finances, and foreign relations, not less than in the ministry and Diet which were already distinct. This was a movement of the Magyars — the dominant

race in Hungary—and it aroused the jealousy of the Croats and Slavonians, who were already offended by the use of the Magyar language in
the Diet and courts of law. Jellachich, Ban of Croatia, raised an army
in support of the imperial government. The democrats of Vienna, on
the contrary, took part with the Magyars, and prevented the march of
an imperial army into Hungary. Latour, the war-minister, was beaten
to death by the mob, and the emperor fled into Moravia,
leaving his capital in their hands. It was besieged three   Oct., 1848.
weeks and at length taken by storm, by the imperial army, reinforced
by Jellachich and his Croats. Meanwhile the archduke Stephen had resigned his office as Palatine of Hungary, and Count Lemberg, who was
sent by the emperor to dissolve the Diet was assassinated on the bridge
of Pesth. Kossuth, as President of the Committee of National Defense,
became leader of the Revolution.

147. The timid and vacillating Ferdinand I. resigned the imperial
crown, Dec. 2., in favor of his nephew, Francis Joseph. The first care
of the new emperor was the reduction of Hungary, which he committed
to Prince Windischgrätz, the captor of Vienna. At his approach, Kossuth abandoned Pesth, carrying with him the crown of St. Stephen, and
tried, by retreating, to draw the Austrians after him into the interior of
the country. Many Poles threw themselves with zeal into the Hungarian
cause, and the Czar Nicholas offered his aid to Francis Joseph, fearing
lest the success of the rebels should lead to a similar effort in his own
lately subjugated province. The Austrians were nevertheless defeated at
Waitzen and Gran, and encountered every-where a spirited and able resistance. The court at Vienna decreed the extinction of Hungarian
nationality; the Diet at Debreczin retorted by deposing the House of
Hapsburg-Lorraine, and proclaiming a Republic with Kossuth at its head.
An overwhelming force was now concentrated from the north, west, and
south upon Hungary. Windischgrätz was superseded by the brutal field-
marshal Haynau, who had lately ended the insurrection in Lombardy.
His victory at Temesvar crushed the hopes of the patriots; Kossuth resigned his office, and Gorgei was made Dictator. The military genius of
Gorgei had been proved on many a battle-field; but he was probably a
traitor at heart—within two days of his appointment he
delivered up his army and artillery to the Russians. All   Aug., 1849.
was lost. Kossuth with a few followers found refuge with the Turks;
and the Sultan refused all the demands of Russia and Austria for their
surrender.

148. Italy, meanwhile, had her full share of revolutions. A secret
league, called Young Italy, organized by Mazzini, had for its object the
expulsion of all foreign rulers from the peninsula. The liberal measures
adopted by Pope Pius IX. at his accession, led to the hope that like

Julius II., though in a happier spirit, he would become the champion of the unity and independence of Italy; and a step in this direction seemed actually to have been taken by the formation of a Customs-union between Sardinia, Tuscany, and the States of the Church. In almost all the Italian states, as in Germany, representative constitutions were granted, after more or less resistance, to the demands of the people. The Sicilians elected the Duke of Genoa to be their king, and for more than a year maintained a war for independence against the odious government of Ferdinand V. of Naples.

149. In Austrian Italy, the archduke Rainer was viceroy, and Marshal Radetzki, a veteran of eighty-two years, commanded the armies. In March, 1848, an insurrection broke out in Milan; barricades were erected, and a four days' fight resulted in the defeat of the Austrians. Charles Albert of Sardinia marched with his whole army to the aid of the insurgents, occupied Milan, and pursued Radetzki to a strong position between the Mincio and the Adige, where he waited, hoping that the sovereignty of upper Italy might fall into his hands without a blow. The Austrian garrisons of Brescia and several important places surrendered to the insurgents; Venice expelled her foreign rulers and proclaimed a restoration of the Republic. In June and July, both Lombardy and Venice declared themselves annexed to Sardinia. Meanwhile Radetzki, being reinforced, was able to resume the offensive. After a victory at Custozza he recovered Milan; and in spite of the brave resistance of Garibaldi and his volunteers, all Lombardy submitted before the middle of August to the Austrian rule. Venice was only reduced by a severe and disastrous siege of more than a year, during which the Austrians lost 20,000 men chiefly by the fevers occasioned by the malaria of the marshes. Aug. 22., 1849.

A. D. 1848.

150. In the spring of 1849, Radetzki invaded Sardinia, and gained so signal a victory at Novara, that Charles Albert in despair resigned his crown to his son Victor Emmanuel II., who immediately made a truce with the Austrians. The liberal dispositions of the Pope, meanwhile, were far outrun by the demands of the people. The latter clamored for a declaration of war against Austria, in the interest of the Lombard insurgents. Attempting to conciliate all sides, Pius was suspected of favoring the foreign tyrants. His minister, Count Rossi, was murdered; and he himself was attacked in his palace on the Quirinal, which was taken by storm, but not until the Pope had escaped in a servant's livery and found refuge at Gaëta. Garibaldi entered Rome with an army of Italian volunteers; a general Constituent Assembly was opened, whose first act was to depose the Pope and proclaim a Roman Republic. The chief mover was Mazzini, who with Armellini and Saffi constituted the executive power of the new Republic. Prince

Feb., 1849.

Charles of Canino, a son of Lucien Bonaparte, was another of the leaders, but his cousin, the French president, disavowed his proceedings, and sent an army to the aid of the Pope. Marshal Oudinot was defeated by Garibaldi before the walls of Rome, but he gained time by negotiations until reinforcements could arrive, and the city was taken, July 3, 1849. Mazzini and Garibaldi escaped, and a government was reëstablished in the name of the Pope, who, however, chose to remain at Gaëta until April, 1850, rather than occupy his capital under foreign protection.

RECAPITULATION.

During 350 years of Turkish rule, bands of Greek mountaineers and Klephts maintained a partial independence. Society of Hetæria (founded before 1798, revived, 1816) concerts plans of revolt. Hostility of the Holy Alliance. Proclamation by Ypsilanti; massacre of Greeks at Constantinople; destruction of sacred Band at Dragaschan; bravery of Klephts at Thermopylæ. Congress at Epidaurus adopts provisional government. Massacre at Scio. Death of Marco Bozzaris. Arrival of Byron and other *Philhellenes.* Invasion of Morea by Mehemet Ali; capture of Missolonghi and Athens. Victory of English, French, and Russian fleets at Navarino. Invasion of Turkey by the Czar. Treaty of Adrianople recognizes the independence of the Greeks. Otho of Bavaria reigns thirty years as King of Hellas, and is superseded by George of Denmark. Conquest of Syria by Ibrahim Pacha calls for interference of the western powers. Treaty of London restores Crete and Syria to Turkey. English influence predominant at Constantinople.

Embarrassments of Louis Philippe. Death of the Duke of Orleans. Intervention in domestic affairs of Spain, where Carlists and Christines dispute the crown after the death of Ferdinand VII. Reform banquets threaten the French government. Guizot at head of the ultra-royalist, Thiers of the moderate or constitutional party. Military interference occasions the outbreak of revolution. The royal family escape. Provisional government declared. National workshops opened. Attempt to control them leads to riot, during which Cavaignac is Dictator. Louis Napoleon Bonaparte becomes President.

Accessions of Victoria in England, Ernest Augustus in Hanover, Frederic William IV. in Prussia, Oscar in Sweden, Frederic VII. in Denmark. Revolt of Schleswig-Holstein with the aid of the Germans. Revolutions of 1848 extend to Prussia, Austria, Hungary, Switzerland and all the German and Italian states. King of Prussia refuses the imperial crown. Croats and Slavonians of Hungary fight against the Magyars, while revolutionists in Austria take their part. Flight of the emperor, assassination of Latour at Vienna and of Lemberg at Pesth. Siege and storm of Vienna by imperial army. Abdication of Ferdinand I., accession of Francis Joseph. Hungarian Republic proclaimed; Kossuth governor. Russians invade Hungary; Haynau in command of the Austrians gains a victory at Temesvar; Görgei, Dictator, betrays his trust. Kossuth is a fugitive and the revolution is ended.

"Young Italy" seeks deliverance from foreign rule. Customs-union between Rome, Sardinia, and Tuscany. King of Sardinia aids Lombardy and Venice in their revolt against Austria. Victory of Radetzki at Custozza; submission of Lombardy; siege and surrender of Venice. Charles Albert of Sardinia, defeated at Novara, abdicates in favor of Victor Emmanuel II. Murder of Count Rossi, capture of the Quirinal palace and flight of the Pope. Roman Republic proclaimed by Mazzini and Garibaldi. Rome retaken by the French army and the Pope reinstated.

THE SECOND FRENCH EMPIRE.

151. France, warned by her bitter experience of revolutions, looked with dread to the new election which the constitution had appointed for

M. H.—27.

the spring of 1852, and the more because the law as it stood forbade the reëlection of the present ruler. Few men ever less resembled the first Napoleon than his nephew and representative. Yet the accident of his birth — or rather, perhaps, the death of his cousin, the king of Rome — made him a political adventurer, and engaged him in the enterprise of reviving the empire of the Bonapartes. Bolder in scheming than in action, his habits were those of a studious recluse, rather than of a leader of men; and the attempts at Strasbourg and Boulogne had proved him more capable of conceiving perilous enterprises than of carrying them into execution. Long years of study during his imprisonment and exile had made him proficient in theories of state-craft and of national defense; his state papers during his presidency had been marked by profound ability. He would perhaps have been considered rather the secretary than the author of the *coup d'état*, had it not ended by placing a crown upon his head.

152. Though many men of high character and illustrious rank would willingly have consented to a renewal or prolongation of the president's term of office, none would connive at any illegal act to secure that end. Therefore during the autumn of 1851, several offices in the government, the army, and the National Guard were filled by persons of doubtful or discreditable history, but who were wholly subservient to the will of Bonaparte. Chief of these were the Count de Morny, General St. Arnaud, who was made minister of war, Maupas, prefect of police, and Magnan, commandant of the army about Paris. Two adventurers, named Fleury and Persigny — men who had all to gain and nothing to lose — had important though less conspicuous parts. On Monday evening, Dec. 1, the president held his usual reception at the palace of the Elysée. When the guests had retired, Morny, Maupas, and St. Arnaud remained for a final consultation. Other members of the plot were already in action. In the darkness and silence of the night, seventy-eight persons including the principal generals and statesmen of France, were seized at their own houses and carried away to prison. A great military force was massed between the Elysée and the Tuileries. Offices of newspapers were occupied by soldiers. At the government printing-house, the printers, under a strong guard of police, set up the proclamations which were to be distributed before daylight.

153. When morning dawned, the walls were found covered with the announcements: "The National Assembly is dissolved; universal suffrage is reëstablished; the elective colleges are summoned to meet Dec. 21. Paris is in a state of siege." These were followed by an address to the people, proposing a responsible chief for ten years; and to the soldiers, reminding them of the neglect they had suffered under Louis Philippe, and promising a renewal of their ancient glory. At the same hour, in

the remotest provinces, the telegraph announced a revolution accomplished at Paris, and described the joy of that sleeping city in a change of which it had not even dreamed. The Deputies, meeting on the morning of Dec. 2, resolved that the President had forfeited his office by illegal acts of violence. They were arrested A. D. 1851. to the number of 235, and conveyed in felons' carts to various prisons. The Supreme Court, having likewise ordered the impeachment of the President, was expelled by an armed force. The resistance, however, was feeble, for to the prosperous classes any rule was better than anarchy. Victor Hugo and a few other deputies who had escaped arrest, organized a committee and erected a barricade. On Dec. 4, an army of 48,000 men was converged upon the city. A multitude of peaceful spectators regarded the parade from windows and sidewalks, when suddenly, without provocation, the troops began firing into the crowd. Thousands must have fallen. This wanton massacre arose probably from a panic among the troops, aggravated by their enmity to the citizens, and may have formed no part of the general plan; but for the deliberate murder of many hundreds in prison — the transportation of 26,560 to the noxious climates of Cayenne and the African coast, the President and his advisers can not so easily be excused.

154. By the subsequent election, Prince Louis Napoleon Bonaparte was invested with the entire executive power for ten years. The generals and deputies were now released from imprisonment, but Changarnier, Victor Hugo and several others were permanently banished. In a tour through France in the year 1852, the President was every-where greeted with cries of " *Vive l'Empereur!* " Returning to Paris, he directed the Senate to debate the question of a change of government, and submit their decision to the sanction of the people. As before, the masses voted under dictation; scarcely a show of opposition appeared; and the President became "Napoleon III., by the grace of God, and by the will of the people, Emperor of the French." Dec. 2, 1852.

155. The first great event under the second Empire was the war in the Crimea against the Czar. Napoleon felt it necessary to redeem his promise to the soldiers, and at the same time to absorb and gratify the nation by the indulgence of its passion for military glory. Nothing could so conduce to the security of his throne as a close alliance with England, and this he gained by adopting the English policy, usually different from that of France, concerning the Eastern Question. The Turks had a prophecy that their empire in Europe would be overthrown just four hundred years from its establishment. Early in 1853 — the year of prophecy — the Czar made secret proposals to the English government to join him in the partition of the spoils of the "sick man of Europe." These overtures were firmly rejected; and England drew closer her relations with the other great powers, but especially with France, in order to resist any aggression on the part of Russia.

156. Nicholas, having mustered a great fleet and army at Sevastopol, sent Prince Mentschikoff to Constantinople with a peremptory message demanding not only increased control of the holy places of Syria and Palestine, but a protectorate, which would really have involved a sovereignty, over the ten or twelve millions of Russo-Greek Christians inhabiting the Turkish provinces. The insulting manner in which the demand was urged made it seem only a pretext for war, and a few weeks later the armies of the Czar occupied Moldavia and Wallachia by way of "material guarantee." A moving cause of hostilities on the part of Nicholas was his personal resentment against Lord Stratford de Redcliffe, whom he called the "English Sultan," and whose ascendency in the counsels of the Porte was continually thwarting the movements of the Russian embassadors. The firmness of Lord Stratford—added to his power to summon a British fleet from Malta—was of great service in allaying a panic at Constantinople, and encouraging the Turkish ministers to persist in their opposition to the unreasonable demands of the Czar; while a Congress at Vienna of Austrian, Prussian, French, and English embassadors sought to settle the differences between Russia and the Porte by negotiation and thus maintain peace.

157. Their efforts were in vain. In October, 1853, the Sultan declared war; his general, Omar Pasha, promptly crossing the Danube, gained at Oltenitza a victory over the invaders; and in January a four days' assault upon the Turkish lines at Kalafat was followed by a retreat of the Russians. Before this (Nov. 30) a fleet issuing from Sevastopol had destroyed a Turkish squadron in the harbor of Sinope and bombarded the town. Four thousand Turks were slain. The Czar refused even to answer a note addressed to him by the governments at London and Paris, requiring his withdrawal from the Danubian provinces, and stating that his refusal or silence would be considered as cause of war. All

March, 1854. hope of peace being thus at an end, France and England concluded a close alliance with each other and with Turkey, and declared war against Russia. A counter-declaration was made by the Czar, April 11, and Prince Paskiewitch with a great force laid siege to Silistria. Contrary to all expectation, the Turks resisted with such spirit and success that the siege was raised in little more than a month. Another defeat at Giurgevo caused the Russians to abandon the lower Danube and even Moldavia and Wallachia.

158. The special cause of war being thus removed, France and England might have ended the contest, but they resolved, on the contrary, to deprive the Czar of the means for future aggressions by destroying the forts which guarded the harbor and immense military magazines of

Sevastopol. The allied armies were therefore conveyed by sea to the Crimea. The Tartar inhabitants of the country, though professing themselves contented with the Russian rule, betrayed no hostility toward their fellow-Mohammedans or their allies, but readily brought supplies of food, and sold their beasts of burden for the use of the armies. On the 20th of September the strong positions of Prince Mentschikoff on the heights above the Alma were stormed and taken. Then pressing on, the land forces, in concert with the fleet which had followed their movements, occupied the port of Balaklava and proceeded to lay siege to Sevastopol. The defenses of the town, planned and vigorously executed by Colonel Todleben, resisted all assaults for nearly a year.

159. The battle of Balaklava (Oct. 25) is chiefly memorable for the gallant but desperate charge of a cavalry brigade, in obedience to a mistaken order, down a long valley swept from either side and from the end by the enemies' guns; and which resulted in a sacrifice of more than two-thirds of the men. The victory was claimed by the Russians; it revived the courage of their comrades within the walls of Sevastopol, and doubtless prolonged their resistance. At Inkermann, however, a very superior Russian force attacking the British lines was repulsed. The armies of the allies suffered far more from disease than from battle; and the hardships of the British troops were aggravated by the mismanagement of their commissariat—men dying from hunger, sickness, and cold within a few miles of plentiful supplies of clothing, medicines, and stores. Indignation at this state of things led in England to the fall of Lord Aberdeen's ministry, and Lord Palmerston became the responsible head of the government. Meanwhile the misery of the army threw into stronger light the merciful ministrations of Florence Nightingale, an English lady, who, having subjected herself to thorough training in the duties of a nurse, devoted her untiring energies—together with a band of voluntary subordinates—to alleviating the sufferings which she could not prevent.

160. English and French fleets penetrated the Baltic and Polar Seas, but accomplished little beyond the burning of timber and naval stores. During the winter of 1854 and '55 the allies were joined by Austria and Sardinia, and the latter sent a well appointed army of 15,000 men to the Crimea. The sudden death of the Czar, and the accession of his son Alexander II., renewed the hope of peace. The allied nations, however, considered their honor engaged to the capture of Sevastopol, which still repulsed the most resolute assaults. A British fleet entered the Sea of Azov, captured Kertch and Yenikale, and destroyed great quantities of stores and provisions. At length the forts at Sevastopol were reduced almost to heaps of rubbish by a bombardment which lasted from August 16 to September 8. The French succeeded in taking the

Malakoff by assault; the English were less fortunate in their storm of the Redan; but the city being no longer tenable, Prince Gortchakoff retired to the north forts, and destroyed all the shipping in the harbor.

161. The Russians had meanwhile been carrying on a war with the Turks in the Trans-Caucasian provinces, and had made some conquests which counterbalanced the loss of Sevastopol. Under the mediation of Austria, preliminaries of peace were signed at St. Petersburg before the end of 1855, and were confirmed at Paris, March 30, 1856, by the ministers of Great Britain, Russia, France, Sardinia, and Turkey. The last named power was admitted into the European system of states, and the integrity of her dominions was guaranteed; conquests were mutually restored; the Danube and the Black Sea were thrown freely open to the commerce of all nations, but the latter was closed against ships of war. Servia and her native prince, though owning a sort of dependence upon Turkey, were placed under the protection of the five great powers. A few years later Moldavia and Wallachia were erected into a nearly independent state under the name of Roumania. Their sovereign is elected by the people, subject to the approval of the Sultan.

162. In its general discussion of European affairs, the Congress of Paris complained of the continued occupation of the Papal States by French and Austrian troops. Since 1849, the French had occupied Rome, while the Austrian armies held the provinces north of the Apennines known as the "Legations." Neither nation could withdraw without leaving the other absolute ruler of central Italy. Austria, indeed, exercised already a controlling power in every Italian state except Sardinia. The liberal constitution of Naples had been overthrown by Austrian intervention. The duchies of Tuscany, Parma, and Modena were occupied by Austrian forces, whose generals exerted civil as well as military control in contempt of existing laws. Suspected persons were carried away to the fortresses of Mantua or Kufstein, or were even sentenced to death in the name and by the authority of the emperor Francis Joseph. To defeat the Carbonari and other liberal associations, three secret societies, composed of the most unscrupulous characters, armed in support of the government; assured of impunity, they robbed and murdered not only men but women and even children in open day, and neither the papal nor the ducal authorities chose to interfere.

163. The hope of Italy was in the House of Savoy and in the expected intervention of France. Victor Emmanuel, after the battle of Novara (§ 150), might have established an absolute despotism with the favor and support of Austria; he chose rather to reign as a constitutional monarch, and to become the champion of Italian independence. Consequently, when in 1859 hostilities began to threaten, volunteers escaping by stealth from every state in Italy flocked by twenties and hundreds to his camp. Of his five superior generals three were Tuscans. On the other hand, Napoleon III., who derived his power professedly from the will of the people, had manifest grounds of difference with Francis Joseph, who founded his pretensions upon an ancient name, while claiming a control in Italy which his ancestors, even during the existence of the Holy Roman Empire, had never been able to enforce. In opposition to the hereditary theory, the French emperor asserted that of national unity and the solidarity of races, and found his natural allies in the Latin nations of the two peninsulas. In his efforts for the unification of Italy he was ably assisted by Count Cavour, the Sardinian prime minister.

164. On the 23d of April, 1859, the Austrian embassador at Turin demanded the reduction of the Sardinian army to a peace footing; the demand was refused, and on the same day the Austrian forces crossed the Ticino. A French army was already landed at Genoa, and Napoleon, leaving the empress Eugénie as Regent of France in his absence, assumed the command, May 12. The Grand-duke of Tuscany, the Duke of Modena, and the Duchess of Parma fled from their capitals. Victor Emmanuel was declared Dictator of Tuscany; declining that office, he accepted the command of its armies, which were joined with those of France and Sardinia. On the 20th of May the Austrians were defeated in a five hours' battle at Montebello, and again on the 30th and 31st at Palestro. But far more decisive was the victory of the French and Sardinians at Magenta, June 4. General MacMahon coming up with his French reserves at the crisis of the battle, contributed greatly to the result, and he was rewarded by a marshal's *bâton*, with the title of Duke of Magenta. The battle of Marignano, though less important, was also disastrous to the Austrians, and the next day (June 8) Napoleon and Victor Emmanuel entered Milan in triumph.

165. The Austrians now retreated within the "Quadrilateral" formed by the fortresses of Cremona, Peschiera, Verona, and Mantua. The final contest of the war took place at Solferino. The Austrians were again defeated, and on the 8th of July the two emperors met at Villafranca to arrange the preliminaries of a peace. Austria surrendered to France all Lombardy (excepting the fortresses of Mantua and Peschiera) to be presented by Napoleon to Sardinia. The Italian states were recommended to unite themselves in a federal league under the honorary presidency of the Pope. Venetia, though remaining subject to Austria, might become a member of the Confederation. This plan was far from satisfying the demand for national unity. Tuscany, Modena, Parma, and the papal province of Romagna petitioned the king of Sardinia to take them under his dominion. The kingdom of Italy, thus constituted, was increased the following year by the conquest of Sicily by Garibaldi and his volunteers, the capture of Ancona and a great

June 24, 1859.

part of the papal territories, and the flight of the Bourbon king, Francis II., from Naples. A unanimous vote of the people of the Two Sicilies declared their union with the kingdom of Italy under the scepter of

Nov., 1860.

Victor Emmanuel. After a victory at the Garigliano, that sovereign entered Naples and was acknowledged as king of the whole country from the Alps to the southernmost point of Sicily, the city of Rome and its immediate territories being the only exceptions beside Venetia.

166. The next general disturbance of the peace of Europe arose from the Danish Question. The death of Frederic VII. in 1863 ended the Oldenburg line of sovereigns, which had reigned more than four hundred years. The Congress of London in 1852 had provided for the accession, in such an event, of Prince Christian of Schleswig-Holstein-Glucksburg, who had married a grand-niece of the late king. The claims of the elder, or Augustenburg branch of his family to the duchies, were purchased for three and a half millions of dollars, and it was expressly arranged that the ducal as well as the royal dominions should descend to Prince Christian. A party in Germany, since 1848, had strongly desired the independence of the duchies, and this was now joined by Austria and Prussia, whose influence in the Diet at Frankfort secured a vote for the occupation of Holstein by federal troops. The Prussian Legislative Assembly voted that the honor and interest of Germany demanded the recognition and support of the Prince of Augustenburg as Duke of Schleswig-Holstein. But this was only a temporary expedient. Count Bismarck, the Prussian minister, had planned, not only a Prussian naval arsenal at Kiel in Holstein, but the reunion of all Germany with the king his master at its head.

167. Austria was a necessary ally at this stage of the movement, and by subtle diplomacy the court of Vienna was persuaded to join Prussia in an invasion of the disputed duchies, notwithstanding the protest of the Diet, which had appointed Hanover and Saxony to execute the military occupation in the name of the German confederacy. The allied forces under General Wrangel entered Holstein in January, 1864. The Danes were constantly defeated on land, though their fleet kept up a blockade of the Prussian ports and defeated that of the invaders off Heligoland. Not only the duchies, but Jutland itself had to be abandoned by the Danish forces, which concentrated themselves in the islands; but after the bombardment and surrender of Alsen, resistance ceased. By the Peace of Vienna, King Christian resigned Schleswig, Holstein, and Lauenburg, and agreed to recognize whatever government Austria and Prussia should see fit to establish. It now appeared that the claims of the Duke of Augustenburg had been merely a pretext on the part of the two great powers; for they continued to occupy the duchies with military force,

and by the convention of Gastein allotted Schleswig and Lauenburg to
Prussia, and Holstein to Austria. (Aug., 1865.)

168. Since 1859 the Prussian armies had undergone a complete reorganization under Count von Roon. The infantry were armed with the
needle-gun, and the whole military system had been brought to the highest degree of efficiency. Austria clung to her old weapons and traditions,
while in diplomacy also she had no match for the far-seeing and resolute
intellect of Bismarck. The short and decisive struggle for leadership in
Germany was now approaching. By a personal conference with Napoleon
III. at Biarritz, Bismarck ascertained that France would not interfere.
England was known to desire peace at any price. Russia was under
recent obligations to Prussia for active assistance against the Poles.
Italy became the close ally of Prussia, moved partly by the refusal of
Francis Joseph to sell Venetia to Victor Emmanuel. General La Mar-
mora said in a dispatch to Berlin: "Piedmont began in 1859 the task
of freeing Italy with the noble aid of France. We desire that within no
distant period that task may be accomplished . . . perhaps by a war
of independence fought side by side with that nation which represents
the future of the German people in the name and on the principle of
an identical nationality." It was agreed not to end the war until Italy
had acquired Venetia, and Prussia a corresponding increase of territory
in Germany.

169. Saxony, Hanover, and Hesse refusing to take part in the war, all
three countries were occupied by Prussian troops. The blind King
George of Hanover was allowed only twelve hours to choose between
alliance against Austria and war with Prussia. In the battle of Langen-
salza the Hanoverians were victorious, but they were soon
surrounded by fresh reinforcements of the Prussians, and   June, 1866.
the king was compelled to surrender not only his army but his crown.
He was permitted to "fix his residence, at His Majesty's pleasure, any-
where except in the realm of Hanover," and the conquered territory now
formed the needed link between the severed provinces of East and West
Prussia. In western Germany the army of General Manteuffel was opposed by the forces of the Confederacy under princes Charles of Bavaria
and Alexander of Hesse; while in the east, where the more important
action took place, the Crown Prince and his cousin, Prince Frederic
Charles, "wrestled their way" through the mountains of the Saxon and
Silesian frontiers into Bohemia, where they were met by the main Austrian
army under Marshal Benedek. At Aschaffenburg the Prussians gained
an easy victory, owing to the large proportion of Venetian troops in the
Austrian contingent, who, rather than fight their friends and allies, sought
the earliest opportunity to surrender.

170. The Prussians then occupied Frankfort without resistance, and proceeded to exact enormous contributions "by right of conquest." In case the last ten millions of thalers were delayed, General Manteuffel threatened bombardment and plunder, though the rights of the "Free City" were under the especial protection of international law. The states of southern Germany had in the field double the number of men that Prussia could oppose to them; and their failure even to check the progress of Manteuffel, proved what Bismarck had charged—the inefficiency of the Confederation. Meanwhile in Bohemia the two princes, by a series of hard-won but decisive victories, had gained command of the Iser and upper Elbe. In the neighborhood of Königsgratz, Marshal Benedek, with his whole Austrian force of 200,000 men, lay awaiting their

July 3, 1866. arrival. The furious combat which followed takes its name from the village of Sadowa—one of many which were included in the battle-field. Here, as every-where, the terrible swiftness and precision of the Prussian fire prevailed even over the valor and discipline of the Austrians; while the Austrian cavalry, hitherto the most celebrated in Europe, was driven to flight by the Uhlans. A storm of wind and rain prevailed through the day. Late in the afternoon the Prussian guards seized Chlum, the center of Benedek's position, and kept it against three resolute attacks by superior numbers. This decided the battle. A large portion of the Austrian cannon, with 20,000 prisoners, were taken. An equal number of men lay dead upon the field.

171. As a consequence of the victory of Sadowa, Venetia was ceded to the emperor of the French, to be given by him to Victor Emmanuel. The king of Italy had been far less fortunate than his ally. He had been defeated with great loss (June 24) at Custozza; and on the day of the battle in Bohemia, Garibaldi and his volunteers were worsted at Monte Suello. But the unity of Italy was accomplished in the same stroke with that of Germany. The Venetians, by an almost unanimous vote and by a personal welcome, accepted Victor Emmanuel as their sovereign, and a thanksgiving for the great event was celebrated in the Church of St. Mark.

172. In Germany the victories of Prussia in the "Seven Weeks' War" were confirmed by the Treaty of Prague. The German Confederation was dissolved. Austria acquiesced in the aggrandizement of Prussia and engaged to take no part in the reconstruction of Germany, while she paid twenty millions of thalers toward Prussian expenses in the war. The ascendency among the German states, enjoyed for nearly six hundred years by the House of Hapsburg, was transferred to the more ancient* but hitherto less celebrated House of Hohenzollern.

---

*The sovereigns of Prussia trace their lineage to Count Tassilo of Hohenzollern, who died A. D. 800. Subsequent members of the family became burgraves of Nuremberg, margraves of Brandenburg, and dukes of Prussia. The Hapsburgs date from A. D. 1096.

173. Confining himself to the government of his hereditary dominions, Francis Joseph sought by a series of wise and needed reforms to raise them from the state of prostration and despair to which they had been brought by the terrible reverses of war. His finances were ruined, his armies nearly annihilated, and the several nationalities which had been forcibly united under his scepter were ready to revolt against an absolute policy which deprived them of civil and religious rights. The hopes of the Liberals were revived by the appointment of the Saxon Baron von Beust as President of the Imperial Council. Representative assemblies, now reëstablished, gave to the people their just share in the burdens and privileges of government. Hungary had her own Diet and a separate ministry with Count Andrassy at its head, though united with Austria under the same sovereign, and having her part in the common interests of the Empire by means of a joint assembly known as "The Delegations," composed of sixty members from each parliament, and meeting alternately at the two capitals. In 1867, Francis Joseph received the crown of St. Stephen at Pesth, and the next year an imperial decree changed the title of his dominion to the "Austro-Hungarian Monarchy," recognizing the separate nationality of his subjects east of the Leitha.

174. The constitution of Austria thus approaches nearly to that of England, where a ministry chosen from the party having a majority in Parliament, is responsible for all the acts of the government. The magnates and clergy naturally resist, but the emperor has been firm and constant in his adherence to the new policy. In a single session of the Reichsrath, or Austrian Parliament, despotisms of a thousand years were swept away. Marriage and education were A. D. 1867, '68. made independent of priestly control; and all classes, religions, and nationalities were declared equal before the law. Probably such complete reforms were never before accomplished in so short a time, unless we except the acts of the French National Assembly in August, 1789. But in France all existing institutions were then plunging down a steep descent into chaos, while in Austria a new and better order has taken the place of the old, and conflicting opinions have produced no outward disturbance of the public peace. In 1870 the Concordat with the Pope, already disregarded in the acts above mentioned, was formerly annulled, and perfect toleration was established.

RECAPITULATION.

Coup d'État of 1851 makes Louis Napoleon President for ten years of the French Republic. In 1852 he becomes Emperor; in 1854 joins England in war against Russia for the preservation of the Ottoman dominions. The Czar Nicholas seizes the Danubian provinces, rejects the intercessions of the Congress of Vienna, orders an attack upon the Turkish fleet and fort at Sinope. His armies are defeated in Wallachia, compelled to raise the siege of Silistria, and withdraw from the Danube. French, English, and Turkish forces invade the Crimea, gain a victory at the Alma, and lay siege to Sevastopol. Charge of the Light Brigade at Balaklava—a sanguinary and indecisive battle. Repulse of the Russians at Inkermann. Sufferings of British soldiers alleviated by Florence Nightingale and her assistants. Austria and Sardinia become allies in the war. Death of Nicholas, accession of Alexander II. in Russia. Conquests of the British in the Sea of Azov—of the Russians between the Caspian and Black seas. Bombardment and surrender of Sevastopol. Peace of Paris.

Supremacy of Austria in Italy. King of Sardinia is champion of liberal institutions and of Italian nationality. Napoleon III. joins the French army in Italy; allied forces defeat the Austrians at Montebello, Palestro, Magenta, and Solferino. Peace of Villafranca adds Lombardy to the kingdom of Victor Emmanuel. By annexation of the central duchies and conquest of the Two Sicilies, that kingdom covers the whole peninsula except Venetia and the States of the Church, A. D. 1861.

Diet at Frankfort interferes in the settlement of Holstein, upon the death of Frederic VII. of Denmark. Austria and Prussia conquer Schleswig, Holstein, and Lauenburg, which are ceded by King Christian at Peace of Vienna. Prussia then obtains the alliance of Victor Emmanuel in a war against Austria with the purpose of expelling the Hapsburgs at once from Germany and Italy. Kingdom of Hanover is overthrown, and its territories serve to consolidate the Prussian dominions. Progress of Manteuffel in western Germany unchecked by forces of the Diet. Frankfort occupied and despoiled. Two royal princes carry on the war in Bohemia, opposed by Benedek. Decisive victory at Sadowa. Misfortunes of Victor Emmanuel at Custozza and Monte Suello counterbalanced by the success of his ally; Venetia added to his kingdom. Dissolution of the German Confederacy. Austria becomes a constitutional monarchy; recognizes the distinct nationality of Hungary. Liberal reforms under Chancellor von Beust.

THE BRITISH EMPIRE IN THE EAST.

175. A complete account of European trading settlements in Asia would be foreign to the purposes of this history; but the rise of British dominion in India, Australia, Borneo, and New Zealand — among the most remarkable series of events in the last two centuries — must be briefly narrated. For a hundred years from its foundation the English East India Company confined itself to commerce, content to obtain sites for its forts and warehouses by the grant of the Mogul emperors, and to defend them by a small guard of soldiers from the attacks of the fierce Mahrattas. The successive decline of the Portuguese, Dutch, and French interests left the trade with the great peninsula almost exclusively in its hands. Of the three English Presidencies (Book IV., § 132), the chief was at Calcutta, which, from a petty village on the Hooghly, presented to the company by Aurungzebe, grew to a magnificent city of palaces, and ultimately became the capital of Hindustan. The French had two Presidencies — one at Pondicherry and one on the Isle of France.

176. The Mogul Empire in Asia during the eighteenth century was in a condition nearly corresponding to that of the "Roman Empire" in Europe. Its pretensions were unabated, but the power that had enforced them had declined; and the twenty-one nations of the Hindu peninsula owned little more allegiance to the court of Delhi than did Frederic II. of Prussia to that of Vienna. The ruling race, it will be remembered, was

Mohammedan, and thus alien in religion from the great mass of the people which held fast the ancient Hindu superstitions. The contending chiefs continually sought foreign alliances in their wars with each other, and thus the English and French became engaged, usually on different sides, in Indian hostilities.

177. The idea of replacing the Mogul by a European dominion originated with the French, who also were the first to train *Sipahis* (Sepoys) or native soldiers to serve under European officers. This was a necessary step to the subjugation of India, for beside the impossibility of transporting troops enough from Europe to conquer so vast and distant a territory, the climate of Hindustan would be fatal to the long continued existence of a foreign army. The Seven Years' War between England and France gave a fresh impulse to the long rivalry between their colonies in India. Madras was besieged and taken by the governor of the Isle of France, and Dupleix, governor of Pondicherry, captured Arcot from the native prince of the Deccan, who was an ally of the English. Arcot, a city of 100,000 inhabitants, was retaken by Robert Clive, a young Englishman who had begun his career as clerk in the counting-house of the company, but whose daring genius found more congenial exercise in the field, and ultimately made him ruler of all British India. Having captured Arcot with only five hundred men, he successfully defended it against a force of 10,000 natives, and was rewarded with a commission as lieutenant-colonel.   A. D. 1746.

178. A few years later Surajah Dowlah, native viceroy of Bengal, took Calcutta and crowded most of the British residents, numbering 146, into a noisome dungeon known as the "Black Hole," where most of them died of suffocation in a single night. Clive, with only 3,000 men, recovered the English capital, took Hooghly by storm, and gained so decisive a victory over Surajah Dowlah's army of 50,000 at Plassy, that he is commonly considered the founder of the British-Indian Empire. From this point the French dominion built up by Dupleix rapidly fell; and within another hundred years the English had subdued the great peninsula and become the rulers of 180 millions of people. This was effected partly by interfering in the quarrels of the native princes, partly by direct purchase of the sovereignties of the several Nizams and Rajahs, who were secured in larger revenues than they themselves had been able to extort from their ill governed estates.

179. The policy of Clive was pursued and extended by Warren Hastings, who, upon the reconstruction of the Company's dominions in 1773, became Governor-General of India. During his administration Hyder Ali, the native Sultan of Mysore, who had been the fiercest opponent of the English, was reduced to submission. Both Clive and Hastings amassed enormous wealth in India; and though their government was more just

and merciful than that of the native despots, there is no doubt that it was stained by acts of oppression which were wholly indefensible under any Christian code of morality. The conduct of each was made the subject of investigation by the British parliament; and though both were acquitted, in view of their great and brilliant services — perhaps, too, of the insufficiency of evidence — Clive was driven to despair and to suicide, and Hastings spent his later years in retirement.

180. Hitherto the British dominions in India had been governed exclusively by the trading company chartered by Queen Elizabeth. Upon the motion of Mr. Pitt, a Board of Control was established in 1784 by Act of Parliament, rendering the officers in India responsible in some measure to the home government; and by degrees a far more humane and liberal policy began to prevail. War continued many years with Tippoo Saib, who had succeeded not only to his father's sovereignty of Mysore, but to his implacable hatred of the English. The French, who had never ceased to resent their expulsion from India, and hoped that the British might as easily be deprived of their Asiatic, as they had lately been of their American possessions (Book IV., §§ 196–298), entered warmly, though secretly, into the plans of Tippoo. In 1792, the sultan was so far humbled that he begged for peace, and gave up his two sons as hostages; in 1799 the war was renewed, and he fell, bravely fighting on the walls of his capital, Seringapatam.

181. Successive wars with the Mahrattas, the wild Goorkas of the Nepaulese mountains, and the Pindarries of the interior, ended in enormous additions to the Company's territories; and in 1819, its commerce was greatly extended by the foundation of an English colony at Singapore, near the southern extremity of the Malay peninsula, as a market for the rich productions of the Indian Archipelago. In 1833, the Company's charter expired, and though the government of Hindustan was again conferred upon it for twenty years, the trade which it had monopolized was thrown freely open to all British subjects. Among the most important consequences of this change was the extension of the opium traffic with China. The government of that empire, which had barely endured the slow and moderate operations of the company, was alarmed by a sudden increase of the supply of opium in the markets and by its effect upon the habits of the people, who were already fatally addicted to its use. Its importation was prohibited by imperial edict; but the Chinese merchants, who were sharers in the profits, encouraged a smuggling trade, and the connivance of officials was easily bought. The government, incensed at these proceedings, ordered the British merchants to be blockaded in their warehouses at Canton until they consented to give up all the opium in their possession, amounting, it is said, to a value of ten millions of dollars.

182. This and other acts of hostility led to a war of two years, during which Canton was taken by the British, but ransomed for six millions of dollars; Amoy, Ning-po, and several other towns were bombarded and captured. After several deceptive negotiations which were undertaken merely to gain time, the Chinese were at length humbled into submission; and a treaty was signed before Nankin, ceding the island of Hongkong to the British, throwing open the ports of Can-   Aug., 1842. ton, Amoy, Foochoo, Ning-po, and Shanghai to foreign trade and the residence of European consuls, and engaging the emperor of China to pay twenty-one millions of dollars as war-indemnity. This treaty, however questionable the acts which led to it, is remarkable as the first of a series of events which have opened the oldest of empires to the intercourse of other nations long excluded.

183. During the same year, the British ended a war with the Afghans. It had been undertaken, A. D. 1838, in the interest of Shah Sujah, a deposed chief, who, when reinstated upon his throne at Cabul proved such an intolerable tyrant that he was murdered by his subjects. In the terrible hardships of their march through the deserts of Scinde and the Bolan mountain pass, the British soldiery showed a heroism worthy of a better cause. They gained many victories, and were established as victors in Cabul, but a revolt of the Afghans, in which several of the English leaders were murdered, compelled a retreat. Married officers and their families, numbering about one hundred Europeans, were left as hostages with Akbar Khan. The retreating army was nearly annihilated by the treachery of the natives and the severity of the climate in midwinter. The hostages were only rescued by a fresh invading force under General Pollock. Afghanistan was left without settled government. The important province of Scinde on the lower Indus—formerly a dependency on the sovereigns of Cabul—was conquered in 1843 by Sir Charles Napier, who became its governor.

184. Of much greater importance was the conquest of the Sikhs, the military rulers of the Punjab. This battle-ground of Afghan and Hindu, the highway of Persian and Tartar invaders, had been probably ever since its invasion by Alexander of Macedon a scene of perpetual rapine and strife. The Sikhs had a religion distinct from that of either Hindus or Mohammedans; by theory it was almost as mild and non-combative as that of the Friends or Quakers; but nature and circumstances were more powerful than tenets, and they formed a fierce, turbulent, and formidable body, of which every member seemed born to the use of lance and spear. The Afghan war stirred up old enmities between the Sikhs and the English; and late in 1845 a large army of the former crossed the River Sutlej and invaded the British province. They were four times defeated with heavy loss, and beside paying seven and a half millions of dollars as war-indemnity, were compelled to leave their boy-king under the guardianship of the English, who were to rule the country during his minority by a special Council at Lahore.

185. Within a few months of the signing of the treaty, the whole dominion of the Sikhs was annexed to the British Empire, the young king being pensioned from his hereditary revenues. The Sikhs, naturally incensed, renewed the war, and were still more decisively overthrown. A celebrated diamond, known as the Koh-i-noor, or Mountain of Light, which for centuries had been supposed to exert a mysterious power in preserving the dominion of its possessor, was taken from them and added to the crown-jewels of the English queen. Sir Henry Lawrence, as Superintendent of the Punjab, undertook the difficult task of reconciling the conquered people to the government so illegally set up. Such was the kindliness and justice of his policy that in five years peace, order, and prosperity had succeeded to long ages of strife. Even the warlike chiefs were won to acquiescence, and their sons flocked eagerly to English colleges, in order to prepare themselves for honorable positions in the civil or military service. The great mass of Hindus and Mohammedans who had been subject to the Sikhs, easily submitted to a rule which gave them greater security of life and property than they had ever before enjoyed. So effectually was the great work of pacification accomplished, that during the terrible scenes of 1857, soon to be described, the Punjab was the rallying point of British authority; and the Sikhs were the most loyal subjects of the queen. But for their fidelity her empire in India would probably have been overthrown.

186. In 1856 the great kingdom of Oude was annexed to the British dominions. Its Rajah, or king, was one of the most odious of the native tyrants, and had been repeatedly threatened with dethronement both for his oppression of his own people and for his violation of treaties with the English. The event perhaps hastened a crisis which had been long apprehended — the mutiny of the Sepoys. It was, indeed, almost incredible that a mere handful of Europeans could have maintained and increased their ascendency, during so many years, over hundreds of millions of people of acute and active minds, in a climate exhausting and often fatal to the ruling class. It was still more wonderful that their power, when shaken by a wide-spread rebellion, should have been promptly and thoroughly reëstablished. The native troops employed by the East India Company numbered 232,224. Better paid, fed, and equipped than they had ever been by their Hindu rulers, they were usually contented, and their relation to their English officers was that of childlike obedience and confidence. But they were intensely superstitious, and a fancied affront to their religion wounded them at a vital point. For their new Enfield rifles, received from England in 1856, they were provided with cartridges supposed to contain beef-tallow. The use of this article was impossible to any devout Hindu; several regiments objected, and the government immediately complied with their wishes by suppressing the cartridges.

187. The discontent aroused by this and other causes, continued, however, to spread, especially among the regiments in Bengal, Oude, and the province of Delhi. The middle and lower classes of the people joined the Sepoys in rebellion; but the chiefs and great landholders, who better understood the English power, and had more to lose by public disturbances, generally remained loyal to the government. At Delhi and Meerut nearly all the European residents, including women and children, were massacred. Delhi became the capital of the insurgents; it was besieged three months by a small British army and finally taken by storm. Its king, or "emperor," was transported to Burmah Sept., 1858. and his two sons were put to death. In June, Sir Hugh Wheeler had been attacked in Cawnpore by the Sepoys lately under his own command, now led by Nana Sahib, rajah of Bithoor. Two hundred English soldiers withstood a siege of seventeen days; but at length, half their number being slain, the rest surrendered the place upon condition of being permitted to retire down the Ganges with the 600 British residents. The treacherous permission was quickly violated. No sooner had the embarkation begun, than the retreating column was attacked by the Sepoys and every man was slain. The women were crowded together for three weeks in one narrow room, but upon the approach of General Havelock for their relief, they too were murdered, and the mangled remains were thrown into a well.

188. Though armed with the most improved weapons and long drilled by British officers, the Sepoys proved no match for their opponents. Outnumbering the little army of Havelock five, eight, and even ten times, they were constantly defeated, and the monster who led them saw his own palace occupied by the English. Having buried the dead at Cawnpore, Havelock pressed on to Lucknow, the capital of Oude, where a Scotch regiment was besieged by a large native army. The arrangements for its defense had been most skillfully made by Sir Henry Lawrence, already mentioned as peacemaker in the Punjab, and lately the governor of Oude. His noble and useful life was ended by a shot at the beginning of the siege. Colonel Inglis, succeeding to the command, continued the resistance with no less constancy. Havelock, in advancing from Cawnpore, gained four victories over the insurgents, but his few hundreds of men were so exhausted that they were compelled to fall back, and the garrison of Lucknow were reduced almost to despair. At length Havelock, being reinforced, was able to recross the Ganges and his presence renewed the courage of the besieged. Still it was impossible

M. H.—28.

to withraw from the place; and it was not until the arrival of Sir Colin

Nov., 1857.

Campbell, nearly five months from its first investment, that the survivors were rescued. General Havelock, worn out by his exertions and anxieties, died a few days before the abandonment of Lucknow. The baronetcy and pension bestowed upon him by the gratitude of his queen, came too late.

189. The capture of Lucknow the following spring by Sir Colin Campbell virtually ended the rebellion, though occasional fighting took place during the summer. An important Act of Parliament transferred the government of India from the Company to the Crown. The queen now appoints the Governor-General, or Viceroy, who represents her in Calcutta; and a Council of fifteen members, presided over by the Secretary of State for India, has superseded the Board of Control. English influence is probably more predominant than ever, by reason of the social changes which have in a great degree broken up the superstitions of the higher classes. Young men of rank and wealth are educated at English colleges or in London, while English governesses are admitted even to the secluded apartments of Hindu women. The cruel and degrading observances of the old religion are losing their prevalence among the educated classes; and even the division of castes promises to give way before the demands of modern civilized life. Railways, telegraphs, newspapers, and even common schools have begun to bring the great mass of the Hindu population into community of ideas with the western world.

190. Within a century Great Britain has established another dominion in the East — more extensive and perhaps yet to be more important than that of India itself. The shores of the vast island, or rather continent, of Australia were explored by the Dutch early in the seventeenth century, but its interior was unknown to Europeans until after

A. D. 1772.

Captain Cook's visit to its south coast had suggested the possibility of finding room and sustenance upon its broad untilled acres for the surplus, and especially the criminal, population of Great Britain. In January, 1788, a fleet of eleven ships bearing a thousand persons, mostly convicts, arrived at Sydney Cove, in what has been pronounced the finest harbor in the world. Having survived the perils resulting from the loss of a store-ship, and the consequent scarcity of food, the colony began to flourish, though its wretched and disorderly elements seemed to afford a most unpromising foundation for a new state. The labor of the settlers belonged to the government; for their crimes had forfeited all civil privileges. These felons, however, were useful pioneers; for they cleared the wildernesses, made roads, built bridges, and constructed many other public works which lightened the tasks of the free settlers. Some of the early governors lacked the wisdom and benevolence which their difficult task required; but under the humane administration of Governor Macquarie (A. D. 1810–1821) the convicts made rapid advances toward reformation. Many who had been driven into crime by the cruel pressure of want, in the overcrowded cities of England, gladly embraced the opportunity to lead a better life, and some of these were even chosen to magistracies in the colony.

191. The thirty years following Governor Macquarie's resignation were marked by a great increase in the number of free colonists. Australian wool had been found equal to the finest fleeces of Germany or Spain, and the flocks of sheep could already be numbered by millions. The transportation of convicts both to Australia and Van Diemen's Land was discontinued; but thousands of the honest poor were aided by the government to emigrate, and so many persons of character and wealth were induced to colonize by the increased facilities of travel and the hope of gain, that the population increased more than tenfold. The original colony of New South Wales was divided, Victoria being set off on the south and Queensland on the north, while Van Diemen's Land and South and West Australia have also been organized at different times under distinct governments.

192. The third period of Australian history was marked by the discovery of gold in the south-eastern provinces, May, 1851. At first the wild excitement threatened the ruin of the colonies; for flocks, herds, and farms were abandoned, and food became scarcely procurable at famine prices. Ships in port were deserted by officers and seamen; all regular industries ceased for a time, but the consequent peril and distress at length brought people to their senses. Society was reorganized; security returned, and the throngs of settlers drawn from foreign parts added to the commercial prosperity of the country. Melbourne, the capital of Victoria, though founded so lately as 1837, now numbers nearly 200,000 inhabitants and has become the seat of a university. Sydney, the older capital of New South Wales, though outstripped in population by the rapid growth of its rival, has also a university, and is the seat of the metropolitan bishopric. Railroads and telegraphs are multiplying year by year; and a submarine cable unites Australia and Van Diemen's Land — now officially called Tasmania — to London.

193. The British possessions in the Eastern Hemisphere have been increased of late years by the formation of eight colonies in New Zealand. The three islands composing the group so called, cover more space than England, Scotland, Ireland, and Wales; while in richness of soil, healthfulness of climate, and grandeur and variety of scenery they are unsurpassed by any country in the world. The first European settlements in New Zealand were made by deserters from whale-ships visiting the South Pacific. The fine timber of its forests attracted more permanent settlers; and English missionaries from 1814 introduced Christianity and the elements of civilization among the Maoris, or native New Zealanders. Cannibalism and all the worst features of heathenism speedily disappeared, and at present nearly all the Maoris are nominally Christian. Most of them can read and write, some are even highly educated, and newspapers are published in their native language.

194. In 1840 the chiefs of the two principal islands acknowledged the supremacy of the queen of England. But disputes concerning the title to lands occasioned a four years' war, A. D. 1843-1847; and hostilities have been renewed at intervals within the last ten years. The intelligence of the Maoris, their skillful use of fire-arms and their knowledge of inaccessible mountain-fastnesses make them dangerous enemies; but their numbers are rapidly diminishing, and at no distant day the population will doubtless be wholly European. The islands are rich in coal, copper, iron, and gold.

195. Another English settlement in the eastern seas is wholly owing to private enterprise. Mr. James Brooke with his own yacht explored the coast of Borneo in 1838, and formed the project of civilizing its savage tribes, as well as of clearing its rivers and bays of the pirates who preyed upon the commerce of the Indian archipelago. Finding the Rajah of Sarawak engaged in a war with his subjects, he aided in putting down the rebellion, and so gained the confidence of the Sultan of Borneo that he was intrusted with the government of the province. The natives were surprised and conciliated by a wiser and more beneficent rule than they had ever yet experienced. With the aid of a British frigate and her boats, Mr. Brooke waged a war of extermination upon the pirates; and rendered such service to the commerce of that region that the home-government appointed him its regent in Borneo. In 1847 the neighboring small island of Labuan was added to his dominion, forming an important English naval station in those distant seas, especially since the discovery of great deposits of coal.

RECAPITULATION.

English East India Company, chartered for purposes of trade, becomes engaged in native wars and lays the foundation of a great British dominion. Decline of the Mogul Empire; independence of its parts. The French train Sepoys to serve in their armies; capture Madras and Arcot. Clive recovers and defends Arcot; recaptures Calcutta, and overthrows Surajah Dowlah at Plassy; becomes Governor of Bengal. Warren Hastings, Governor-General, conquers Hyder Ali; is impeached for extortion and oppression. Wars with Tippoo Saib, with Mahrattas, Goorkas, and Pindarries end in favor of the English. Singapore founded. Exclusive rights of the Company expire. War with China occasioned by the opium trade, terminates in cession of Hong Kong and opening of five other ports to the English. Disastrous war with the Afghans. Conquest of the Sikhs. Annexation of Oude. Mutiny of the Sepoys and rebellion of Hindu people. Massacres at Delhi and Cawnpore. Siege and relief of Lucknow. Death of Havelock. Government of India assumed by the queen of Great Britain.

Convict settlements in Australia and Van Diemen's Land, succeeded by free colonies.

Discovery of gold; rapid growth of Sydney and Melbourne. Colonization of New Zealand. *Maoris* Christianized. Their wars with the whites. Mineral wealth of the country. Settlement and improvement of Borneo. English coaling station at Labuan.

AMERICAN AFFAIRS.

196. The forty years following the Peace of 1814 with Great Britain were to the United States a period of material growth and prosperity, such as no other country probably has ever known. Famines in Germany in 1816 and 1817 gave an impulse to emigration; and from that time onward an ever increasing current has set toward the American ports from the European continent and the British islands. Those who, by reason of the frequent wars, the oppressive military systems, or the overcrowded population of the old world, were placed at a disadvantage in the struggle for life, found here an ample field for enterprise; and their labor was of inestimable value in developing the resources of the new continent. The Erie Canal, which in 1826 connected the Hudson with the Great Lakes, brought the inexhaustible grain-fields of the Mississippi basin nearer to the hungry multitudes of Europe. The use of steam for transportation on land, rivers, and even oceans, is drawing the whole world into a community of interests; but nowhere have its effects been more important than in the vast extent of the American Republic. The magnetic telegraph — largely an American invention — has annihilated the barriers opposed by space to the communication of thought; and its greatest triumph was reached when in 1858 a cable, laid under the waters of the North Atlantic, united the two hemispheres. The first cable failed to transmit messages after a few months; but a second, laid in 1866, has been a perfect success. Since then submarine telegraphs in successful working have established instant communication between the remotest regions of the globe.

197. The general peace of the United States was hardly interrupted by the wars with the Sacs of the north-western frontier or the Seminoles of Florida; though the latter, protected by their dense and noxious everglades, were subdued only by a seven years' contest. Florida had been ceded by Spain in 1819, upon the United States undertaking to pay the debts of the Spanish government to American citizens, and to relinquish their claims to Texas, which on account of the colony of La Salle (Book IV., § 130) had been regarded by the French as part of Louisiana. In 1822, Mexico became finally independent of Spain, and after a series of revolutions, adopted a federal constitution modeled upon that of the more northern republic. This constitution was abolished in 1833 by the President Santa Anna; and the people of Texas, many of whom were immigrants from the United States, thereupon declared their separation from Mexico. War followed, in which Santa Anna was taken prisoner and compelled to acknowledge the independence of Texas, A. D. 1836. This republic then sought admission into the United States, but for eight years it was refused. In 1844, by electing President Polk, the Americans were understood as giving their vote for the annexation of Texas, which accordingly took place by act of Congress, the following year.

198. Upon receiving news of this transaction, the Mexican government withdrew its minister from Washington, and prepared for war. General Taylor, on the other hand, occupied Texas with an "American" army, gained several victories over superior numbers of Mexicans, and, crossing the Rio Grande, took by siege and storm the strong city of Monterey. General Kearney, meanwhile, with only 1,800 men, captured Santa Fé and took possession of the whole province of New Mexico; then pushing across the continent with a squad of cavalry, aided Commodore Stockton in the capture of San Gabriel, which completed the conquest of California. This had been partly effected by Captain Fremont, who, with a corps of engineers, had been engaged in exploring a new route to Oregon when the war broke out. The brilliant victory of General Taylor at Buena Vista, with the conquest by Colonel Doniphan of the province of Chihuahua, established the power of the United States over northern Mexico. Two weeks later, General Scott, landing at Vera Cruz, took by storm the strong castle of San Juan de Ulloa and soon afterward began the toilsome ascent from the coast to the capital. Santa Anna awaited him with 12,000 men in the pass of Cerro Gordo, but was defeated and put to flight, leaving several important cities and fortresses to fall into the hands of the Americans. Proceeding with his march, Scott encountered, at the entrance to the plateau of the City of Mexico, another and larger army which Santa Anna had with great energy gathered to oppose his progress. This also was defeated in the battles of Contreras and Cherubusco; and the storming of Molino del Rey and the castle of Chapultepec compelled the surrender of the capital.

Aug., 1846.

199. Santa Anna fled the country. A treaty of peace at Guadalupe Hidalgo fixed the boundaries between the two Republics at the Rio Grande and the Rio Gila; but as a partial compensation for the vast territory ceded by Mexico, the United States agreed to pay fifteen millions of dollars and assume the debts of the Mexican government to American citizens. Toward the end of the war, gold was discovered in a river bed of California. The deposit was soon found to be extremely rich, and a tide of immigration set in from every part of the civilized world. The lawless character of many of the adventurers had an unfavorable effect in the formation of the new society; but "vigilance committees" of the best citizens undertook the preserva-

Feb., 1848.

tion of order. San Francisco, from an obscure Spanish "mission," became a prosperous city and the metropolis of the Pacific coast.

200. The enormous extension of territory gained by the United States gave a new impulse to forces within their limits which already tended to disunion. The people of the south and west were engaged in agriculture, those of the north-east mainly in commerce and manufactures. The former favored free trade, which secured the best market for their products; the latter desired to impose heavy duties on foreign merchandise, in order to "protect" their own fabrics. These conflicting interests had already embittered the theoretical discussion of state and national rights; the south insisting on the independence of the several states, the north, on the centralization of power in the federal government, as a guarantee of peace and the maintenance of a dignified attitude toward foreign nations. As early as 1832, South Carolina, asserting her sovereign rights, had attempted to "nullify" an act of Congress concerning the tariff. The firmness of President Jackson, and a compromise, accepted by Congress on the motion of Henry Clay of Kentucky, averted the danger for a time.

201. The chief fire-brand of discord was negro slavery, which prevailed in the states south of the Ohio and Potomac Rivers, while it had been abolished, so far as it ever existed, in the north. With regard to their own institutions, the rights of the several states were fully recognized, but upon the question of introducing slavery into newly acquired territories, violent differences arose. On the admission of Missouri in 1821, a law was passed limiting the future extension of that institution to regions south of 36° 30′ north latitude. California now asked admission to the Union with a constitution prohibiting slavery. Again a compromise was proposed by Mr. Clay and accepted by Congress, but without allaying the general discontent. California was admitted as a free state. The question of slavery in the remainder of the territories acquired from Mexico was left to their inhabitants whenever a state constitution should be adopted. In 1854, the same policy was extended to the two territories of Kansas and Nebraska, which had been part of the Louisiana Purchase; the "Missouri Compromise" being thus repealed. Hence arose a violent struggle for the possession of Kansas by actual settlement — ended after six years by the adoption of a free constitution.

202. The line between North and South became deeper than ever in 1860, when among four candidates for the Presidency, Abraham Lincoln received the electoral votes of all but one of the free states. A plan cherished for thirty years by a few southern leaders was now put in execution. In December, 1860, a convention in South Carolina declared the secession of that state from the American Union. Its example was followed within a few months by Mississippi, Florida, Alabama,

Georgia, Louisiana, Texas, Virginia, Arkansas, North Carolina, and Tennessee. Before the last four states had formally joined the movement, the "Secessionists" in convention at Montgomery, Alabama, had elected Mr. Jefferson Davis to be their President, and had organized a government for the "Confederate States of North America." Several heads of the new departments had held high positions in the Federal Union, and had used their official authority to scatter its army to remote frontiers and its navy to the most distant seas, while they transferred great stores of arms to southern arsenals. Added to this, from the different constitution of society north and south, a greater number in the latter had sought commands in the army and navy; so that the South had at first an immense advantage in her highly trained officers, many of whom took the part of their native states against the federal government. Such was the condition of affairs when Abraham Lincoln, reaching the capital by a secret journey to elude a plot for his detention or assassination at Baltimore, pledged himself by his inaugural oath to the most difficult task ever assumed by man — to "preserve, protect, and defend the constitution of the United States."

Feb., 1861.

203. Within six weeks Fort Sumter in Charleston harbor was taken by the Confederates. War thus begun, the President called for 75,000 men and an extra session of Congress. The confederate government issued letters of marque to all privateers who would prey upon federal commerce; the President, in return, declared the southern ports in a state of blockade. The summer of 1861 was disastrous to the Federals, but with unabated energy Congress voted half a million of men and five hundred millions of dollars for the prosecution of the war. The Confederates were sustained by the hope of active alliance with England and France, encouraged by their recognition as belligerents by those powers, and by the shelter afforded to their privateers. In November, 1861, Messrs. Mason and Slidell, their envoys to England and France, were seized on board the British mail-steamer *Trent* and conveyed as prisoners to the United States; but the government at Washington disavowed the act and surrendered them upon the demand of the English embassador.

204. Late in 1861 the capture of Confederate works at Hatteras Inlet, Port Royal Entrance, and Tybee Island gave to the Federals a long line of sea-coast. In 1862 an important series of victories opened to them the towns and forts on the Mississippi as far south as Vicksburg; and in April New Orleans was taken by the fleet of Commodore Farragut, accompanied by an army under General Butler, who took military possession of the city. The fiercest fighting of this year was in Virginia, where two movements toward Richmond were repulsed in a long and terrible series of battles which have never been surpassed in the numbers engaged or in the sacrifice of life. Washington, too, was threatened, and Maryland was invaded by Lee; but he was defeated at South Mountain and at Antietam, and compelled to evacuate Harper's Ferry. At the beginning of the war, President Lincoln had declared that he had neither the right nor the disposition to alter the domestic institutions of the southern states. But in withdrawing from the Union, the seceding states had relinquished their rights to the protection of the federal constitution. On the first day of 1863, all persons held to servitude in those states were declared free and invited to enter the federal armies or fleets.

205. The first four days of July, 1863, were the turning point in the war. A great invading army under General Lee was defeated in a three days' battle at Gettysburg, Pennsylvania, and pursued into Virginia. On July 4, Vicksburg surrendered to General Grant; four days later, Port Hudson, the last remaining post on the Mississippi, likewise yielded, and the great river was open from its source to the Gulf. In September the federal army under Rosecrans was defeated and shut up for two months in Chattanooga in south-eastern Tennessee. It was relieved by Grant, who in three days' hard fighting drove General Bragg from his strong positions on Lookout Mountain and Missionary Ridge. The exhaustion of war was now most severely felt by the southern people, whose ports were closed, and whose available resources had never been as many and various as those of the north. The United States, on the other hand, were burdened with a debt nearly half as great as that of Great Britain which had been accumulating two hundred years — differing, however, from the English debt in having for its security the unmeasured and inexhaustible resources of a comparatively new continent.

206. Appreciating the situation, the people of the north made vigorous preparation for the final conflict. Grant received the title of Lieutenant-General with the command of all the armies of the Union. A simultaneous forward movement was made in May, 1864, by the army of the Potomac toward the James, and by Sherman from Chattanooga to the Atlantic. The former, by the tremendous Battles of the Wilderness and a series of flanking movements, crowded the army of Lee backward upon Richmond and Petersburg, which were both besieged by the federal forces. The Confederates were able to repulse all direct attacks upon the towns; but their railway connections were cut off and they were enclosed in an ever narrowing circle. General Early, marching down the Shenandoah Valley, attempted a counter movement upon Washington, but he was driven back, and the valley laid waste to prevent its affording supplies. Sherman, meanwhile, by several hard-fought battles had advanced to Atlanta, which he took by two months' siege, and then swept through Georgia to the sea. Savannah surrendered, December 21. The *Alabama*, the *Georgia*, and the *Florida*, all English-built Confederate cruisers, were captured this year, to the great advantage of federal commerce.

207. The reëlection of President Lincoln in November, 1864, expressed the unchanging resolution of the north, and the campaign of 1865 opened with still greater disparity of forces. Sherman moved into South Carolina, and by dividing the confederate armies, compelled Charleston and Columbia to surrender on the same day. The United States forces were now concentrated about the army of Lee. After a defeat at Five Forks, the Confederate Government took flight from Richmond, which was soon occupied by the Union troops. Lee's army, marching southward, was compelled to surrender near Appomattox Court House.

208. The war was ended, and April 14, the fourth anniversary of its beginning, was appointed as a day of general thanksgiving. Late at night its joy was turned into mourning by news of the assassination of the President. But this crime did not avail to destroy the peace so long desired and happily restored. The vice-president, Andrew Johnson, took the oath of the highest office within a few hours of Mr. Lincoln's death, and all the operations of government went on without interruption.

209. The remaining forces of the Confederacy were surrendered within a few weeks; its president became a prisoner. Four of its eleven states, having been occupied in part by federal forces, had already formed governments approved by the Congress at Washington. The rest repealed their ordinances of secession, and accepted an amendment in the Federal Constitution prohibiting "slavery or involuntary servitude, except as a punishment for crime." Two subsequent amendments extended all the rights of citizenship — even to the holding of civil offices — to the persons lately released from slavery.

210. Thus ended the great civil war — one of the most destructive of life and property that history is compelled to record. No fewer than 600,000 persons are supposed to have perished in the two great armies; and if all those disabled and maimed for life were added, the victims would probably number a million. The federal government emerged from the contest with a debt of nearly three thousand millions of dollars, which probably did not represent one-half of the expenses of the war, shared as these were by states, counties, towns, and individual persons, and aggravated by the immense destruction of property by armies and navies, and the withdrawal of three millions of persons, north and south, from the productive industries.

211. The claims of the United States against Great Britain for shelter and encouragement afforded to confederate cruisers, threatened the peace of the two countries, but in 1871 the treaty of Washington referred these claims to a Board of Arbitration composed of five commissioners from neutral nations, who met accordingly at Geneva in June, 1872. The

danages awarded by the Board were promptly acknowledged and provision made for their payment by the British government.

212. The only attractive feature of the war is found in the efficient efforts of private liberality to relieve suffering. First among organizations was the Sanitary Commission, whose expenditures amounted to millions, and whose faithful agents were found in every camp and on every battle-field, carrying to the wounded or sick of both armies comforts which it was impossible for the government to afford. Medical science surpassed itself in the construction of ambulances and the invention of the most skillful methods of alleviating distress; and so well was this appreciated in Europe, that a noble emulation led to an International Convention at Geneva for abating the barbarities of war. Most of the great powers agreed to concede neutral   A. D. 1864. rights to every house in which the wounded were sheltered and to all persons employed in attending them. The sufferers themselves while disabled are regarded as neutrals. This humane agreement, so far as it has been observed, has greatly alleviated the miseries of a state of war.

213. The American Union now embraces thirty-seven states and ten territories, bound together by more than 60,000 miles of railways, while its lines of telegraphs if extended would reach more than three times around the globe. The completion of a railroad across the continent and the establishment of a line of steamers from San Francisco to Yokohama and Hong Kong has brought the old empires of China and Japan into intimate connection with the great Republic of the West. At the same time this increase of commerce and travel has led to a serious crisis in the relations of the government with the Indians of the interior. These savages decline to accept "reservations" of unprofitable land in lieu of their unlimited hunting-grounds; and they have undoubted cause of complaint in the conduct of many commissioners and traders. Yet it is certain that the continent is destined to be the abode of civilized man, and to sustain millions of industrious beings instead of idle and scattered savages. About one-fourth of the Indian tribes have become civilized, and have settled to the cultivation of the soil. One-tenth of the whole Indian population are citizens of the United States. If the dealings of the white men with these prior occupants of the continent had been always characterized by justice and humanity, the Modoc War would never have occurred and the Indian Question would be nearer to a peaceful solution.

RECAPITULATION.

The United States largely populated by immigration from Europe; their prosperity increased by railways and telegraphs. Wars with native tribes. Texas secedes from the Mexican Republic and seeks admission to the United States. Its annexation causes a war with Mexico. Victories of Generals Taylor, Kearney, and Scott. City of Mexico captured. Territories of New Mexico, Arizona, California, Nevada, Utah, and Colorado added to the United States. Gold discovered in California.

Conflicting interests in the United States. Disruption averted for a time by compromise. Disputes concerning the extension of slavery. California admitted into the Union and the Missouri Compromise repealed. Contest for Kansas. Election of Abraham Lincoln. Secession of South Carolina and ten other states. Confederate States organized with Jefferson Davis as their president. Surrender of Fort Sumter. Blockade of the southern ports. Recognition of the Confederates by England and France. Capture and surrender of their envoys to Europe. Victories of Union forces on the Atlantic and Mississippi. Capture and military occupation of New Orleans. Richmond and Washington alternately threatened. Proclamation of freedom to slaves in the seceded states. Union victories at Gettysburg, Vicksburg, and Port Hudson; opening of the Mississippi. Defeat of Federals at Chickamauga; siege of Chattanooga — raised by Grant who becomes Lieutenant-General. His march to Richmond; defeat of Early in the Shenandoah Valley. Sherman's capture of Atlanta and Savannah, Charleston and Columbia. Reëlection of President Lincoln; surrender of Richmond and of Lee's army. Assassination of the President; inauguration of Johnson. Reconstruction of the Union. Settlement of "Alabama Claims" against Great Britain by arbitration at Geneva. American organizations for relief of the wounded, imitated in Europe by International League.

Intercourse of United States with China and Japan by Pacific Railway and steamers. War with the Modocs and doubtful relations with other Indian tribes.

Decline and Fall of the French Empire.

214. The first two years of the American War witnessed an invasion of the neighboring Republic of Mexico by the combined forces of England, France, and Spain. Its main purpose was to exact payment for debts and reparation for injuries inflicted upon subjects of those nations during a civil war of three years' standing; but the emperor of the French had a further aim — to set up a sort of protectorate of the "Latin Race" in America — which was encouraged by the apparently hopeless disruption of the United States. Hence the French commissioner refused to meet those of England, Spain, and Mexico, when the latter had proposed to settle the questions in dispute by peaceful conference, and insisted on marching to the capital. The alliance was therefore broken off, and the English and Spanish troops were recalled; while the French, joined by some of the revolutionary Mexican forces, declared war against the government of President Juarez. They were reinforced by several regiments under General Forey who assumed the command; and having taken Puebla by siege, occupied the capital in June, 1863. Here a Council of Notables, under a controlling French influence, declared in favor of a hereditary empire as the future government of Mexico; and subsequently chose Maximilian, a brother of the Austrian emperor, to be their sovereign.

215. Monterey became the capital of the republican government under Juarez. The emperor Maximilian and the empress Carlotta entered the City of Mexico in June, 1864. War went on with varying success between the conflicting governments; several important towns being taken by the Republicans. In 1866, the interests of Napoleon III. and the urgency of the United States, required the withdrawal of his forces from Mexico, and he advised Maximilian to seek his own safety by abdication. The Austrian prince refused, however, to abandon those Mexican leaders who had risked their lives in his cause; though, as the event proved, one at least was animated by less honorable motives. The last of the French troops departed in March, 1867. Two months later, the town of Queretaro, where the emperor was then residing, was betrayed to the Juarists by General Lopez, the commandant appointed by Maximilian. The unfortunate emperor was shot by order of Juarez, June 19. Mexico, though constantly disturbed, has ever since maintained its republican constitution.

216. The rapid and brilliant movement of the Seven Weeks' War had disappointed Napoleon, while it awakened uneasiness in France. The emperor had long foreseen the contest; but he had expected that Prussia would require his assistance and would buy it with the provinces on the left of the Rhine, which he chose to designate as the "natural boundary" of France. His minister at Berlin indeed put in a claim to the Rhine provinces as compensation to France for the increased power of Prussia; but on Bismarck's reply that the claim was "inadmissible" it was immediately withdrawn. Count Benedetti then presented a scheme for the annexation of Belgium to France — the latter in return to oppose no obstacle to the subjection of all southern Germany to Prussia. This paper, in the handwriting of the French embassador, was laid aside for future use by the far-seeing Chancellor. Napoleon then attempted a quiet purchase of Luxembourg from the king of Holland, who was always in want of money, and to whom the province was of little value. Unfortunately for the scheme, Luxembourg belonged to the North German Confederation and was garrisoned by Prussian troops. Germany protested, and the bargain was abandoned; for though a party in France clamored for war, the emperor knew that a complete rearming of his troops was necessary before he could meet the Prussians in the field. The war of 1866 had clearly shown the superiority of the breech-loading fire-arms, which the French military officers had not then decided to adopt.

217. A revolution in Spain hastened the crisis which was to change the whole states-system of Europe. Isabella II. had reigned as a constitutional sovereign since 1843. Her government, if so it could be called, had been carried on by an ever-shifting succession of generals and favorites; and civil war had come to be almost the normal condition of the country. In 1868, Gonzales Bravo came to the head of affairs. He summarily arrested and banished seven of the most distinguished generals, as well as the Duke and Duchess of Montpensier, the latter of whom, it will be remembered (§ 198), was sister of the queen. Rebellion instantly broke out in the army, where each of the banished generals had adherents, and the queen's troops were defeated in the field. She herself had repaired to St. Sebastian under pretense of sea-bathing, but really to be near the French frontier in order to consult her ally, the emperor, who was at Bayonne. Upon news of her disaster she crossed the border and was assigned a residence at Pau. A provisional government was organized at Madrid, and the Bourbon dynasty was declared at an end. Serrano, one of the banished generals, was placed at the head of the new ministry.

218. A few of the best men in Spain desired a republic; but a majority preferred a liberal monarchy, and then followed a search for a king. Candidates were easy to find. The Duke of Montpensier pressed his claims with money and influence. A grandson of Don Carlos, the queen's uncle (§ 157), revived the old Salic theory, and announced himself to Spain and the courts of Europe as King Charles the Seventh. The French imperial party urged the young Prince of Asturias, then eleven years of age, through whom it expected to govern Spain.

June, 1870. His mother abdicated in his favor, but the Spanish nation refused to receive him. The king of Portugal declined the offered crown both for himself and his brother. The choice of the Spaniards then fell upon Prince Frederic of Hohenzollern-Sigmaringen, younger brother of the Prince of Roumania, and a very distant relative of the king of Prussia. The French court made no objection to this choice; but when, in the summer of 1870, it became known that the invitation had been transferred to Frederic's eldest brother, Leopold, the war-party at Paris suddenly denounced his candidacy as a Prussian aggression.

219. For ten years the French emperor had been balancing two opposite theories of government. *Caesarism*, or imperialism, through which he had personally undertaken to "guarantee order to France," could only be maintained by a continual succession of victories in war, or at least by a commanding attitude in the diplomacy of Europe. Opposed to the theory of "personal government" was the English system by which the ministry are held responsible for all the royal acts, and are removable at any time by a "vote of want of confidence" on the part of the legislative body. The decline of the emperor's health gave strength to the anti-imperialists; to conciliate them a committee of the Senate was charged with the preparation of a new representative constitution, which was to be promulgated on the centennial of the birth of Napoleon

Aug. 15, 1869. I. Brilliant celebrations had been appointed for this occasion; but the emperor's illness, the absence of the empress and her son in Corsica, and above all the death of Marshal Niel, Aug. 13, cast a gloom over the day which accorded well with the prophecies that the year 1869 was to be fatal to the power of the Bonapartes. Under the new constitution Emil Ollivier was commanded to form a parliamentary ministry; and it comprised several men of high character who had been opponents of the *coup d'état* and of the imperial government. The new system was submitted to a *plebiscite*, and as usual a great majority voted *yes*, though one-sixth of the army were opposed. It had been industriously declared by the official journals that the "Empire is peace," and that the consequence of a negative vote would be a war for the Rhine frontier. The reverse was true.

220. In vain the king of Prussia assured the French government that he knew nothing of the candidacy of Prince Leopold; and that he had no power to command or forbid the prince's acceptance of the Spanish crown. In vain Leopold himself withdrew his name, as soon as he heard of the excitement at Paris. The French embassador, Benedetti, demanded from the king an apology for having permitted the candidateship, and a pledge that it should never again occur. At this crisis the secret proposal of Benedetti in 1867 was published by Bismarck (see ¿ 216), and occasioned great excitement throughout Europe; especially in Great Britain, whose government had guaranteed the independence of Belgium. The English Foreign Office demanded from Napoleon III. the most ample securities for his observance of Belgian neutrality in the struggle which was too evidently impending. On the very day of Leopold's resignation, French troops began their march toward the Rhine. On the 15th, war was declared. Nothing could have put so effective a finishing touch to German nationality. Whatever jealousy of Prussia had existed in southern Germany was silenced; Bavaria, Wirtemberg, and Baden put their armies at the disposal of King William.

July 12, 1870.

221. The Crown Prince of Prussia assumed command of the German army at Spires, while Napoleon III., having named the empress Eugénie regent during his absence, repaired with his son to the army at Metz. Only when the French van-guard stood on the German border, did the generals take a just estimate of their resources. There was a great deficiency of horses; and of those actually with the army great numbers had been let out for months to farmers and were unfit for service. Proposals for feeding the army were only received on the 28th of July. The number of men by actual count was less than half the nominal strength of the divisions. In short the French nation had been "plunged into war with not one single arm of the naval or military service really prepared;" and a French officer has declared from personal knowledge that "whole divisions went into action in a literally famishing condition." On the other hand the Prussian army was drilled, fed, and equipped to the highest degree of efficiency, and when joined by the South German forces had more than twice the numbers of its opponents. Its highly trained officers were more familiar with the roads and deep-cleft, narrow valleys of north-eastern France than were the French themselves; for a minute study of European topography was a most important part of the "war-play" of their military schools. It is not surprising that the war was an almost uninterrupted succession of German victories.

222. The first action was an attack (Aug. 2) upon a small Prussian outpost on the heights above Saarbrücken; only remarkable from the presence of the French Prince Imperial to receive his "baptism of fire," and for the first serious trial of the *mitrailleuse*, a new invention in field-artillery, from which tremendous results were expected. The Prussians retired to their next post as soon as the "hail-storm" of shot became inconvenient. On the 4th the French were repulsed from the German lines at Weissemburg; on the 6th, MacMahon was disastrously defeated at Wörth, and Frossard between Saarbrücken and Forbach.

223. On this fatal 6th of August, bulletins posted on the Bourse at Paris announced the annihilation of the Crown Prince's army and a glorious victory to the French. Rumor, swiftly following, not only declared this a falsehood, but whispered that the ministers had invented it for their own private account in order to speculate in the public funds. The palace of Ollivier was mobbed by an indignant crowd demanding true information from the seat of war. As yet only the defeat at Weissemburg was known, but the next day the disasters at Wörth and Forbach were also announced. The excitable Parisians were plunged into extreme despondency and discontent with the ministry. The empress convened the Senate and Corps-Législatif on the 9th. Ollivier's speech was interrupted by a storm of opposition, and his cabinet immediately resigned. A new "Ministry of Public Defense" was formed under the presidency of Count Palikao. Marshal Lebœuf, commanding under the emperor, resigned, and Bazaine was placed at the head of the armies. He was terribly defeated, however, before Metz, again less decisively at Mars-la-Tour, and most completely at Gravelotte (Aug. 14, 16, 18), and was shut up in Metz by a superior German force.

224. Strasbourg had meanwhile been invested by Badenese troops aided by the Prussian *landwehr* or militia. Napoleon, no longer commanding except in name, joined the army which MacMahon was concentrating at Chalons, either to cover Paris, now threatened by the Crown Prince of Prussia, or to march to the relief of Bazaine. The latter movement was chosen; and the effort of the Germans was then to entrap the French between the Meuse and the Belgian frontier, which they could only cross by surrendering their arms (see ½ 220). The great decisive combat took place at Sedan. The French were completely surrounded and driven into the town, where the whole army by a capitulation, Sept. 2, became prisoners of war. The emperor, by letter, surrendered himself to the king of Prussia, and was assigned a resi-

Sept. 1, 1870.

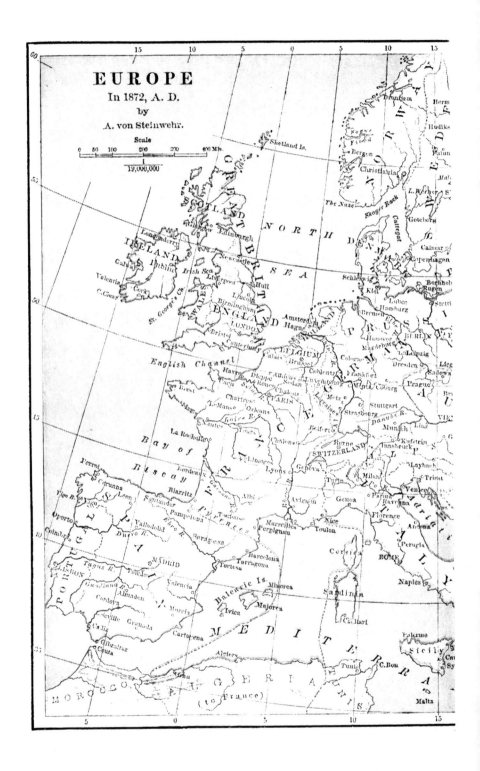

EUROPE

In 1872, A. D.

by

A. von Steinwehr.

Scale

0   50   100   200   300   400 Mls.

19,000,000

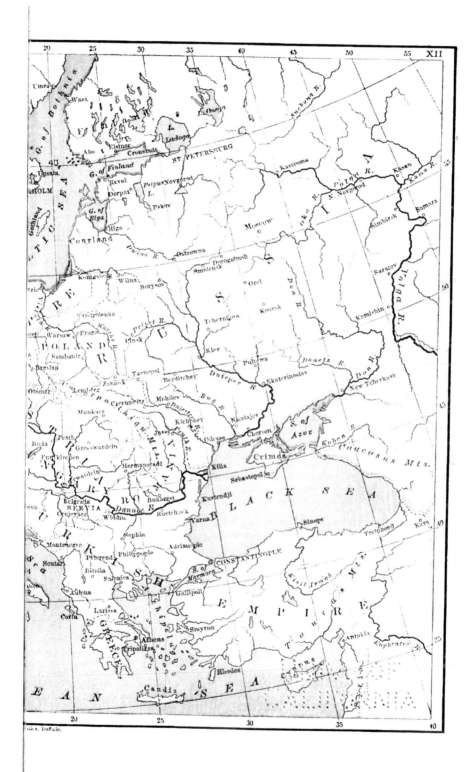

dence at Wilhelmshöhe in Hesse Cassel, where his uncle Jerome had lived as king of Westphalia. The fortress of Sedan, with 70 *mitrailleuses*, 480 cannon, 10,000 horses, and 108,000 men fell into German hands.

225. In the terror which reigned at Paris, General Trochu, an honest and able soldier, but no favorite with the imperialists, was appointed governor of the city, and zealously prepared for its defense. The outer moat was filled with water and a fleet of gun-boats was collected in the Seine. The *Guard Mobile* was drawn in from the provinces; sailors and 9,000 custom-house officials were armed, and with the National Guard made a total of 400,000 men. Firemen were telegraphed from the provincial cities, and arrived to the number of 60,000, imagining that some great conflagration had broken out. The work of provisioning Paris for a siege began; 80,000 Germans resident in the city were expelled, and the inconvenience and suffering, thus occasioned, aroused that national enmity which is the most mélancholy result of the war.

On the announcement of the news from Sedan in the Corps-Legislatif, Jules Favre arose and declared that the "Empire had ceased to exist." Troops of the National Guard and crowds of people thronged the square around the Palais Bourbon, demanding the fall of the Bonapartes. The empress regent, deserted by all her domestics but one, fled from the Tuileries and took refuge with her son in England. A provisional government was formed with Trochu at its head, and with Messrs. Arago, Crémieux, Favre, Ferry, Gambetta, and others for its ministers.

226. The new government would gladly have arranged a peace, to be ratified by the French nation as soon as there should be time to consult it. But a difficulty had arisen. The king of Prussia had already placed Alsace and part of Lorraine under German administration, and demanded their permanent cession as the price of peace. The French government refused to give up "an inch of its land or a stone of its fortresses," though intimating that the fortunes of war might require from it some concession in money. M. Thiers, then 73 years of age, made a pilgrimage to the courts of London, St. Petersburg, Vienna, and Florence, asking mediation and moral support for France. The sovereigns were reminded that the king of Prussia had constantly declared his hostility to be, not with the French nation, but with its emperor, who had injured and insulted him. Now that Napoleon III. had been deposed by the will of the people, it was claimed that the cause of war no longer existed. The same views were urged by Favre in his interviews with Bismarck at Ferrières, Sept. 18–20; but the German armies were already surrounding Paris, and the Crown Prince took up his quarters at Versailles on the last day of the conference.

227. The French capital, under Louis Philippe and Napoleon III., had become a gigantic fortress, which for size and strength has probably had no equal since Babylon. Its walls were thirty-three feet high and twenty miles in length, and were surrounded by a moat or ditch forty feet in width. Sixteen detached forts formed a girdle of defense at distances of several miles from the walls. The reduction of such a place taxed all the resources of the art of war, while its defense, embarrassed by the necessity of feeding and sheltering two millions of people, exhausted even French ingenuity and the multiplied inventions of the nineteenth century. The underground telegraphs having been cut, intelligence was only conveyed to the outer world by balloons and carrier-pigeons — the latter bearing a single quill containing a scrap of silken paper on which had been photographed many thousands of words. M. Gambetta, ascending from Paris in a balloon, joined several of his colleagues at Tours, and as Minister of War and the Interior became in fact the dictator of four months of the war. The imperial forces had been either destroyed, scattered, or shut up in besieged towns. The government at Tours ordered under arms every Frenchman between 20 and 40 years of age. Garibaldi and his two sons offered themselves to the service of the Republic, and the former was assigned to the command of the irregular troops of the Vosges. Cavalry recruits were found even in the free Bedouin bands of the African desert. Eleven camps of instruction were formed in various parts of France. The unflinching zeal of the French people contradicted the too prevalent belief that the corruption of the "Lower Empire" had extended to the heart of the nation.

228. The fall of Strasbourg, after a bombardment which shattered its beautiful Cathedral-towers and destroyed its library, sent a thrill of grief and rage throughout France. A month later, Metz, with the whole army of Bazaine, including three marshals, fifty generals, 6,000 inferior officers, and 173,000 men, with an immense train of artillery, surrendered to the Prussians. It had been more than three hundred years a French town (Book III., §§ 168, 172). The towns and fortresses of northern France fell rapidly into the hands of the Germans. After their victory at Amiens, Rouen and the excellent harbor of Dieppe were opened to them. Orleans had already been taken, and recovered by General d'Aurelles de Paladines in the battle of Coulmiers. The movement of the victorious general for the relief of Paris was thwarted by the advance of Prince Frederic Charles, and Orleans was again occupied by German troops. The government emigrated from Tours to Bordeaux. Three tremendous efforts were made by the army in Paris to break through the investing lines, but all were repulsed.

Both besiegers and besieged suffered severely from the intense cold of an uncommonly rigorous winter; and this was aggravated in Paris by the want of wood, coal, and gas. On the 27th of December the Prussian batteries opened fire from the heights of Sèvres, Meudon, Clamart, and

Chatillon. Starvation was added to the horrors of bombardment; and nearly five thousand people died every week within the walls.

229. Meanwhile a great but peaceful change was effected in the constitution of Germany. Delegates from Bavaria, Wirtemberg, Baden, and Hesse Darmstadt were instructed to propose in the North German Diet a union of all the states and free cities in a new German Confederation. But the events of 1866 had proved this plan inadequate to the wants of Germany. King Louis II. of Bavaria cut the Gordian knot by a letter received at Versailles, Dec. 3, in which, after consultation with his fellow-sovereigns and the burgomasters of the free cities, he invited the king of Prussia to assume the title of German Emperor. The North German Parliament sent its address of assent and congratulation by the hands of its president, Herr Simson, who in 1849 had been charged with a similar embassy to King Frederick William IV. (§ 145.) This time the imperial crown was accepted, and in a hall of the palace of Versailles, still resplendent with the magnificence of Louis XIV., King William I. was solemnly invested with the new dignity. The Jan. 18, 1871. act was announced to the German people in a proclamation which declared that the king assumed the imperial title from considerations of duty to the Fatherland, hoping to deserve the title "Semper Augustus," not by conquests in war, but by the blessings and benefits of peace.

230. Famine had now reduced the fair, proud city of Paris to the humiliation of a surrender, and on the night of the 26-27 of January the bombardment ceased. The forts of the outer circle were surrendered with all their stores and munitions; and unless the war should close within a month, the entire army of Paris were to be prisoners. An armistice of three weeks gave the French people time to organize a government competent to conclude a permanent peace; but as great hopes were still entertained of the relief of Belfort by the army of the East under Bourbaki, that department was especially excepted. Writs were issued for the election of a Constituent Assembly. The delegation at Bordeaux, by an independent decree, declared all persons ineligible who had held any official relation to the Second Empire. This was the act of Gambetta; and when the government at Paris, upon the protest of Bismarck, annulled the decree the Dictator resigned. The choice of representatives indicated an overwhelming popular demand for peace. The Assembly met at Bordeaux, Feb. 12; a provisional Republic was proclaimed, and M. Thiers, as the most prominent representative of the peace party, was elected its chief Executive by a large majority.

231. Meanwhile the army of the East had been overwhelmed with disasters. Bourbaki, defeated in a three days' battle before Belfort, lost his reason, and the command devolved upon General Clinchy. When news of the armistice arrived by the telegraph, the exception in the case of the Department of the East was most unfortunately omitted; and the French general, attempting to open negotiations with Manteuffel, was taken at a great disadvantage. No alternative was left but a retreat into Switzerland, and this was accomplished during the first four days of February, 1871. The wretched train of 85,000 men, worn with fatigue, privation, and disease were received with warm hospitality. Deprived of their arms and war-materials, they were distributed throughout the cantons; and private charity did more than the governments could have done for their relief.

232. On the 26th of February, preliminaries of peace were signed at Versailles. France ceded Alsace and German Lorraine to the new Empire and agreed to pay five thousand millions of francs as war indemnity. All the French troops except a garrison of 40,000 in Paris retired south of the Loire. A detachment of the German army entered Paris, March 1; but left it on the third. Their departure was followed by a still greater calamity than their presence. In the confusion attending the close of the siege, some troops of the National Guard, acting without orders, seized a great number of cannon and dragged them to the heights of Montmartre, where they intrenched themselves and resisted the efforts of General Vinoy to dislodge them. They were joined by troops of the line; and Vinoy withdrew his forces from Paris for the protection of the Assembly, which now transferred its sittings from Bordeaux to Versailles. The insurgents organized a government at the Hotel de Ville, and are henceforth to be known as the *Commune.*

233. A conflict of interests had already arisen between the large towns and the country districts; and the Assembly had undertaken to discriminate in favor of the latter by limiting the freedom of elections in the towns. Moreover there was a strong monarchical element in the Assembly, while the cities universally favored a republic. The Commune at Paris declared itself the champion of municipal freedom, and it had the sympathy of strong parties in the other towns. But unhappily the best men who opposed the Versailles government were overborne by that revolutionary element which France has learned by bitter experience to dread (§ 140). The worst people seized power and robbed the banks in order to obtain means of maintaining themselves by force. The troops of the two governments fought for the possession of the forts south of Paris; those of the Commune were several times routed with great loss. The government at Versailles was compelled to ask permission of the Germans to increase its army north of the Loire, and the return of French prisoners of war was hastened. The unhappy contest wrought greater injury to Paris than had been effected by the German shells. As victory inclined to the Assembly, the Communists avenged themselves for certain defeat by setting fire to the Louvre, the Tuileries, and the

Palais Royal, and by pulling down the great column of the Place Vendôme, the proudest monument of the First Empire. The venerable Archbishop of Paris and other hostages were shot; a number of Dominican monks were murdered. At length all the forts were in the hands of the Versailles government, the insurgents were driven from their last position in the Cemetery of Père la Chaise; May 28, 1871. and the *Commune* was ended. A terrible vengeance was exacted by the Court Martial at Versailles, which ordered multitudes of men and even women, convicted of having part in the violent proceedings in Paris, to be put to death.

234. In ten months one empire had fallen, and another, of different materials and organized on wholly different principles, had arisen in Europe. The kingdom of Italy without having taken any part in the general contest, had reaped, perhaps, its most important advantage. Rome had been abandoned by its French protectors in August, 1870, and the next month it was quietly occupied by the troops of Victor Emmanuel. The Pope was confirmed in the possession of the Leonine City (Book I., § 64), and in all his honors and dignities as head of the Roman Church; but the territories formerly under his sovereignty were declared to be part of the kingdom of Italy, after a vote of the people had expressed, with scarcely a dissentient voice, their desire for annexation. The government of the kingdom was transferred to the ancient capital, July 1, 1871.

235. After the resignation of Prince Leopold (§ 220) the Spanish crown was accepted by Amadeo, Duke of Aosta and second son of King Victor Emmanuel of Italy. He was crowned, Dec. 30, 1870, and gave his assent to a liberal constitution which established civil and religious freedom in a nation so long under the curse of despotism. The new reign had continued, however, little more than two years when Amadeo found the difficulties of his position between the party which desired yet greater changes and the Carlists, who were supported by perpetual intrigues of the priests, too great for endurance; and suddenly resigned the crown, Feb. 11, 1873. A republic was then proclaimed.

RECAPITULATION.

French war in Mexico. Maximilian of Austria chosen Emperor. Upon the withdrawal of French troops he is defeated and shot at Queretaro. Reëstablishment of Republic under Juarez. Napoleon III. seeks compensation for aggrandizement of Prussia in Seven Weeks' War. Fall of the Spanish Bourbons. Flight of Isabella II. Rival claimants to the crown; Leopold of Hohenzollern accepts it, subject to the will of the Spanish people. New liberal constitution in France; Ollivier chief minister. King of Prussia refusing to render account to France of Prince Leopold's candidacy, Napoleon declares war. Unprepared condition of the French army. Its repeated disasters. Riot in Paris upon receipt of false intelligence. Palikao succeeds Ollivier. Battle of Sedan results in captivity of Napoleon III. and his army. Trochu governor of Paris; preparations for its defense.

Flight of the empress; provisional government under Trochu. Peace prevented by annexation of Alsace and Lorraine to Germany. Four months' siege of Paris. Delegation of the Government of National Defense at Tours, afterward at Bordeaux. Creation of an army south of the Loire. Fall of Strasbourg and Metz. Ineffectual efforts of the besieged army to break out of Paris.

Establishment of a new German Empire under William I. Paris is reduced by famine and bombardment. Its surrender. Three weeks' armistice. Constituent Assembly meets at Bordeaux. A republic organized with Thiers at its head. Bourbaki's army *interned* in Switzerland. Treaty of Versailles cedes Alsace and Lorraine and burdens France with a ruinous war indemnity. Communist insurrection in Paris. Three months' war between the two governments ended by victory to the Assembly. Rome occupied by Victor Emmanuel. Temporal sovereignty of the Popes overthrown. Reign and resignation of Amadeo in Spain. Spanish Republic proclaimed.

QUESTIONS FOR REVIEW.

Book V.

BOOKS RECOMMENDED FOR MORE EXTENSIVE READING.

Gibbon's Decline and Fall of the Roman Empire. Milman's Edition.
Finlay's History of Greece under the Romans.
    "   History of Greece from its Conquest by the Crusaders to its Conquest by the Turks.
    "   History of the Byzantine Empire, A. D. 717-1057.
    "   History of the Byzantine and Greek Empires.
Stanley's History of the Eastern Church.
Milman's History of Christianity.
    "   History of Latin Christianity.
Sismondi's History of the Italian Republics.
Parke Godwin's History of France.
Michelet's History of France.
Martin's History of France. (The last named may supersede all others for readers of French.)
Voltaire's Age of Louis XIV.
    "   Life of Charles XII.
    "   " " Peter the Great.
Guizot's History of Civilization.
Bryce's Holy Roman Empire.
Raumer's History of the Hohenstaufen.
Coxe's House of Austria.
Froissart's Chronicles.
Memoirs of Philip de Comines.
Kirke's Life of Charles the Bold.
Major's Life of Prince Henry the Navigator.
Prescott's Reign of Ferdinand and Isabella.
    "   Conquest of Mexico.
    "   Conquest of Peru.
    "   Edition of Robertson's Charles the Fifth.
    "   Life of Philip the Second.
Motley's Rise of the Dutch Republic.
    "   United Netherlands.
    "   Life of J. van Olden Barneveldt.
Ranke's History of Germany during the Reformation.
    "   History of the Popes.
Hübner's Life and Times of Sixtus V.
Weiss' History of French Protestant Refugees.
Pressensé's History of Protestantism in France.
Memoirs of the Duc de St. Simon.
D'Aubigné's History of the Reformation.
Campbell's Life of Petrarch.
Villari's Life of Savonarola.
Grimm's Life of Michael Angelo.
Trollope's History of the Commonwealth of Florence.
Roscoe's Life of Lorenzo dé Medici.
    "   Life of Leo X.
Dyer's History of Modern Europe.
Turner's Anglo Saxons.
Palgrave's Normandy and England.
Thierry's Norman Conquest.

Freeman's Norman Conquest.
Knight's Popular History of England.
Miss Strickland's Lives of the Queens of England.
   "   "   Lives of the Queens of Scotland and of English Princesses
    connected with the Succession. (To be consulted chiefly for illustrations of
    manners and customs—with great caution as to characters.)
Hume's History of England to A. D. 1688.
Macaulay's History of England from the Accession of James II.
   "   Essays on Bacon, Milton, Hampden, Hastings, Sir Wm. Temple, *et al.*
Carlyle's Life and Letters of Oliver Cromwell.
Froude's History of England from the Death of Wolsey to the Death of Elizabeth.
Mahon's History of England from the Peace of Utrecht to the Peace of Versailles.
Molesworth's History of England from A. D. 1830.
Thackeray's Lectures on the Four Georges.
Mrs. Oliphant's Sketches of the Reign of George II.
Jesse's Life and Reign of George III.
Campbell's Lives of the Lord Chancellors.
   "   Lives of the Chief Justices of England.
Bancroft's History of the United States.
Parkman's Pioneers of France in the New World.
     "   Jesuits in North America.
     "   Discovery of the Great West.
     "   Conspiracy of Pontiac.
     "   Oregon Trail.
Palfrey's History of New England.
Irving's Mahomet and His Successors.
    "   Conquest of Granada.
    "   Life of Columbus.
    "   Life of Washington.
Sparks' Diplomatic Correspondence of the American Revolution.
    "   Lives of Washington, Franklin, G. Morris, *et al.*
De Tocqueville's Democracy in America.
Carlyle's Frederic the Great.
    "   French Revolution.
Lamartine's Girondists.
Thiers' History of the French Revolution.
    "   The Consulate and the Empire.
Lanfrey's Life of Napoleon.
Kinglake's War in the Crimea.
Malet's Overthrow of the Germanic Confederation.
Hozier's Seven Weeks' War.
The Austro-Hungarian Empire and the Policy of Count von Beust. By an Eng-
    lishman.
Rüstow's War for the Rhine Frontier.
Lectures on Modern History, by Dr. Arnold, Prof. Goldwin Smith, Prof. Seelye.
Bulwer's Historical Characters.
Mrs. Jameson's Historical Portraits.

*Among numberless works of imagination illustrative of History, the following
may be especially recommended :*

Southey's Roderick, the Last of the Goths.
Tasso's Jerusalem Delivered. Fairfax's Translation.

Dante's Divine Comedy. Longfellow's Translation and Notes.
Camoens' Lusiad.
Byron's Marino Faliero.
Scott's Historical Novels.
Bulwer's Rienzi, the Last of the Tribunes.
" The Last of the Barons.
Kingsley's Amyas Leigh, or Westward, Ho!
" Two Years Ago.
" Hereward, the Last of the Saxons.
George Elliot's Romola.
Dickens' Barnaby Rudge.
Dickens' Tale of Two Cities.
Goethe's Goetz of Berlichingen.
" Egmont.
Schiller's Mary Stuart.
" Maid of Orleans.
" William Tell.
" Don Carlos.
" Wallenstein, Coleridge's Translation.
Henry Taylor's Philip van Artevelde.

APPENDIX A

DEVELOPMENT OF THE SWISS CONFEDERATION.

1. Alliance of III. primitive Cantons: Schwytz, Uri, Unterwald (Pure democracy) . . . . A. D. 1291
2. Alliance of IV. Forest Cantons (Waldstätten): Schwytz, Uri, Unterwald, Lucerne 1332
3. Alliance of V. Cantons: Schwytz, Uri, Unterwald, Lucerne, Zurich (Domination of the burghers) 1350
4. Alliance of VIII. Cantons. Accession of Glaris and Zug, 1352; of Berne 1353
5. Confederation of XIII. Cantons. Accession of Fribourg and Soleure, 1481; Basle and Schaffhausen, 1501; Appenzell 1513
    Foreign military service
    Reformation.
    Aristocratic rule. Decline and Revolution.
6. Helvetic Republic, one and indivisible. The Cantons suppressed, under influence of the French Directory 1798
7. Act of Mediation. XIX Cantons. Accession of St. Gall, Grisons, Argovie, Thurgovie, Tessin, and Vaud, under influence of Napoleon 1803
8. Treaty of 1815. Confederation of Sovereign States, under influence of the Holy Alliance. XXII Cantons. Accession of Valais, Neuchâtel, and Geneva 1815
9. Federal Constitution, voted by the Swiss People without foreign influence, XXII Cantons forming XXV States, all democratic republics, September 12 1848

B.—*Page* 104.

HOUSES OF VALOIS AND ORLÉANS.

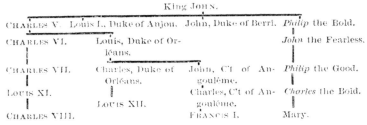

King JOHN.

CHARLES V.   Louis I., Duke of Anjou.   John, Duke of Berri.   *Philip* the Bold.

CHARLES VI.   Louis, Duke of Or-   *John* the Fearless.
léans.

CHARLES VII.   Charles, Duke of   John, C't of An-   *Philip* the Good.
Orléans.   goulême.

Louis XI.   Charles, C't of An-   *Charles* the Bold.
goulême.

Louis XII.

CHARLES VIII.   FRANCIS I.   Mary.

N. B.—Kings of France are in capital letters, Dukes of Burgundy in italics.

C.—*Page* 296.

THE SPANISH SUCCESSION.

PHILIP III.

Anne of Austria, m. *Louis XIII.*   PHILIP IV., m. Eliz. of   Mary Anne, m. FER-
France.   DINAND III.

Louis XIV., m. Maria Theresa.   CHARLES II.   Marg't Theresa, m. LEOPOLD I., who
m. (2d) Mary Anne of Neuberg.

Louis Dauphin.   Mary Antoinette, m.   JOSEPH I. CHARLES VI.
Elector of Bavaria.

Louis.   PHILIP V.   Joseph Ferdinand, Electoral Prince of Bavaria.

N. B.—Emperors are in large capitals, Kings of Spain in small capitals, Kings of France in italics.

D.—*Page* 304.

HANOVERIAN SUCCESSION.

James I. of England.

Charles I.   Elizabeth, m. Frederick V., Elector Palatine.
Henrietta Maria, m. D. of Orleans.   Sophia, m. Duke of Brunswick Luneburg, aft.
Elector of Hanover.

Anne Marie, m. Victor Amadeus,   George Lewis, Elector of Hanover, became
D. of Savoy.   George I., King of Great Britain.

Charles Emmanuel, Duke of Savoy.

It will be seen that the House of Savoy was one step nearer to the English throne than that of Brunswick or Hanover. The latter succeeded by the Act of Parliament excluding Romanists.

INDEX.

461

468

CPSIA information can be obtained at www.ICGtesting.com
Printed in the USA
LVOW07*1531250116

472162LV00010B/112/P